Palgrave Law Masters

Torts

PALGRAVE LAW MASTERS

Series Editor Marise Cremona

Torts

Alastair Mullis
Dean of Norwich Law School
University of East Anglia

and

Ken Oliphant
Senior Lecturer at Cardiff Law School
Cardiff University

Series Editor: Marise Cremona
Professor of European Commercial Law
Queen Mary Centre for Commecial Law Studies
University of London

First edition 1993
Reprinted twice
Second edition 1997
Reprinted
Third edition 2003
Published by
PALGRAVE MACMILLAN
Houndmills, Basingstoke, Hampshire RG21 6XS
and 175 Fifth Avenue, New York, N.Y. 10010
Companies and representatives throughout the world

ISBN 0–333–96379–2

This book is printed on paper suitable for recycling and made from fully managed and sustained forest sources.

A catalogue record for this book is available from the British Library.

A catalogue record for this book is available from the Library of Congress.

10   9   8   7   6   5   4   3   2   1
12   11   10   09   08   07   06   05   04   03

Printed and bound in Great Britain by
Creative Print & Design (Wales), Ebbw Vale

Contents

Part IV   INTERFERENCE WITH REPUTATION

Part V   GENERAL PRINCIPLES OF TORTIOUS LIABILITY

Preface

Torts make headline news. From mass disasters like Hillsborough to scandal-mongering in the popular press, torts are seldom far from the front pages. Yet, despite its human interest, the law of torts is notoriously difficult for students.

We aim in this book to provide an accessible introduction to the law of torts. We cover the basic principles of the law and examine them in the context of those torts which most commonly feature in degree courses. In doing so, we hope to stimulate thought about the complexities of the subject and about tort law's role in society.

In this third edition, we have extensively revised many sections of the book to take account of developments since 1997, of which the most important is perhaps the implementation of the Human Rights Act 1998. The updated text includes analysis of the first cases to discuss the Act's provisions and of relevant decisions of the European Court of Human Rights. Other important developments have also been incorporated, including crucial House of Lords decisions in the areas of causation, mental injury, public authority liability, defamation, vicarious liability and damages. We have expanded the chapter on product liability to allow consideration of the first cases on the Consumer Protection Act 1987, the Act's statutory modification, and recent decisions of the European Court of Justice on the European Directive that the Act implements.

In preparing the new edition, we have benefited greatly from discussions with former colleagues at King's College, London, and new colleagues at University of East Anglia and Cardiff, and we thank them for their help and encouragement. Mark Lunney and John Murphy read sections of the new text and made helpful comments, for which we are very grateful. We must also express our gratitude to Rebecca Mashayekh, our editor, and Ann Edmondson who copy-read our text very thoroughly indeed. Alastair Mullis's special thanks go to Camilla, Lara and Max, and Ken Oliphant's to Annelise, for helping them to retain at least some small sense of what is really important in life.

As in previous editions, 'he' and 'she' are used in alternating parts of the book to indicate a person of indeterminate gender.

We have endeavoured to state the law on the material available to us on 1 October 2002.

ALASTAIR MULLIS
KEN OLIPHANT

Table of Cases

Table of Statutes

1 Introduction

1.1 What Is a Tort?

'Tort' is the French word for wrong. (Other terms derived from this root are the adjective 'tortious', the adverb 'tortiously' and 'tortfeasor', the name for a person who commits a tort.) Yet, just as all dogs are animals but not all animals are dogs, so all torts are wrongs but not all wrongs are torts. To make sense of this conundrum, we must distinguish (a) civil wrongs from criminal wrongs; (b) equitable civil wrongs from common law civil wrongs; and (c) the different varieties of common law civil wrongs, some of them known as 'torts', some going under different names.

Criminal and Civil Wrongs

If I punch you in the face, that is both a crime and a civil wrong (both the crime and the tort of battery). The one event gives rise to two legal responses. First, I may be prosecuted by the state for committing the criminal offence and, if found guilty by the court, made to pay a fine to the state, sent to prison or punished in some other way. Secondly, I may be sued by you in the civil courts (the County Courts or the High Court) and, if found liable, ordered to pay you a sum of money (damages) or to change my behaviour in the future (by an injunction). Unlike criminal proceedings, civil actions are brought by individuals, not (generally) the state. Furthermore, it is those individuals, not the state, who stand to benefit directly from a court judgment against the defendant. Because of this, and because the defendant who is held liable is not exposed to the stigma of a criminal conviction, civil actions are possible in many circumstances in which no criminal liability arises. It should be noted, however, that not all crimes give rise to concurrent tortious liability: this is true especially of so-called victimless crimes (e.g. possession of drugs) which have no effect upon other people.

Some would press the distinction between criminal and civil law further and say that the criminal law is designed to punish the defendant while the civil law aims only to vindicate the claimant's rights, but we should not pursue doctrinal purity at the expense of practical convenience. Medieval English law certainly knew no such purity. Criminal proceedings were originally instituted by individuals, for the law enforcement arm of the state did not develop until much later. Furthermore, many proceedings we would now recognise as civil were at least semi-criminal in character: the unsuccessful defendant would be punished as well as being obliged to pay damages, while the defendant who failed to appear in court would not only lose her case but would also be liable to arrest and imprisonment (see Maitland, 1936, pp. 39–40). In view of these beginnings, and of the pragmatic nature of English lawyers throughout history, it is no surprise that the modern criminal and civil law borrow elements from each other. Thus a criminal court may order the guilty party to pay compensation to the victim under s. 35 of the Powers of Criminal Courts Act 1973 as well as passing a criminal sentence. Conversely, the damages awarded by a civil court may include a punitive element designed not to vindicate the claimant's rights but to punish the defendant for her wrongdoing (see 22.2).

Equitable and Common Law Wrongs

Within the category of civil wrongs, history obliges us to make a fundamental distinction between wrongs at common law and wrongs in equity (see Baker, 2002, ch. 6). Before 1875, two distinct court systems existed side by side. The first to evolve had been the common law courts of the King's Bench and Common Pleas. The law applied in these courts was embodied in the 'forms of action', the verbal formulas written on the 'writs' purchased from the Chancellor's office (the Chancery) which authorised citizens to commence an action. In order to mount successful proceedings, litigants of the period had to ensure that the form of words inscribed on the writ matched the substance of their complaint. In the case of the writ of trespass to the person, for example, this required them to establish that, in the florid language of the writ, they had been beaten, wounded and maltreated by force and arms, against the King's peace. With the passage of time, the forms of action became more or less set in stone. Such rigidity in the law led to injustice because litigants were denied the remedy they deserved simply because none of the existing forms of action covered their case.

It was to remedy this injustice that the equitable jurisdiction was developed. (The common law's response to the same problem was to recognise the flexible 'action on the case', yet even this did not go far enough and the writ system was finally abolished by the Judicature Act 1873.) Some of the victims of such injustice took to petitioning the King for help, and in time these petitions came to be passed on to the Chancellor who proved willing to grant relief in some cases where the common law provided no remedy. The grant of this relief was at first purely discretionary, but after a while a body of established rules and principles evolved. A primary concern of these rules was to lay down the circumstances under which property, whose official 'legal' title was held by one person, should be held on trust for another. They thus laid the foundation for our modern law of trusts. For present purposes, the rules are significant for their recognition of a class of equitable wrongs. Examples of equitable wrongs might include an employee 'stealing' a trade secret from her employer in the hope of selling it to a rival, or a company director accepting a bribe to ensure that the company enters into contracts with a particular supplier. The remedies that equity gave in respect of these wrongs differed from the normal common law remedy of damages: the employee might be subjected to an injunction forbidding her to pass on the trade secret to anyone else, while the company director might be required to 'account for' (hand over) the value of the bribe she received.

This equitable jurisdiction, and these equitable remedies, grew up outside the common law courts; however, the Judicature Act 1875 'fused' the two separate systems so that, from that time on, both common law and equitable principles were applied by the same courts. Nevertheless, and despite the views of many judges who – like Lord Diplock in *United Scientific Holdings Ltd* v. *Burnley Borough Council* [1978] AC 904, 925 – believe that 'the waters of the confluent streams of law and equity have surely mingled now', most commentators continue to regard breach of equitable duty as entirely distinct from the civil wrongs at common law. The result is not only that the subjects are treated in different textbooks (breach of equitable duty being consigned to books on equity and trusts), but also that certain equitable remedies, particularly the account of profits made by a wrongdoer, are generally held not to be available in respect of common law wrongs (cf. Birks, 1991). Yet there is one cause of action which seems to straddle both categories. The origins of the law of confidence are in equity, but there is a new tendency to treat breach of confidence as a tort (see, e.g., *Douglas* v. *Hello! Ltd* [2001] QB, 967, 998 per Sedley LJ; cf. the reservations previously expressed by North, 1972). By developing the law of confidence, the courts have been able to increase the level of protection afforded by English law to the right of privacy under art. 8 of the European Convention for the Protection of Human Rights and Fundamental Freedoms (see further 20.1), with which they must now ensure that their decisions are compatible (Human Rights Act 1998, s. 6; see 1.4). The full implications of the judicial recognition of this hybrid 'equitable tort' are yet to be worked out, but any development that reduces the hold of anachronistic legal distinctions is to be applauded.

Torts and Other Common Law Wrongs

Common law wrongs themselves come in different varieties, breach of contract, tort and unjust enrichment being the most familiar. This subdivision of the common law wrongs was unknown to the early common law and only took shape closer in time to the modern era when lawyers looked to impose some order on the many disparate forms of action that history had bequeathed them (see Baker, 2002, pp. 401–2). Their first move was to seize upon a body of law dealing with undertakings or promises and, sharply differentiating breach of promise from other forms of wrong, to develop a set of rules that we recognise today as our law of contract. A comparable, and ongoing, endeavour has been the attempt to formulate a law of unjust enrichment by drawing together a variety of causes of action, many of which had previously been considered to be rather anomalous appendages to the law of contract, torts or equity (see Birks, 1985). The common element of such cases is that the defendant has acquired a benefit which the law requires her to surrender to the claimant. The law of tort is what is left behind after cases of breach of contract and unjust enrichment have been withdrawn from the list of common law wrongs and may be accurately described as 'our residual category of civil liability' (Gilmore, 1974, p. 87).

1.2 **The Classification of Torts**

The status of the law of tort as our residual category of civil liability means that it consists of a 'rag-bag' of disparate cases which very often have little connection with one another. For this reason, it is very difficult to elaborate general principles of the law of tort to match those of the law of contract, which are to be found in any textbook on the subject. The considerations raised by a road traffic accident are very different from those raised by a smear campaign of a public figure conducted in the popular press, which in turn are very different from those raised by industrial action taken by disgruntled employees. All these incidents might lead to liability in the law of tort, but it would be impossible to apply the same principles in relation to each. So when we turn to modern works on the law of tort, we find chapters dealing with principles said to be common to all torts intermixed with discussions of the divergent rules applicable to different kinds of case. These rules are generally listed under the name of a particular tort, but they may come under a heading which groups together a number of different torts. These groupings may be justified on the grounds that the torts are all relevant in a particular context (e.g. 'Liability for Land and Structures'), that they all serve to protect a particular interest (e.g. 'Interests in Reputation'), that they can all be traced back to one of the early common law's forms of action (e.g. 'Trespass'), or that they share a common mental element (e.g. 'Intentional Wrongs').

The different torts that we can identify today often overlap with one another in their application. They are a mixture of 'hand-me-downs' from the age of the forms of action, abolished by the Judicature Act 1873, whose names recall the names of the original writs (e.g. trespass), and later creations, both judicial and legislative. These later judicial creations were attempts to draw together different instances of liability recognised under the old forms of action. The most notable of these is the tort of negligence, which united a variety of instances of liability for damage caused by negligence and was recognised as a fully-fledged tort in its own right only in 1932 (see 2.1). Since that time it has done the work of a number of the older torts and has become the favoured head of claim for many claimants, being the purest expression recognised by the law of the moral notion that wrongdoers should pay for their wrongs.

1.3 **The Organisation of This Book**

This book conforms to type in giving separate treatment to the general principles of tortious liability (Part V) and to the various discrete torts (Parts I–IV). In dealing with the latter, we start with the tort of negligence

(Part I) which merits this prime position by virtue of its present practical importance and its tendency with the passage of time to subsume the other torts under its mantle. When we come to dealing with the remaining torts, we make no pretence of completeness: this is a student book and the torts covered in depth are those that typically feature in tort courses in university. We have omitted detailed coverage of areas of the law that are generally found in the syllabuses of other subjects (thus conversion has been left to the commercial lawyers and intimidation, conspiracy, etc., to courses on labour law). Despite these exclusions, we have been left with a wide-ranging though ramshackle body of law, as befits tort law's status as the great dustbin of civil liability.

To impose some order on this expanse of materials, we have looked at the various torts in terms of the interests they may be said primarily to protect, dealing in turn with interests in the person and personal property (Part II), interests in land (Part III) and interests in reputation and privacy (Part IV). We preface our discussion of the torts selected under each heading with a few words on the extent to which negligence provides protection in each area, and on the continuing importance of the other torts in furnishing additional relief. One major interest has been largely omitted: that in financial well-being. As financial well-being is largely dependent on one's ability to exploit one's labour, goods and land, it is protected by those torts that provide relief in respect of physical interference with the person and personal property (Part II) and with land (Part III). Other torts provide relief even where there has been no physical interference with these interests, as where *I pass off* my goods as yours so that I can sell at a better price or where *I conspire* with militant workers to picket your factory and cause you to cease trading by *intimidating* you with threats of personal violence. The torts of passing off, conspiracy, intimidation and the like are omitted for the reason given above, namely that they are best left to be considered in depth in other, more specialised works. Liability in respect of pure economic loss sustained as a result of another's negligence is, however, dealt with in the chapters on negligence (see ch. 5).

1.4 **Torts and Human Rights**

A new stage of the development of the law of tort began on 2 October 2000. This was the date on which the Human Rights Act 1998 came into effect. Bringing about change in the law of tort was perhaps not the foremost concern in the mind of the legislator, though there was a lot of discussion – both in and out of Parliament – as to whether the Act would enable the courts to fashion a remedy in tort for invasions of privacy. Nevertheless, it is clear that the Act will have a pervasive effect on tort law, much of which will have to be re-examined to ensure that it is human-rights compatible.

For our purposes, the central provision of the Act is to be found in s. 6(1), which states: "It is unlawful for a public authority to act in a way which is incompatible with a Convention right." The Act defines 'Convention rights' by reference to specific provisions of the European Convention for the Protection of Human Rights and Fundamental Freedoms and certain protocols added to it (s. 1). Amongst the most important of these are the right to life (art. 2), the right not to be subjected to inhuman or degrading punishment (art. 3), the right to liberty and security (art. 5), the right to respect for private and family life (art. 8), the right to freedom of expression (art. 10), and the right to the protection of property (art. 1 of the First Protocol). Certain parts of the Convention do not feature in the Act's definition of 'Convention rights' because the Act already contains equivalent provisions.

The effect of the Act on the law of tort is two-fold. First, in what may be termed the Act's 'vertical' effect, it allows any person who is the victim of a public authority's breach of its section 6 duty to bring proceedings against the authority under the Act (s. 7) and, at the court's discretion, to recover damages if this is necessary by way of 'just satisfaction' (s. 8). It is also possible for victims of a public authority's unlawful act under s. 6 to rely upon their Convention rights in other legal proceedings, for example, those brought against them by the authority (ss. 7(1)(b) and (6)). The nature and scope of the new cause of action against public authorities is considered further in 7.3–4.

Secondly, in what may be termed the Act's 'horizontal' effect, it appears that one may rely upon one's Convention rights even in litigation against another private person. This is because the courts are included within the Act's definition of 'public authority' (s. 6(3)) and so must comply with the duty imposed on all public authorities by s. 6(1). The result is that the courts must ensure that *all* their decisions are human-rights compatible, whoever the litigants are, and not just when public authorities are involved. Consequently, it seems that the courts will be required to develop the common law where it does not currently give full weight to Convention rights. This obligation may be regarded as the counterpart of the courts' *express* obligation under the Act to read and give effect to *legislation* in a way which is compatible with Convention rights (s. 3(1)). But the obligation to develop *the common law* is not express: everything depends upon how the courts' s. 6 obligation is interpreted. Already, a range of different opinions has been expressed, with some arguing for 'full horizontality', whereby the violation of Convention rights would automatically be actionable even if perpetrated by a private person (see, e.g., Wade, 2000), and others that the court's duty is only to see that *its procedures* are Convention compliant, and not to develop the substantive law at all (see, e.g., Buxton, 2000). Most likely, the courts will adopt an intermediary position – 'limited horizontality' – which will require them to develop the substantive common law except insofar as this would undermine 'the measure of certainty which is necessary to all law' (*Douglas v Hello! Ltd* [2001] QB 967, 1002 per Sedley LJ). Indeed, in the case of *Venables v News Group Newspapers Ltd* [2001] 1 All ER 908, Dame Elizabeth Butler-Sloss P seems to have taken precisely this approach, stating (p. 918):

'[The] obligation on the court does not seem to me to encompass the creation of a free-standing cause of action based directly upon the articles of the convention ... The duty of the court, in my view, is to act compatibly with convention rights in adjudicating upon existing causes of action, and that includes a positive as well as negative obligation.'

Clearly, this contemplates not only the limitation of tortious liabilities that threaten Convention rights, for example, by increasing the scope of the available defences (the negative obligation) but also the incremental development of existing causes of action so as to protect Convention rights (the positive obligation). It is too early to determine exactly how the courts will fulfil these obligations, but in the rest of this book we shall summarise the developments to date and consider the directions along which English tort law, under the influence of the Human Rights Act, may develop further in the future.

Summary

1.1 A tort is a civil, as opposed to criminal, wrong. The category of civil wrongs contains breaches of contract and equitable wrongs as well as torts.

1.2 Different torts deal with different types of wrongful conduct and developed, often haphazardly, over the course of time. This makes it difficult, if not impossible, to identify general principles about the law of tort.

1.3 In this book, we look at (a) the tort of negligence, the most important tort in both theory and practice; (b) a selection of other torts arranged according to the interest they primarily protect; and (c) such general principles as do exist.

1.4 The passage of the Human Rights Act 1998 will have a significant effect on the law of tort. Its 'vertical effect' is to enable victims of a public authority's violation of their 'Convention rights' to bring a new statutory action against the authority. Its 'horizontal effect' is to require the courts to act compatibly with Convention rights in developing the law, whether in cases involving public authorities or not.

Part I

The Tort of Negligence

2 Negligence: Introduction

2.1 **Origins**

It all began in August 1928. The scene was Minchella's cafe in Paisley, near Glasgow. A certain Mrs Donoghue had gone in for a drink. This is her story: a friend bought her a bottle of ginger beer; she began to drink it; then, as her friend topped up her tumbler, she watched in horror as the decomposed remnants of a snail floated out with the ginger beer; she suffered shock and an upset stomach. Now Mrs Donoghue's injuries may seem of less than earth-shattering importance to us today, but it is to these unlikely beginnings that the modern law of negligence owes its existence. Mrs Donoghue, unable to sue Minchella in the law of contract because she had not bought the bottle herself (there was no 'privity of contract'), brought an action in tort against the manufacturer, Stevenson. She alleged that he had been negligent in producing the drink. In response, Stevenson denied that those injured by a negligently manufactured product had any right to recover damages outside certain exceptional categories (e.g. inherently or patently dangerous products like firearms). The case reached the House of Lords, which found in favour of Mrs Donoghue. It was not a unanimous decision: two powerful dissents were registered. Neither was the decision of the majority clear and unambiguous in every respect: was it to be a rule confined to defective products or was it to have wider effect? Today, however, its status is unquestioned and its effect plain for all to see, for *Donoghue* v. *Stevenson* [1932] AC 562 is the case that changed the face of the law of negligence.

Up to that time, liability for negligent conduct had been recognised only in certain carefully defined circumstances, for example where innkeepers were careless in looking after property in guests' rooms or where fire damage resulted from negligence. The courts allowed actions for damages in these cases because – they said – the special circumstances gave rise to a 'duty of care'. The significance of *Donoghue* v. *Stevenson*, and of Lord Atkin's speech in particular, was that it sought to unify these disparate duties of care in a single general theory. Lord Atkin noted (pp. 579–80) that the courts had previously been 'engaged upon an elaborate classification of duties' as they existed in various fact situations, and urged them to recognise that 'the duty which is common to all the cases where liability is established must logically be based upon some element common to the cases where it is found to exist'. He continued:

'[I]n English law there must be and is some general conception of relations giving rise to a duty of care, of which the particular cases found in the books are but instances. The liability for negligence ... is no doubt based upon a general public sentiment of moral wrongdoing for which the offender must pay. But acts or omissions which any moral code would censure cannot in a practical world be treated so as to give a right to every person injured by them to demand relief. In this way rules of law arise which limit the range of complainants and the extent of their remedy. The rule that you are to love your neighbour becomes in law: You must not injure your neighbour, and the lawyer's question: Who is my neighbour? receives a restricted reply. You must take reasonable care to avoid acts or omissions which you can reasonably foresee would be likely to injure your neighbour. Who then, in law, is my neighbour? The answer seems to be persons who are so closely and directly affected by my act that I ought reasonably to have them in contemplation as being so affected when I am directing my mind to the acts or omissions which are called in question.'

2.2 **The Elements of the Tort of Negligence**

Negligence is a common word, referring to a type of fault, that is often treated as synonymous with 'carelessness'. But since *Donoghue* v. *Stevenson* it has also become the name of a self-contained tort with its own internal framework of rules. The elements of liability in the tort of negligence can be outlined as follows:

(a) the defendant must owe the claimant a *duty of care*;
(b) the defendant must be in *breach* of that duty (i.e. she must be careless or negligent);
(c) the breach of duty must *cause* the claimant loss;
(d) the loss caused must not be too *remote* (i.e. it must be foreseeable);
(e) the defendant must not be able to raise any *defence* to the claimant's action.

   This list of requirements makes it plain that it can be misleading simply to talk of liability for negligence. In the first place, in negligence (which is descended from the action on the case and is not a form of trespass: see 1.1) damage is the gist of the action; there is no liability for negligence 'in the air', only for negligently causing harm. Secondly, *factual responsibility* for negligently causing harm cannot be equated with *legal responsibility*: it is not every harmful result of one's negligence for which one must pay damages. Although Lord Atkin appealed in his 'neighbour principle' to our moral intuitions which suggest that there should be general recognition of tortious liability for harm caused by negligence, he himself stressed the need for 'rules of law ... which limit the range of complainants and the extent of their remedy'. Legal responsibility is thus determined by the concepts of the duty of care and remoteness of damage (and to a certain extent also causation), and by the law relating to defences. Because they have the function of limiting legal responsibility for negligently inflicting injury, those concepts and the various defences can be thought of as limitation mechanisms or control devices in the tort of negligence, keeping liability for (factual) negligence within acceptable bounds.

The distinction between questions of factual and legal responsibility is not clear-cut – even the factual questions of negligence, i.e. breach of duty, and causation are determined within a framework of legal principle, while the 'duty' question raises factual issues of foreseeability and not just issues of law – but it is nevertheless useful for pedagogical purposes. It also has great practical importance, even in a modern system in which questions of fact are determined by a judge rather than a jury. First, questions of law may be dealt with in preliminary proceedings in advance of trial of the factual issues, thereby saving unnecessary expense in calling witnesses, compiling expert reports, etc. (especially where it transpires that the claimant has no case in law). A very common example of this is the striking-out application, in which the defendant makes a pre-emptive attack against the claimant's action, contending that it would reveal no arguable case in law even if the claimant were to make out all the factual allegations; typically the assertion is that there was no duty of care. Secondly, rights of appeal are more extensive in relation to questions of law than questions of fact. Although many of the key questions of what we have been calling 'factual' responsibility in reality relate to *inferences* from primary facts (e.g. as to whether the care exercised by the defendant was reasonable), and can hence be attacked on grounds other than that they were 'plainly wrong', the judge's conclusions on such questions are entitled to respect and should not be rejected simply because the appellate court might itself have ruled differently. Conversely, in relation to questions of law, the appellate court must impose its own view. The treatment of certain preconditions of liability, especially that of 'duty', as questions of law rather than fact enables appellate courts to keep the scope of liability within acceptable bounds, not only by overruling errant decisions but also and more importantly by setting down binding guidelines for use in subsequent cases.

2.3 Negligence: A Developing Tort

In terms of legal history, the tort of negligence is of comparatively recent birth and it remains in its adolescence. It lacks many of the characteristics of a mature system of law, most notably a settled conceptual apparatus and a set of reasonably clear boundaries. In many areas, the question whether liability may arise has yet to be determined. Courts encountering unprecedented claims must grapple with concepts (of duty, causation, remoteness, etc.) which all too often lack any fixed meaning and all too rarely provide a clear answer as to whether a claim should be allowed. This has produced a certain scepticism about the way judges decide cases in the tort of negligence. Some feel that conceptual language is used inconsistently and instrumentally, in order to give an aura of legal respectability to decisions reached on non-legal (policy) grounds. The following, typically bold expression of this view comes from a judgment of that leading judicial sceptic, Lord Denning (*Lamb* v. *Camden LBC* [1981] QB 625, 636):

> 'The truth is that all these three, duty, remoteness and causation, are all devices by which the courts limit the range of liability for negligence ... As I said recently ... "it is not every consequence of a wrongful act which is the subject of compensation." The law has to draw a line somewhere. Sometimes it is done by limiting the range of persons to whom a duty is owed. Sometimes it is done by saying that there is a break in the chain of causation. At other times it is done by saying that the consequence is too remote to be a head of damage. All these devices are useful in their way. But ultimately it is a question of policy for the judges to decide.'

Lord Denning perhaps puts his case too strongly, for it would be wrong to suggest that judges feel free to disregard rules laid down in previous cases and to impose whatever solution they feel is warranted in terms of public policy. Nevertheless, his words stand as a useful indication of the imprecision that surrounds the use of the key concepts in the tort of neligence and of the scope that this imprecision allows for judges to give effect to policy choices.

We should not ignore, however, the extent to which there exists a bedrock of settled principle in the modern law of negligence. The typical cases of everyday legal practice – cases of accidents on the roads or at the workplace – give rise to few legal difficulties: the issue between the parties is more likely to concern questions of fact than questions of law. In this, the 'core' area of negligence, the law is simplicity itself: the person who carelessly injures the person or property of another is liable to compensate for that loss. *Factual* responsibility is equated with *legal* responsibility. Only when we move from the core to peripheral areas of the tort – to cases involving more problematic forms of loss, or omissions rather than positive acts, etc. – do the principles become more complex as the courts struggle to contain liability within acceptable bounds, to limit the scope of legal responsibility for factually causing harm through a lack of care. Here the language of the law reports becomes more abstract and conceptual, and it is difficult to discriminate between the technical-legal employment of certain terms and their purely rhetorical use. In some cases technical-legal definitions of some precision do in fact exist, or may at least be posited, albeit that they can only be identified after stripping away several layers of unnecessary and unrevealing abstraction (see especially the discussion of 'proximity' at 3.5). Elsewhere, however, especially where a case presents novel features, the analysis may amount to no more than a vague appeal to what is reasonable in the circumstances (see 3.6). This perhaps is inevitable in an area of law that is still relatively young and continues to develop rapidly, and, far from being cause for exasperation or despair, accounts in large measure for the fascination of the subject, for study of the modern law of negligence inevitably entails a creative engagement with the principles of justice and the concerns of public policy that shape the law in the light of changing social conditions.

2.4 The Objectives of Negligence Law

Negligence law may be seen as embodying the principle of corrective justice, i.e. that one who wrongfully causes another harm should correct that injustice by the payment of compensation (see especially Weinrib, 1995). But, although the 'righting of wrongs' must be regarded as the central tenet of the tort of negligence (and perhaps of all liability in private law), it is possible to identify certain secondary objectives which serve to temper the law's pursuit of its goal of corrective justice; to see the modern law of negligence as concerned purely with corrective justice is to pay scant regard to its vibrant complexity. The law is shaped not only by 'principle' but also by considerations of public policy which fluctuate in the light of changing social conditions.

A number of secondary objectives may be posited for the tort of negligence: vindication of the claimant's rights, denunciation of the defendant's wrong, education of people generally as to proper standards of safety, the peaceful settlement of disputes arising from the accidental infliction of injury, etc. (for a review, see Williams, 1951). But the two most often cited objectives of negligence law are compensation and deterrence, and it is these that we now proceed to consider in more detail.

Compensation

The provision of compensation is so central to the tort of negligence that it is often regarded as *the* objective of the tort, rather than just as one of its policies. Yet it is helpful to view it as one of many policies pursued in the tort of negligence, for this emphasises that in some circumstances the goal of compensation may be outweighed by other, competing considerations.

It is important to be clear what we mean when we talk of compensation. 'Compensation' is the goal both of the tort of negligence and of the social security system, but the meaning of the term varies according to the context. In the former, it is part of a regime of corrective justice; in the latter, part of a regime of distributive justice. This is reflected in two ways. First, the payment of compensation in negligence depends on a finding that the claimant's loss was caused by fault. In the context of social security, fault is generally irrelevant. Thus we can say that, whereas tort damages are awarded as a matter of individual responsibility, social security benefits are paid as a matter of social responsibility. Secondly, the amount of compensation paid differs according to the context. Damages are designed to compensate for *loss*: the sum awarded is that needed to restore the claimant, as nearly as possible, to the position she would have been in but for the defendant's negligence. Social security benefits, in contrast, aim to compensate for *need*, and benefits are generally limited to the amount necessary to sustain the recipient at an acceptable standard of living.

This is not to say that there has been no cross-fertilisation between the notions of compensation adopted in negligence and social security respectively. Entitlement to social security payments may depend on proof that the claimant's injuries were caused by someone else's fault. This is the case under the Criminal Injuries Compensation Scheme, which provides for the payment of compensation in respect of personal injury attributable to a criminal offence, the arrest of a suspect or the prevention of crime. Awards, formerly assessed in the same way as common law damages, are now made according to a scale of tariffs but remain broadly comparable to damages in terms of size and can be seen as compensating for loss rather than need (see Criminal Injuries Compensation Act 1995). It is also conceivable that social security benefits should be earnings-related rather than flat-rate (as has in the past been the case), and to that extent should compensate for loss rather than need, but the political desire to constrain public expenditure and encourage private provision against the misfortunes of life resulted in the abolition of the earnings-related components of such benefits (see Ogus *et al.*, 1995, pp. 20–1).

Conversely, concerns of social responsibility that underpin the compensation objectives of the social security system have also had an influence on the development of the law of tort, both in the tort of negligence and elsewhere. Certain tort doctrines (the vicarious liability of employers for the torts of their employees, see ch. 21; liability for the breach of strict statutory duties imposed in the workplace, ch. 15) serve to direct losses away from individuals towards defendants whose 'deep pockets' can more easily bear the cost, irrespective of whether they were personally at fault. The influence of such considerations is evident within the tort of negligence itself, notably in the observed tendency of the courts to characterise blameless and inevitable slips as negligence in contexts in which liability insurance is compulsory or common (see 8.3). In fact, these social welfare concerns are also apparent in the introduction of compulsory liability insurance for drivers of motor-vehicles (1933; see now Road Traffic Act 1988, s. 145) and employers (Employers Liability (Compulsory Insurance) Act 1969). But there is an inevitable tension between these social values and the notions of individual responsibility that are entrenched in tort law, which (at least nominally) pits individual claimant against individual defendant. (The reality, however, is that almost 90 per cent of claims are defended by the nominal defendant's insurer: Pearson, 1978, vol. 2, para. 509.) This tension has been heightened by a number of attempts to expand the scope of the duty of care into areas in which popular sentiment has it that the 'victim' should take responsibility for what has occurred. Thus the so-called 'socks' school of psychiatry expresses scepticism about the expansion of liability for psychiatric illness, relying upon its defining tenet that sufferers are best left to 'pull their socks up' (cf. ch. 4). The recognition of duties to protect claimants from third parties, or even from themselves, has also led to claims that we are undermining individual responsibility and inculcating a 'pass the buck' mentality in a 'something for nothing' society (cf. ch. 6). All in all, according to some commentators, we have developed 'a culture of complaintiffs' (Weir, 1996, p. vi).

This popular backlash against the increasing modern tendency to 'pass the buck' and 'chase the bucks' should not, however, divert attention away from society's need to develop a humane, efficient and coherent system of compensating those whose suffering and needs warrant redress. We may doubt whether principles of tort law, in which negligence plays the central role, properly merit a place in such a system. Tort may be seen to be adrift in the 'high Cs' – costly, cumbersome, confrontational and capricious. It is too expensive, takes too long, concerns itself with 'winning' rather than 'justice', and limits compensation to those injured by another's fault (denying it to the victims of 'pure' accidents regardless of the severity of their condition or the extent of their needs). Perhaps compensation should be regarded as a matter exclusively of social responsibility, and the relevant principles of tort law swept away to make space for the introduction of a 'no-fault' compensation scheme offering real compensation to all those suffering from disability. We return to such questions, and consider them in more detail, in ch. 12.

Deterrence

Doubts as to the success of negligence as a mechanism of compensation have prompted some to seek an alternative justification for it in the goal of deterrence (see Cane, 1999, pp. 361–92). They argue that negligence has a major role to play in the prevention of accidents as actual and potential liability costs encourage people to take care in what they do and drive them away from activities that are fraught with unnecessary danger. Thus, if a manufacturer of fizzy drinks thinks that the installation of an Acme Patent Snailguard on her bottling line will reduce the risk of consumers suffering food poisoning, and hence reduce her liability costs, she will have an incentive to go ahead and have one fitted. And if she finds that she still cannot produce the drink without an unacceptable risk of food poisoning, the liabilities she incurs may force her to raise her prices to an extent that she is no longer be able to compete in the market ('market deterrence': see Calabresi, 1970, ch. 5). Nowadays, these arguments are most often made by lawyer-economists, who view the law as a series of incentives designed to promote a state of economic efficiency in which the wealth of society is maximised; the function of negligence thus becomes 'the deterrence of *inefficient* accidents' (Posner, 1992, p. 202; emphasis added). Looking at the law exclusively in these terms is regarded by many as morally disreputable, because it pays no heed to individual rights, which ought not to be sacrificed in the public interest (see Dworkin, 1986, ch. 8). In any case, attempts to evaluate the law of negligence in terms of economic efficiency tend to rely on too many unproven assumptions for them to be of significant practical value (although occasional references to the economic analysis literature will be made in the course of this book).

Again the key question is whether negligence law, and tort law as a whole, performs a deterrent function better than its alternatives. It seems odd at first sight that the threat of liability, which operates indirectly and materialises only where a lack of care results in injury, should be more effective than the 'direct' or 'specific' deterrence achieved by regulation backed up with criminal sanctions; the latter not only allows for liability even where the carelessness fortuitously causes no harm but also enables standards of safe conduct to be specified with a measure of precision quite beyond negligence, where the injunction is simply to take such care as is reasonable in the circumstances. Against this, it may be said that government regulation cannot deal with the complexity and constantly fluctuating circumstances of life and attaches insufficient importance to individual views as to what risks are worth running (see Calabresi, 1970, ch. 6). No conclusive view can be drawn from the evidence on this question (for an excellent survey, see Dewees *et al.*, 1996), but it may perhaps be accepted that such evidence as there is at least puts the burden of proof on those who would replace negligence liability for personal injury with a no-fault compensation scheme to show that other mechanisms are in fact apt to maintain the standards of safety that modern society demands.

Summary

2.1   In *Donoghue* v. *Stevenson*, the House of Lords recognised for the first time a general rule of liability for harm caused by negligence. As a result, it became possible to talk of a tort of negligence.

2.2   Notwithstanding this general rule, liability for the consequences of careless-ness is limited by the requirements of the duty of care, causation and remoteness, and by the various defences that the defendant might raise.

2.3   The tort of negligence is of comparatively recent birth and it is still developing; the precise scope of liability for negligence is still uncertain in a number of key respects.

2.4   Negligence law reflects the principle of corrective justice, but it has been shaped by a variety of competing social policies (e.g. deterrence of accidents, compensation of the victims of accidents).

Exercises

2.1   What was the significance of *Donoghue* v. *Stevenson*?

2.2   In addition to showing that the defendant was in fact negligent, what else must the plaintiff in a negligence action establish?

2.3   What is the difference between 'policy' and 'principle'? Should judges be concerned with both?

2.4   What impact has the desire to compensate the needy had on the development of the tort of negligence? Why should the courts ever want to deny the claim to compensation of someone injured by another's negligence?

2.5   What role might the tort of negligence have in accident prevention? Is there a danger of going too far?

3 The Duty of Care Concept

3.1 The Nature of the Duty of Care Concept

Not every instance of carelessness resulting in harm will lead to liability in the tort of negligence. Liability is limited by reference to various 'control devices' (see 2.2) of which the most significant is the duty of care. The existence of a duty of care is a precondition of liability in negligence; it is what transforms *factual* responsibility for carelessly causing harm into *legal* responsibility.

In most cases encountered in practice – e.g. cases of foreseeable physical injury suffered in accidents at work or on the roads – the existence of a duty of care is clearly established by the authorities (see *Alcock* v. *Chief Constable of South Yorkshire Police* [1992] 1 AC 310, 396). The only question will be whether the defendant was *in fact* negligent (in breach of duty). In such cases, the moral imperative expressed by Lord Atkin in his 'neighbour principle' points towards liability on the part of the person at fault. But other cases are not so simple. Deviation from the 'typical' case of physical injury caused by positive act, by one private individual to another, may necessitate a more cautious approach to the imposition of liability and bring the duty of care issue 'into play'. There may be doubts as to whether the loss of which the claimant complains should be recoverable (especially in cases of mental injury or pure economic loss). Alternatively, the doubts might concern the way in which the claimant's loss was caused (especially where it results from the defendant's statement or omission). Or they might arise because the defendant is a public authority, not a private individual.

The duty of care concept marks out these cases – the 'atypical' cases – in which it cannot be taken for granted that the defendant should pay compensation for carelessly caused harm. And it determines whether the special circumstances of these cases are sufficient to outweigh the claimant's moral claim to compensation. Hence the concept's role is essentially negative. As Lord Goff stated in *Smith* v. *Littlewoods Organisation Ltd* [1987] 1 AC 241, 270, 'nowadays ... the broad general principle of liability for foreseeable damage is so widely applicable that the function of the duty of care is not so much to identify cases where liability is imposed as to identify those where it is not'. The duty of care question is raised in order to deny liability even where the defendant was at fault, and even if that fault caused the claimant harm. To deny the existence of a duty of care is to shield the defendant from liability no matter how culpable her carelessness and no matter how severe the claimant's injury.

3.2 **Testing the Existence of a Duty of Care**

How do we know when a duty of care will be recognised? The courts have wavered between different approaches to this question. In *Caparo Industries* v. *Dickman* [1990] 2 AC 605, 616, Lord Bridge described the 'traditional' approach as follows:

> 'Traditionally the law find the existence of the duty in different specific situations each exhibiting its own particular characteristics. In this way the law has identified a wide variety of duty situations, all falling within the ambit of the tort of negligence, but sufficiently distinct to require separate definition of the essential ingredients by which the existence of the duty is to be recognised.'

From the time of *Donoghue* v. *Stevenson* onwards, however, the courts began to find the traditional approach wanting. It lacked any basis in principle for determining whether the frontiers of liability should be pushed forward or the *status quo* maintained. So judges sought to identify the principles by which the existence of a duty of care could be determined.

The most celebrated of such attempts was made by Lord Wilberforce in delivering the opinion of the House of Lords in *Anns* v. *London Borough of Merton* [1978] 1 AC 728, 751–2. He laid down a two-stage test of the existence of a duty of care:

> 'First one has to ask whether, as between the alleged wrongdoer and the person who has suffered damage, there is a sufficient relationship of proximity or neighbourhood such that, in the reasonable contemplation of the former, carelessness on his part may be likely to cause damage to the latter, in which case a prima facie duty of care arises. Secondly, if the first question is answered affirmatively, it is necessary to consider whether there are any considerations which ought to negative, or to reduce or limit, the scope of the duty or the class of person to whom it is owed or the damages to which a breach of it may give rise.'

The most natural interpretation of this passage is that it lays down a presumption of liability where the defendant, in the circumstances in which she found herself, *ought to have foreseen* injury to the claimant. This will be a question of fact to be determined by the judge in every case. The judge then has to decide whether to decline to allow recovery on grounds of public policy. This interpretation of Lord Wilberforce's words found favour for some time and judges soon began to adopt them enthusiastically as a simple test of liability in negligence. Subsequently, however, the courts expressed dissatisfaction with this way of proceeding and resorted instead to a more cautious, case-by-case approach reminiscent of that taken prior to the great decision in *Donoghue* v. *Stevenson* [1932] AC 562 (see 3.3).

So what was wrong with Lord Wilberforce's two-stage test? Essentially, the problem was that it provided the springboard for a massive expansion of liability in the late 1970s and early 1980s. The first stage of Lord Wilberforce's test presented no hurdle to litigants at all: almost everything in life is foreseeable if you have a vivid enough imagination. This meant that the courts were left to restrict the scope of negligence liability by reference to the policy considerations that come in at the second stage of Lord Wilberforce's test. In fact, judges proved unwilling to let matters of public policy stand in the way of their understandable sympathy for the injured plaintiffs in court before them. As Lord Keith subsequently observed (*Rowling* v. *Takaro Properties Ltd* [1988] AC 473, 501):

'[A] too literal application of the well-known observation of Lord Wilberforce in *Anns* ... may be productive of a failure to have regard to, and to analyse and weigh, all the relevant considerations in considering whether it is appropriate that a duty of care should be imposed.'

In key cases such as *McLoughlin* v. *O'Brian* [1983] 1 AC 410 and *Junior Books* v. *Veitchi Co Ltd* [1983] 1 AC 520 (see 4.2 and 5.3), judges roundly condemned the policy arguments which were said to justify restrictions on liability. The 'floodgates' argument (see 3.6), in particular, was dismissed in cavalier fashion ('I believe that the "floodgates" argument ... is, as it always has been, greatly exaggerated': *McLoughlin* v. *O'Brian* [1983] 1 AC 410, 442 per Lord Bridge). The results were twofold. First, the courts recognised duties of care in a wide variety of situations that had not previously come before the courts (e.g. in respect of 'wrongful birth': see 7.2). Secondly, and more controversially, judges used the two-stage test as a justification for recognising duties of care whose existence had previously been denied, thereby casting aside restrictions on liability that had been recognised in older cases (particularly in the context of economic loss and omissions). It was this tendency that raised judicial concerns and prompted a 'retreat from *Anns*'. As Lord Brandon commented in *Leigh & Sillivan Ltd* v. *Aliakmon Shipping Co Ltd* [1986] AC 785, 816, it was an error to use the test 'as a means of re-opening issues relating to the existence of a duty of care long settled by past decisions'.

3.3 *Caparo* and the Retreat from *Anns*

Unhappy with the way things were shaping up, courts in the late 1980s and early 1990s sought to reverse many of the developments of the previous 20 or so years. This led to a so-called 'retreat from *Anns*'. In a series of decisions (beginning perhaps with *Peabody Donation Fund* v. *Parkinson* [1985] AC 210), appellate courts warned against the lazy reliance upon too simple a test of liability, and sought to reassert limits on the scope of liability that had traditionally been recognised in the caselaw (e.g. in the areas of pure economic loss, mental injury and omissions). These decisions insisted that the questions of 'foreseeability' and 'proximity', apparently run together by Lord Wilberforce, be clearly separated out, and that the concept of 'proximity' be dissected to reveal 'the narrower but still identifiable principles ... [on the basis of which] ... liability can properly be imposed' (*Smith* v. *Littlewoods Organisation Ltd* [1987] 1 AC 241, 280 per Lord Goff).

The decisive moment in this trend was the speech of Lord Bridge in *Caparo Industries* v. *Dickman*. He suggested that the courts should abandon 'the modern approach' of looking for a single general principle underlying the tort of negligence and revert to 'the more traditional categorisation of different specific situations as guides to the existence, the scope and limits of the varied duties of care which the law imposes.' His approach depended upon a 'pragmatic' evaluation of the exact circumstances of every individual case, but certain general observations could be made. In a passage of great influence and importance, he explained (pp. 617–18):

> '[I]n addition to the foreseeability of damage, necessary ingredients in any situation giving rise to a duty of care are that there should exist between the party owing the duty and the party to whom it is owed a relationship characterised by the law as one of 'proximity' or 'neighbourhood' and that the situation should be one in which the court considers it fair, just and reasonable that the law should impose a duty of a given scope on the one party for the benefit of the other. But ... the concepts of proximity and fairness embodied in these additional ingredients are not susceptible of any such precise definition as would be necessary to give them utility as practical tests but amount in effect to little more than convenient labels to attach to the features of different specific situations which, on a detailed consideration of all the circumstances, the law recognises pragmatically as giving rise to a duty of care of a given scope.'

Although it appears that Lord Bridge intended in this passage to rule out any simple recourse to a universal formula for determining the existence of a duty of care, subsequent decisions have seen him as laying down a three-stage test for recognition of the duty under which the questions of 'foreseeability', 'proximity' and 'fairness, justice and reasonableness' replace the two stages of the discredited *Anns* inquiry. This trend is probably too well-established to buck at the present time, but it should be remembered that the so-called '*Caparo* principles' represent no more than useful shorthand in indicating the *types* of factors which determine whether a duty of care will arise. The principles provide a *framework* for inquiry into the existence of the duty by identifying the principal *stages* of that inquiry, but they do not in themselves provide a practical test of the duty; treating them as such is likely to produce the same liability 'beanfeast' as was alleged to follow from *Anns*. The following explanations are an attempt to rationalise the role of the key elements of the *Caparo* principles, although it must be admitted that judicial expressions of opinion on this issue are often inconsistent and that this attempt therefore has elements of prescription as well as mere description.

3.4 Foreseeability

The claimant must fall within the class foreseeably put at risk by the defendant's failure to exercise due care and skill. The same requirement is expressed by the principle that the defendant must be in breach of a duty of care owed to the claimant rather than to the world at large: what singles the claimant out is that she was the foreseeable victim of the defendant's wrong. The rule serves to weed out claims by those whose injury is regarded as far-fetched in much the same way as the *Wagon Mound* rule of remoteness of damage weeds out heads of damage that are unforeseeable consequences of the defendant's negligence (see ch. 10). Like the remoteness rule, the issue it raises is primarily one of fact, and this stage of the duty inquiry may therefore be termed the question of 'factual duty' (cf. Clerk and Lindsell, 2000, para. 7–07).

The most famous elaboration of the principle that only the foreseeable claimant can recover damages in negligence is that attempted by Cardozo J in the New York Court of Appeals in *Palsgraf* v. *Long Island Rail Road* 248 NY 339 (1928). The case also provides a memorable example of the principle at work. Mrs Palsgraf was injured while standing on a railway platform. Some distance away, commotion had broken out as a man, running to catch a train that was beginning to move out of the station, was pushed on board by railway employees. The man dropped an apparently innocuous paper package. In fact, it contained fireworks and exploded on contact with the ground. The shock waves caused heavy metal scales near to Mrs Palsgraf to topple over and strike her, causing her injury. (Or were the scales merely knocked over in the commotion? See Prosser, 1953.) The majority of the court held that the railway employees owed her no duty of care as she was not a foreseeable victim of their negligence; it was not enough that their negligence exposed others to risk. Cardozo J explained:

'One who seeks redress at law does not make out a cause of action by showing without more that there has been damage to his person. If the harm was not willful [*sic*], he must show that the act as to him had possibilities of danger so many and so apparent as to entitle him to be protected against the doing of it though the harm was unintended. The victim does not sue derivatively, or by right of subrogation, to vindicate an interest invaded in the person of another. He sues for a breach of a duty owing to himself.'

In England, the same sort of analysis was soon to appeal to the House of Lords in the case of *Bourhill* v. *Young* [1943] AC 92. The case arose out of a motorcycle accident. The motorcyclist, John Young, who was killed, had been travelling too fast and had collided with a car a short distance away from where Mrs Bourhill was standing. She was eight months pregnant at the time of the accident and she alleged, in a suit against Young's estate, that hearing the impact and seeing the pool of blood afterwards had caused her to miscarry and to suffer nervous shock. The House of Lords found that Young could not have been expected to foresee that anyone in the position of Mrs Bourhill could be affected. The following words of Lord Wright call to mind the reasoning of Cardozo J (p. 108):

> 'John Young was certainly negligent in an issue between himself and the owner of the car which he ran into, but it is a different issue whether he was negligent *vis-à-vis* the appellant. She cannot build upon a wrong to someone else. Her interest, which was in her own bodily security, was of a different order from the interest of the owner of the car.'

The requirement of the foreseeable claimant has attracted criticism on the grounds that, as between innocent victim and careless injurer, the equities favour the former (see Fleming, 1998, p. 159). It may also be criticised in that the test of foreseeability is easily manipulated and may serve merely to obscure the policy considerations that have caused the courts to develop the law as they have. One learned overseas observer, a former President of the New Zealand Court of Appeal, has detected signs that 'the English Courts are coming to speak of reasonable foresight in a deliberately artificial sense' and has warned of the need to take care lest the concept be 'employed to conceal the fact that the decision is one of policy rather than one as to what was reasonably foreseeable in fact' (*South Pacific Manufacturing Co* v. *New Zealand Security Consultants & Investigations Ltd* [1992] 2 NZLR 282, 295 per Cooke P). This temptation most frequently arises in cases involving so-called 'secondary' victims. Even the most typical of tort cases may involve losses that extend beyond the immediate victim of the tortfeasor. Those who suffer as a result of a car accident may include those injured in rescue attempts, the bystanders who suffer psychiatric illness as a result of witnessing the scenes of carnage, the relatives who have to spend time and money to care for their disabled family members and the taxpayer whose contributions fund the emergency services and the National Health Service (NHS). None of these 'ripple effect' losses can be regarded as far-fetched. Nevertheless, some types of secondary victims (e.g. rescuers) habitually gain compensation in the courts on the grounds that they are foreseeable claimants, while others (e.g. bystanders, like Mrs Bourhill, who suffer nervous shock) are regarded as unforeseeable and have to go without. In fact, this has nothing to do with the probability of loss to the various parties; rather it reflects the law's view of the desert of each and the consequences of recognising liability. This was seen clearly by Andrews J when, in his dissenting judgment in *Palsgraf*, he derided the manipulation of the foreseeability device in such cases as 'merely an attempt to fit facts to theory'.

The better approach, evident in many recent decisions, is to distinguish such issues of legal policy from the factual duty question, i.e. the question of foreseeability. These issues relate to the question of 'legal' or 'notional' duty (cf. Clerk and Lindsell, 2000, para. 7–06), whose existence determines whether liability is *in principle* capable of arising on facts analogous to those in the present case (given for instance the nature of the claimant's loss, the means by which it was caused and the identity of the parties). The legal duty question has two components – 'proximity' and 'fairness, justice and reasonableness' – to which we now turn our attention.

3.5 **Proximity**

The requirement that the claimant stand in a relationship of proximity with the defendant is now of central importance in the tort of negligence. Although 'proximity' was once equated with 'reasonable foreseeability' (such that a relationship was presumed to be proximate wherever it was reasonably foreseeable that negligence by one party might cause harm to another: see the discussion of *Anns* above at 3.3), it has now assumed an independent existence, and acts in many cases as the primary determinant of whether a duty of care will arise. Its meaning, however, must be considered elusive. It is not to be interpreted literally as referring to 'closeness' either in time or space: its use is as a legal term of art. Yet, even understood as such it may conceal more than it reveals, for there is a tendency to affirm the presence or absence of proximity on the facts of an individual case without adequate explanation. There is considerable truth in Weir's wry observation (1991) that 'Proximity is now the key word, though it doesn't open many doors'.

Yet the meaning of proximity need not remain obscure. It is no more than what Lord Bridge described in *Caparo* as a 'convenient label' identifying 'the features of different specific situations which ... the law recognises pragmatically as giving rise to a duty of care' (see 3.3). It is an error to regard it as having an immutable core meaning such as to give it utility as a practical test of whether a duty arises; rather it is the generic name for *all* the more specific – and practically useful – tests for the existence of the duty which have been established in different types of case. Different 'proximity principles' apply in different duty situations. In what we have been calling the 'typical' or 'core' cases of negligence – cases of personal injury caused by the positive act of a private individual – the proximity rules generally add nothing to the requirement of foreseeability (albeit that the question of proximity remains theoretically distinct: see *Marc Rich & Co AG* v. *Bishop Rock Marine Co Ltd, The Nicholas H* [1996] AC 211): it may be said that it is the reasonable foreseeability of injury that establishes the necessary proximity. But as we move towards the problematic peripheral areas of the tort – towards cases involving different forms of loss, or an omission rather than a positive act, or some other 'atypical' feature – 'proximity' imposes a more substantial hurdle. For example, where the claimant complains of mental injury as a result of witnessing an accident, a number of new proximity requirements arise: the claimant must show a proximate relationship (i.e. a close tie of love and affection) with the 'primary victim' of the accident; she must have been 'proximate' to the accident (literally, this time) in time and space, etc. (see further ch. 4). Equally, in cases where the claimant's loss is purely economic, the authorities hold that there can be no proximity between the parties unless the defendant has 'voluntarily assumed responsibility' for the performance of a particular task (see further ch. 5). Here, it is the voluntary assumption of the responsibility that establishes the necessary proximity.

The concept of proximity thus refers to the established legal rules – varying from one duty situation to another – that determine whether liability is *in principle* capable of arising. These rules can only be found in the caselaw, so the first injunction to the negligence lawyer is: 'see how far the authorities have gone' (*Hedley Byrne & Co* v. *Heller & Partners* [1964] AC 465, 526 per Lord Devlin). Analysis of the caselaw need not, of course, reveal a clear answer, for there may be disagreement as to the precise scope of a rule in a particular case (did it depend on factors (a), (b) *and* (c), or just (a) and (b)?). Nevertheless, the court must ultimately take a view on this question, and determine whether or not the authorities conclusively establish the presence or absence of proximity in the case at hand. If the matter is as yet unresolved (e.g. if the case is a novel one), the court must decide whether or not to recognise a relationship of proximity in the new situation. In such a case, there is a good deal of overlap between the second and third stages of Lord Bridge's approach in *Caparo* v. *Dickman*, for the court should only conclude that a relationship of proximity exists where the imposition of liability would be 'fair, just and reasonable'.

In general, the courts have adopted a cautious approach to the recognition of new relationships of proximity: the range of duty situations should only be extended, as one Australian judge has put it, 'incrementally and by analogy with established categories' (*Sutherland Shire Council* v. *Heyman* (1985) 157 CLR 424, 481 per Brennan J). Yet 'incrementalism' has its own dangers and two caveats are necessary. First, to say that extensions of the scope of the duty of care should be allowed only incrementally is not to indicate the principles which determine *whether* such extensions should be allowed: it merely prescribes that those principles should be narrowly defined. The need to identify the relevant principles remains. As one of the leading practitioners' works states, incrementalism should be seen to 'support rather than supplant the development of principles as the basis for determining the existence and scope of the duty of care' (Clerk and Lindsell, 2000, para. 7–21). Secondly, there is a danger that the principles by which step-by-step expansions of the duty are permitted will reflect arbitrary features of previously decided cases rather than the essential merits of the claimant's action against the defendant; liability may turn upon history rather than justice. In short, as an Irish judge has astutely noted, 'the verbally attractive proposition of incremental growth ... suffers from a temporal defect – that rights should be determined by the accident of birth' (*Ward* v. *McMaster* [1988] IR 337, 347 per McCarthy J). This concern may however be alleviated if judges are prepared to allow a measure of flexibility – and sensitivity to the underlying merits of the claim – in the development of rules at the proximity stage.

3.6 Fairness, Justice and Reasonableness

A duty will only be recognised where it is fair, just and reasonable to hold the defendant liable to the claimant. Like the question of proximity, the question of fairness reflects matters of legal policy. Where proximity deals with principles already developed in the caselaw, consideration of the fairness of the claimant's case allows the court to raise matters of policy on an *ad hoc* basis. Fairness is 'raw' policy; proximity is policy 'crystallised' into legal principle.

The courts have not always been prepared openly to acknowledge the extent to which policy choices influence their decisions. Understandably, many judges have been keen to play down their political role by emphasising that their task is merely to apply principles developed over the course of time in case after case. They recognise that they have no special training or democratic mandate to determine issues of social or economic policy and that a trial involving only two parties may deny a hearing to many with a legitimate interest in its outcome. The best-known elaboration of this position is found in Lord Scarman's speech in *McLoughlin* v. *O'Brian* [1983] 1 AC 410, 430:

> 'By concentrating on principle the judges can keep the common law alive, flexible and consistent, and can keep the legal system clear of policy problems which neither they, nor the forensic process which it is their duty to operate, are equipped to resolve. If principle leads to results which are thought to be socially unacceptable, Parliament can legislate to draw a line or map out a new path.'

This approach may be criticised for trusting too much in Parliament's willingness to intervene where the common law produces injustice and Lord Scarman's speech attracted a sharp rebuke from Lord Edmund Davies in the very same case. The latter asserted that 'public policy issues *are* "justiciable"' (p. 428) and it seems that the current House of Lords would agree. Indeed, in a series of recent decisions, their Lordships have embarked upon an open and full discussion of policy considerations relevant to the question whether it was fair, just and reasonable to impose a duty of care (e.g. in *White* v. *Jones* [1995] 2 AC 207 (see 5.6), *X (Minors)* v. *Bedfordshire County Council* [1995] 2 AC 633 (see 7.3), and *Barrett* v. *Enfield London Borough Council* [2001] 2 AC 550).

Such issues of fairness arise in two types of case. First, they must be invoked where the proximity issue is unresolved by binding precedent (as where the situation before the court is novel). Here it is up to the claimant to demonstrate the fairness of recognising a duty. A typical strategy is to reinforce the claimant's basic claim to corrective justice by reference to the 'secondary purposes' of negligence liability (see 2.4), e.g. by alleging that denial of duty would deprive a certain class of people of all prospect of compensation, there being no 'alternative avenue of protection' (see *White* v. *Jones*; Stapleton, 1995), or would remove the primary mechanism for deterring a certain type of wrongdoing. Secondly, where the court accepts that there is proximity between the parties, considerations of whether it is fair, just and reasonable to allow a claim may serve to rebut the prima facie inference of a duty of care, provided that the courts do not simply allow the defendant a 'blanket immunity', which would appear to be contrary to the Human Rights Act 1998 (see 3.7). Here attention is often directed at the so-called 'floodgates' and 'overkill' arguments, which we now turn to consider in more detail.

'Floodgates'

The so-called floodgates argument has often been deployed as a justification for the refusal to recognise alleged liabilities in negligence. However, despite the frequent judicial recourse to the argument, there is considerable confusion as to what it stands for and what weight should be attached to it (see 3.2). The argument takes many different forms (see Bell, 1983, ch. 3) and it is not always clear in which sense a court means to use it. Sometimes it focuses attention on the administration of the courts and points to the risk that the courts, were they to allow a particular type of claim, might be swamped with more claims than they could handle. This form of the argument seems rather weak, for the more people that suffer a particular wrong, the more reason there is for the courts to redress it. Another variation of the floodgates argument commands greater respect. This focuses on the defendant and asks whether it is fair to expose her to liability. A court may find that it is not fair where the extent of the liability would be too great ('excessively burdensome') or too indeterminate: as the American judge Cardozo J remarked, in a phrase that has often been adopted in English decisions, the courts should be wary of imposing 'liability in an indeterminate amount for an indeterminate time to an indeterminate class' (*Ultramares Corpn* v. *Touche* 174 NE 441, 444 (1931)).

The floodgates argument is becoming increasingly linked with fears about the ability of the liability insurance industry to cope with the demands placed on it. Such fears warrant serious attention, for the ability of the tort of negligence to furnish the victims of accidents with compensation depends on the efficient operation of the liability insurance market. Without insurance, the process of compensation through the tort of negligence would effectively grind to a halt. The principal fear is that the continuing expansion of the tort of negligence threatens to 'overload' the liability insurance system. Insurers are now exposed to potential liabilities of such an extent that they have become wary of undertaking new business (see Alexander, 1972) They are also concerned for their continued existence, because their liabilities under policies they have already issued may considerably exceed their estimates, which may not have taken account of recent developments in the law. Furthermore, the liabilities that insurers face have become increasingly indeterminate in size, especially as a result of the recent judicial willingness to allow claims for so-called 'ripple effect' losses suffered by an unpredictable number of 'secondary victims' of accidents (see Stapleton, 1991). This indeterminacy inhibits insurers in the necessary task of adjusting their premiums in line with the risks they take on, with the result that insureds who are better able to forecast their own liabilities may opt to self-insure; if they do so in sufficient numbers, the insurance market will simply 'unravel' (see Priest, 1987).

Although the courts have repeatedly held that the existence of liability insurance is in itself no reason for upholding a damages claim against the insured (see *Davie* v. *New Merton Board Mills Ltd* [1959] AC 604; *Morgans* v. *Launchberry* [1973] AC 127), the above analysis suggests that the difficulty of insuring against excessive and indeterminate liabilities may make it unfair to recognise a duty of care. Admittedly, insurance-based arguments are rarely deployed explicitly by the courts. But such arguments do seem to have a certain force and have on occasion been invoked, e.g. in *Caparo Industries plc* v. *Dickman* [1990] 2 AC 605, 643 where Lord Oliver warned against the imposition of a duty of care on company auditors for fear of opening up 'a limitless vista of uninsurable risk'. In the light of continuing concerns about the health of the Lloyd's of London insurance market, we may expect courts increasingly to make the link between the floodgates argument and the so-called 'insurance crisis'.

The Danger of Overkill

Just as the floodgates argument warns of the risk of pursuing a policy of *compensation* too single-mindedly, the overkill argument points out the deleterious consequences that arise if the *deterrent* effect of negligence liability is too great. The argument was considered in some depth by Lord Keith in *Rowling* v. *Takaro Properties Ltd* [1988] AC 473, 502. His Lordship explained:

> 'It is to be hoped that, as a general rule, imposition of liability in negligence will lead to a higher standard of care in the performance of the relevant type of act; but sometimes not only may this not be so, but the imposition of liability may even lead to harmful consequences. In other words, the cure may be worse than the disease.'

In 'the overkill scenario', those threatened with liability respond by taking unnecessary safety precautions or by giving up a socially beneficial activity altogether. Impressed by the risk of such detrimentally defensive conduct, the House of Lords has ruled that it is not fair, just and reasonable to impose a duty on local authorities in discharging their functions *vis-à-vis* the prevention of child abuse (*X (Minors)* v. *Bedfordshire County Council* [1995] 2 AC 633) or on the police in their investigation of crime (*Hill* v. *Chief Constable of West Yorkshire* [1989] AC 53; but see 3.7 below). Another example is provided by *The Nicholas H* [1996] AC 211, in which their Lordships decided that considerations of fairness also precluded any claim in negligence by cargo owners after the loss at sea of a vessel that had recently been surveyed and certified as fit to sail by an international maritime classification society. According to Lord Steyn, who spoke for the majority of the House of Lords, the classification society's performance of its public role, as a 'non-profit-making entity, created and operating for the sole purpose of promoting the collective welfare, namely the safety of lives and ships at sea', might be jeopardised by the threat of liability. Classification societies might be induced to adopt 'a more defensive position', e.g. by declining to take on high-risk business, where their services were most necessary, or by diverting their resources away from their primary task of saving lives and ships. This risk (among others) outweighed the countervailing argument, advanced by Lord Lloyd (dissenting), that the recognition of a duty would induce classification societies to take due care in surveying vessels, promoting safety at sea and thereby addressing concerns within the shipping community about declining standards.

There is some evidence that the overkill argument is being approached with greater scepticism than before, (see, e.g., *Barrett* v. *Enfield London Borough Council* [2001] 2 AC 550, considered below at 7.4). In the past, it seemed all too often to be the case that the courts simply relied upon speculation and second-hand knowledge, e.g. as the alleged 'liability crisis' in the USA (on which, see Huber, 1988). Not untypical is the following dictum of Purchas LJ (*Greater Nottingham Co-operative Society Ltd* v. *Cementation Piling and Foundations Ltd* [1989] QB 71, 95):

> 'That this is a field in which the law has properly applied policy restrictions [on the scope of liability] is justified by a glance at the position reached on the other side of the Atlantic where damages awarded in respect of medical and surgical negligence is, it is believed, affecting the proper execution by surgeons of their professional tasks to the detriment of the patients.'

In the absence of real evidence of such questions, reliance upon overkill arguments can only be speculative and intuitive, and the risk of inconsistency is high. For example, although the House of Lords in *Hill* was swayed by the danger that the risk of liability might induce police officers to adopt a detrimentally defensive frame of mind in investigating crime, it had previously rejected such arguments in respect of officers at a training camp for young offenders (*Home Office* v. *Dorset Yacht Co Ltd* [1970] AC 1004). Memorably dismissing any analogy with US authority where the overkill argument had succeeded, Lord Reid stated (p. 1033):

> 'It may be that the public servants of the State of New York are so apprehensive, easily dissuaded from doing their duty, and intent of preserving public funds from costly claims, that they could be influenced in this way. But my experience leads me to believe that Her Majesty's servants are made of sterner stuff.'

As now seems to be widely recognised, there are considerable doubts about the strength of the overkill argument in some of the situations in which it is employed. Courts should be reluctant to dismiss otherwise deserving claims for damages on the basis of grounds as flimsy as a mere 'glance at ... the other side of the Atlantic' and should bear in mind Lord Browne-Wilkinson's prescription that 'the public policy consideration which has first claim on the loyalty of the law is that wrongs should be remedied and that *very potent* counter-considerations are required to override that policy' (*X (Minors)* v. *Bedfordshire County Council* [1995] 2 AC 633, 749; emphasis added).

3.7 The Impact of the Human Rights Act 1998

The enactment of the Human Rights Act 1998 is likely to have some impact on the way in which the courts approach duty of care issues. However, it seems at present that they will maintain the existing framework of the *Caparo* principles – though for a while even this was placed in doubt (see below) – and that no radical change to existing practice will be required.

It will be recalled that the courts, as 'public authorities' under the Act, must act compatibly with Convention rights in reaching their decisions (see 1.4). This is the basis of the Act's so-called 'horizontal' effect, that is, its impact even in proceedings brought by one private individual against another. Inevitably, the *substantive* rights in the Convention – for example, the right to life (art. 2) and the right not to be subjected to inhuman or degrading punishment (art. 3) – will affect decisions as to whether or not a duty of care arises in particular contexts, perhaps being brought in under the question of fairness, justice and reasonableness. It may be, for instance, that the courts will have to review their blanket denial of any duty to rescue, which is now subject to only limited exceptions, in view of their obligation to uphold the right to life (see 6.7). The impact of substantive Convention rights on particular duty situations is considered, where appropriate, in the chapters that follow.

Here, our concern is with the impact of the apparently *procedural* right to a fair trial in art. 6 of the European Convention. Recent decisions of the Court of Human Rights indicate that, despite appearances, art. 6 goes beyond purely procedural matters and applies also to the substantive law. In *Osman* v. *United Kingdom* [1999] 1 FLR 193, the Court made a number of fundamental criticisms of the role of the duty of care concept in English law, finding that the striking-out of a claim on the basis of 'no duty' was on the facts a violation of the right of access to a court which was to be implied into art. 6. Fortunately, the evidence of more recent decisions from Strasbourg is that the Court has resiled significantly from the hostile stance it adopted in *Osman*, and recognises the legitimacy of the English courts' basic approach to duty of care questions.

Article 6(1) of the European Convention states: 'In the determination of his civil rights and obligations or of any criminal charge against him, everyone is entitled to a fair and public hearing within a reasonable time by an independent and impartial tribunal established by law.' As these procedural guarantees would be meaningless if there were no right of access to a court, the Strasbourg court has read such a right into art. 6 by way of necessary implication (*Golder* v. *United Kingdom* (1975) 1 EHRR 524). Where violation of the right of access is alleged, the Court approaches the matter in two stages. First, it determines whether art. 6 is applicable by considering whether there is an arguable basis for the applicant's contention in domestic law. If this is resolved in the applicant's favour, the Court must then address the question of compliance and decide whether there was a violation of the right to a court on the facts. What is decisive here is whether the applicant's right to a court was actually restricted and, if so, whether such restriction served a legitimate aim and was a proportionate means of achieving that aim (*Ashingdane* v. *United Kingdom* (1985) 7 EHRR 528).

We shall now consider how the above principles were applied by the Court in the *Osman* decision. The case arose out of the fatal shooting of a man whose son had become an object of infatuation to the killer, a former teacher at the boy's school named Paget-Lewis. Over a period of several months, Paget-Lewis had pursued a campaign of harassment against the boy and his family, in the course of which he caused damage to their property. These incidents were reported to the police, who interviewed Paget-Lewis and other teachers at the boy's school. Eventually, the police decided that there was sufficient evidence to make an arrest, but by this time Paget-Lewis had moved away from the area and the police did not succeed in arresting him. Some months later, Paget-Lewis returned to the area and, in a violent attack, wounded the boy and killed his father. In subsequent proceedings, the claimants (the boy and his mother) alleged that the police had been negligent in failing to prevent Paget-Lewis from carrying out the attack. The police sought to strike out the claim as disclosing no cause of action and in *Osman* v. *Ferguson* [1993] 4 All ER 344 their application was successful before the Court of Appeal, which found, applying the decision of the House of Lords in *Hill* v. *Chief Constable of West Yorkshire Police*, that it would not be fair, just and reasonable to impose a duty of care on the police in respect of their investigation of crime. However, when the claimants brought an application under the European Convention, the Strasbourg court ruled that the English Court of Appeal had violated their right of access to a court under art. 6. (For other aspects of this decision, see 7.4.)

The reasoning of the ECtHR on this point is perhaps not entirely transparent, but two threads of analysis may be identified. First, the ECtHR seems to have considered that the striking-out procedure employed in the domestic courts (see further 2.2) deprived the Osmans of their right to a full trial of their action on the merits. Secondly, to complement this procedural concern, there was some suggestion that the domestic law of negligence might fall foul of art. 6 *as a matter of substantive law*, in that the Court of Appeal's reliance upon the third stage of the *Caparo* test (fairness, justice and reasonableness) effectively allowed the police a blanket immunity from liability, which was a disproportionate and therefore unjustifiable restriction on the Osmans' right of access to a court. Neither aspect of the judgment struck English lawyers as terribly convincing, for the right of access to a court presupposes that the claimant has some 'right' that can be vindicated there, and the denial of duty on grounds of fairness, justice and reasonableness meant that there was no right on which art. 6 could bite. As Lord Browne-Wilkinson explained, 'a holding that it is not fair, just and reasonable to hold liable a particular class of defendants whether generally or in relation to a particular type of activity is not to give immunity from a liability to which the rest of the world is subject. It is a prerequisite to there being any liability in negligence at all that as a matter of policy it is fair, just and reasonable in those circumstances to impose liability in negligence' (*Barrett* v. *Enfield London Borough Council* [2001] 2 AC 550, 559). Further, once it was conceded that there was no right in substantive law, it would be pointless to require the action to go to full trial as the most the Osmans could have got was 'a declaration that, apart from the public policy preventing suits against the police, they would have had a claim in negligence against the police' (ibid.).

Despite the flaws in the Court of Human Rights' analysis, the English courts responded by adopting a much more cautious approach to striking-out than previously, especially where the case turned on considerations of fairness, justice and reasonableness (see further 7.3). In the meantime, it seems, there was considerable behind-the-scenes lobbying of the Strasbourg court with the result that, in two recent decisions delivered on the same day, the Court seems to have retreated significantly from the position it adopted in *Osman. Z* v. *United Kingdom* [2001] 2 FLR 612 and *TP and KM* v. *United Kingdom* [2001] 2 FLR 549 were cases that arose out of the decision of the House of Lords in the group of appeals reported under the name *X (Minors)* v. *Bedfordshire County Council* [1995] 2 AC 633. Both concerned the responsibilities of local authority social services departments in deciding whether or not to take children deemed to be at risk of abuse into their care. The cases are considered in more detail below (7.4). What is important here is to note that the House of Lords had struck out actions in negligence against the local authorities whose decisions were impugned, relying on the third stage of the *Caparo* approach. From this point of view, the domestic decision seemed indistinguishable from that of the Court of Appeal in *Osman* v. *Ferguson*. But, instead of following its *Osman* ruling, the Court of Human Rights stated that its earlier decision had been based on an understanding of the domestic law of negligence which had had to be 'reviewed'. On the procedural question, the court accepted that the striking-out procedure did not in itself offend the principle of access to court, as it merely addressed the question whether, if their factual allegations were assumed to be true, the applicants had an arguable cause of action in law. Once the House of Lords had ruled that they had no arguable case in law, the applicants could no longer claim any right under art. 6 to a hearing on the facts. On the substantive question, the Court accepted that the test of fairness, justice and reasonableness was an 'intrinsic element of the duty of care' and that ruling out a claim for failure to satisfy that test did not amount to the operation of an immunity.

This seems to be a pretty comprehensive backtracking from the worrying implications of the *Osman* case, but we should not assume too quickly that art. 6 has no relevance at all to decisions on the question of duty in English law. Even in its two recent decisions, the ECtHR seems to have proceeded on the basis that a finding of 'no duty', although it did not amount to the operation of an immunity, did not preclude further scrutiny of the domestic court's decision under art. 6 , though it found on the facts that the House of Lords had carefully weighed up the policy reasons for and against the imposition of liability on the local authorities in the circumstances of the cases with which it was concerned. The implication seems to be that the English courts will have to consider the policy arguments afresh each time they are raised, even if (as in *Osman* v. *Ferguson*) they consider the facts of the case indistinguishable from those of a binding authority. How this can be squared with the doctrine of precedent is not immediately apparent.

Decisions of the Court of Human Rights must be taken into account by the domestic courts where a question arises of a person's Convention rights, but they are not strictly binding on them (Human Rights Act 1998, s. 3). Nevertheless, it is likely that they will endeavour to apply Convention rights in a manner that is consistent with the Strasbourg jurisprudence, and that they will at least pay lip-service to the art. 6 decisions. Now that the Court of Human Rights has gone some considerable way to addressing domestic concerns about its *Osman* decision, it seems that the domestic courts can continue to approach questions of duty in much the same way as before, with the minor qualification that questions of fairness, justice and reasonableness will have to be assessed anew on every occasion that they arise.

Summary

3.1 The existence of a duty of care is a precondition of liability in the tort of negligence. In cases where the positive acts of a private individual cause physical damage, the existence of such a duty can be presumed, but in other cases the question whether a duty of care exists may be problematic.

3.2 The courts have wavered between different approaches to the question when a duty of care will be recognised. In *Anns*, Lord Wilberforce advanced a presumption of a duty of care where the parties were in a relationship of proximity such that it was reasonably foreseeable the defendant's negligence would injure the plaintiff. This approach led to a rapid expansion of the scope of liability in negligence.

3.3 The last several years have seen a retreat from *Anns* in an attempt to restrict the scope of liability for negligence. Rather than seeking a single general principle of liability, the courts have reverted to the traditional approach of identifying different specific situations in which a duty of care arises. The situations share a number of common features.

3.4 First, the claimant must have been a foreseeable victim of the defendant's negligence (the question of 'duty in fact').

3.5 Secondly, the claimant must stand in a relationship of proximity with the defendant (the first aspect of the 'legal' duty question). The requirement of 'proximity' has no fixed and immutable content, and is merely a convenient label for identifying the features of those situations which give rise to a duty of care.

3.6 Lastly, it must be fair, just and reasonable to hold the defendant liable to the claimant (the second aspect of the 'legal' duty question). The courts have restricted liability under this heading by reference to a number of policy considerations (e.g. the floodgates and overkill arguments).

3.7 The introduction of the Human Rights Act 1998 is likely to have some effect on the way in which courts approach questions of duty. The 'substantive' Convention rights should be taken into account in determining whether or not a duty of care arises. The apparently procedural right of access to a court under art. 6 of the Convention, despite some indications to the contrary in the Court of Human Rights' decision in *Osman* v. *United Kingdom*, seems broadly consistent with the *Caparo* approach to the existence of a duty.

Exercises

3.1 What purpose does the duty of care concept serve?

3.2 What considerations do you think Lord Keith had in mind when he said that 'a too literal application of the well-known observation of Lord Wilberforce in *Anns* ... may be productive of a failure to have regard to, and to analyse and weigh, all the relevant considerations in considering whether it is appropriate that a duty of care should be imposed' (*Rowling* v. *Takaro Properties Ltd*)?

3.3 What differences are there between the approaches of the courts to the duty of care concept at the beginning of the 1980s, at the beginning of the 1990s, and at the beginning of the new millennium?

---

4 Mental Injury

4.1 Introduction

The area of liability for mental injury is one of the most controversial in the modern law of negligence. Traditionally, the courts were reluctant to allow claims for what was dismissively termed 'nervous shock', fearing a flood of all-too-easily fabricated claims and misguidedly thinking that psychiatric illness was less serious than physical injury. Advances in medical science have now largely dispelled former prejudices about the reality of psychiatric illness (*McLoughlin* v. *O'Brian* [1983] AC 410, 433 per Lord Bridge: 'no less real and frequently no less painful and disabling'), and generated confidence in the ability of medical practitioners to diagnose it accurately and root out false claims (Law Commission, 1998, paras. 3.31–2). The law has consequently had to re-evaluate its position too, though not perhaps as quickly and fully as some critics would have hoped (see, e.g., Mullany and Handford, 1993). There are still several significant respects in which liability for mental injury is more restrictive than that for physical harm, especially in the context of so-called 'secondary victims'. As one Australian judge has wryly observed, it has been a case of the law 'marching with medicine but in the rear and limping a little' (*Mount Isa Mines Ltd* v. *Pusey* (1970) 125 CLR 383, 395 per Windeyer J).

It is well-established that one who suffers physical injury as a consequence of another's negligence can recover compensation for the mental consequences of that injury. The award is described as one for 'pain and suffering' (see 22.6). But where the claimant's injuries are purely mental, it is normally necessary to show that they amount to a 'positive psychiatric illness' (*McLoughlin* v. *O'Brian* [1983] AC 410, 431 per Lord Bridge). The tort of negligence does not generally recognise claims in respect of 'mere' grief, anxiety, distress or fear unaccompanied by physical injury (*Hicks* v. *Chief Constable of South Yorkshire Police* [1992] 2 All ER 65: Hillsborough victims' fear of death; *Reilly* v. *Merseyside Regional Health Authority* (1995) 6 Med LR 246: claustrophobia and fear from being trapped in lift). In this respect, negligence may be contrasted with the torts of intentional trespass to the person – assault, battery and false imprisonment – which are actionable without proof of damage, meaning that awards of damages for mental distress are quite permissible and, indeed, commonplace (see generally ch. 13). It should be noted, however, that the negligent performance of a service may give rise to liability for mental distress where it is undertaken under a contract of which it was a major or important object to give the client pleasure, relaxation or peace of mind (*Farley* v. *Skinner* [2001] UKHL 49, [2001] 4 All ER 801: negligence of surveyor in investigating likely noise from airport close to house client was intending to buy).

Whether the claimant's mental condition amounts to a positive (i.e. recognised) condition is a matter for the court after hearing expert evidence from psychiatrists. As the medical profession's understanding of psychiatric conditions develops, so the law may recognise new varieties of nervous shock. Since the late 1980s, attention has focused upon post-traumatic stress disorder (PTSD), the condition at the centre of many high-profile law suits around that time (the actions arising from the sinking of the ferry *Herald of Free Enterprise* in Zeebrugge harbour, the fire at King's Cross Underground station and the Hillsborough football stadium disaster are prominent examples). The condition is provoked by an event of an exceptionally threatening or catastrophic nature and may manifest itself in a variety of symptoms, including sleeping disorders, tension and depression. PTSD for the first time received judicial recognition in the litigation following the Hillsborough tragedy in which 96 fans were crushed to death as a result of overcrowding (*Alcock* v. *Chief Constable of South Yorkshire* [1992] 1 AC 310). The understandable recent focus on PTSD should not, however, cause us to overlook other forms of psychiatric illness – e.g., anxiety and depressive disorders – which are perhaps more common consequences of mental trauma.

It should be noted that the term 'mental injury' is also apt to describe cases where a sudden shock triggers physical damage, as where a traumatic event triggers a heart attack. In *Bourhill* v. *Young* [1943] AC 92, the plaintiff (a pregnant woman) suffered a miscarriage after coming upon the scene of a road accident in which the defendant motor cyclist was killed. The House of Lords held that she was owed no duty of care. The court's reasoning is perhaps not as transparent at that to be found in the more recent caselaw, but undeniably it was important that the plaintiff was put in no danger of physical impact by the accident, had no prior relationship with the deceased, and was considered – on account of her pregnancy – to be unusually vulnerable to mental trauma. These factors would no doubt dictate the same result if the case were to be decided again today, and it is submitted that the approach adopted by the courts in cases of psychiatric illness is equally applicable to cases where mental trauma produces a physical injury. This outcome is especially desirable given uncertainty within the medical profession as to whether particular conditions arising from mental trauma are more appropriately regarded as physical or psychiatric in nature (see especially *Page* v. *Smith* [1996] 1 AC 155, in which doubts as to the exact nature of the condition known as myalgic encephalomyelitis (ME) or chronic fatigue syndrome (CFS) were noted but considered irrelevant to the outcome of the case).

4.2 The Distinction between Primary and Secondary Victims

A fundamental distinction is now drawn between 'primary' and 'secondary' victims, though the Law Commission (1998, para. 5.45) has noted that there is 'confusing inconsistency' as to how the line should be drawn. The following definitions are adopted here: a primary victim is a person who was within the zone of physical danger created by the defendant's negligence, i.e. someone who might foreseeably have suffered physical harm, but who only actually suffers mental injury; a secondary victim is a person who suffers mental trauma as a result of someone else's physical injury, or as a result of fear that such injury might occur. Broadly speaking, liability to secondary victims is more restrictive than liability to primary victims, being limited by a number of proximity requirements which do not apply to claims by the latter. These are explored in more detail below (4.3).

At one time or another, the term 'primary victim' – or its equivalent, 'participant' – has been applied to various categories of claimant other than those physically endangered by the defendant's negligence. In *Alcock* v. *Chief Constable of South Yorkshire Police* [1992] 1 AC 310, 407–8, Lord Oliver stated that a person effecting a rescue necessitated by the defendant's negligence was also 'involved, either mediately or immediately, as a participant' in the accident itself, and not merely a witness to it, as was the person who acted as an innocent agent in bringing about an accident which was really someone else's fault. As we shall see, the House of Lords subsequently ruled that Lord Oliver's dictum did not accurately state the law applying to rescuers, who it now appears are only primary victims if actually exposed to physical danger in the course of the rescue (*White* v. *Chief Constable of South Yorkshire Police* [1999] 2 AC 455; see 4.5).

This still leaves a number of cases in which the primary/secondary victim distinction (as defined above) does not work because *no one* is physically endangered by the defendant's negligence. The most obvious example is employment-related stress, claims which the courts have begun to allow in the last few years. In the leading case (*Hatton* v. *Sutherland* [2002] EWCA Civ 76, [2002] ICR 613), the Court of Appeal treated these as a variety of primary victim claim (para. 21, per Hale LJ), but a better basis for the employer's duty in such cases is an assumption of responsibility for the employee's mental health arising as a necessary incident of the employment relationship. Analogous assumptions of responsibility may warrant the recognition of a duty to prevent psychiatric illness in the context of a number of other established relationships, e.g. between doctor and patient.

In *W* v. *Essex County Council* [2001] 2 AC 592, 601, Lord Slynn remarked that 'the categories of those claiming to be included as primary or secondary victims are not as I read the cases finally closed. It is a concept to be developed in different factual situations'. It is respectfully submitted, however, that the categories of primary and secondary victims need to be defined with a measure of precision, and that it is a mistake to impose the terminology on the various new types of claim – e.g. for occupational stress – which are now coming before the courts. There is a clear risk that judicial attempts to restrict liability to secondary victims will become redundant if too many claimants are treated as primary victims. If there is to be an expansion of liability for psychiatric illness beyond the accepted categories, this must be on a principled basis – with the principle justifying the new liability clearly articulated (e.g. an assumption of responsibility for the claimant's mental health).

4.3 Primary Victims

Where the claimant is personally exposed to the risk of physical harm it is sufficient that some form of personal injury – whether occasioned by physical or psychiatric means – be foreseeable. It is not necessary to show that injury *by shock* was itself foreseeable. This was determined by the House of Lords in its decision in *Page* v. *Smith* [1996] 1 AC 155, disapproving a dictum of Lord Denning in *King* v. *Phillips* [1953] 1 QB 429, 441 that 'the test for liability for shock is foreseeability of injury by shock'. Lord Denning's approach held good in the witness or 'secondary victim' cases to be considered below, but had no place in relation to claims brought by 'primary victims'.

Page v. *Smith* concerned a car crash described as being 'of moderate severity'. The plaintiff was driving with due care when, suddenly and without warning, the defendant, coming in the opposite direction, turned into his path. The impact caused some physical damage to the cars but none to the occupants. Three hours later, however, the plaintiff felt exhausted and took to his bed. The exhaustion continued and the plaintiff never fully recovered. At the time of appeal, and despite the lapse of almost eight years, the plaintiff had not yet returned to work. The diagnosis was the recrudescence of the condition known as myalgic encephalomyelitis or chronic fatigue syndrome; the plaintiff had suffered from a mild form of this sporadically in the past, but it now became an illness of chronic intensity and permanency. The principal defence was that it was not reasonably foreseeable that a person of normal fortitude would have suffered psychiatric injury in such circumstances. The House of Lords, by a bare majority (Lord Keith and Lord Jauncey dissented), held that this was irrelevant. Lord Lloyd, who delivered the leading speech, held that where *injury by physical means* was foreseeable the plaintiff could be regarded as a 'primary victim' of the accident and it was not necessary to show that *injury by psychiatric means* was also foreseeable; it made no difference that the plaintiff might have been abnormally susceptible to the onset of ME/CFS, for this affected only the foreseeability of injury by psychiatric means, not the foreseeability of injury *howsoever caused*. Lord Lloyd added that in these primary victim cases there was no need for the plaintiff to satisfy the various proximity requirements applicable to claims brought by secondary victims.

Page v. *Smith* is a subtle case that requires careful attention. It has a twofold significance. First, it makes clear the importance of the distinction between the person within the 'area of impact' or 'zone of danger' (i.e. at risk of injury by physical means) and the witness, with liability to the former being much easier to establish. But the question of what constitutes the area of impact or zone of danger is far from straightforward. Suppose a fire in the engines of an aeroplane causes it to crash in a residential area after the pilot has struggled for minutes to keep it in the air (see Trindade, 1996, p. 24). Are all those with such fragile personalities that they suffer anxiety disorder from seeing the aircraft's descent and fearing it might crash onto them to be regarded as primary victims? If so, it appears that a very large number of claims might arise out of a single incident. It seems likely that the courts will try to avoid such an outcome by defining the relevant zone of danger in narrow terms. Secondly, the decision in *Page* v. *Smith* elaborates the nature of the harm that must be foreseeable in order to satisfy the test of remoteness of damage. In laying down that the claimant need generally show only the foreseeability of some personal injury, whether by physical or psychiatric means, the case seems to put forward a rule applicable to all personal injury, not just to mental harm (see further ch. 10).

4.4 Secondary Victims

As has been indicated, the courts have adopted a restrictive approach towards those who suffer mental injury from witnessing another person's exposure to physical danger ('secondary victims'). In order to prevent a flood of claims arising from a single incident, they have limited the scope of the duty of care owed to secondary victims by requiring them to satisfy a number of special proximity requirements – and a stiffer test of foreseeability than applies to primary victims.

The foundations for the modern approach to the resolution of secondary victim claims were laid in the speech of Lord Wilberforce in *McLoughlin* v. *O'Brian* [1983] AC 410, which was endorsed by the House of Lords in its decision in the case of the Hillsborough relatives, *Alcock* v. *Chief Constable of South Yorkshire Police* [1992] 1 AC 310. Lord Wilberforce had adopted a conservative approach, in which he began by asking how far the previous decisions had gone in recognising claims by secondary victims, and then considered whether public policy warranted an incremental expansion in the class of claims that would be allowed. In his view, the existing caselaw showed that there were three key limitations on the scope of the duty of care. These related to 'the class of persons whose claims should be recognised; the proximity of such persons to the accident; and the means by which the shock was caused' ([1983] AC 410, 422). There had to be a close relationship between the plaintiff and the primary victim, the plaintiff had to be proximate to the accident in time and space, and the injury had to come through sight or hearing of the event. In the case before him, the plaintiff did not fall exactly within these established categories, as she had seen the accident victims – members of her close family – in the casualty ward of the hospital to which they were taken, and had not witnessed the accident itself. But Lord Wilberforce was prepared to allow an incremental development in the law so as to enable a claimant who came upon the immediate aftermath of the accident, even if not at the actual scene, to satisfy the requirement of proximity in time and space.

The rest of the House of Lords agreed with Lord Wilberforce's resolution of the case in the plaintiff's favour, but adopted a rather different approach. Where Lord Wilberforce proceeded by analogy with decided cases, and was prepared to allow only incremental developments beyond what had previously been decided, the other members of the House rejected what they saw as arbitrary and rigid limitations on liability, Lord Bridge urging that 'we should resist the temptation to try yet once more to freeze the law in a rigid posture which would deny justice to some who ... ought to succeed' (p. 443). The majority of the House preferred to start from the presumption that liability should arise wherever the plaintiff's psychiatric injury was the reasonably foreseeable consequence of the defendant's negligence, and would only have limited liability on an ad hoc basis where policy militated against recovery in the instant case. (Lord Scarman dissented on this point, pursuing his rather idiosyncratic argument that concerns of public policy have no place in private law adjudication: see 3.6.)

Although these differences of approach were undoubtedly present in *McLoughlin*, they were ignored in *Alcock*, where the House of Lords unanimously chose to adopt Lord Wilberforce's analysis. *McLoughlin* v. *O'Brian* remains, however, a classic illustration of the two broad types of approach to establishing a duty of care later identified by Lord Bridge in *Caparo* v. *Dickman* [1990] AC 605 (see 3.2). Ironically, however, it was Lord Wilberforce, whose speech in *Anns* gave most impetus to the recognition of duties of care on the basis of a single general principle, who adopted a cautious, incremental approach in *McLoughlin*, and Lord Bridge, who in *Caparo* advocated the incremental approach, who wanted to apply a simple test of foreseeability, reined in by policy only on a case-by-case basis.

We shall now consider in more detail the requirements that must be satisfied if a secondary victim is to establish a duty of care.

Foreseeability of Psychiatric Illness

The claimant must first demonstrate that it was reasonably foreseeable that a person of normal fortitude would have suffered psychiatric illness as a result of the defendant's negligence (*Page* v. *Smith* [1996] 1 AC 155, 189 per Lord Lloyd). Where the psychiatric illness results only by reason of an abnormal sensitivity (i.e. in circumstances in which a normal person would not have been affected), no liability will arise. In *Bourhill* v. *Young* [1943] AC 92, the plaintiff was a pregnant woman who alleged that she suffered a miscarriage as a result of witnessing an accident in which the defendant motorcyclist was killed. She heard the accident occur, and came immediately to the scene where she saw the blood left on the road by the dead man. She was not related to him in any way. Five weeks later, she suffered a miscarriage. On those facts, the House of Lords held that it was not reasonably foreseeable that a person of normal fortitude (or 'customary phlegm', as Lord Porter put it: [1943] AC 92, 117) would have suffered nervous shock. Their Lordships considered, on perhaps less-than-convincing evidence, that her pregnancy made her abnormally vulnerable and that other passers-by would have had the fortitude to withstand the traumatic scenes.

This is a stricter test of foreseeability than applies generally in the tort of negligence. Usually it is enough that *the claimant's* injury was foreseeable, not injury to some hypothetical person of normal fortitude, and it is well-established there may be a duty to take special precautions for those who are abnormally vulnerable (see *Haley* v. *London Electricity Board* [1965] AC 778: roadworks to be rendered safe for blind people). As we have seen (4.3), this reformulated foreseeability test does not apply to primary victims, who need only show that some injury, whether physical or psychiatric, was the foreseeable consequence of the defendant's negligence. It is applied to secondary victims' claims because policy considerations dictate that liability in such cases should be kept within narrow bounds.

It is important to realise, however, that the claimant's abnormal susceptibility to injury does not preclude the recovery of damages altogether. Once *some* psychiatric harm is foreseeable to a person of normal fortitude, a person whose abnormal susceptibility aggravates the injury sustained is entitled to recover to the full extent of her loss (*Brice* v. *Brown* [1984] 1 WLR 997).

Proximity of Relationship

The secondary victim must establish a 'close tie of love and affection' with a person injured or endangered by the event in question. The most detailed analysis of this issue is to be found in the decision of the House of Lords in *Alcock* v. *Chief Constable of South Yorkshire Police* [1992] 1 AC 310, one of the cases that arose out of the Hillsborough football stadium tragedy. This was a test case, consolidating a number of separate appeals that exemplified the different legal issues raised by hundreds of actions brought in the aftermath of the tragedy by friends and relatives of those caught in the crush at the Leppings Lane end of the ground. The diagnosis in each case was of post-traumatic stress disorder. Various relationships with those in the Leppings Lane pen were represented, including those between children, grandchildren, brothers and fiancés. The House of Lords held that they all had to be subjected to the requirement of a close tie of love and affection.

Precisely how one measures love and affection is an issue on which their Lordships were silent. It appears that the courts are entitled to presume the existence of the requisite ties in certain relationships, such as those of parent and child, spouses and – going beyond the relationships specified by Lord Wilberforce in *McLoughlin* – fiancés (p. 398, per Lord Keith). Their Lordships denied, however, that the relationship between brothers is such as to allow the same presumption to be made, for the quality of relationship between siblings is recognised to vary enormously, and it was for this reason that the claim of one of the Hillsborough plaintiffs was dismissed. In these and other relationships, the claimant must lead evidence to prove a special bond of affection existed between her and the victim. (Is the judiciary ready to hear our courtrooms swell with the sounds of wailing and gnashing of teeth on the part of claimants seeking to establish their love for the deceased?) In fact, in another action brought by a Hillsborough relative, a half-brother of one of the deceased, the court did accept that there was the necessary tie of love and affection, describing the family in question as 'very close-knit' (*McCarthy* v. *Chief Constable of South Yorkshire Police*, unreported; noted in *Daily Telegraph*, 12 December 1996). Conversely, in the case of relationships in which a special bond is to be presumed, it is open to the defendant to seek to rebut the presumption of liability, for example by showing that a married couple had fallen out several years ago and were virtual strangers. As Weir (1992) has pointed out, 'this will be very messy in practice', and risks causing 'perplexity to advisers and embarrassment to litigants' (p. vi).

Although in the majority of cases the claimant will have to prove the existence of a special bond of affection between herself and the primary victim, the House of Lords was not prepared to rule out the possibility that a mere bystander might recover if the circumstances of a catastrophe occurring close-by were especially horrific. By way of example, Lord Ackner envisaged a passer-by who witnesses a petrol tanker careering out of control into a school in session and bursting into flames, and commented that he would not exclude the possibility of liability on such facts (p. 403). He failed to explain, however, why they would be regarded as more horrific than the terrible events at Hillsborough. Subsequently, the Court of Appeal has indicated that it is not prepared to recognise a duty to a mere bystander even in the case of an exceptionally horrific accident. In *McFarlane* v. *EE Caledonia Ltd* [1994] 2 All ER 1, the plaintiff brought an action alleging PTSD arising out of the Piper Alpha disaster in which a blazing inferno engulfed an oil platform in the North Sea, killing 164 people. The plaintiff had witnessed the scenes from a support vessel which was engaged in the effort to fight the fire and came within 100 metres of the rig. One of the grounds on which he submitted he was owed a duty of care by the owners of the rig, who accepted responsibility for the fire, was that the fire was exceptionally horrific. He relied upon the dictum of Lord Ackner noted above. The Court of Appeal declined to follow the learned Lord of Appeal, citing objections both practical and principled. In the first place, there was no scale against which could be measured the horror generated by any particular accident. In addition, Lord Ackner's unexpressed premise – that recovery should be allowed in particularly horrific cases because it was more foreseeable that psychiatric damage would result – effectively reduced the duty of care issue to the single general principle of foreseeability, an approach that is now discredited.

Can a claimant establish a close tie of love and affection with an item of property? Some support for an affirmative answer to this question can be derived from the decision in *Attia* v. *British Gas* [1988] QB 304. Mrs Attia, having earlier in the day let the gasman in to install central heating, returned home to find her house in flames. She alleged that she suffered a serious psychological reaction as a result. The Court of Appeal accepted that liability for psychiatric damage might arise in such circumstances. It considered that, as the gas company undeniably owed a duty not to cause physical damage to the house, the question of whether the plaintiff could claim also for psychiatric damage was simply one of remoteness, in relation to which the only relevant consideration was the foreseeability of her injury. This analysis may be criticised in that the question of whether a duty is owed must be addressed in relation to each of the different types of loss suffered by the claimant. The fact that she can recover for *some* loss (e.g. property damage or personal injury) does not entail that she can recover for *all* her losses purely on satisfying the court of their foreseeability. A more satisfactory basis for the decision is that a person's home is of such emotional significance that its loss is comparable with, though not to be equated to, the loss of a loved relative (cf. Law Commission, 1998, para. 2.49). Focusing on the emotional attachment to the property rather than on its mere ownership would also obviate the need for unfortunate discriminations between the owners of property and others (e.g. their children) who might suffer equal shock and loss but lack any legal interest in the family home.

Proximity in Time and Space

The original requirement that the claimant had to suffer mental injury as a result of experiencing the traumatic event unfold was relaxed in *McLoughlin* v. *O'Brian* [1983] AC 410. It is now sufficient that she comes upon its 'immediate aftermath'. The issue of what counts as an accident's immediate aftermath remains problematic despite attempts to clarify it in the leading cases, and seems destined to be approached in an intuitive and impressionistic fashion.

In *McLoughlin* v. *O'Brian,* the plaintiff suffered nervous shock after a car crash involving her husband and three children. One child was killed; the others were badly injured. Mrs McLoughlin had been at home at the time the accident happened. She was told the grim news an hour or so afterwards by a friend who drove her to the hospital. There, she saw the surviving members of her family – bruised and battered, covered in grime – and heard their sobs and screams. Subsequently, she suffered the condition of which she complained. Although Mrs McLoughlin had not actually gone to the scene of the crash but only to the hospital, the House of Lords was content to treat her as having come upon the accident's immediate aftermath. It appears that a decisive consideration was that, at the time of her visit, the injured family members 'were in the same condition [as they had been immediately after the accident], covered with oil and mud, and distraught with pain' (p. 419, per Lord Wilberforce). If they had been washed and cleaned and operated upon, it seems that the necessary element of immediacy would have been lacking (*Jaensch* v. *Coffey* (1984) 155 CLR 549).

In *Alcock*, the House of Lords held that the immediate aftermath did not extend to cover those who had attended at temporary mortuaries some nine hours or more after the disaster in order to identify bodies. Lord Jauncey distinguished *McLoughlin* v. *O'Brian* on the basis that the lapse of time in the Hillsborough case was much greater and that the visits were made not for the purpose of rescuing or giving comfort to a victim, but purely for the purposes of identification (pp. 423–4). His Lordship warned, however, against attempting to draw up any exhaustive catalogue of examples that would fall within the immediate aftermath and his words should not be treated as precluding claims by those who do not come upon the aftermath in order to make a rescue or give comfort. Thus the woman who returns home to find the charred body of her husband, electrocuted by a defectively wired product, should be able to argue she had come upon the immediate aftermath of the accident. Unlike the plaintiffs in *Alcock*, she would have had no chance to steel herself in advance of exposing herself to the tragic scenes.

Proximity of Perception

The basic rule is that the claimant must personally perceive the shocking event or its immediate aftermath. In *McLoughlin*, Lord Wilberforce contrasted cases where an accident, or its immediate aftermath, was witnessed in person with those in which the victim was told of the accident by a third party. Only in the former type of case did he consider that liability would arise (see further *Ravenscroft* v. *Rederiaktiebølaget Transatlantic* [1992] 2 All ER 470 (note)). He reserved his judgment on the question of whether watching live television coverage of an accident, or employing any other 'equivalent of sight or hearing', would suffice. The issue subsequently came before the House of Lords in *Alcock*. On the facts, the House concluded that those plaintiffs who had only viewed the disaster on television or listened on the radio, or who had merely been told about it, were barred from recovering for that reason. Their Lordships urged that the interpolation of television coverage between event and observer robbed the scenes of their sudden impact upon the senses. All their Lordships, however, confined their decision to the facts in front of them and Lord Ackner was prepared to accept that there might be occasions on which television pictures would have at least as great an impact on observers as actual presence at the scene. An example of such a case would, he said, be where parents viewed live television pictures of a special event of children travelling in a hot-air balloon in which the balloon suddenly burst into flames and plummeted to the ground (p. 405). Perhaps the crucial distinguishing factor in this case is that the parents knew their children would be injured whereas in the Hillsborough case the television viewers, unable to make out recognisable individuals in the crowd, merely feared that their friends and relatives would be caught up in the crush.

There remains some uncertainty as to whether the person communicating distressing news can be liable for mental injury suffered as a consequence. Two types of case can be imagined. The first is where the defendant passes on erroneous information about the fate of the claimant's close relative. In Australia, it has been held that a duty of care can arise in such circumstances, and liability was imposed where state authorities told the plaintiff falsely that her husband had been admitted to an asylum (*Barnes* v. *Commonwealth* (1937) SR (NSW) 511). The issue has not yet arisen in England, though the existence of the duty was conceded in *Allin* v. *City & Hackney Health Authority* [1996] 7 Med LR 91 where the plaintiff recovered damages for PTSD she developed after being told that her baby had died during childbirth; six hours later, she learnt that the child was actually still alive. The second case is where the communicant tells no lies but pays no regard for the claimant's sensibilities, e.g. by giving unnecessarily gory details of a loved one's death or by printing or broadcasting close-up pictures of the death. Recognition of a duty in such circumstances may be thought particularly undesirable because, quite apart from the questions of free speech it would raise (see Dziobon and Tettenborn, 1997), it is difficult to square with the lack of any duty owed by the person actually responsible for the death (see *Alcock*, above). The matter remains to be tested in English law, though the existence of a duty was conceded in one case before the Court of Appeal, *AB* v. *Tameside & Glossop Health Authority* [1997] 8 Med LR 91, where patients of the defendant health authority complained of the way in which they had been told of the very remote risk that they had been infected by a health worker who had been diagnosed as HIV positive. There was no liability on the facts because the patients failed to show any failure to exercise reasonable care.

Injury Must be Caused by Shock

In the case of a secondary victim, it is necessary to show that the mental injury was occasioned *by shock*. It is not enough that the harm be caused by a series of events that result in the gradual accumulation of pressures on the nervous system. In *Alcock*, Lord Ackner stated that, in his opinion, the absence of any 'shock' would preclude liability where a spouse was worn down by caring for a tortiously-injured husband or wife and where a parent was distressed by the wayward conduct of a tortiously brain-damaged child (p. 400; see also p. 407, per Lord Oliver). The need for a shock was confirmed by the decision of the Court of Appeal in *Sion* v. *Hampstead Health Authority* [1994] 5 Med LR 170, where the plaintiff, alleging negligence in the hospital treatment of his son after a motorcycle accident, stayed at his bedside for a period of two weeks, during which he saw his son deteriorate in health, fall into a coma and die. The court struck out his claim for damages for the psychiatric illness he claimed to have suffered as a result, partly on the basis that the illness could not be regarded as resulting from shock but only from a process which continued for some time (cf. *Tredget* v. *Bexley Health Authority* [1994] 5 Med LR 178, where the two days between the birth and death of the plaintiff's baby constituted 'effectively ... one event').

Claims Against the Primary Victim

In *Alcock*, Lord Oliver expressed the view that a defendant who imperilled or injured herself would owe no duty to those who suffered mental injury as a result, and hence there would be no liability on the part of a son who, watched by his mother, negligently walked in front of an oncoming motor vehicle (p. 418). The issue subsequently arose for decision by the High Court in *Greatorex* v. *Greatorex* [2000] 1 WLR 1970, where the claimant, a fire-fighter, attended at the scene of a car accident in which his son was injured by his own negligence. After a thorough review of the policy considerations, Cazelet J concluded that the arguments against the son owing a duty of care in such circumstances outweighed those in favour. But the matter cannot be regarded as finally settled, and it is submitted that there are flaws in Cazelet J's analysis. For a start, the learned judge was needlessly concerned that the imposition of a duty would represent an undue interference with a person's right to self-determination, entailing, for example, a potential liability where a father committed suicide and his son discovered the body. Here it must be remembered that negligence is the *unreasonable* exposure of another to the risk of harm. If the law recognises a right to self-determination, it can hardly regard the exercise of that right as unreasonable – except perhaps where the person committing suicide deliberately sets out to shock. Furthermore, Cazelet J's other main fear – that litigation between family members would be 'potentially productive of acute family strife' (p. 1986) – seems equally misplaced once it is acknowledged that there is nothing to stop family members suing each other for physical injuries. Here the judge seems guilty of a failure to treat psychiatric harm as potentially as severe in its impact as physical harm, and of a suspicion that it can too easily be faked. On both counts, he is out of line with the preponderance of opinion in both medicine and the law (see 4.1). In these circumstances, it seems that there is no convincing reason to deny the existence of a duty, all the more so when one recognises the injustice that may result where a third party shares responsibility for the shocking event with the primary victim: if the latter is exempted from liability, the burden of compensation will fall entirely on the former, even if her fault was comparatively minor.

4.5 Other Categories of Claim

As indicated above (4.2), the categories of primary and secondary victim do not necessarily cover all those who suffer mental injury as a result of another's negligence. Over time, it has been argued that a number of different types of claim merit separate recognition, mainly in an effort to get around the proximity requirements that must be satisfied in the case of secondary victims. These further categories of claim are considered in the following subsections.

Unwitting Agents of Misfortune

In *Dooley* v. *Cammel Laird & Co* [1951] 1 Lloyd's Rep 271, a crane was lifting a heavy load when the rope which was carrying it snapped, and the load fell into the hold of a ship in which people were working. In *Galt* v. *British Railways Board* (1983) 133 NLJ 870, a train driver rounded a bend and suddenly saw two railway workers on the track in front of him. The crane operator in the first case, and the train driver in the second, both recovered damages for 'nervous shock' consequent on their fears for those they had imperilled, though fortunately no one suffered physical injury in either incident. In *Alcock*, Lord Oliver explained the result of the cases on the basis that, though neither plaintiff had been in a relationship of love and affection with those in the zone of physical danger, they had done more than simply witness the incidents: both could be regarded as the unwitting agent of what had occurred, albeit without any negligence on their part (pp. 407–8).

The House of Lords has now treated such claims as at least arguable in its decision in *W* v. *Essex County Council* [2001] 2 AC 592. The aspect of the case that concerns us now is the claim by the parents of children who were sexually abused by a foster-child placed in their home by the defendant local authority. The parents alleged negligence on the part of the council, and claimed that they had suffered psychiatric injury on finding out about the abuse. Dismissing the council's strike-out application, the House of Lords ruled that the parents had an arguable case insofar as their psychiatric injury flowed either from a feeling that they had brought the abuser and the abused together or from a sense of responsibility for not detecting earlier what was happening. Although they were referred to the Court of Appeal's decision to the contrary in *Hunter* v. *British Coal Corporation* [1999] QB 140, their Lordships were not persuaded that the parents had to have seen the abuse itself or discovered evidence of it 'immediately' after its occurrence (p. 601, per Lord Slynn). Given the divergent views that have been expressed in this area, it is to be hoped that the House of Lords shortly gets the chance to rule definitively on the status of 'unwitting agents', after a full trial on the merits.

Rescuers

In *Alcock*, Lord Oliver considered that the rescuer ought also to be considered as a 'participant' in the events that resulted in mental injury, and not merely as a witness to them, and therefore did not have to satisfy the proximity requirements applied in secondary victim cases. This approach was followed in the subsequent decision of the Court of Appeal in *McFarlane* v. *EE Caledonia Ltd* [1994] 2 All ER 1, though the court found that the acts done by the plaintiff were not in fact sufficient to warrant his treatment as a rescuer. But, in *White* v. *Chief Constable of South Yorkshire Police* [1999] 2 AC 455, a bare majority of the House of Lords ruled that rescuers were not in any special position in claiming for mental injury suffered in the aftermath of an accident.

White was the test case brought by police officers who had been on duty at the time of the Hillsborough football stadium disaster and suffered PTSD as a result. More than 150 officers had sought compensation for mental illness resulting from their experiences on that day. Acting on the advice of its insurers, the South Yorkshire Constabulary settled 14 of the claims which were brought by officers who had actually gone into the fenced pens at the Leppings Lane end of the ground in an effort to save fans from the crush. The test case that then proceeded related to officers who had been involved in the disaster operation but who had not themselves gone into the pens. Following its earlier decision in *McFarlane*, the Court of Appeal [1998] QB 254 ruled that the key question was whether the individual plaintiffs were to be regarded as rescuers having regard to the role that each of them played in the disaster operation. If they were, they were owed a duty of care regardless of the fact that they were in no way exposed to physical danger themselves, nor related to any of the fans caught in the crush. The House of Lords, however, stated that the Court of Appeal's approach was erroneous. Treating rescuers as in a special category of their own would offend the ordinary person's notions of distributive justice by favouring the police, even as members of a wider class of rescuers, over the bereaved relatives whose claims had already been rejected by the House of Lords in *Alcock* (p. 510, per Lord Hoffmann). It was necessary to show that the rescuer had actually been exposed to physical danger in the rescue attempt. An example was provided by the well-known case of *Chadwick* v. *British Railways Board* [1967] 1 WLR 912, where the plaintiff risked physical injury by climbing into the wreckage after a major railway disaster in order to give aid to those trapped inside (though Waller J did not appear to attach any particular significance to this consideration in his judgment). In a powerful dissent, Lord Griffiths took a different view of what the public, and the bereaved relatives, would regard as just: 'I think better of my fellow men than to believe that they would, although bereaved, look like dogs in the manger upon those who went to the rescue at Hillsborough' (p. 465). Both he and Lord Goff took the view that it was artificial and unnecessary to require the police to show that they had been in physical danger.

The effect of the majority's decision is that rescuers, unless actually exposed to physical danger in the course of the rescue, are to be treated as normal secondary victims for the purposes of the law on mental injury. Only rarely will they be able to satisfy the proximity requirements applying to secondary victims generally because there will usually be no prior relationship between them and the primary victim. Exceptionally, however, even professional rescuers may be in a situation where they are called to the scene of an accident involving a close relative (see *Greatorex* v. *Greatorex*, 4.4 above, where the claim failed for other reasons).

Workplace Accidents

A second line of argument adopted by the Court of Appeal in *White* was that, like rescuers, employees exposed to traumatic events in the course of their employment by their employers' negligence fell into a special category of claimant. This provided an alternative basis upon which the Hillsborough officers might succeed even if they were not to be classified as rescuers. But when the case went on appeal, the House of Lords again took a different view (Lord Griffiths dissenting), ruling in effect that the claimant's contract of employment with the defendant could not be used to get around the proximity restrictions on claims by secondary victims. It was not enough to point to the duty of all employers to take reasonable steps to safeguard their employees from harm, as this begged the question of whether the duty extended to the type of injury for which the employee was claiming (p. 505, per Lord Hoffmann). This was to be assessed by applying the normal criteria, and the Hillsborough police officers were not to be exempted from the *Alcock* tests simply because the disaster was caused by the negligence of other officers. The contrary analysis would produce 'striking anomalies', with the police given rights denied to others who had rendered assistance, including first aid volunteers, ambulance officers and perhaps doctors who happened to be in the crowd and stayed out of moral, rather than legal, obligation (p. 506, per Lord Hoffmann).

Occupational Stress

A somewhat different analysis is adopted where an employee suffers a recognised psychiatric condition as a result of occupational stress. The first successful claim of this nature was *Walker* v. *Northumberland County Council* [1995] 1 All ER 737, where Colman J found that the defendant employer, having been warned of the plaintiff's nervous exhaustion when overwork brought on a first mental breakdown, ought to have foreseen and guarded against a second breakdown on the plaintiff's return to work. The existence of the employer's duty in respect of stress was subsequently confirmed by the decision of the Court of Appeal in four conjoined appeals reported as *Hatton* v. *Sutherland* [2002] EWCA Civ 76.

The Court of Appeal's starting point, in a judgment delivered by Hale LJ, was that '[t]here are no special control mechanisms applying to claims for psychiatric (or physical) illness or injury arising from the stress of doing the work the employee is required to do. The ordinary principles of employers' liability apply' (para. [43]). In applying these principles, the 'threshold question' was whether it was reasonably foreseeable that the individual employee would suffer that particular kind of harm, having regard to any special susceptibility to psychiatric illness that ought reasonably to have been known to the employer. If this threshold was crossed, it was immaterial whether or not an employee of normal fortitude would have succumbed to the stress. But Hale LJ emphasised that the threshold question was not too easily to be answered in the affirmative, observing that '[a]n employer is usually entitled to assume that the employee can withstand the normal pressures of the job unless he knows of some particular problem or vulnerability' (ibid.). In effect, the employer can take a reactive approach to stress-related illness, with the onus being on stressed employees to reveal the state of their mental health. The employer 'does not generally have to make searching enquiries of the employee or seek permission to make further enquiries of his medical advisers' (ibid.). It therefore appears that the employer owes no duty in the typical case of an employee who deliberately covers up her stress because she does not want to appear unable to cope (*Pratley* v. *Surrey County Council* [2002] EWHC 1608).

Hale LJ's judgment provides very welcome guidance in a difficult area, especially for employers who need practical advice as to how they can comply with their legal obligations. She notes, for example, that '[a]n employer who offers a confidential advice service, with referral to appropriate counselling or treatment services, is unlikely to be found in breach of duty' (para. [43]). But it must be said that her analysis of the conceptual nature of the employer's duty leaves something to be desired. In her view, the situation was governed by 'ordinary principles of employers' liability' and the claim was simply one for breach of the employer's contractual duty of care. It was a claim by a primary victim in contract, and was to be distinguished from tortious claims brought by primary victims, who were '*usually* those within the foreseeable scope of physical injury' (para. [21]; emphasis added). With respect, it must be said that this analysis is very difficult to reconcile with the reasoning of the House of Lords in *White* v. *Chief Constable of South Yorkshire Police*, where the issue was 'nervous shock' suffered by employees. Their Lordships made it clear that the 'ordinary principles of employers' liability' could not be relied upon to show that a duty arose in respect of psychiatric rather than physical harm: whether it did so or not was to be assessed in the light of general principles of negligence (see above). It is unclear why a different approach should be warranted where the illness is caused by stress as opposed to shock. At the very least, the Court of Appeal in *Hatton* was guilty of ignoring the normative question of whether the employer's duty of care *should* extend to stress-induced illness. It must also be said that it is disingenuous to rely upon the employer's duty being contractual rather than tortious because, in the absence of express promise, the two duties are generally regarded as co-extensive. Here, the Court of Appeal offers no explanation of why the contractual duty should go further than the duty in tort.

In fact, *Hatton* contains hints of a broader principle – tortious rather than contractual in nature – which underpins the courts' treatment of the stress cases. Hale LJ observed in passing that the circumstances of some primary victims in tort did not fit the 'usual' description involving a foreseeable risk of physical harm, but were 'akin to those of primary victims in contract' (para. [21]). She did not explain further, but it seems likely that she had in mind a principle of assumption of responsibility acting as the foundation for both the employer's contractual duty to safeguard employees from stress and a variety of duties arising in non-contractual situations.

Assumption of Responsibility for Mental Health Generally

The courts have allowed or recognised the possibility of claims for negligently-inflicted psychiatric injury suffered in a variety of situations not covered by the above categories. Schools must take reasonable care to protect their pupils from bullying, whether on school premises or elsewhere, and may be liable for psychiatric illness suffered by a victim of bullying (*Bradford-Smart* v. *West Sussex County Council* [2002] EWCA Civ 7: no negligence on the facts). Hospitals and other providers of medical services also owe a duty of care to their patients which stretches to the psychiatric consequences of negligent treatment. Hence, a woman was able to recover damages for the psychiatric illness she suffered when her hospital's negligence lead to her giving birth in extremely traumatic circumstances (*Farrell* v. *Merton, Sutton and Wandsworth Health Authority* (2001) 57 BMLR 158), while a group of plaintiffs who had been treated for dwarfism with human growth hormone were entitled to sue the Department of Health for psychiatric illness consequent upon their anxiety at finding out that the treatment had exposed them to the risk of infection with Creutzfeldt-Jacob Disease, there being no way of knowing whether they were incubating the disease or not (*The Creutzfeldt-Jakob Disease litigation* (1997) 41 BMLR 157). Equivalent duties may arise in other professional contexts too, which explains why solicitors were unsuccessful in their attempt to strike out a claim against them by their client, who alleged that their negligent preparation of his defence in criminal proceedings had resulted in his wrongful conviction, subsequently reversed, and then in mental illness (*McLoughlin* v. *Grovers (a firm)* [2001] EWCA Civ 1743). More esoterically, a stage hypnotist was found liable to a person volunteering to undergo hypnotism during his performance, when this caused her psychiatric injury by triggering memories of childhood sexual abuse (*Howarth* v. *Green*, unreported, 25 May 2001, Leveson J).

The principle underlying these decisions remains obscure. In some, the courts have relied upon the argument that the claimant was a primary victim of the defendant's negligence, but – for reasons explained more fully above (4.2) – we prefer to reserve this terminology for cases in which the claimant is foreseeably exposed to the risk of physical harm. Its use in other contexts too often does no more than express a conclusion that the claimant was owed a duty of care, and substitutes for proper analysis of the duty's basis. A more convincing analysis is that the defendants in the above cases had assumed responsibility for the claimants' mental health by entering a relationship – e.g. between school and pupil, doctor and patient, employer and employee – which the law recognises as giving rise to duties of care more extensive that those arising between strangers. This at least provides a loose framework for analysis of the cases, including the stress cases considered above, though it must be admitted that some anomalies remain. Why, for example, should the employer's duty extend to the protection of employees from stress (*Hatton* v. *Sutherland*) but not from 'nervous shock' (*White* v. *Chief Constable of South Yorkshire Police*)? Our feeling is that this area of law is in the very early stages of development, and that the correctness of even apparently invulnerable decisions of the appellate courts may have to be reconsidered as the judiciary goes through the process of refining the applicable principles.

4.6 Reform

Many of the original fears accounting for judicial reluctance to accept claims for negligently-inflicted mental injury have now been dispelled. The nature of psychiatric illness is more fully understood, and the medical profession more confident of its ability to provide accurate and consistent diagnoses. Consequently, the danger of fraudulent and exaggerated claims has receded. This in turn has allowed a proper recognition of the seriousness of psychiatric illness, and it is no longer thought appropriate to denigrate the moral fibre of sufferers and to urge them simply to 'pull themselves together'. Nevertheless the floodgates argument continues to exert a significant influence on the development of the law relating to mental injury. In *McLoughlin*, for instance, Lord Wilberforce (while accepting that the fears aroused by the floodgates argument were often exaggerated) thought it necessary to impose proximity restrictions on liability for nervous shock 'just because 'shock' in its nature is capable of affecting so wide a range of people' (pp. 421–2). These sentiments were echoed by the House of Lords in *Alcock* and used as a justification for the restrictive approach adopted.

The Law Commission (1998), in a thorough review of liability for psychiatric illness, has recognised the diminishing force in an age of increasing medical sophistication of policy arguments that rest upon the risk of fraudulent and exaggerated claims or conflicting medical opinions. It notes that medical and legal experts working in the field now give due recognition to 'the seriousness of psychiatric illness and how it can be as debilitating as physical injury, if not more so' (para. 6.7n). Such arguments were of insufficient weight to warrant serious contemplation of any proposal that liability for psychiatric illness be abandoned, or – less drastically – denied to mere witnesses. Yet the Law Commission accepted that the floodgates argument retained considerable force, above all because 'the dividing line between what level of mental disturbance does and does not amount to a psychiatric illness is a matter of degree not kind and ... the concept of psychiatric illness has widened significantly over the past few years ... [T]he adoption of a simple foreseeability test would or could result in a significant increase in the number of claims which, at least at this point in time, would be unacceptable' (para. 6.9). For this reason, the Law Commission by and large endorsed the current state of the law, while suggesting slight refinements in particular areas.

The Law Commission's main recommendations related to secondary victims, as it saw no need to interfere with the law relating to primary victims as laid down in *Page* v. *Smith*. It proposed, first, that liability to secondary victims should continue to be restricted in order to prevent a mass of claims arising from a single event (which the Law Commission saw as the major concern underlying the floodgates argument). The reasonable foreseeability of psychiatric illness should not be sufficient to give rise to a duty of care. Secondly, secondary victims establishing a close tie of love and affection with a primary victim of the accident should no longer have to satisfy the requirements of proximity in time and space and proximity of perception. In the Law Commission's view, these requirements were 'unduly restrictive' because the need to establish a close tie of love and affection was itself sufficient to undermine the floodgates objection. Furthermore, they made it necessary to distinguish between claimants on grounds that appeared arbitrary and unjust, especially given medical recognition that 'where there is a close tie of love and affection between the plaintiff and the immediate victim, the plaintiff's proximity to the accident or its aftermath is not always a relevant factor in determining his or her reaction to it' (para. 6.10). To ensure that the courts did not simply invent new restrictions on mental injury claims to replace those the Law Commission wished to abolish, the Commission proposed the recognition of a new statutory duty of care in relation to psychiatric illness, with its elements – not including proximity to the accident or direct perception of it – fully spelt out in the statute (para. 6.20). Thirdly, the list of qualifying relationships would be put on a statutory footing and extended beyond parents, children and spouses to encompass brothers and sisters as well as unmarried partners, including those in a stable homosexual relationship. For those not on the list (e.g. close friends), it would still be open to prove a close tie of love and affection with the immediate victim (paras. 6.26–7). Lastly, amongst a number of more specific recommendations, the Law Commission proposed the abandonment of the 'shock' requirement in claims by secondary victims, as it was difficult to justify different treatment for negligently-inflicted psychiatric illness which occurred over a number of years (para. 5.33), and the removal of the bar against claims where the defendant was the primary victim, as the threat such claims posed to the right to self-determination was adequately addressed by giving the courts a residual discretion not to impose a duty of care where this would not be just and reasonable because the defendant had chosen to cause her own death, injury or imperilment (para. 5.43). The Law Commission declined to make specific proposals in relation to liability for psychiatric illness suffered through stress at work, preferring to allow the law to develop on a case-by-case basis, and it also preferred to leave open the question of liability to bystanders, noting that attitudes to liability for psychiatric illness were liable to change over time and that it might in future be thought right that a secondary victim should have a claim even in the absence of a close tie of love and affection (para. 7.15).

The Law Commission's desire to leave substantial areas of the law on negligently-inflicted mental injury for judicial development gives its report something of the feel of a temporary fix. For now, it insists on a close tie of love and affection in claims by secondary victims, but it would leave the courts room to develop liability to mere bystanders. The Report, as Wheat (1998, p. 216) has commented, is 'modest in its proposals' but at least has the merit of recognising that the common law 'has taken a wrong turn' and cannot be justified in its present form. This is now accepted even by the House of Lords, which in *White* v. *Chief Constable of South Yorkshire Police* described this area of the law as 'a patchwork quilt of distinctions which are difficult to justify' (p. 500, per Lord Steyn), making 'an ugly ruck' in the law's fabric (p. 506, per Lord Hoffmann). Yet their Lordships absolved themselves of any responsibility for retrieving the situation, which after all was of their own making, Lord Steyn stating that it was for Parliament to undertake the task of radical law reform and that 'the only sensible general strategy for the courts is to say thus far and no further' (p. 500). This explicit acknowledgement that the law is beyond judicial repair makes legislative reform even more pressing, and it is to be hoped that it will be pursued in the near future, whether along the lines suggested by the Law Commission or otherwise.

Summary

4.1 Cases of what lawyers have traditionally called 'nervous shock', i.e. psychiatric illness and other personal injury caused by mental trauma, have given rise to significant difficulties in the modern law of negligence and the courts have adopted a cautious and restrictive approach to the recognition of a duty of care.

4.2 A fundamental distinction is now drawn between 'primary' and 'secondary' victims, with liability to the latter restricted by a number of proximity requirements. A primary victim is one who was within the zone of physical danger created by the defendant's negligence. A secondary victim is a person who suffers mental trauma as a result of witnessing someone else's injury or imperilment.

4.3 To make out a claim as a primary victim, it is only necessary to show a foreseeable risk of physical injury resulting from the defendant's negligence, and not that some specifically psychiatric injury was foreseeable. It is not necessary to satisfy the various proximity requirements imposed in secondary victim cases.

4.4 To make out a claim as a secondary victim, it is necessary to show a foreseeable risk of some specifically psychiatric injury resulting from the defendant's negligence, and to satisfy the requirements of proximity of relationship, proximity in time and space, and proximity of perception.

4.5 At various times, it has been argued that a number of different types of claim merit separate recognition, mainly in an effort to get around the proximity requirements that apply to secondary victim claims. It is now established that rescuer cases do not fall into a category on their own. A principle of assumption of responsibility provides a framework for analysing various cases that do not fit into the primary/secondary victim categories.

4.6 The Law Commission (1995), in a thorough review of liability for psychiatric illness, has by and large endorsed the current state of the law, while suggesting a relaxation of the proximity requirements applying to secondary victim claims, and other slight refinements in particular areas.

Exercises

4.1 Is psychiatric illness to be treated as an unexceptional type of personal injury in respect of which the sole criterion of liability is foreseeability or is it a type of injury that requires the scope of the duty of care to be limited? If the latter, what is it about psychiatric illness that calls for a restrictive approach?

4.2 What is the importance of the distinction between the 'primary' and 'secondary' victims?

4.3 In what circumstances might brothers and sisters of a deceased claim damages for mental injury after witnessing her death? What evidence about their relationship with the deceased would they have to produce in court?

4.4 Must the claimant in a mental injury action always actually see the traumatic event in person? What if the claimant is blind?

4.5 Two years ago a fatal train crash occurred at Thames Junction. The 7.20 a.m. from Fleet was directed down the wrong track through the negligence of a railway employee and ploughed into a group of workers laying new track. Three of the workers were killed; two were seriously injured. Only G escaped being caught in the impact, though she had felt sure that she was doomed. None of the passengers in the train, driven by H, was hurt. J, the station supervisor and the twin sister of one of those killed, had watched the accident as it happened on closed circuit television; she proceeded bravely to coordinate the rescue attempts from her office with the aid of the television cameras. It took several hours to recover the bodies of the dead and wounded from the wreck. As they were laid by the side of the track, relatives were allowed to approach. K saw her daughter wracked with pain and attempted to give her comfort; L saw the lifeless body of her son and kissed him farewell. Railway staff refrained from telling K that her daughter, having been designated look-out, was partly responsible for the injuries suffered. The whole proceedings, from the moment of the crash on, were observed by M, a five-year-old child. G, H, J, K L and M all suffered post-traumatic stress disorder as a consequence of their experiences. N, the lover of one of those injured in the crash, nursed her loved one slowly back to health but herself suffered a nervous breakdown as a result of the strain which this caused. Advise the parties as to their rights and liabilities in tort.

5   Economic Loss

5.1 **What Is 'Pure Economic Loss'?**

The tort of negligence provides compensation for all sorts of losses that are financial in nature. If you were to be run over by a negligent car driver, you would get damages not only for your physical injuries (your pain and suffering, etc.) but also for the financial consequences of those injuries. Hence you would be able to recover in respect of any medical costs incurred and any wages lost. However, when the courts are faced with loss that is *purely* economic in nature – that is, which does not stem from any physical damage to the claimant or her property – their approach is very different. The courts have so restricted liability for pure economic loss that it is possible to state as a general rule that it is not recoverable in the tort of negligence.

The crucial distinction is between (recoverable) *consequential* economic loss and *pure* economic loss (not generally recoverable), as is illustrated by the instructive case of *Spartan Steel and Alloys Ltd* v. *Martin & Co Ltd* [1973] QB 27. Martin & Co were building contractors carrying out road works near Spartan Steel's metal-processing plant. Their men were careless in digging up the road and damaged the electricity cable running to the plant. The power was cut off for several hours. Spartan Steel sued Martin & Co for their lost profits. The Court of Appeal allowed the claim only in part. The majority of the court made the following distinction. The profits lost on the metal that was being processed at the time the electricity was cut off were recoverable. This metal was actually damaged by the power cut and so these profits could be regarded as consequential economic loss stemming from physical damage to the plaintiff's property. The rest of Spartan Steel's loss, however, was purely economic. This loss arose from the fact that Spartan Steel was not able to process other lots of metal in the time the power was off: it did not stem from damage to any of these lots. Admittedly, the electricity cable had been damaged, but the cable belonged to the electricity board, not to Spartan Steel: to recover financial loss you have to establish that it was caused by physical damage to your own person or property (see further *Leigh & Sillivan Ltd* v. *Aliakmon Shipping Co Ltd* [1986] AC 785, but note the Carriage of Goods by Sea Act 1992, s. 2).

The courts' adoption of a general 'no recovery' or 'exclusionary' rule for pure economic loss is explained by a number of underlying policy considerations. The floodgates argument has perhaps been most influential: the principal fear is that liability might extend to an indeterminate class of claimants, in an indeterminate amount, thereby imposing an undue burden upon the defendant. In *Hedley Byrne & Co.* v.

Heller & Partners Ltd [1964] AC 465, 536–7, Lord Pearce explicitly acknowledged that the risk of indeterminate liability justified restrictions on the scope of the duty of care:

> 'How wide the sphere of the duty of care in negligence is to be laid depends ultimately upon the courts' assessment of the demands of society for protection from the carelessness of others. Economic protection has lagged behind protection in physical matters where there is injury to person and property. It may be that the size and the width of the range of possible claims has acted as a deterrent to extension of economic protection.'

The same concern was identified and developed by Lord Denning in *Spartan Steel* itself (p. 38):

> 'If claims for economic loss were permitted for this particular hazard there would be no end of claims. Some might be genuine, but many might be inflated or even false.'

In Lord Denning's view, it was best to leave the losses to lie where they fell rather than concentrating them on the defendant: if the losses were small, they might without hardship be absorbed by the victims themselves; if they were serious, then the victims ought themselves to have taken out insurance by way of protection against that risk.

5.2 Defective Product Economic Loss

We must now elaborate our definition of pure economic loss to take into account the question of defective products. The courts insist that the manufacturer of a defective product will be liable only in respect of damage that the product causes to another's person or property. If a product is simply no good, or merely physically deteriorates, even if it blows up and destroys itself, any financial loss that results is purely economic. In short, a defect does not constitute 'damage'. So, while Mrs Donoghue's claim for compensation for being ill after drinking that fabled bottle of ginger beer would today be unanswerable, she would not be entitled to recover the cost of a replacement bottle of ginger beer, that cost arising solely from the bottle's defective nature.

Three decisions of the House of Lords stand out as being of first rate importance: *Anns* v. *Merton LBC* [1978] AC 728, *D & F Estates* v. *Church Commissioners* [1989] AC 177 and *Murphy* v. *Brentwood DC* [1991] 1 AC 398. Each raised the question of defective product economic loss in relation to the construction of buildings (for application of the same principles to defective goods rather than buildings, see, e.g., *Muirhead* v. *International Tank Specialities Ltd* [1986] QB 507). In *Anns*, the House of Lords had held that, where the defective nature of the building's foundations had caused subsidence, then cracks that consequently appeared in the walls of the building might be regarded as 'material, physical damage' (p. 759, per Lord Wilberforce). The plaintiff, who had proceeded against the local authority which had the power to supervise the work, was allowed to recover the cost of remedying the damage to the building so as to avoid a 'present or imminent danger to the health or safety of the persons occupying it' (p. 760, per Lord Wilberforce). In *D & F Estates*, however, the House of Lords disputed Lord Wilberforce's categorisation of the loss in such cases as arising from 'material physical damage' and held that the loss was purely economic because it was attributable solely to the defective condition of the building. In *D & F Estates*, the action was brought against the builder who was directly responsible for the defective work, and so it was not necessary for the House of Lords to rule on the correctness of its earlier decision in *Anns*; nevertheless, the decision in *D & F Estates* effectively undermined the reasoning in *Anns*, and it was perhaps inevitable that the House of Lords would exercise its power to overrule that decision when the opportunity presented itself. That opportunity arose in *Murphy* v. *Brentwood DC* [1991] AC 398, which like *Anns* concerned the liability of a local authority in respect of alleged negligence in supervising the construction of a dwelling. The property was eventually acquired by the plaintiff, who suffered loss on its subsequent sale after defects in the foundations had been discovered following the appearance of cracks in the walls of the house. The House of Lords followed its decision in *D & F Estates* and treated the cracks and subsidence as merely the manifestation of a defect in the building, not as damage; accordingly, the money Mr Murphy lost on the subsequent sale of his house was purely economic and fell within the scope of the general 'no recovery' rule.

The decisions of the House of Lords in *D & F Estates* and *Murphy* leave a number of loose ends to be tied together. In the following paragraphs, we look at two – the availability of preventative damages and the complex structures argument – before considering the question of reform. But we should also draw attention to a further matter, to be discussed in more detail below, namely the extent to which the recognition of liability under the rule in *Hedley Byrne & Co* v. *Heller & Partners Ltd* [1964] AC 465 may serve to undermine the general 'no recovery' rule adopted in those decisions (see 5.3).

Preventative Damages

An alternative explanation of *Anns*, which did not depend upon the classification of the loss in that case as arising from 'material physical damage', was that there should be a limited exception to the general 'no recovery' rule applicable to pure economic loss where it was necessary to incur the cost of repair work in order to prevent the occurrence of anticipated physical damage. Under this approach (adopted by the Supreme Court of Canada in *Winnipeg Condominium Corp No 36* v. *Bird Construction Co* (1995) 121 DLR (4th) 193), liability might arise in respect of 'dangerous' defects, but not in respect of pure defects of quality. The award of 'preventative damages' in such cases might be thought to have intuitive appeal in so far as it allows a property owner to claim damages in order to avert personal injury or damage to *other* property without having to wait until the loss is sustained: it reflects the common-sense maxim that prevention is better than cure.

In *Murphy*, however, the House of Lords rejected an argument that the decision in *Anns* should be upheld on this limited basis. Their Lordships appear to have taken the view that damages in respect of the cost of preventative repair work were not warranted because, if the property owner had decided to wait until physical damage was sustained, it would not have been appropriate to compensate for the cost of remedying that damage. In such a case, the owner's knowledge of the defect was enough to neutralise the danger because she would have the option of repairing the defect or abandoning the building as unfit for habitation. In either case, the loss sustained was in essence a purely economic loss. As Lord Bridge explained, 'because the danger is now known ... the defect becomes merely a defect in quality' (p. 475). His Lordship continued:

'If a builder erects a structure containing a latent defect which renders it dangerous to persons or property, he will be liable in tort for any injury to persons or damage to property resulting from that dangerous defect. But, if the defect becomes apparent before any injury or damage has been caused, the loss sustained by the building owner is purely economic.'

Their Lordships' analysis here is difficult to follow and appears to be somewhat questionable. In so far as it rests on an assumption that the occupier who knows the full extent of the defect yet continues to occupy the building is the author of her own misfortune, the analysis seems to rest on principles of causation and voluntary assumption of risk; yet these principles only bar claims by those who voluntarily and unreasonably run the risk of injury, and we may doubt whether these conditions are truly satisfied here (see 9.4 and 11.3). Is the homeowner who, lacking the financial means to effect a repair or to move to alternative accommodation, continues in occupation after discovery of a dangerous defect really to have no recourse against the builder? The Court of Appeal has apparently found this prospect unpalatable and in *Targett* v. *Torfaen Borough Council* [1992] 3 All ER 27 declined to treat *Murphy* as barring a claim by an occupier who was injured by a known defect on the premises. Sir Donald Nicholls V-C noted (p. 37) that

'knowledge of the existence of a danger does not always enable a person to avoid the danger. In simple cases it does. In other cases, especially where buildings are concerned, it would be absurdly unrealistic to suggest that a person can always take steps to avoid a danger once he knows of its existence, and that if he does not do so he is the author of his own misfortune'.

In his view, the real question was whether 'it is reasonable for the plaintiff to remove or avoid the danger, and unreasonable for him to run the risk of being injured by the danger' (ibid.). It is submitted that the Vice-Chancellor's approach is entirely convincing and that it substantially undermines the reasons for the House of Lords' rejection of a doctrine of preventative damages in *Murphy*: if homeowners might in appropriate cases recover compensation for damage suffered as a consequence of a known defect, then there should also be a remedy for those homeowners who have both the prudence and the means to effect repairs before damage is sustained.

In any case, there are indications that the House of Lords' rejection of a doctrine of preventative damages was somewhat equivocal. Lord Bridge was apparently prepared to contemplate an exception to the general rule if a dangerous defect in a building should threaten to injure those in neighbouring houses or on the street: in such circumstances, he thought that the owner might be able to recover the cost of demolition or repair work effected to remove the danger to third parties. Although Lord Oliver expressed doubts whether it was right to admit such an exception, Lord Bridge's suggestion has since been followed by the High Court in *Morse* v. *Barratt (Leeds) Ltd* [1992] Const LJ 158. In that case, the defendant property developers were held liable for the cost of repairing a stone retaining wall at the rear of their development which had become liable to collapse as a result of their negligence. The wall had become a danger to users of the highway, and the plaintiff residents of the development were entitled to recover the cost of making the wall safe and thereby protecting themselves against liability to highway users. This leaves the law in a puzzling state for it seems that, while a property owner may be expected to abandon her property to save herself from physical harm, she is not expected to bear the costs of demolition work to protect those on adjacent land from such a risk.

The Complex Structures Argument

The decisions in *D & F Estates* and *Murphy* leave a further potential loophole for claimants to exploit. This centres upon the 'complex structures' argument first advanced by Lord Bridge in *D & F Estates* v. *Church Commissioners* [1989] AC 177 and developed by Lord Bridge and other members of the House of Lords in *Murphy* v. *Brentwood District Council* [1991] 1 AC 398, esp. 470, 476–9 and 497. The argument suggests a qualification to the general rule preventing recovery in respect of any physical deterioration of a product which arises out of a mere defect: certain products might be analysed as 'complex structures' made up of several separate and distinct component items of property, such that the owner would be able to sue in respect of *damage* to one component part caused by a *defect* in another. Such damage would not be considered pure economic loss and would be recoverable under normal *Donoghue* v. *Stevenson* principles. Doubts exist as to the circumstances in which the complex structures analysis might operate. Lord Bridge in *Murphy* suggested that it might apply if a defective central heating boiler in a house were to cause a fire damaging the house and that the owner might therefore recover damages from the boiler manufacturer. However, the House of Lords in *Murphy* was adamant that the complex structures argument had no place in the case before it: it could not be said that the cracks in the walls of Mr Murphy's house were damage to a part of the building separate from the defective foundations which were the root of the problem. It seems that the argument depends upon a number of factors, among them whether the component causing the damage came from a supplier different from that of the rest of the product and whether the component might be replaced without doing structural damage to the rest of the product. But whether the argument will find favour with the courts, and (if so) precisely how it will be applied, is as yet uncertain (see Fleming, 1989b; Grubb and Mullis, 1991).

Reform

What is the justification for applying the 'no recovery' rule to defective product economic loss? In the context of pure economic loss generally, the principal fear seems to be that recognition of a duty of care would open up a 'liability in an indeterminate amount for an indeterminate time to an indeterminate class' (*Ultramares Corpn* v. *Touche* 174 NE 441, 444 (1931), per Cardozo J). Yet the fear of indeterminate liability loses its force in the context of defective products, for the amount of the loss attributable to the defect is normally limited by the value of the product itself, while the class of potential claimants is limited to the owner of the product for the time being. In fact, an entirely distinct consideration of public policy is raised in relation to defective products, namely the danger of subverting key doctrines of the law of contract and hence of upsetting the settled expectations of those engaged in business dealings. Allowing the purchaser of a defective product to sue the producer in tort in respect of a merely qualitative (as opposed to dangerous) defect would effectively expose the producer to 'the obligations of an indefinitely transmissible warranty of quality' ([1991] 1 AC 398, 480 per Lord Bridge). The scope of the producer's liability would no longer be limited by the contractual doctrine of privity. Perhaps we should pause for thought before urging the courts to take such a dramatic step. As Lord Keith observed in *Murphy*, 'in what is essentially a consumer protection field ... the precise extent and limits of the liabilities which in the public interest are imposed on builders and local authorities are best left to the legislature' (p. 472).

In fact, the legislature has already acted to address the plight of homeowners in Mr Murphy's situation (although the material facts of his case arose before the legislation came into effect). By s. 1 of the Defective Premises Act 1972, architects, builders and others 'taking on work for or in connection with the provision of a dwelling-house' may be held liable to owners of those dwellings if they fail to carry out their work in a workmanlike or professional manner and this failure results in the building being unfit for habitation (query whether this extends to local authorities who approve the plans of a proposed development). The Act only applies to 'dwellings'; commercial properties are excluded. Also excluded are houses erected under schemes approved by the Secretary of State. Such schemes, notably the 'Buildmark' scheme run by the National House Building Council, for a long time covered virtually all newly built homes, and the effect of this exclusion in practice was therefore to limit the operation of the Act to renovations and improvements. It now seems, however, that the NHBC no longer seeks ministerial approval for its schemes, with the result that purchasers under the schemes retain their statutory remedy (see Clerk and Lindsell, 2000, para. 7–125). The Act imposes a limitation period of six years from the completion of the relevant work, which contrasts unfavourably with the position at common law where the six-year limitation period only begins to run from the date at which the loss is sustained. (In so far as defective product economic loss is recoverable, the loss is deemed to arise when the defect becomes evident and thereby affects the value of the property: see *Invercargill City Council* v. *Hamlin* [1996] AC 624.) The Law Commission in its report (1970b) which formed the basis for the Act had stated that the new legislation it proposed was not intended to prevent further development of the common law, but the House of Lords in *Murphy* thought it unwise to add at common law to the statutory obligations. Lord Bridge's view was typical (pp. 480–1):   .

> 'It would be remarkable to find that similar obligations in the nature of a transmissible warranty of quality, applicable to buildings of every kind and subject to no such limitations or exclusions as are imposed by the 1972 Act, could be derived from the builder's common law duty of care.'

The existence of the statutory remedy may well be enough to deflate further pressure for recognition of a common law action against the builder, and enable the English courts to justify their approach in an area in which many Commonwealth jurisdictions have taken a contrary view. Indeed, in *Invercargill City Council* v. *Hamlin* [1996] AC 624, the Privy Council accepted that the New Zealand courts might legitimately decline to follow *Murphy* given the absence of any legislation equivalent to the 1972 Act in that country: the decision whether or not to recognise a duty of care reflected policy considerations that might be expected to vary from one country to another, in the light *inter alia* of the legislative background (see also *Bryan* v. *Maloney* (1995) 128 ALR 163 (Australia); *Winnipeg Condominium Corp No 36* v. *Bird Construction Co* (1995) 121 DLR (4th) 193 (Canada; liability for dangerous defects only)).

5.3 Exceptional Liability for Pure Economic Loss

Over the years, the courts have recognised a number of exceptions to the rule against recovery for the negligent infliction of pure economic loss, but the only exceptions of lasting and general significance derive from the decision of the House of Lords in *Hedley Byrne & Co* v. *Heller & Partners Ltd* [1964] AC 465. The case considered the liability of a bank in respect of an inaccurate credit reference. Hedley Byrne, a firm of advertising agents, was engaged to conduct an advertising campaign by a certain company, Easipower Ltd. In the course of this engagement, Hedley Byrne became personally liable under a number of contracts for advertising time and space. As a precautionary measure, the firm had its bank check Easipower's creditworthiness by writing to Heller & Partners, Easipower's bankers. Heller & Partners replied, in a letter marked 'without responsibility', that Easipower was in a sound business position. This turned out to be false and Hedley Byrne lost several thousands of pounds under the contracts when Easipower went into liquidation. Hedley Byrne sued Easipower's bankers to try to recover this money. Its claim was rejected by the House of Lords on the grounds that Heller & Partners had successfully excluded any liability to Hedley Byrne by making it clear that they supplied the information requested 'without responsibility'. The House of Lords did, however, accept (by a bare majority) that the bankers would have been liable for Hedley Byrne's pure economic loss had they not made this disclaimer of responsibility. Furthermore, their Lordships were unanimous that there would be cases outside the banker–creditor context in which liability for pure economic loss would be imposed.

This was a major breakthrough. Although the courts had previously recognised liability for pure economic loss resulting from misrepresentation in the tort of deceit, negligence is not sufficient to make out liability in deceit (*Derry* v. *Peek* (1889) 14 App Cas 337) and the Court of Appeal (Denning LJ dissenting) had ruled in *Candler* v. *Crane, Christmas & Co* [1959] 2 QB 164 that no liability would arise in the tort of negligence. The latter decision was overturned by *Hedley Byrne* and the dissent of Denning LJ approved. The House of Lords did not, however, found itself directly upon the duty of care of broad scope recognised in *Donoghue* v. *Stevenson*. Instead it sought to develop a narrow exception to the 'no liability' rule by building incrementally upon an existing principle by which liability for carelessness might arise. This principle was one of equity rather than tort law: the principle that in a fiduciary relationship the fiduciary must take reasonable care of the interests of the beneficiary (*Nocton* v. *Lord Ashburton* [1914] AC 932; this obligation is in fact only one of the incidents of the fiduciary duty, which also entails, for example, the obligation to account for profits: see *Boardman* v. *Phipps* [1967] 2 AC 46). The House of Lords took the view that there were other analogous 'special relationships' in which a duty to take care at common law – a duty, in this context, to speak carefully and not merely honestly – might arise.

This landmark decision paved the way for judicial recognition of liability for pure economic loss in a variety of situations. A surveyor employed to value a house for a building society to determine whether it is adequate security for a prospective mortgage may owe a duty of care not only to the building society but also to the prospective mortgagor who proceeds with the purchase in reliance upon the valuation (*Smith* v. *Eric S*

Bush [1990] AC 831). An accountant may be held liable to a takeover bidder who effects a takeover in reliance upon a specially prepared audit statement (*Morgan Crucible Co* v. *Hill Samuel Bank* [1991] Ch. 259), but not, it seems, to shareholders who are simply sent a copy of the annual audit required by statute (*Caparo Industries* v. *Dickman* [1990] 2 AC 605). When acting as a referee for a former employee or agent, an employer owes the latter a duty of care (*Spring* v. *Guardian Assurance* [1995] 2 AC 296). So, too, does an environmental health officer who advises the owners of a guest house to make costly alterations or risk closure of their business (*Welton* v. *North Cornwall District Council* [1997] 1 WLR 570; but note the doubts expressed by Sir Richard Scott v-c in *Harris* v. *Evans* [1998] 1 WLR 1285, 1301). Of all these and similar applications of the rule in *Hedley Byrne* v. *Heller*, however, perhaps the most significant has been its application to acts as well as representations. In *Henderson* v. *Merrett Syndicates Ltd* [1995] 2 AC 145, the House of Lords held that 'the principle extends beyond the provision of information and advice to include the performance of other services' (p. 180, per Lord Goff); applying the principle in *Hedley Byrne*, the House of Lords held that managing agents in the Lloyd's of London insurance market owe a duty of care to the 'names' who subscribe to their syndicate.

Not all the subsequent cases which allowed recovery for pure economic loss were brought under the *Hedley Byrne* umbrella. In the rapid expansion of liability for negligence that occurred in the 1970s and early 1980s, some courts took a more radical approach and claimed to base liability on normal *Donoghue* v. *Stevenson* principles, rather than on the narrower rule in *Hedley Byrne* (see *Ministry of Housing and Local Government* v. *Sharp* [1970] 2 QB 223; *Ross* v. *Caunters* [1980] Ch 297). The high-water mark came with the problematic case of *Junior Books Ltd* v. *Veitchi Co. Ltd* [1983] AC 520, in which a majority of the House of Lords imposed liability in respect of defective product economic loss representing the cost of replacing a negligently laid floor. The action was brought by the owner of premises, who had engaged contractors to do construction work, against the defendant subcontractor, whom the owner had nominated to lay the floor. It subsequently transpired that the plaintiff had already settled a contractual claim against the main contractors, subject to an agreed limitation of liability (Atiyah, 1995, p. 383n; this evidence was not before the House of Lords). The case therefore raised in stark form the question of whether it was right to allow the tort remedy to bypass limitations of liability and other protections built into the contractual structure. Reaction to *Junior Books* was largely hostile and since that time there has been a marked retrenchment of liability in this area. In a series of cases, the Court of Appeal declined to apply the decision, finding it distinguishable on the facts (see *Muirhead* v. *International Tank Specialities Ltd* [1986] QB 507; *Simaan General Contracting Co* v. *Pilkington Glass Ltd (No 2)* [1988] QB 758; *Greater Nottingham Co-operative Society Ltd* v. *Cementation Piling and Foundations Ltd* [1989] QB 71). Consigning the case to what appeared to be early oblivion, Lord Bridge described it (in *D & F Estates*) as depending upon a 'unique' relationship between the parties and asserted that 'the decision cannot be regarded as laying down any principle of general application in the law of tort' (p. 202). Nevertheless, his Lordship has more recently suggested that *Junior Books* might now be regarded as falling within the scope of *Hedley Byrne* (see *Murphy* v. *Brentwood District Council* [1991] AC 398, 481) and it may well be that the case warrants renewed attention on that account (see 5.7).

We must now turn to the important question of the ingredients of the *Hedley Byrne* liability. These cannot be identified by reference to *Hedley Byrne* alone, as their Lordships in that case were initiating a major departure in the law and were able to predict its subsequent development to only a limited extent. It is only through practical experience of the application of the rule in *Hedley Byrne* that a complete and coherent view of the law can be derived. The position adopted here is that there is in fact *a set* of principles based upon the central notion of a special relationship – rather than a single general principle – that give rise to a duty to take care in protecting another's purely economic interests. In addition to (a) the type of relationship exemplified by *Hedley Byrne*, in which there is *direct reliance* upon a voluntary assumption of responsibility by the defendant to the claimant, there are cases of (b) *indirect reliance*, i.e. reliance upon the defendant's assumption of responsibility to a third party, and (c) *indirect loss without reliance*, where the defendant's failure to fulfil a responsibility assumed towards a third party causes loss to the claimant without the claimant's having acted in reliance upon the assumption of responsibility at all. It can be seen that the latter two categories are derived from and parasitic upon the first in that they depend upon the existence of a special relationship in which responsibility is assumed by the defendant, albeit to a third party and not to the claimant.

5.4 Direct Assumption of Responsibility

A duty of care may arise in respect of pure economic loss on the basis of the defendant's voluntary assumption of responsibility to the claimant. The basic principle is that the defendant is taken to assume responsibility to the claimant by their jointly entering into a special relationship (sometimes said to be one which is 'equivalent to contract') in which the claimant reasonably relies upon the defendant's careful exercise of special skill, knowledge or authority. The concepts here are not, however, used entirely consistently, and it is necessary to spend some time elaborating the meaning and interrelationship of the concepts of voluntary assumption of responsibility, special relationship, special skill, and reasonable reliance.

Voluntary Assumption of Responsibility

The concept of voluntary assumption of responsibility was apparently invoked by the House of Lords in *Hedley Byrne* in order to pre-empt the argument that, given that the defendant bankers had no duty to answer the credit inquiry, they could have no duty to exercise due care if they chose to respond. This reasoning was exposed as fallacious by the House of Lords. Recognition of a duty to exercise due care where an answer was in fact given was quite consistent with there being no legal compulsion to respond at all. The point was put clearly by Lord Reid in a well-known passage (p. 486):

> 'A reasonable man, knowing that he was being trusted or that his skill and judgment were being relied upon, would, I think, have three courses open to him. He could keep silent or decline to give the information or advice sought: or he could give an answer with a clear qualification that he accepted no responsibility for it or that it was given without that reflection or inquiry which a careful answer would require: or he could simply answer without any such qualification. If he chooses to adopt the last course he must, I think, be held to have accepted some responsibility for his answer being given carefully, or to have accepted a relationship with the inquirer which requires him to exercise such care as the circumstances require.'

The original purpose of the concept of a voluntary assumption of responsibility was therefore to explain how liability might arise in relation to a gratuitous undertaking, and it was not originally intended to function as a means of limiting the situations in which the duty might arise or the parties to whom the duty might be owed. Now that it seems to have acquired the latter purposes, the circumstances in which responsibility will be treated as assumed must be specified. It has been said that the words should be 'understood ... as referring to a conscious assumption of responsibility for the task rather than a conscious assumption of legal liability to the plaintiff for its careful performance' (*White* v. *Jones* [1995] 2 AC 207, 274 per Lord Browne-Wilkinson; see also Lord Nolan at p. 293). This formulation has the merit of emphasising that the responsibility is imposed by law and is therefore not precluded by the defendant's failure consciously to advert to it (*Williams* v. *Natural Life Health Foods Ltd* [1998] 1 WLR 830, 835 per Lord Steyn) or even by the defendant's purported refusal to accept any responsibility at all (see further *Smith* v. *Eric S Bush* [1990] AC 831, considered below at 5.4). However it fails to account for the special position – relative to the world at large – of *the person to whom the responsibility is assumed* and thus runs the risk of opening the floodgates to a multitude of claims from an indeterminate number of claimants. It is better to regard the responsibility as assumed to the claimant by the voluntary act of entering into a special relationship with her, and as a legal incident of that relationship, in which the claimant is distinguished from the world at large by virtue of her reciprocal dealings with the defendant (i.e. by an element of 'mutuality').

A Special Relationship ('Equivalence to Contract')

The voluntary assumption of responsibility arises 'internally from the relationship in which the parties [have] chosen to place themselves' and is 'a reflection of the relationship in question' (*White* v. *Jones* [1995] 2 AC 207, 287 per Lord Mustill; his Lordship dissented from the final decision, but his analysis of the authorities is still most convincing). It cannot arise purely out of *the situation* in which the claimant and defendant found themselves, for example, whereby the claimant was foreseeably affected by the defendant's acts or foreseeably relied upon the defendant's words. Lord Devlin placed considerable emphasis on this point in the course of his exemplary analysis in *Hedley Byrne* itself of the 'sort of relationship which gives rise to a responsibility' (p. 529):

> 'I do not understand any of your Lordships to hold that it is a responsibility imposed by law upon certain types of persons or in certain sorts of situations. It is a responsibility that is voluntarily accepted or undertaken, either generally where a general relationship, such as that of solicitors and client or banker and customer, is created, or specifically in relation to a particular transaction.'

The relationship, as Lord Devlin makes clear, may be either general or specific. In addition to the examples he gives of the former, we may add the relationships (among others) between employer and employee (in which the former is under a duty – continuing even after employment has been terminated – to take reasonable care while acting as the latter's referee: *Spring* v. *Guardian Assurance* [1995] 2 AC 296) and between underwriters managing an insurance syndicate and the members of (i.e. investors in) that syndicate (see *Henderson* v. *Merrett Syndicates Ltd*, below). Whether a relationship will arise in the absence of such a continuing relationship, i.e. in relation to a specific transaction, depends upon whether the parties engage in dealings of a bilateral and reciprocal character. It is this element of 'mutuality' (as it was termed by Lord Mustill in *White*, p. 283) that creates the special relationship between the parties and makes their relationship different from that between the defendant and others who might foreseeably suffer economic loss as a result of the defendant's carelessness. Lord Mustill explained how such mutuality had formed the basis for the special relationship, arising in relation to a specific transaction, in *Hedley Byrne* (p. 287):

> 'this relationship was bilateral, being created on the one hand by the acts of the plaintiffs in first asking for a reference in circumstances which showed that the bankers' skill and care would be relied upon and then subsequently relying upon it; and on the other hand by the bankers' compliance with the request.'

In Lord Mustill's analysis, the plaintiff company's request was particularly important in demonstrating the 'active role' the plaintiff had played in the transaction and indeed in 'initiating' the relationship. Without such a request, there would have been no mutuality and (we may add) no simple mechanism for limiting the class of those to whom the responsibility was undertaken.

The relationship between the parties 'may or may not be contractual in nature' (*Henderson* v. *Merret Syndicates Ltd* [1995] 2 AC 145, 180 per Lord Goff). It may arise in relation to pre-contractual negotiations (see *Esso Petroleum Co Ltd* v. *Mardon* [1976] QB 801; and note the concurrent liability under Misrepresentation Act 1967, s. 2) or even, as in *Hedley Byrne* itself, in relation to dealings which do not have a contract as their object. But the relationship must be at least 'equivalent to contract'. This notion was propounded by Lord Devlin in *Hedley Byrne* (p. 529); he indicated that there would be the necessary equivalence 'where there is an assumption of responsibility in circumstances, in which, but for the absence of consideration, there would be a contract'. Although consideration need not, therefore, pass from claimant to defendant, this is not to say that in cases outside contract the law entirely ignores what the defendant stands to gain from the transaction. This may be relevant to the court's determination of whether the reciprocal dealings are apt to give rise to legal responsibility or are purely social in character, a point to which Lord Devlin also adverted (p. 529):

'It may often be a material factor to consider whether the adviser is acting purely out of good nature or whether he is getting his reward in some indirect form. The service that a bank performs in giving a reference is not done simply out of a desire to assist commerce. It would discourage the customers of the bank if their deals fell through because the bank had refused to testify to their credit when it was good.'

The requirement of a contractual or equivalent relationship has the merit of emphasising the need for dealings of a bilateral and reciprocal character and of thereby serving to limit the scope of the liability owed. But it also highlights a possible tension between the principles of contract and those of tort. Two issues are raised. First, if there is a contract between the claimant and the defendant, is it necessary and desirable for the law to recognise a tort claim as well? If concurrent liability were to arise, it may be that the claimant would be able to pick and choose according to which cause of action – tortious or contractual – were more beneficial (e.g. in relation to the question of remoteness where tort is more generous than contract, allowing liability even for 'extremely unlikely results' on the basis of their reasonable foreseeability where contract requires 'a very substantial degree of probability': *Koufos* v. *C Czarnikow Ltd* [1969] 1 AC 350, 388–9 per Lord Reid). Secondly, if there is *no* contract between the parties, is it right that the law of tort should impose liability in respect of what may be a gratuitous undertaking, or an obligation undertaken contractually *vis-à-vis* a third party? These questions are considered further below (see 5.7).

Special Skill, Knowledge or Authority

The requirement that the defendant exercise a special skill (or employ special knowledge or authority) serves to limit the extent to which the liability arising under *Hedley Byrne* v. *Heller* might subvert central doctrines of the law of contract. It restricts the scope of the remedy in tort and channels liability to professionals and others who might be expected to have insurance to protect themselves against possible liabilities.

The general principle was first formulated by Lord Morris in *Hedley Byrne* (pp. 502–3):

> '[I]f someone possessed of a special skill undertakes, quite irrespective of contract, to apply that skill for the assistance of another person who relies upon such, a duty of care will arise.'

A restrictive interpretation of this principle was given by the Privy Council in *Mutual Life and Citizens Assurance Co* v. *Evatt* [1971] AC 793. The opinion of the majority was that liability should be restricted to those who give advice in a professional capacity: architects, surveyors, accountants and the like. Applying that rule, the Privy Council held that the plaintiff was not entitled to damages from his insurance company who had carelessly given him false information about the financial stability of an associated company in which he invested: the defendant was not in the business of giving advice about investments. A dissenting opinion was offered by Lord Reid and Lord Morris. In their view, it was sufficient that considered advice was sought from a businessman in the course of his business, which was clearly the case on the facts before them. This more expansive conception of *Hedley Byrne* liability has been preferred in the English courts to the narrow view of the majority. It was applied in *Esso Petroleum Co Ltd* v. *Mardon* [1976] QB 801, in which Esso was held liable under the *Hedley Byrne* doctrine, as well as under s. 2(1) of the Misrepresentation Act 1967, to the owner of a petrol-filling station whom it had negligently advised about the likely profitability of his investment in the station.

This broader view of *Hedley Byrne* liability was effectively confirmed in the House of Lords in *Spring* v. *Guardian Assurance* [1995] 2 AC 296 in which an employer was held to owe a duty of care in writing a reference about a former employee or equivalent. The plaintiff had recently been engaged as a 'company representative', acting in a self-employed capacity, for Guardian Assurance. Seeking to go into business as an insurance agent on his own, he applied to become a company representative of another insurance firm, which requested a reference from Guardian Assurance. The latter was bound to provide this under the relevant regulatory regime (governed by LAUTRO). The reply (which the trial judge found to have been carelessly compiled) amounted to a 'kiss of death' as it called the plaintiff's honesty into question. The plaintiff's job application was rejected, as were two further applications made to other companies who received the same reference. A majority of the House of Lords (Lord Keith dissenting) held that the former employer owed a duty of care on the facts and that the case should be remitted to the Court of Appeal to determine whether the plaintiff had suffered loss as a result of the established breach of duty (Lord Lowry dissented on this last point). Their Lordships held that there were no reasons of public policy that precluded the imposition of liability. They could not imagine that this would have a significantly adverse effect upon the willingness of employers to give references, or upon the frankness of disclosure in those references. Nor did the fact that employers have a defence against liability in defamation prevent liability in negligence, for liability in defamation is in crucial respects more stringent than that in negligence, giving rise to the need for special defences not available elsewhere in the law of tort (see ch. 20).

Although Lord Slynn and Lord Woolf held that liability arose without express reliance upon *Hedley Byrne* principles, those principles formed the basis of the decision of Lord Goff, with whom Lord Lowry agreed on this point. Lord Goff carefully refrained from approving the approach of the majority in *Mutual Life*, noting the 'formidable' dissent of Lord Reid and Lord Morris and that the case had attracted 'serious criticism'. Nevertheless he stated that the result in the case before him was consistent with the majority's reasoning: 'the skill in preparing a reference in respect of an employee falls as much within the expertise of an employer as the skill of preparing a bank reference fell within the expertise of the defendant bank in *Hedley Byrne* itself' (p. 320). It seems that Lord Goff regarded the defendant's 'special skill' as crucial to the imposition of liability, provided that the phrase was understood in a broad sense to include special knowledge or the ability to acquire knowledge (p. 318). In fact, even this may not be broad enough. In *Spring*, the defendant undoubtedly possessed knowledge that was 'special' relative to the enquirer, but it is difficult to see how that can be the basis of a duty owed to the subject of the reference. In relation to that person, what is special about the position of the former employer is that the latter provides the reference with special *authority*, namely as a former employer, and the subject of the reference has no opportunity to challenge any inaccuracy. There is an imbalance of power between them. The notion of 'special skill' must therefore be broad enough to encompass not only special knowledge but also special authority in the sense described.

One issue yet to be resolved satisfactorily is whether *Hedley Byrne* liability might arise outside the business context, where a mere social acquaintance possesses or claims special skill. This question was raised in *Chaudhry* v. *Prabhakar* [1988] 3 All ER 718. A young woman sought the advice of a friend in buying a second-hand motor car. He recommended a car he had seen in the garage of a panel-beater, notwithstanding obvious signs that it had been involved in an accident. She took his advice and gave him money to make an initial payment for the car, paying the balance directly to the seller. The case concerned the standard of care owed by the friend giving the advice; it was conceded that the friend did owe a duty of care, under the law of principal and agent, as he was acting as a gratuitous agent. As the existence of the duty was conceded, the case is at best of limited authority, although two out of three members of the Court of Appeal accepted that the concession was correctly made and that the rule in *Hedley Byrne* v. *Heller* represented an alternative basis for the duty. May LJ doubted this, and the issue cannot be taken to have been finally resolved.

Reasonable Reliance

Reliance is a problematic concept: there is a sense in which all negligence cases involve reliance, 'as every motorist relies upon every other motorist in the vicinity to drive carefully' (*Muirhead* v. *International Tank Specialities Ltd* [1986] QB 507, 527 per Robert Goff LJ). Here, however, the concept of reliance bears a narrower meaning: it refers to the claimant's reliance upon the defendant's exercising special skill, knowledge or authority which the defendant has undertaken to apply to the claimant's benefit. In other words, there must be *specific* reliance upon the defendant's voluntary assumption of responsibility, not merely the *general* reliance exhibited in Robert Goff LJ's motorist example. In the case of the negligent provision of information or advice, the claimant must act upon the information or advice in question; in the case of the negligent provision of services, the claimant must entrust the conduct of her affairs to the defendant. Such reliance serves to 'consummate' the reciprocal relationship between claimant and defendant that has previously been initiated by the claimant (*White* v. *Jones* [1995] 2 AC 145, 288 per Lord Mustill). It also provides the necessary causal link between the defendant's negligence and the claimant's loss. In cases where the claimant's reliance is unreasonable, this may negate the causal connection (or alternatively provide the basis for a defence of *volenti* or contributory negligence).

5.5 **Indirect Reliance**

In the cases to which we now turn, the claimant suffers loss through reliance upon the defendant's assumption of responsibility to another person with whom the defendant is in a direct relationship. Although it is possible that the defendant might assume responsibility to both that other and the claimant, it seems that liability can arise when the responsibility is assumed only to the former, i.e. when there is no course of reciprocal dealings and hence no relationship between claimant and defendant. This may be regarded as problematic, as it deprives the courts of a ready mechanism for limiting the range of claims (hence raising the fear of indeterminate liability). Furthermore, it may be thought to distort the economic incentives on service providers (including advisers) who are held liable without having any opportunity to negotiate payment for their services or, in appropriate cases, exemption from liability. This raises fears of overkill as service providers resort to unduly defensive practice, or even withdraw from certain fields of activity altogether (see Bishop, 1980). Indeed, a government inquiry has warned that professionals faced with increasing liabilities might carry out unnecessary checks on their work, which serve no purpose other than to protect themselves in the event of a claim, or reject categories of clients who seem to raise particular risks, or even leave the profession altogether, to the detriment of the British business community which depends on having highly qualified professional advisers (Likierman, 1989).

Given the dual fears of indeterminate liability and overkill, it should be no surprise that the courts have proceeded cautiously in this type of case. Yet, although the results of cases have so far kept the scope of liability in check, the leading cases in this area have tended to employ tests of the necessary proximity between claimant and defendant that are too vague to provide a workable test of when a duty of care will arise, promote *ad hoc* decision-making, keep alive the possibility of an expansion in the sphere of liability, and thereby result in unnecessary litigation and concomitant uncertainty in the insurance markets.

The crucial case is *Caparo Industries* v. *Dickman* [1990] 2 AC 605, in which the issue before the House of Lords was whether accountants performing their statutory task of auditing company accounts at the end of the business year could be held liable to those who invest in the company in reliance upon the accounts and suffer losses as a consequence. Their Lordships held that no liability arose on the facts, saying that the purpose of the statutory audit was to enable shareholders to monitor the performance of the board of directors, not to enable them – or members of the investing public generally – to purchase shares with confidence. (In fact, the government which introduced the statutory requirement had precisely the latter purpose in mind: see Mullis and Oliphant, 1991.) They declined to follow the Court of Appeal in drawing a distinction between the first purchase of shares by the plaintiffs, who were then simply members of the investing public generally, and the purchase of subsequent tranches of shares at a time when the plaintiffs had of course become shareholders. But their Lordships accepted that liability might arise in exceptional circumstances, for example, where the auditor made specific representations to a particular investor in anticipation of a proposed takeover. Of course, where the audit is required for different purposes – for example, in order to assist regulatory supervision of a trade or profession – the auditor may well owe a duty of care to whoever is intended to rely upon it. In *Law Society* v. *KPMG Peat Marwick* [2000] 1 WLR 1921, the Court of Appeal ruled that auditors of solicitors' accounts owe a duty to the Law Society, to whom solicitors must make annual reports so as to facilitate the Society's exercise of its regulatory powers and, more specifically, to enable it to protect the contents of the Compensation Fund which makes awards to the victims of solicitors' dishonest conduct.

The actual decision in *Caparo* was undoubtedly cautious, and indeed was criticised as excessively cautious by those worried by the absence of any alternative legal incentive on auditors diligently to pursue their role as company 'watchdogs' (Mullis and Oliphant, 1991). But their Lordships based their decision on an interpretation of *Hedley Byrne* v. *Heller* that might be regarded as rather vague. According to Lord Bridge, for instance, the necessary proximity resided in the following requirements (p. 621; the other members of the House of Lords adopted very similar tests):

'that the defendant knew that his statement would be communicated to the plaintiff, either as an individual or as a member of an identifiable class, specifically in connection with a particular transaction or transactions of a particular kind ... and that the plaintiff would be very likely to rely on it for the purpose of deciding whether or not to enter on that transaction or on a transaction of that kind.'

This language is so imprecise as to make us ask why the test was not satisfied in *Caparo*. The auditors undoubtedly knew that their statements would be communicated to a 'class' of individuals, namely shareholders, and they undoubtedly knew that some members of that class would rely upon the information in relation to 'transactions of a particular kind' (further share purchases). The suspicion is that the House of Lords was guilty of somewhat manipulative reasoning in deciding that the group of shareholders was too wide to constitute 'a class' and that the purchase of shares was not a matter of sufficient specificity to count as 'a particular kind' of transaction.

Aside from its imprecision, the principal difficulty with the test employed is its liability to collapse into a test of mere foreseeability. Their Lordships clearly allowed that the duty might arise from the *inferential* knowledge of the defendant, i.e. what the defendant *ought to know*, and it is easy to slip from this into an acceptance that one *ought to know* things which are foreseeable with a certain degree of probability. If the liability of auditors is to be kept within reasonable bounds, it is necessary to test the existence of the duty by reference to factors which are more concrete than the notions of foreseeability and probability. It is submitted that the concept of voluntary assumption of responsibility, arising out of a reciprocal relationship between the parties, provides a more precise mechanism with which to determine the existence and extent of liability. The result in *Caparo* might itself be justified on this basis, in that there was no reciprocal relationship between auditor and investor: the auditor was engaged by the company and undertook responsibility only to the company. This reasoning would also allow the exceptional imposition of liability upon auditors who have direct dealings with a prospective take-over bidder, as was countenanced in *Caparo* (cf. *JEB Fasteners Ltd* v. *Marks, Bloom & Co* [1981] 3 All ER 289). More problematic is the case where a corporate 'predator', having already made one offer to the shareholders of the target company, makes a further, higher offer in reliance upon representations by financial advisers contained in the 'defence documents' prepared by the directors of the target company. The existence of a reciprocal relationship might perhaps be inferred from such facts, in that the course of events was initiated by the plaintiff's first bid for the company and that, although the defence documents were addressed to shareholders of the target company, it is well known that one of their purposes is to induce the bidder to raise its offer (cf. *Morgan Crucible Co* v. *Hill Samuel Bank* [1991] Ch. 259).

Another House of Lords decision gives rise to problems of analysis similar to those in *Caparo*. In *Smith* v. *Eric S Bush* [1990] AC 831 (heard with *Harris* v. *Wyre District Council*), surveyors valued a house at the request of a lending institution which passed the information on to its customer, Mrs Smith. The latter purchased the property in reliance upon the valuer's report which had erroneously stated that the property needed no essential repairs. Shortly afterwards, a chimney flue collapsed and crashed through the bedroom ceiling and floor. Mrs Smith sought damages from the valuer, notwithstanding that she had declined to commission a full structural survey of the property and that the report contained a purported disclaimer of liability. In *Harris* v. *Wyre District Council*, the plaintiffs, Mr and Mrs Harris, obtained a loan from their local authority in order to make a house purchase; the house was valued by the authority's own employee who failed to report that the house suffered from serious settlement necessitating major repairs. The Harrises did not see this report, but took the authority's offer of a loan to indicate that the house suffered from no significant defects; like Mrs Smith, they did not commission an independent survey. In each case, the plaintiffs were charged a valuation fee by their lending institution.

The House of Lords held that, in the circumstances of these cases (both of which involved a modest residential property), the valuer owed a duty of care to the potential purchaser (conceded in *Smith* v. *Bush*) and that the attempted disclaimer of liability did not satisfy the requirement of reasonableness imposed by the Unfair Contract Terms Act 1977 (see further 11.4). In looking for the necessary relationship of proximity, their Lordships focused upon two factors: 'The necessary proximity arises from the surveyor's knowledge that the overwhelming probability is that the purchaser will rely on his valuation ... and the fact that the surveyor only obtains the work because the purchaser is willing to pay his fee' (p. 865, per Lord Griffiths). It did not matter that the property valuation was designed to reassure the lending institution that the property in question represented adequate security because it has become common practice for house purchasers to treat such valuations as evidence of the structural soundness of the property and very few go to the additional expense of commissioning a full structural survey. Lord Griffiths added that '[t]here is no question here of creating a liability of indeterminate amount to an indeterminate class', emphasising that '[t]he extent of the liability is limited to the purchaser of the house' and that '[t]he amount of the liability cannot be very great because it relates to a modest house' (p. 865).

Although these cases are sometimes seen as 'three party' cases equivalent to *Caparo*, they are better differentiated from *Caparo* on the basis that each involved a direct assumption of responsibility by the valuer to the house purchaser, cutting across the indirect contractual relationship between the parties (see also the case of the indirect names in *Henderson* v. *Merrett*: 5.7). Although Lord Griffiths expressly doubted the utility of the concept of voluntary assumption of responsibility, it seems that he erroneously thought that it required the defendant's conscious assumption of legal responsibility rather than merely the voluntary entering into a relationship of reciprocal character (see, under 5.4, 'Voluntary Assumption of Responsibility'). In both *Smith* and *Harris*, the element of 'mutuality' which is necessary to create such a relationship seems to have been present: in each case, the plaintiffs *initiated* the reciprocal relationship between the parties by their request for a mortgage and payment of valuation fee, and *consummated* it by relying upon the valuer's (express or implied) representation as to the property's soundness. Seen in this light, the most controversial aspect of these cases is that the House of Lords implicitly regarded the assumption of responsibility as consistent with a contractual framework within which the plaintiffs were given, but declined, the option of entering into a direct relationship with the valuer by commissioning a full structural survey (carrying with it full guarantees). It is, one might think, unusual for the courts to impose a policy of consumer protection where consumers have the ready means of purchasing such protection for themselves.

5.6 **Indirect Loss Without Reliance**

Another exceptional type of case is where the defendant's conduct, for which the defendant has assumed a responsibility towards a third party, causes loss to the claimant without reliance on the part of the latter. Once again, if liability is to be recognised in such circumstances it becomes difficult to limit the scope of the duty, and the fear arises of a flood of claims placing an excessive burden on the defendant. So the courts have proceeded cautiously but have nevertheless recognised a duty in certain exceptional circumstances.

In *White* v. *Jones* [1995] 2 AC 145, the House of Lords had to consider the correctness of the decision in *Ross* v. *Caunters (a firm)* [1980] Ch 297 that solicitors who undertake the task of drawing up a will owe a duty of care to intended beneficiaries left unable to inherit as a result of the solicitors' negligence. As a result of a family quarrel, the elderly testator, Mr Barratt, had excluded his two daughters (the plaintiffs) from his will. Shortly afterwards, there was a reconciliation and Mr Barratt instructed his solicitors to draw up a new will in which his daughters would be named as beneficiaries. His instructions were accepted but the solicitors unreasonably delayed in acting upon them, and had failed to draw up the new will at the time of Mr Barratt's sudden death a couple of months later. Under established principles of the law of succession, the estate could only be divided in accordance with the terms of the existent will: the subsequent instructions to the solicitors were not witnessed and could not take effect as a will. The daughters were therefore deprived of their intended inheritance, and brought an action for damages in negligence. By a majority of 3–2, the House of Lords held that the solicitors owed the intended beneficiaries a duty of care and could be held liable to indemnify the plaintiffs for their loss of expectation.

The primary significance of this case is that it allows liability for the negligent provision of a service which was undertaken at the request of a third party and caused loss without any specific act of reliance by the plaintiffs (but note Lord Nolan's reservations on this last point, below). As Lord Goff stated, the case did not fall within the standard *Hedley Byrne* v. *Heller* special relationship (p. 262):

'[T]here is great difficulty in holding, on ordinary principles, that the solicitor has assumed any responsibility towards an intended beneficiary under a will which he has undertaken to prepare on behalf of his client but which, through his negligence, has failed to take effect in accordance with his client's instructions. The relevant work is plainly performed by the solicitor for his client; but, in the absence of special circumstances, it cannot be said to have been undertaken for the intended beneficiary ... [T]here will have been no reliance by the intended beneficiary on the exercise by the solicitor of due care and skill; indeed the intended beneficiary may not even have been aware that the solicitor was engaged on such a task, or that his position might be affected.'

Nevertheless, the majority of the House of Lords was prepared to allow an incremental expansion of the existing categories of liability for pure economic loss and to fashion a remedy to meet the special circumstances of the case.

What most impressed the majority of their Lordships' House was the practical justice of the plaintiffs' case. In the absence of a tort remedy, there was, as Lord Goff noted, an asymmetry as between loss and remedy (pp. 259–60):

'if such a duty is not recognised, the only person who might have a valid claim (i.e. the testator and his estate) has suffered no loss, and the only person who has suffered a loss (i.e. the disappointed beneficiary) has no claim... It can therefore be said that, if the solicitor owes no duty to the intended beneficiaries, there is a lacuna in the law which needs to be filled.'

To their Lordships, it was immaterial that recognition of the duty would result in a windfall benefit to the estate, which would still distribute the bequest in accordance with the terms of the actual will.

Their Lordships agreed that the duty of care arose from the defendant's voluntary assumption of responsibility for the task of preparing the will, but their speeches reveal small yet significant variations of approach. Lord Goff held that responsibility was *in fact* assumed only to the testator. Nevertheless, in view of the need to fill the lacuna in the law, he was prepared to *deem* the assumption of responsibility to have wider effect: 'the assumption of responsibility by the solicitor towards his client should be held in law to extend to the intended beneficiary' (p. 268). By means of this legal fiction, he was able to disregard the need for any reliance by the plaintiffs upon the defendant's care and skill.

In contrast, both Lord Browne-Wilkinson and Lord Nolan found that the solicitors had voluntarily assumed responsibility by accepting Mr Barratt's instructions: it was up to the law to specify the scope of that responsibility and, in particular, to determine whether it extended to the plaintiffs. Both decided that it did indeed extend to them, Lord Nolan on the narrow ground that there were (on the facts of this case) specific acts of reliance by the plaintiffs who had been 'intimately concerned' in instructing the solicitors to revise the will (they had been in direct contact with the solicitors: p. 295); Lord Nolan appears therefore to have regarded the course of dealings between the parties as crucial in this case and to have treated the case as falling within the straightforward *Hedley Byrne* type of special relationship. Lord Browne-Wilkinson (like Lord Goff), however, preferred not to leave the result dependent upon the actual dealings between the parties on the facts of the case, as in many cases the intended beneficiaries might not even know of the proposed bequest. His approach was to identify a new class of special relationship – by incremental expansion upon the existing classes of relationship, namely the fiduciary relationship and the *Hedley Byrne* special relationship – in which liability depended upon the defendant's voluntary assumption of responsibility in agreeing to perform a task but not upon any specific acts of reliance by the claimant.

The decision cannot be regarded as satisfactory. First, the divergence of approach as between the members of the majority makes it impossible to state the *ratio decidendi* of the case and makes further litigation inevitable, though it appears that the Court of Appeal has adopted the sensible course of treating Lord Goff's opinion as expressing the reasoning of the majority of the House of Lords (see, especially, *Carr-Glynn* v. *Frearsons (a firm)* [1999] Ch 326, 335 per Chadwick LJ). Nevertheless, the narrowness of the ground on which Lord Nolan, the 'swing judge', found for the plaintiffs means that another visit to the Lords may well be required just to resolve the case of the intended beneficiaries who are ignorant of the proposed bequest. Secondly, the interpretation given to the concept of voluntary assumption of responsibility by Lord Browne-Wilkinson and Lord Nolan is so broad as to deprive it of all meaning and utility. Responsibility is assumed in the sense described by their Lordships in the performance of any potentially harmful activity: 'If the defendant drives his car on the highway, he implicitly assumes a responsibility towards other road users' (p. 293, per Lord Nolan). Yet such an interpretation negates the concept's role in specifying the scope of liability in the particular sphere of pure economic loss because it provides no way to limit the class of those to whom responsibility is assumed. The more precise conception of Lord Goff, which requires evidence of a course of dealings between the parties, is to be preferred (see, under 5.4, 'Voluntary Assumption of Responsibility').

It is submitted, therefore, that the rule in *White* v. *Jones* should be interpreted as applying where the defendant assumes responsibility to one person with a view to conferring a benefit upon another, in circumstances where the latter will be without a remedy should the defendant fail to discharge that responsibility. The principle should apply not just to wills but also to such equivalent transactions as the purchase of life insurance designed to benefit the insured's dependants after his death (*Gorham* v. *British Telecommunications plc* [2000] 1 WLR 2129), though not where the arrangements between the parties are designed to exclude or restrict any remedy in damages (cf. *Leigh & Sillivan Ltd* v. *Aliakmon Shipping Co Ltd*

[1986] AC 785). As the duty to the claimant is derivative from the initial assumption of responsibility, it follows that the scope of that duty will reflect the extent of the responsibility assumed, and that the defendant's disclaimer of responsibility may defeat the claimant's action irrespective of whether the latter had notice of it (p. 268, per Lord Goff). Conversely, where responsibility is directly assumed to the claimant under normal *Hedley Byrne* principles, it would seem that she must have notice of the disclaimer if it is to have effect. The duty is designed to fill a lacuna in the law, and hence will not be imposed where the disappointed beneficiary has an equally-good alternative remedy, as in the case of a will which contains a drafting error which can be formally rectified by invoking the appropriate statutory procedure (*Walker* v. *Geo H Medlicott & Son (a firm)* [1999] 1 WLR 727). The same applies where the intending benefactor discovers the defendant's negligence whilst still alive but fails to take reasonable steps to ensure the rights of the intended beneficiaries (*Gorham* v. *British Telecommunications plc* [2000] 1 WLR 2129), and *a fortiori* where she still retains the means to perfect the transaction or provide some equivalent benefit, as in the case of a typical *inter vivos* gift (see *Clarke* v. *Bruce Lance & Co (a firm)* [1988] 1 WLR 881). But there may be exceptional cases of *inter vivos* transactions in which the ability to perfect the transaction has been irretrievably lost, and it appears that the rule might apply in such circumstances, for example, where a solicitor's negligence results in a settlor conferring benefits under an irrevocable deed of settlement to someone other than the intended beneficiary, or where solicitors retained by an employer in order to draft an effective tax avoidance scheme for the benefit of employees are negligent with the result that the scheme is ineffective and the tax payable (*Hemmens* v. *Wilson Browne (a firm)* [1995] Ch 223, per Judge Moseley QC).

5.7 Hedley Byrne and the Contract–Tort Boundary

Having surveyed the principal headings under which liability for pure economic loss may exceptionally arise, we now turn to the difficult questions which result from the interplay of principles of contract and tort in this area. Questions of the contract–tort boundary – of that area of law termed 'contorts' by one commentator (Hedley, 1995) – arise in cases of concurrent liability and in other cases in which an action in tort might be thought to 'short-circuit' a set of contractual arrangements. This might be the case where to recognise a tort liability would give the claimant the benefit of a gratuitous undertaking, or a contractual undertaking contained in a contract to which the claimant was not privy. We here consider these issues in turn.

The question of concurrent liability was authoritatively addressed by the House of Lords in *Henderson* v. *Merrett Syndicates Ltd* [1995] 2 AC 145. The case involved a multiplicity of claims arising out of the near-collapse of the Lloyd's of London insurance market in the early 1990s. At this time, many Lloyd's syndicates sustained heavy losses, partly as a result of unprecedented liabilities for storm damage following hurricanes in the USA, and called upon their members (known as 'names') to make good the losses. The names alleged negligence on the part of the managing agents who organised the affairs of the syndicates. Their claims fell into two groups: those brought by the so-called 'direct names', i.e. those who were in a direct contractual relationship with the managing agents, and those brought by the 'indirect names', i.e. those who were linked with the managing agents indirectly through a contractual chain (the names had contracted with 'members' agents', who had in turn contracted with the managing agents). The House of Lords held that in both types of case the managing agents had assumed a direct responsibility to the names. Lord Goff, who delivered the leading speech, emphasised the reciprocal nature of the relationship between names and managing agents (p. 182):

> 'The managing agents have accepted the names as members of a syndicate under their management ... The names ... gave authority to the managing agents to bind them to contracts of insurance and reinsurance and to the settlement of claims.'

In such circumstances, a prima facie duty of care arose.

This conclusion was, however, subject to consideration of the relevance of the contractual context. The case of the direct names required the House of Lords to decide whether the plaintiffs should be limited to their claim under the contract or free as an alternative to pursue a concurrent remedy in tort. This was in the interest of some of the plaintiffs because of the more favourable limitation period applying to the claim in tort (six years from the date of loss, rather than from the date of the breach of contract). The defendants relied upon a well-known statement of Lord Scarman in the decision of the Privy Council in *Tai Hing Cotton Mill Ltd* v. *Liu Chong Hing Bank Ltd* [1986] AC 80, 107 where he said:

> 'Their Lordships do not believe that there is anything to the advantage of the law's development in searching for a liability in tort where the parties are in a contractual relationship.'

The House of Lords rejected the implicit premiss of this view, which saw 'the law of tort as supplementary to the law of contract, i.e. as providing for a tortious liability in cases in which there is no contract', holding that it was the law of tort that was fundamental ('the general law': p. 193, per Lord Goff). Although 'the contract can modify and shape the tortious duties which, in the absence of contract, would be applicable' (p. 206, per Lord Browne-Wilkinson, who delivered a short concurring speech), the tortious liability is presumed to survive unless 'so inconsistent with the applicable contract that ... the parties must be taken to have agreed that the tortious remedy is to be limited or excluded' (p. 194, per Lord Goff). Such agreement might be inferred where the contract specifies duties which are less extensive than those in tort, but this was not the case in *Henderson*, and the plaintiffs were therefore to be left to choose whichever remedy was more advantageous to them (e.g. in relation to limitation periods).

If the relationship between claimant and defendant is not contractual, is it desirable for the law to recognise a tort claim on the basis that the relationship is nevertheless 'equivalent to contract'? In the classic example of such a relationship identified by Lord Devlin in *Hedley Byrne* – namely 'where there is an assumption of responsibility in circumstances, in which, but for the absence of consideration, there would be a contract' – it might be thought that recognition of a tort liability would effectively undermine the requirement of consideration in contract. Other central doctrines of contract law might be under similar threat. The case of the indirect names in *Henderson* provides an example, because, notwithstanding the reciprocal nature of their relationship with the managing agents, the contractual link between them was so structured as to give the names contractual rights only against their agents (the members' agents) and to limit the contractual liability of the managing agents to their sub-agency agreement with the members' agents. In short, there was no privity of contract: the plaintiffs' contractual rights arose under one contract; the defendants' contractual duties arose under another.

Lord Goff's approach to this problem in *Henderson* was to start with the propositions identified above, namely that the law of tort is the general law but that tortious duties may be displaced by the contrary agreement of the parties. He suggested that the existence of a contractual chain structured so as to avoid privity between claimant and defendant would often enable such agreement to be inferred, for example, in the case of subcontracting under an ordinary building contract:

'in many cases in which a contractual chain comparable to that in the present case is constructed it may well prove to be inconsistent with an assumption of responsibility which has the effect of, so to speak, short circuiting the contractual structure so put in place by the parties.' (p. 195; cf. *Simaan General Contracting Co* v. *Pilkington Glass Ltd (No 2)* [1988] QB 758)

However, Lord Goff denied that the agreements in the present case were inconsistent with the defendant's prima facie assumption of responsibility to the plaintiffs, commenting only that, in this respect, the facts of the present case were 'most unusual'.

Lord Goff provides little guidance as to the factors that are relevant in determining when an assumption of responsibility will be permitted to 'short-circuit' a contractual chain. He declined to pass substantive comment upon the problematic case of *Junior Books Ltd* v. *Veitchi Co Ltd* [1983] 1 AC 520 (considered above, 5.3) in which specialist subcontractors were held to have assumed responsibility directly to the owners of premises then under development, despite the fact that their contractual rights and liabilities arose only in respect of the main contractor. Nevertheless, and despite Lord Goff's opinion that there might be inferred an agreement to exclude tort liability in the ordinary case of subcontracting under a building contract, the decision may be justified on the basis that there was a mutuality of relationship between the building owner and the subcontractor (the former having nominated the latter to perform the work) and that the latter was a specialist, exercising a special skill, who might be expected to have insurance against such loss. The extent to which this analysis might serve to undermine the basic 'no recovery' rule in *Murphy* v. *Brentwood District Council* [1991] 1 AC 398 remains to be seen. This is perhaps the most crucial of the questions left unresolved by the House of Lords in its recent attempts to define the scope of the exceptional liability for pure economic loss under *Hedley Byrne* v. *Heller* and other related principles.

Summary

5.1 Pure economic loss is financial loss not consequent upon damage to the claimant or her property.

5.2 Any harm that a defective product causes to itself is pure economic loss: a claim can generally only be made in respect of a defective product if it damages *other* property. Parliament has, however, created a statutory liability in respect of defective dwellings (Defective Premises Act 1972).

5.3 Exceptionally, liability for pure economic loss is recognised under the principle in *Hedley Byrne* v. *Heller* and related principles.

5.4 The basic principle of *Hedley Byrne* v. *Heller* provides that a person may assume a legal responsibility to another when they enter into a special relationship in which the latter reasonably relies upon the former's careful exercise of special skill, knowledge or capacities.

5.5 By an analogous principle, it appears that a duty may be owed to a person who suffers loss through reliance upon the defendant's assumption of responsibility to a third party.

5.6 By another analogous principle, the defendant's assumption of responsibility to one person, with a view to conferring a benefit upon another who would otherwise be without a remedy, may be deemed to extend to the latter.

5.7 Questions of the contract–tort boundary arise in cases of concurrent liability and in other cases in which an action in tort might be thought to 'short-circuit' a set of contractual arrangements.

Exercises

5.1 Is the loss suffered in the following examples to be counted as pure economic loss:

    (a) A's hotel is damaged by fire. It has to close for repairs. A suffers a loss of profits as a consequence.

    (b) B's hotel has to close for repairs after the plaster on the dining room ceiling collapses, damaging furniture underneath. It takes one week to replace the furniture and two further weeks to have the room replastered. B suffers a loss of profits as a consequence.

    (c) C, a newsagent, is injured in a car crash and has to close the shop for two months while she recuperates. She suffers a loss of profits as a consequence. D, who delivers newspapers for C, suffers a loss of earnings while the shop is closed.

5.2 Lord Wilberforce in *Anns* classified the loss suffered by the plaintiff in that case as 'material, physical damage'. Discuss.

5.3 In *Spartan Steel*, Edmund Davies LJ (dissenting) stated that 'an action lies in negligence for damages in respect of pure economic loss, provided that it was a reasonably foreseeable and direct consequence of failure in a duty of care.' In *Junior Books*, Lord Roskill suggested that Edmund Davies's reasoning might be preferred to that of the majority of the Court of Appeal in *Spartan Steel*. Do you think it would?

5.4 In what circumstances (a) was pure economic loss recoverable in 1983 and (b) is it recoverable now?

5.5 How is the concept of a 'voluntary assumption of responsibility' understood by (a) Lord Griffiths in *Smith* v. *Eric S Bush*, (b) Lord Goff in *Henderson* v. *Merrett*, and (c) Lord Browne-Wilkinson in *White* v. *Jones*? Does the concept have any utility?

5.6 Why should the courts adopt a restrictive approach to the recovery of damages for negligently inflicted pure economic loss? Would the argument in favour of liability be stronger or weaker if the loss were *intentionally* inflicted?

5.7 P is a keen wine collector who used to seek advice from Q, a wine consultant, who gave her advice without payment as P was a friend. Q negligently advised P to keep cases of Woolloomooloo White, an Australian wine which she already possessed, far too long. When P opened the first bottle, she found that the wine had turned to vinegar. Her tasting of other bottles confirmed that all of them were spoiled. She was doubly dismayed as she had arranged to sell a couple of cases of the wine at a large profit. Q had also advised P to put in a bid at auction for some very old wine labelled Château Mutton. P succeeded in buying the wine for £500 but later discovered that Q had confused the name of the wine at the auction for that of a far superior producer, Château Mouton. The wine turned out to be undrinkable. P also had in her cellar two cases of English table wine, Chateau Strand and Chateau Aldwych, which she had received as a gift. These also turn out to be spoiled. This time the cause is a mould which was present in the corks of the bottles. The corks in the bottles of Chateau Strand had been produced for the winery by R Ltd. Those in the bottles of Chateau Aldwych, also produced by R Ltd, had been inserted by Q by way of replacement of the original corks after the bottles had come into P's possession. Advise the parties as to their rights and liabilities in tort.

6 Omissions

6.1 **Introduction**

In formulating his general statement of principle in *Donoghue* v. *Stevenson*, Lord Atkin took as his starting point the biblical command that you are to love your neighbour, alluding to the parable of the good Samaritan (Luke 10: 29–37). Some 40 years or so later, Lord Diplock returned to that parable to illustrate the limits of the 'neighbour' principle, particularly in the context of omissions. According to Lord Diplock, although the priest and the Levite who passed by on the other side of the road might attract moral censure, they would have incurred no civil liability in English law (*Home Office* v. *Dorset Yacht Co* [1970] AC 1004, 1060).

The traditional approach of the common law has been to adopt the general rule that there is no liability for omissions or, to put it another way, that there is no duty to act to prevent harm. This approach is premised upon a highly individualist political theory which holds that people should be concerned purely and simply with their own self-advancement and not subject to legal liability for failing to intervene for the benefit of others. This, the theory suggests, is the most effective way of maximising individuals' freedom of action (see Smith and Burns, 1983). In addition to the fear of unduly burdening individuals, another justification for the general rule of no liability for omissions is the pragmatic concern that there may be no reason for holding any particular defendant liable for harm she could have prevented rather than all the others who were just as able to intervene. Why pick on the priest and the Levite when countless others might have passed by on the road to Jericho that celebrated day?

With the advance of community values, evident in particular in the institution of the welfare state, a categorical denial of liability for omissions looks out of touch with modern reality. Conscious of this, judges have begun to admit exceptions to the general rule. The exceptions have arisen where the two responses identified above – 'Don't burden me' and 'Why pick on me?' – are weakest. Thus, for instance, it does not seem unfair to burden an employer with the duty actively to take precautions for the safety of her workforce (see, e.g., *Paris* v. *Stepney Borough Council* [1951] AC 367: provision of personal protective equipment), as it was for her benefit that they were exposed to danger in the first place. Furthermore, this provides a clear reason for picking on the employer rather than, say, those passing by in the street who see that the working practices are unsafe yet do nothing about it. Yet, despite the growing number of cases of liability for omission, the general rule of no liability remains. In cases which fall outside the exceptions, often labelled cases of 'pure' omissions, people can ignore their moral responsibilities towards others without legal sanction. It is, for instance, quite unthinkable that there should be 'liability in negligence on the part of one who sees another about to walk over a cliff with his head in the air and forbears to shout a warning' (*Yuen Kun Yeu* v. *A-G of Hong Kong* [1988] AC 175, 192 per Lord Keith). The implementation of the Human Rights Act 1998 may well make it easier to find a duty of affirmative action in particular fact-situations, but it seems unlikely that it will induce the courts to abandon their insistence upon a general rule of no liability for omissions (see 6.7).

The exceptional cases in which the courts have imposed liability for omission defy easy categorisation. It is nevertheless possible to identify a number of factors which trigger the imposition of a duty of affirmative action in different types of case, and which may indeed overlap on the facts of an individual case. It is these factors which, together or in isolation, may provide the element of proximity necessary for the recognition of a duty of care. We now proceed to consider a number of these factors in turn.

6.2 **Voluntary Assumption of Responsibility**

In stark contrast to the law of tort, the law of contract is all about imposing duties of affirmative action. Accordingly, it is no surprise that the courts are most willing to hold people liable in tort for their negligent omissions in cases where they have agreed, expressly or impliedly, to take on a responsibility for the benefit of others. Hence, where a decorator agrees to lock the premises on leaving but neglects to do so, this may amount to a breach of a duty of affirmative action owed to the occupier who may recover as damages the value of any goods stolen by thieves during the decorator's absence (see *Stansbie* v. *Troman* [1948] 2 KB 48). Similarly, a police officer who agrees to stand close-by while a fellow officer visits a violent prisoner in the cells owes a duty to come to her aid if she is attacked (*Costello* v. *Chief Constable of Northumbria Police* [1999] ICR 730). Another example is the duty of sporting bodies, in licensing events in which there is a plain risk that participants might suffer physical injury, to ensure the availability of appropriate medical facilities and assistance (*Watson* v. *British Boxing Board of Control Ltd* [2001] QB 1134). In such circumstances, the fact that the defendant has freely undertaken the responsibility can be taken to indicate that she regards her conduct as advancing her own interests, and the 'Don't burden me' objection is therefore weakened. Furthermore, where the defendant induces reliance upon her conduct by others, then lets them down, it may be said that she has actually made their position worse, not merely failed to render a benefit.

Responsibility may be assumed by acceptance of a particular office or position, or simply on an *ad hoc* basis. Where a swimmer encounters trouble at sea and is in peril of drowning, the lifeguard has a duty to intervene which arises by virtue of her accepting her position of responsibility; ordinary bystanders, under no such obligation (irrespective of their swimming ability), might nevertheless assume responsibility on that particular occasion if they were to embark on a rescue or go in search of assistance. At what point in time does the rescuer assume a responsibility towards the person in danger? There is a divergence of opinion on this issue in other jurisdictions (see Fleming, 1998, pp. 164–5), but no clear English authority. At one extreme is the view that only if the rescuer should carelessly inflict fresh injury on the person in danger would liability arise. At the other extreme is the opinion that the duty arises at the moment the rescue is commenced or at least when the rescuer takes charge of the situation (e.g. by pulling the drowning person from the water). Perhaps the strongest view, however, is that the rescuer assumes responsibility for the rescue as soon as her intervention induces reliance by others which is detrimental to the interests of the person in danger (e.g. by discouraging others from coming to her aid). It is the adverse impact of the rescuer upon the position of the person in danger that justifies the imposition of the duty.

The English cases have not spoken with a single voice on this issue, partly because it has arisen mainly in the context of the duties owed by the emergency services, where special considerations of public policy arise and the position is not strictly analogous to that of the private individual who embarks upon a rescue (see 7.3–4). In *Capital & Counties plc* v. *Hampshire County Council* [1997] QB 1004, the Court of Appeal ruled that the fire brigade had no common law duty to answer calls to fires or to take reasonable care in responding to calls it had accepted, Stuart-Smith LJ remarking that '[i]f therefore they fail to turn up or fail to turn up in time because they have carelessly misunderstood the message, got lost on the way or run into a tree, they are not liable' (p. 1030). Furthermore, a fire brigade did not assume responsibility to the owner or occupier of premises merely by attending at the fire ground and fighting the fire, even where the senior officer actually took control of the fire-fighting operation. In *Kent* v. *Griffiths* [2001] QB 36, by contrast, the Court of Appeal held that the ambulance service did assume responsibility to the person to whose aid they were summoned by a 999-call and could be held liable where that person's condition was aggravated by the failure of the ambulance to arrive in good time. The court distinguished *Capital & Counties* on the basis that the ambulance had been called for the claimant alone, and nobody else would be affected whether it turned up on time or not, whereas the fire service might on occasion have to sacrifice the claimant's property in the interests of the wider community. Because the public policy considerations arising in these cases are so specific, they do not really provide much guidance in relation to the position of the rescuer who is a true volunteer. There is perhaps a closer analogy with the facts in *Barrett* v. *Ministry of Defence* [1995] 1 WLR 1217, where the Court of Appeal decided that the person taking charge of the situation where the deceased fell unconscious through excessive drinking thereby assumed a responsibility to him. In that case, though, the incident occurred on the defendant's premises, and the deceased had been drinking alcohol provided by the defendant, so the duty might well have arisen even in the absence of any specific assumption of responsibility on the defendant's behalf.

6.3 **Protection of the Vulnerable**

The premise of individualistic political theory – that people are best off if left to their own devices – is clearly false when applied to particular groups of vulnerable people. In such cases, a social or moral responsibility will often fall upon certain others who stand in a continuing relationship with the vulnerable person (close family, health care practitioners, etc.). And the law of tort may regard this as sufficient warrant for the imposition of a concurrent *legal* responsibility.

The most obvious example of such a responsibility is that owed to very young children. Infants are manifestly vulnerable in that they are incapable of looking after themselves. Thus, parents and those *in loco parentis* must take steps to ensure that children in their care are reasonably safe, and a teacher who after class lets a small schoolchild wander off onto a busy main road, without adult supervision, may be held liable if the child is run over (*Barnes* v. *Hampshire County Council* [1969] 1 WLR 1563). Those with mental disabilities have an equal claim to special consideration and it is clear that medical staff in mental hospitals owe a duty to prevent the patients harming themselves. The same duty arises where a mentally-ill person is in official custody, whether after arrest or whilst on remand or serving a prison sentence (*Kirkham* v. *Chief Constable of Greater Manchester Police* [1990] 2 QB 283: suicide of mentally-ill remand prisoner). In fact, such are the psychological pressures acting on the mind of those who have been imprisoned that a duty of care will arise once a particular prisoner has been identified as a suicide risk, even if not suffering from mental illness. In *Reeves* v. *Commissioner of the Police for the Metropolis* [2000] 1 AC 360, the House of Lords allowed a claim by the widow of a remand prisoner who, whilst in police custody awaiting trial, had asphyxiated himself with a ligature he had fashioned from his shirt and threaded through the cell door hatch, which had been inadvertently left open. To the police's knowledge, the deceased had made two previous suicide attempts, the more recent being at the magistrate's court on the very morning of his death, but the doctor who examined him on his arrival at the police station found no evidence of psychiatric disorder or clinical depression. Their Lordships considered that the police had correctly conceded that they owed the deceased a duty of care, which Lord Hoffmann described as 'a very unusual one, arising from the complete control which the police or prison authorities have over the prisoner, combined with the special danger of people in prison taking their own lives' (p. 369). The point at issue on the appeal was whether the deceased's free and deliberate act in taking his own life broke the chain of causation and relieved the police of responsibility for the death. On this, the House of Lords ruled that it was not open to the police to argue that the occurrence of the very act which they ought to have prevented interrupted the causal chain (see further 9.4), though it made a 50 per cent reduction in damages for contributory negligence. Recognition of a duty in such circumstances accords with the state's obligation to protect the right to life of persons in custody arising under art. 2 of the European Convention.

The Strasbourg jurisprudence accepts, however, that the duty only arises where there is a 'real and immediate risk' of suicide (*Keenan* v. *United Kingdom* (2001) 33 EHRR 913), and it appears entirely consistent with that caselaw for the English Court of Appeal to rule that there was no duty to take special precautions in the case of an apparently run-of-the-mill drunk who had been arrested for disorderly conduct and placed in the cells until he sobered up (*Orange* v. *Chief Constable of West Yorkshire Police* [2001] EWCA Civ 611, [2001] 3 WLR 736). The police were not responsible when he used his belt to make a noose with which he took his own life.

6.4 Acts of Third Parties and Relationships of Control

Just as the basic rule is that I have no duty to protect others from harm, so too I generally have no responsibility for the actions of others. A third party's intervention is normally sufficient to break the chain of causation between the defendant's negligent conduct and the claimant's injury. Exceptionally, however, the law recognises a positive duty to control the actions of another person arising out of a relationship with that person. In some of these exceptional cases, the third party lacks the capacity to count as a new intervening cause of the claimant's injury. Cases involving very young children again provide the best example: as very young children lack the capacity to take full responsibility for their actions, those looking after them cannot justifiably abandon them to their own devices. Thus, in *Carmarthenshire County Council* v. *Lewis* [1955] AC 549, the House of Lords held a local authority liable for its failure to secure a school playground which allowed a small child to wander onto the road, causing a lorry to swerve and crash; the driver was injured.

Other exceptional cases involve liabilities arising in respect of harm caused by third parties who are fully responsible for their own actions. Such actions are normally sufficient to break the chain of causation, but the law meets this difficulty by recognising an exceptional duty to control the third party in question. Where such a duty is imposed, the liability is based upon a weaker form of causal connection than is usually required, namely the provision of the means or opportunity for a third party to bring about the harm. The defendant's liability is not, strictly speaking, for *causing* the harm, but for *occasioning* it (see Hart and Honoré, 1985, pp. 194–204).

Liabilities of this description – where a special duty of care allows the defendant to be held liable merely for occasioning, rather than causing, harm – are currently very restricted in scope. One of the few unequivocal instances of such liability is where the defendant is charged with the task, as a matter of public safety, of holding the third party in lawful custody. Hence, prison authorities may be held responsible for harm caused by one inmate to her fellows while in custody, and even for harm caused to those in the vicinity in the course of an escape from custody. In *Home Office* v. *Dorset Yacht Co* [1970] AC 1004, Borstal officers had, in breach of instructions, left their charges unsupervised while on a training exercise. A number of young offenders made good their escape; in the course of this they damaged a yacht. The House of Lords held the Home Office vicariously liable for the damage. It would, however, have been excessive to have burdened the custodians with responsibility for all the harm subsequently done by the escapees and Lord Diplock, whose speech seems the one most in tune with current judicial attitudes, made it clear that he would impose liability only in respect of harm caused in the course of the escape, at roughly the same time and in the vicinity. Thus it seems that the Home Office would not have been liable if the complaint had been that the escapees had some weeks later robbed a post office in another part of the country.

In the course of the decision, Lord Pearson advanced the proposition that 'control imports responsibility'. This should not be taken to mean that the defendant's mere *ability* to control the activities of a third party is sufficient foundation for a duty of care. The *obligation* to control is limited to a narrow set of control relationships (e.g. that between prisoner and custodian). For instance, although it may be said that the police – through their powers of arrest – may exercise a degree of control over those suspected of criminal activities, they do not stand in any relationship of control with those suspects (except for any period in which the latter are actually in police custody). So the police are not generally responsible for injuries inflicted by suspects whom they unreasonably fail to arrest. In *Hill* v. *Chief Constable of West Yorkshire* [1989] AC 53, an action was brought against the police by the estate of one of the victims of the so-called 'Yorkshire Ripper', Peter Sutcliffe. The House of Lords held that the police were not in a relationship of proximity with the deceased, distinguishing the *Dorset Yacht* case on the grounds that Sutcliffe had never been taken into police custody (see further 7.4).

The result would appear to be the same where the authorities have released a dangerous person into the community, at least where they had no reason to know of an immediate risk to a particular individual. In *Palmer* v. *Tees Health Authority* [2000] PIQR P1, the defendant health authority discharged a psychiatric patient from its care even though he had admitted that he had sexual feelings towards children and claimed that a child would be murdered after his discharge. A year after his release from hospital, but while still an out-patient, he abducted, sexually assaulted and murdered the claimant's four-year-old daughter. Striking out the claimant's action for damages, the Court of Appeal stated that there was insufficient proximity to found a duty of care. At the very least, it was necessary to show that the victim could have been foreseen as particularly at risk. The court reserved its opinion on the case where the victim was identified or identifiable in advance, for example, as a child in the abuser's household (p. P12, per Stuart-Smith LJ). Similarly, in *K* v. *Secretary of State for the Home Department* [2002] EWCA Civ 983, the Court of Appeal decided that the Home Secretary owed no arguable duty to a woman who was raped by a foreign national with a known history of sexual offences, who was subject to a deportation order but had been released from detention for reasons that were never satisfactorily explained. Laws LJ stated (at [29]) that it would have been 'contrary to principle' to treat the defendant's knowledge that another person posed an especially grave risk of harm to the public at large as supplying the relationship of proximity between claimant and defendant that was necessary to create a duty of care: 'A defendant does not become the world's insurer against the grave danger (where the danger is general) posed by a third agency, which he might control but does not, by virtue only of the fact that he appreciates that the danger exists'. The position might, of course, be different if the danger is specific to an identifiable individual.

6.5 Creation of a Source of Danger

A more general consideration giving rise to a duty of affirmative action is the defendant's creation of a source of danger. This is the basis of the driver's obligation, after being involved in an accident, to stop and render assistance to the injured, even if blameless, and of the manufacturer's duty to recall or warn of dangerous products (*Rivtow Marine Ltd* v. *Washington Iron Works* [1974] SCR 1189). In such cases, it can be said that the defendant has not merely failed to render a benefit to the claimant but has actually, albeit over an expanded 'time-frame', made her worse off by exposing her to the risk of harm.

This principle may also apply where the danger is sparked off by a third party. The classic example is *Haynes* v. *Harwood* [1935] 1 KB 146: the defendant's employee, the driver of a horse-drawn cart, left the horses unattended in the street. The horses bolted when an unknown third party threw a stone at them. The plaintiff policeman saw the horses galloping down the street and grabbed them to bring them to a halt and thereby protect the general public from danger; in doing so, he suffered injuries. The Court of Appeal held the defendant liable, notwithstanding the intervention of the third party. In the language we have adopted, the defendant had *occasioned* injury to the plaintiff by creating a new danger which was foreseeably sparked off by the third party.

It is not enough that foreseeable intervention by a third party might create a danger: the circumstances of the case must give rise to a *special* risk. In *Topp* v. *London Country Buses (South West) Ltd* [1993] 1 WLR 976, the Court of Appeal declined to accept that vehicles left unattended in the street would meet this requirement, even in the extreme circumstances of the case. During licensing hours one evening, a minibus used for public transport was left unattended outside the White Horse public house in Epsom, its keys still in the ignition. At around closing time, persons unknown (possibly from the pub, although the trial judge stated that there was 'no evidence' of this) commandeered the bus and drove off down the street, erratically and without headlights. Shortly afterwards, it careered out of control and fatally collided with the deceased. The Court of Appeal upheld the decision of the trial judge, May J, that a parked minibus was no more a source of danger than any other vehicle on the road and was clearly distinguishable from such obvious sources of danger as '[a] startled horse or a spilt paraffin lamp or a substantial quantity of fireworks stored in an unlocked garden shed'. Further, the learned judge submitted that to treat the defendant's minibus as, in the circumstances, especially alluring would require the courts to make impossible distinctions in the future, for example as to 'the relative allurements of (say) a blue Volvo estate, a Ford GTi, ... or a pink VW beetle, to mention but a few'. What then is the difference between an unattended vehicle and unattended horses? Perhaps it is that horses, if left unattended, might present a danger even without the involvement of an independent third party, whereas a car will usually be harmless until driven away.

Liability might well arise, however, where a vehicle owner hands over the car to a person who is plainly drunk, and the latter then runs over the claimant (*P Perl (Exporters)* v. *Camden London Borough Council* [1984] QB 342, 359 per Robert Goff LJ). In such a case, the use of the car by the drunken driver, entailing an obvious danger to other road users, is actually authorised by the owner. Would the drunken driver have an action against the owner if injured in the same collision? It is submitted that the owner should bear some portion of the responsibility, subject of course to a deduction for the driver's contributory negligence, at least where the driver's intoxication is so extreme as to blind her to her inability to drive safely. The situation is obviously different where the intoxicated claimant is a passenger in the defendant's vehicle, not its driver. A taxi-driver's responsibility, for example, is to drive safely and to set clients down where they can safely alight, and not to ensure that they are in a fit state to get to their destination without suffering injury, so there was no liability where the plaintiff, who was clearly drunk, got out of the defendant's taxi and was struck by another vehicle as he tried to cross the road immediately afterwards (*Griffiths* v. *Brown* [1999] PIQR P131).

To be distinguished from cases where a drunk is encharged with a dangerous thing are cases where the claimant is exposed to the dangers of drink. As alcohol may be consumed safely within certain limits, which are best ascertained by each drinker personally, the scope of the duty here is more restricted than where a special danger arises from the conjunction of drink with an independent factor; the person responsible for a bar owes no duty to stop customers drinking to excess, but may have to assume a responsibility for their care if they lapse into unconsciousness. This analysis prevailed in *Barrett* v. *Ministry of Defence* [1995] 1 WLR 1217, where the deceased drowned in his own vomit after a drinking spree at the mess bars of the naval base on which he was stationed. The Court of Appeal ruled that the base commander, although guilty of a failure to enforce disciplinary regulations against excessive drunkenness, did not have a duty in tort to prevent the deceased's alcohol abuse. But when he lapsed into unconsciousness and a duty officer arranged for him to be taken by stretcher to his room, this amounted to an assumption of responsibility and the officer should have taken steps to ensure that he was lying in a safe position. The defendant was held liable subject to a reduction in damages of two-thirds to reflect the deceased's contributory negligence. *Barrett* was distinguished in the later case of *Jebson* v. *Ministry of Defence* [2000] 1 WLR 2055, where the plaintiff soldier was injured in the course of drunken japes whilst returning from a night out on the town organised by his camp commander. The injury was sustained when the plaintiff tried to climb onto the canvas roof of the lorry provided as transport for the occasion, as it was in motion, but lost his footing and fell. No one had been formally put in charge of the returning soldiers whom the commander should have foreseen would be drunk and rowdy. The Court of Appeal found that the lack of any supervision amounted to a breach of duty, and allowed the plaintiff's claim for damages subject to a 75 per cent reduction for contributory negligence. The commander had impliedly undertaken responsibility for the soldiers' safety on the return trip, and this responsibility extended to taking reasonable precautions against the risk of self-inflicted injury from drunken behaviour.

6.6 Owners and Occupiers of Land

The privilege of owning or occupying land carries with it certain obligations and may warrant the imposition of a duty of care in respect of those foreseeably injured by events or activities on the land. As Lord Nicholls has stated, 'In cases involving the use of land, proximity is found in the fact of occupation. The right to occupy can reasonably be regarded as carrying obligations as well as rights' (see *Stovin* v. *Wise* [1996] AC 923, 931). Whether or not the occupation of land serves *in all cases* to satisfy the requirement of proximity is, however, a disputed question, as the following discussion will reveal.

A number of different types of case must be distinguished as the scope of the duty – and indeed its source – may vary from one to another. We should note immediately that the liability of landowners to those who come onto their land and are injured by the state of the land is governed by statute (see ch. 13), though it seems probable that the tort of negligence would have developed to impose similar liabilities. Liability towards those on neighbouring property or on the public highway arises at common law but is governed by a variety of legal principles. In so far as the injury arises out of the action of natural forces on the defendant's land, liability is well established in the torts of both negligence and nuisance, and it seems that little turns upon the claimant's choice of cause of action (see *Goldman* v. *Hargrave* [1967] AC 645). Cases where the harm is caused by the actions of third parties on the defendant's land have, however, caused more problems, for they elicit the individualistic response that one person ought not be held responsible for the actions of another.

A distinction may be drawn between cases in which harm to those on adjoining land is caused by visitors on the defendant's property and those involving trespassers. In the former type of case, the choice to allow the visitors onto the land can be taken as evidence of a benefit derived from their presence, and it may be regarded as appropriate to impose a corresponding burden in the form of an obligation to supervise their activities. Consider the case of a football club that allows known hooligans into its ground for a match, appreciating that there is a risk that they will tear up lumps of concrete for use as missiles as the terracing is in a state of disrepair. If the hooligans were to throw the lumps of concrete at police gathered in the street beside the ground, injuring some of them, it is probable that the club would be held liable for their actions. The club after all derived the benefit of the admission fees paid by the hooligans (see *Cunningham* v. *Reading FC Ltd* (1991) *The Times*, 22 March).

Different considerations apply where the harm is caused by trespassers. Here, the case for liability is much weaker, but a breach of duty may nevertheless be found in exceptional circumstances. This was accepted by the House of Lords in *Smith* v. *Littlewoods Organisation Ltd* [1987] AC 241. In that case, a fire was started by vandals on the site of a disused cinema bought by Littlewoods, who wanted to locate a supermarket there. The fire spread to neighbouring properties, causing serious damage, and the owners of those properties sued the supermarket chain. All members of the House of Lords agreed that liability could be imposed for the acts of trespassers on one's land only in exceptional circumstances, and that those circumstances were not present on the facts of the case. However, the approach of the various judges differed significantly.

Lord Goff adopted the traditional approach favoured by Lord Bridge in *Caparo* (see 3.3). First of all, he denied that there was any general duty placed on owners or occupiers of property to take reasonable precautions against the wrongdoing of third parties. This seems tantamount to a denial that the mere occupation of land supplies the necessary element of proximity between the parties (cf. the view of Lord Nicholls in *Stovin* v. *Wise*, cited above). His Lordship then explained how to identify the exceptional cases in which liability might arise (p. 280): 'having rejected the generalised principle, we have to search for special cases in which, upon narrower but still identifiable principles, liability can properly be imposed'. In his view, the caselaw identified two such principles. In the first place, where a landowner has knowledge, or means of knowledge, that intruders have created the risk of fire on her property, she may be liable for failing to take reasonable steps to prevent any such fire damaging neighbouring property. On the facts before him, he could see no reason why Littlewoods should have known that vandals were creating a fire risk; it was not enough to point to a foreseeable possibility that this might have been the case. The second principle applied where a landowner creates, or allows to be created, an unusual source of danger on her land. Lord Goff illustrated this principle by considering the case of a villager deputed to buy the fireworks for the village Guy Fawkes night display who stores the fireworks in an unlocked garden shed. He suggested that the villager might be liable if mischievous children from the village were to sneak into the shed and, playing with the fireworks, start a fire which burns down the neighbouring house. However, he concluded that an empty cinema was not an unusual danger in the nature of a stock of fireworks.

Whereas Lord Goff made an effort to isolate a number of rules governing the liability of landowners for the acts of third parties, the other members of the House of Lords spoke in much more generalised terms. The common theme of these other speeches was that the outbreak of fire was not sufficiently likely to justify holding Littlewoods liable, particularly in view of the burdensome nature of the precautions necessary to stop the vandals: only a 24-hour guard would have been likely to prevent the fire. As Markesinis (1989) points out, it is not clear whether these other Law Lords dismissed the claim for damages because Littlewoods owed its neighbours no duty of care or because, although there was a duty of care, Littlewoods' behaviour could not have been regarded as unreasonable. Markesinis claims the latter is the better interpretation of the speeches (consistently with Lord Nicholls' view that proximity is found in the fact of occupation: see *Stovin* v. *Wise*, above) and suggests that, where the burden of precautions is less, the courts might well hold a landowner liable. More ambitiously, Markesinis claims that the majority opinion heralds 'an unnoticed revolution'. In his view, the case is a significant forward step towards a generalised liability for omissions and 'may mark a new beginning for the law of negligence'. However, it is unlikely that the case will be regarded as authority for a general duty outside the area of the liability of landowners and the categorical denial of liability for 'pure' omissions seems no less insistent now than ever before.

6.7 Impact of the Human Rights Act 1998

It seems unlikely that the general picture outlined above will be greatly affected by the implementation of the Human Rights Act 1998, and the general rule of no liability for omissions will no doubt survive, though perhaps admitting of more exceptions than before. The Act creates a statutory remedy against public authorities that act incompatibly with a person's Convention rights, and states that, for these purposes, 'an act' includes a failure to act (s. 6(6)). In fact, though there is no equivalent provision in the Convention itself, the Strasbourg court has for some time recognised that positive obligations do arise thereunder, ruling, for example, that the police and prison authorities have a positive obligation under art. 2 (right to life) to adopt preventative measures to protect an identified individual whose life is known actually or imputedly to be at real and immediate risk, whether from the criminal acts of a third party (*Osman* v. *United Kingdom* [1999] 1 FLR 193) or from the individual's propensity for injuring herself (*Keenan* v. *United Kingdom* (2001) 33 EHRR 913: suicide of mentally-ill prisoner), and that local authority social services departments must take positive steps to ensure that individuals within their jurisdiction – particularly children and other vulnerable persons – are not subjected to inhuman or degrading treatment contrary to art. 3 (*Z* v. *United Kingdom* [2001] 2 FLR 612). These decisions will no doubt be persuasive authority when it falls on the English courts to determine the scope of the positive obligations placed on public authorities by the Human Rights Act.

It is argued elsewhere in this book (7.3–4) that the common law liabilities of public authorities are likely to develop to match those under the Act, and make recourse to the statutory remedy unnecessary. The effect of any such development should not be overestimated, however, as it appears that a public authority's duty to take positive steps will not ordinarily arise unless the claimant can be identified as an individual who is at real and immediate danger, and not merely in the same position as the public at large. In *K* v. *Secretary of State for the Home Department* [2002] EWCA Civ 983 (see 6.4), the claimant argued that her rape by the man released from Home Office detention amounted to inhuman or degrading treatment under art. 3 of the Convention, which the Home Office had culpably failed to prevent, and that the common law should be interpreted so as to protect her Convention rights by allowing a claim in negligence. (As the relevant events took place before the Convention's incorporation into English law, she could not rely upon the statutory remedy in the Human Rights Act itself.) The Court of Appeal disagreed, finding that the denial of a duty of care for lack of proximity, in cases where the claimant was not known in advance to be at special risk, was entirely consistent with the jurisprudence of the ECtHR (see, especially, *Bromiley* v. *UK* (Application 33747/96), 29 November 1999, unreported: declaration of inadmissibility where a woman was murdered by a psychopath who had been released from prison on home leave). The principles governing the liability of various specific public authorities are considered in more detail in section 7.4, below.

Claims against private persons are less likely to be affected by the incorporation of Convention rights into English law. Admittedly, the Strasbourg court has ruled that the obligation on signatory states to secure those rights to everyone in their jurisdiction (art. 1) entails a positive duty to have in place a legal framework which provides effective protection for them, which may require the recognition of civil remedies against private persons who perpetrate or threaten rights violations (see, e.g., *Young, James and Webster* v. *UK* (1980) 4 EHRR 38: right to remedy for unfair dismissal on grounds of non-membership of trade union). But this reasoning seems as yet to have been applied only where Convention rights have been violated by the positive acts of a private person, and not where the latter is only guilty of an omission. Effective protection of fundamental Convention rights may require the availability of a civil remedy against the person who violates them by positive misfeasance, but it is quite another thing to insist on a remedy against the third party who could have intervened to prevent this, or to require recognition of a general duty of rescue that is enforceable in private law. Civilian jurists, accustomed to legal systems in which private individuals are required to intervene if they come across a person whose life is in danger, no doubt regard recognition of such a duty as essential to the protection of the right to life. But, as Wright (2001, pp. 142–3) has observed, the lack of any consistent approach even within civil law jurisdictions as to whether failure to rescue should attract civil as well as criminal liability itself militates against treating a remedy in damages as mandatory under the Convention. In the circumstances, it therefore seems unlikely that the English courts will feel impelled under the Human Rights Act to develop the law of negligence so as to incorporate a duty of affirmative action of general scope.

Summary

6.1   The courts have been wary of imposing liability for omissions because they fear unduly burdening individuals and recognise the pragmatic difficulty of determining which of those who could have intervened should be held liable. Nevertheless, liability has been recognised in exceptional cases.

6.2   A duty to protect another person may arise by virtue of one's voluntary assumption of responsibility to the other (either in the course of a particular office or position or on an *ad hoc* basis).

6.3   A duty to protect another person may arise by virtue of a relationship (e.g. a family relationship) with a vulnerable person (e.g. an infant).

6.4   Although a third party's intervention will normally break the chain of causation between the defendant's negligent conduct and the claimant's injury, the law exceptionally recognises a positive duty to control the actions of another person (e.g. where there is a 'control' relationship) and thereby accepts a liability for 'occasioning' harm (a weaker form of causal responsibility).

6.5   The defendant's creation of a special source of danger may also create a duty of affirmative action, and the defendant may be liable for the acts of a third party who sparks off the danger.

6.6   The defendant's occupation of land may warrant the imposition of a duty of care in respect of those foreseeably injured by events or activities on the land. The precise scope of this duty is disputed.

6.7   Under the Human Rights Act, the positive obligations of public authorities are expanded in scope, but it seems unlikely that the courts will feel impelled to recognise a general duty of rescue on private individuals coming across another person whose life is in danger.

Exercises

6.1   Is this an area of the law where the courts have adopted, in the words of Lord Bridge in *Caparo*, the 'modern approach' of looking for a single general principle that can be applied in all cases, or is it one in which they have preferred the 'traditional approach' of developing the law incrementally and by analogy with established heads of liability?

6.2   Will the law, in any circumstances, impose liability for failing to shout a warning at someone who is about to walk over the edge of a cliff?

6.3   What is the significance of the decision of the House of Lords in *Smith* v. *Littlewoods Organisation Ltd*?

6.4   Might liability in negligence arise in the following circumstances?

(a)   A fails to brake as she approaches an intersection in her car and crashes into B.

(b)   C receives a telephone call to say that her daughter, who ought to have been at school, is standing in the middle of a busy road. C does nothing. D is injured when she swerves to avoid the girl. (Would it make any difference whether the girl was aged 5 or 15?)

(c)   E sells F a pistol. Before F leaves the premises, she tells E that she plans to shoot her mother. E does nothing. F is in fact mentally ill and she shoots her mother later that day.

7   Special Duty Problems: Particular Parties

Special duty problems arise not only out of the nature of the loss and the way it was caused but also out of the identity of the parties. We deal here first with two classes of claimant that call for special consideration: rescuers, whose cases raise questions of foreseeability, of the fairness justice and reasonableness of recognising a duty, and of defences; and unborn children, in respect of whom it was unclear for some time whether any duty was owed at all. Then we turn to look at the special rules that govern the liability of public authorities, concentrating on the common law but noting also the new remedy created by the Human Rights Act 1998. The trend here has been to cut back on the limitations on liability that were formerly recognised by the courts. A comparable development is the recent abolition of the 'immunity' previously enjoyed by members of the legal profession in respect of their conduct of cases in court, to which we turn in the final section of this chapter.

7.1 **Rescuers**

The courts' sympathy for those who have selflessly exposed themselves to danger for the sake of others, allied with their desire not to deter people from undertaking rescues, has caused them to adopt a generous stance in respect of claims brought by rescuers. It is possible to discern a general leniency in the courts' application of the formal requirements for liability in the tort of negligence. Thus rescuers injured whilst responding to an emergency situation are invariably held to be foreseeable victims of the negligence of those who caused the emergency in the first place. As the American judge Cardozo J remarked: 'Danger invites rescue. The cry of distress is the summons to relief. The law does not ignore these reactions of the mind in tracing conduct to its consequences. It recognises them as normal. It places their effects within the range of the natural and probable' (*Wagner* v. *International Railway Co* 232 NY 176, 180 (1921)).

A similar leniency is apparent when it comes to consideration of the defences that might be raised against those injured in a rescue attempt: courts are very loath to say that a rescuer was contributorily negligent or voluntarily assumed the risk of injury, or indeed that her actions negatived any causal connection between her injury and the defendant's negligence (see chs 9 and 11). These issues were canvassed in the leading case of *Baker* v. *TE Hopkins & Son Ltd* [1959] 1 WLR 966. Dr Baker had descended into a well containing poisonous fumes in an attempt to rescue two workers who were feared to be in difficulty. The rope by which the doctor was lowered into the well became caught and both he and the workers were fatally overcome by the fumes. An action in respect of the doctor's death was brought against the employers of the dead workers. The Court of Appeal allowed the claim. First, it held that the doctor was owed a duty of care as it was reasonably foreseeable that, if the employees were imperilled, someone would seek to rescue them from their peril. Secondly, it denied that principles of causation or the law relating to defences barred the action. The court emphasised especially that a rescuer will very rarely be found to have been contributorily negligent. Such a finding would only be appropriate where the rescuer's conduct was 'so foolhardy as to amount to a wholly unreasonable disregard for his own safety' (per Willmer LJ; for an example of a case where such a finding was made, see *Harrison* v. *British Railways Board* [1981] 3 All ER 679).

A number of more particular issues arise in relation to the so-called 'rescuer' cases. First, are 'professional rescuers' like members of the fire brigade owed the same duty as that owed to ordinary people who undertake to assist someone in peril? English courts have declined to apply a 'fireman's rule' akin to that adopted in several US states by which liability is denied on the basis that fire officers are trained and paid out of public funds to deal with the very risk that eventuated and that it would therefore be unduly burdensome to charge private individuals with the cost of their injuries (see *Ogwo* v. *Taylor* [1988] AC 431). Nor do they distinguish between the 'ordinary' risks inherent in fire-fighting and 'exceptional' risks, created by some unusual feature of the fire (e.g. one relating to the state of the premises in question), which the defendant is able to eliminate by warning or otherwise: in *Ogwo*, the House of Lords declined to disadvantage the professional rescuer relative to the ordinary member of the public by limiting liability to cases involving exceptional risks of that description. The same approach has also been applied in relation to psychiatric injury where police officers, in the Hillsborough football stadium tragedy, were exposed to horrific scenes in the course of the rescue attempt. The House of Lords rejected an argument that special rules applied to professional rescuers, following the principle in *Ogwo* (*Frost* v. *Chief Constable of South Yorkshire Police* [1999] 2 AC 455). Lord Goff noted, however, that 'in considering whether psychiatric injury suffered by a plaintiff is reasonably foreseeable, it is legitimate to take into account the fact that the plaintiff is a person, such as for example a policeman, who may by reason of his training and experience be expected to have more resilience in the face of tragic events in which he is involved, or which he witnesses, than an ordinary member of the public possesses who does not have the same background', though that was not a factor in the wholly exceptional case before him (p. 471; see also p. 511, per Lord Hoffmann).

Secondly, can a rescuer recover damages from the person imperilled if the latter was negligent in exposing herself to danger? In *Harrison* v. *British Railways Board* [1981] 3 All ER 679, the plaintiff (a train guard) injured himself in his attempt to assist another person who, while trying to board a moving train, found himself in difficulty. Boreham J held that the plaintiff was entitled to recover damages (subject to a reduction for his contributory negligence): there was no reason to deny the existence of a duty of care simply because the defendant was also the person imperilled. Implicit in this conclusion is the premiss that the duty owed to the rescuer is an independent duty, not merely one derived from that owed to the person imperilled (see *Videan* v. *British Transport Commission* [1963] 2 AB 650; cf. 4.4).

Lastly, does a rescuer owe a duty of care to others who intervene when the rescuer's attempts to assist the person imperilled prove unsuccessful? This issue was considered in the Canadian case of *Horsley* v. *Maclaren* (1972) 22 DLR (3d) 545. The case concerned a boating accident: a guest on Maclaren's vessel fell overboard and Maclaren tried to manoeuvre the boat in order to carry out a rescue; this was unsuccessful and another guest, Horsley, dived in to do what he could; both guests died. The Supreme Court of Canada held that on the facts Maclaren had not been negligent. If he had been, however, the court would have been prepared to hold him liable to Horsley provided that his rescue attempts had placed the first guest in a 'new situation of peril' (per Ritchie J) distinct from the peril to which he was originally exposed. While it seems equitable that one rescuer should be liable to another, the 'new situation of peril' requirement imposed by the Supreme Court may be too restrictive. Liability should not be limited only to a case in which the defendant, by increasing the danger to the claimant, has made a second rescue attempt more likely; it should also arise in a case where the defendant makes the rescue attempted by the second rescuer more risky than it would otherwise have been, for example, where the captain of a rescue vessel assisting at an oil rig fire approaches unreasonably close to the blaze and thereby exposes the crew to danger (see *McFarlane* v. *EE Caledonia* [1994] 2 All ER 1, 10 per Stuart-Smith LJ). It should be noted that in such a case the captain's negligence might negate any causal connection between the fault of the party responsible for the fire and the injuries suffered by those on board the vessel (ibid.).

7.2 The Unborn Child

In the case of children born after suffering congenital disabilities, the only requirement is that injury to the mother was reasonably foreseeable; there is no need to establish that the unborn child was a foreseeable victim of the defendant's negligence. This rule is set out in the Congenital Disabilities (Civil Liability) Act 1976 which was implemented because of confusion as to the rights of the unborn child at common law. It is now clear, however, that a claim could have been brought at common law in respect of births occurring prior to that reform (*Burton* v. *Islington HA* [1993] QB 204) although – even allowing for the fact that the limitation period does not run against a child until she reaches the age of majority – it seems likely that any new claim of this nature would be time-barred. Only the statutory claim is possible in respect of births since the Act came into effect.

The liability under the Act is derivative in that the child's claim is dependent upon the defendant owing a duty of care to the parent; however, there is no need to prove that the parent suffered actionable injury (s. 1(3)). The derivative nature of the action is also evident in the rule that the child's claim may be reduced to reflect the parent's share of responsibility for the disability (s. 1(7)). Similarly, there is no right to recover where either or both the parents (but not just the father if he is the defendant) knew of the risk of the child's disability before she was conceived (s. 1(4)). The child may sue her own father, but she can only recover damages from her mother where the latter's negligence occurred while driving a motor vehicle (s. 2); in such a case, the desire to maintain harmonious relations between mother and child is outweighed by the recognition that the mother will carry compulsory insurance against such an eventuality.

The Act only applies to those who suffer congenital disabilities as the result of another's tort. It does not cover 'wrongful life' claims by those whose disability is attributable to natural causes but who allege negligence on the part of a doctor who could have prevented the birth in the light of the likely extent of the child's disability. At common law, such claims were held to be contrary to public policy by the Court of Appeal in *McKay* v. *Essex Area Health Authority* [1982] QB 1166. The court in that case rejected an action for damages by an infant who was born disabled after her mother contracted German measles during pregnancy, and claimed that the mother's doctor should have advised her of the baby's condition and thereby given her an opportunity to seek an abortion. The court also held that the 1976 Act excluded the possibility of such claims in respect of any birth subsequent to its coming into effect.

To be distinguished from a 'wrongful life' claim is one in respect of a 'wrongful birth' (see generally Mullis, 1993). In such an action, it is the parents who sue in respect of the financial, psychological and other consequences of giving birth to a child whom they would rather not have had and whose birth should have been avoided by the defendants. In *Emeh* v. *Kensington and Chelsea and Westminster Area Health Authority* [1985] QB 1012, the Court of Appeal accepted that all foreseeable losses of that nature were recoverable, but the House of Lords subsequently took a more restrictive view in the case of *McFarlane* v. *Tayside Health Board* [2000] 2 AC 59. In their Lordships' view, the costs of raising a healthy child were to be treated as offset by the joys of parenthood. As Lord Millett observed (pp. 113–14; see also p. 97, per Lord Hope, and p. 105, per Lord Clyde):

'[T]he law must take the birth of a normal, healthy baby to be a blessing, not a detriment. In truth it is a mixed blessing. It brings joy and sorrow, blessing and responsibility. The advantages and the disadvantages are inseparable. Individuals may choose to regard the balance as unfavourable and take steps to forgo the pleasures as well as the responsibilities of parenthood. They are entitled to decide for themselves where their own interests lie. But society itself must regard the balance as beneficial. It would be repugnant to its own sense of values to do otherwise. It is morally offensive to regard a normal, healthy baby as more trouble and expense than it is worth.'

For this reason, the House of Lords ruled, the parents of a healthy infant, who was conceived after the father had undergone a vasectomy and been negligently advised that he was sterile, could not recover damages for the basic costs of raising the child, though (Lord Millett dissenting) the mother was entitled to damages for the pain, suffering and inconvenience of pregnancy and childbirth. Their Lordships also expressed somewhat differing views as to the extent to which the mother could recover for loss of earnings and out-of-pocket expenses associated specifically with the pregnancy and birth. Subsequently, the Court of Appeal ruled that the right to recover damages for loss of earnings did not extend to earnings foregone when the mother decided to stay at home in order to care for her child (*Greenfield* v. *Irwin* [2001] 1 WLR 1279).

Two exceptional situations do not, however, fall within the scope of the *McFarlane* ruling. First, where a child is born with substantial disabilities following an unwanted pregnancy, for which the defendant's negligence was responsible, the parents may recover damages to the extent to which the disabilities increase the cost of raising and maintaining the child (*Parkinson* v. *St James and Seacroft University Hospital NHS Trust* [2001] EWCA Civ 530, [2002] QB 266). The additional costs are treated as going beyond those which have to be set off against the benefits of having a child. In the case in question, Hale LJ emphasised that this analysis did not in any way involve treating a disabled child as less valuable than a healthy child: 'It simply acknowledges that he costs more' (at [90]). Secondly, where the unwanted pregnancy results in the birth of a healthy child to a disabled mother, she is entitled to recover the additional costs resulting from *her* disability (*Rees* v. *Darlington Memorial Hospital NHS Trust* [2002] EWCA Civ 88, [2002] 2 WLR 1483). The damages may be regarded as necessary to enable her to discharge the ordinary tasks of parenthood and merely involve putting her in the same position as an able-bodied mother (ibid., at [21]–[22], per Hale LJ).

The doctor's duty in respect of an unwanted birth is only to the patient and the patient's partner for the time being, not to subsequent partners. In *Goodwill* v. *British Pregnancy Advisory Service* [1996] 2 All ER 161, the Court of Appeal struck out an action brought by a woman who had become pregnant in the course of a sexual relationship commenced some three year's after a vasectomy operation on her partner. She alleged negligence on the part of the defendants, who had arranged the operation, in advising her partner that he no longer needed to use any other method of contraception; she had relied upon this 'warranty of permanent infertility' in removing her contraceptive coil, thereby exposing herself to the risk of pregnancy, of which the defendants should have warned, when there was a spontaneous reversal of the vasectomy. The Court of Appeal, raising what might be called the 'Don Juan scenario', held that it could not be the policy of the law to impose a duty towards the indeterminately large class of partners with whom the patient might have a sexual relationship in the future and rejected the plaintiff's claim.

7.3 Public Authorities: General Issues

No special principles govern the liability of public authorities except in spheres in which they are exercising a public function. Like every other employer, a public authority owes a personal duty of care to its employees, and can be held liable where an employee suffers injury because of defective equipment, the lack of a safe system of work, or the dangerous state of the workplace. Similarly, there is no problem with holding a public authority vicariously liable where one employee negligently injures another in the course of employment, or breaches some other established duty of care (e.g., where a hospital doctor treats a patient negligently or a council van-driver carelessly causes a road accident). But there is a sphere of activity in which public authorities are performing a distinctively public role and given, as a matter of public law, powers and duties not shared with ordinary individuals. An authority's public law duties may be enforced by an application for judicial review but to get compensation a person injured by the exercise or non-exercise of public law powers and duties must bring an action for damages. So the question arises whether, and in what circumstances, a public law power or duty can give rise to a parallel duty of care in private law.

Two sets of difficulties arise. First, there is the danger that the courts might intrude unduly in the workings of a body which forms part of the democratic process (see 'Justiciability and Discretion', below). Secondly, the application of the normal three-stage approach for determining the existence of a duty of care may be influenced by the public role which the authority is performing. On one hand, if as a matter of public law the authority is given powers and duties in order to protect those in the position of the claimant from injury, that may be found to give rise to the proximity of relationship that must be proved at the second stage of the *Caparo* approach. On the other hand, the need to conserve public funds and ensure that public authorities carry out their functions most effectively may mean that it is not fair, just and reasonable to impose a duty of care on them (see 'Ordinary Duty Questions', below.) It is evident that these considerations pull in different directions, some *pro*, others *contra* liability. Until the past few years, it appeared that the factors that militated against the imposition of liability were given greater weight by the courts, as public authority liability was kept within narrow bounds. There are signs, however, that a change of direction has occurred in the last few years, and that the reluctance to hold public authorities liable in negligence is diminishing. No doubt this has at least something to do with the criticisms the European Court of Human Rights made of the English courts in its decision in *Osman* v. *United Kingdom* [1999] 1 FLR 193, and with the implementation of the Human Rights Act 1998, which, by exposing public authorities to a direct action for violation of Convention rights, has made it somewhat futile to limit their liabilities at common law.

Justiciability and Discretion

We begin with the 'public law dimension' of actions against public authorities. The basic concern here is that a private law claim for damages may not be the appropriate means by which to challenge the actions and decisions of a public authority. In the first place, the decisions made by a public authority may require a more wide-ranging investigation than is possible in the courtroom. No court is equipped, for example, to decide whether the Home Office is right to operate an 'open' borstal policy and, as part of it, to take young offenders away from safe confinement in highly secure institutions on training exercises (cf. *Home Office* v. *Dorset Yacht Co Ltd* [1970] AC 1004). This decision requires the balancing of considerations that the courts are scarcely able to identify never mind weigh: How much does it cost to operate an open borstal system as opposed to a closed one? Should the object of the system be to punish young offenders or to rehabilitate them? What additional risks are imposed on the local community by allowing young offenders more freedom of movement? Such is the diversity of the issues that might be relevant that it is inconceivable that the two parties represented in court would raise them all. Matters like these should be decided only after a public enquiry has given all interested parties an opportunity to air their views. This suggests a second reason why courts should stay clear of cases that raise these matters: the decisions made by public authorities are often the product of the democratic process and it would be unconstitutional for the courts to undermine this by challenging those decisions. This consideration is particularly weighty when the public authority in question is elected, for example, a local council. Where this is the case, the authority is accountable to its electorate and there is a strong argument for saying that the electorate alone should pass judgment on it.

These concerns are all too familiar to public lawyers. As a matter of public law, actions of public authorities under statute are not reviewable by the courts unless *ultra vires* (i.e. in excess of their power or discretion). Is it necessary in a private law action for damages to show that the public authority acted in an *ultra vires* fashion? Different judicial answers have been given to this question. According to a well-known dictum of Lord Diplock, '[t]he public law concept of ultra vires has replaced the civil law concept of negligence as the test of the legality, and consequently of the actionability, of acts or omissions of government departments or public authorities done in the exercise of a discretion conferred on them by Parliament' (*Home Office* v. *Dorset Yacht Co Ltd* [1970] AC 1004, 1067). More recently, however, Lord Browne-Wilkinson has doubted the utility of employing concepts of public law in relation to a private law claim: 'I do not believe that it is either helpful or necessary to introduce public law concepts as to the validity of a decision into the question of liability at common law for negligence' (*X (Minors)* v. *Bedfordshire County Council* [1995] 2 AC 633, 736–7). His Lordship pointed out that Lord Diplock's dictum was potentially misleading, for in public law a decision could be *ultra vires* for reasons which had no relevance to the question of negligence (see further *Rowling* v. *Takaro Properties* [1988] AC 473, where the Privy Council accepted that a government minister had acted without negligence, albeit in excess of his powers, in basing a particular decision on an irrelevant consideration). In Lord Browne-Wilkinson's view, Lord Diplock's words did no more than stipulate that the exercise of a statutory discretion could not be impugned unless it was so unreasonable that it fell altogether outside the ambit of the discretion (i.e. was unreasonable in what public lawyers know as the *Wednesbury* sense). To avoid confusion in such matters, his Lordship preferred in a private action for damages to employ the concepts of *justiciability* and *excess of discretion* rather than that of *vires* (cf. Craig, 1999, pp. 860–75).

It is submitted that the concepts of justiciability and excess of discretion relied upon by Lord Browne-Wilkinson represent twin legal responses to a single policy consideration, namely the need to protect public authorities against inappropriate judicial scrutiny of their actions. The question of justiciability arises at the duty stage and requires the court to ask whether the subject matter of the case raises 'policy' issues which the court is not competent to determine. This turns upon a distinction, introduced by Lord Wilberforce in *Anns* v. *Merton London Borough Council* [1978] AC 728, between a public authority's formulation of a policy and its operation of that policy. According to Lord Wilberforce, the more 'operational' the matter before the court is, the easier it is for the court to regard the public authority as owing a common law duty of care (although the ordinary duty requirements of proximity and fairness must also, of course, be satisfied). He considered the difference between policy and operational matters was probably one of degree. Subsequent decisions have made clear that the distinction is not self-executing and that the ultimate question is always whether the subject matter of the case is fit for judicial scrutiny ('justiciable'). As Lord Keith has said:

> '[T]his distinction does not provide a touchstone of liability, but rather is expressive of the need to exclude altogether those cases in which the decision under attack is of such a kind that a question whether it has been made negligently is unsuitable for judicial resolution, of which notable examples are discretionary decisions on the allocation of scarce resources or the distribution of risks.' (*Rowling* v. *Takaro Properties Ltd* [1988] AC 473, 501)

Although there is no simple rule by which 'policy' may be distinguished from 'operational' matters, it is possible to identify a number of conventional heads of 'policy', most notably the allocation of scarce resources and the imposition of risks on sectors of the community for a wider public benefit. Hence, in *Home Office* v. *Dorset Yacht Co Ltd* [1970] AC 1004, to choose an illustrative example, it is clear that the decision of the Home Office to operate an open borstal system was a policy matter and hence unchallengeable in the courts: it involved the deliberate exposure of local residents to the risk of damage in the pursuit of a higher social purpose, the rehabilitation of offenders. By way of contrast, however, the carelessness of the borstal officers in going off to bed and thereby leaving their charges to their own devices, contrary to regulations, was an operational matter and it was appropriate to hold the Home Office liable for it.

It seems that questions of justiciability will only rarely play a decisive role at the duty stage of the inquiry, especially given the current reluctance of the courts to reach a conclusion of 'no duty' in actions against public authorities (see 'Ordinary Duty Questions', below). Except in very clear cases of policy formulation, they are likely to be repackaged as questions of *discretion* under the heading of breach of duty. Only if a public authority has exceeded the scope of its discretion will a finding of breach be warranted. In deference to the public authority's position in the democratic process, the usual test of reasonable care is in this context replaced by the test of *Wednesbury* unreasonableness by which the court does not simply substitute its view of what was reasonable for that of the authority, and intervenes only on the basis that *no* reasonable authority would have acted in such a way (cf. *Associated Provincial Picture Houses Ltd* v. *Wednesbury Corporation* [1948] 1 KB 223). This deferential attitude may be compared with that adopted by the courts through the mechanism of the *Bolam* test in relation to doctors and other professionals (see 8.4; cf. Bowman and Bailey, 1986). Because a public authority's exercise of its discretion can only be impugned after consideration of its reasonableness in the circumstances of the case, the question of discretion is essentially one of fact. It can therefore only be determined at full trial and, unlike the question of justiciability, is not suitable for resolution in a striking-out application.

Ordinary Duty Questions

As elsewhere in the tort of negligence, the ordinary requirements of foreseeability, proximity, and fairness, justice and reasonableness must be satisfied if a public authority is to be found to owe a duty of care. An action against a public authority may raise exactly the same special duty problems which make it necessary to restrict the scope of the duty of care in an action against a private individual or a company. Thus, for example, the *type of loss* suffered by the claimant (Did it flow from physical damage or was it purely economic?) and the *character of the defendant's conduct* (Was it a positive act or a mere omission?) may throw doubt upon the existence of the necessary element of proximity between the parties. Additionally, the particular position and role of the public authority may make it unfair, unjust and unreasonable to impose liability, even where proximity can be established.

One of the most important questions for the courts in this area has been to determine when the fact that a public authority has been statutorily empowered or obligated to perform a particular task, and given funds for that purpose, will give rise to a duty of affirmative action. In *Stovin* v. *Wise* [1996] AC 923, 952, Lord Hoffmann urged caution in recognising such duties:

> 'It is one thing to provide a service at the public expense. It is another to require the public to pay compensation when a failure to provide the service has resulted in loss To require payment of compensation increases the burden on public funds. Before imposing such an additional burden, the courts should be satisfied that this is what Parliament intended.'

The key question, then, is the legislative intent. It seems, at the very least, that the statute must be one which was designed to protect a determinate class of person against a particular type of loss. Hence, the power of local authorities to inspect building work arising under the public health legislation does not give rise to a cause of action on the part of property developers in relation to pure economic loss, whatever the position with the regard to residents whose personal safety is at risk (*Governors of the Peabody Donation Fund* v. *Sir Lindsay Parkinson & Co* [1985] AC 210). Similarly, a 'regulator' established to maintain a register of deposit-taking companies owes no duty to those suffering loss through the fraudulent mismanagement of registered companies, for the regulator exercises only a 'quasi-judicial' power to determine whether the company should be allowed to trade and this can only be construed as for the benefit of the public generally, not of any particular class (*Yuen Kun Yeu* v. *Attorney-General of Hong Kong* [1988] AC 175). The approach of the courts here is very similar to that taken in the separate tort of breach of statutory duty (see ch. 15), and in his speech in *Stovin* v. *Wise* Lord Hoffmann indicated that the same result would normally ensue in both torts: 'If the policy of the Act is not to create a statutory liability to pay compensation, the same policy should ordinarily exclude the existence of a common law duty of care' (p. 953).

Lord Hoffmann made the further point that it was fundamental to distinguish between statutory duties and powers. Liability for failure to exercise a statutory power could only be rare as the element of discretion in the exercise of a power 'must be some indication that the policy of the Act conferring the power was not to create a right to compensation', and there would have to be 'exceptional grounds for holding that the policy of the statute requires compensation to be paid to persons who suffer loss because the power was not exercised' (p. 953). Lord Hoffmann was not prepared, however, to accept the proposition that 'a statutory "may" can never give rise to a common law duty of care', though he considered that for a duty to arise the court would have to be satisfied that 'it would in the circumstances have been irrational not to have exercised the power, so that there was in effect a public law duty to act'.

Even where these hurdles can be surmounted, it must still be asked whether it would be fair, just and reasonable to recognise a duty of care.

Until the last few years, the courts were very conscious of the need to protect limited public funds against the flood of claims that might perhaps be released by the recognition of a duty of care, and of the importance of ensuring that public authorities are able to devote themselves to the performance of their statutory functions without constantly having to look over their shoulders to guard themselves against the risk of liability (the overkill argument). The outcome was a very restrictive approach to the liability of public authorities in the performance of their public functions, as exemplified by such landmark cases as *Hill* v. *Chief Constable of West Yorkshire* [1989] AC 53 (conduct of police investigations), *X (Minors)* v. *Bedfordshire County Council* [1995] 2 AC 633 (social services' responsibilities to vulnerable children), *Stovin* v. *Wise* [1996] AC 923 (highway authority's maintenance of public roads), and *Capital & Counties plc* v. *Hampshire County Council* [1997] QB 1004 (fire brigade's response to emergencies).

In 1998, however, the European Court of Human Rights expressed criticism of the way in which the English courts had restricted the scope of the duty of care owed by public authorities by reference to broad consideration of public policy (*Osman* v. *United Kingdom* [1999] 1 FLR 193; the particular context was the conduct of police investigations). The Strasbourg court's judgment is considered in more detail elsewhere in this book (3.7), and for now it is sufficient to note that, whatever interpretation of *Osman* ultimately proves to be correct, the clear message it sent to the English courts was that they had been wrong to afford public authorities an immunity from negligence liability in extensive areas of their activities. The English courts responded, though without acknowledging that the *Osman* decision – which was not (then) officially part of English law at all – had influenced their approach in any way. That it did so, however, is beyond dispute. Where previously the English courts had frequently disposed of claims against public authorities on preliminary striking-out applications, on the basis that it was not necessary to have a full trial to demonstrate that there was not even arguably a duty of care (see, especially, *Hill* v. *Chief Constable of West Yorkshire* and *X (Minors)* v. *Bedfordshire County Council*), they now urge extreme caution in the use of this pre-emptive tactic: 'in an area of the law which [is] uncertain and developing (such as the circumstances in which a person can be held liable in negligence for the exercise of a statutory duty or power) it is not normally appropriate to strike out' (*Barrett* v. *Enfield London Borough Council* [2001] 2 AC 550, 557 per Lord Browne-Wilkinson).

There seems also to have been a change of approach in the courts' attitude to the applicable policy considerations. Recent cases exhibit a marked disinclination to exclude any duty of care on grounds of public policy, and factors which were once considered sufficient to do so are now accorded much less significance. Typical is the way in which the fear of overkill, which was crucial in leading the House of Lords to its conclusion of 'no duty' in the cases of *Hill* v. *Chief Constable of West Yorkshire* and *X (Minors)* v. *Bedfordshire County Council*, is now said to be 'normally ... a factor of little, if any, weight' (*Barrett* v. *Enfield London Borough Council*

[2001] 2 AC 550, 568 per Lord Slynn). If such factors are still to count at all, it seems that this must be in determining whether there is a breach of the public authority's duty of care, and not whether there is a duty in the first place.

The implementation of the Human Rights Act 1998, which came into effect in October 2000, will no doubt prove to have cemented these developments. As indicated above, since the Act creates a statutory remedy for the violation of Convention rights by public authorities, it may be regarded as futile to limit the remedy for common law negligence. In any case, if the victims of public authority negligence were to find that their only remedy arose under the Act, that could be perceived as an indictment of the common law's ability to keep pace with social change, and it is to be doubted whether the courts would allow any such perception to arise.

7.4 Public Authorities: Specific Contexts

In this section, we shall consider the state of the law in specific contexts in which the issue of public authority liability has arisen, paying particular attention to the recent trend towards the relaxation of restraints on the scope of the duty of care.

The Police

There is no question that a police officer, like anyone else, may be liable in tort where her negligent acts result in injury to another. By s. 88 of the Police Act 1996, the chief constable of the area may be vicariously liable for these acts, in which case damages will be paid out of the police fund (see ch. 21). In order to avoid undue interference with the exercise of police discretion, the police's liability is restricted to the operational sphere of their activities; as is the case with other public institutions, their activities in the policy sphere are non-justiciable. In *Rigby* v. *Chief Constable of Northamptonshire* [1985] 1 WLR 1242, a building owner claimed against the police after they had used inflammable CS gas to smoke out a gunman holed up in the property, a ploy which achieved its aim but also succeeded in causing serious fire damage to the building. Taylor J relied on Lord Wilberforce's distinction between the policy and operational spheres of activity to hold that he could not impugn the police force for equipping itself with inflammable CS gas even though a non-flammable alternative was available: this was a policy decision. However, he did hold the police liable in negligence for failing to have firefighting equipment in attendance at the time they used the gas: this, evidently, was a matter falling within the operational area.

More difficult than cases like *Rigby* which involve the direct infliction of injury by means of a positive act are cases of police nonfeasance. In principle, a claim against the police in respect of an allegedly negligent omission may succeed if it falls within one of the established categories of proximity (e.g. a care or control relationship). Thus, the police may assume responsibility to witnesses who give them confidential tip-offs, and so be held liable if their negligence exposes the witnesses' identities and makes them the target of reprisals (*Swinney* v. *Chief Constable of the Northumbria Police* [1997] QB 464: no liability on the facts found at the subsequent trial). Those taken into custody are also owed a duty of care by the police, which extends to the taking of steps to reduce the risk of self-inflicted harm (*Reeves* v. *Metropolitan Police Commissioner* [2000] 1 AC 360). In addition, by a duty analogous to that arising in the *Dorset Yacht* case (see 6.4), the police may be liable where their negligence allows a prisoner to escape, doing damage to the property of those in the area in the process. However, the domestic courts for some time maintained that the police could not be held liable to those who simply suffered harm from criminal activities which they alleged the police should have prevented. This conclusion was reached by the House of Lords after considering the issue in a case brought by the estate of the last victim of Peter Sutcliffe, the so-called 'Yorkshire Ripper', a mass-murderer who conducted a campaign of terror against young women in Yorkshire from 1975 to 1980 (*Hill* v. *Chief Constable of West Yorkshire* [1989] AC 53). The claim failed both for want of the necessary ingredient of proximity and also for a variety of policy reasons which made it unfair, unjust and unreasonable to recognise a duty of care. On the question of proximity, Lord Keith distinguished the case before him from the *Dorset Yacht* case on the basis that Sutcliffe had never been in police custody, while 'Miss Hill [the victim] was one of a vast number of the female general public who might be at risk from his activities but was at no special distinctive risk'. By way of contrast, in the *Dorset Yacht* case the Home Office's open Borstal policy had exposed local residents to the additional risk of injury in the course of any escape. On the question of fairness, justice and reasonableness, Lord Keith listed a number of policy reasons for allowing the police substantial immunity from suit. First, the fear of liability might cause the police to carry out their tasks in a detrimentally defensive frame of mind. (It seems that borstal officers are made of sterner stuff: in the *Dorset Yacht* case, Lord Reid expressly dismissed the argument that they might be dissuaded from doing their duty by the fear of liability.) Secondly, many cases would concern the exercise of discretion as to the way an investigation should proceed: this could not be called into question by the courts. Thirdly, the time, trouble and expense put into the defence of claims, even those that were totally meritless, would represent a significant diversion of police manpower and attention from their task of suppressing crime.

The decision in *Hill* was followed by the Court of Appeal on a number of occasions, for example, to justify the conclusion of 'no duty' where it was alleged that the police, without adequate investigation of the scene, dismissed an emergency 999 call as a false alarm and enabled burglars to make off with the plaintiff's property (*Alexandrou* v. *Oxford* [1993] 4 All ER 328). In *Osman* v. *Ferguson* [1993] 4 All ER 344, a teenage boy was subjected to harassment by a former schoolteacher who had developed an obsession with him. The police investigated but took the view that the man was not a serious danger to the boy or his family (the Osmans). He subsequently killed the boy's father in an attack with a firearm in which the boy was also wounded. The Court of Appeal was prepared to accept that there was a relationship of proximity between the parties, but ruled out any claim on the basis of the policy considerations identified in *Hill*. Unsuccessful in the English courts, the Osmans took their case to the European Court of Human Rights, which in *Osman* v. *United Kingdom* [1999] 1 FLR 193 took the view that the Court of Appeal had violated the Osmans' rights under art. 6 of the Convention by applying a blanket immunity which had the effect of depriving them of any effective access to a court. But the Court of Human Rights found that there was no breach of the Osmans' rights under art. 2 of the convention (right to life), as there was in fact no reason why the police should have known that their lives were at real and immediate risk.

The ruling on art. 2 has very significant implications for English law, even if the Osmans were not actually successful on this point before the Court. The Court recognises that, in principle, the police have a positive obligation to take preventative measures to protect an identified individual whose life they know or ought to know is at real and immediate risk. The Human Rights Act itself provides a mechanism for the payment of compensation for failure to comply with the obligation (ss. 7–8), but there is every reason to think that the common law will also adapt. In other contexts, the courts have distanced themselves from the idea of blanket immunities and have apparently moved towards a position in which they treat resource-constraints and the danger of defensive practice in looking at the question of breach, not duty. There is every likelihood that they will do so here as well.

The Emergency Services

Here too we find some restrictive decisions on the scope of the duty owed, followed by hints of a more relaxed approach in more recent years. Most significant of the restrictive decisions is *Capital & Counties plc* v. *Hampshire County Council* [1997] QB 1004. This was a consolidated appeal arising from incidents involving three separate fire brigades. In the *West Yorkshire* case, the plaintiffs' chapel was destroyed by a fire which they alleged would have been put out but for the fire brigade's failure to ensure that its fire hydrants were in working order and their location properly signed. In the *London* case, the claim was that the fire brigade had left the scene of an explosion on land next to the plaintiff's premises without inspecting the latter, which were severely damaged when smouldering debris from the explosion later caused a fire to break out on them. In the *Hampshire* case, the fire brigade attended a fire on the plaintiff's premises and its fire officer ordered the automatic sprinkler system to be switched off. This was a negligent mistake which had the result of allowing the fire to spread, destroying the plaintiff's premises entirely. The Court of Appeal found for the defendants in two of the three claims. Delivering the judgment of the court, Stuart-Smith LJ identified three fundamental principles. First, 'the fire brigade are not under a common law duty to answer the call for help and are not under a duty to take care to do so. If therefore they fail to turn up or fail to turn up in time because they have carelessly misunderstood the message, got lost on the way or run into a tree, they are not liable' (p. 1030). That disposed of the *West Yorkshire* and *London* cases. Secondly, simply going to the scene and embarking on fighting the fire did not involve any assumption of responsibility by the fire brigade to individual property owners, for 'the fire brigade's duty is owed the public at large to prevent the spread of fire and that this may involve a conflict between the interests of various owners of premises. It may be necessary to enter and cause damage to A's premises in order to tackle a fire which has started in B's' (p. 1036). Lastly, however, a fire brigade could be held liable for a positive act of misfeasance which created a new danger that materialised and caused damage that would not otherwise have been sustained. This was what had occurred in the *Hampshire* case, where the fire officer had switched off the automatic sprinklers at a time when the fire was already contained, and it was only this negligent act which had allowed the fire to get out of control.

In *OLL Ltd* v. *Secretary of State for Transport* [1997] 3 All ER 897, May J followed this approach in considering the duty of care owed by the coastguard. In an action for contribution between tortfeasors, it was alleged that the coastguard had been negligent in misleading independent rescuers as to the likely location of a group of children who had got lost at sea whilst on a canoeing expedition. Striking out the claim, the judge stated that there was 'no obvious distinction between the fire brigade responding to a fire where lives are at risk and the coastguard responding to an emergency at sea' (p. 905). The coastguard therefore had no duty to respond to an emergency call, and could not be held liable if, having chosen to respond, their response was negligent. Only if, as in the *Hampshire* case (above), the coastguard's positive intervention had resulted in greater harm than would have occurred if it had not intervened at all could it be held liable, but that was not the case on the facts before the court.

In a more recent case brought against the ambulance service, however, the Court of Appeal declined to follow *Capital & Counties* and recognised that the service had a private law duty to respond expeditiously once it had accepted an emergency call (*Kent* v. *Griffiths* [2001] QB 36). Here, the claimant had suffered an asthma attack and her doctor, attending at her home, called for an ambulance to take her immediately to hospital. The local ambulance service took the call and agreed to attend at once, but for reasons that were never satisfactorily explained the ambulance's arrival was considerably delayed, and the claimant suffered a respiratory arrest and consequent brain damage that would probably have been averted had the ambulance attended in reasonable time. The trial judge found that the delay was unreasonable and his decision that the ambulance service was in breach of its duty of care was upheld by the Court of Appeal. Distinguishing the case before it from *Alexandrou* v. *Oxford* [1993] 4 All ER 328 (see 'Police', above) and *Capital & Counties plc* v. *Hampshire*

County Council [1997] QB 1004, the court denied that the situation of the ambulance service was truly analogous to that of the police or the fire brigade. Whereas the duty of the police and the fire brigade was primarily to the public at large, whose interests might prevail over those of the person requesting assistance, in the present case it was only the claimant whose interests fell to be considered. In fact, the correct analogy to make was not with the police or the fire brigade but with hospitals and other parts of the health service, and it was therefore clear that the ambulance service owed the claimant a duty of care once it had accepted the call made on her behalf. Lord Woolf added that, even in a situation where the duty to the claimant might conflict with that owed to others, as in an accident after which a number of people need transporting to hospital, it might be better to allow for the pressures under which the ambulance service was acting at the breach of duty stage than by denying the existence of any duty of care at all. Logically, it is submitted, the same approach ought also to apply to the other emergency services.

Social Services

The potential liabilities of local authority social services departments in dealing with vulnerable children have been considered by the courts on several occasions in recent years, and here too we see the pattern of an initial attempt to restrict the scope of the duty owed, followed by later decisions which take a broader view. In *X (Minors)* v. *Bedfordshire County Council* [1995] 2 AC 633, two of the five appeals consolidated before the House of Lords were on this issue. (For consideration of the other appeals, see 'Education', below.) In the *Bedfordshire* case, the five plaintiffs were brothers and sisters who claimed that they had suffered ill-treatment and ill-health as a result of their local authority's negligent failure to act quickly enough in putting them on the child protection register and taking them into care. In the *Newham* case, a mother and daughter claimed damages for anxiety neuroses allegedly suffered as a result of the local authority erroneously taking the child into care on the recommendation of its social worker and psychiatrist, who had misunderstood what the daughter had said to them in an interview. The cases came to the House of Lords on a preliminary striking-out application and their Lordships ruled that the claims should indeed be struck out as revealing no arguable cause of action, having failed at the third stage of the *Caparo* approach (fairness, justice and reasonableness). In their Lordships' opinion, a variety of considerations made it unfair to allow the claims to proceed, paramount amongst them being the danger of overkill: 'if a liability in damages were to be imposed, it might well be that local authorities would adopt a more cautious and defensive approach to their duties ... [M]oney and human resources will be diverted away from the performance of the social service for which they were provided' (p. 750, per Lord Browne-Wilkinson). Furthermore, private citizens had alternative means of ensuring that local authorities properly discharged the responsibilities in question (statutory appeals procedures, the right to petition the local authority ombudsman), although it had to be admitted that none of these provided for a right to compensation. These considerations of public policy themselves warranted the conclusion that neither the councils nor their employees owed the plaintiffs any duty of care. An additional reason for rejecting the claim of vicarious liability in the *Newham* case was that the psychiatrist and social worker who were alleged to have been negligent had been retained only to advise the council, and not the plaintiffs, and had therefore assumed responsibility only to the former.

Since this decision, the issue of social services liability has twice come before the House of Lords and on each occasion *X (Minors)* v. *Bedfordshire County Council* has been distinguished. In *Barrett* v. *Enfield London Borough Council* [2001] 2 AC 550, the House of Lords declined to strike out a claim relating not to the decision whether or not to take the claimant into care but to his allegedly-negligent treatment thereafter, over the whole of the period in which he was in care (some 16 years). The result was the same in *W* v. *Essex County Council* [2001] 2 AC 592, where the claim was brought by members of a family into which the council placed a child in its care for fostering. The foster child proceeded to commit sexual assaults against the other children in the family. It was alleged that the council had acted negligently, because its files indicated the risk of such assaults, and that both the assaulted children and their parents had suffered psychiatric injury as a result. The judge at first instance had declined to strike out the claims by the children, and there was no appeal against this decision, and the House of Lords was only concerned with the claim by the parents, to whom it found the council did owe an arguable duty of care.

What to make of these decisions is not an easy matter. The least radical interpretation is that they simply reflect the House of Lords' renewed determination to ensure that the power of strike-out is used only in the clearest and most obvious cases, and to insist on a full trial in areas – like that of social services liability – in which the law is still developing and a wide variety of policy considerations have to be weighed. But it is submitted that the significance of *Barrett* and *W* goes beyond this, because they cast doubt not only on the use of the striking-out procedure in *X* but also on the House of Lords' approach in that case to the substantive questions of fairness, justice and reasonableness. All the indications are that, on the facts of the later cases, the House of Lords attached very little significance to the policy considerations relied upon in *X*, as typified by Lord Slynn's remark in *Barrett* that the overkill argument was entitled to 'little, if any, weight' (p. 568). If this is so, then *X* is very much out of tune with the rest of the caselaw on social services liability, perhaps sufficiently so as to encourage some enterprising lawyer to think of taking a *Bedfordshire*- or *Newham*-type case once more before the Lords.

In any new litigation on such facts, of course, the claimant's position will be bolstered by the implementation of the Human Rights Act. The extent of a local authority's social services department's duty under s. 6 of the Act has been made clear by the decisions of the European Court of

Human Rights arising out of the two unsuccessful appeals in *X (Minors)* v. *Bedfordshire County Council,* which was of course decided before the Act came into effect. In the *Bedfordshire* case, the Strasbourg court ruled that there had been a violation of art. 3 of the Convention as the State had breached its positive obligation of protecting the children from inhuman or degrading treatment, and it was immaterial that the ill-treatment was administered by a private individual provided this ought to have been foreseen by the authorities (*Z* v. *United Kingdom* [2001] 2 FLR 612). In the *Newham* case, the court ruled that there had been a violation of art. 8 of the Convention (right to respect for family life) in that the local authority had failed to make full disclosure of the information upon which it relied in taking the daughter into care; if it had done so, mother and daughter could well have been reunited more quickly (*TP and KM* v. *United Kingdom* [2001] 2 FLR 549). The court accepted, however, that the initial decision to take the daughter into care had a legitimate basis which was not affected by the mistake made by the social worker and psychiatrist in their difficult task of interpreting what the daughter was saying to them. These decisions are not binding on the English courts, but there seems no reason to doubt their interpretation of the Convention rights in question. If the facts of these cases were repeated today, there would be every prospect of a successful action for compensation under ss. 7–8 of the Human Rights Act, though the trend of recent decisions suggests that the House of Lords might simply admit that the law of negligence has changed since its decision in *X (Minors)* v. *Bedfordshire County Council* and allow a claim at common law as well.

Education

In *X (Minors)* v. *Bedfordshire County Council,* the House of Lords had already taken a broad view of the duties of local authorities in providing appropriate education for children with special needs, notwithstanding its restrictive approach in the social services appeals. In two of the three 'education' appeals in that case ('*Dorset*' and '*Hampshire*'), the alleged negligence was basically the same, viz. the unreasonable failure to provide special schooling for a child who was subsequently recognised to have particular needs. The nature of the loss alleged in the two cases, however, differed: in *Dorset,* it was the cost of private special needs schooling; in *Hampshire,* in which the child had remained at an ordinary state school, it was psychological injury, under-achievement and the significant restriction of vocational prospects. In the final case ('*Bromley*'), the local authority was said to have acted unreasonably in placing a child in special schooling unnecessarily, with consequent impairment of his personal and intellectual development. The actions brought against the local authorities included claims of both direct and vicarious liability, the latter based on the alleged negligence of educational psychologists and other employees involved in the assessment of the plaintiffs' educational needs. Following its reasoning in the social services appeals, the House of Lords struck out the direct actions to the extent to which they relied on authorities' bare failure to provide appropriate education to the plaintiffs, as required by the Education Acts 1944 and 1981. It would not have been fair, just and reasonable to recognise a private law duty of care because this would cut across the statutory mechanisms established to ensure that the legislator's purposes were achieved. But, in *Dorset*, where the plaintiff had also relied upon the allegedly-negligent advice provided by the council's 'psychology service', their Lordships thought that it would be wrong to strike out the claim until all the facts were known, and they took the same view of the claims of vicarious liability made in the various cases. Unlike social workers and psychiatrists asked to investigate suspected child abuse, educational psychologists and others assessing special educational needs faced no obvious conflict of interests: the duty to the child was entirely consistent with the duty to the local authority. Lord Browne-Wilkinson, who delivered the leading speech, cautioned however that further investigation of the facts might reveal the need to limit or exclude the duty of care owed by the councils and their employees if this would impede local authorities' performance of their statutory duties.

With 'education cases' thus given the green light to proceed to full trial, it was not long before the House of Lords was again faced with the duty issues it half side-stepped in *X (Minors)* v. *Bedfordshire County Council* – this time in a case which, having gone to trial, required a final determination of those issues. In *Phelps* v. *Hillingdon London Borough Council* [2001] 2 AC 619, the claim was for loss of earning potential and other financial losses resulting from the negligent failure of the defendant's educational psychologist to identify and treat the plaintiff's learning difficulties or dyslexia whilst she was a pupil at the defendant's school. In the House of Lords, a panel unusually consisting of seven Lords of Appeal ruled that the claim was legally sound and that the plaintiff, having succeeded on the facts at trial, was therefore entitled to damages. There was some apparent disagreement as to whether the plaintiff's dyslexia was a personal injury, and consequently as to whether her claim was for pure economic loss, but it is clear that, however her loss was classified, it was actionable in negligence. The policy factors identified in *X* did not preclude the recognition of a duty of care on the psychologist's part, or the imposition of vicarious liability on the council. (Lord Slynn even went to so far as to suggest that, if the psychologist was doing something which would have given rise to a duty if done privately, the fact that it was done in pursuance of the local authority's statutory duties was immaterial: p. 654.) As Lord Clyde, with whom the rest of the House of Lords agreed, observed (p. 672):

'I am not persuaded that there are sufficient grounds to exclude these claims even on grounds of public policy alone. It does not seem to me that there is any wider interest of the law which would require that no remedy in damages be available. I am not persuaded that the recognition of a liability upon employees of the education authority for damages for negligence in education would lead to a flood of claims, or even vexatious claims, which would overwhelm the school authorities, nor that it would add burdens and distractions to the already intensive life of teachers. Nor should it inspire some peculiarly defensive attitude in the performance of their professional responsibilities. On the contrary it may have the healthy effect of securing that high standards are sought and secured.'

In addition, it could not be said that the imposition of a duty of care would lead to a conflict of interest, because the duty to the pupil 'would march hand in hand' with the duty to the council (p. 666, per Lord Nicholls). Given this decision on the vicarious liability of the local education authority, it was not necessary for their Lordships to express a concluded view as to whether the authority might ever owe a direct duty of care to a pupil, and they preferred to leave this issue to be resolved on the proven facts of a future case.

Highway Authorities

Unlike the statutory powers and duties considered above, the statutory duties of a highway authority are capable of being enforced in a tortious action for breach of statutory duty (see, generally, ch. 15). Section 41(1) of the Highways Act 1980 imposes on every highway authority the duty to maintain the highways for which it is responsible, and it is expressly contemplated that breach of the duty is actionable in damages (s. 58). The duty is expressed in absolute terms, but it is a defence under the Act that the authority had taken reasonable care to ensure the highway was not dangerous for traffic (s. 58). The duty applies only to the maintenance of the fabric of the road in good repair and does not extend to the erection of traffic signs (*Lavis* v. *Kent County Council* (1992) 90 LGR 416), the accumulation on the road of ice and snow (*Goodes* v. *Sussex County Council* [2000] 1 WLR 1356), or dangers on land adjoining the highway (*Stovin* v. *Wise* [1994] 1 WLR 1124, CA), unless these affect the condition of the highway itself, for example, where a blocked drainage ditch overflows and causes a flood (*Thoburn* v. *Northumberland County Council* (1999) 1 LGLR 819). Because s. 41 is of limited scope, those injured on the roads have on occasion sought to sue the highway authority for common law negligence relating to the exercise of their wide-ranging powers under other sections of the Act and the performance of their general duty to ensure road safety under Road Traffic Act 1988, s. 39. Here there is less indication than in the contexts considered above that the courts are embarking upon a new, pro-claimant phase of liability.

In *Stovin* v. *Wise* [1996] AC 923, the House of Lords took a very restrictive approach to recognition of common law duties to complement the statutory duty under s. 41. The plaintiff was injured in an accident at a junction which presented an unusual danger because of the presence of a visual obstruction on adjoining land. Because the obstruction was next to, but not on, the road, the statutory duty under s. 41 did not apply, though the highway authority had a statutory power to order the obstruction's removal. By a bare majority, however, the House of Lords ruled that this power did not give rise to a duty of care at common law as there were no exceptional grounds to indicate that the policy of the statute entailed the provision of compensation to people injured in the circumstances of the case. In addition, it could not be said it had been 'irrational' for the authority not to have ensured the removal of the obstruction in question because its decision whether to proceed with the work, and also how and when it should be done, raised budgetary questions and fell within the scope of the authority's discretion. As Lord Hoffmann remarked, 'the court is not in a position to say what an appropriate standard of improvement would be. This must be a matter for the discretion of the authority' (p. 958).

Stovin v. *Wise* limits the liability of highway authorities at common law where the claimant relies simply upon the authority's failure to exercise its statutory powers. Only if this can be regarded as 'wholly unreasonable' – a very stiff test – will liability arise (*Larner* v. *Solihull Metropolitan Borough Council* [2001] RTR 32: no liability on the facts). But this does not entail an equally restrictive approach where the claim is that the authority had created the danger in question, and not merely failed to make the highway safer (*Kane* v. *New Forest DC* [2002] 1 WLR 312: new footpath emerging at a foreseeably dangerous point of the road).

The cases here do not provide evidence for the same 'sea change' in the law of public authority liability that has occurred in the contexts considered above. This seems largely to be because the specific victim in highway cases is unlikely to be foreseeable, in contrast with many of the cases in which liability has been imposed. Even with the implementation of the Human Rights Act, it is unlikely that there will be a significant change of the law in this area, for the Strasbourg jurisprudence suggests that positive duties entailed by the Convention rights arise only where the public authority knows or ought to know of a real and immediate risk to particular individuals (*Osman* v. *United Kingdom* [1999] 1 FLR 193).

7.5 The Legal Profession

For some time, the courts maintained that barristers and solicitors had an effective immunity against liability for negligence in presenting their client's case in court (*Rondel* v. *Worsley* [1969] 1 AC 191) and in pre-trial work that was intimately connected with the presentation of the case in court (*Saif Ali* v. *Sidney Mitchell & Co* [1980] AC 198). When rights of audience in the higher courts were extended to solicitors, the immunity was recognised by statute, which provided that solicitors were entitled to the same immunity as barristers (Courts and Legal Services Act 1990, s. 62). But, in *Arthur J S Hall & Co (A Firm)* v. *Simons* [2002] 1 AC 615, a seven-strong panel of the House of Lords reconsidered its earlier decisions, and abolished the immunity – unanimously in respect of the conduct of civil proceedings, and by a majority of four to three in respect of criminal proceedings.

In its decisions in *Rondel* v. *Worsley* and *Saif Ali* v. *Sidney Mitchell*, the House of Lords had identified a number of policy arguments in favour of the immunity. First, an advocate owes an overriding duty to the court which, on occasion, may conflict with her duty to the client. If the latter were able to sue for negligence, this might inhibit the lawyer and detract from the administration of justice. Secondly, removing the immunity might have the effect of inducing barristers to break the 'cab rank' rule, by which they (but not solicitor-advocates) are bound to provide their services for any client who will pay their fees. Fear of vexatious claims might induce them to pick and choose their clients in order to avoid those who seemed intent on airing a grievance whatever the merits of their case, yet many apparently hopeless cases turn out, after a full and fair hearing, to be well-founded. Thirdly, there was an analogy with the immunity accorded to witnesses in court cases, which was necessary to ensure that they came forward and spoke freely without fear of being sued, even unsuccessfully. Lastly, a suit alleging negligent conduct of a trial would amount to a collateral challenge to the correctness of the original decision, grafting onto the criminal appeals system 'a sort of unseemly excrescence', and producing in the civil justice system 'litigation upon litigation with the possibility of a recurring chain-like course of litigation', contrary to the principle of finality in litigation (*Rondel* v. *Worsley* [1969] 1 AC 191, 250–1 per Lord Morris).

In *Hall* v. *Simons*, the House of Lords took a different view of these police arguments. In themselves, they were not particularly strong, nor supported by empirical evidence, and not even cumulatively did they warrant the retention of the immunity. The position of advocates in respect of possible conflicts of duty was no different from that of many other professionals (e.g. doctors) who did not enjoy an equivalent immunity (p. 680, per Lord Steyn; pp. 688–9, per Lord Hoffmann), and there was no reason to think that their 'divided loyalty' would lead to 'defensive lawyering' detracting from the administration of justice, especially given the wide range of judicial powers (e.g. wasted costs orders against advocates personally) designed to keep the resources expended on a case proportionate to its value and importance (p. 693, per Lord Hoffmann). The argument based on the cab rank rule was also of little substance, as barristers could seek summary dismissal of vexatious claims by disgruntled clients, and would no doubt continue to provide representation for those who needed it. In any case, the cab rank rule did not apply to solicitor-advocates. In addition, the witness analogy was inapt because that immunity was based on the fear that witnesses might not come forward if they thought they might be sued, and did not apply to lawyers who had assumed a responsibility to their client for reward (p. 698, per Lord Hoffmann). Finally, the public interest in preventing the re-litigation of court decisions could be satisfactorily protected by the exercise of the inherent judicial power to strike out any claim that constituted an abuse of procedure. In the case of a collateral civil challenge to a criminal conviction (which a minority of the House of Lords would never have allowed, because of the important public duty performed by defence lawyers), it would almost always be necessary to show that the conviction had been set aside by the criminal courts before a civil action could proceed.

The decision reflects the courts' current hostility to the manipulation of the duty requirement so as to create effective immunities from liability in negligence. The approach they have now adopted seems to meet the criticisms made of the English law of negligence by the European Court of Human Rights in the *Osman* case (see 3.7 and 7.3), though the Human Rights Act had not actually come into force at the time of when *Hall* v. *Simons* was decided. But it is important to realise that the decision only applies to the lawyer's liability to her own client, and that the general principle remains that a lawyer owes no duty to the other side in a private transaction (*Gran Gelato* v. *Richcliff* [1992] 1 All ER 865; *aliter* if the lawyer 'voluntarily assumes responsibility' to the other side: *Al-Kandari* v. *JR Brown & Co* [1988] QB 665), and that, in criminal proceedings, neither the Crown Prosecution Service (CPS) nor its lawyers owe a duty to those who are prosecuted, for example, to discontinue prosecution and ensure their release from custody once the evidence against them is revealed to be unsound (*Elguzouli-Daf* v. *Commissioner of Police of the Metropolis* [1995] QB 335). Whether the courts will maintain these 'no duty' situations after the implementation of the Human Rights Act remains to be seen, especially in the case of the CPS, which owes a duty to respect Convention rights as a public authority under the Act. It may also prove necessary to review the application of witness immunity to paid expert witnesses (*Stanton* v. *Callaghan* [2000] QB 75), for the reasoning of at least some of their Lordships in *Hall* v. *Simons* suggests that the policy reasons for the immunity of witnesses generally do not apply in their case (see, further, Cane, 1996, p. 237).

Summary

7.1 Rescuers are invariably held to be foreseeable claimants and are rarely defeated by claims that they unreasonably exposed themselves to the risk of injury.

7.2 Two types of action are currently available in respect of pre-natal negligence. First, there is the action under the Congenital Disabilities (Civil Liability) Act 1976 brought by a child born with a disability as a result of negligence. Secondly, there is the common law action for 'wrongful birth' brought by the parents of a child who would not have been born but for the defendant's negligence. Neither under the common law nor under the 1976 Act is it possible for a disabled child to bring a 'wrongful life' action claiming she should not have been born.

7.3 Judicial reluctance to recognise liability on the part of public bodies has led to the imposition of a requirement of 'justiciability' in respect of actions brought against public bodies in respect of their public functions, as well as the frequent invocation of policy considerations (e.g. the overkill argument) to justify the refusal to recognise a duty of care.

7.4 A recent trend to loosen the restrictions on the duties of care owed by public authorities is evident from an analysis of the liabilities of public authorities in specific contexts (the police and emergency services, social services, educational provision and highway maintenance).

7.5 Barristers and solicitors now owe their clients a duty of care even with regard to the conduct of litigation or to preliminary matters which are intimately connected with the conduct of a case in court.

Exercises

7.1 Is the duty of care owed to a rescuer a 'derivative' duty or one owed to her in her own right? What difference does it make?

7.2 In what circumstances will the birth of a child give rise to an action in negligence? In what circumstances will the conception of a child give rise to such an action?

7.3 Should the courts allow an action for 'wrongful life'?

7.4 A local authority is empowered by statute to supervise and control the operations of builders with a view to maintaining proper standards of health and safety and has set up an inspectorate to perform this task. One of the inspectors, A, carelessly fails to spot that a certain house is built on defective foundations. The house subsequently falls down and injures its occupier, B. Advise the parties as to their rights and liabilities in tort. Would it make any difference if B's house had not been inspected because (a) for budgetary reasons, the authority had decided to suspend all inspections, or (b) the authority's lawyers had misinterpreted the relevant statute and advised the authority that it was not in fact entitled to carry out on-site inspections.

7.5 Assess the strength of the 'overkill' argument in relation to lawyers, the police and public authorities generally.

7.6 In what circumstances is the interest in the finality of litigation considered relevant to an action in negligence? Whose interest is it? What weight should the courts attach to it?

8   Breach of the Duty of Care

8.1 Introduction

Under the heading of breach of a duty of care the question is not whether the defendant should be held liable for her negligence (which is the question in relation to duty, causation and remoteness), but whether the defendant was in fact negligent in the first place. Negligence consists in falling below the standard of care required in the circumstances to protect others from the unreasonable risk of harm. This is judged in relation to the position in which the defendant found herself: it is easy to be wise after the event, but the court should not let hindsight influence its judgment as to what the defendant ought to have done in the circumstances. It follows that, where knowledge of the risks involved in particular activities has developed over the course of time, the defendant's conduct should be assessed in the light of the state of knowledge at the time she acted, not that at the date of trial. In *Roe* v. *Minister of Health* [1954] 2 QB 66, the plaintiffs had become paralysed after being injected with anaesthetic which had been contaminated by disinfectant. The anaesthetic had been stored in ampoules placed in the disinfectant; the latter had seeped into the ampoules through invisible cracks. At the date of the injuries, 1947, this was not generally considered possible. In the Court of Appeal, Denning LJ stressed that later developments in scientific knowledge should be ignored in assessing the culpability of the defendants (p. 84): 'We must not look at the 1947 accident with 1954 spectacles'.

8.2 The Objective Standard of Care

In general, the law requires defendants in negligence actions to measure up to an objective standard of care demanded by the activity in question and declines to accept excuses that are founded on the defendant's inability to measure up to that standard. The question to be asked is, 'What level of care and skill was required by the activity which the defendant was pursuing?' rather than 'What could this particular defendant have done?'. As Lord Macmillan put it in the case of *Glasgow Corporation* v. *Muir* [1943] AC 448, 458 the objective standard 'eliminates the personal equation and is independent of the idiosyncrasies of the particular person whose conduct is in question'. The reason for this approach was clearly expressed by the great American judge and jurist, Oliver Wendell Holmes (1881):

> 'The standards of the law are standards of general application. The law takes no account of the infinite varieties of temperament, intellect and education which make the internal character of a given act so different in different men. It does not attempt to see men as God sees them ...

[W]hen men live in society, a certain average of conduct, a sacrifice of individual peculiarities going beyond a certain point, is necessary to the general welfare. If, for instance, a man is born hasty and awkward, is always having accidents and hurting himself or his neighbours, no doubt his congenital defects will be allowed for in the courts of Heaven, but his slips are no less troublesome to his neighbours than if they sprang from guilty neglect. His neighbours accordingly require him, at his proper peril, to come up to their standard, and the courts which they establish decline to take his personal equation into account.'

This general rule holds true when we are concerned with those whose lack of skill, experience or intelligence leads them to injure others. In the leading English case, *Nettleship* v. *Weston* [1971] 2 QB 691, a learner-driver failed to straighten the steering-wheel after turning a corner and ran into a street lamp; her driving instructor was injured. The Court of Appeal held her liable to the instructor, finding that she had fallen below the standard expected of a qualified and experienced driver; it was irrelevant that she as a learner might not be able to attain that standard. However, it appears that age and certain other physical characteristics will be taken into account. In *Mullin* v. *Richards* [1998] 1 WLR 1304, two 15-year-old schoolgirls were 'fencing' each other with plastic rulers. One of the rulers snapped and a splinter hit one of the girls in the eye. In her action against her classmate, the Court of Appeal held that the test to apply was whether an ordinarily prudent and reasonable 15-year-old schoolgirl, not being of adult years, would have realised in the circumstances that her actions gave rise to a real risk of injury. On the facts, it could not be said that she would: play fencing was common in the school, and the girls had never been warned about it or told of any injuries occasioned by it. It should be noted, however, that this was a case of a child's game, and a different conclusion may be warranted where the child undertakes an adult activity knowing that it demands the skills of an adult. If a 15-year-old tearaway were to hot-wire a motor-car and drive it off, she would be measured against the standard of care reasonably to be expected of a qualified adult driver without any allowance for her age.

A further element of subjectivity may intrude into the ostensibly objective standard applied by the courts where the defendant has a physical or mental disability. In *Mansfield* v. *Weetabix Ltd* [1998] 1 WLR 126, the defendant lorry driver was out on the road when he suffered a hypoglycaemic episode due to a glucose deficiency and, without realising it, progressively lost consciousness of what he was doing. Whilst in this state but still retaining some control over his actions, he drove his vehicle into the plaintiffs' shop and caused extensive damage. In the action for damages that followed, the Court of Appeal rejected the submission, based on the judgment of Neill J in *Roberts* v. *Ramsbottom* [1980] 1 WLR 823, that the driver could escape liability only if he demonstrated that his actions were wholly beyond his control at the relevant time. This was the approach of the criminal law to the defence of automatism, but it had no place in the civil law. In civil law, the standard to be applied was that of a reasonably competent driver with the impairment in question. The assessment was whether the defendant had in fact matched that standard taking account of, amongst other things, whether or not it was reasonable to expect him to have ceased driving on becoming aware of the condition. Because, in the case before the court, the defendant had been unaware of the gradual onset of his condition, it could not be said that he was culpable and hence in breach of duty. In *Roberts* v. *Ramsbottom*, by contrast, the defendant had 'continued to drive when he was unfit to do so and when he should have been aware of his unfitness' (pp. 832–3) and Neill J's decision may be regarded as correctly decided on that ground, notwithstanding his erroneous comments about the standard of care.

Where a person holds herself out as possessing a special skill over and above that of reasonable people, then she will of course be expected to live up to the standard she has represented she can attain. It would be no excuse for the surgeon whose piercing of your ears resulted in an infection to say that you were not entitled to demand more in the way of hygiene or competence than you would expect had you visited a jeweller instead. However, a jeweller performing the same service need not match the standards of a surgeon, because ear-piercing is not an activity that requires surgical skill (*Philips* v. *Whiteley (William) Ltd* [1938] 1 All ER 566), while a practitioner of alternative medicine is not to be assessed according to what would be expected of an orthodox medical practitioner (*Shakoor* v. *Situ* [2001] 1 WLR 410; see further 8.4).

8.3 **Application of the Objective Standard**

Many commentators have discerned a progressive raising of the objective standard in the course of the last century which they attribute to the spread of liability insurance (see Tunc, 1983). Though such matters rarely receive explicit judicial recognition, the phenomenon was identified with characteristic candour by Lord Denning in his judgment in *Nettleship* v. *Weston* [1971] 2 QB 691, 699–700:

> 'The high standard imposed by the judges is, I believe, largely the result of the policy of the Road Traffic Acts. Parliament requires every driver to be insured against third-party risks. The reason is so that a person injured by a motor-car should not be left to bear the loss on his own, but should be compensated out of the insurance fund. The fund is better able to bear it than he can. But the injured person is only able to recover if the driver is liable in law. So the judges see to it that he is liable, unless he can prove care and skill of a high standard ... Thus we are, in this branch of the law, moving away from the concept: "No liability without fault". We are beginning to apply the test: "On whom should the risk fall?" Morally the learner-driver is not at fault; but legally she is liable to be because she is insured and the risk should fall on her.'

There is no doubt that such considerations, whether expressed or not, lie behind the modern tendency of the courts to treat inevitable lapses of concentration or judgement as deviations from the standard of the reasonable person. It should be noted, however, that occasionally a judge will swim against the tide by arguing that not every careless slip can give rise to liability (especially in emergencies and other situations demanding split-second judgements: see *Wooldridge* v. *Sumner* [1963] 2 QB 43).

Cases involving lapses of concentration or judgement present few problems for the courts, for the defendant would be almost bound to admit that she had done something wrong and that she could think of no justification for her actions. However, as we move away from simple lapses of attention into the area of accidents that might have been avoided with a bit of foresight, things become more complicated. In these cases, it might be that the defendant can argue that she thought she could not be expected to behave differently to guard against possible injury to the claimant. Taking risks with our own and others' personal welfare and property is part of everyday existence. Indeed, life would be impossible if we did not do so. The point was put graphically by Asquith LJ in *Daborn* v. *Bath Tramways* [1946] 2 All ER 333, 336: 'if all the trains in this country were restricted to a speed of 5 miles an hour, there would be fewer accidents, but our national life would be intolerably slowed down'. The question the law of negligence must confront then is: 'Just how much is the law to require us to do in order avoid causing harm to others?'.

The precautions we should take to guard against injury to others depend on the circumstances of the case. The more likely injury is to result, and the greater the severity of that injury if it does result, the more we should do to eliminate the risk. On the other hand, if the costs of eliminating the risk exceed the benefits to be gained from doing so, then it might be reasonable to do nothing. This has been expressed as a mathematical formula by the American judge, Learned Hand J (*United States* v. *Carroll Touring Co* (1947) 159 F 2d 169). Where the probability of injury occurring is P, the extent of the likely loss is L and the burden of taking precautions to eliminate the risk is B, liability will arise if $B < PL$ (in other words, if the seriousness of the risk, assessed by combining the factors on the right-hand side of the equation, outweighs the burden of eliminating it). This is known as the 'Learned Hand formula'.

While English courts might deride such an approach for its veneer of scientific infallibility, the cases show that they attach significance to the same factors as feature in the 'Learned Hand formula', namely (a) probability, (b) the severity of the possible loss, and (c) the burden of eliminating the risk of loss.

Probability of Harm

All other things being equal, the greater the probability of harm resulting from the defendant's conduct (measured from the defendant's standpoint), the more likely it is that the conduct will be judged negligent. Two superficially-conflicting decisions on the issue of whether a cricket club can be held liable for damage caused by balls hit out of the ground provide a clear illustration. In *Bolton* v. *Stone* [1951] AC 850, the plaintiff was struck by a cricket ball whilst standing on the road outside the defendants' cricket ground. The ball had travelled approximately 100 yards before it hit her, clearing a 17-foot-high fence. In her subsequent action for damages, the main question was whether the defendants had been in breach of duty in failing to take more effective steps to prevent such an occurrence. The evidence was that the ball had cleared the fence and landed on the road no more than six times in 30 years, and that no one had ever been hit before. On that basis, the House of Lords ruled that the risk of damage to road-users was so small that it had been reasonable for the defendants to have taken no further steps to prevent the danger. It was not enough that the defendants knew it was possible that batsmen might hit the ball out of the ground from time to time, and therefore that there was a conceivable possibility that someone might be hit. In *Miller* v. *Jackson* [1977] QB 966, by contrast, the evidence before the Court of Appeal was that balls were hit out of a different cricket ground, and into neighbouring gardens, several times each season. As this presented a much greater risk of injury, the court ruled that the club which played at the ground was guilty of negligence on every occasion a ball came over the fence and caused injury.

It is important to note that the probability of harm is not considered in isolation, but only in conjunction with the other elements of the Learned Hand equation. Even in the cricket cases summarised above, the likelihood of injury was assessed in the light of the gravity of the possible harm and the cost of the precautions necessary to guard against it. In *Bolton* v. *Stone*, for example, it was crucial that the defendants' ground was large enough to be safe for all practical purposes, and that their perimeter fence could not safely have been raised any higher. It is for this reason that it is not possible to stipulate precisely how likely the possible harm must be before a defendant is regarded as negligent: everything here is relative. If the gravity of potential harm is very great, and the relevant precautions easy to take, it may be negligent to ignore even a quite far-fetched risk of injury.

Gravity of the Potential Injury

To quantify the risk of harm attributable to the defendant's conduct, the probability of the loss occurring must be combined with its potential severity if it occurs. Other things being equal, the more serious the potential harm, the more a reasonable person can be expected to do to avoid it, and the stronger the inference of negligence if the defendant does nothing. As Morris LJ has observed, '[t]he law expects of a man a great deal more care in carrying a pound of dynamite than a pound of butter' (*Beckett* v. *Newalls Insulation Co Ltd* [1953] 1 All ER 250, 255). Indeed, there are some contexts in which the possible consequences of an accident are so grave that the duty to take reasonable care 'may fall little short of absolute obligation' (*Davie* v. *New Merton Board Mills Ltd* [1959] AC 604, 620 per Viscount Simonds).

In considering the extent of the injury to which the defendant's negligence may give rise, the court must take account of any factors peculiar to the claimant which, as the defendant knows or ought to know, might aggravate that injury. In *Paris* v. *Stepney Borough Council* [1951] AC 367, the plaintiff was struck in the eye by a metal splinter whilst working for the defendant council as a car mechanic. In fact, as the council knew, he was already blind in the other eye and the consequence of the accident was that he lost his sight altogether. In its defence, the council argued that it was not the ordinary practice of garage-owners to supply safety-goggles to their mechanics, but the House of Lords held that this was immaterial: the consequences of losing the sight of one's only good eye were far worse than losing the sight of one of two good eyes, and the council therefore had to take extra precautions in respect of the plaintiff than it would for its other mechanics. On the facts, its failure to provide safety-goggles for the plaintiff was negligent. Contrary to the view which had prevailed in the Court of Appeal, a reasonably prudent employer would take account not only of disabilities that increased the probability of an accident but also of those which increased the gravity of the consequences of such an accident.

Cost of Precautions

Once quantified, the risk of harm must be weighed against the burden or cost of eliminating or reducing the risk. The question for the court is whether the reasonable person in the defendant's position would have taken the necessary precautions. The duty to prevent injury is not absolute, and the mere fact that there was an opportunity to remove or reduce the risk does not mean that it was negligent not to do so, for the cost of precautions might be excessive relative to the magnitude of the risk. 'Cost' here is to be construed broadly. It refers not only to such matters as the defendant's out-of-pocket expenditure on safety improvements, but also to any benefits that would be forgone if the defendant took the steps necessary to eliminate the risk. In *Latimer* v. *AEC Ltd* [1953] AC 643, the defendant's factory was flooded and the water, mixed with oil from channels in the floor, left the floor exceedingly slippery. The trial judge held that in these circumstances the factory should have been shut down until the floor was made safe. The House of Lords overturned the judge's ruling on the grounds that the circumstances did not demand that the employer take such a drastic step. It should be noted, however, that even where it is unreasonable to expect the defendant to eliminate a particular risk altogether, it is still necessary to take reasonable precautions to reduce its extent (*Williams* v. *Birmingham Battery Co* [1899] 2 QB 339, 345 per Romer LJ).

Where appropriate, the court should also take account of the cost to society as a whole of making the defendant give up some generally beneficial activity. The social utility of the defendant's conduct may be such as to justify the creation of an otherwise unreasonable risk of harm. As Asquith LJ has observed, '[t]he purpose to be served, if sufficiently important, justifies the assumption of abnormal risk' (*Daborn* v. *Bath Tramways Motor Co Ltd & Trevor Smithey* [1946] 2 All ER 333, 336). In *Watt* v. *Hertfordshire County Council* [1954] 1 WLR 835, for example, the plaintiff fireman was crushed by a heavy lifting jack whilst en route to the scene of a car crash in which a woman had been trapped under a vehicle. The jack was on castors, and it rolled across the floor of the truck in which the plaintiff was riding when the driver was forced to brake suddenly. The truck in question was not fitted to carry the jack, but the specially-adapted lorry was out on another call at the relevant time. The Court of Appeal found that the defendants had acted reasonably in the circumstances and rejected the plaintiff's action for damages, Denning LJ remarking that '[t]he saving of life or limb justifies taking considerable risk' (p. 838).

8.4 Common Practice

The cost–benefit analysis performed by the court in assessing whether defendants have acted unreasonably is not to be regarded as merely an economic calculation: it requires the court to weigh up matters such as the value of human life and limb which cannot be reduced to a simple arithmetical quantity. It is necessary, therefore, for the court to exercise a value judgement in the light of prevailing community standards. For this reason, and also in recognition of the need to defer to expert or more qualified opinion, the courts attach great importance to the common practice of those involved in the activity in question. Where it is common practice to take certain precautions in the course of a particular activity, the failure to take those precautions creates a strong inference of negligence, rebuttable only on presentation of convincing reasons why the precautions were unnecessary. Conversely, where the defendant does take all the precautions commonly adopted by others in her field of activity, this on its own will often be sufficient evidence that all reasonable care was taken.

Although common practice may be relevant in asking what the defendant might reasonably have done, it is not decisive. The courts reserve the power to set standards for a field of activity and do not limit themselves merely to reflecting the standards of those engaged in that activity. Thus, in the context of industry, the courts have on occasion declared an industry-wide practice to be negligent and have insisted that standards be raised across the board. A progressive judgment in this respect is that of Mustill J in *Thompson* v. *Smith Shiprepairers Ltd* [1984] QB 405, a case concerning industrial deafness suffered by workers in shipyards. Mustill J proceeded on the basis that 'the defendants simply shared in the indifference and inertia which characterised the industry as a whole' (p. 417), but made it clear that one employer was not exonerated merely by proving that other employers were just as negligent. His view was that there were certain cases in which an employer might be penalised for failing to take the initiative in seeking out developing knowledge of possible risks and precautions. He emphasised, however, that the obligation placed on employers should not be too demanding (p. 416): 'The employer must keep up to date, but the court must be slow to blame him for not ploughing a lone furrow.'

Where an action in negligence is brought against a professional (e.g. a doctor, architect or lawyer), the test is whether the defendant complied with a 'responsible body of opinion' in the profession in question. This is known as the *Bolam* test, named after the case in which McNair J explained the issue of a doctor's liability in negligence to a jury in substantially those terms (*Bolam* v. *Friern Hospital Management Committee* [1957] 1 WLR 582). There may, of course, be conflicting views as to the appropriate practice to adopt, but it is enough that the defendant complies with one such view; the fact that a contrary view exists is regarded as irrelevant. The body of opinion with which the defendant complies must, however, be 'responsible'. In *Bolitho* v. *City and Hackney Health Authority* [1998] AC 232, Lord Browne-Wilkinson emphasised this element of the *Bolam* test, explaining that 'the court has to be satisfied that the exponents of the body of opinion relied upon can demonstrate that such opinion has a logical basis' (pp. 241–2). He suggested, however, that it would only rarely be the case that a court would find a body of medical opinion not to be responsible. (For an example, see *Hucks* v. *Cole* [1993] 4 Med LR 393.) In *Shakoor* v. *Situ* [2001] 1 WLR 410, the question arose in an action brought against a practitioner of traditional Chinese herbal medicine. Here the court ruled that it was not enough to consider whether the defendant had exercised the degree of skill appropriate to his 'art', for it was necessary to take account of the fact that he was offering an alternative to the orthodox medicine practised in this country. Practitioners of alternative medicine had a duty to ensure that any remedy they prescribed was not actually or potentially harmful, and to discharge this duty they had to take steps to keep up to date with reports in orthodox medical journals (e.g. by subscribing to an association which would search the relevant literature on their behalf), not merely rely upon the remedy's traditional use. On the facts, however, the court found that there was nothing in the orthodox medical journals to indicate that the remedy prescribed by the defendant was improper.

Although the *Bolam* test was developed in the particular context of medical negligence, it has now been applied to all professions or callings which require special skill, knowledge or experience (*Gold* v. *Haringey Health Authority* [1988] QB 481, 489 per Lloyd LJ; see, for example, *Edward Wong Finance Co Ltd* v. *Johnson Stokes & Master* [1984] AC 296: solicitors).

8.5 Proof of Negligence

Claimants may face an uphill struggle in proving that the defendant's negligence was responsible for the harm they have suffered. Often the scale of the task will be immense. In the litigation arising out of the use of the anti-arthritis drug, Opren (see *Davies* v. *Eli Lilly & Co* (1987) 137 NLJ

1183), the plaintiffs had to hire a team of scientific, medical, pharmaceutical and legal experts to plough through literally millions of documents released to them by the manufacturer of the drug. Furthermore, in many cases the claimants will have to rely on the defendant releasing information to them (e.g. as to the tests to which a new pharmaceutical product was subjected): unscrupulous defendants might attempt to destroy documents unfavourable to their case rather than comply with a court order for the disclosure of such evidence. The plight of claimants in such cases has prompted innovation on the part of Parliament and the courts to ensure just claims are not defeated by evidential difficulties. In the area of substantive law, legislative reform of the law of product liability was motivated in part by this concern (see ch. 14). At a procedural level, Parliament has made rules of disclosure more stringent over the last century. The response of the courts to the same problem can be seen in the doctrine of *res ipsa loquitur* ('the accident tells its own story').

The classic exposition of the doctrine is that of Erle CJ delivering the judgment of the Court of Exchequer Chamber in the case of *Scott* v. *London and St Katherine Docks Co* (1865) 3 H&C 596. The plaintiff had been injured when struck by six bags of sugar which fell on him from above when he walked under a crane. The crane was being used by the defendants' servant to lower the sugar to the ground from the defendants' warehouse. At trial, the plaintiff gave no explanation of how the accident had happened, with the result that the trial judge directed the jury to find for the defendants on the grounds that there was no evidence of negligence on their part. The plaintiff appealed and the case eventually came before the Court of Exchequer Chamber to determine if there should be a new trial. The court held that there should, applying the following proposition of law (p. 601):

> 'There must be reasonable evidence of negligence, but, where the thing is shown to be under the management of the defendant, or his servants, and the accident is such as, in the ordinary course of things, does not happen if those who have the management of the machinery use proper care, it affords reasonable evidence, in the absence of explanation by the defendant, that the accident arose from want of care.'

This passage makes it clear that two requirements must be met before the rule comes into operation. In the first place, the thing causing the accident must be 'shown to be under the management of the defendant or his servants'. This would be the case where you were driving your car when it suddenly swerved across the road, colliding with oncoming traffic. However, if the car had been driven by a friend to whom you had lent it, it could not be said to have been under your management and the doctrine could not be raised against you. Erle CJ's second requirement was that 'the accident is such as, in the ordinary course of things, does not happen if those who have the management of the [thing] use proper care'. Whether this requirement is satisfied will depend on all the circumstances. Thus, for example, the inference of negligence if you slip on yoghurt spilt on the floor will be stronger where the accident takes place in a supermarket rather than an office block, for in the former case the owners should have known that spillages would not be infrequent and should have taken precautions to deal with them as soon as they occur (compare *Ward* v. *Tesco Stores Ltd* [1976] 1 WLR 810 with *Bell* v. *Department of Health and Social Security* (1989) *The Times*, 13 June).

Views have differed as to the effect of the doctrine of *res ipsa loquitur* and the law on the subject remains murky. Two diametrically opposed positions have attracted the most support (see Atiyah, 1972). One school of thought holds that the proposition lays down no new rule of law but merely reflects the common-sense view that, in some circumstances, the likelihood that an accident was caused by the defendant's negligence is so great that it is not necessary for the claimant to explain exactly how the accident came to occur. Accordingly, if Erle CJ's requirements are met, it is permissible for the court to infer from the occurrence of an accident that it was probably caused by the defendant's negligence. The opposing view is that the doctrine of *res ipsa loquitur* is a distinct legal rule which casts the legal burden of proof on the defendant when certain requirements are met. This burden requires the defendant to do one of two things. One course is for her to explain precisely how the accident happened, for once the facts are known the maxim can have no application: it is simply a matter of deciding whether those facts support the allegation of negligence or not. If she cannot do this, she may take the second course of trying to prove that she took all reasonable care irrespective of the cause of the accident. As, on this view, the burden of proof lies with the defendant, the judge must resolve any doubt she has as to whether the defendant's negligence caused the accident in favour of the claimant rather than the defendant. The extent of the hurdle facing the defendant can be gauged from *Henderson* v. *Henry E. Jenkins & Sons* [1970] AC 282. Mr Henderson had been killed after the brakes on the defendant's lorry had failed. The defendant firm produced evidence that the lorry had been inspected in accordance with the manufacturer's instructions; however, the House of Lords held that, in order to prove it had exercised all reasonable care, the firm should have produced evidence that the lorry had never carried loads that might have corroded the brake pipes.

Despite this apparent House of Lords authority that the effect of the doctrine is to reverse the legal burden of proof, the Privy Council has subsequently expressed a preference for the alternative view in *Ng Chun Pui* v. *Lee Chuen Tat* [1988] RTR 298. This is to be regretted. As Atiyah (1972) has pointed out, there is good reason for allowing an exception to the general rule that it is up to the claimant to prove her case on the balance of probabilities in precisely those cases identified by Erle CJ in which the thing causing the accident was under the control or management of the defendant. In such cases, the claimant may face grave evidential difficulties as she will have no information as to the precautions the defendant took in using the thing. A shift in the burden of proof would help to redress this imbalance.

Summary

8.1 'Negligence' or 'breach of duty' consists in falling below the standard of care required in the circumstances to protect others from the unreasonable risk of harm.
8.2 Negligence does not connote personal fault but merely the failure to comply with the standard of conduct to be expected of a reasonable person pursuing the activity in question; lack of skill or experience is no defence.
8.3 Breach of duty consists in creating an unreasonable risk of harm. The creation of the risk of harm will be *unreasonable* unless it is outweighed by the cost to the defendant of reducing the risk or by the social utility of the defendant's conduct.
8.4 The existence of a common industrial or professional practice creates a standard against which to judge the defendant. However, deviation from that practice is not conclusive of negligence, and neither is compliance conclusive of lack of negligence.
8.5 Where the claimant alleges that the defendant was negligent in causing an accident but does not know how the accident occurred, she may be aided by the doctrine of *res ipsa loquitur*. The way the doctrine operates is disputed.

Exercises

8.1 What does it mean to describe the standard of care as 'objective'? When can the courts take account of factors peculiar to the defendant?

8.2 Is the ratio of *Nettleship* v. *Weston* that, although women drivers are unable to match up to the standards of their male counterparts, they should be judged by those standards for the purposes of the tort of negligence? If not, what is the ratio of that case? Is it fair?

8.3 What is the 'Learned Hand formula'? Is it employed by the English courts?

8.4 Is it ever legitimate to ignore a very sizeable risk of harming another person? If so, in what sort of case?

8.5 To what extent is the plea 'Well, everybody else does it' sufficient to rebut an allegation of negligence?

8.6 What is the doctrine of *res ipsa loquitur*? Is it a doctrine at all? If so, what effect does it have?

8.7 A owns a medical supplies business and employs a number of van drivers to deliver the supplies to hospitals throughout the country. In the aftermath of a mining disaster in South Wales, she receives an emergency request for supplies from a local hospital. Unfortunately, all her regular drivers are away making deliveries in France and, rather than arrange for one of them to be flown back, she reluctantly decides to drive the van herself although it is some time since she has driven. On the way, the brakes of A's van fail and it crashes into a car travelling in the opposite direction. B, the driver of that car, is badly hurt; A escapes unharmed. There is some evidence that a van driver who drove regularly would have been able to control the vehicle and avoid the collision. It seems that the brake failure was caused by a hole in an unusually corroded part of the brake pipe which would only have been visible had the pipe been removed from the van. In fact, A, following the practice of other firms, had not done so, though she had complied with the manufacturer's advice that the visible parts of the pipe be inspected regularly. It is not clear whether the van had previously been used to carry any corrosive chemical agents. Advise the parties as to their rights and liabilities in tort.

9   Causation

Causation is a central, but elusive, concept in the law of tort. In the tort of negligence, the claimant is required to prove that the defendant's negligence caused her to suffer actionable damage, and there is an equivalent causation requirement for most other torts as well. In the vast majority of cases causation presents no problems. In a small minority, however, the questions raised are ones that have taxed lawyers and philosophers for centuries.

9.1 Causation in Fact and the 'But For' Test

If you were to witness a car accident and afterwards note down all the details that you could remember, your list would include some factors that were causally relevant to the accident and some that were not. Among the former, you might count the treacherously icy condition of the road, the fact that the driver of one of the cars had evidently been drinking and the failure of a faulty traffic light to turn to red. Conversely, the registration numbers of the vehicles involved, the colour of the victims' hair and the clothes they were wearing could not be treated as causally relevant. The presence of these factors was in no way *necessary* for the accident to happen.

The notion of a 'necessary condition' is crucial to the issue of causal relevance or, as it is often called, causation in fact. When we stipulate that a factor must be a necessary condition of the harm in question, we mean that it must be a necessary member of a set of conditions which together are sufficient to produce that harm. If you were to throw a lighted match into the waste-paper basket, your action would be treated as the cause of the fire: it is plain that what you did was necessary to complete a set of conditions (which also includes the presence of inflammable material in the basket and oxygen in the atmosphere) jointly sufficient to produce the fire.

In seeking to identify what is a cause in fact and what is simply irrelevant, courts often rely on the so-called 'but for' test. This poses the question: would the claimant not have suffered harm but for defendant's negligence (i.e. in the absence of defendant's negligence, would she have avoided the harm)? The case of *Barnett* v. *Chelsea and Kensington Hospital Management* [1969] 1 QB 428 is frequently cited as an example of how the test is applied. In that case, the plaintiff's husband had experienced persistent vomiting after drinking some tea and had gone to the casualty department of a hospital. The duty doctor refused to see him and Mr Barnett subsequently died from arsenical poisoning. The court found that the doctor's refusal to see Mr Barnett, though negligent, was not a cause in fact of his death. It was considered causally irrelevant, for there was little or no chance that effective treatment could have been given in time anyway. To put it another way, Mr Barnett's drinking the poisoned tea would have brought about his death whether or not he was treated in hospital.

The 'but for' test demands, then, a hypothetical inquiry into what would have happened if the defendant had acted without fault. Paradoxically, as Prosser and Keaton (1984, p. 265) have noted, to determine causation in fact we must look at what did not in fact occur. This entails consideration not only of how the *defendant* should have acted but also of how the *claimant* would have reacted to the defendant's hypothetical conduct. To be taken into account are both purely physical reactions, for example, how the claimant would have responded to proper medical treatment, and reactions reflecting the claimant's deliberate choice. Hence, where the defendant employer's breach of duty consisted in the failure to provide a safety harness to a worker who fell 70 feet to his death from scaffolding, it was necessary for his widow to establish that he would have worn the harness if it had been provided (which she was unable to do on the facts: see *McWilliams* v. *Sir William Arrol & Co* [1962] 1 WLR 295).

It is not enough that the damage results from the defendant's conduct: it must result from *the wrongful aspect* of the defendant's conduct. This general rule was stated by Lord Hoffmann in *South Australia Asset Management Corp* v. *York Montague Ltd* [1997] AC 191, 213: 'the law limits liability to those consequences which are attributable to that which made the act wrongful'. So where, for example, the defendant's alleged negligence consists in driving with faulty brake-lights, this cannot be treated as the factual cause of a head-on collision in which the defendant's vehicle is involved: the accident would have occurred even if the defendant's brake lights had been in full working order (see further *The Empire Jamaica* [1957] AC 386).

In order to determine whether the claimant's loss results from the aspect of the defendant's conduct which constitutes a breach of duty, it is necessary to determine precisely the scope of that duty and the risks against which its imposition is designed to guard. In the *South Australia* case, the issue was the extent of a surveyor's liability in respect of the negligent overvaluation of property, in circumstances in which the loss was increased as a result of market falls occurring between the date of the valuation and the date of trial. In three separate actions consolidated before the House of Lords, the plaintiff was the lender who had advanced money to the purchaser on security of the property; on the purchaser's default, the plaintiff sought to recover the money advanced by selling the property but a shortfall remained. On a simple 'but for' approach, it might be said that, if the plaintiffs would not have continued with the transaction if they had known the property's true value, they would not have been affected by the market falls at all and should therefore be entitled to recover in respect of the entire amount of the shortfall. The House of

Lords rejected this argument, however, on the basis that, as the defendants had only undertaken to provide the plaintiffs with information as to the value of the properties, not advice concerning the contemplated loans, they could only be liable 'for the consequences of the information being inaccurate' (p. 213, per Lord Hoffmann). The defendants' liability was that portion of the loss that was attributable to the inaccuracy of the valuation, and was limited to the difference between the amount of the negligent overvaluation and the actual value of the property at that time; any additional loss was attributable only to the market fall. One of the cases before the House of Lords may be employed to illustrate this principle. The plaintiff lender advanced £1.75 million on security of property negligently overvalued at £2.5 million and actually worth only £1.85 million; after the borrower defaulted, the property realised only £0.95 million. Although the plaintiff's total loss was the difference between the sum advanced and that recovered (i.e. £0.8 million), only £0.65 million was held to be attributable to the inaccuracy of the valuation, being the difference between the erroneous valuation and the actual value at that time; the rest of the loss was exclusively attributable to the collapse of prices in the property market. This rule will no doubt lead to increased certainty in a difficult area of legal practice, but it must be said that it seems to owe less to strict considerations of legal principle than to a policy that the risk of market fluctuations should be borne primarily by speculators in the marketplace. (For criticism of the decision, see Stapleton, 1997.)

9.2 Multiple Causation

The 'but for' test is generally a good guide as to whether a given factor was a cause in fact. However, it is not a perfect guide. As Hart and Honoré (1985, p. 113) point out, the test's major defect is that it rests on the assumption that there was, at the moment in question, only one set of conditions sufficient to bring about the claimant's injury. Where this is not so – in cases of 'multiple causation' – the test will produce misleading answers. Thus, if two raging fires converge and together burn down your house, applying the 'but for' test would lead to the absurd conclusion that neither fire was the cause provided that each was sufficient to cause the damage: whichever one we imagine not to have happened, we could only conclude that the damage would have resulted anyway. In these cases, it is generally accepted that the law puts aside the 'but for' test and addresses the more fundamental matter of whether the factor in question was necessary to complete a set of conditions together sufficient to produce the result. Looked at this way, it is clear that each fire was a cause of your house burning down, assuming that each fire, together with other conditions such as the way the wind was blowing and the presence of dry leaves on the ground, made a material contribution to the causal process that brought about the damage. Accordingly, if each fire was started through the negligence of different people, each of them would be jointly and severally liable for the harm. If one fire was attributable to natural causes, however, it is far from clear that the person who negligently started the other fire should be liable for the entire loss. Could she not argue that, although her fire was a cause of the harm, the damages that she was liable to pay should be reduced in view of the inevitable destruction of the house by the natural fire? The difficulties arising in this context from the interplay of principles of causation and of the assessment of damages have yet to be satisfactorily resolved by the courts.

Two types of case involving multiple causation can be distinguished. First, there are instances of 'cumulative' causation, as in the example above where two fires converge on a house. The two fires contribute to a single causal process which results in the destruction of the house. The leading case is *Bonnington Castings Ltd* v. *Wardlaw* [1956] AC 613. Here, the plaintiff contracted pneumoconiosis after working for several years in the defendant's workshop, where he was exposed to silicone dust. The dust came from two sources, one innocent, one guilty in the sense that it was attributable to the defendant's breach of duty. The medical evidence was that pneumoconiosis was caused by the gradual accumulation of silicone dust in the lungs, and that it could not be ascribed wholly to either innocent or guilty dust. In these circumstances, the House of Lords ruled that the correct test to apply was whether the guilty dust made a material contribution to the disease. In effect, it had to be proved only that the guilty dust made up a more than negligible proportion of the total amount of dust to which the plaintiff was exposed. It was unnecessary to show that the guilty dust was the sole cause of the disease, nor even that the plaintiff would not have suffered the disease if there had been no guilty dust. On the facts, the plaintiff won. The decision confirms that, where the claimant's injury arises from cumulative exposure to a single causal agent and the defendant's negligence is responsible for a proportion of that claimant's exposure, it is appropriate to set aside the 'but for' test of causation and apply instead the test of material contribution. This does not mean, however, that the defendant is responsible for the whole of the claimant's injury, for it may be that the damages the defendant is liable to pay are reduced so as to reflect the proportion of the exposure for which she was responsible. In *Holtby* v. *Brigham & Cowan (Hull) Ltd* [2000] 3 All ER 421, the claimant suffered asbestosis as a result of cumulative exposure to asbestos dust in the workplace; this occurred over the course of various periods of employment with different employers. It was common ground that asbestosis was a progressive condition that developed in proportion to the quantity of asbestos inhaled. The Court of Appeal ruled that each employer's liability should be limited to reflect the extent to which it contributed to the claimant's total exposure to asbestos, and assessed each employer's share of responsibility on a 'time-exposure' basis. It is crucial to note that *Holtby* was a case in which all the substantial contributions to the claimant's exposure involved negligence. Whether the same analysis is to be applied to a situation where, as in *Bonnington*, there are both innocent and guilty contributions to that exposure remains to be seen.

Secondly, there are cases involving 'pre-empted' or 'overtaken' causes. A famous textbook example of this type of case is where a traveller, about to set out across the desert, has a lethal dose of poison put into her water keg by one enemy and the keg emptied by a second; ignorant of this, she sets out on her journey, during the course of which she dies. The 'but for' test again threatens to mislead: if the keg had not been poisoned, the traveller would have died of thirst, while, alternatively, if the keg had not been emptied, she would have died from the poison. However, this is not a case like that of the converging fires where we can say that both factors were a cause, for the traveller in fact died of thirst and not of poison. In cases of this sort, we would say that the plan of the first enemy was 'pre-empted', 'overtaken' or 'neutralised' by that of the second. The secret here, as Wright (1985) points out, is to ask what actually happened, not what might have done.

Cases in which the claimant suffers successive injuries, the effects of which overlap, cause significant difficulties of analysis in this context. In fact, the question that arises is not generally one of causation, namely whether the defendant caused actionable injury to the claimant: there is no doubt but that *some* actionable injury has occurred. Rather, the question is what value to attach to that injury, i.e. it is a question of the assessment or quantification of damages. Where the action is brought in respect of the second of the two injuries, the rule is that one must take one's victim as one finds her. In *Performance Cars* v. *Abraham* [1962] 1 QB 33, the plaintiff's Rolls-Royce was involved, in the space of two weeks, in two collisions each of which was caused by the fault of a different person. Either collision on its own would have necessitated a respray of the car. In an action against the second tortfeasor, the Court of Appeal rejected the owner's claim for the cost of the respray on the grounds that the loss did not flow from the defendant's wrongdoing: at the time of the second collision, the vehicle was already in need of a respray.

Where the action is brought in respect of the first of two successive injuries, the courts have adopted a pragmatic distinction between cases in which the second injury is tortious and those in which it is innocent. In *Baker* v. *Willoughby* [1970] AC 467, the plaintiff was first run down by the defendant's negligent driving, suffering a stiff leg, and then shot in the same leg in a hold-up, after which the leg had to be amputated. With his stiff leg, the plaintiff had suffered a loss of mobility and a consequent reduction in his earning capacity; the loss of the leg, on its own, would have been sufficient to produce that same (and greater) loss of mobility and reduced earning capacity. The House of Lords rejected the argument that the defendant's negligence could only be regarded as the cause of that loss up to the time of the second incident, the second injury 'obliterating' the effect of the first. Lord Reid, speaking for the majority of the court, held that both injuries were concurrent causes of the disability from the time of the shooting onwards and that the defendant therefore remained liable in respect of the period after the shooting. He thus treated the issue purely as one of causation and ignored the principle that, in assessing damages, the aim is to put the claimant into the position she would have been in had the tort not happened. This aspect of his speech attracted much criticism in the subsequent decision of the House of Lords in *Jobling* v. *Associated Dairies* [1982] AC 794. This case differed from *Baker* in that the second injury was the onset of a natural disease and not the tortious conduct of a third party. The defendant employers had been responsible for injuring the plaintiff's back and thereby reducing his earning capacity. Subsequently, the disease rendered the plaintiff totally unfit for work. Again the House of Lords had to consider whether the defendants continued to be liable for that reduced earning capacity in respect of the period after the second event, the onset of the disease. This time their Lordships took account of the aim of an award of damages and held that the plaintiff would be over-compensated if able to recover for the continuing loss. Accordingly, the defendants' liability ceased at the time of the onset of the disease. Yet, although the members of the House of Lords criticised the reasoning of Lord Reid in *Baker*, they accepted that that case might be correctly decided on its facts and were not prepared to rule out the possibility that the result reached in *Baker* might be appropriate in cases involving successive tortious injuries. This seems fair: as Lord Keith pointed out in *Jobling*, where two successive tortfeasors are liable to the plaintiff, 'it would be highly unreasonable if the aggregate of both awards were less than the total loss suffered' (p. 815).

9.3 Causal Indeterminacy

In typical cases of negligence, for example, where the claimant is injured in a car accident, proof of factual causation is a simple matter: witness accounts and physical examination of the accident scene will make it tolerably clear what happened. But, as we move away from paradigmatic instances of negligence liability, we come across cases in which no number of witnesses could produce evidence enabling us to determine unequivocally how the claimant was injured. We have entered the realm of scientific or medical uncertainty.

An illustration of the difficulties that can arise is provided by the litigation in the USA arising out of the use in the Vietnam war of the chemical Agent Orange, a defoliant employed as part of a modern-day 'scorched earth' policy by the US Army (see *Agent Orange Litigation*, 597 F Supp 740 (1984)). After the war, veterans claimed that exposure to the chemical as it was sprayed over the forests of Vietnam had caused them serious health problems and had produced congenital disabilities in their children. They sought to pin responsibility on the various manufacturers of Agent Orange whom they alleged had improperly failed to warn of the risks inherent in the use of the chemical. However, the veterans faced an uphill battle in making out a case for compensation for, although there was evidence that the incidence of health problems of those exposed to Agent Orange was abnormally high, there was no evidence that any individual had suffered those problems as a consequence of that exposure rather than through natural causes. Nor was there evidence as to which company had manufactured the particular quantities of Agent Orange with which each individual came into contact. These difficulties of establishing causation in individual cases forced the veterans to settle out of court for a level of compensation that fell far short of their original expectations.

The Agent Orange case neatly illustrates two different problems that claimants might face in seeking to establish causation. First, there is the problem of the 'indeterminate claimant'. This arises in cases where, in a group of people suffering similar injuries, it is not clear whose injury resulted from the defendant's negligence as opposed to some other, non-tortious factor. This difficulty faced many of those involved in the Agent Orange litigation, as there was a pre-existing 'background risk' of contracting, without any contact with the chemical at all, many of the conditions from which the claimants suffered. Secondly, there are cases in which each of a number of defendants is known to have injured a proportion of the class of victims but there is no way of identifying the individuals for whose injury each is responsible. Such cases present the problem of the 'indeterminate defendant'. Again, the Agent Orange litigation provides an illustration: there was no evidence available with which to prove that it was one manufacturer rather than another that had produced the particular quantities of Agent Orange to which individual veterans had been exposed.

The normal rules of civil proof may produce injustice in such cases. Ordinarily, the claimant must prove on the balance of probabilities that it was the defendant's negligence that caused her injury, i.e. that the defendant's negligence was more likely than not to have been the (or a) cause. But the scientific or medical uncertainty may be such as to prevent *all* those in the claimant group from recovering damages, even though it is absolutely certain that *some* in that group had indeed suffered tortious injury. This not only deprives those within the affected group of what might be thought reasonable compensation, but also weakens the incentive on those in the position of the defendant to take due care. The same is true where the scientific or medical uncertainty makes it impossible to identify which defendant was responsible for which claimant's injury: the result may be that none of the claimants recovers and all of the defendants get off scot-free.

These problems of causal indeterminacy do not arise only in the context of group claims; they may be repeated at the level of the individual claimant. The state of scientific or medical knowledge may be such that it is unknowable whether the claimant was injured by the defendant's negligence or by some innocent alternative cause (the problem of the indeterminate claimant), or whether it was Defendant A rather than Defendant B, both of whom have negligently exposed the claimant to the same risk of injury, who actually caused the claimant's injury (the problem of the indeterminate defendant).

In such cases, the urge to depart from the traditional approach to proving causation is strong, and we shall consider in turn two alternative approaches that have been explored in English law.

Liability for Increasing the Risk to which the Claimant is Exposed

In *McGhee* v. *National Coal Board* [1973] 1 WLR 1, the House of Lords took a decisive step away from the traditional requirement that the claimant must prove on the balance of probabilities that her injury was caused by the defendant's negligence, and substituted instead the weaker casual requirement that the defendant's negligence must be shown to have increased the risk to which the claimant was exposed. As we shall see, for some considerable time this decision was misunderstood by the courts in such a way as to obscure its radical departure from tradition, but the House of Lords (in *Fairchild* v. *Glenhaven Funeral Services* [2002] UKHL 22) has now confirmed that *McGhee* did indeed break new legal ground, albeit only in a strictly limited set of cases in which scientific or medical uncertainty makes it impossible to determine the true cause of the claimant's injury.

In *McGhee*, a worker in a brick kiln contracted industrial dermatitis through exposure to brick dust. The risk of dermatitis was a part of the job of a kiln worker, as exposure to brick dust in the kilns was inevitable, but the defendant employers had negligently increased the period of exposure by failing to provide showering facilities at the workplace with the result that the brick dust was left caked on the bodies of the kiln workers until they got home. In contrast with *Bonnington Castings Ltd* v. *Wardlaw* [1956] AC 613 (see 9.2), it was unclear whether the plaintiff contracted dermatitis as a result of his cumulative exposure to the brick dust or as the result of a single abrasion caused by the dust. In the latter eventuality, orthodox theory suggested that it was necessary to prove that this abrasion occurred whilst the plaintiff was on the way home from work, but this was not a matter which was susceptible to definitive proof. In a radical response to these evidential difficulties, the House of Lords found for the plaintiff on the basis that the increase in the risk of dermatitis could be treated as having made a substantial contribution to the injury. For Lord Wilberforce, in cases where the defendant had negligently increased the risk of injury to the plaintiff but there was no evidence that this had actually affected the plaintiff, the burden of proof should be reversed; as this burden was *ex hypothesi* impossible to discharge, the loss would inevitably fall on the defendant. The other members of the House of Lords reached the same result without reversing the formal burden of proof. In *Wilsher* v. *Essex Area Health Authority* [1988] AC 1074, the House of Lords declared that Lord Wilberforce's approach was contrary to principle, and held that he must be regarded as having dissented from the approach of the majority in *McGhee*, which was to be preferred. The crucial question, therefore, was how the majority's reasoning was to be interpreted. In *Wilsher*, the House of Lords took the conservative view that the majority in *McGhee* 'laid down no new principle of law whatever' (p. 1090, per Lord Bridge) and had simply made a factual inference that the increased exposure to brick dust resulting from the defendant's negligence was probably a materially contributing cause of the plaintiff's dermatitis. In its more recent decision in *Fairchild* v.

Glenhaven Funeral Services [2002] UKHL 22, the House of Lords (Lord Hutton dissenting on this point) has now declared that this interpretation of *McGhee* was wrong.

In *Fairchild*, the House of Lords considered three separate appeals in which the question was whether, and in what circumstances, a claimant who sustains mesothelioma through exposure to asbestos dust in the workplace, during separate periods of employment with different employers, can recover damages. Medical science cannot yet determine the exact process by which mesothelioma is contracted, and it was accepted before the House of Lords that there was no reason to prefer either one of two rival theories: first, that mesothelioma is an 'indivisible' disease which is triggered on a single unidentifiable occasion when one or more asbestos fibres initiate a process whose effects only become apparent some 10–40 years later; secondly, that it is a condition which requires cumulative exposure to asbestos and develops only when that exposure reaches a critical level. Before the case reached the Lords, the Court of Appeal had ruled that the scientific uncertainty was such as to prevent any of the claimants proving on the balance of probabilities that their mesothelioma was caused during any particular period of employment, and that all the claims against the former employers therefore had to fail ([2001] EWCA Civ 1881). The claimants' appeal against this decision was allowed by the House of Lords. 'Any other outcome,' said Lord Nicholls (at [36]), 'would be deeply offensive to instinctive notions of what justice requires and fairness demands.'

Their Lordships ruled that, in the particular circumstances of the cases before them, it was necessary to depart from the ordinary approach to proof of causation and treat the contribution of each employer to the risk to which the claimants were exposed as making a material contribution to their injury. In effect, this seems to have been to accept 'a lesser degree of causal connection' than is ordinarily required (at [38], per Lord Nicholls), with the fact of exposure to risk, in breach of duty, being all that it was necessary for the claimants to prove. Although in one sense it was unjust to impose liability on a defendant who could not be shown to have caused the claimant's injury, this injustice was 'heavily outweighed by the injustice of denying redress to a victim' of such conduct (at [33], per Lord Bingham), bearing in mind especially each of the defendants' admitted breach of duty. Their Lordships emphasised that the occasions on which it would be appropriate to adopt this alternative approach to causation would be rare, though they did not identify in precise terms what those occasions might be, preferring to allow the law to develop on a case-by-case basis.

In fact, *Fairchild* is not as radical a decision as *McGhee*, though the break with traditional approaches to causation is more clearly acknowledged in the more recent case. In *Fairchild*, the House of Lords was in effect dealing with the problem of the indeterminate defendant, in which it was accepted that each claimant had been tortiously injured, and the only question was which of two or more guilty defendants, each of whom had exposed the claimants to the risk which eventuated, was actually responsible for the injury. The injustice of holding each of the defendants liable in such a case was small. But, in *McGhee*, it was not clear that the plaintiff had been tortiously injured at all: an innocent explanation of his injury was also possible. This was akin to the case of the indeterminate claimant, and it must be said that the policy reasons for favouring McGhee over others who could not prove their injury was caused by negligence – rather than by some other, innocent factor – are not immediately apparent.

The limits of the *McGhee/Fairchild* doctrine are plainly illustrated by the subsequent decision of the House of Lords in *Wilsher* v. *Essex Area Health Authority* [1988] AC 1074. Although we now know the House of Lords' interpretation of *McGhee* in that case to have been wrong, it appears to have been correctly decided on its facts. Their Lordships were presented with a situation in which a premature baby was given negligent treatment in the defendant's hospital and subsequently lost his power of sight. The medical evidence was inconclusive as to whether the negligence was actually the cause of the blindness, as the boy was born with a number of other conditions which might also have produced the same result. Applying *McGhee*, the trial judge and Court of Appeal (by a majority) found for the boy on the basis that the defendant's negligence had materially increased the risk of his going blind and could therefore be held to have contributed to his blindness. The House of Lords allowed the defendant's appeal, ruling that the boy had failed to establish that the defendant's negligence was a more likely cause of his blindness than some other, innocent factor. In view of the understanding of *McGhee* that has now prevailed, it appears that the distinction between the two cases is that, in *McGhee*, the risk that eventuated was substantially the same as that created by the defendant's breach of duty, while in *Wilsher* the injury could have been caused by a number of quite different factors, only one of which was the defendant's negligence.

Damages for Loss of a Chance

An alternative approach to the problem of causal indeterminacy is the award of damages for 'loss of a chance'. The question whether such damages are available in English law was raised before the House of Lords in *Hotson* v. *East Berkshire Area Health Authority* [1989] AC 750. There, a teenage boy who had fallen from a tree in his school playground was taken to hospital, where staff negligently failed to appreciate the extent of his injuries with the result that he did not receive the appropriate treatment for several days. Afterwards, the boy was found to be suffering from a permanent disability (avascular necrosis) in his hip joint. The medical evidence was that the fall had probably caused such damage that prompt treatment would have made no difference, but there was a 25 per cent chance that his initial injuries were not so serious and that he would have responded if treated without delay. On this evidence, it was clear that the boy would fail to satisfy the burden of proving on the balance of probabilities that his disability was caused by medical negligence;

consequently, the claim was presented as one for the loss of his chance of a full recovery and the damages sought were limited to 25 per cent of amount to which the boy would have been entitled had full liability been accepted. This argument succeeded at trial and before the Court of Appeal, but was robustly rejected by the House of Lords: on the facts before the House, it was necessary to prove on the balance of probabilities that the injury itself resulted from the negligence. Nevertheless, the House of Lords declined to reject the idea of damages for loss of a chance altogether, citing *Kitchen* v. *Royal Air Force Association* [1958] 1 WLR 563 as an example of a case in which such damages might be awarded. In that case, solicitors negligently failed to commence an action on behalf of their client within the limitation period and were held liable for the amount of the client's claim discounted by the probability of its success. What is more, Lord Bridge even went so far as to observe that, '[i]n some cases, perhaps particularly medical negligence cases, causation may be so shrouded in mystery that the court can only measure statistical chances' (p. 782). But he denied that the case before him was of that description: at the time of the defendant's negligence, the probability was that the avascular necrosis was already inevitable and that medical treatment could have made no difference.

The decision in *Hotson* leaves the law on loss-of-chance damages in a rather confused state, but matters are clarified somewhat if we make a fundamental distinction: between cases where the claimant can prove no loss resulting from the defendant's negligence other than a loss of a chance, and those where the claimant establishes some tortious injury and seeks damages for the consequences of that injury. In assessing the quantum of damages, it is perfectly orthodox – indeed, necessary – to measure the probability of each possible consequence of the injury and to adjust the award accordingly (see generally ch. 22). In that context, it is permissible to talk of the award of damages for loss of a particular chance, for example, the chance that the claimant, but for the accident, would have embarked upon a new and particularly lucrative career. But the loss-of-chance analysis has no role to play in determining whether the claimant has established the causal link between the defendant's breach of duty and her injury which is an essential element of liability in negligence. Here, the claimant must prove the existence of the causal link on the balance of probabilities or she has no claim at all. This all-or-nothing question of causation is logically prior to that of quantum, for it makes no sense to value the claimant's claim until it is clear that she in fact has an action. As Lord Bridge explained in *Hotson*, '[u]nless the plaintiff proved on a balance of probabilities that the delayed treatment was at least a material contributory cause of the avascular necrosis he failed on the issue of causation and no question of quantification could arise' (p. 782).

The distinction between issues of causation and quantum calls for particular care in cases of pure economic loss, for the actionable damage is not so readily identifiable here as in cases of physical harm (see Coote, 1998). In *Kitchen*, the client's actionable injury was properly analysed as the loss of the claim, and the cause of action accrued at the time of that loss. The probability of success was taken into account only in putting a value upon that injury, i.e. in relation to quantum, not causation. The same principle was applied when a solicitor's negligence caused a client to miss out on the opportunity of a favourable business deal (*Allied Maples Group Ltd* v. *Simmons & Simmons* [1995] 1 WLR 1002; *pace* Lunney, 1996–97): the deal had been 'a substantial chance rather than a speculative one' (p. 915, per Stuart-Smith LJ), and the client had therefore 'lost something of substance' (p. 925, per Hobhouse LJ) so it was necessary only to value that loss, taking account of the probability of the deal actually being concluded. The statutory claim for loss of dependency under the Fatal Accidents Act 1976 (see ch. 22), which is in effect a claim for pure economic loss, raises equivalent issues: the dependant must establish a cause of action by proof, on the balance of probabilities, that the deceased was killed by the defendant's wrongful act and that she stood in a relationship of dependency with the deceased; in assessing the value of that dependency, however, a discount should be made to reflect the probability of its continuing (*Davis* v. *Taylor* [1974] AC 207; on the facts, however, the claimant failed altogether as she had been separated from her husband at the time of his death, with no significant prospect of a reconciliation).

The question that remains is whether there is any mileage in Lord Bridge's apparent suggestion that cases where causation is 'shrouded in mystery' may warrant a different approach. There is a possible distinction between cases like *Hotson*, where on the balance of probabilities the plaintiff was already 'doomed' at the time of the defendant's negligence (the fall had probably caused such serious damage that there was nothing the doctors could have done), and other cases where the claimant's fate was still hanging in the balance. But whether there is any reason of policy for distinguishing the two classes of claimant is to be doubted.

Evaluation

In its *Fairchild* decision, the House of Lords showed a commendable willingness to depart from traditional causal doctrines where their application would have resulted in injustice. No doubt, there will be further attempts to persuade their Lordships to endorse similar innovations in other cases of causal indeterminacy. But there is a risk that, by seeking to avoid one form of injustice, the courts will simply create another. In our view, it is fundamental to liability in tort that the claimant can prove her injury resulted from another's wrongful act. Without this, there is nothing to distinguish her from the countless others who suffer injury or illness through no one else's fault, and no pressing need to impose liability on a defendant who, though admittedly in the wrong, cannot be shown to have caused any injury at all. It is submitted therefore that the application of the *Fairchild* decision should be limited to cases raising the problem of the indeterminate defendant, in which the claimant can prove that her injury resulted from another's wrongful act but cannot identify which of a number of wrongdoers was responsible. Here the policy considerations are very different from those that apply where there is a competing, innocent explanation for the claimant's injury, for (by definition) none of the wrongdoers is innocent. Some support for departing from orthodoxy in such cases is provided by the decision of the House of Lords in *Baker* v. *Willoughby* (see 9.2), where the issue was also the allocation of responsibility between different wrongdoers.

In fact, there is at least one English case that appears to have been decided on the basis of the approach advocated here. In *Fitzgerald* v. *Lane* [1987] QB 781, a pedestrian suffered a disabling injury after being struck successively by two negligently-driven vehicles; the injury was caused by a single impact but it could not be determined which this was. On the facts, the Court of Appeal decided to apportion responsibility for the injury equally between the two negligent drivers even though, in the case of the second driver, it could not be shown on the balance of probabilities that he had caused or contributed to the injury. (The matter was not addressed when the case came before the House of Lords: [1989] AC 328.) The Court of Appeal's decision received some tentative approval in the House of Lords in *Fairchild*, as did a number of overseas decisions dealing with hunting injuries sustained in circumstances in which there is no evidence as to which of two weapons, both discharged negligently, fired the guilty bullet. In the United States and Canada, the courts have found each of the negligent hunters liable and apportioned the loss equally between them (*Summers* v. *Tice* 199 P. 2d 1 (1948); *Cook* v. *Lewis* [1952] 1 DLR 1), and it appears that the House of Lords now envisages the adoption of a comparable approach in England. A further extension of the same approach might lead to the recognition of a 'market share' theory of liability – already adopted by the Californian Supreme Court – by which manufacturers of a defective generic product might be held liable in proportion to their market share when it is not clear which of them was the manufacturer of the product that had actually injured the claimant (*Sindell* v. *Abbott Laboratories*, 607 P 2d 924 (1980): generic pharmaceutical drug). What is notable about all these examples is that they involve uncertainty not about the aetiology of a disease but about the circumstances of the individual claimant, and would therefore involve an extension of the *Fairchild* doctrine beyond cases of scientific uncertainty with which the House of Lords was concerned in that case. It is submitted, however, that the policy considerations recognised by the House of Lords are of equal weight in all cases raising the problem of the indeterminate defendant and hence that such an extension would indeed be desirable.

9.4 Legal Causation

When we seek to identify the cause of a particular event, we do not ordinarily try to compile a list of all its factual causes. What we do is pick out one or other of them as particularly significant. Thus, in the example of the car accident given above, we might say that the cause of the accident was the icy road surface or drunken driving, but it would not be particularly illuminating to isolate the fact that all the cars involved had petrol in their tanks, even though, indisputably, this was a necessary condition for the accident. Not everyone will pick out the same factors: our choice is determined by who we are and what we are trying to prove, as is shown by the following example (see Honoré, 1983): a man lives with his wife in an unhappy marriage, comes home drunk, quarrels with her, takes out a revolver which he possesses without a licence, and shoots her, whereupon she consults a quack who treats her unsuitably and she dies. To a marriage reformer, the cause of her death is the state of divorce law; to a teetotaller, it is drink; to a pacifist, possession of the weapon; to an upholder of medical interests, the activity of the quack. Ordinary people, however, have no time for this dry intellectualism: their response is more instinctive. Headlines in the tabloid press would declare 'Wicked husband in brutal wife murder', and this would no doubt be the common response. By and large, the law takes the tabloid line.

The 'tabloid line' reflects a highly individualistic political theory which demands that people take full responsibility for their deliberate actions and trusts in their ability to control the physical world around them. Accordingly, in selecting the legal cause from a number of factual causes, the law grants special status to deliberate human acts. Furthermore, it homes in on the deliberate human act that most closely precedes the outcome in question and will generally look no further for its cause. In doing so, the law assumes that the choice whether or not to bring about the outcome lay entirely in the hands of the last actor: it refuses to let her 'pass the buck' and will not hold anyone else responsible for her actions. One product of this approach is that the defendant remains fully liable even where the claimant's loss is partly attributable to a pre-existing state of affairs (e.g. the claimant's pre-existing susceptibility to injury: see the 'thin skull' rule, 10.4). In *The Sivand* [1998] 2 Lloyd's Rep 97, the defendant's tanker negligently collided with and damaged the plaintiff's dock. The plaintiff engaged contractors to effect the necessary repairs, but a second accident occurred while the work was being done when the contractors' barge capsized because the seabed was unable to support the weight of its stabilising legs. This was an eventuality that the contractors could not reasonably have been expected to foresee. In deciding that the defendants' negligence was the cause of the second accident as well as the first, making them liable for the contractors' additional costs, the Court of Appeal emphasised that the second accident resulted from the pre-existing condition of the seabed, not from an independent intervening event like an earthquake. Although the accident could not have been foreseen, it did not 'break the chain of causation'.

The special status accorded to voluntary human action is especially clear in the tendency to treat deliberate interventions by third parties, and deliberate risk-taking by the claimant, as intervening acts negativing any causal connection between the defendant's wrongdoing and the claimant's injury. (Note that the Latin phrase *novus actus interveniens* is often used to denote an intervening act which negatives causal connection.) According to Hart and Honoré (1985), 'the free, deliberate and informed act or omission of a human being, intended to exploit the situation created by defendant, negatives causal connection' (p. 136). Hence, where the defendant local authority flooded the plaintiff's home, which had to be vacated during repairs, and squatters entered the vacant property and caused damage, the local authority could not be said to have caused the plaintiff's loss (*Lamb* v. *Camden London Borough Council* [1981] QB 625). Although there is a tendency in such cases to view the reasonable foreseeability or likelihood of the intervention as the test of *novus actus interveniens* (see, in particular, *Home Office* v. *Dorset Yacht Co* [1970] AC 1004, 1030 per Lord Reid), the stronger modern view is that the voluntary character of the intervention suffices to negative causal connection irrespective of how foreseeable it was. Exceptionally, however, the courts may recognise a special duty to prevent a third party causing harm. In such cases, the defendant is not strictly speaking the *cause* of the harm, but the law accepts as sufficient a weaker causal relationship, namely that in which the defendant is said by Hart and Honoré to *occasion* the harm (as in the *Dorset Yacht* case: see further 6.4).

Of course, not all deliberate acts intervening between a defendant's wrongdoing and the claimant's injury will negative causal connection. Acts of irresponsible agents such as infants and those with mental disabilities will rarely do so (see *Kirkham* v. *Chief Constable of Greater Manchester* [1990] 2 QB 282). Nor will even the deliberate acts of a responsible agent unless they can be regarded as 'voluntary'. What is voluntary is to be assessed taking account of the pressures under which the intervening act occurs, and acts done to remedy the situation the defendant has negligently created will not normally be accorded this status, even if they cause further injury. The classic example is the rescuer who suffers injury in the course of a rescue attempt necessitated by the defendant's negligent imperilling of another, in which context the courts have repeatedly rebuffed attempts to invoke the *novus actus* doctrine (see *Haynes* v. *Harwood* [1935] 1 KB 146; *Ward* v. *T E Hopkins & Son Ltd* [1955] 3 All ER 225; and 7.1 above). Similarly, where an accident victim undergoes remedial surgery, any additional injury suffered in the course of the operation will still be regarded as a consequence of the initial accident, provided the treatment is appropriate and carried out with reasonable care (*Hogan* v. *Bentinck West Hartley Collieries (Owners) Ltd* [1949] 1 All ER 588, 595 per Lord Normand).

A case that illustrates the principle, as well as demonstrating the tendency of the courts to obscure the issue by recourse to bewildering metaphors, is *The Oropesa* [1943] P 32. Two ships, the *Oropesa* and the *Manchester Regiment*, had been involved in a collision at sea for which they were both partly to blame. The weather was rough and, in view of the damage his ship had sustained, the master of the *Manchester Regiment* feared she might not stay afloat. He began to ferry his crew across to the *Oropesa* by boat; on its second trip, with the master and the deceased crew member whose family brought the action on board, the boat overturned and the deceased was drowned. The Court of Appeal had to consider whether the act of setting off in the boat negatived the causal connection between the negligence of the *Oropesa* and the death of the deceased. In reaching the conclusion that it did not, Lord Wright, who delivered the leading judgment, explained his approach in the following cryptic, but oft-cited, passage (p. 39): 'To break the chain of causation it must be shown that there is something which I will call ultroneous, something unwarrantable, a new cause which disturbs the sequence of events, something which can be described as either unreasonable or extraneous or extrinsic.' As Hart and Honoré remark, 'It would have been simpler to say that the acts were done partly for self-preservation and partly in pursuance of what was at least a moral duty to save the lives of those on board' (p. 148).

It is not only deliberate acts intended to exploit the situation created by the defendant that may negative causal connection: reckless or negligent interventions can, on at least some occasions, have the same effect. Whether a negligent act breaks the chain of causation is, however, a question of fact for the court, and it can be extremely difficult to predict the result on the facts of an individual case. For example, where the claimant undergoes remedial surgery after an accident caused by the defendant's negligence, and suffers further injury as a result, the defendant may be relieved of responsibility if the operation is ill-advised (*Hogan* v. *Bentinck West Hartley Collieries (Owners) Ltd* [1949] 1 All ER 588) or carried out without reasonable care and skill (*Rahman* v. *Arearose Ltd* [2001] QB 351). But, in other contexts, the courts have been more reluctant to hold that mere negligence negatives causal connection. In *Rouse* v. *Squires* [1973] QB 889, a lorry jack-knifed as a result of its driver's negligence and caused an obstruction of the road; shortly afterwards, a second lorry, driven at excessive speed, was unable to brake in time to avoid the obstruction and skidded into the deceased, who had stopped to offer assistance. The Court of Appeal held that the second driver's negligence did not relieve the first driver of all responsibility for the death, of which he remained a joint cause. Cairns LJ, however, distinguished those (like the second driver) whose negligence consisted in driving too fast or not keeping a proper lookout from 'those who deliberately or recklessly drive into the obstruction' (p. 898).

Knightly v. *Johns* [1982] 1 WLR 349 may be regarded as falling within Cairns LJ's exception. The plaintiff police motorcyclist was injured in the aftermath of an accident caused when the first defendant negligently overturned his motor-vehicle at the exit from an underground carriageway. The defendant police inspector, arriving to take charge at the scene, forgot to close off the tunnel at its entrance and ordered the plaintiff to ride back down it, against the flow of traffic (the other carriageway being closed for maintenance), in order to do so. The plaintiff was struck by an oncoming motorist who was driving without negligence. The Court of Appeal held that the defendant driver could not be regarded as responsible for the plaintiff's injury. Stephenson LJ accepted that not every intervening error or act of folly would negative causal connection, but ruled that the folly here was so out of the ordinary as to have that effect: 'too much happened here, too much went wrong, the chapter of accidents was too long and varied to impose on the first defendant liability for what happened to the plaintiff' (p. 367).

The same principles apply where the intervening act is not that of a third party but that of the claimant. In *McKew* v. *Holland & Hannan & Cubitts (Scotland) Ltd* [1969] 3 All ER 1621, as a result of the defendant's admitted fault, the plaintiff suffered an injury which left his left leg liable to give way suddenly and without warning. Shortly afterwards, the plaintiff lost control of the leg while descending a steep flight of stairs that did not have a handrail; to avoid falling headfirst, he threw himself from the stairs but broke his right ankle on landing. The House of Lords accepted that his decision to jump, while perhaps an error of judgement, was not such as to break the chain of causation given the need for a split-second reaction to the danger; only an action that was 'so utterly unreasonable that even on the spur of the moment no ordinary man would have been so foolish as to do what he did' would have such an effect (p. 1624, per Lord Reid). Nevertheless, their Lordships ruled that the causal connection was negatived by the plaintiff's prior conduct in unreasonably placing himself in a position where he might be confronted with an emergency. Lord Reid stated: 'if the injured man acts unreasonably he cannot hold the defender liable for injury caused by his own unreasonable conduct. His unreasonable conduct is novus actus interveniens' (p. 1623). This dictum should not be thought to entail that any intervening fault whatsoever on the part of the claimant will negative causal connection, for that would undesirably trespass upon the defence of contributory negligence. It is submitted that only conduct amounting to a reckless disregard for the claimant's personal safety should have this effect.

In exceptional circumstances, causal connection may be negatived by a natural event rather than an intervening human action. If the ambulance taking the accident victim to hospital is hit by a falling tree, causing her additional harm, there is no prospect of attributing this further injury to the person who was responsible for the initial accident; it was a mere coincidence, simply her bad luck. The test here is whether the conjunction of the two accidents was reasonably foreseeable. An example is provided by *Carslogie Steamship Co* v. *Royal Norwegian Government* [1952] AC 292): the plaintiff's ship, the *Heimgar*, was damaged in a collision caused by negligence attributable to the defendant government; temporary repairs rendered her seaworthy but, while steaming to the USA for permanent repairs, she suffered further damage in a heavy winter storm. It was held that the storm damage was a 'supervening event' and not in any sense a consequence of the collision; therefore the defendant could not be held responsible for the loss of chartered hire for the period in which the heavy-weather damage was being repaired. As Hart and Honoré point out, regardless of whether the storm could be regarded as unforeseeable in itself, it was mere coincidence that it happened to damage the vessel while *en route* for repairs (pp. 164–8).

In summary, causal connection between the defendant's negligence and the claimant's injury is negatived if the injury results from (a) a voluntary intervening act by the claimant or a third party; (b) a grossly negligent or reckless intervening act by the claimant or a third party (but not usually where there is negligence of a lesser degree); or (c) an abnormal natural occurrence. This, essentially, is the thesis advanced by Hart and Honoré. The most common attack on the thesis is that it introduces policy considerations into what should be a purely factual concept (see, for instance, Wright, 1985). However, Hart and Honoré are surely right in maintaining that the process of selection from among causally relevant factors is appropriately termed 'causal' because it merely reflects the distinction we make in ordinary speech between 'mere conditions' and 'the cause' of an event. This, of course, is not to insist that the causal enquiry is value-free. Indeed, as our values change, it may be possible to discern some difference in our, and the law's, use of causal language. Thus it may be that the advance of collective values at the expense of the individualistic values of pre-welfare state Britain may prompt the law to relax its insistence that deliberate acts negative causal connection and to hold responsible those who provide the opportunity for others deliberately to cause harm. To some extent, this has already happened with regard to landowners and public authorities (see 6.6 and 7.3–4).

Summary

9.1 The defendant's negligence will be treated as a 'cause in fact' of the claimant's injury if it was a necessary element of a set of conditions together sufficient to produce that injury. The 'but for' test is often employed as a simple guide as to whether the requirement of causation in fact is satisfied.

9.2 The 'but for' test is not able to deal with cases of multiple causation and in such cases we have to employ the underlying notion of causation in fact. However, even if the defendant's action is treated as causally relevant, it may be that the policy of the law relating to the assessment of damages requires the court to take account of the fact that the claimant's loss would have occurred in any event because of some other (non-tortious) factor.

9.3 The claimant must prove, on the balance of probabilities, that her loss was caused by negligence rather than by natural causes. Exceptionally, however, in cases where it is impossible to establish how the claimant's injury occurred, it may be enough to show that the defendant's negligence exposed the claimant to a risk of the same type that eventuated.

9.4 Not all causes in fact are treated as the cause of the claimant's loss in law. An intervening act or event may negative causal connection ('break the chain of causation') between the defendant's negligence and the claimant's injury.

Exercises

9.1 What is the 'but for' test? Does it always identify all the factors that may be treated as the cause of the claimant's loss? Does it identify them specifically enough or do we need to supplement it with different principles of causation?

9.2 How, if at all, can *Baker* v. *Willoughby* be reconciled with *Jobling* v. *Associated Dairies*?

9.3 Your employer is required to issue you with a safety harness when you work above ground level but has never done so. You are pig-headed and there is a chance that you would have refused to use one even if it was provided. If you were injured in a fall that would have been avoided had you been wearing a harness, how would a court decide if your injury was caused by your employer's neglect?

9.4 Explain the difference between the problem of the indeterminate claimant and the problem of the indeterminate defendant. Should the same considerations govern both?

9.5 How do the courts decide if the causal connection between the defendant's negligence and the claimant's loss is negatived by an intervening act or event?

9.6 Is there sufficient causal connection in the following situations:

    (a)   A hits B and leaves her on the beach where she is drowned by the incoming tide.

    (b)   C hits D and leaves her on the beach where she is murdered by a robber.

    (c)   E crashes her car into a lamp post. A police officer negligently directs traffic around the obstruction and a collision ensues in which F is killed.

    (d)   G carelessly leaves the door of her house unlocked. Thieves walk in, break down a thin partition wall and steal property from H's house next door.

9.7 To what extent do the law's principles of causation reflect matters of policy?

10 Remoteness of Damage

10.1 The *Wagon Mound* Test of Remoteness

In order to recover damages in respect of injury caused by another's negligence, you must establish that injury of that type was a reasonably foreseeable consequence of the negligence. This rule was laid down by the Privy Council in the case *Overseas Tankship (UK) Ltd* v. *Morts Dock & Engineering Co Ltd, The Wagon Mound* [1961] AC 388; although the English courts were not in strict law bound by the decision, it was nevertheless reasonably foreseeable that they would accept the principle, as one contemporary commentator wryly predicted (Goodhart, 1966). The rule is one of a number of mechanisms by which the law limits liability for the consequences of one's negligence; most notable among the others are the principles concerning selection from among causally relevant factors and those concerning the existence and scope of the duty of care.

In *The Wagon Mound*, a fire started in Sydney Harbour had damaged a wharf belonging to the plaintiffs. The fire had begun when oil, which had carelessly been allowed to overflow from the defendant's ship, the *Wagon Mound*, was accidentally set alight. The Privy Council held that, while it was foreseeable that the oil spillage might foul the plaintiffs' wharf, it was not foreseeable that the oil would be set alight and cause fire damage to the wharf. The claim in respect of fire damage was disallowed. It was not enough that some damage to the plaintiffs' wharf was foreseeable; the plaintiffs had to establish that damage of the type that actually occurred was foreseeable.

The justification for the rule is that it ensures that the defendant is not penalised excessively for her default. Under the law as it stood before the *Wagon Mound* decision, it appeared that a defendant would be held liable for all the consequences of her negligence so long as they were 'direct'. This requirement, which was attributed to the decision of the Court of Appeal in *Re Polemis* [1921] 3 KB 560, strikes many as obscure and seems to do no more than reiterate the fact that an intervening act or event may negate the causal connection between the defendant's wrongdoing and the claimant's loss (for an alternative analysis of *Re Polemis*, see Clerk and Lindsell, 2000, para. 7–139). In *The Wagon Mound*, Viscount Simonds suggested that the rule in *Re Polemis* might give rise to 'palpable injustice' (p. 422):

'[I]t does not seem consonant with current ideas of justice or morality that, for an act of negligence, however slight or venial, which results in some trivial foreseeable damage, the actor should be liable for all consequences, however unforeseeable and however grave, so long as they can be said to be "direct".'

The *Wagon Mound* rule of remoteness applies elsewhere in the law of tort, for instance in the law of nuisance and under the rule in *Rylands* v. *Fletcher* (1868) LR 3 HL 330 (see *Cambridge Water Co* v. *Eastern Counties Leather Co* [1994] 2 AC 264). However, it does not apply where the defendant intends to inflict injury on the claimant: in torts such as deceit and the economic torts, in which intentional injury is the gist of the tort, the claimant can recover in respect of all the direct consequences of the defendant's wrong under the rule in *Re Polemis* (see *Smith New Court Securities Ltd* v. *Scrimgeour Vickers (Asset Management) Ltd* [1996] 4 All ER 796).

10.2 The Concept of Foreseeability Examined

Foreseeability in the context of the *Wagon Mound* rule of remoteness plays a rather different role from when it is employed in order to determine whether a defendant was negligent (in breach of duty). Its place in the latter enquiry is as one of a number of factors – others being the gravity of the possible injury and the burden of guarding against it – which must be considered before we can say whether certain behaviour was reasonable or not. The degree of foreseeability required before the defendant is branded negligent varies in relation to those other factors: running a risk of a certain probability will be reasonable in some circumstances but not in others. In contrast, the stipulation that the harm the claimant has suffered must be of a type that was reasonably foreseeable requires the court to look at the issue of foreseeability in isolation.

That foreseeability is used in different senses in these two contexts is established by the case of *Overseas Tankship (UK) Ltd* v. *The Miller Steamship Co, The Wagon Mound (No. 2)* [1967] 1 AC 617. This arose out of the same set of circumstances as the first *Wagon Mound* decision, but dealt with a claim by a different plaintiff. The fire in Sydney Harbour damaged not only the wharf belonging to Morts Dock, the plaintiffs in the first action, but also ships belonging to The Miller Steamship Co, the plaintiffs in the second. As we have seen, the Privy Council held in the first case that it was not reasonably foreseeable that the oil would be set alight and cause fire damage to the wharf. In the second case, different evidence was led, causing the trial judge to take a different view of the facts of the case. He held that it was in fact reasonably foreseeable that the oil might catch fire and the Privy Council held that he was perfectly entitled so to do. The trial judge went wrong, however, in going on to hold that this risk was too small to attract liability. This was an error because, once it had been decided that fire damage was a reasonably foreseeable possibility, the question was whether a reasonable person would have run that risk. In determining this, the degree of risk could not be looked at in isolation but had to be considered in the light of other factors such as the cost of averting the danger. The trial judge had not appreciated this and, while he had correctly analysed foreseeability in the remoteness context, he had fallen into error when it came to looking at it from the point of view of breach of duty. On the facts of the case, as the risk was not far-fetched, and as it could have been eliminated without expense simply by stopping the discharge, the Privy Council held the defendant shipowners liable (see Dias, 1967).

10.3 **Foreseeable Type of Loss**

As we have seen, the claimant must show that the type of loss she suffered was reasonably foreseeable. It was for this reason that the plaintiffs in the first *Wagon Mound* case failed: their actual loss (the fire damage to the wharf) was of a different type from that which was foreseeable (damage by oil fouling). However, while the claimant must prove that loss of the type she suffered was reasonably foreseeable, she need not prove that loss of the same extent was foreseeable.

It will be readily apparent that the crucial question is how widely defined is the relevant 'type of harm'. The lack of clear guidance on this question of definition has caused the courts to adopt a variety of different approaches, from the narrow and restrictive to the generous and expansive. The case of *Tremain* v. *Pike* [1969] 1 WLR 1556 provides an example of the narrow definition of the relevant type of harm. The plaintiff, a herdsman at the defendants' rat-infested farm, came into contact with rats' urine in the course of his employment and contracted Weil's disease. His claim for damages was rejected by the High Court: Payne J held that the defendants ought to have foreseen the possibility of some illness or infection arising from the infestation but decided that the contraction of Weil's disease itself was unforeseeable and therefore too remote to be actionable. Such an approach will strike many as inequitably restrictive, given the defendant's undoubted negligence and the plaintiff's lack of alternative recourse in respect of his injury.

More recently, however, the House of Lords has signalled a much more expansive approach, at least in cases involving personal injury rather than property damage. In *Page* v. *Smith* [1996] AC 155 (see further 4.3), the House of Lords had to determine precisely what harm had to be foreseeable in a case involving 'nervous shock'. By a majority, their Lordships denied that *The Wagon Mound* entailed that the risk of nervous shock should be specifically foreseeable (albeit that the desirability of limiting the number of claims by 'secondary victims' necessitated, as a matter of policy, a more restrictive approach at the duty stage in such cases) and effectively treated personal injury as a single, indivisible type of harm. Lord Lloyd (with whom Lord Ackner and Lord Browne-Wilkinson agreed) stated that it was necessary to satisfy only the following test of foreseeability, namely 'whether the defendant can reasonably foresee that his conduct will expose the plaintiff to the risk of personal injury, whether physical or psychiatric' (p. 197). He added: 'There is no justification for regarding physical and psychiatric injury as different "kinds of damage".' His Lordship did not specifically advert to *Tremain* v. *Pike* or any other case taking a narrow approach to the 'type of harm' criterion in relation to personal injury, but such cases may now be regarded as impliedly overruled.

In contrast with cases of personal injury, cases of property damage must still, it seems, be subdivided into a set of different types. The *Wagon Mound* decision provided that damage by fire is a different type of harm from damage by fouling, while the Privy Council's criticism in that case of *Re Polemis* (in which a plank falling into a ship's hold unexpectedly caused a fire) suggests that fire damage is a different type of harm from impact damage. The more expansive approach adopted in cases of personal injury, relative to that applied where the loss is property damage, may be justified on the basis of the comparative value of the interest to be protected. The law rightly values personal integrity above the interest in property. In addition, the more restrictive approach to property damage may also reflect the fact that first-party insurance against loss of or damage to property is much more common than that against personal injury.

10.4 Foreseeable Kind of Accident

In addition to establishing that she has suffered loss of a reasonably foreseeable kind, the claimant must also prove that the accident causing her loss fell within the scope of the risk created by the defendant's negligence, i.e. that the accident, not just the injury, was a reasonably foreseeable consequence of the negligence (see, further, Stauch, 2001). This was the approach adopted by the House of Lords in the recent case of *Jolley* v. *Sutton London Borough Council* [2000] 1 WLR 1082. Here, the plaintiff was one of two teenaged boys who came upon and decided to repair an abandoned boat that had been left lying on the defendant's property for more than two years, during which time it was exposed to the elements and became derelict and rotten. Using a car jack to raise the boat so that they could repair the holes in its bottom, the boys worked on their project in their spare time until one day when the boat toppled off the jack and landed on the plaintiff who was working underneath. He suffered serious spinal injuries and was left a paraplegic. In his subsequent action for damages against the council, as occupier of the land in question, the council accepted that there had been a risk that children playing on the boat might suffer injury, for example by falling through a rotten section of planking, and hence that it had been negligent in allowing the boat to remain derelict on its premises for so long. But it disputed whether the accident that occurred was within the scope of this risk, especially as it could not be proved that the boat's falling off the jack was attributable to its derelict or rotten condition. Although the defendant council succeeded before the Court of Appeal, the House of Lords took a much broader view of the risks created by the defendant's negligence, bearing in mind in particular the ingenuity of children in finding unexpected ways of doing mischief to themselves (p. 1093, per Lord Hoffmann). The risk for which the defendant council was responsible was that children would meddle with the boat at the risk of some physical injury, and it was clear that the risk which eventuated fell within that general description.

In *Jolley*, the House of Lords refuted criticism of its earlier decision in *Hughes* v. *Lord Advocate* [1963] AC 837. There, road works being carried out by the Post Office were left unattended during a teabreak. There were paraffin lights around the site. Two boys sneaked on to the site to play. One of them knocked over a lamp which fell into a manhole and caused a violent explosion; the boy was badly burnt. The House of Lords accepted that the explosion had been unforeseeable but held that the boy's injury was not too remote as it was reasonably foreseeable that he might have been burnt by the oil in the lamp. The foreseeable risk that did not eventuate and the unforeseeable risk that did were both of the same type. As Lord Guest remarked, 'I cannot see that these are two different types of accident. They are both burning accidents and in both cases the injuries would be burning injuries' (p. 356). Expressed in those terms, it is clear that the decision in *Hughes* was perfectly consistent with that in *Jolley*: the risks created by the negligence included that of a burning accident and it was a burning accident that occurred.

More problematic is the decision of the Court of Appeal in *Doughty* v. *Turner Manufacturing Co Ltd* [1964] 1 QB 518. In that case, the plaintiff suffered burns in an accident at work when the cover of a cauldron of molten liquid was inadvertently knocked into the cauldron. The cover reacted with the molten liquid and caused an explosion in which the plaintiff was injured by liquid dispelled from the cauldron. The Court of Appeal held that, even accepting that injury might foreseeably have resulted from splashing caused by the cover's falling into the cauldron, the actual events that occurred were wholly unforeseeable and hence too remote from the original inadvertence (see also *Crossley* v. *Rawlinson* [1982] 1 WLR 369). In retrospect, this seems an unduly narrow application of the requirement that the kind of accident injuring the claimant must be reasonably foreseeable. In fact, it seems to ignore that the question is whether the *kind* of accident was foreseeable, and not whether the precise circumstances of the accident were foreseeable. In *Jolley*, the House of Lords emphasised that a 'broad description' of the relevant risk was to be adopted (p. 1093, per Lord Hoffmann) and, applying this to *Doughty*, it was surely enough that a 'scalding accident' of some description occurred, even though on the facts it was by (unforeseeable) explosion rather than by (foreseeable) splashing.

In cases of personal injury, provided the kind of accident causing the injury is reasonably foreseeable, it is immaterial whether it was attributable to psychiatric or physical processes (see *Page* v. *Smith* [1996] AC 155 and 10.3).

10.5 **The 'Thin Skull' Rule**

The 'thin skull' rule is a potentially significant exception to the requirement that the type of harm suffered by the claimant must have been reasonably foreseeable. Where the claimant suffers foreseeable injury as the result of the defendant's negligence and this triggers off an unforeseeable reaction which is attributable to the claimant's pre-existing susceptibility, there is authority to suggest that she can recover in respect of both foreseeable and unforeseeable consequences of the negligence. In such cases, the principle enunciated by Lord Parker CJ in the leading case of *Smith* v. *Leech Brain & Co Ltd* [1962] 2 QB 405 is that 'a tortfeasor takes his victim as he finds him'. The case concerned an accident at the defendant's iron works in which Mr Smith was hit on the lip and burnt by a piece of molten metal. As he had a premalignant condition, he was abnormally susceptible to cancer; shortly afterwards a cancerous growth, which proved to be fatal, formed at the site of the burn. The court allowed Mr Smith's widow to recover damages in respect of his death regardless of the unforeseeable nature of his fatal cancer; it was sufficient that the burn he had suffered was reasonaby foreseeable. In the view of the court, the Privy Council in *The Wagon Mound* did not have any intention of making inroads into the 'thin skull' doctrine.

Two interpretations of this decision are possible. The narrow view is that it is wholly entailed by the *Wagon Mound* approach, which provides that if damage of a particular type is reasonaby foreseeable it is immaterial that the extent of the damage sustained is not. Given that personal injury must now be treated as a single, indivisible type of harm (see *Page* v. *Smith*), it appears that the deceased in *Smith* v. *Leech Brain* did indeed suffer a foreseeable type of harm, for the court accepted that personal injury *of some type* was foreseeable; the unforeseeable cancer was a matter affecting only the *extent* or gravity of that injury. The alternative and more expansive view is that the decision in *Smith* v. *Leech Brain* represents an exception from the *Wagon Mound* doctrine, applicable where a foreseeable loss triggers another loss, of a different and unforeseeable type, as a result of the pre-existing susceptibility of the claimant or the claimant's property. Suppose the defendant were negligently to drop a plank into the hold of the claimant's ship (cf. *Re Polemis*: see 10.1). It is foreseeable that the plank might fall upon the claimant's goods in the hold, causing them damage. But if the bottom of the hold were unsound and should spring a leak, causing water damage to the goods, this would seem to be damage of a different sort. Should the claimant be able to recover in respect of the unforeseeable water damage on the basis that it was triggered by the conjunction of the foreseeable impact and the pre-existing unsoundness of the hold? It is submitted that the claimant should not recover in such a case for, on such facts (as in many cases of property damage), the damage is best regarded as a commercial risk against which the claimant might be expected to take out insurance. Accordingly, the first interpretation of *Smith* v. *Leech Brain* is to be preferred.

10.6 **Impecuniosity**

Where the claimant incurs expenses in seeking to mitigate a loss sustained as a result of the defendant's negligence, those expenses that are attributable exclusively to the claimant's impecuniosity or lack of financial means are deemed too remote. In *Liesbosch Dredger (Owners)* v. *Edison (Owners)* [1933] AC 449, a vessel called the *Edison* negligently caused the loss of a dredger known as the *Liesbosch*. The *Liesbosch* was under contract to carry out certain work and, in order to complete these contracts, the owners of the *Liesbosch* were obliged to secure the use of a substitute dredger. In the long run, it would have been cheaper to buy the substitute rather than hire it, but the financial position in which the owners found themselves initially precluded this. The House of Lords declined to allow the owners to recover the hire charges, limiting their damages to the cost of acquiring a replacement dredger; the hire charges were incurred as a result of their want of means and as such were too remote or, alternatively, they resulted from an independent cause. The decision apparently contradicts the principle of *The Wagon Mound* that, if the type of harm suffered is foreseeable, its precise extent is immaterial, and it is perhaps best considered as a somewhat anomalous exception to that principle.

The rule is capable of operating very harshly on the facts of individual cases, and it is no doubt for this reason that *The Liesbosch* has been distinguished on numerous subsequent occasions. The most significant restriction on its application is where the extra expense incurred by the claimant can be ascribed to commercial good sense or general financial prudence, and not exclusively to her lack of means. In *Dodd Properties (Kent) Ltd* v. *Canterbury City Council* [1980] 1 WLR 433, the plaintiffs sought compensation in respect of damage caused to their garage by the defendants' building operations nearby. The damage was suffered in 1970 but the plaintiffs postponed carrying out repairs until after judgment had been given against the defendants in 1978, by which time the cost had soared. One of the reasons for this delay was the fact that the plaintiffs were very short of cash. The trial judge followed *Edison* in holding that the delay was due to the plaintiffs' impecuniosity, and therefore they could only recover the cost of repairs as it would have been in 1970. The Court of Appeal reversed this ruling, Megaw LJ distinguishing *Edison* on the grounds that '[t]he "financial stringency" which would have been created by carrying out the repairs was merely one factor among a number of factors which together produced the result that commercial good sense pointed towards deferment of the repairs' (p. 453). Among the other factors was the concern that, if the defendants were not found liable, the plaintiffs' limited resources might be better spent on another project.

The reasoning in the *Dodd Properties* case was extended to a non-commercial situation in the Privy Council case of *Alcoa Minerals of Jamaica Inc* v. *Broderick* [2002] 1 AC 371. In that case, corrosive dust from the defendant's smelting plant caused damage to the roof of the plaintiff's house. This amounted to an actionable nuisance. He claimed damages from the defendant, but did not begin work on the roof for so long as the defendant disputed liability. The cost of repairs rose by more than fourfold in the course of four years as a result of rapid inflation and the fall of the Jamaican dollar, and the question for the Privy Council was whether the plaintiff was entitled to recover the increased amount. On the facts, it was obviously foreseeable that a person in the plaintiff's position might not have the means to repair serious damage to his house and that he would only be able to do so if he established liability and recovered damages. It was reasonable for him to postpone the repairs until he was sure that the defendant would be liable for them.

The Privy Council distinguished *The Liesbosch* on the basis that, there, there were two separate heads of damage – the cost of purchasing a new dredger and the cost of hiring a temporary replacement – and the latter head could be separated from the first and regarded as attributable to the plaintiff's impecuniosity; by contrast, in the case before the Privy Council the only head of damage was the cost of repairing the building. With respect, it must be submitted that this analysis is unconvincing. There is no reason to distinguish the claimant who cannot afford to buy a replacement, and incurs additional hire charges, from the claimant who cannot afford to undertake repairs. Both have equal cause to wait until it is clear that the defendant will pay damages sufficient to cover the cost. Indeed, this appears already to have been accepted by the Court of Appeal which, in a decision of great practical importance, declined to apply *The Liesbosch* to the very common situation in which a motor-car is negligently damaged and has to spend some time off-road for repairs, during which period its owner is obliged to hire a substitute. In *Mattocks v. Mann* [1993] RTR 13, the repairers would not release the plaintiff's vehicle until she paid for the repairs, but she could not afford to do so until she received her damages from the defendant's insurers and so had to extend the period during which she hired a substitute. The Court of Appeal found that her actions had been entirely reasonable in the circumstances and allowed her to recover the full amount of the hire charges.

Given the substantial inroads that have now been made into the *Liesbosch* principle, it would be desirable if the House of Lords were to state authoritatively that there is no special impecuniosity rule, and that the only question is whether the claimant has acted reasonably in mitigating her loss. It is a matter of regret that the Privy Council did not undertake a fundamental reconsideration of the relevant principles when the opportunity arose in the *Alcoa Minerals* case (see further Coote, 2001).

Summary

10.1 The claimant must establish that her loss was of a type that was the foreseeable consequence of the defendant's negligence. This is known as the *Wagon Mound* rule of remoteness.

10.2 The use of the concept of foreseeability in this context is rather different from its use as one of the factors determining whether the defendant was in breach of duty.

10.3 It is not enough that some loss to the claimant was the foreseeable consequence of the defendant's negligence: the same type of loss as that suffered by the claimant must have been foreseeable. The categorisation of different 'types' of loss has proved problematic.

10.4 It must also be established that the accident causing the claimant's loss fell within the scope of the risk created by the defendant's negligence, i.e. that the accident was of a kind that was a reasonably foreseeable consequence of the negligence.

10.5 The 'thin skull' rule, by which the claimant is allowed to recover in respect of the unforeseeable consequences of the defendant's negligence when those consequences were attributable to the claimant's pre-existing susceptibility, is of uncertain status in the modern law and arguably adds nothing to what is entailed by the *Wagon Mound* rule of remoteness.

10.6 Where the claimant incurs expenses in seeking to mitigate a loss sustained as a result of the defendant's negligence, those expenses that are attributable exclusively to the claimant's impecuniosity may be deemed too remote, but not those that can be ascribed to general financial prudence.

Exercises

10.1 What is the difference between the *Wagon Mound* and *Polemis* tests of remoteness? Which torts take which test?

10.2 How does the role of the concept of foreseeability in the context of remoteness of damage differ from its role in the context of breach of duty?

10.3 According to what criteria do the courts decide if the harm that eventuates is of the same type as that which was foreseeable?

10.4 What is the 'thin skull' rule? Does it apply to 'thin wallet' cases (i.e. those in which the claimant's loss is aggravated by her own impecuniosity)?

---

11   Defences

The defences we consider below are in fact of general application in the law of tort, but we deal with them here partly for convenience and partly because they are most frequently encountered in practice in the context of negligence litigation.

11.1 Voluntary Assumption of Risk: Introduction

We begin by looking at what is popularly known as the 'free will' defence, which arises where the claimant is found to have voluntarily assumed the risk of injury. In fact, this label indicates a group of related defences rather than any single principle. The defence of consent, which arises most frequently in relation to intentional interference with the person, is considered elsewhere (see 16.7). Here we shall consider waivers of liability (exclusions and disclaimers) and the defence expressed by the Latin maxim *volenti non fit iniuria* (see 11.2 and 11.3). The former deal with actual agreements to assume the risk of negligent injury; the latter with conduct from which it may be inferred that the claimant willingly took that risk upon herself. Unlike contributory negligence, which functions only as a partial defence, both doctrines act as a total defence to tortious liability.

The free will defences have played a significant role in the history of tort law though that role has decreased in recent times (see Cornish and Clark, 1989, pp. 499–500, 509–10). The product of an earlier and more individualistic age, the defences were used to shield entrepreneurs in post-Industrial Revolution Britain from claims by the victims of increasing industrialisation. Employees injured as a result of dangerous conditions at work were held to have voluntarily assumed the risk of that injury on the grounds that they were aware of the dangers; no heed was paid to the economic pressures that forced them to endure those conditions. Equally, the railway companies protected themselves against claims from passengers hurt in train crashes by issuing tickets only on terms that the companies were not to be liable for such injury. Gradually, however, the tide turned. The courts realised the harsh social consequences of regarding employees as having 'volunteered' to work in dangerous conditions: this could only be true if the employees had accepted additional wages as 'danger money' (see *Bowater* v. *Rowley Regis BC* [1944] KB 476). And reform of the defence of contributory negligence, making it a partial defence by providing for apportionment of responsibility between the parties, further reduced the role of the free will defences which were seen as harsh and inflexible on account of their 'all-or-nothing' basis.

The modern era has also seen the introduction of various statutory limitations upon the operation of the common law's free will defences. The most important of these, the Unfair Contract Terms Act 1977, is considered below (see 11.4); a couple of other notable examples are noted here. By the Road Traffic Act 1988, s. 149, the defences of exclusion of liability, disclaimer of responsibility and *volenti non fit iniuria* are declared to be unavailable in actions for negligence brought by any passenger in a compulsorily-insured vehicle against the driver of that vehicle. This rule seems to rest on the underlying sentiment that, as any damages award would be met out of the considerable resources of an insurance company, it would be unduly harsh to prevent even an extremely foolhardy passenger from recovering anything at all. It remains possible, however, to raise contributory negligence, for example, against a passenger who accepts a lift from a driver who is clearly drunk (cf. *Owens* v. *Brimmell* [1971] QB 859). Another statutory restriction on the free will defences is to be found in the Consumer Protection Act 1987, s. 7, which prohibits reliance upon any provision which purports to exclude or limit the liability imposed by the Act in respect of damage caused by defective products. The statute does not expressly advert to the defence of *volenti* and the predominant view is that this defence may be raised in an action under the Act (see 14.7).

Before going on to consider the elements of the defences of waiver of liability and *volenti non fit iniuria*, it must be stressed that the question whether the defendant has been careless at all must be considered prior to the question whether the claimant, by reason of her agreement or conduct, should be precluded from recovering compensation for the consequences of any carelessness. This has not always been appreciated by the courts, who on occasion have made erroneous and unnecessary use of the principles of voluntary assumption of risk. This fault is particularly evident in cases which deal with injuries suffered by participants in, or spectators at, sporting events. The issue was fully discussed in *Wooldridge* v. *Sumner* [1963] 2 QB 43 in which a professional photographer covering the National Horse Show sought to recover damages after being knocked down by the defendant's horse; the horse had been taken too fast into a corner by its rider and had careered into a seating area. The Court of Appeal denied that principles of voluntary assumption of risk had any application: the only question was whether the rider had taken reasonable care in the circumstances. Because the circumstances were those of a fast-moving competition, not every error of judgement or lapse of skill would amount to a departure from the standard of the reasonable participant. Something akin to a reckless disregard of the spectator's safety was required and the rider's conduct fell far short of this.

The court's preference for analysing these cases in terms of breach of duty rather than voluntary assumption of risk has the important practical consequence of preventing the result of the case from depending on the identity of the claimant: as the free will defences can only be employed against responsible agents who have the capacity to assume the risk in question, where does this leave the infant spectator struck in the face by the football or the passer-by outside the ground hit when the ball is kicked over the fence? If liability to such claimants is to be denied, it can only be on the basis that the defendant did nothing wrong rather than that the claimant voluntarily assumed the risk.

11.2　Voluntary Assumption of Risk: Waivers of Liability

A person may voluntarily assume the risk of harm by agreeing in advance not to sue the person by whose negligence the harm is caused. Often this agreement will be contained in a contract as an exclusion clause: one only has to think of the small print on airline tickets or car-hire forms for an example. However, there need not be any contract and it will be sufficient that the claimant freely exposes herself to the risk after being informed that the defendant takes no responsibility for any harm that occurs; this is known as a disclaimer of reponsibility. Thus, if the claimant enters premises after seeing a notice stating that entry is at her own risk, or relies upon financial information or advice after being told that this was given without responsibility, then she will be denied compensation if she is injured on those premises or loses money as a result of relying upon the information or advice (subject to the operation of the Unfair Contract Terms Act – see 11.4). The underlying reason for giving effect to these non-contractual disclaimers is that the defendant might have relied on the claimant's agreement to those terms in placing herself in a position of potential liability (see Jaffey, 1985). As in the law of contract, the existence of the requisite agreement is tested objectively. It is not necessary that the claimant *in fact* consented to – or even took notice of – the provision in question. The question is only whether the defendant took reasonable steps to communicate the disclaimer to her (*Ashdown* v. *Samuel Williams & Sons Ltd* [1957] 1 QB 509).

Strictly speaking, exclusions and disclaimers are dependent upon the existence of an agreement to waive one's legal rights, not merely to run the risk of injury. Indeed (in contrast with the defence of *volenti*) the claimant need not have any knowledge of the precise risk that may eventuate provided that there is a clear intention to absolve the defendant from liability for harm howsoever it is caused. The waiver may be express or implied; in the latter case, a number of surrounding circumstances may be relevant in deciding whether the claimant has truly agreed to give up the right to sue. In *Nettleship* v. *Weston* [1971] 2 QB 691, the plaintiff agreed to give informal driving instruction to the defendant in a car owned by the defendant's husband. He had previously enquired whether he was insured against injury in the event of an accident, and had been told (correctly) that he was. He suffered injury when the defendant, owing to her inexperience, crashed the car. The court declined to accept the defence that the plaintiff had voluntarily assumed the risk of injury. Far from being a case in which the plaintiff had expressly waived his rights to sue, his request for information about the insurance position showed that he had no intention of bearing his own loss if there was an accident.

Where parties are linked together by a chain of contracts and subcontracts, the effectiveness of exclusions of liability contained in those contracts is prima facie restricted by the doctrine of privity of contract. But strict adherence to the doctrine has caused commercial inconvenience and given rise to attempts to circumvent the privity requirement (for a discussion of the resultant problems in the law of contract, see McKendrick, 2000, ch. 7.2). In the law of tort, two issues arise. First, when, if ever, may the claimant in a tort action be bound by an exclusion clause in the defendant's contract with a third party? In principle, it should be possible for the contractual exclusion to the third party to act concurrently as a non-contractual disclaimer of responsibility to the claimant, at least where the latter has reasonable notice of it (see, e.g., *Smith* v. *Eric S Bush* [1990] AC 831; in the exceptional cases in which the duty to the claimant is derived by extension from a voluntary assumption of responsibility by the defendant to a third party, it seems that it may not even be necessary for the claimant to have notice of the relevant exclusion or disclaimer: see *White* v. *Jones* [1995] 2 AC 145, 268 per Lord Goff, considered above at 5.6). Secondly, can the defendant seek to evade the doctrine of privity of contract by taking advantage of an exclusion clause in the claimant's contract with a third party? This is a more difficult question. English law knows no doctrine of vicarious immunity (*Scruttons Ltd* v. *Midland Silicones Ltd* [1962] AC 446), but the courts have shown a great deal of ingenuity in discovering collateral contractual relationships between claimant and defendant in order to give effect to the exclusion (see especially *The Eurymedon* [1975] AC 154). A simpler solution, however, is to treat the exclusion accepted by the claimant as relevant to the question whether it is fair, just and reasonable to recognise a duty of care. Although this approach is most evident in the cases dealing with pure economic loss, there is no reason why it should not be applied to cases of physical damage as well (see *Norwich City Council* v. *Harvey* [1989] 1 All ER 1180; cf. the approach of the Supreme Court of Canada in *London Drugs Ltd* v. *Kuenhe & Nagel International Ltd* (1992) 97 DLR (4th) 261). Another way of enabling the defendant to benefit from an exclusion clause in a contract to which she is not party is provided by s. 1 of the Contracts (Rights of Third Parties) Act 1999, though this only applies where the contract purports to benefit a person who is expressly identified in the contract by name, by reference to a class, or by description (see further McKendrick, 2000, ch. 7).

11.3 *Volenti non fit iniuria*

The Latin maxim *volenti non fit iniuria* states that those who voluntarily accept the risk of injury through another's negligence have no legal claim if the risk eventuates. The scope of this defence is not clearly defined and has generated much debate. Although it has sometimes been doubted whether the defence may be raised in an action for negligence (see, e.g., *Wooldridge* v. *Sumner* [1963] 2 QB 43, 70 per Diplock LJ), there is unambiguous modern authority that it can (see, e.g., *Morris* v. *Murray* [1991] 2 QB 6). There is still controversy, however, as to whether the conceptual basis of the defence is the claimant's implied consent to run the risk of injury, or simply the unreasonableness of her conduct. It is submitted here that there is ample authority for bringing both types of case within the scope of the *volenti* doctrine.

The defence may be analysed as having three elements: knowledge of the risk in question (in Latin, the *sciens* element); a voluntary exposure to the risk (the *volens* element); and – most elusively – an *assumption* of the risk. Let us take the knowledge requirement first. This serves to distinguish the defence from that of exclusion or other waiver of liability (see *White* v. *Blackmore* [1972] 2 QB 651). A notice at the entrance to farmland stating 'The owner disclaims all liability for injury howsoever caused' would be effective as a waiver of liability (subject to the Unfair Contract Terms Act), but in order to trigger the defence of *volenti* it would have to specify the type of risk that would be encountered by the entrant (e.g. 'Danger! There is a big and bad-tempered bull in this field. Enter at your peril.'). The claimant must have actual knowledge of the risk. It is not enough that such knowledge may be imputed to her on the basis that a reasonable person in her position would have known of the risk; nor is it enough, in a case where the claimant is intoxicated at the relevant time, that she would have known of the risk if sober, for she must be 'capable of appreciating the risks' (*Morris* v. *Murray* [1991] 2 QB 6, 16 per Fox LJ, see below).

Secondly, the claimant must *voluntarily* expose herself to the risk. The concept of voluntariness here is given a narrower definition than it has in the criminal law where it refers to the conscious control of a person's bodily movements. In tort, the term refers to the absence of constraints upon the person's freedom of action. For instance, an act will be non-voluntary if it is done in order to avert danger to life or limb (see especially the so-called 'rescuer' cases: 7.1). In *Haynes* v. *Harwood* [1935] 1 KB 146, horses left unattended in a public place by the defendant's servant were startled and ran off down a crowded street. The plaintiff police constable saw that people in the street were in considerable danger and averted that danger by grabbing hold of the horses and bringing them to a stop. As a result of this act of bravery he suffered injury. The court ordered the defendant to pay him compensation, declining to find that the constable had voluntarily exposed himself to the risk of harm. In such cases, the defendant's conduct, although deliberate, is not 'voluntary'.

Finally, we turn our attention to the meaning of the key phrase 'assumption of liability'. This entails something more than that the claimant freely exposed herself to the risk of injury. She must do something that warrants the conclusion that the loss should be left to fall on her if the risk eventuates. Precisely what this might be is not entirely clear from the authorities. The narrowest view is that there must be an express or implied waiver of liability by the claimant. But a contrary and, it is submitted, better view, suggests that the risk may be assumed even in the absence of a waiver in two types of case: first, when the claimant either agrees that the defendant should do the very thing which was alleged to constitute the negligence; secondly, when the claimant exhibits a reckless disregard for her personal safety going beyond mere contributory negligence.

Must There Be a Waiver of Liability?

In *Nettleship* v. *Weston* [1971] 2 QB 691, 701 Lord Denning MR stated: 'Nothing will suffice short of an agreement to waive any claim for negligence'. However, this view must be treated with some caution. In the first place, it gives rise to certain doctrinal difficulties. If, as he seems to assert, the defence of *volenti* is no more than a subcategory of the defence of waiver, it is hard to see the justification for the other requirements of the defence. One can effectively waive liability for negligently inflicted injury 'howsoever caused', so why should the defence of *volenti* require knowledge on the part of the claimant of the type of risk to be encountered? Additionally, the fact that the defence of *volenti* may be negated by constraints on the claimant's action which render her conduct non-voluntary seems to contradict the rule, applicable to contractual waivers and probably to notices, etc., as well, that only a very limited range of factors (e.g. incapacity) will negate agreement to an exclusion or disclaimer. Even putting these doctrinal difficulties aside, it is submitted that Lord Denning's approach does not satisfactorily account for the actual application of the doctrine in many of the decided cases (see especially *Morris* v. *Murray* [1991] 2 QB 6, below) and that the search for even an implied waiver of liability often leads to artificiality. The following analysis proceeds therefore on the basis that other factors more satisfactorily account for the application of the defence than a simple waiver of liability.

Agreement to the Conduct Constituting the Negligence

It appears that the defence of *volenti* is triggered where the claimant consents to the defendant's performance of the very act or acts alleged to constitute negligence (and not merely to acts which may or may not be performed negligently). In *Imperial Chemical Industries Ltd* v. *Shatwell* [1965] AC 656, two brothers, George and James Shatwell, were employed by ICI as shotfirers, whose job it was to detonate explosives at a quarry belonging to the company. One day, when testing a series of some fifty explosives wired together, they found that one of the detonators in the circuit must have been a dud. They decided to test the detonators by passing an electrical current through each of them in turn. The law's mythical 'reasonable man' might have thought it safer to retreat some distance before doing this, but the Shatwell brothers, acting contrary to company regulations, carried out the testing from close at hand. The predictable result was an explosion in which both men were injured. George commenced legal proceedings against ICI, alleging the company was vicariously liable for James's negligence. The House of Lords ruled that George had voluntarily assumed the risk of injury and hence could recover nothing, emphasising the brothers' deliberate disobedience of the company rules and their knowledge of the risk involved. We might go further and suggest that this was a particularly strong case of *volenti* because George had in fact agreed to every aspect of the conduct that he subsequently alleged to amount to negligence.

Reckless Exposure of Oneself to the Risk of Injury

Although cases like *ICI* v. *Shatwell* may legitimately be seen as based upon consent, not specifically to relieve the defendant of liability but to the defendant's performance of the relevant acts, others are not amenable to this analysis: at most, the claimant can be said to have consciously and voluntarily encountered the risk that the defendant might act negligently. But this is not decisive of the question of whether the claimant has forfeited the right to sue for that negligence. It is submitted that the answer to this question, in the residual category of cases with which we are now concerned, turns simply upon the reasonableness of the claimant's conduct. The defence can have no application where she acts reasonably, even if aware of the risk that the defendant might act without due care and skill (see *Nettleship* v. *Weston*). Nor ought it to intrude on that sphere in which it is enough to reduce the level of damages payable to reflect the claimant's contributory negligence. There are, however, some cases in which the claimant's lack of care for her own safety goes beyond mere negligence and amounts to recklessness. Because apportionment of liability under the Law Reform (Contributory Negligence) Act 1945 must reflect the claimant's 'share' in responsibility for the damage, courts are not able to rule that even an extremely foolhardy claimant has been 100 per cent contributorily negligent (for then responsibility for the accident would rest entirely with the claimant and not be shared at all). Nevertheless, the same result may be achieved through the defence of *volenti*.

A clear example of this type of case is provided by *Morris* v. *Murray* [1991] 2 QB 6. The plaintiff and defendant, after drinking all afternoon at public houses, agreed to go flying in the defendant's light aircraft, which was kept at a local flying club. It seems that shortly after take-off the defendant lost control of the aircraft, which stalled and then dived to the ground. The defendant was killed and the plaintiff severely injured. At the autopsy, the defendant was found to have drunk the equivalent of 17 whiskies prior to the flight (more than three times the limit permitted for a car driver). In the plaintiff's action for damages, the defendant's estate raised the plea of *volenti*, and this was held to be good by the Court of Appeal. The plaintiff had embarked upon the flight without compulsion and, despite his intoxication, with adequate knowledge of the risks involved: he was 'merry' rather than 'blind drunk'. This amounted to 'great folly' and was distinguishable from a case in which the claimant accepted a lift in a motor vehicle from a person who was clearly drunk (cf. *Dann* v. *Hamilton* [1939] 1 KB 509, which held that *volenti* did not apply in such circumstances; motoring cases are now governed by the Road Traffic Act 1988, s. 149: see 11.2). As Fox LJ explained (p. 17):

> 'It seems to me . . . that the wild irresponsibility of the venture is such that the law should not intervene to award damages and should leave the loss where it falls. Flying is intrinsically dangerous and flying with a drunken pilot is great folly. The situation is very different from what has arisen in the motoring cases.'

The emphasis here, in determining whether the plaintiff had assumed the risk of injury, is not so much on any agreement to absolve the defendant from liability but on the plaintiff's recklessness (or 'wild irresponsibility') in exposing himself to risk (cf. the approach of Stocker LJ, who emphasised the requirement of consent). It is submitted that this is the better approach, and that in such cases the *volenti* defence is the legal equivalent of the 'playing with fire' doctrine in popular morality: if you play with fire, you cannot complain if you get your fingers burnt.

11.4 Unfair Contract Terms Act 1977

The scope of the various defences involving a voluntary assumption of responsibility is significantly restricted by the Unfair Contract Terms Act 1977. Although its name may suggest otherwise, the Act in fact applies to liabilities in tort as well as contract, and casts its net over non-contractual provisions such as notices that attempt to limit liability, as well as over contract terms. Put briefly, the Act operates against all attempts to exclude or limit business liability for negligence. This short definition has three elements which we consider in turn – 'exclusions and limitations', 'business liability', and 'negligence' – before turning to the question of the effect the Act has when it does in fact apply.

Exclusions and Limitations

A defendant might attempt to exclude or limit her liability in various ways. In many cases, the most prudent course would be to make it an express term of a contract with the claimant that she should agree to waive any rights against the defendant in the event that she should be injured by the defendant's fault. If contracting with the claimant is not practicable, then the defendant might put up a notice to the same effect where it will be seen by the claimant. For instance, a landowner might place a sign at the entrance to her grounds making it clear that those coming on to her land do so at their own risk. These are obvious attempts to exclude liability. Less obvious are ingenious efforts to avoid the operation of the Act by trying to prevent any duty of care coming into existence at all, rather than by seeking to exclude liability in respect of an admitted breach of duty. You will recall that liability under the rule in *Hedley Byrne* v. *Heller* is often said to depend on an 'assumption of responsibility' by the defendant towards the claimant. Could all those facing possible *Hedley Byrne*-type liabilities escape the operation of the Act by the simple expedient of telling people who might rely on their advice 'I assume no responsibility towards you'? The answer – it is now clear – is 'No'. In *Smith* v. *Eric S Bush* [1990] AC 831; see also 5.4), the surveyor who prepared the valuation report that Mrs Smith relied on in purchasing her house put words to that very effect on the front of his report, but the House of Lords declined to accept the argument that the Unfair Contract Terms Act could not bite on such a provision. Their Lordships took the view that, if the effect of a provision was to exclude or limit liability, it did not matter one jot how it was phrased.

Business Liability

The scope of the Act, in so far as it applies to liabilities in negligence, is restricted to cases of 'business liability'. This phrase is given a technical definition in s. 1(3) of the Act. Originally, the Act applied to all liabilities arising out of business activities or from the occupation of premises used for the occupier's business purposes, with 'business' referring not only to commercial ventures but also to the activities of public bodies. In 1984, the reference to liabilities arising out of the occupation of 'business premises' was amended to take account of the objections of farmers who thought it unfair that they should not be entitled to exclude their liabilities towards members of the public strolling across their fields and who threatened to restrict access to their land in response. Section 1(3) was accordingly amended, by the Occupiers' Liability Act 1984, so as to ensure that those injured on account of the dangerous state of land they had entered for recreational or educational purposes might be prevented from suing the landowner by an appropriate notice: liability in such circumstances would no longer be regarded as a 'business liability'. However, the amendment makes it clear that, where granting access to land for recreational or educational use falls within the business purposes of the occupier, the Act still applies. Hence, while Farmer Giles is free to exclude his liability towards those who wander through his fields without worrying about the provisions of the Act, Lord Fauntleroy cannot do the same to those who pay an entrance fee to stroll through his ornamental gardens.

Negligence

A brief glance at the Act gives the impression that it only prevents the exclusion or limitation of liabilities in the tort of negligence. This is somewhat misleading, because s. 1(1) of the Act gives an extended definition of the word 'negligence'. As well as covering liabilities in the tort of negligence, the word also refers to breach of all other common law duties to take reasonable care as well as to breach of the common duty of care imposed by the Occupiers' Liability Act 1957. Curiously, 'negligence' is not said to cover breach of the duty owed to trespassers imposed by the Occupiers' Liability Act 1984. Perhaps this is because this duty is a legal minimum that cannot ever be restricted at all (see 13.8).

Effect of the Act

Having considered the circumstances in which the Act will apply, let us turn now to look at what effect the Act has in such circumstances. This can be dealt with briefly. Everything depends on the type of loss of which the claimant complains. Where that loss is death or personal injury, the Act prevents any exclusion or limitation of liability at all (s. 2(1)). Where the claimant merely suffers property damage or pure economic loss, then s. 2(2) allows the defendant to exclude or restrict her liability, but only in so far as the contractual term or notice in question satisfies the requirement of reasonableness (i.e. that it was fair and reasonable that the term should be included in the contract or, in the case of a notice, that it was fair and reasonable to allow reliance upon it: s. 11). It is not possible exhaustively to catalogue all the factors that may be taken into account in assessing the reasonableness of an exclusion or restriction of liability: different factors will be relevant depending on the circumstances. An example of how this enquiry is carried out can be found in *Smith* v. *Eric S Bush*, in which the House of Lords considered the reasonableness of the surveyors' attempted exclusion of liability. In deciding that the notice was not reasonable, their Lordships took account of the inequality of bargaining power favouring the surveyors, the 'low-risk' nature of the task they were performing and the ease with which they could obtain liability insurance. Had the property been destined for commercial use, however, their Lordships felt that the result might have been different.

11.5 Contributory Negligence

Until 1945, contributory negligence operated like voluntary assumption of risk to bar a plaintiff's claim completely. This rule, which operated no matter how trivial the plaintiff's fault, came to be regarded as unduly harsh and the courts devoted considerable ingenuity to defeating its effect. Pressure for reform was met with the introduction – in the Law Reform (Contributory Negligence) Act 1945 – of a new regime that gave a court freedom to reduce an award of damages 'to such an extent as the court thinks just and equitable having regard to the claimant's share in the responsibility for the damage' (s. 1(1)). As we have seen (11.3), the word 'share' prevents the claimant being found 100 per cent contributorily negligent.

The defence does not depend on the claimant owing the defendant a duty of care: the only question is whether she took due care for her own safety. This is assessed according to an objective standard, attaching weight to much the same factors as determine whether a defendant was in breach of duty. Hence, the degree of care demanded of someone placed in an emergency situation by the defendant's negligence is lower than that demanded of one who can respond in a considered fashion (see *Jones* v. *Boyce* (1816) 1 Stark 493). Cane (1999, p. 46) has suggested that '[t]he test of negligence as applied to the conduct of plaintiffs is more "subjective" than the test of negligence applied to defendants', and that 'the courts are more prepared to acquit plaintiffs of negligence on grounds of their personal abilities and characteristics (and so avoid the need to reduce their damages) than they are to acquit defendants on such grounds (with the result that the plaintiff is deprived of compensation)', but it is important to note that no such distinction exists in strict law. (The Pearson Commission (1978, vol. 1, para. 1077) did propose a statutory rule that children under 12 should never have their damages reduced for contributory negligence when injured by a motor vehicle, but this has not been enacted.) It would be entirely understandable, however, if there were a tendency to be lenient in the application of the strict legal principles to injured claimants seeking compensation not from a private individual but, as is nearly always the case, from a faceless insurance company.

The words of the statute make it clear that the rules of contributory negligence only operate where there is some causal link between the claimant's conduct and the harm she suffers: if she is injured in a head-on car crash, it would be no defence for the negligent driver of the other vehicle to point to the fact that she had been driving without brake lights. To rely upon the defence, it must be shown that the claimant's injury was a foreseeable risk of her carelessness for her own safety. In *Jones* v. *Livox Quarries* [1952] 2 QB 608, the Court of Appeal found that the plaintiff was guilty of contributory negligence in riding on the towbar at the back of a moving vehicle. He was injured when another vehicle ran into him from behind. He accepted that his own conduct was foolhardy, but argued that the only foreseeable risk was that he would fall off the vehicle. The Court of Appeal disagreed, finding that the accident was indeed one of the risks foreseeably created by his negligence, though his riding on the towbar could not have been regarded as a contributory cause of his injury if (say) he had been hit in the eye by a shot from a negligent sportsman (p. 616, per Denning LJ).

The operation of the statute is not excluded where the claimant's conduct is deliberate rather than conventionally negligent, though the claimant's intentional acts may 'break the chain of causation' and so relieve the defendant of all liability for her loss (see 9.4). Where it is the defendant's duty to protect the claimant from such acts, there will be no break in the causal chain but damages may yet be reduced under the 1945 Act (see, e.g., *Reeves* v. *Commissioner of the Metropolitan Police* [2000] 1 AC 360: damages reduced by 50% where police negligence gave the deceased the opportunity to commit suicide in his cell).

The defence of contributory negligence represents a powerful weapon in the hands of the defence during the out-of-court settlement process (see 22.5). In one survey of personal injury cases, it was found that the claimant's contributory negligence was taken into account in almost half (45 per cent) of all settlements, though only 7 per cent of claimants were found to have admitted any responsibility for their injury at the outset of their case (Harris *et al.*, 1984, pp. 91–2). As judges are left with a great deal of discretion as to the appropriate level of deduction to make in individual cases, raising the defence may contribute to the uncertainty playing on the claimant's mind and induce her to accept an early, and hence low, offer of settlement. Claimants in personal injury litigation are typically risk-averse 'one-shotters', unlike the 'repeat-playing' insurance companies who in over 90 per cent of cases represent the nominal defendant (see further Genn, 1987). Their concern is not only that they might lose their case if they push on to trial, but also that they might not win it handsomely enough. If the defendant has made an official offer of settlement (CPR, Part 36), and if the damages eventually awarded to the claimant are lower than that figure, then the court will penalise the claimant for continuing with her case by declining to make the usual order for costs against the losing defendant in respect of the period after the offer was made. In such circumstances, the more uncertainty surrounding the claimant's prospects of success, the greater the 'downside risk' will weigh in her mind. The difficulty of predicting what deduction, if any, will be made for contributory negligence adds considerably to that uncertainty.

Things are improved somewhat by the courts' willingness to lay down fixed percentage reductions in certain frequently occurring types of case, a practice first approved by the Court of Appeal in *Froom* v. *Butcher* [1976] QB 286. The court suggested a standard 25 per cent deduction where a driver or passenger injured in a car crash would have escaped injury had she been wearing a seat-belt, with 15 per cent as the appropriate figure where she would have still suffered some injury, albeit not so severe. In *Capps* v. *Miller* [1989] 1 WLR 839, the Court of Appeal adopted these guidelines for use in cases of failure to wear a motorcyclist's crash helmet, suggesting a 10 per cent reduction where the helmet is worn but the strap is not done up. Use of these fixed percentage reductions is to be applauded because they make it more difficult for defence lawyers and insurance claims adjusters to pressurise injured claimants into accepting unduly low offers of settlement.

11.6 Illegality

According to the Latin maxim, *ex turpi causa non oritur actio*, no action can be founded on an unlawful act. It would undermine the authority of law if unlawful activity were condoned by the award of damages to those who break the law. Furthermore, depriving law-breakers of a remedy in damages might serve to make them think twice about pursuing their wrongful conduct. Yet the law does not go so far as to brand all those who have in the past engaged in unlawful conduct, or even those engaging in unlawful conduct at the time of their loss, as 'outlaws' for the purposes of tortious compensation. It would be draconian, for instance, to disallow wholly a claim for damages following a traffic accident just because the claimant was breaking the speed limit at the time the defendant negligently veered into her path. Sometimes illegality will defeat a claim and sometimes it will not, and the question of when precisely it will do so has provoked much controversy.

The Law Commission (2001) has stated its view that the law on illegality in tort is 'unclear and sometimes confusing', with no single approach attracting unqualified assent (para. 5.15). In broad terms, the English courts have varied between two approaches: some have applied a 'public conscience' test, asking whether allowing recovery would be an affront to the public conscience; others have declared it impossible to determine an appropriate standard of care where two parties to a joint illegal enterprise have absolved each other from acting according to normal standards (the 'no standard of care' approach). The latter approach can be illustrated by reference to a popular hypothetical example in which two safeblowers set out to burgle a house, only for one of them to detonate the explosives too soon, injuring the other. In such a case, it is alleged, it would be impossible for a court to prescribe what precautions the burglars should have taken for they have no way of knowing how burglars might respond to the exigencies of the situation (footsteps upstairs, police sirens wailing in the distance, etc.). In *Pitts* v. *Hunt* [1991] 1 QB 24, the majority of the Court of Appeal expressed a preference for the 'no standard' approach, at least in the case of a joint criminal enterprise. The plaintiff, Pitts, and his friend, Hunt, had spent the night drinking at a disco before setting off home on a motorcycle, driven by Hunt with Pitts riding pillion. Encouraged by Pitts, Hunt drove in a dangerous manner designed to frighten other road users. The motorcycle crashed: Hunt was killed and Pitts was injured. The Court of Appeal held that Pitts's claim for damages against Hunt's estate was barred by the defence of illegality; in the view of the majority of the court, it was impossible to set a standard of care for a course of criminal conduct. Dillon LJ expressly rejected the public conscience test as unsatisfactory: first, the reaction of the public to the compensation of wrongdoing plaintiffs might be affected by irrational considerations (such as factors of an emotional nature); secondly, it was impossible to draw a graph of moral turpitude that would separate those plaintiffs who should succeed from those who should not. It may be objected, however, that, whatever the defects of the public conscience test, the 'no standard' approach of the majority is also flawed (see the powerful arguments of Brennan J in *Gala* v. *Preston* (1991) 172 CLR 243). It is a fiction to say that it is impossible to determine a standard of care for those involved in unlawful ventures: even if we take the case of the safeblowing burglars, it is not hard to see that, by any standard, it is careless for the burglar with the plunger to detonate the charge while the other is attaching gelignite to the safe. Furthermore, the courts are well used to altering their view of the conduct required of the defendant in the light of the exigencies of her situation: a police officer engaged in a high-speed car chase need not obey the same rules of the road as ordinary drivers. In any case, the 'no standard' approach can have no application where the claimant was engaged in a solo criminal venture, as in *Vellino* v. *Chief Constable of Greater Manchester* [2001] EWCA Civ 1249 (below).

In truth, the courts have responded to the problem of the wrongdoing claimant in a way that is more intuitive than reasoned and, to this extent, their approach may be thought to approximate to the 'public conscience' test. A number of factors seem to be of particular importance. First, the court may take account of the interest which the law broken is designed to protect. Where the claimant's wrongdoing consists in a breach of a law passed for her own benefit, the court is unlikely to deprive her totally of her remedy. This argument is most likely to succeed in the context of workplace accidents arising out of an agreement between employer and employee to 'cut corners' in breach of the law relating to health and safety at work (see *Progress and Properties* v. *Craft* (1976) 135 CLR 651).

Secondly, the relative fault of the parties seems to be a material consideration: the defence is more likely to arise where the claimant's conduct involves real moral turpitude rather than, say, the breach of a merely administrative regulation. Conversely, where the defendant's wrongdoing goes beyond mere negligence and amounts to recklessness or gross negligence, this may preclude the operation of the defence. This seems to be the best explanation of the striking decision of the Court of Appeal in *Revill* v. *Newbery* [1996] QB 567 in which the septuagenarian defendant was held liable in damages to the plaintiff burglar whom he unintentionally shot while trying to deter the latter from breaking into his allotment shed (see also 13.8). The Court of Appeal, in a decision that attracted much adverse press comment, declined to apply the defence of illegality but upheld the trial judge's decision to reduce the level of damages by two-thirds on account of the plaintiff's contributory negligence. Although the court made allowance for the fact that the defendant's judgement was clouded by fear, it held that his actions went so far beyond what was reasonable force in the circumstances as to be clearly dangerous and bordering on the reckless (p. 580, per Millet LJ), given especially that the defendant had fired from inside the shed through a hole in the door and was effectively blindfolded in that he had no means of knowing for sure whether the gun was pointing at anyone. It should not be concluded, however, despite some rather ambiguous remarks in the decision, that the use of excessive force in self-defence or the prevention of crime will always amount to an actionable civil wrong: such conduct may well result in a criminal liability for the defendant (although it did not here: Mr Newbery was acquitted) but it is a different matter to allow the claimant to recover damages for injuries sustained in the course of the criminal enterprise.

Lastly, the closeness of the link between the claimant's injury and her unlawful conduct is a matter to be taken into account. In the example of the safeblowing burglars (above), the injured party would be unable to recover if she was blown up by her colleague: her injury would have been sustained in the course of criminal conduct. Neither would she get compensation if she sustained her injury in a crash which brought to an end their high-speed getaway: this was a risk that she brought upon herself (see *Ashton* v. *Turner* [1981] QB 137). However, she would probably succeed in a suit against her accomplice if the latter crashed the getaway car well away from the scene of the crime when there was no longer any immediate pressure to avoid detection: in this case, her injury would be merely coincidental to her wrongdoing.

In *Vellino* v. *Chief Constable of Greater Manchester* [2001] EWCA Civ 1249, [2002] 1 WLR 218, the Court of Appeal indicated that circumstances sufficient to bring into play the maxim *ex turpi causa non oritur actio* might also lead the court to the conclusion that there was no duty of care on grounds of fairness, justice and reasonableness, i.e. under the third part of the test in *Caparo* v. *Dickman*. On this basis, a majority of the court ruled against a habitual criminal who was injured when he jumped from the window of his second floor flat in an effort to evade arrest by the police; as there was no duty, it did not matter that the police knew he had done the same in the past yet failed to take reasonable care for his safety. (This was also an alternative ground for the decision in *Clunis* v. *Camden and Islington Health Authority* [1998] QB 978, below.) In a recent consultation paper, the Law Commission (2001) accepted the correctness of the 'no duty' analysis, but went on to argue that illegality should not act as a *defence* in cases where the claimant suffers personal injuries in the course of an illegal activity. With respect, it must be said that this seems a pointless distinction: the issue of substance is whether claimants should be denied a remedy on grounds of their criminal conduct, and whether this is achieved at the duty stage or by means of a discrete defence is neither here nor there.

So far we have looked at cases in which illegality bars the claimant's claim in its entirety. In other cases, the courts have ruled out only part of the claimant's claim on the grounds that it would offend public policy to allow recovery of particular heads of damage (e.g. where the claimant requests damages for loss of earnings derived from her career as a burglar: see *Burns* v. *Edman* [1970] 2 QB 541). The courts would describe their approach to this sort of case as pragmatic, though others would regard it as merely arbitrary. A striking example is *Meah* v. *McCreamer* [1985] 1 All ER 367, [1986] 1 All ER 943. The litigation arose out of a car crash caused by McCreamer's negligence, in which Meah suffered brain damage which brought on a change in personality. Some years later, Meah perpetrated a number of violent sexual attacks, for which he was convicted and imprisoned; he was also successfully sued by two of the victims of the assaults. In two successive cases against McCreamer, he sought damages first in respect of the time he spent in prison and then in respect of the compensation he was required to pay his victims. Although both claims were founded on the same criminal conduct, Woolf J allowed only the first, disqualifying the second as offensive to public policy.

His decision to allow damages for the consequences of conviction was subsequently doubted by the Court of Appeal in *Clunis* v. *Camden and Islington Health Authority* [1998] QB 978. There, the plaintiff had killed another man in a sudden and unprovoked attack shortly after his release from the hospital in which he was being detained under the Mental Health Act. He subsequently pleaded guilty to manslaughter by reason of diminished responsibility, then brought an action for damages against the health authority that had – negligently, he alleged – released him into the community when he was still a danger, and thereby started the chain of events that resulted in his imprisonment. The Court of Appeal ruled that, since his claim arose out of his commission of a criminal offence, when he knew what he was doing, it fell foul of the maxim *ex turpi causa non oritur actio* and would not be entertained. The decision might have been different if, in the criminal proceedings, the plaintiff had been given the special verdict of not guilty by reason of insanity on the basis that he had been unaware of what he was doing.

Summary

11.1 The defence of voluntary assumption of risk operates as a total bar to the recovery of damages. It only comes into play if the defendant was in fact careless and care should be taken not to invoke the defence unnecessarily in cases where the defendant has done nothing wrong. The role of the defence has diminished as a result of legislative changes.

11.2 A person may voluntarily assume the risk of harm by agreeing in advance not to sue the person by whose negligence the harm is caused (e.g. by accepting a contractual exclusion clause or a non-contractual disclaimer of liability).

11.3 The Latin maxim *volenti non fit iniuria* expresses a related principle by which a person may be held to have voluntarily accepted the risk of injury through another's negligence. It requires proof of knowledge of the risk in question, a voluntary exposure to the risk, and (most elusively) an 'assumption' of the risk.

11.4 The ability of the defendant to make out a defence of voluntary assumption of risk has been restricted by the Unfair Contract Terms Act 1977. The Act, which applies to cases of business liability, prevents exclusion or limitation of liability for negligently causing death or personal injury, and subjects exclusions or limitations of liability in respect of other losses to a test of reasonableness.

11.5 Since 1945, the defence of contributory negligence has operated to reduce, by an amount considered just by the court, the damages recovered by a claimant who shared responsibility for her injury.

11.6 Where the claimant was engaged in unlawful activity at the time of her injury, she may be barred from recovering damages by the defence of illegality (e.g. in the case of a joint unlawful venture).

Exercises

11.1 In what circumstances will the defence of voluntary assumption of risk arise? Is the defence based exclusively on agreement?

11.2 Do you agree with Lord Reid (in *ICI* v. *Shatwell*) that voluntary assumption of risk is 'a dead or dying defence'? If so, why is this the case?

11.3 Would the case of *Hedley Byrne* v. *Heller* (see 5.3) still be decided the same way now that the Unfair Contract Terms Act 1977 has come into force?

11.4 What advantages are there in developing a set of tariffs to deal with commonly recurring types of contributory negligence?

11.5 What significance, if any, is attached to the fact that the claimant in a tort action was engaged in illegal activities at the time when the injury was sustained?

11.6 Is the law justified in precluding entirely any claim by a young man injured in a tragic accident, albeit one which resulted from his fooling around on a motorcycle after an evening's drinking (*Pitts* v. *Hunt*), at the same time as recognising a liability in damages to the burglar shot by a terrified septuagenarian who was merely defending his property (*Revill* v. *Newbery*)?

11.7 F and G, both aged 14, decide to go cycling on their tandem one afternoon. After cycling for a while, they decide to stop for some liquid refreshment and go into an off-licence where they are served by H. F asks for a six-pack of Lodgers Extra Strength lager for each of them, adding jokingly that 'Cycling up the hills should be a good deal easier after drinking that lot.' H sells them the lager. F and G get back on their tandem and cycle several more miles, drinking as they go. Rather the worse for alcohol, they decide to start a 'Mexican wave', which involves each of them in turn standing up on the pedals and waving her hands in the air. As they are doing this, F, who is steering, loses control of the tandem and both are involved in a head-on collision with J. J's car is dented and one of the tyres is punctured. Nevertheless, J decides to drive F and G to the hospital. However, on the way, she loses control of the car because of the punctured tyre. The car crashes into a ditch, causing extensive damage to the bodywork but no further injury to those in the car. J asks her neighbour K, who is a keen DIY car-repairer, if she would fix the bodywork on his car. K replies that she 'will have a go.' K makes a mess of the job and J has to have the car repaired professionally at considerably greater cost than would have been necessary before K had done any work on it. Advise the parties as to their rights and liabilities in tort.

Interference with the Person and Personal Property

Part II

Interference with the Person and
Personal Property

12 Interference with the Person and Personal Property

12.1 Overview

Having considered the tort of negligence, we begin now our discussion of the remaining torts that feature on the typical tort syllabus. As we stated above, these are to be grouped according to the interests they may be said primarily to protect (see 1.3). Here we deal with torts that protect against interference with the person and personal property. Subsequent parts of the book deal with interests in land (Part III) and interests in reputation and privacy (Part IV). In each of these areas, we consider the impact made by the tort of negligence and the distinctive contribution made by other tortious causes of action.

In the context of interference with the person and with personal property, the rise of the tort of negligence has had a very significant impact. As a practical matter, negligence now tends to marginalise the older common law torts. As a matter of strict law, its rise has led the courts to regard the distinctive features of other torts as anomalous, and consequently to eliminate those features. However, a number of older common law torts continue to play a valuable role in the law today. The most important of these are listed below:

Trespass to the person is the label affixed to a group of torts, actionable without proof of damage, which deal with 'direct' violations of the person or of personal liberty. The group consists of *assault, battery* and *false imprisonment*. These are considered in ch. 16.

Wrongful interference with goods (not considered elsewhere in this book) is also a name given to a group of torts, this time dealing with injury to personal property rather than to the person. Among them are *trespass to goods*, which consists in any unjustified 'direct' interference with goods (e.g. snatching your wallet, kicking your dog or ramming your car) and *conversion*, which consists in unjustified and wilful taking away, detention, disposal or destruction of goods in a manner inconsistent with the rights of another. If nothing done to the goods is inconsistent with another's rights, the only action is in trespass. Thus my stealing your ball is both a trespass and conversion, but my grabbing your ball to throw it at someone else is only a trespass, for I am not questioning your rights over it.

Liability for animals, an example of strict liability (i.e. liability without fault), developed in the early days of the common law. It was expressed in two common law rules, the first concerning *cattle trespass*, the second dealing with the infliction of harm by dangerous animals whose vicious propensity was known – actually or imputedly – by their keeper (the *scienter* action). The old common law actions have been abolished, and the principles of strict liability in relation to the keeping of animals codified, by the Animals Act 1971.

As we have observed, the emergence of the tort of negligence, and of the ideology that underpins it, has influenced the legal development of the other torts and led to their marginalisation in practice. These processes are evident when we consider the relationship between negligence and trespass to the person. The influx of notions of negligence into the legal definition of trespass is traced below (see 16.1). As trespass became increasingly assimilated to negligence, it was tempting to regard as anomalous those exceptional cases in which liability might arise in the former but not in the latter (e.g. where the claimant suffers no damage). The result has been an attempt to eradicate those anomalies by treating unintentional interference with the person as giving rise to liability in negligence alone (*Letang* v. *Cooper* [1965] 1 QB 232; see 16.2) As a matter of practice, however, negligence had long since supplanted trespass as the principal action for personal injuries. Although negligence could not be regarded as a comprehensive and self-contained tort until *Donoghue* v. *Stevenson*, liability for negligence in various contexts was established centuries before. In such contexts (e.g. running-down cases on the highway), it was preferable for plaintiffs to frame their actions in negligence, as the scope of the action of trespass was limited and uncertain. Crucially, there were doubts as to whether the requirement of trespass that the interference be caused by 'direct' means was satisfied where a collision on the highway was caused by negligence rather than by wilful conduct (see Baker, 2002, pp. 412–13). By way of contrast, actions for negligence came to be allowed in respect of both 'direct' and 'indirect' damage (see *Williams* v. *Holland* (1833) 10 Bing 112) and so the risk of losing one's case on the pleadings was reduced.

Weir (1992) has noted wryly that 'Negligence is always trying to edge out the other torts ... [but] ... a few torts have managed to survive the competition' (p. 313). The torts considered in the subsequent chapters of this part of the book may be numbered among them. They are not mere historical relics. The various forms of trespass to the person (see ch. 16) retain a practical importance in the protection of civil liberties and the vindication of individual rights. Furthermore, various statutory torts provide a more satisfactory remedy than the tort of negligence. One reason for this is that the availability of an action in negligence may be limited by restrictions on the scope of the duty of care (as was the case in relation to occupiers' liability: see ch. 13). Another reason is that a number of statutes impose liability that is 'strict', in the sense that negligence on the part of the defendant need not be established (see chs 14 and 15).

12.2 Fault-Based and Strict Liability

When considering the role of fault in tort liability throughout history, three phases can be distinguished.

1. Early tort actions seem little concerned with fault. This was probably because the age was unmechanical and it was difficult for people at the time to conceive of harm being caused other than intentionally. If the fact that the defendant took all reasonable care was recognised as an excuse, this does not appear in the law reports of the time (see Baker, 1990, pp. 456–9).

2. With increasing industrialisation all this changed. Accidents at the workplace and on the roads, railways and shipping routes became frighteningly common. Infant industry, its existence still perceived as precarious, feared being crippled by liabilities imposed by the law of tort. To limit these liabilities, it adopted the standard 'No liability without fault'. Where industry was not threatened, by contrast, liability might well be recognised as strict, as was the case with the *scienter* action.

3. The advent first of workers' compensation schemes (1897) and then of the social welfare state (1946) reflected a change in society's attitudes to its responsibilities for the unfortunate. Industry was now established and producing enough wealth to safeguard its future even if it were exposed to an increased level of tortious liabilities. Many people came to feel that industry had a responsibility towards those who were injured by its activities, irrespective of whether anyone was at fault. In a startling piece of judicial innovation, the courts in *Rylands* v. *Fletcher* recognised strict liability in respect of damage caused by the escape of water from a reservoir used to power the defendant's mill (see ch. 19). The courts also began to recognise liability for the breach of strict statutory duties imposed upon employers and others, even when no statutory remedy was prescribed (see ch. 15). The spirit of reform has enveloped the legislature as well, notably in the field of product liability (see ch. 14).

The rationale of strict liability is that it is unfair for the community at large to benefit at the expense of the individual. The community benefits from risky activities carried out in industrial and other spheres, activities which have their inevitable cost in the injuries suffered by employees, consumers and others. The wealth generated by industry could well be employed to provide compensation for the victims of the machine age. The rationale of strict liability can be contrasted with that of negligence. Whereas the latter focuses upon the defendant's wrong and treats that as the reason for requiring him to compensate the victim, strict liability accepts that the defendant's conduct might be blameless – even for the public benefit – but nevertheless requires him to compensate the victim as the price of pursuing his activities. The compensation paid may be viewed as a tax on, or licence fee for, those activities.

12.3 Compensation for Personal Injuries

As we have just seen, a more general response to increasing welfarism than the recognition of strict liability in certain areas was the introduction of workers' compensation schemes and subsequently of social security benefits. Once the principle of compensation out of public funds and irrespective of fault became established, a collision of ideals between the social welfare state and the common law of tort was inevitable. The continuing relevance of the law of tort as a means of providing compensation for personal injuries was now open to doubt.

The centrepiece of any discussion of the role of tort law in compensation for personal injury is the report of a Royal Commission on Civil Liability and Compensation for Personal Injury, chaired by Lord Pearson, which was presented to Parliament in 1978. The Commission had been set up in 1972 amid public concern about the Thalidomide cases. These cases had fuelled debate about the place of tort law in modern society and had stimulated a number of calls for the abolition of tort law. Providing ammunition for those making such calls were the reports of government-appointed teams of inquiry in New Zealand (1967) and Australia (1974), both chaired by Mr Justice Woodhouse. The reports concluded that tort claims in respect of personal injury should be abolished and replaced by comprehensive schemes providing compensation irrespective of whether anyone else could be proved to be responsible for the injury. These factors generated the expectation that the Pearson Commission would recommend the abolition of the tort system in respect of accidental injury. However, this was not to be.

The Pearson Commission took the view that its terms of reference precluded it from considering whether tort should be abolished. It had been directed to consider when and how compensation should be paid in respect of death or personal injury caused at work, on the roads, by defective products or services, on other people's premises or otherwise through the acts or omission of another. Because a large proportion of injuries, notably many of those suffered in the home, fell outside these terms, the Commission felt unable to recommend a comprehensive scheme dealing with all personal injury. Having reached this controversial conclusion, it was inevitable that the Commission would base its detailed recommendations on the assumption that tort should continue to have a major role in any accident compensation strategy. As the Commission pointed out, unless a comprehensive compensation scheme were in operation, 'the abolition of tort for personal injury would deprive many injured people of a potential source of compensation, without putting anything in its place' (vol. 1, para. 275). Accordingly, the Pearson Commission recommended the retention of a 'mixed system' of accident compensation.

12.4 The Mixed System of Accident Compensation

The mixed system that the Pearson Commission wished to perpetuate was and is one in which social security is the primary method of providing compensation and the role of tort law is supplementary. As a system of compensation, tort law suffers from a number of limitations in comparison with social security, being of limited scope, costly and prone to delay. In terms of the scope of its coverage, it is social security which ensures that the needs of the vast majority of those who have been injured are met. The Pearson Commission found that, whereas over 1.5 million of those suffering personal injury each year receive social security payments, only 215 000 (6.5 per cent) of them obtain tort damages. Those whose condition stems from illness rather than accident are particularly unlikely to recover in tort. As Stapleton (1986a) points out, even those who suffer from 'man-made disease', and who are therefore potential tort claimants in that they at least have a defendant to pursue, may find their case runs up against insurmountable obstacles. In particular, it may prove impossible to establish more than the fact that exposure to a certain substance *may* cause injuries of the sort suffered by the claimant, which is not sufficient to satisfy the causal requirement that the claimant was *in fact* injured in a certain manner (see 9.3).

In terms of cost, tort again suffers in comparison: lawyers charge breathtaking fees, insurance companies devote considerable resources to handling claims and valuable court time is taken up with determining liability and assessing damages. Taking all such factors into account, the Pearson Commission estimated that the operating costs of the tort system amount to about 85 per cent of the value of tort compensation payments; the equivalent figure for social security was about 10 per cent. These costs suggest that tort law is an inefficient means of channelling compensation to accident victims. The same story emerges from a consideration of the length of time it takes for accident victims to receive compensation. Although, according to the Pearson Commission, almost half of all tort claims are settled within a year, those alleging substantial losses often take considerably longer (frequently more than five years). A long delay before receiving compensation may place considerable demands on the resources of the victim, especially as he may be in no condition to work, and may detrimentally affect his quality of life. This is exacerbated in the case of those whose condition may actually require them to spend money: someone who is crippled after an accident, for instance, may have to make alterations to his house in order to get about it freely. By way of contrast with the law of tort, victims of accidents or illness begin to receive social security benefits as soon as they need them.

Advocates of the tort system would argue, however, that the expense of running the system is justified. Adherents to notions of corrective justice, for example, maintain that those injured by another's fault have a claim to greater compensation than the bare minimum support provided by the social security system, even if their injuries are similar to those of people who have to make do without such support. (This view seems to underpin much of the Pearson Commission's thinking; contrast Cane, 1999, ch. 7.) A different school of thought holds that the expense of the tort system is warranted on the grounds that the threat of liability serves to deter wrongdoing and leads to the most efficient utilisation of society's resources. For a comprehensive analysis of the competing theories, see Cane, 1999, ch. 18.

12.5 **The Pearson Commission Proposals**

As the Pearson Commission thought that recommending a comprehensive compensation system was beyond its remit and was committed to the continuation of a mixed system, its proposals for reform were rather limited. They amount to an effort to tinker with the tort system rather than a major overhaul. The Commission's aims were fourfold: (a) to make sure that tort compensation did not overlap with social security payments; (b) to give priority within the tort system to the most seriously injured and ensure that their interests were adequately looked after; (c) to introduce pockets of strict liability; and (d) to consolidate or extend 'no-fault' schemes of limited scope in certain areas.

(a) The Prevention of 'Overlap'

In a mixed system of compensation, there is a danger that benefits from one source will simply duplicate those from another. The result is overcompensation. To guard against the possibility of overlap between the two partners in the mixed system of compensation approved by the Pearson Commission, the Commission made a number of recommendations: the value of social security payments should be deducted in full from damages awards (implemented in part by the Social Security Act 1989; see 22.9); private medical expenses should only be recoverable where the plaintiff could show that for medical reasons it was reasonable to incur them (not implemented); and the value of being maintained by the NHS (the 'hotel element') should be taken into account in the assessment of damages (implemented by Administration of Justice Act 1982, s. 5; see 22.7).

(b) Prioritising the Most Serious Cases

The Pearson Commission aimed to give priority within the tort system to those who would need it most by making radical changes to the law relating to the assessment of damages (see ch. 22). First, many minor cases were to be removed from the system altogether by imposing a threshold in relation to non-financial loss. The Commission recommended that no damages should be recoverable for non-financial loss suffered during the first three months after the date of injury. Its rationale for this restriction was that it would leave the tort system free to concentrate on serious and continuing losses. Secondly, the Commission recommended that no damages for non-financial loss should be recoverable for permanent unconsciousness: the award of such damages could perform no useful purpose because the plaintiff would not be able to derive enjoyment from their use. Thirdly, the Commission proposed that, in cases of death or serious and lasting injury, compensation for post-trial financial losses should be paid on a periodic basis rather than in a single lump sum. The extra expense which would result from the operation of a system of periodic payments would be justified by the fact that the plaintiff would be more accurately compensated for what he had lost, namely his income, and better protected in the event of a change in his circumstances. None of these proposals has as yet been implemented.

(c) Strict Liability

The Pearson Commission considered that, in general, negligence should remain as the basis of liability in tort. However, the Commission recommended the introduction of strict liability regimes in respect of rail transport, defective products, vaccine damage, and things and activities involving exceptional risks (see Cane, 1999, pp. 87–9). The rationale behind this piecemeal approach is unclear; certainly, it was never fully explained by the Commission. Its reasons for emphasising the role of 'fault' as a precondition of tort liability seem largely sentimental and amount to little more than a repeated assertion that it would be unfair to hold those who cause accidents innocently liable to their victims. This ignores both the justifications for the imposition of strict liability (see 12.2) and the fact that much tort liability is already strict (e.g. breach of statutory duty: ch. 15; vicarious liability: see ch. 21). Even the tort of negligence manifests some characteristics of strict liability, for the standard of care it demands is that of the reasonable person and this may result in the imposition of liability even though there was nothing a particular defendant could have done to prevent the injury in question (see 8.2).

The only area in which the Pearson Commission's proposals on strict liability have properly been implemented is that of product liability, on which the UK was required to act as a matter of EC law (see ch. 14). In relation to vaccine damage, the government, on which the strict liability was to fall, pre-empted the Commission's proposals by announcing that, subject to certain qualifications, severely vaccine-damaged children would be given lump sum payments of £10 000 (now increased to £30 000). Cane (1999) comments that the preferential treatment of vaccine-damaged children as compared with other disabled children seems to owe more to political action than any satisfactory moral distinction (p. 90):

> 'It appears that in this case, as in some others, preferential treatment for a small group was the result of a well conducted political campaign which played on public sympathy for particularly heart-rending cases.'

(d) 'No Fault' Compensation Schemes

The Pearson Commission advocated the consolidation or extension of 'no fault' compensation schemes in three areas. 'No fault' provides accident victims with compensation regardless of whether their injuries were the result of anyone else's fault. In this, it resembles strict liability. It differs from strict liability, however, in that the money paid as compensation comes from a central fund rather than directly from the person who caused the accident. The Pearson Commission approved the basic structure of the existing industrial injuries scheme, although it recommended some improvements. (Currently, the scheme is administered as part of the social security system, offering Disablement Benefit in the form of a weekly pension for those suffering a medically-assessed degree of disability in excess of 14 per cent for more than 15 weeks.) It suggested that a new scheme be introduced for those injured on the roads. This has not been done, although the issue was raised again for consideration in a Lord Chancellor's Department consultation paper (1991), which provisionally recommended the introduction of no-fault compensation only for injuries valued at less than £2500; this too seems unlikely to be implemented. Finally, the Pearson Commission submitted that a new social security benefit should be introduced for severely handicapped children (not implemented). In each of these areas, injured people were to retain their rights to tort compensation.

12.6 **Comprehensive Compensation Schemes**

The piecemeal approach of the Pearson Commission to the institution of no fault compensation schemes contrasts with efforts to implement comprehensive schemes elsewhere. As we have noted, the introduction of such schemes was first seriously considered in the common law world in New Zealand and Australia. The New Zealand accident compensation scheme was introduced in 1974 by legislation that at the same time abolished any claim to compensatory damages in tort for accidental personal injury; proposals to introduce a similar scheme in Australia were scuppered shortly afterwards as a result of a change in government.

The New Zealand scheme set out to achieve compensation and deterrence objectives (see 2.4) more effectively than under a mixed system. Its fundamental precept was that of comprehensive entitlement to compensation. Compensation was to be paid to all those suffering 'personal injury by accident'. This phrase included injuries suffered because of medical misadventure as well as occupational disease, though not ill health generally. The compensation provided by the scheme was to be paid on a periodic basis for the whole duration of the incapacity and it was to be earnings-related. However, a limit was set to awards in respect of lost income at 80 per cent of pre-accident earnings subject to an overall maximum figure; the scheme's focus upon pre-accident earnings meant that no allowance could be made for prospects of promotion or other contingencies. Provision was made for the award of lump sums up to specified maximums in respect of non-financial losses. The scheme was to be financed by levies on employers, the self-employed and vehicle licence holders, as well as out of general taxation. This allowed a deterrence element to be built into the scheme. Employers with good safety records could have a proportion of their contributions to the scheme refunded, while those with bad safety records might incur penalty rates (though some remain sceptical about the effectiveness of these mechanisms).

The scheme became the envy of many in other countries. Its combination of the principle of comprehensive entitlement with administrative costs that proved to be very low (around 6 per cent of the sums paid out) led to it being treated as a model of enlightened reform. In so far as the scheme attracted criticism, it was for failing to go far enough, and many pressed for its extension to all cases of disease as well as accidental injury. Such calls were quickly silenced when the scheme ran into financial difficulties in the mid-1980s which saw it teetering on the brink of bankruptcy and necessitated an immediate and dramatic increase in the level of premiums. In retrospect, it appears that these difficulties were largely the fault of the scheme's administrators, who had reduced the level of premiums without taking account of the fact that the scheme was still 'maturing': in the first 15 years or so, it was to be anticipated that the cost of the scheme would rise as increasing numbers of continuing liabilities were brought forward from year to year, although costs could be expected to stabilise once the scheme reached a plateau of maturity, i.e. when liabilities dropping off the books in any given year matched the new liabilities that were taken on.

The perception at the time, however, at least of the incoming (conservative) National government, was that entitlements to compensation under the scheme were too generous and needed to be more carefully limited in scope than before. In an effort to cut costs, the Accident Rehabilitation and Compensation Insurance Act 1992, described in its preamble as '[a]n Act to establish an insurance-based scheme to rehabilitate and compensate in an equitable and financially affordable manner those persons who suffer personal injury', made several significant reforms. First, it abolished the right to recover a lump sum in respect of non-pecuniary losses, replacing it with a weekly independence allowance for those left with significant disabilities. Secondly, it gave a restricted definition to the concept of compensable personal injury in order to reduce uncertainty about the scope of entitlement to compensation and to reverse the effect of a number of judicial decisions which had had the effect of extending the right to compensation in various respects (e.g. in relation to medical misadventure, mental injury and stress). Lastly, the scheme was to be financed by premiums levied upon the ordinary taxpayer as well as upon those who subsidised the original scheme, while provision was made for the 'experience rating' of premiums, in an effort to promote the deterrence objectives of the scheme more effectively than under the previous system of penalties and bonuses.

From 1999–2000, there was a short-lived experiment with the partial privatisation of the scheme. Employers no longer paid a levy to the state-run Accident Compensation Corporation but instead purchased compensation cover for work-related injuries on the open market. The experiment was brought to an end when the Labour party returned to government in 2000. Shortly afterwards, the new government introduced legislation which, with effect from 1 April 2002, restored lump-sum compensation for permanent impairment in place of the weekly independence allowance introduced in 1992 (Injury Prevention, Rehabilitation, and Compensation

Act 2001). The scheme now appears to have put its financial problems behind it, and continues to attract cross-party political support, as well as that of the principal employer and employee representative bodies.

Summary

12.1   The emergence of the tort of negligence has put other torts concerned with interference with the person and personal property into the shade. Many of the latter have been assimilated to negligence in some measure. Nevertheless, they retain practical importance in some fields (e.g. the protection of civil liberties). Furthermore, tort liabilities imposed by statute may be more stringent than those in negligence.

12.2   Although the ideology expressed by the tort of negligence has dominated legal thinking since the time of the Industrial Revolution, the welfare values of the last hundred years or so have questioned whether fault should be a prerequisite of liability. The result has been the judicial recognition and legislative creation of pockets of strict liability.

12.3   Increasing welfarism has also focused attention on the way accident victims are dealt with by society. The role of tort law in providing compensation for personal injury, and its relationship with social security, was considered by the Pearson Commission.

12.4   The Pearson Commission recommended the retention of a mixed system of compensation for personal injuries in which social security would play the major role, but tort law would continue to provide – at a cost – higher levels of compensation for the privileged few.

12.5   The reforms proposed by the Pearson Commission were designed to ensure there was no overlap between tort damages and social security benefits, to prioritise the most serious cases in the tort system and to introduce areas of strict liability and no fault compensation. Many of these proposals have yet to be implemented.

12.6   A more radical solution than that found in the Pearson Report would be the institution of a comprehensive no fault compensation scheme. In such a scheme, an example of which exists in New Zealand, the entitlement to compensation would be available even to those whose injuries were not caused by fault and the awards would be paid from public funds.

Exercises

12.1   What is strict liability? Can its imposition ever be justified?

12.2   What was the Pearson Commission? What were the principal recommendations that it made? Did these recommendations go far enough?

12.3   What is meant by talk of the 'mixed system' for compensation for personal injuries? Does every part of that system perform the task of compensating the needy satisfactorily? Does any part of that system perform any other tasks? (Please specify.)

12.4   What reforms would you advocate for the system of compensation for personal injuries?

13 Occupiers' Liability

13.1 Introduction

This chapter is concerned with the liability of an occupier of premises for injury caused or damage done to persons or their property while on the premises. The law in this area is now statutory and is governed by the 1957 and 1984 Occupiers' Liability Acts. This chapter does not deal with the situation where things done on the occupiers' premises affect other premises; this is the province of the law of 'nuisance' and *Rylands* v. *Fletcher* (see chs 18 and 19). The 1957 and 1984 Acts replaced a somewhat complex regime of common law, distinct from that developed from *Donoghue* v. *Stevenson*, under which an occupier owed different standards of duty depending on the status of the person who came onto his land. Those entering under a contract were owed the highest duty, while progressively lower duties were owed to those entrants the law classified as invitees, licencees or trespassers. The position today is that the Occupiers' Liability Act 1957 governs liability to lawful visitors and the 1984 Act governs the duty owed to those entrants loosely referred to as 'trespassers'. In the first part of this chapter we will examine the Occupiers' Liability Act 1957.

13.2 Scope of the Occupiers' Liability Act 1957

The 1957 Act abolishes the common law categories and provides that all lawful entrants are owed the same 'common duty of care'. This duty is owed by the occupier to his visitors 'in respect of dangers due to the state of the premises or to things done or omitted to be done on them' (s. 1(1)(a)).

Before analysing the central concepts of occupier, visitor and common duty of care, a number of points should be made about the scope of the Act. First, the duty is imposed on the occupier of 'premises', a term which has been interpreted very broadly. Premises clearly include buildings, houses and all real property. Further, s. 1(3)(a) of the Act states that the duty applicable to the occupier of premises applies equally to a person occupying or having control over 'any fixed or moveable structure, including any vessel, vehicle or aircraft (s. 1(3)(a)). Thus, while immoveable property is clearly within the Act, so too are moveable objects such as ships and aircraft. Other less permanent structures such as scaffolding, a diving board and even a ladder may, where they can be regarded as moveable structures, also fall within the definition. Literally, it would seem that the Act could cover claims arising out of the defective conditions of cars or other motor vehicles but in practice such claims are more likely to be pleaded as ordinary negligence claims. In any case, the issue is not likely to be of much practical significance for there is little if any difference between the duty of care in negligence and the common duty of care arising under the Act. Secondly, the obligations of an occupier extend beyond a duty not to cause personal injury to a visitor and cover damage to property suffered on the premises whether the property be that of the visitor or of a person who is not himself the visitor (s.1(3)(b)). Thirdly, liability under the Act may arise in respect of both acts and omissions. Thus, not only is an occupier liable for defects in the premises created by his own negligence but he may also be liable for defects in the premises created by another but which he has failed to remedy.

More difficult is the question whether the Act covers so-called 'activity' duties as well as 'occupancy' duties. At common law, the tripartite classification of lawful entrants into contractual entrants, invitees and licensees did not provide a complete picture of the law as the courts also drew a distinction between cases arising out of the state of the premises (the so-called 'occupancy' duty) and cases arising from activities being carried out on the premises (the 'activity' duty). It was only in respect of accidents arising out of the state of the premises that the special rules of liability were applied. Where the accident arose from activities being carried out on the premises, the ordinary rules of negligence were applied (see, for example, *Abbot* v. *Dunster* [1954] 1 WLR 58, 62; *Fairchild* v. *Glenhaven Funeral Services Ltd* [2002] 1 WLR 1052, paras 109–21). Of course, the common law relating to the liability of an occupier to his lawful entrants has now been replaced by the 1957 Act. However, it is not entirely clear whether the distinction between activity and occupancy duties has survived the Act. On the one hand, s. 1(1) provides that the rules provided by the Occupiers' Liability Act 1957 shall have effect, 'in place of the rules of the common law, to regulate the duty which an occupier of premises owes to his visitors in respect of dangers due to the state of the premises or to things done or omitted to be done on them'. On the other hand, s. 1(2) provides that the rules shall regulate 'the nature of the duty imposed by law in consequence of a person's occupation or control of premises'. While s. 1(1), if read literally, would appear to cover all conduct of an occupier on his premises, the same cannot be said of s. 1(2) which does not seem apt to cover the activity duty. Although the position is not entirely certain, the better view is that unless the accident arises out of the state of the premises, or out of an activity that affects the condition of the premises, the Act does not apply, and liability if it exists at all must arise under the common law of negligence or some other statutory provision (*Revill* v. *Newbery* [1996] QB 567; *Fairchild* v. *Glenhaven Funeral Services Ltd* [2002] 1 WLR 1052 (CA)). In most cases it will not matter whether the case is pleaded in negligence or under the Act as there is little if any difference between the duty of care in negligence and the common duty of care as applied to current activities. However, where the defect in the premises was not created by the occupier but by another person, then unless a relationship of, for example, employer and employee exists, liability for failure to remedy the defect can only exist under the Act for it is only his role as occupier that puts the defendant under any responsibility to make the premises safe (*Fairchild* v. *Glenhaven Funeral Services Ltd* [2002] 1 WLR 1052).

13.3 Who is an Occupier?

The Act does not attempt a definition of 'occupier', but instead, in s. 1(2), provides that an occupier is a person who would have been treated as such at common law. The leading case on the definition of an occupier is *Wheat* v. *Lacon* [1966] AC 552. In that case the defendants were owners of a public house, the management of which they entrusted to a manager. By virtue of the service agreement, the manager was entitled to live in a flat above the public house and to take in paying guests. There was no direct access between the pub and the flat, both parts having separate entrances. W and his wife were paying guests of the manager. W was fatally injured when he fell down an unlit and defective staircase in the flat. W's wife sued the defendants and the main issue was who was in occupation of the flat. The House of Lords held that, in determining who the occupier was, the important question was who had sufficient degree of control over the premises such that he ought to be under a duty of care to those who come lawfully onto the premises. Applying this test the court said that the defendants were to be treated as occupiers for the purposes of the Act.

Although it is clear that the important question is one of control, it is more difficult to determine what is a sufficient degree of control for the purposes of the Act. While an owner in occupation would no doubt have sufficient control, *Wheat* v. *Lacon* makes clear that an absentee owner may also retain sufficient control to be an occupier. In Lord Denning's speech in *Wheat* v. *Lacon*, he said that the defendants, although not in actual occupation, retained sufficient control because they had only granted a contractual licence to the manager to occupy the flat and had retained a right to enter to do repairs. This right was enough to make them occupiers. If, however, the defendants had let the flat to the manager, granting him a right of exclusive occupation, they would not have been occupiers of the flat for the purposes of the Act. However, where one person has a right of occupation over premises but the owner still has a right or duty to keep it in repair, then the owner is liable to take reasonable care for the safety of those present on the premises (Defective Premises Act 1972, s. 4).

Wheat v. *Lacon* makes clear a further point, namely that it is possible for two or more persons to be in occupation, for the purposes of the Act, at the same time. Thus, if the plaintiff had sued the manager it appears from the speeches of Lords Denning, Morris and Pearson that they would have held the manager also to be in occupation.

To conclude, the question of occupation is to be decided in each case on the particular facts having regard specifically to the degree of control exercised by the defendant over the premises. As has been seen, particular legal relationships or the fact of absentee ownership cannot be conclusive one way or the other but are no doubt factors to be taken into account.

13.4 **Who is a Visitor?**

The occupiers' duty under the 1957 Act is owed to lawful visitors. The Act does not define visitors but provides in s. 1(2) that a visitor is a person who would at common law have been treated as an invitee or licensee. These two categories cover a wide range of entrants and essentially encompass all those who enter with the express or implied permission of the occupier.

While this group is very wide the Act also makes specific provision for other classes of entrant who were not invitees or licensees at common law and these deserve some mention. First, at common law, those entering under a contract (such as hotel guests or workmen carrying out building work), although not classified as invitees or licensees, were nevertheless afforded a high degree of protection. Section 5(1) of the 1957 Act provides that in the absence of a specific term of the contract dealing with the duty owed to the contractual entrant there will be implied a term that he is owed the common duty of care. The parties are, however, free to negotiate different terms which may provide that a more or even less onerous duty is owed. Terms which seek to limit or exclude the duty may, of course, fall foul of the Unfair Contract Terms Act 1977 (see 11.4).

Secondly, s. 2(6) provides that 'persons who enter premises for any purpose in the exercise of a right conferred by law are to be treated as permitted by the occupier to be there for that purpose, whether they in fact have his permission or not'. Thus, a police officer entering a house in the execution of a warrant to search or a fire-fighter entering to put out a fire are within the Act. Section 2(6) was not, however, intended to expand the range of persons who are to be treated as visitors. Thus, those using a public (*McGeown* v. *Northern Ireland Housing Executive* [1995] 1 AC 233) or private (*Holden* v. *White* [1982] 2 WLR 1030) right of way, who were not treated as either licensees or invitees at common law, are not, because of s. 2(6), to be treated as visitors. That is not to say, however, that those using private or public rights of way are wholly without protection. A person using a *private* right of way may be owed a duty under the Occupiers' Liability Act 1984 and a person using a *public* right of way may have an action against the owner of the land over which the right of way exists for breach of the ordinary duty of care in negligence (*Thomas* v. *British Railways Board* [1976] QB 912). But, as the House of Lords made clear in *McGeown* v. *Northern Ireland Housing Executive*, the owner's liability in respect of both public and private rights of way will only arise in respect of positive misfeasance; he is under no duty to maintain any right of way in a safe condition. Such a conclusion was justified by Lord Keith on the ground that

> 'rights of way pass over many different types of terrain, and it would place an impossible burden upon landowners if they not only had to submit to the passage over them of anyone who might choose to exercise them but were also under a duty to maintain them in a safe condition.'

Whether the acquisition of a public right of way over a path always extinguishes the common duty of care that would otherwise be owed to the occupier's visitors is not clear. Owners of shopping malls, to which the public are obviously invited, often dedicate land as a public right of way. In the absence of the right of way, visitors to the mall would obviously be 'visitors' for the purposes of the 1957 Act. It is surely absurd to suggest that merely by dedicating access to such shops as a public right of way the owners could evade liability for injury caused by the state of the premises.

As already mentioned, invitees and licensees were those people who entered with the express or implied permission of the occupier. Where the occupier *expressly* invites a person onto his premises, it is generally clear that that person is a lawful visitor for the purposes of the Act. Significant problems may, however, arise in determining whether a person has the *implied* permission of the occupier to be on the occupier's premises.

It is a question of fact whether or not a person's entry has been impliedly permitted and the onus of proving this rests on the person who asserts it (*Edwards* v. *Railway Executive* [1952] AC 737, 747 per Lord Goddard CJ). To take a simple example, a person who walks up an occupier's front path with the intention of paying a social visit, or of trying to sell something to the occupier, will be treated as having the occupier's implied permission to be there (*Robson* v. *Hallet* [1967] 2 QB 939). It may be that even where he enters for his own purposes, for example if his hat is blown off into the occupier's front garden and he enters to retrieve it, he will still be held to be a visitor. However, it is clear that a licence, whether express or implied, can be withdrawn provided this is done clearly and that the licensee is given a reasonable time to leave the premises.

When we move from the rather obvious examples mentioned above, it is somewhat more difficult to discern when the courts will hold that a person's entry has been impliedly permitted. The courts have on a number of occasions made it clear that such permission should not be implied lightly. Thus, mere knowledge that persons are entering the occupiers' premises will not generally be enough (*Edwards* v. *Railway Executive*). What must be shown is that in spite of this knowledge the occupier took no steps or took insufficient steps to keep the visitor out. This can be illustrated by the case of *Lowery* v. *Walker* [1911] AC 10. People were in the habit of using the defendant's field as a shortcut on their way to the railway station. Although the defendant gave them no express permission to do so, he knew they used it as a short cut and he took no steps to stop them. The defendant, without any warning, put a savage horse into the field which attacked and injured the plaintiff. On the facts, the House of Lords held that the plaintiff was a lawful visitor.

Where children are concerned, the courts have been rather readier to imply permission than they have in the case of adults, particularly where the child has been 'enticed' onto the land by some attractive object or plaything (see, for example, *Cooke* v. *Midland Great Western Railway* [1909] AC 229: a railway turntable). This willingness to imply a licence is attributable to at least two factors: first, until relatively recently trespassers were treated very harshly by the law, and, second, children are often meritorious, or at least attractive, claimants. Since the enactment of the Occupiers' Liability Act 1984 trespassers are treated far less harshly than they had been at common law and it is probable, therefore, that courts will feel under less pressure to imply the fictitious licences that were necessary to do 'justice' in the past.

Two further problems in relation to implied permission deserve mention. The first arises where, in contravention of an express prohibition by an employer in occupation of certain premises, an employee or independent contractor invites onto the premises a person who is then injured. This situation arose in *Ferguson* v. *Welsh* [1987] 1 WLR 1553 where the House of Lords held that in such circumstances the injured person would be a lawful visitor *vis-à-vis* the employer provided he honestly and reasonably believed that the employee or independent contractor was entitled to invite him onto the premises. In *Ferguson* v. *Welsh* a local council engaged S to do some demolition work. The contract between them expressly prohibited S from subcontracting the work. In breach of this, S arranged with W to do the work. The plaintiff, who was working for W, was injured as a result of unsafe working practices being adopted. One of the issues considered by their Lordships was whether, *vis-à-vis* the council, the plaintiff was a lawful visitor. The House of Lords held that he was. The plaintiff had no reason to know anything about the details of the contract between the council and S and thus it was reasonable for him to believe that both S and W were entitled to invite him onto the premises.

Secondly, even where a person has the permission of an occupier to enter premises such permission may be limited by time, space or circumstance. As Scrutton LJ said in *The Calgarth* [1927] P 93, 100 'when you invite a person into your house to use the stairs, you do not invite him to slide down the bannisters'. However, the application of this limitation has been approached in a common-sense way. In one case, for example, a customer in a public house wandered into a private part of the building looking for a lavatory, and in so doing fell down some stairs and suffered injury. The court held he was not behaving unreasonably in looking where he was looking, even though he had no express permission to be there, and that, therefore, he remained a lawful visitor (*Gould* v. *McAuliffe* [1941] 2 All ER 527n).

13.5 **The Common Duty of Care**

Section 2(1) of the Occupiers' Liability Act 1957 provides that the duty which an occupier owes his visitor is the common duty of care. This is defined in s. 2(2) as 'a duty to take such care as in all the circumstances of the case is reasonable to see that the visitor will be reasonably safe in using the premises for the purposes for which he is invited or permitted by the occupier to be there'. This duty, as Lord Denning pointed out in *Roles* v. *Nathan* [1963] 1 WLR 1117, is really the same as the ordinary duty of care in negligence and thus the factors mentioned in the chapter on breach of duty (ch. 3), such as the nature of the danger, the length of time the danger was in existence, the steps necessary to remove the danger and the likelihood or otherwise of an injury being caused, are equally relevant here. However, the Act also draws attention to two specific matters that are to be taken into account when considering the degree of care required.

First, s. 2(3)(a) provides that 'an occupier must be prepared for children to be less careful than adults'. This gives statutory recognition to a fact of life that the courts have always taken into account, namely, that what may not be a danger to adults may nevertheless be a danger to a child. Thus the courts have held that it is careless for a local authority to plant a shrub with poisonous berries in a public park to which children have access, because it is known that children are attracted by bright berries and may try to eat them (*Glasgow Corporation* v. *Taylor* [1922] 1 AC 44). Were an adult to eat one of the berries it is unlikely that the court would allow recovery because it is simply not foreseeable that an adult would act in such a foolhardy way. Whether or not something is likely to attract a child and therefore become a danger in circumstances where it would not be a danger to an adult, is a question of fact to be decided in the light of all the circumstances. What needs to be emphasised is that where an occupier knows, or ought to know, that children are in the habit of frequenting a particular place he must take account of that fact, and may be required to take greater care than he would do if children did not have access. Having said that, the courts have made it clear that occupiers may in some circumstances be entitled to rely on children being supervised by their parents: an occupier should not have to be an insurer for irresponsible parents. Thus, while it may be expected that young children will be left unaccompanied in designated play areas, it is less foreseeable that they will be left to wander wasteland or building sites (*Phipps* v. *Rochester Corporation* [1955] 1 QB 450). As Devlin J said in that case:

'[T]he responsibility for the safety of little children must rest primarily on the parents; it is their duty to see that such children are not allowed to wander about by themselves, or at least to satisfy themselves that the places to which they do allow their children to go unaccompanied are safe for them to go to. It would not be socially desirable if parents were, as a matter of course, able to shift the burden of looking after their children from their own shoulders to those of persons who happen to have accessible bits of land.'

The second specific matter highlighted in the Act is found in s. 2(3)(b), which provides that 'an occupier may expect that a person in the exercise of his calling will appreciate and guard against any special risks ordinarily incident to it, so far as the occupier leaves him free to do so'. This subsection was extensively considered by the Court of Appeal in *Roles* v. *Nathan*. A central heating boiler produced a great deal of smoke when lit. On the advice of a heating engineer, two chimney sweeps were engaged to clean the flues. The engineer warned the sweeps of the dangers presented by fumes when the boiler was lit and told them not to clean the flues at such a time. The sweeps however disregarded this warning and were subsequently killed by the fumes given off. The action brought by their widows failed because, as Lord Denning put it, 'the householder could reasonably expect the sweeps to take care of themselves so far as any dangers from the fumes are concerned'. This was a special risk ordinarily incident to the work of a sweep. If, however, the sweeps had been injured by the collapse of a bench on which they were sitting in their teabreak, the occupier may well have been liable. The risk of a bench breaking is not one ordinarily incident to a sweep's work and, thus, there is no reason why the sweeps should not in such a case be treated as any other visitor.

Section 2(3)(b) will not automatically absolve the occupier from liability when a person 'exercising his calling' is injured. This is illustrated by its application to cases where firemen have suffered injury while fighting a fire on the defendant's premises. In *Salmon* v. *Seafarer Restaurants* [1983] 1 WLR 1264 firemen were injured at a fire negligently started by the occupier in his fish and chip shop. The defendants sought to argue that there is always some risk involved in fire-fighting and that they should only be liable where they failed to warn the firemen of some exceptional risk not ordinarily incident to the job. Woolf J, however, rejected this argument and stated that an occupier would be liable where

> 'it can be foreseen that the fire which is negligently started is of a type which could first require firemen to extinguish the fire and where because of the nature of the fire they will be at risk even though they exercise all the skill of their calling'.

The majority of states in the United States have adopted a different approach. Relying on concepts such as assumption of risk by the firefighter, a desire to avoid imposing overburdensome liability on the occupier, and the danger of discouraging property owners from seeking assistance from emergency services, courts have generally held that firemen (extended to police officers and other professional 'risk-takers': *Berko* v. *Freda* (1983) 459 A 2d 663 (police officers); *Anicet* v. *Gant* (1991) 580 So 2d 273 (public employee caring for violent insane persons)) cannot recover unless the defendant's negligence creates undue risks of injury beyond those inevitably involved in fire-fighting (*Krauth* v. *Geller* (1960) 157 A 2d 129).

In considering whether the occupier has discharged the common duty of care, s. 2(4) of the Act lists two further matters to be taken into account.

First, s. 2(4)(a) provides that 'where damage is caused to a visitor by a danger of which he had been warned by the occupier, the warning is not to be treated without more as absolving the occupier from liability, unless in all the circumstances it was enough to enable the visitor to be reasonably safe'. Clearly if a notice is illegible or unintelligible it will not be enough and, in considering this, account must be taken of the capabilities of those who the occupier knows or ought to know are likely to see or hear the warning. Even if the warning is clear, this may not be enough to comply with the occupier's duty which is to make the premises reasonably safe. If, for example, to reach the occupier's front door his visitors have to cross a bridge over a river on his land and the bridge is rotten, the occupier is unlikely to be absolved from liability by putting up a notice warning that the bridge is rotten. This does not enable his visitors to be reasonably safe if it is the only way to get to the front door. Conversely, if there are two bridges, only one of which is safe, and a notice which says, 'this bridge is dangerous, use the other one', the occupier may not be in breach of his duty towards his visitors because the warning enables them to be reasonably safe (*Roles* v. *Nathan*, per Lord Denning).

Secondly, s. 2(4)(b) provides:

'where damage is caused to a visitor by a danger due to the faulty execution of any work of construction, maintenance or repair by an independent contractor employed by the occupier, the occupier is not to be treated without more as answerable for the danger if in all the circumstances he had acted reasonably in entrusting the work to an independent contractor and had taken such steps (if any) as he reasonably ought in order to satisfy himself that the contractor was competent and that the work had been properly done.'

This section was considered by the House of Lords in *Ferguson* v. *Welsh* where their Lordships rejected the plaintiff's argument that, having regard to s. 2(4)(b), the council had failed to discharge the common duty of care which they owed to him. In so doing, their Lordships considered a number of problems concerning the interpretation of that section. First, the plaintiff had argued that the council should not be able to rely on the section because the work it had engaged S to do was 'demolition' and this was not within the ambit of the section which refers to 'any work of construction, maintenance or repair'. In rejecting this argument the House of Lords held that 'a broad and purposive' approach should be taken to the meaning of these words and that 'demolition' was embraced by the word 'construction'. Second, it was argued that an occupier did not discharge the common duty of care where he employed someone he knew or ought to have known was incompetent. While this argument was accepted as correct in principle, it was rejected on the facts of the case. There was not enough evidence to suggest that the council ought reasonably to have doubted the honesty or competence of S. Had the council known that S was in the habit of adopting dangerous working practices, it is unlikely that it would have been held to have discharged the common duty of care. Finally, it was argued that the council ought to have supervised the conduct of the work. Again, this was rejected on the facts. The council did not have any reasonable grounds to suspect S was anything other than competent and this was not the type of work where supervision would ordinarily be required. However, there may be cases where work is of such technical difficulty that the occupier's common duty of care will not be discharged unless a specialist is employed to supervise the work and to make sure that it is completed properly.

Section 2(4)(b) is of course merely an example of the circumstances that may be relevant in determining whether the common duty of care has been discharged by an occupier who has employed an independent contractor. While the provision is limited in its terms to the case of an independent contractor who is employed to carry out works of construction, it is clear that in any case where an occupier employs an independent contractor he does not thereby automatically discharge his duty of care to a lawful entrant (*Gwilliam* v. *West Hertfordshire Hospitals NHS Trust* [2002] EWCA Civ 1041). The question remains whether in all the circumstances the occupier took reasonable care to ensure that the entrant would be reasonably safe in using the premises to which he had been invited. Though s. 2(4)(b) can only be directly applied where the independent contractor is employed to carry out works of construction, the Court of Appeal in *Gwilliam* v. *West Hertfordshire Hospitals NHS Trust* [2002] EWCA Civ 1041 held that it could be applied by analogy in other cases where an occupier had employed an independent contractor, e.g. to provide entertainment at a children's fair. Thus, it was a relevant question in determining whether the occupier had discharged the common duty of care whether the contractor employed was competent. In deciding whether a contractor was competent matters such as the experience and reliability of the contractor were clearly relevant. However, the fact of insurance may also be a relevant factor since 'if the firm did not hold themselves out as being insured this would reflect on their ability to meet any claim and, in addition, suggest that they were unlikely to be a reputable firm' (*Gwilliam* v. *West Hertfordshire Hospitals NHS Trust* [2002] EWCA Civ 1041, para. 15, per Lord Woolf LCJ).

13.6 Defences

Defences are dealt with generally in Chapter 11 and as a result only matters specifically relevant to the liability of occupiers are mentioned here.

First, by s. 2(5), the Act expressly preserves the general defence of *volenti non fit iniuria*. Secondly, the Act does not specifically mention whether a visitor's own lack of care can be taken into account in reducing damages. However, the courts have in a number of cases applied the Law Reform (Contributory Negligence) Act 1945 to reduce damages. Thus, it seems clear the defence of contributory negligence is available to an occupier. Finally, s. 2(1) of the Act specifically allows an occupier the freedom 'to extend, restrict, modify or exclude his duty to any visitor or visitors by agreement or otherwise'. However, such freedom is limited in three important ways. The first, and most important limitation is by the Unfair Contract Terms Act (see 11.4). The second limitation is found in s. 3(1) of the Occupiers' Liability Act 1957, which provides that, where an occupier is bound by contract to permit persons who are strangers to the contract to enter or use the premises, he owes them the common duty of care and the occupier cannot by that contract restrict or exclude this duty. Thus, if A puts K up as a lodger in his flat, he cannot stipulate that he will not be liable for any injury suffered by any person visiting K as a consequence of a defect in the premises. Finally, where a visitor is a 'contractual entrant' the occupier's ability to limit his liability to his visitor may be restricted by the Unfair Terms in Consumer Contracts Regulations 1994 (see McKendrick, 2001).

13.7 Liability to Trespassers

The law governing the duty owed by an occupier to a trespasser was left unaltered by the 1957 Act. Until the House of Lord's decision in *BRB* v. *Herrington* [1972] AC 877, an occupier was only liable to a trespasser if it could be proved that he had done some act intending to harm the trespasser or with reckless disregard for the trespasser's safety (*Addie & Sons (Collieries)* v. *Dumbreck* [1929] AC 358). The harshness of this principle was to a large extent alleviated by the House of Lords in *BRB* v. *Herrington*, where it was held that trespassers were owed the 'common duty of humanity'. Their Lordships did not, however, make clear precisely what they meant by this and in particular how it differed from the ordinary duty of care in negligence or the duty arising under the 1957 Act. Subsequent cases indicated that the duty was somewhat higher than the old common law duty owed to trespassers but lower than the ordinary duty of care in negligence. Dissatisfaction with the uncertainty of the principle led the then Lord Chancellor, Lord Hailsham, to ask the Law Commission to consider, 'in the light of the decision of the House of Lords in *BRB* v. *Herrington*, the law relating to liability for damage or injury suffered by trespassers'. The Law Commission recommended that legislation was needed to clear up the uncertainty (Law Commission, 1976) and the Occupiers' Liability Act 1984 was the result.

13.8 The Occupiers' Liability Act 1984

The Occupiers' Liability Act 1984 replaces the common law as laid down in *Herrington* (s. 1(1)). It places the occupier ('occupier' having the same meaning under the 1984 Act as it does under the 1957 Act: s. 1(2)) under a duty to 'persons other than his visitors' to take such care as is reasonable in all the circumstances to see that they do not suffer injury on the premises provided certain conditions are satisfied. In this section we use the term 'trespasser' as shorthand for 'persons other than [the occupier's] visitors'. However, note that the Act does in fact apply to more than just 'trespassers': the duty is owed to 'persons other than his visitors'. Thus, in addition to those who enter an occupier's premises without that person's express or implied permission (trespassers properly so called), the Act also applies to those using private rights of way (*Holden* v. *White* [1982] 2 WLR 1030) and those exercising rights under National Parks and access to the countryside legislation (National Parks and Access to the Countryside Act 1949 and Countryside and Rights of Way Act 2000), but not to those using the highway (Occupiers' Liability Act 1984, s. 1(7)).

As is the case under the 1957 Act, the duty owed under the 1984 Act is owed in respect of any risk of people suffering injury by reason of 'any danger due to the state of the premises or to things done or omitted to be done on them' (s. 1(1)(a)). In *Revill* v. *Newbery* [1996] QB 567, the Court of Appeal held that the Act did not apply where the defendant carelessly shot the plaintiff burglar who was trying to get into his shed. Although the Act could apply to dangers arising both from the state of the premises and from activities conducted on the land where those activities affected the state of the premises, s. 1(1)(a) was only intended to impose liability on an occupier *qua* occupier. Here the fact that he was an occupier was irrelevant to his liability.

The duty owed under the 1984 Act does not, unlike under the 1957 Act, extend to damage done to the entrant's property (s. 1(8)). Thus, if A entered B's land as a trespasser riding his scrambling bike, and due to a danger on B's land A fell off, he may be able to recover for any personal injury suffered in the accident but cannot recover for any damage done to the bike. Presumably in such a case the common law position accepted in *Herrington* would apply to the property damage though it is somewhat unsatisfactory to talk in terms of a breach of the duty of common *humanity* where only property damage is suffered.

The Act provides in s. 1(3) that a duty is owed by an occupier to a trespasser provided:

'(a) he is aware of the danger or has reasonable grounds to believe that it exists;

(b) he knows or has reasonable grounds to believe that the other is in the vicinity of the danger concerned or that he may come into the vicinity of the danger ...; and

(c) the risk is one which in all the circumstances of the case, he may reasonably be expected to offer the other some protection.'

The phrasing of ss. 1(3)(a) and 1(3)(b) creates some difficulty. Does a duty only arise if the occupier had *actual* knowledge of the existence of the danger and a similar knowledge of the presence or likely presence of the trespasser? Or, is it enough that a reasonable person would have, or ought to have, such knowledge? The language used is unclear, providing as it does that the occupier must know or be aware or 'have reasonable grounds to believe' that the danger exists and that the trespasser is in the vicinity or is likely to come into the vicinity. The better view is that the occupier must either have *actual* knowledge of the danger or actual knowledge of facts from which a reasonable person would draw the inference that the danger existed and that the person was in the vicinity or was likely to come into it. This is not the same as saying that it is enough that a reasonable person ought to know of the danger and likely presence of the trespasser.

This view is supported by the decision of the Court of Appeal in *White* v. *St Albans City Council* (1990) *The Times*, 12 March. The plaintiff was injured while taking a short cut to get to his car, which was parked in the defendants' car park. Although the defendants were aware of the danger and had taken steps to prevent any injury arising from it by blocking off access to the short cut, they had no evidence that the short cut was ever used to get to the car park. The court held that s. 1(3)(b) was not satisfied. Further, the court acknowledged that this would have been the case even if a reasonable person in the position of the occupier would have been aware that the short cut was in fact used.

The content of the duty owed under the 1984 Act is governed by s. 1(4). This provides that the occupier owes a duty to 'take such care as is reasonable in all the circumstances of the case to see that [the trespasser] does not suffer injury on the premises by reason of the danger concerned'. The duty owed is akin to the ordinary duty of care in negligence and, as a result, unlike under *BRB* v. *Herrington*, questions of the resources of the individual defendant will be irrelevant. However, in considering whether the duty has been breached, it is to be remembered that what constitutes reasonable care will vary according to the circumstances. Thus, for example, the duty will be less easily breached with respect to a burglar than with respect to a child who wanders into an occupier's garden to have a look at the fish in a pond.

By virtue of s. 1(5), the duty owed may be discharged when warning of a danger is given. As is the case under the 1957 Act, a warning will not in every case be sufficient to discharge the duty owed by an occupier. However, it is more likely to be effective to discharge the duty owed to a trespasser than to a lawful visitor. The reason for this is that whereas a lawful visitor may have no choice but to run the risk of being injured on the premises, the trespasser will usually have that choice.

In principle, the general defences available to an action in negligence should also be applicable to an action under the 1984 Act. However, some doubt was cast on this by the unsatisfactory decision of the Court of Appeal in *Revill* v. *Newbery* (criticised by Weir, 1996b). While the court accepted that an occupier sued by a trespasser could plead contributory negligence, it refused to allow the defendant to plead *ex turpi causa non oritur actio* (see 11.6). By enacting s. 1, Parliament made clear that an occupier cannot treat a burglar as an outlaw. Indeed, it set out the scope of the duty that an occupier owes a trespasser. Yet, the court held, to allow the defendant to rely on the defence would have the effect of turning burglars into outlaws.

It is true that Parliament did decide that trespassers should not, as a class, be treated as outlaws. But it is does not follow from the fact that

Parliament recognised a duty to trespassers generally, that the behaviour of some trespassers can never be so bad that their claims ought not to be totally barred. The existence of a duty of care and any defence barring a claim based on that breach of duty are logically distinct. Thus, it is submitted that there should have been no reason why the defendant should not have been entitled to rely on the defence. This point becomes stronger when account is taken of the fact that the 1984 Act was enacted to protect 'innocent trespassers', such as those who accidentally blunder onto another's property, and children. It hardly seems likely that Parliament would have bothered to enact a statute mitigating the 'harshness' of the common law just to protect someone like the plaintiff in *Revill*.

Finally, it should be noticed that the Act makes no provision as to whether the duty owed to trespassers can be excluded. As a matter of policy it could be argued that the duty imposed by the Occupiers' Liability Act 1984 should be seen as an irreducible minimum imposed by the law which cannot be excluded. The problem with such an argument is that in certain circumstances, it would leave a lawful visitor, to whom the duty has been properly excluded in a worse position than a trespasser. This may lead lawful visitors, where there is an exclusion clause, to seek to argue that they are trespassers. The courts could deal with this problem either by holding that the duty under the 1984 Act can be excluded, or, and, it is argued, this is the better solution, by holding that the 1984 Act provides an irreducible minimum duty which cannot be excluded as against either visitors or trespassers.

Summary

13.1   The law relating to the liability of an occupier of premises for injury caused or damage done to persons or their property while on the occupier's premises is governed by the Occupiers' Liability Acts 1957 and 1984. These Acts replace a complex regime of common law rules distinct from that developed from *Donoghue* v *Stevenson*.

13.2   The Occupiers' Liability Act 1957 governs the liability of occupiers to their lawful visitors and certain other entrants in respect of dangers due to the state of the premises and to things done or omitted to be done on them.

13.3   An occupier is a person who has sufficient degree of control over the premises such that he ought to be under a duty of care to those who come onto the premises. It is possible for more than one person to be an occupier. An occupier need not live in the premises of which, for the purposes of the Act, he is an occupier.

13.4   A 'lawful visitor' is a person who enters with the express or implied permission of the occupier. The Act also expressly provides that persons entering premises under a contract and those entering as of right are afforded the same protection as lawful visitors. An occupier may limit permission to enter.

13.5   The duty owed by an occupier to his lawful visitors is the common duty of care. This is very similar to the ordinary duty of care in negligence. The Act requires two specific matters to be taken into account when considering the standard of care required. These are, first, that children may be less careful than adults and, second, that a person should guard against risks ordinarily incident to his calling. In considering whether the duty has been discharged, regard is to be had to any warning given. Furthermore, in considering whether an occupier is to be held liable for acts of an independent contractor, regard must be had to his selection and supervision of the independent contractor.

13.6   The same general defences available in an action under the ordinary law of negligence apply with regard to the Occupiers' Liability Act 1957. An occupier may extend, restrict, exclude or modify his liability to a lawful visitor, to the extent that the law leaves him free to do so. The Unfair Contract Terms Act, s. 3 (1) of the Occupiers' Liability Act 1957 and the Unfair Terms in Consumer Contracts Regulations 1994 substantially curtail this freedom.

13.7   The law relating to the liability owed to trespassers is now governed by the Occupiers' Liability Act 1984. The Act replaces the common law test as laid down by the House of Lords in *BRB* v *Herrington*.

13.8   Occupiers owe a duty of care to trespassers and certain other entrants in respect of dangers due to the state of the premises and to things done or omitted to be done on them. The duty is only owed to a trespasser if the criteria set out in s. 1(3) are satisfied. The standard of care imposed is to take reasonable care to see that the trespasser does not suffer injury while on the premises.

Exercises

13.1   How is 'occupier' defined for the purposes of the Occupiers' Liability Acts 1957 and 1984?

13.2   Would an action against the manager have succeeded in *Wheat* v. *Lacon*?

13.3   Were all their Lordships in *Wheat* v. *Lacon* agreed on the basis on which the defendants were occupiers *vis-à-vis* the plaintiff's husband?

13.4   How is 'lawful visitor' defined for the purposes of the 1957 Act? Why are those persons exercising a public or private right of way not lawful visitors?

13.5   In what circumstances will the courts hold that an entrant has the implied permission of the occupier to be there? Why are the courts more ready to find such permission exists in the case of children than in the case of adults?

13.6   What factors, along with those specifically mentioned in the Act, will the courts take into account when considering whether or not the common duty of care has been broken?

13.7   Was it fair in *Phipps* v. *Rochester Corporation* to refuse to allow the child to recover anything? Would a different approach have been fairer?

13.8   A fire-fighter is injured at a fire negligently started by the occupier. What factors will be relevant in deciding whether or not the occupier is liable?

13.9   In what circumstances would it be unreasonable, (a) for an occupier to entrust work to an independent contractor? (b) for an occupier not to supervise an independent contractor?

13.10   Is property damage recoverable under the 1984 Act? If it is not recoverable under the Act, would an action succeed at common law?

13.11   What degree of 'knowledge' must be possessed by the occupier before a duty will be owed to a trespasser?

13.12   Is it possible to exclude the duty imposed upon an occupier by the 1984 Act?

14 Product Liability

14.1 Product Liability at Common Law

The most famous product liability case is perhaps the most famous in all of the law of tort: no defective product has ever since achieved the notoriety of Mrs Donoghue's bottle of ginger beer and its alleged contents, the decaying remnants of a snail. In deciding that case, Lord Atkin laid down the following test of liability for products in the common law of negligence (*Donoghue* v. *Stevenson* [1932] AC 562, 599):

'[A] manufacturer of products which he sells in such a form as to show he intends them to reach the ultimate consumer in the form in which they left him, with no reasonable possibility of intermediate examination, and with the knowledge that absence of reasonable care in the preparation or putting up of the products will result in injury to the consumer's life or property, owes a duty to that consumer to take that reasonable care.'

The case allowed consumers rights against manufacturers of defective products that they lacked under the law of contract. Contract law provided consumer plaintiffs with very powerful remedies against those defendants with whom they could establish privity of contract. Most significantly, contractual remedies were available even where the defendant was in no way at fault as liability for breach of contract is, in general, strict. The common law of contract was buttressed by the Sale of Goods Act (now of 1979, as amended) which implied terms into contracts of sale that the goods sold were of 'satisfactory quality' and reasonably fit for any purposes made known by the buyer to the seller (ss. 14–15). However, the doctrine of privity of contract limited the value of contractual remedies in two respects. In the first place, liability could only arise in favour of someone who had 'bargained for' the goods. That is why Mrs Donoghue was unable to sue in contract: her bottle of ginger beer had been bought for her by a friend. Secondly, it is the seller of the goods, not the manufacturer, who is held liable to the consumer in the law of contract. Had Mrs Donoghue bought the bottle of ginger beer herself, it would have been Minchella, the cafe-owner, and not the manufacturer, who would have had to compensate her. The cafe-owner would then have had to sue his supplier, initiating a series of actions for breach of contract which would continue until the 'contractual chain' led to the manufacturer. This is at best a clumsy way of fixing liability on the manufacturer and is unfair to any seller who cannot identify his supplier or whose supplier has gone out of business. Suing in tort avoids both these problems.

The development of the tort of negligence served the interests of consumers well. Although in theory the burden of establishing fault lay on the consumer, in practice the presence of a defect in a product gave rise to an inference of negligence. Furthermore, it was no excuse for a manufacturer to say that his quality control system was as good as it could be and the defect could only be the result of human error: through the doctrine of vicarious liability, the manufacturer would be liable for the errors of his employees. These principles were relied upon in the Australian case of *Grant* v. *Australian Knitting Mills* [1936] AC 85, which went on appeal to the Privy Council. Mr Grant had suffered a severe skin complaint after wearing a new pair of woollen underpants and he sued the manufacturer, alleging that traces of chemicals used in the manufacturing process had been left in the wool. The Privy Council found that Mr Grant was entitled to damages and Lord Wright, who delivered the advice of the Privy Council, described how the case was approached (p. 101):

'If excess sulphites were left in the garment, that could only be because someone was at fault. The appellant is not required to lay his finger on the exact person in all the chain who was responsible, or to specify what he did wrong. Negligence is found as a matter of inference from the existence of the defects taken in connection with all the known circumstances.'

The 70 years since *Donoghue* v. *Stevenson* have shown that the courts have preferred to uphold the spirit of Lord Atkin's 'neighbour principle' rather than seek a literal application of his words quoted above. Failure to fit in with Lord Atkin's precise words has not resulted in a total denial of liability: courts have assured themselves of a degree of flexibility to meet the circumstances of each case. Hence the possibility of intermediate inspection, for example, will not prevent a duty of care from arising, although it may cause the harm caused by a product to be regarded as too remote (see *Aswan Engineering Establishment Co* v. *Lupdine Ltd* [1987] 1 WLR 1).

14.2 Reform: The Consumer Protection Act 1987

Despite these developments, well-publicised tragedies arising from the use of defective products stimulated pressure for legislative reform. In particular, the Thalidomide tragedy of the late 1950s and early 1960s, in which hundreds of babies were born without limbs as an unforeseen side-effect of a drug their mothers had taken during pregnancy, gave rise to public concern and prompted consideration of the issue by law-review bodies. Ultimately, reform was accomplished as part of EC law. A 'Product Liability' Directive (85/374/EEC) was adopted in 1985, obliging member states to implement its provisions in their domestic legislation. This was done in the UK by Part I of the Consumer Protection Act 1987.

The goals of the new statutory products liability regime were spelled out in the recital to the European Directive: '[l]iability without fault on the part of the producer is the only way of solving the problem, peculiar to our age of increasing technicality, of a fair apportionment of the risks inherent in modern technological production'. Yet, despite this nod towards consumer protection, the Directive's legal foundation was art. 100 of the EEC Treaty (now art. 94 EC), which provided for the harmonisation of the laws of member states so as to improve the functioning of the common market. In a series of recent decisions promulgated on the same day, the European Court of Justice has ruled that this legal basis precludes individual member states from implementing a more stringent form of liability than that established by the Directive (*European Commission* v. *France*, Case C-52/00, 25 April 2002, and *European Commission* v. *Greece*, Case C-154/00, 25 April 2002) or even maintaining in force pre-existing national provisions which afford greater consumer protection than under the Directive (*Sanchez* v. *Medicina Asturiana SA*, Case C-183/00, 25 April 2002). Differences in levels of consumer protection in different member states might distort competition between traders and impede the free movement of goods.

Sceptics have argued that, in terms of consumer protection, the new scheme is flawed because it is no easier to prove that a product is defective than to prove that it was negligently manufactured (especially when the effect of the development risks defence is considered as well: see 14.7 and Stapleton, 1986b). On the other hand, proponents of the reform claim that the new scheme provides a speedier and therefore cheaper remedy for consumers (see Jolowicz, 1987). In any case, the British consumer will be left no worse off than before: the statutory remedy exists alongside the existing remedies in contract and tort. Thus, those injured by a product they themselves have bought, for example, will still be able to sue for breach of the implied warranty of quality in the contract of sale.

One final introductory point to note about the Consumer Protection Act is that, under EC law, it must fully implement all the provisions of the Directive. Should it not do so, the European Court of Justice can call upon the UK to amend its legislation. The UK has sought to avoid this by inserting an 'interpretation clause' in the Act: s. 1(1) states that Part I of the Act shall be construed 'as is necessary in order to comply with the product liability Directive'. This clause was intended to allow courts to comply with EC law by adopting a generous interpretation of any provision in the statute that appears, on its face, to be too narrow. Given that the obligation to interpret domestic legislation so as to give effect to principles of EC law also arises under EC law itself, it may be appropriate in some cases to go straight to the wording of the Directive, and to refrain from analysis of the equivalent provisions of the Act – at least where there is no clear conflict between the two (see, e.g., *A* v. *National Blood Authority* [2001] 3 All ER 289).

14.3 Meaning of 'Product'

The basic definition of a product is found in section 1(2) of the Act:
' "product" means any goods or electricity and ... includes a product
which is comprised in another product'. This last limb of the definition
encompasses the component parts of larger products as well as the raw
materials of which products are made: if you were to buy a car, the engine
and tyres would be regarded as products no less than the car as a whole,
and you would be able to sue the manufacturers of these component parts
if the parts were defective and caused you injury. The same would be true
with regard to the manufacturers of the metal and tyre rubber used as raw
materials if the defect were traced to them. In both cases, however, you
would have an alternative claim against the car-maker, which is
particularly important where you do not know who supplied the
components or raw materials.

'Goods', in turn, is defined in the Act: s. 45(1) says the term is to include
'substances, growing crops and things comprised in land by virtue of being
attached to it and any ship, aircraft or vehicle'. The precise limits of the
definition of 'goods', and therefore of the definition of 'products', will be
hard to determine. Take, first of all, the case of buildings and building
materials. On its face, the definition of 'goods' seems to encompass these
things on the basis that a building is a thing attached to land. However, it
is arguable that a building is better regarded as 'land' itself, rather than a
thing 'attached to land'. This interpretation is supported by the Directive,
art. 2 of which defines 'products' as meaning all moveables, which it
contrasts with immoveables, although it allows that moveables remain
products even if incorporated into an immoveable. From this, it appears
that the building materials (the bricks, beams, tiles, etc.) that are used in
constructing a building were, being moveables, meant to be covered by the
Directive, even where incorporated into a building. Conversely, the
building itself, being an immoveable, falls outside the scope of the
Directive, and therefore of the Consumer Protection Act.

A second hard case concerns the information contained in goods like
books and computer software (see generally Stapleton, 1989; Whittaker,
1989). A much-debated example is the chemistry textbook which misstates
the chemicals to be mixed together in a particular experiment, causing an
explosion when followed to the letter. A number of commentators (e.g.
Howells, 2000, para. 4.55; Nolan, 2002, para. 19.43) argue that such cases
are outside the scope of the legislation because information is not itself a
product and does not become a product even if conveyed in concrete form
– for example, in a book or on a computer disk. It may be objected,
however, that the book and computer disk can themselves be regarded as
products, whose defectiveness lies in the unsafe information they contain.
Maintaining the contrary entails the wholly unwarranted exclusion from
the strict liability regime of a whole class of products, like traffic lights and
smoke alarms, whose main or only purpose is to provide safety
information. There is simply no basis for this in the legislation. Indeed,
the legislation itself contemplates at least one case of liability for defective

information, namely, where injury results from following misleading instructions provided with an otherwise safe product (see 14.4). One can sympathise with the intuitions of those who object to the imposition of liability in respect of information published to the world at large, given especially the unlikelihood of the common law recognising a duty in such a case (see *Candler* v. *Crane, Christmas & Co* [1951] 2 KB 164, 183 per Denning LJ). But such concerns are best allayed by reference to notions of causation and contributory negligence, for in most cases in practice it will be unreasonable to rely upon such information without making independent inquiries. It would be wrong to meet this concern by artificially restricting the meaning of 'product' under the legislation.

One difficulty does however remain: strict liability applies only to defective products, not defective services, and this fundamental distinction may be blurred if information or advice is taken to be part-and-parcel of a product simply because it is conveyed in concrete form. As Howells (2000, para. 4.54) has urged: 'Just because advice is put down on paper should not change the liability regime'. The Product Liability Directive was not intended to impose strict liability on doctors in respect of their prescriptions, lawyers for their written opinions, and architects for their drawings. In borderline cases, it will therefore be necessary for the courts to decide whether what the defendant has supplied is in reality a product or a service, bearing in mind such considerations as the scale of production, the extent to which specifications are varied according to the needs of the individual purchaser, and whether or not the information or advice was conveyed pursuant to a relationship of professional and client.

Another type of product calling for special comment is game and agricultural produce. In the original Act of 1987, this was to fall within the new strict liability regime only if it had undergone an industrial process (CPA s. 2(4); in fact, the Directive spoke here only of an *initial* process, with no indication that it had to be industrial). As a result of concerns raised in the 1990s by evidence that bovine spongiform encephalopathy (BSE) can be transmitted from cattle to humans, a new Directive (EC 99/34) extended the scope of the existing Product Liability Directive to include primary agricultural products, causing a consequential amendment to the UK legislation (by the Consumer Protection Act 1987 (Product Liability) (Modification) Order 2000/2771). Whether the human victims of BSE-infected beef would have benefited from this provision had it been implemented in time may, however, be doubted because it would be practically impossible to prove precisely who, several years previously, had supplied the beef that caused the illnesses in question.

14.4 Meaning of 'Defect'

The Consumer Protection Act does not hold a producer liable for all the harm caused by his products: he may only be liable if his product is defective. It is more accurate to speak of liability under the Act as 'defect liability' rather than 'strict liability'. The test of defectiveness is found in

s. 3(1): 'there is a defect in a product ... if the safety of the product is not such as persons generally are entitled to expect'. Four preliminary points should be noted. In the first place, the test refers to the safety of a product, not to its usefulness. The Act gives no remedy in respect of products that simply do not work: for this, the consumer must look to the law of contract. Secondly, the test is framed in terms of public expectations rather than in terms of whether the producer exercised reasonable care and skill (the test in negligence). It is perfectly possible for a product to be regarded as defective even though the producer took all reasonable steps to ensure its safety. Thirdly, the court must consider what the public is entitled to expect: the test is one of legitimate expectations, which are not necessarily the same as actual expectations. Lastly, what the public is entitled to expect depends in part on what information is in the public domain. So, in *A* v. *National Blood Authority* [2001] 3 All ER 289, the case arising out of the use in transfusions of blood contaminated with the Hepatitis C virus, Burton J found that there was at the relevant time no public understanding or acceptance of the infection of transfused blood and so concluded that the public was entitled to expect that the blood would be safe. Of course, once the public has been educated as to the risks associated with a particular product, their legitimate expectations may well be reduced.

In determining what consumers are entitled to expect about the safety of a product, 'all the circumstances shall be taken into account'. This is the phrase used in s. 3(2), which goes on to list certain of those circumstances. In paragraph (a), there is a list of a number of factors which relate to the way the product is marketed or presented (see Schlechtriem, 1989). It seems that the way a product is advertised may be held to affect the legitimate expectations of consumers. If, for example, a car of a particular model is marketed as having advanced anti-locking brakes, it might be regarded as defective if its brakes were in fact no better than those in the standard model. This paragraph also requires regard to be had to any instructions or warnings accompanying the product: a product that is potentially dangerous may be perfectly safe if used correctly. For instance, many drugs are lethal if taken in large quantities: these would not be regarded as defective if the correct dose were clearly stated and a warning against exceeding that dose prominently displayed. But the steps taken to convey the warning or advice to consumers need only be proportionate to the risk. In *Worsley* v. *Tambrands Ltd* [2000] PIQR P95, where the claimant alleged that she had suffered toxic shock syndrome (TSS) from use of the defendants' tampons, Ebsworth J ruled that a short warning about TSS appearing on the box, cross-referenced to health advice on a leaflet inside, was sufficient. It was not necessary to print the full advice on the outside of the package to guard against the possibility that a consumer might throw the leaflet away. Paragraph (b) refers to the use one might reasonably expect the product to be put to. The wording of this paragraph makes it clear that a product may be regarded as defective because its misuse was predictable. Hence, bottles of drugs might be declared defective if not fitted with child-proof tops. Finally, paragraph (c) requires the court to look at the time the product was supplied by the producer: the fact that products supplied more recently have additional safety features built in as standard does not require the court to hold an old product to be defective simply because it lacks those features. If a car were marketed today with no safety belts, it would undoubtedly be regarded as defective; however, a vintage car would not be so regarded as the importance of safety belts was not recognised at the time the car was supplied by its manufacturer.

The public is not entitled to expect that every product will be totally safe. Some products (knives, fireworks, etc.) are inherently dangerous but they are not defective so long as the risks are kept to a minimum and appropriate instructions are provided for their use. Whether or not such a product is defective will depend upon the likelihood and severity of the injuries that might be suffered, weighed against the benefits to be derived from the product's use, and the practicality of giving further warnings or instructions. In *Abouzaid* v. *Mothercare (UK) Ltd* (2001) *Times*, 20 February the claimant was injured when trying to fit the defendants' sleeping bag over his younger brother's pushchair. The sleeping bag was intended to be attached to the pushchair by pulling elasticated straps around it and fastening them with a buckle. As the claimant pulled the straps taut, the elastic slipped from his hand and the recoil caused the buckle to hit him in the eye. The Court of Appeal found that the product was defective because there was an appreciable risk that this might happen, yet no warning had been supplied to this effect. The court attached great significance to the serious consequences that might flow from an injury to the eye: the result might have different if the worst which could have occurred was an impact of elastic on the hand (at [27], per Pill LJ). By contrast, where a group of claimants alleged they had suffered burn injuries from being scalded by excessively-hot coffee sold at the defendant's restaurants, Field J ruled that the coffee was not a defective product as the public expected precautions to be taken against the risk of scalding injuries only in so far as it remained possible to buy hot drinks at temperatures at which people wanted to drink them (*B* v. *McDonald's Restaurants Ltd* [2002] EWHC 490).

This risk-utility inquiry is appropriate in every case where the allegation is of a 'design defect' in respect of a standard product (i.e. one which corresponds with the producer's specifications). As the approach here is very similar to that undertaken in the tort of negligence, which also applies a risk-utility approach, some commentators have doubted whether the remedy under the Act is any more effective than that at common law (see, e.g., Owen, 1996), especially when the effect of the 'development risks' defence is taken into account (see 14.7). But, if a product turns out to present an unacceptable risk of injury, it will be regarded as defective even if the producer could not reasonably have been aware of the risk at the time of supply (*Abouzaid* v. *Mothercare (UK) Ltd* (2001) *Times*, 20 February, where liability arose under the statute but not at common law; see further 8.1). In addition, even though the producer may benefit from the development risks defence where the risks were truly unknowable, this remains a far cry from fault-based liability because it is immaterial that he took reasonable steps to ascertain the risks or even that he acted upon what then appeared to be the best scientific or technical advice (see further 14.7 below).

There is perhaps more scope for liability under the Act in respect of 'manufacturing defects' or other cases of non-standard products (where the product in question possesses a harmful characteristic that sets it apart from the 'standard' model). Yet even at common law, as we have seen, the courts have proved themselves very ready to impose liability where something has gone wrong in the production process, treating the presence of the defect as raising a strong inference of negligence. But, in negligence, it is theoretically open to the producer to argue that some product variation is inevitable and that it is not unreasonable to supply products of a particular type even though a few of them might not be as safe as the others. This may not prevent liability arising under the Act. In *A* v. *National Blood Authority* [2001] 3 All ER 289, the claimants had been infected with the Hepatitis C virus when they received transfusions of blood which had been obtained from the defendants. The latter argued that it could not reasonably be expected that every batch of their blood would be free from contamination, as contamination was an unavoidable risk in a small minority of cases. So the public was only entitled to expect that there had been 'legitimately expectable' testing and precautions; they should not 'expect the unattainable'. This submission was rejected by Burton J, who ruled that its effect was 'to reformulate the expectation as one that the producer will not have been negligent or will have taken all reasonable steps' (p. 335) and hence to undermine the strict liability that the legislation was intended to introduce.

It should be noted, however, that *A* was a case in which the risk of contamination was not generally known. The public was therefore entitled to expect that blood used for transfusions would be 100 per cent clean. Where, by contrast, a degree of product variation is accepted by the general public, the situation may well be different. This is one possible explanation for the decision of Ian Kennedy J in *Richardson* v. *LRC Products Ltd* [2000] PIQR P164. Here the action was brought against the manufacturer of a condom which split as the claimant had sex with her husband; the claimant consequently conceived and claimed damages for the unwanted pregnancy. The learned judge ruled that the mere fact that the condom had split did not prove that it had been defective: although it was naturally enough the user's expectation that a condom would not fail, the manufacturer had never claimed that no condom would ever fail and 'no-one has ever supposed that any method of contraception intended to defeat nature will be 100 per cent effective' (p. P171).

14.5 Who Can be Liable Under the Act?

The primary liability under the Act is upon the producer of a product. 'Producer' is defined in s. 1(2) as one who manufactures a product, or wins or abstracts it, or carries out any process upon it to which essential characteristics of the product are attributable. This definition gives rise to a number of complexities which centre around the crucial distinction drawn in s. 1(2) between products which have been 'manufactured, won or abstracted' and those which have not. In the case of products not 'manufactured, won or abstracted', liability under the Act will only arise if 'essential characteristics' of that product are attributable to any process which has been carried out on it. This leaves us with a three-stage inquiry. First, we have to ask whether the product we are concerned with has been manufactured, won or abstracted. Secondly, if the answer to that question is 'No', we have to determine whether any 'process' has been carried out upon the product. Lastly, in such cases we have to decide whether that process has given the product certain 'essential characteristics'.

To conduct the first part of our enquiry, we have to know what the words 'manufactured, won or abstracted' mean. Clearly anything that is man-made comes within the meaning of 'manufactured': the word itself means, literally, 'made by hand' but clearly extends to things made by machine. It seems equally clear that substances like coal that are mined come within the definition of those that are 'won or abstracted'. On the other side of the line come agricultural products, which are neither won nor abstracted but may be processed (see below). Beyond these paradigm cases, there is considerable doubt as to where to draw the line between those products which are, and those which are not, 'manufactured, won or abstracted'. In order to ensure effective consumer protection, courts should be encouraged to take a broad view of this phrase so that, for example, blood taken for transfusion should be treated as 'abstracted' from the blood donor.

Passing over these difficulties, we discover more obscurity when we come to the second stage of our enquiry. At this stage we have to ask whether a product which has not been 'manufactured, won or abstracted' has had any process carried out on it. Shells washed up on the seashore are certainly not 'manufactured, won or abstracted': if they are polished, can they be said to have undergone a process? Again, courts should be encouraged to adopt a generous interpretation: anything that is done deliberately to a product, in an attempt to adapt it for some use, should count as a process.

The third issue is whether the process carried out on the product has given it 'essential characteristics'. This phrase gives rise to enormous problems of definition. Take the simple example of a carrot. Is it an essential characteristic of a carrot bought from the supermarket that it has had its leaves removed and all the dirt shaken off it? What if it has been sorted into a selection of carrots of the same size and put in a plastic bag? Or if it has been peeled and washed? Or grated? Our intuition tells us that the fact that carrots have been grated is an essential characteristic of those carrots. Equally, we are inclined to view a carrot bought from the supermarket as just a carrot unless we have paid more for it because it has, for instance, been peeled and washed. However, when it comes to formulating a rule to distinguish these cases, and to apply to borderline cases, we come unstuck. It seems likely the courts will address this issue in a very impressionistic way, relying on the notorious 'elephant test': 'Don't ask me to describe it, but I know one when I see one'.

The justification for 'channelling' liability to the producer of the products is that he is best placed both to absorb the loss (typically by taking out insurance) and to do something about the defect by making his product safer. However, a number of other people may, depending on the circumstances, be treated as equivalent to the actual producer of a product and be held liable under the Act. These are anyone who 'has held himself out to be the producer of the product' (e.g. supermarkets who sell 'own-brand' goods), anyone who imported the product in question into the EC ('the importer'), and anyone who has at any time supplied the defective product to another. In the case of suppliers, liability will arise only if they are unable to identify their supplier or, alternatively, the importer or actual producer of the product. These provisions are found in s. 2(2)–(3) of the Act.

14.6 Who Can Recover Under the Act?

As a general rule, anyone who suffers personal injury or property damage that is caused by a defective product may recover to the full extent of his loss. The Act makes no distinction between those who are injured while using the product and those who are mere bystanders injured by someone else's use of the product. The main restrictions on the right to recover relate to property damage. No compensation may be awarded in respect of property damage in three cases. The first case is given in s. 5(2): where the damage is to the product itself or to any product supplied with the product in question comprised in it, no liability arises under the Act. This provision means that, if you buy a car which is fitted with a faulty engine that blows up, you cannot claim under the Act for the cost of a replacement engine: the engine is 'the product itself'. Neither can you recover for the cost of repairing the bodywork should that be damaged by the explosion: this is damage to a product (the car) which was supplied with the defective product (the engine) 'comprised in it'. This corresponds to the rule in the common law of negligence that damage to the product itself is pure economic loss and not recoverable (though note the possibility that at common law certain things might be regarded as 'complex structures' so that damage to one part of the structure, even though caused by another part of the same structure, would still be regarded as damage to 'other property': see 5.2). The second case in which property damage gives rise to no liability is where the damaged item is not both of a type that is ordinarily intended for private use and intended by the plaintiff mainly for his own private use (s. 5(3)). Hence, a barrister has no claim under the Act if a leaky pen damages his courtroom attire, but he would have if the pen were to damage the clothes he uses for lazing about the house. The final case is where the total property damage complained of is valued at no more than £275. This case is dealt with by s. 5(4) of the Act, the purpose being to cut out trivial claims for property damage.

The simple word 'cause', of course, obscures a great many complicated issues (see ch. 9). Of particular note in the present context is its use in Civil Law countries, in which it encompasses rules of remoteness or 'legal cause'. It would seem to be possible for an English court to justify applying the *Wagon Mound* foreseeability rule in cases under the Act, and perhaps the principle of *volenti non fit iniuria* too, on the grounds that these rules are entailed by the word 'cause' (see chs 10–11).

14.7 Defences

The Act lists a number of specific defences in s. 4(1)(a) to (f):

(a) '[T]he defect is attributable to compliance with any requirement imposed by or under any enactment or with any Community obligation...'

Suppose a statute requires children's toys to be coated with a certain flame-resistant substance. Many children prove allergic to the substance and suffer severe rashes. The manufacturer would have a defence under this paragraph. However, if the statute did not require, but merely permitted, him to use that substance, the defence would not avail him. The statutory permission would, however, almost certainly be conclusive proof that the product was not defective.

(b) '[T]he person proceeded against did not at any time supply the product to another...'

'Supply' is the term used in the 1987 Act, although the Directive uses the phrase 'put into circulation'. According to the definition in s. 46(1) of the Act, supplying goods covers not only selling, hiring out or lending the goods but also making a gift of them, as well as other specified acts done in connection with them. Initially, it seems that this defence was designed to deal with the case where the product is stolen from its place of manufacture, but it clearly applies in other situations as well, for example, where the product injures an employee whilst still on the production line. The question of waste products is more problematic. It is clear that strict liability may arise if the manufacturer were to sell his waste products or even to give them away, but the discharge of waste into (say) a river appears not to fall within the meaning of 'supply' under the 1987 Act. Nevertheless, it is arguable that it counts as putting the waste product into circulation under the Directive (see further Stapleton, 1994, pp. 337–9), and it seems that the general interpretative obligation in s. 1(1) may require the English courts to give 'supply' a wider meaning than that which the seemingly-exhaustive wording of s. 46(1) prima facie suggests.

A product may be supplied or put into circulation even though it never leaves the manufacturer's control, as where a patient receives hospital treatment involving use of medicine or some other preparation made up in the hospital dispensary. It follows that, on such facts, the hospital authority would not be able to avail itself of the defence (*Veedfald* v. *Århus Amtskommune* [2001] ECR I-3569).

(c) The supply was not with any business motive falling within s. 4(1)(c).

Liability only attaches to those who supply products with what might loosely be called a business motive. This result is ensured by s. 4(1)(c) which allows a defendant a defence that he at no time supplied the product in the course of business or with a view to profit. Thus, if you give your home-made jam to be sold off for charity in the local church fête, you will not be liable under the Act if it makes those who eat it sick, though you may still be liable in the common law of negligence. Equally, if you bring back souvenirs from your holiday in Australia which you give to your relatives, you will face no liability under the Act if they prove to be dangerous even though you have imported and supplied the goods. However, the supply of a product may be in the course of business even though no charge is levied for it, as in the case of a product which is manufactured at the public expense and used in connection with medical treatment on the National Health Service (*Veedfald* v. *Århus Amtskommune* [2001] ECR I-3569).

(d) The defect did not exist in the product at the time it was supplied by the defendant.

This defence protects a manufacturer whose product has become dangerous because it has been interfered with after it has left his control. However, certain products should be designed so they cannot be interfered with (e.g. containers for prescription drugs should have child-proof tops) and a product might be regarded as defective because it lacks this design feature.

(e) '[T]he state of scientific and technical knowledge at the [time the product was supplied by the producer] was not such that a producer of products of the same description as the product in question might be expected to have discovered the defect if it had existed in his products while they were under his control...'

This is the most important and controversial defence of all. Often known as the 'development risks' defence, it was included in the Directive after enormous pressure from manufacturers, particularly in the pharmaceutical industry. They alleged it would be unfair to hold them liable for risks (e.g. the side-effects of a particular drug) they could not be expected to detect, and that to do so would impede technological innovation. Member states were left to choose whether or not they would include this defence in their domestic legislation; the UK was among those countries that did.

At first glance, the form in which the defence appears in the Consumer Protection Act seems more generous to producers than the Directive would allow. Whereas the Directive stipulates that the defence will only avail a producer where 'the state of scientific and technical knowledge at the time when he put the product into circulation was not such as to enable the existence of the defect of the defect to be discovered' (art. 7), the defence in s. 4(1)(e) of the Act requires only that the state of knowledge was such that 'a producer of products of the same description as the product in question might be expected to have discovered the defect'. On its own, this could be seen as more generous than the Directive in that it asks what might reasonably be expected of producers of a particular product rather than what was possible given the state of scientific knowledge. However, in infringement proceedings brought against the United Kingdom by the European Commission (*European Commission* v. *United Kingdom* [1997] All ER (EC) 481), the European Court of Justice ruled that there was no clear conflict between the Act and the Directive. The UK courts could be relied upon to interpret s. 4(1)(e) so as to achieve the result which the Directive had in view, in accordance with their general interpretative obligation under s. 1(1). In particular, contrary to the argument advanced by the Commission, s. 4(1)(e) did not make the defence available simply because a producer in the industrial sector in question could not reasonably have been expected to know of the risk: the question was whether *any* scientific and technical data that was 'accessible' at the time the product was put into circulation was such as to enable the existence of the defect to be discovered. Whether or not scientific and technical information is accessible appears to depend upon its place of origin, and the language and circulation of the publications in which it is carried, so that (to use an example suggested by Advocate General Tesauro) the defence would not be precluded by proof that a brilliant researcher in Manchuria had identified the defect in a Chinese-language scientific journal which was not disseminated outside the region at the relevant time. (The same would also apply to unpublished research retained within the laboratory or research department which carried it out: *A v National Blood Authority* [2001] 3 All ER 289, 327 per Burton J, who noted (p. 326) that the Advocate General's example might not work if the product were one for which Manchuria were especially known.) Provided the information is accessible, however, it is immaterial that it represents the most advanced level of scientific and technical knowledge that exists, even (it appears) if at the time it was considered an eccentric view.

If the existence of a defect is known to be theoretically possible, this prevents the defendant from relying upon the development risks defence even if there is no known way of discovering its presence in an individual product or of preventing its occurrence. An argument to the contrary was rejected by Burton J in *A* v. *National Blood Authority* [2001] 3 All ER 289, where the defendants had known of the risk that some batches of their blood might be contaminated by the Hepatitis C virus but claimed that contemporary screening techniques did not allow them to identify whether any particular batch was contaminated. Deciding that the development risks defence did not apply on such facts, the learned judge stated (p. 342): 'Once the *existence of the defect* is known, then there is the risk of that defect materialising in any particular product'.

(f) The defect in the product is wholly attributable to the design of another product in which it was comprised or to compliance with instructions given by the producer of that other product.

Note that, even though a manufacturer who supplies component parts or raw materials to another to be incorporated into a more complex product may escape liability under the Act by virtue of this defence, he may yet be liable under the common law. This may be so if he should have known better than the subsequent producer and pointed out the errors of his ways.

Outside the s. 4 defences, the defendant may also rely on the defence of contributory negligence. Express reference is made to this defence in s. 6(4). Yet the defence of *volenti non fit iniuria*, which often arises on the same facts, is not mentioned at all in the Act: it may be that it is encompassed by the concept of 'legal cause'. One defence is expressly ruled out by the Act: by virtue of s. 7, the defendant cannot rely on any provision that purports to exclude or limit liability under the Act.

Summary

14.1 At common law, consumers have remedies in respect of harm caused by defective products under the law of contract (within the constraints imposed by the doctrine of privity) and the tort of negligence.

14.2 The Consumer Protection Act 1987 was enacted in order to comply with the European 'Product Liability' Directive, which was a response to public concern after disasters such as the Thalidomide tragedy. Its most notable feature is that it removes the need for those injured by a product to establish fault on the part of the producer. The extent to which the Act will in practice improve on the common law of negligence is, however, disputed.

14.3 Under the Act, 'product' means any goods or electricity, including component parts and raw materials. The term 'goods' probably includes building materials (but not the buildings into which they are incorporated) and sources of information such as books and computer software.

14.4 The test of defectiveness under the Act is whether the product is as safe as persons generally are entitled to expect (the 'public expectations' test). This test is the source of many criticisms of the Act which allege it is insufficiently radical. Such criticisms have most force in the context of design defects.

14.5 The primary liability under the Act is upon the producer of a product, though 'own-branders', importers and suppliers (in some circumstances) may be held liable.

14.6 Anyone who suffers injury or property damage caused by a defective product can recover under the Act, though there are some limitations on the recovery of property damage.

14.7   The Act lists a number of specific defences, of which the most important and controversial is the 'development risks' defence. The exclusion of liability under the act is prohibited.

Exercises

14.1   What are the comparative advantages and disadvantages of the law of contract and the tort of negligence as remedies in respect of defective products?

14.2   Does the Consumer Protection Act 1987 actually advance the interests of consumers?

14.3   What problems does the definition of 'product' under the Act give rise to?

14.4   Explain how design defects differ from manufacturing defects. Do the courts approach them in the same way? If not, why not?

14.5   What goals were the framers of the legislation trying to achieve in selecting those who could be liable under the new products liability regime?

14.6   What do the limitations imposed on the recovery of property damage under the Act tell us about the interests that the law is trying to protect?

14.7   What is the 'development risks' defence? Should it be allowed?

14.8   What improvements, if any, could still be made to the law of product liability?

---

15   Breach of Statutory Duty

15.1 **Introduction**

Each year Parliament enacts a substantial number of statutes that impose duties on public bodies, private individuals and others. Some of these statutes specifically create a detailed scheme of civil liability of a tortious nature. The Occupiers' Liability Acts 1957 and 1984, the Animals Act 1971 and the Consumer Protection Act 1987 are all examples. Claims brought under these statutes are often described as actions for breach of statutory duty. While there is nothing inherently wrong with this description, claims under these statutes do not create any of the problems normally associated with the tort of breach of statutory duty. The creation of an express tortious action in these cases is clear and the person who has suffered loss has his remedy in the statute.

Our concern in this chapter is with those statutes that impose duties but are either silent on the question whether Parliament intended a civil action to lie for breach of that duty, or provide some other sanction for such a breach. If the breach of the statute is determined to give rise to an action then the common law treats this as a nominate tort (*Thornton* v. *Kirklees Metropolitan BC* [1979] QB 626, 642). The difficulty faced by the courts is to determine which statutes do, and which do not, give rise to such liability. A tortious remedy is obviously available where Parliament has made express provision for it, but it does not follow from the fact that Parliament has included no provision for such a remedy that none exists.

It might be thought that, given the enormous volume and disparate coverage of modern legislation, Parliament would articulate clearly whether or not it intends there to be a civil remedy. Unfortunately, it does not always do so. It is true that Parliament does sometimes make clear that no civil remedy lies for breach of statute (for examples, see: Health and Safety at Work Act 1974, s. 47(1); Safety of Sports Grounds Act 1975, s. 13; Guard Dogs Act 1975, s. 5(2)(a)). There are also examples where a statute states expressly that breach of duty constitutes a tort (Building Act 1984, s. 38; Resale Prices Act 1976, s. 25(2), (3); Race Relations Act 1976, s. 57; Sex Discrimination Act 1975, s. 66). Too often, however, legislation is enacted that makes no express provision either in favour or against the provision of a civil remedy. The difficulty which this failure to provide for the consequences of a statutory breach presents the courts prompted Lord Du Parcq to say in *Cutler* v. *Wandsworth Stadium Ltd* [1949] AC 398, 410:

'To a person unversed in the science or art of legislation it may well seem strange that Parliament has not by now made it a rule to state explicitly what its intention is in a matter which is often of no little importance, instead of leaving it to the courts to discover by a careful examination and analysis of what is expressly said, what that intention may be supposed probably to be ... I trust, however, that it will not be thought impertinent ... to suggest respectfully that those responsible for framing legislation might consider whether the traditional practice, which obscures, if it does not conceal, the intention which Parliament has, or must be presumed to have, might not be safely abandoned.'

Lord Du Parcq's suggestion has not, unfortunately, been taken up. It may be that this is for political reasons: Staughton LJ suggested in the Court of Appeal in *M* v. *Newham BC* [1994] 4 All ER 602, 627 that it might be politically embarassing to make clear in a statute that there should be no common law remedy where a public authority fails to perform its statutory duty. Whatever the reason, the difficulty of ascertaining Parliament's intention remains and it is with that issue that this chapter is concerned.

15.2 Inferring the Existence of the Tort

The problem that the courts face in any case where the statute is silent on whether or not there should be a civil remedy is to discern the intention of Parliament on a matter that has not been expressly resolved by the language of the statute. The courts must determine whether Parliament did or did not *intend* to confer an action on this particular claimant. Although the factors to be considered by the court in answering this question are relatively well settled, their application in any particular case is unlikely to be straightforward. Indeed Lord Denning protested in one case that, '[t]he dividing line between the pro-cases and the contra-cases is so blurred and so ill-defined that you may as well toss a coin to decide it' (*Ex Parte Island Records Ltd* [1978] Ch 132, 135). A number of attempts have been made to bring some order and consistency to the problem of whether or not a civil remedy was intended.

In some early cases on breach of statutory duty, courts went so far as to hold that where Parliament has created a duty by statute the common law should provide a remedy to a person injured by breach of it (*Couch* v. *Steel* (1854) 3 El & Bl 402). Thus Coke said, 'whensover an act of Parliament doth generally prohibit any thing the party grieved shall have his action for his private reliefe' (2 Inst 163). A relatively modern expression of this approach can be found in the judgment of Greer LJ in *Monk* v. *Warbey* [1935] 1 KB 75. His Lordship said (p. 81), 'prima facie a person who has been injured by the breach of a statute has a right to recover damages from the person committing it unless it can be established by considering the whole of the Act that no such right was intended to be given'. However, to the extent that this dictum ever represented the law, it can no longer be supported.

Until recently the approach most favoured by the courts was based on the application of two presumptions which were first stated by Lord

Tenterden CJ in *Doe dem. Murray, Lord Bishop of Rochester* v. *Bridges* (1854) 1 B & AD 847. There he said (p. 859):

'[A]nd where an Act creates an obligation, and enforces the performance in a specified manner, we take it as a general rule that performance cannot be enforced in any other manner. If the obligation is created, but no mode of enforcing its performance is ordained, the common law may, in general, find a mode suited to the particular nature of the case.'

Modern support can be found for this approach in *Lonrho Ltd* v. *Shell Petroleum Co Ltd* [1982] AC 173. However, in *Lonrho* Lord Diplock, with whom the other Lords agreed, articulated two exceptions to the presumption against actionability where the statute provides a specific mode of enforcement, e.g. through a criminal penalty (p. 185):

'One starts with the presumption ... that "where an Act creates an obligation, and enforces the performance in a specified manner ... that performance cannot be enforced in any other manner" ... there are two exceptions to this general rule. The first is where ... it is apparent that the obligation or prohibition was passed for the benefit or protection of a particular class of individuals ... The second exception is where the statute creates a public right (i.e., a right to be enjoyed by all those of Her Majesty's subjects who wish to avail themselves of it) and a particular member of the public suffers ... "particular, direct and substantial" damage "other and different from that which was common to all the rest of the public".'

The approach may be justified on the basis that the presumptions tell the legislature how a court will respond to the use of different legislative drafting techniques. The court assumes that the legislature knows what the presumptions are and, if it gives no express direction as to actionability, it is assumed that the legislature has done this with full knowledge of what the judicial response will be.

In several of the most recent cases, courts have emphasised that Lord Tenterdon's presumptions are merely 'indicators' of Parliament's intention and have adopted a much more fluid approach to the recognition of private rights of action, treating a number of factors or indicators as relevant to the discovery of the legislative intent (*X (Minors)* v. *Bedfordshire County Council* [1995] 2 AC 633, 731; *Olotu* v. *Home Office* [1997] 1 All ER 385). No one indicator is conclusive in favour or against liability. As Lord Browne-Wilkinson made clear in *X (Minors)* v. *Bedfordshire CC*, 'There is no general rule by reference to which it can be decided whether a statute does create such a right of action but there are a number of indicators' (see also *Olotu* v. *Home Office* [1997] 1 All ER 385, 393 per Lord Bingham CJ). Thus, as is the case in the tort of negligence (when deciding whether a duty of care is owed), determining whether an action lies for breach of statutory duty is a complex question.

The courts will have regard to several indicators that may be treated as more or less compelling according to the circumstances. In the next section we consider some of the factors that the courts are likely to consider in any particular case.

15.3 Ascertaining Parliament's Intention

Where the Statute Provides an Alternative Method of Enforcement

Where a statute provides for a penalty to be paid for a breach of the duty a presumption will arise that this was the only remedy intended. In *Atkinson* v. *Newcastle and Gateshead Waterworks Co* (1877) LR 2 Ex.D 441 the defendants were, by s. 42 of the Waterworks Clauses Act 1847, under a duty to keep water in their pipes under a certain pressure. Failure to comply with this section subjected the defendants to a penalty of £10. In breach of the section the defendants failed to maintain this pressure, as a result of which firemen were unable to save the plaintiff's house from being gutted by fire. The plaintiff brought an action for damages for breach of the section. The Court of Appeal held that the plaintiff's action failed since the penalty was intended to be exclusive. It cannot have been the case, according to the court, that Parliament intended the defendants to become 'gratuitous insurers of the safety from fire ... of all the houses within the district over which their powers were to extend'. Such a 'presumption' may also exist where the statute provides an administrative remedy by way of complaint to a minister or some administrative tribunal (*Scally* v. *Southern Health and Social Services Board* [1992] 1 AC 294).

Where the Statute is Passed for the Benefit of a Particular Class of Persons

Where a provision is passed for the benefit of a particular class of persons the traditional view is that an action for breach of statutory duty will lie. In *Groves* v. *Lord Wimborne* [1898] 2 QB 402, a workman was injured because of a failure to fence a dangerous piece of machinery. The Court of Appeal held an action would lie for damages despite the fact that the statute provided only for a penalty. Section 5(3) of the Factory and Workshop Act 1891 (see now Provision and Use of Work Equipment Regulations 1998 (S1 1998/2306, reg. 11) provided that, '[a]ll dangerous parts of the machinery ... shall either be securely fenced, or be in such position or of such construction as to be equally safe to every person employed in the factory as it would be if it were securely fenced'. This section, the court said, was passed for the benefit and protection of a specified group, namely employees. In the words of Vaughan Williams LJ, 'where a statute provides for the performance by certain persons of a particular duty, and someone belonging to a class of persons for whose benefit and protection the statute imposes the duty is injured by failure to perform it, prima facie, and, if there be nothing to the contrary, an action by the person so injured will lie against the person who has failed to perform the duty'. So also in *Ex Parte Island Records Ltd* [1978] Ch 132, a majority of the Court of Appeal held that musicians had a right of action for breach of s. 1 of the Dramatic and Musical Performers' Protection Act 1958. Section 1 provides that 'if a person knowingly – (a) makes a record, directly or indirectly from or by means of the performance of a dramatic or musical work without the consent in writing of the performers ... he shall be guilty of an offence under this Act'. Although the only 'remedy' provided by the Act was a criminal penalty, the Court held that the Act was passed for the protection of a particular class of individuals, namely musical performers, and therefore an action would lie for breach of statutory duty.

Where, however, the duty is imposed for purposes of a general or social nature and not for the benefit of a particular class an action will not generally lie. So in *Atkinson* v. *Newcastle and Gateshead Waterworks Co*, the obligation to maintain the water in the pipes at a certain pressure was held to be owed to the public in general and not to any member of the public whose property was damaged as a result of the breach. One of the leading cases on this point is *Cutler* v. *Wandsworth Stadium Ltd* [1949] AC 398, which raised the question whether an action for breach of statutory duty lay in respect of breach of s. 11(2)(b) of the Betting and Lotteries Act 1934. This section provided that 'the occupier of a licensed track ... shall take such steps as are necessary to secure that ... there is available for bookmakers space on the track where they can conveniently carry on bookmaking in connection with dog races run on the track'. The appellant, a bookmaker, claimed injunctions prohibiting the respondents from excluding him from the track and also requiring them to secure a space for him where he could conveniently carry on bookmaking. The House of Lords refused to grant the injunctions sought. The purpose of the Act was to protect the public interest by regulating the operation of betting at dog tracks. Any benefit which accrued to bookmakers was wholly incidental to this purpose. The Act was not intended to confer a right upon an individual bookmaker who presented himself at the stadium to demand a place on the track.

While the question whether a statute was passed for the benefit of a particular class of persons is undoubtedly treated by the courts as a relevant factor in deciding whether a civil action for breach of statutory duty was intended, it is important for two reasons not to give too much emphasis to this question. First, as was made clear by the House of Lords in *X (Minors)* v. *Bedforshire CC* [1995] 2 AC 633, the mere fact that legislation is introduced primarily for the protection of a limited class of persons does not mean that a cause of action will always exist. Such a 'purpose' is only a 'pointer in favour of imputing to Parliament an intention to create a private law cause of action' (p. 378, per Browne-Wilkinson). Other factors may militate against the existence of a cause of action (cf. *R* v. *Deputy Governor of Parkhurst Prison, ex parte Hague* [1992] 1 AC 58). Second, whether or not a statute is held to have been passed for the benefit of a particular class of persons or the public at large is inevitably a question of impression. In *Cutler*, for example, was it not strongly arguable that the Act had been passed for the benefit of bookmakers, among others? It could legitimately be said that bookmakers constituted a sufficiently identifiable group and possessed sufficiently common interests to constitute a defined group. As we have already mentioned, the real issue in all these cases is whether Parliament intended not merely to benefit a class of the public but to create a cause of action for breach of statutory duty.

The Availability of Alternative Remedies

Where the statute creates a duty but makes no provision as to the method of enforcement, it is not always the case that the injured person will be without remedy. He may for example have, apart from any possible remedy for breach of statutory duty, an alternative remedy of a private or public law nature. Where this is the case, the question arises whether the existence of the alternative remedy precludes a remedy for breach of statutory duty.

Where there is an existing private law remedy, the prevailing view seems to be that Parliament cannot have intended to provide an action for breach of statutory duty. So, for example, in *Scally* v. *Southern Health and Social Services Board* [1992] 1 AC 294 the House of Lords (adopting the reasoning of Kelly LJ in the Court of Appeal [1991] 4 All ER 573n) held that no remedy in damages for breach of statutory duty lay for breach of an employer's statutory duty to give his employee information about pensions and pension schemes (Contracts of Employment and Redundancy Payments Act (Northern Ireland) 1965, s. 4(1)). A full and effective remedy already existed in the form of recourse to a tribunal which was empowered to order that the information be given. So too in *Phillips* v. *Britannia Hygenic Laundry Co* [1923] 2 KB 832, the Court of Appeal decided that breach of the Motor Car (Use and Construction) Order 1904, which governed the conditions to be met by motor cars on the highway, did not give rise to an action for breach of statutory duty. One of the reasons given by the court for refusing to impose such liability was that rights of road users 'have always been sufficiently protected by the common law' (per Bankes LJ).

It is suggested that this reluctance to recognise a claim for breach of statutory duty where an alternative remedy already exists is sensible. Where there is already a remedy in damages it is unlikely that Parliament intended to duplicate that remedy. However, it should be noted that the availablity of an alternative private law remedy has never been treated as decisive. As Ormrod LJ made clear in *McCall* v. *Abelesz* [1976] QB 585, such a 'formula, though useful, must be cautiously applied for it purports to do just what Lord Simonds declined to do in *Cutler's Case*, namely to formulate a set of rules' (p. 595). So, for example, an action was held to lie in *Groves* v. *Lord Wimborne* [1898] 2 QB 402 notwithstanding that an action would have existed in negligence for breach of the employer's non-delegable duty and in *Monk* v. *Warbey* [1935] 1 KB 75, where the defendant allowed an uninsured driver to drive a vehicle without insurance contrary to Road Traffic Act 1930, s. 35 (see now Road Traffic Act 1988, s. 143), this was held to give rise to an action for breach of statutory duty notwithstanding the fact that the plaintiff had a private law remedy in negligence against the (uninsured) driver. It may be, as Weir (2000, p. 200) has pointed out, that the decision is justifiable because it fits well into the policy of the law that 'victims of *negligence* on the highway should not only be entitled to compensation, but should actually receive it'. However, the case was distinguished in *Richardson* v. *Pitt Stanley* [1995] QB 123 (criticised by O'Sullivan, 1995) where the Court of Appeal held that the Employers' Liability (Compulsory Insurance) Act 1969, which made it an offence for an employer to fail to insure against liability for injury sustained by its employees in the course of their employment, did not give rise to an action for breach of statutory duty. One of the reasons given was that the employer's liability for the injury was already well provided for under the common law, whereas in *Monk* v. *Warbey* the owner of the motor vehicle would, absent the statute, have had no direct liability to the injured party.

Where the only remedy is a 'public law' remedy via an application for judicial review the cases are less consistent. In *R* v. *Deputy Governor of Parkhurst Prison, ex parte Hague* [1992] 1 AC 58 Lord Jauncey considered the existence of a public law remedy was relevant to the question whether an action for breach of statutory duty was intended and refused to find that breach of the Prison Rules was actionable at the instance of the plaintiff. A similar conclusion was reached by the Court of Appeal in *Olotu* v. *Home Office*, where the plaintiff had, in breach of the Prosecution of Offences Act 1985 and reg. 5(3)(a) of the Prosecution of Offences Act (Custody Time Limits) Regulations 1987, been detained for 81 days after the expiry of her custody time limit. The court, in that case, treated the availability of public law proceedings for habeas corpus and mandamus as a 'strong indicator' that no action for breach of staturory duty was intended. However, in other cases the existence of the general remedy of judicial review has not deterred the courts from finding that a statute was intended to give rise to an action for damages. There is much to be said for the approach taken in *Hague*. Parliament must surely be presumed to know of *all* existing remedies, whether of a private or a public law nature. It seems unsatisfactory to ignore the existence of such rights in considering whether or not Parliament intended there to be an action for breach of statutory duty. Yet against that it might be argued that the public law remedy is of little use to the claimant who wants damages rather than, say, mandamus.

The Ambit of Discretion

In considering whether an action should lie, the courts have in a number of cases given considerable weight to the nature of the duty imposed on the defendant. Where the duty imposed is of a very broad nature giving a large measure of discretion to the person on whom the duty is imposed it is unlikely to give rise to an action for breach of statutory duty. Thus, in *X (Minors)* v. *Bedfordshire CC* one of the reasons for refusing to allow an action for failure to bring care proceedings (Children and Young Persons Act 1969, s. 2) or for failing to take a child into care (Child Care Act 1980, s. 2) was that the duties imposed were made conditional upon the exercise by the local authorities of subjective judgement that they had good grounds for doing so. Lord Browne Wilkinson (p. 379) found it

> 'impossible to construe such a statutory provision as demonstrating an intention that even where there is no carelessness by the authority it should be liable in damages if a court subsequently decided with hindsight that the removal, or failure to remove, the child from the family either was or was not "consistent with the duty to safeguard the child".'

It will be recalled that in the tort of negligence, when considering the liability of public authorities, courts have drawn a distinction between policy and operational decisions (see 7.3). Broadly speaking it is only in respect of the latter that a duty of care can arise. Similarly, where a statute entrusts policy matters to a particular person or body, it is unlikely that a court will find that any duty thereby imposed gives rise to an action for breach of statutory duty. As Lord Browne-Wilkinson said in *X (Minors)* v. *Bedfordshire CC* (p. 371):

> 'Where Parliament has conferred a statutory discretion on a public authority, it is for that authority, not for the courts, to exercise the discretion; nothing which the authority does within the exercise of the discretion can be actionable at common law. If the decision complained of falls outside the statutory discretion, it *can* (but not necessarily will) give rise to a common law liability. However, if the factors relevant to the exercise of the discretion include matters of policy, the court cannot adjudicate on such policy matters and therefore cannot reach the conclusion that the decision was outside the ambit of the statutory discretion. Therefore a common law duty of care in relation to the taking of decisions involving policy matters cannot exist.'

By way of contrast to cases where the statute grants a wide discretion, the courts have shown themselves willing to infer the existence of the tort where a penal statute enacts a safety standard to protect against personal injury (an area of considerable practical importance, see, for example, *Groves* v. *Lord Wimborne* [1898] 2 QB 402). The willingness of the courts to allow an action in the case of industrial safety legislation probably stems, at least in part, from a desire to give monetary compensation to an injured workman and to ensure that employers do not evade safety standards imposed by statute (see also *Monk* v. *Warbey* [1935] 1 KB 75 in the context of road traffic cases). Whatever the reason, most industrial safety legislation has been interpreted to give rise to an action for the tort of breach of statutory duty (actionability is to be presumed in relation to regulations under the Health and Safety at Work Act unless the contrary is stated: s. 15). Where, on the other hand, the effect of allowing an action for breach of statutory duty would be to protect the claimant against an economic loss the courts have been markedly less willing to find that a civil action was intended. In *Cutler*, for example, to have given bookmakers a right of action would have protected the bookmaker against an economic loss, i.e. the loss of business as a result of being excluded from the track (see also *Richardson* v. *Pitt-Stanley*).

Where the Enactment is Purely Regulatory

Where an enactment is purely regulatory, contravention of a duty laid down by the statute is unlikely to give rise to an action for breach of statutory duty. As Lord Browne-Wilkinson said in *X (Minors)* v. *Bedfordshire CC* (p. 364):

> 'Although the question is one of statutory construction and therefore each case turns on the provisions of the relevant statute, it is significant that your Lordships were not referred to any case where it has been held that statutory provisions establishing a regulatory system or a scheme of social welfare for the benefit of the public at large had been held to give rise to a private right of action for damages for breach of statutory duty.'

Thus, in *Hague*, for example, Lord Goff, in deciding that breach of the Prison Rules was not actionable, gave as a reason that the Prison Rules are 'regulatory in character and were never intended to confer private rights on prisoners in the event of breach'. So too in *Olotu*, the Court of Appeal, in holding that there could be no action for breach of the custody time limit prescribed under s. 22 of the Prosecution of Offences Act and regulation 5(3)(a) of the Prosecution of Offences Act (Custody Time Limits) Regulations 1987, laid considerable stress on the regulatory function of the provisions. The object of the Act and regulations made thereunder was to expedite the prosecution of criminal offences and, if such expedition was lacking, to ensure that defendants did not languish in prison for excessive periods. The elaborate scheme of duties backed up by administrative procedures made it impossible to infer that Parliament intended there also to be a cause of action for breach of statutory duty.

The Insurance Position

A factor which has occasionally been relied upon by a court is the insurance position. In *Atkinson*, for example, the Court of Appeal was clearly influenced by the burden that would be imposed on the defendant if it was to allow an action for breach of statutory duty. The effect of allowing such an action would be to make the defendants gratuitous insurers against fire of all the houses in their area (see also *Capital & Counties plc* v. *Hampshire County Council* [1997] QB 1004). In this situation it was thought that the householder was a better loss bearer than the defendants because he was more likely to have insurance and to be able to obtain it more cheaply to cover such an eventuality. Similarly, the courts have generally been unwilling to allow a civil action for breach of any road traffic legislation. This unwillingness reflects the view that to allow an action in such cases may be too harsh on the defendant. For example, having a defective rear light is an offence under road traffic legislation. This is the case even where the light has gone out while the defendant is driving the motor vehicle and had no way of knowing that the light was no longer functioning. The refusal to allow an action in such cases may also reflect the view that the claimant can easily acquire insurance to protect himself against non-negligent accidents and the loss should, therefore, fall on him. Against this, it might be argued that the defendant will be, or should be, insured and, as he is also the cause of the loss, that he is the more suitable loss-bearer. This view can be seen reflected in *Monk* v. *Warbey* [1935] 1 KB 75. The Court of Appeal held in that case that the failure to insure was actionable and its decision is surely justifiable on the basis that the very purpose of the section was to ensure that third-party insurance was available to protect accident victims. Where, as here, that insurance had not been taken out the court was justified in giving the victim the additional protection of an action against the owner of the vehicle. *Monk* v. *Warbey* is, however, almost the only case where a breach of road traffic legislation has been held to give rise to an action in tort and it seems unlikely that such actions will be extended any further.

Where the Statute Creates a Public Right and the Claimant Suffers Special Damage

In *Lonrho* Lord Diplock mentioned a second exception to the 'presumption' of non-actionability where the statute provides a penalty. This arose according to his Lordship where the statute creates a public right and a particular member of the public suffers 'special' damage. It is not, however, altogether clear in what circumstances this 'exception' is to apply. The widest view would treat all criminal and administrative law duties as creating public rights, any violation of which causing special damage would be actionable by the individual affected. The actual decision in *Lonrho* shows that this is too broad an interpretation of Lord Diplock's words. An Order in Council had been made making it a criminal offence to supply oil to what was then Southern Rhodesia. It was alleged by the plaintiffs that, in breach of this Order, the defendants had supplied oil to Southern Rhodesia. The plaintiffs argued that as a result of this they had suffered loss and claimed damages in respect of the breach. The House of Lords held that the plaintiffs had no civil action for breach of this Order. Lord Diplock, delivering a speech with which the other Lords agreed, held that no public right was created. The whole purpose of the Order was to withdraw a pre-existing right, i.e. to trade with Southern Rhodesia, and not to create a right to be enjoyed by the general public.

While it is the case that not every breach of a 'public' right causing special damage gives rise to liability, the exact circumstances in which such a breach does give rise to liability is far from clear. More detailed discussion of this point should be sought in specialist texts: see Stanton (1986).

15.4 Elements of the Tort

Persons Protected and Risk Covered

Once it has been determined that an action for breach of statutory duty lies the court must decide whether the damage suffered is recognised by the statute in question. This is a question of judicial interpretation. The leading case is *Gorris* v. *Scott* (1874) 9 Exch 125. An Order was made in pursuance of the Contagious Diseases (Animals) Act 1869 requiring sheep or cattle being transported by ship from any foreign ports to ports in Great Britain to be put in pens of certain dimensions. The defendant did not have any such pens on board his ship and the plaintiff's sheep were washed overboard in a storm and drowned. The plaintiff brought an action for damages for breach of the Order. The court held that the action failed. The statute had been passed, according to the judges, merely for 'sanitary purposes, in order to prevent animals in a state of infectious disease from communicating it to other animals with which they might come into contact'. The purpose of the statute was not to prevent them being drowned. So too, in *West Wiltshire District Council* v. *Garland* [1995] Ch 297 it was held that the statutory duty of a district auditor (s. 15 Pt III Local Government Finance Act 1982) gave rise to a civil action by the local authority whose accounts were audited by him, but no duty was owed to an individual officer of the authority since Parliament intended that district auditors should be able to criticise local authority officers without fear of an action.

The Duty Imposed

Second, it must be considered what the content of the duty imposed is and whether, on the facts, such duty has been broken. The answer to this question depends upon the interpretation of the statutory language used. The wide variety of language used in different statutes has meant that a variety of different standards have been imposed. Some statutes impose strict or even absolute duties; others, however, impose more qualified, 'negligence' duties. There is no rule of thumb used to determine which duty has been imposed. Each statute must be construed carefully to determine what the standard imposed is. The following cases are illustrative.

Statutes imposing absolute standards are rare. However, an example of an absolute duty can be seen in the case of *Galashiels Gas Co Ltd* v. *Millar* [1949] AC 275 (HL, Sc). By s. 22(1) of the Factories Act 1937 it was provided that 'every hoist or lift shall be properly maintained'. The House of Lords held that the section imposed an absolute duty to maintain a lift in an efficient state. Proof of any failure in a lift mechanism, therefore, established a breach of duty, even if it was impossible to foresee the failure before the event or explain it afterwards. Here liability is truly independent of fault.

More often a statute will impose a qualified duty: e.g. to do what is 'practicable' or 'reasonably practicable'. There are many reported cases which interpret qualified standards of this type. Space considerations, however, preclude full consideration being given to these. The point that must be recognised is that it is always necessary to turn to the statute to discover what the content of the duty imposed on the defendant is. One case may be cited by way of illustration. In *McCarthy* v. *Coldair Ltd* [1951] 2 TLR 1226 an employee fell when a short ladder he was ascending slipped. He claimed that his employer was in breach of what became s. 29(1) of the Factories Act 1961, which provided that '[T]here shall, so far as is reasonably practicable, be provided and maintained safe means of access to every place at which any person has at any time to work' (see now Workplace (Health, Safety and Welfare) Regulations 1992, reg. 12). The employer was held to be in breach of his duty. It was accepted by the court that it would not ordinarily be reasonably practicable to station a man at the foot of a short ladder, because this would be a disproportionately expensive way of avoiding a small risk. However, in light of the fact that the ladder was being used on a semi-glazed floor which had been splashed by paint, the court felt that the risk was greatly increased such that it would be reasonably practicable to take the steps suggested by the worker.

15.5 **Reform**

The approach taken by English courts to the question whether an action for breach of statutory duty lies has been the subject of criticism. First, it is argued that adoption of a presumption or 'indicator' approach to determine Parliament's intention is misguided because in most cases the silence of the statute on the question of civil liability points to the conclusion that Parliament either did not have the problem in mind or that it deliberately omitted to provide for it. Secondly, the matters considered by the courts are unhelpful in that they serve to produce no clear result. The courts are thus left with considerable discretion as to whether liability should be imposed. Thirdly, it is hard to explain why it is that the so-called indicators are relevant in assessing Parliament's intention. For example, why should it be the case that an action should be presumed where a duty is owed to a particular class but not where it is owed to the general public. It is surely strange that a duty which Parliament considers to be so important that it provides that it should be owed to the public at large will generally not give rise to an action whereas a less important duty owed to a particular class will, prima facie at least, be presumed to give rise to an action.

As a result of this dissatisfaction various alternatives have been suggested. The Law Commission has argued for a statutory presumption that an action will lie unless express provision to the contrary is made in the statute (Law Commission, 1969). This suggestion attracted severe criticism when placed before Parliament and seems unlikely to be adopted. It does at least have the merit of introducing clarity into a notoriously unclear area but it does so, surely, by imposing an unacceptably wide liability. Moreover the suggested presumption of actionability pays no attention to the areas in which it would operate. Rights and duties should be imposed only where they are shown to be required. The Law Commission proposal ignores this. It might be argued, however, that it would have the merit of focusing Parliament's attention on the question of actionability and would at least answer the criticism that Parliament's intention was being frustrated.

An alternative approach is to regard breach of statutory duty as a particular species of negligence. Any breach of such a duty should be treated either as negligence *per se* or as evidence of negligence. Under this approach, breach of statutory duty would no longer be considered a nominate tort but instead would be subsumed under the tort of negligence. This is the approach favoured in most American jurisdictions (where the view adopted by the majority of States is that breach of a statutory duty is *per se* negligence) and in Canada (where breach of statute is evidence of negligence only). Perhaps the strongest argument in favour of the 'statutory negligence' approach, in either of its forms, is that it gets rid of the necessity for the courts to ascertain what was Parliament's intention. English courts would no longer be able, were such an approach to be adopted, to shield their decisions from public scrutiny behind the presumptions. At present, however, any significant reform seems unlikely.

Summary

15.1 In this chapter we have sought to answer the question when statutes that impose duties but are either silent as to whether a civil action should lie for breach or impose some other form of liability for breach give rise to a civil action for breach of statutory duty.

15.2 In determining whether a statute gives rise to a civil action for breach of statutory duty, the courts seek to determine whether Parliament intended there to be an action.

15.3 In ascertaining the intention of Parliament the courts consider a number of indicators. These include, but may not be limited to: (a) provision of an alternative method of enforcement; (b) a legislative intention to benefit a particular class of persons; (c) the availability of alternative remedies independent of the statute; (d) the ambit of discretion; (e) the regulatory character of the enactment; (f) the insurance position, and; (g) the creation by the statute of a public right, interference with which carries special damage to the claimant.

15.4 Once it has been determined that an action for breach of statutory duty lies, the court must decide whether the damage suffered is recognised by the statute in question. The court must also determine what the content of the duty imposed is.

15.5   A number of proposals have been made to reform the law relating to breach of statutory duty. They have involved either the replacement of the existing presumptions with a new one (Law Commisssion) or treating breach of statutory duty as a particular species of negligence.

Exercises

15.1   I'm the Parliamentary Draftsman,
I compose the country's laws,
And of half the litigation
I'm undoubtedly the cause. (J.P.C., *Poetic Justice*, 1947)

Is this true? (see Williams, 1960, from where this 'poem' is taken)

15.2   What factors do the courts take into account in determining whether a statute gives rise to an action for breach of statutory duty?

15.3   What effect does the existence of a private or public law remedy have on the question whether Parliament intended there to be a civil action?

15.4   What policy considerations, if any, do the courts take into account in considering whether a statute was passed for the benefit of a particular class of persons? Does the fact that a statute was passed to benefit a particular class of persons mean that an action will always lie?

15.5   Why have the courts not imposed civil liability for breach of statutory duty in the area of motor vehicles?

15.6   What proposals for reform have been suggested? Which do you prefer?

16 Trespass to the Person

16.1 **Introduction**

In most societies, protection of an individual's bodily integrity is likely to
rank high on the agenda of interests considered worth protecting. It is
understandable, therefore, that one of the earliest remedies provided by
English law was for forcible wrongs against the person. Such wrongs were
remediable by commencing an action using a writ of trespass. The writ of
trespass emerged in the thirteenth century. It originally existed in a semi-
criminal form and if the defendant did not appear to answer the writ he
would be outlawed while, if convicted, he was liable to a fine or
imprisonment in addition to being liable to the claimant in damages.
However, by the end of the medieval period the tort action had shed its
criminal characteristics. In the civil law the writ of trespass dealt with
direct interference with the person in three types of case which correspond
to the modern torts of assault, battery and false imprisonment.

By the eighteenth century, trespass was differentiated from the other
main writ providing a remedy for tortious misconduct, namely the action
of trespass on the case (later simply called case), by its requirement that
the interference be direct. Case provided a remedy where the harm was
indirectly caused. The tendency in later years, however, has been to
associate case with negligently caused harm and trespass with intentional
wrongs. The main cause of this belief is the fact that the modern law of
negligence is derived from the action on the case. As case was associated
with negligence, so trespass came to be seen as a tort of intention.
However, unlike negligence, which provides a remedy for both indirectly
and directly caused harm, trespass has retained the requirement that the
harm must be directly caused.

16.2 **Trespass and Negligence**

The essence of trespass to the person is that it affords a claimant
protection against direct invasions of his bodily integrity. In this regard
the early common law imposed a very strict responsibility on the
defendant. Although it is doubtful that a person would ever have been
liable in trespass where he was totally without fault, it was certainly once
true that where the claimant had established a direct interference the
defendant would be liable unless he could establish some justification or
excuse. However, in 1959 it was clearly established that in order to succeed
in trespass it was not enough for the claimant simply to prove a direct
invasion of his bodily integrity. In *Fowler* v. *Lanning* [1959] 1 QB 426 the
plaintiff's statement of claim alleged that on a certain date and at a certain

place 'the defendant shot the plaintiff' and that by reason thereof the plaintiff suffered injury. The defendant objected that this statement of claim disclosed no cause of action in that it did not allege that the shooting was intentional or negligent. Diplock J held that to succeed in trespass it was not enough to prove a direct act (the defendant shot me); the plaintiff had in addition to prove that the direct act was done intentionally or negligently.

The result of *Fowler* v. *Lanning* is that, where the injury is unintended, whether it is a direct or indirect consequence of the defendant's act, the claimant will only succeed where he can show that the defendant's conduct was unreasonable (i.e. negligent). Thus, in most cases of unintentional injury the claimant will bring his action in negligence rather than trespass because there is no need in negligence, unlike trespass, to prove that the injury was a direct consequence of the act. To a large extent, therefore, the rules of negligence have overtaken those of trespass where the defendant's act is unintentional.

Difficulties, however, remain in determining the true relationship between trespass and negligence. In particular, can an action for trespass still be brought where the defendant's act was unintentional? This question is important in cases where the claimant suffers no damage because, unlike negligence where *damage* is the gist of the action, the tort of trespass is actionable *per se* (i.e. without proof of damage). The point was considered by the Court of Appeal in *Letang* v. *Cooper* [1965] 1 QB 232. The defendant negligently drove his Jaguar car over the legs of the plaintiff, who was sunbathing in a car park. More than three years after the accident the plaintiff sued the defendant in negligence and trespass. The plaintiff admitted that her action in negligence was time barred by the Limitation Act 1939 but argued that her alternative claim in trespass was not. Her argument succeeded at first instance but was rejected by the Court of Appeal. One reason given for the decision was that the three-year limitation period applicable to actions for personal injury in negligence also applied to *any* cause of action, including trespass to the person, whereby damages for personal injuries were claimed. This part of the decision must now be seen as wrong in light of the decision of the House of Lords in *Stubbings* v. *Webb* [1993] AC 498. Lord Griffiths, who delivered the leading judgment, held that an action for trespass did not fall within s. 11 of the Limitation Act 1980 but within s. 2. Section 11, which provides for a basic period of limitation of three years (which can be extended: sections 14 and 33), applies to 'any action for damages for negligence, nuisance or breach of duty ... where the damages claimed by the plaintiff ... include damages in respect of personal injuries to the plaintiff or other person'. Section 11 was intended to be limited to causes of action for personal injury caused by *accidents*; personal injury caused by a trespass to the person was not accidental and therefore did not come within the section (for a criticism of *Stubbings* v. *Webb*, see Mullis, 1997). An alternative ground for the decision in *Letang* does, however, remain of continuing importance. Lord Denning MR, with whom Danckwerts LJ agreed, held that where the defendant inflicts the injury unintentionally no action would lie for trespass. He agreed with the judgment of Diplock J in *Fowler* v. *Lanning*, but said (p. 240):

'I would go this one step further: when the injury is not inflicted intentionally, but negligently, I would say that the only cause of action is negligence and not trespass. If it were trespass, it would be actionable without proof of damage; and that is not the law today.'

In Lord Denning's opinion, therefore, trespass is truly an intentional tort in that only the intentional application of force can give rise to an action in trespass. Where the act is unintentional, the correct and only cause of action is negligence.

Lord Denning's opinion in *Letang* v. *Cooper*, that a cause of action will only lie in trespass where a person intentionally applies force directly to another, has not found universal support. For example, in the same case, Diplock LJ stated that trespass could be committed negligently but thought that there were no significant differences between an action for unintentional (but negligent) trespass and an action in negligence. Also, in Canada and Australia support still exists for the view that there may be a negligent trespass. While the point still remains open, the better view is that expressed by Lord Denning. In the first place little is lost to the claimant by depriving him of a right to sue in trespass where the application of force is unintentional. If damage is suffered he has an action in negligence. Where no damage is suffered it is almost inconceivable that the claimant would want to bring an action. In the second place, Lord Denning's view achieves a welcome clarification of the law by classifying liability according to the mental state of the defendant.

16.3 **Assault and Battery**

Where one person intentionally and without consent applies force directly to another, this constitutes a battery. Where he intentionally makes a threat that causes another reasonably to apprehend the immediate infliction of a battery on him, that is an assault. It should be noted that in some of the cases courts use the word *assault* to describe what is in essence a *battery*. The reason for this is that most assaults end in a battery and the result is often described as an assault and battery or just an assault. Despite this terminological confusion, the distinction between the two torts is fairly clear. Thus, it is an assault for A to point a loaded gun at B who fears being shot but if A fires the gun and the bullet hits B that is a battery. It is an assault for A to drive a car at B such that B fears being hit but it is a battery to hit him. Often battery and assault go together, but they need not. For example, if A sneaks up behind B without B hearing him and hits him over the head there is a battery but no assault. Similarly if A shakes his fist at B that is an assault but not a battery.

Although extensively analysed in the context of criminal law, the meaning of 'intention' has not been much discussed in tort cases. If it can be shown that it was the defendant's *purpose* to apply force directly to the claimant then liability will be established. Proof that he knew with substantial certainty that the above consequences would occur would also be sufficient to ground liability. However, an intention to *injure* is probably not necessary. Provided it can be established that the defendant intentionally applied force directly to another, then liability is established even if the consequences were not intended (*Wilson* v. *Pringle* [1987] QB 237). More difficult is the question whether recklessness will suffice. There is little or no authority on this question but such as there is (e.g. *Ball* v. *Axten* (1866) 4 F & F 1019) is not inconsistent with the view that recklessness may be sufficient. There is also no English authority on the question whether the transferred intent doctrine, recognised in the criminal law context, applies in trespass actions. American cases have recognised the existence of such a doctrine (*White* v. *Davis* (1982) 18 BR 246 (Bkrtcy, Va)) and some courts have even been prepared to allow the transfer of intention from one intentional tort to another. Thus, in one case (*Altieri* v. *Colasso* (1975) 362 A 2d 798), where the defendant threw a stone in the direction of A intending to frighten (assault) him (A) but hit B the court held the defendant liable to B for battery.

Battery

As we have seen, there is no requirement in establishing a battery that the defendant intended to cause *harm*. All that the claimant need show is that the defendant intended to touch the body of the claimant. This might be thought to give rise to intolerable difficulties. Is it, for example, a battery if I shake your hand in greeting, or if I slap you on the back in congratulations when you tell me your examination results? An early attempt to distinguish acceptable from unacceptable touchings was made by Holt CJ in *Cole* v. *Turner* (1704) 6 Mod 149 where he said 'the least touching of another in anger is a battery'. While there is nothing inherently wrong with this statement, in that if A touches B in anger his act will generally amount to a battery, some behaviour not committed in anger will still be a battery. Examples of such behaviour might include an unwanted kiss or restraining someone to question them, but not restraining them merely to attract their attention (*Collins* v. *Wilcock* [1984] 1 WLR 1172). Despite the fact that the test is plainly inadequate to explain all the cases, Holt CJ's words were held by the Court of Appeal in *Wilson* v. *Pringle* [1987] QB 237 to lay down the appropriate test. Croom Johnson LJ held that for there to be a battery there must be 'something in the nature of overt hostility'. Hostility, he said should not be equated with ill-will or malevolence: an act can be 'hostile' even if not committed in anger. Instead he appears to suggest that it means little more than an objectionable touching. This, it is suggested, is not very helpful: all it does is restate the very question that needs to be answered.

A better approach is that suggested by Robert Goff LJ in *Collins* v. *Wilcock*. There he said that a touching will only amount to a battery where it does not fall within the category of physical contacts 'generally acceptable in the ordinary conduct of general life'. Thus being jostled in the underground during the rush-hour would not be a battery, whereas an unwanted kiss or perhaps an over-exuberant shove in the back may be. Although this approach was thought impracticable by Croom Johnson LJ in *Wilson* v. *Pringle*, Lord Goff (as he has become) restated his views in the House of Lords in *F* v. *West Berkshire Health Authority* [1990] 2 AC 1, 73 where he explicitly rejected any requirement of 'hostility' as unnecessary. It is likely, therefore, that this will be the approach adopted in future cases.

Historically, a cause of action in trespass only lay where the touching was the direct or immediate result of the defendant's act. This requirement was well stated by Blackstone J in *Scott* v. *Shepherd* (1773) 2 Black W 892 where he said, 'where the injury is immediate, an action in trespass will lie; where it is only consequential, it must be an action on the case'. Thus it has been said that, where a person throws a log of timber onto the highway and another person falls over it and is injured, this injury is only consequential and an action for trespass will not lie. By way of contrast, if the log were to hit someone that would give rise to an action in trespass because the contact would be direct and immediate. In the modern law the claimant is still required to show that the touching was the direct result of the defendant's act, but the courts have stretched the concept of directness so far that it is doubtful whether today this requirement provides a substantial hurdle for many claimants. The facts of *Scott* v. *Shepherd* itself illustrate the broad nature of the concept. The defendant threw a lighted squib made of gunpowder into a covered market where a large number of people were collected. The squib fell onto B's stall and he picked it up and threw it onto C's stall; C likewise threw it away and in doing so hit the plaintiff. The court, by a majority, held that an action for trespass would lie. The intermediate acts of B and C were, somewhat surprisingly, found not to have broken the chain of directness between the defendant and the plaintiff.

In the more recent case of *DPP* v. *K* [1990] 1 WLR 1067, K, a 15-year-old schoolboy, took some concentrated sulphuric acid out of a chemistry lesson and went to the lavatory. On hearing footsteps outside the lavatory door he poured the acid into a hand and face drier. Another pupil turned the drier on and was badly burnt when acid spurted out. K was convicted of assault occasioning actual bodily harm. Although the case has subsequently been held to be wrongly decided on another ground, it is no less interesting from our point of view because it appears to have been assumed that the contact was the direct, as opposed to consequential, result of the defendant's act. Surely, this is a case where the touching was consequential on the act of the defendant in putting the acid into the drier. If the case is correctly decided on this point then leaving a log on the highway over which someone falls should also be seen as the direct cause of the claimant's harm, as should the setting of a trap for the claimant. While other, generally older cases, have taken a narrower view as to the meaning to be ascribed to the word 'direct', the requirement no longer appears to be a serious bar to recovery and could be abandoned (as it has been in the United States).

Assault

The essence of an assault is the making of a threat that places the claimant in reasonable apprehension of an immediate battery to himself. It is not every threat, however, that will suffice to give rise to liability. Clearly, if A points a loaded gun at B, the pointing of the gun will suffice. In such a case by virtue of the pointing of the gun the claimant reasonably apprehends the infliction of an immediate battery. Would the position be any different if A, without a gun, had said 'I am going to shoot you dead'? In other words, can the speaking of words amount to an assault? Although such authority as there is is inconclusive, the view most often cited is that of Holroyd J in *R* v. *Mead and Belt* (1823) 1 Lewin 184. He said there that 'no words or singing are equivalent to an assault'. This view reflects the fact that in many cases the uttering of mere words will not give rise to fear of an *immediate* battery. In our example, the speaking of the words 'I am going to shoot you dead' by a person without a gun would probably lack immediacy. The speaker would have to go away, find a gun and then return before he could put the threat into effect.

The fact that mere words are used should not, however, mean that in every situation there will be no assault. For example, if a mugger were to say to his victim, 'your money or I will beat you up' this could amount to an assault even in the absence of any threatening gestures by the mugger. Similarly, if the defendant, who was engaged in beating up A, were to say to the claimant 'you are next', this too could amount to an assault. What is important, therefore, is not how the threat is conveyed but whether what is conveyed is enough to place the claimant in reasonable apprehension of an immediate battery.

Although older English decisions emphasised the immediacy requirement, more recent (criminal) cases suggest that the mood of the courts towards verbal (and non-verbal) threats may be changing. In the case of *R* v. *Ireland* [1998] AC 147 (which involved an appeal against a successful criminal prosecution on three counts of assault occasioning actual bodily harm contrary to s. 47 of the Offences Against the Person Act 1861), the House of Lords held that the making of a large number of telephone calls to three women and remaining silent when they answered was capable of amounting to an assault (see also *Smith* v. *Chief Superintendent, Woking Police Station* (1983) 76 Cr App Rep 234). Such a decision, if applied by a civil court, would effectively make the immediacy requirement redundant. Whether in the light of the enactment of the Protection From Harassment Act 1997 (which would provide protection against such behaviour: ss. 1 and 4) it was wise for the court to stretch the ambit of the crime of assault to punish this defendant must be open to doubt.

Words may not only amount to an assault: they may also have the effect of neutralizing a threat made by a gesture. In *Turbervell* v. *Savadge* (1669) 1 Mod 3, T put his hand on his sword and said to S, 'if it were not assize-time I would not take such language from you'. These words were held to prevent the gesture from amounting to an assault. Their effect was to show that there was no intent. By way of contrast, a phrase such as, 'your money or your life' might (if the threat is sufficiently immediate) be actionable. While the words still negative intent, they do so only by demanding fulfilment of a condition by the claimant. The defendant should not be forced to 'buy' his safety by compliance with a condition and therefore such conditional threats ought to be actionable.

For there to be an assault the claimant must reasonably anticipate the infliction of a battery. Thus, where the claimant has no knowledge of the threat there can be no assault. This point is well illustrated by the American case of *McCraney* v. *Flanagan* (1980) 267 SE 2d 404. The plaintiff brought an action against the defendant for *assault* alleging that he had had intercourse with her without her consent. However, the plaintiff could remember nothing about the alleged assault though it was clear from the physical evidence that intercourse had taken place. The North Carolina Court of Appeals upheld the grant of summary judgment to the defendant. While a *battery* may well have have occured, an *assault* had not. As the court said (pp. 408–9):

> 'The tort of assault occurs when a person is put in apprehension of a [battery] and there is no evidence here that the plaintiff feared, or even knew, that such a contact might occur. She has no recollection at all of the events. Since the interest involved is a mental one of apprehension of contact, it should follow that the plaintiff must be aware of the defendant's act at the time.'

However, there will be an assault if the claimant reasonably anticipates the infliction of a battery even if he is not *in fact* put in a state of fear or terror. It is the claimant's knowledge that is important and not the effect that this knowledge has on his mind.

A related, though distinct, question is whether there is an assault where, although the claimant thinks that the defendant is about to inflict a battery on him, the defendant does not in fact have the necessary means to do so. For example, if a person points an unloaded gun at another does this amount to an assault? In *Stephens* v. *Myers* (1830) 4 Car & P 350 Tindal CJ said, 'it is not every threat, when there is no actual personal violence that constitutes an assault, there must be, in all cases the means of carrying the threat into effect'. This approach finds support in *Blake* v. *Burnard* (1840) 9 Car & P 626 where Lord Abinger CB held that it was not an assault to point an unloaded pistol at another. However, while these cases have not been overruled, other cases (e.g. *R* v. *St George* (1840) 9 Car & P 483) have held that such an act can amount to an assault. In principle, the better view is that expressed in *R* v. *St George*. Where a battery is, in all the circumstances, *reasonably* apprehended this should be enough to constitute an assault.

16.4 False Imprisonment

The tort of false imprisonment is committed when the defendant intentionally and without lawful justification restrains a person's liberty within an area delimited by the defendant. It is not necessary in order to establish the tort that a person be locked up in a prison or restrained within four walls. As was said in the *Termes de la Ley*:

'imprisonment is no other thing but the restraint of a man's liberty whether it bee in the openfield, or in the stocks or in the cage in the street or in a man's own house, as well as in the common gaole; and in all the places the party so restrained is said to be a prisoner so long as he hath not his liberty freely to goe at all times to all places wither he will without baile or mainprise or otherwise.'

Thus, preventing a person from leaving his own house, casting him adrift in a boat or taking hold of him in the street can all amount to false imprisonment.

In order for there to be a false imprisonment the restraint must be total. In *Bird* v. *Jones* (1845) 7 QB 742 the defendants enclosed part of Hammersmith Bridge and put seats in the enclosure for the use of paying spectators of a regatta. The plaintiff insisted on passing along the bridge through the enclosure and climbed over the fence of the enclosure without paying the charge. The defendants then refused to let the plaintiff go forward in the direction he wished to go but told him that he could go back and cross the bridge though not through the enclosure. The court held that this was no false imprisonment. In reaching this conclusion, Patteson J said (pp. 751–2) that there was no imprisonment where 'one man merely obstructs the passage of another in a particular direction, whether by threat of personal violence or otherwise, leaving him at liberty to stay where he is or to go in any other direction if he pleases'.

A difficult decision which at first sight appears to conflict with the decision in *Bird* v. *Jones* is that of *Robinson* v. *Balmain New Ferry Co Ltd* [1910] AC 295. The respondents operated a ferry service between Sydney and Balmain. On the Sydney side a turnstile with an exit and entrance was set up and a notice displayed stating that a penny had to be paid on entering and leaving the wharf. The appellant paid his penny to enter and then changed his mind and sought to leave without paying a further penny. The respondents prevented him from doing so. The Privy Council held that this was not a false imprisonment. How can this be so? Surely it was the case that the plaintiff was wholly restrained within the wharf? If so it would seem to be the case that an action for false imprisonment should have succeeded. One explanation of the case is that the appellant was never completely restrained: he could still have used the ferry, as he had originally intended to do, and gained his freedom unconditionally on the other side. Thus, his contractual path was never closed to him and he was not, therefore, falsely imprisoned.

While this may be a convincing explanation of the case, it is not clear that this was the reason given by the Privy Council for their decision. An alternative view of the reasoning of the court was that there was no false imprisonment because an occupier of premises is entitled to impose reasonable conditions on the manner in which an entrant leaves his premises. On the facts, the Privy Council held that it was reasonable for the ferry company to insist that all persons leaving the wharf paid one penny. The plaintiff had contracted to leave the wharf via the ferry and the payment of one penny was not an unreasonable condition to impose for his leaving by a different route.

A similar case was that of *Herd* v. *Weardale Steel Coal and Coke Co Ltd* [1915] AC 67. A miner employed by the defendants refused, in breach of his contract, to do certain work in his pit. His employers refused to take him to the surface for some time after a cage was available to do so. He sued for false imprisonment. The House of Lords held that his action failed. Clearly, the restraint here was total, the only way out was via the cage to the surface. The court, relying on the decision in *Robinson* v. *Balmain New Ferry Co*, held that the miner had gone down the mine on certain terms and it was not false imprisonment to hold him to the conditions he accepted when he went down. Both cases may, therefore, be authority for the proposition that a landowner's imposition of a reasonable condition on exit may negate false imprisonment.

Such a conclusion is, however, not without difficulty because, if correct, it seems tantamount to recognising an extra-judicial right to imprison for breach of contract. Yet *Sunbolf* v. *Alford* (1838) 3 M & W 247 establishes that English law does not allow a man to be imprisoned for debt. It has been argued, therefore, that these cases are not authority for the proposition that enforcement of a contractual condition may negate false imprisonment but are instead about consent (Tan, 1981). While a person can consent to a deprivation of his liberty (as happened in *Herd* and *Robinson*) he can always, subject to considerations of reasonableness, revoke that consent. A person does not, by consenting to a deprivation of his liberty, tie his hands forever. Thus the issue in *Herd* and *Robinson* was whether the claimants had effectively revoked their consent. It is established law that a revocation of consent need not in every case take immediate effect. The owner of premises who would be unreasonably inconvenienced if required to allow a visitor to leave at once can lawfully restrain him until such time as it is convenient to let him go. It is for this reason that the passenger on a bus has no right to insist on being allowed to alight between stops. This consideration may underlie the decisions in *Herd* and *Robinson* although, as Tan admits, the extent of the delay in these cases must have been close to the limit of what was permissible.

There may be a false imprisonment even in the absence of actual force or direct physical contact. Thus if a police officer informs a person that he is under arrest this, in the absence of lawful justification, will amount to a false imprisonment. It has even been held that requiring a person to come along to a police station and answer some questions may be sufficient. All that is required, therefore, is that there must be some constraint on the person's will such that he believes that he is under restraint. The emphasis is on the impression created in the victim's mind. Given this emphasis it might be thought that a person cannot be falsely imprisoned where he does not know that he is under constraint. However, such a view was rejected in *Meering* v. *Graham-White Aviation Co* (1919) 122 LT 44 where a majority of the Court of Appeal held that knowledge of the constraint was not an essential element of the tort. This view was approved by the House of Lords in a Northern Ireland appeal, *Murray* v. *Ministry of Defence* [1988] 1 WLR 692, although their Lordships made clear that a person who is unaware that he has been falsely imprisoned and has suffered no harm can normally expect to recover no more than nominal damages. Though it is the case that imprisonment is actionable even in the absence of knowledge of the constraint, there must actually be a detention. Thus, it was held in *R* v. *Bournewood Mental Health Trust, ex parte L* [1999] 1 AC 458 that a mentally-ill patient who was sedated and kept in an unlocked room where he was carefully supervised was not detained even though his compulsory detention would have been sought under the Mental Health Act had he attempted to leave the hospital. While it is clearly correct that a detention is required before there can be an actionable false imprisonment, *Bournewood* is by no means easy to reconcile with *Meering* and *Murray* v. *Ministry of Defence*. In both *Meering* and *Bournewood* the imprisonment consisted in the certainty that total restraint would have been enforced had the claimants chosen to leave even though neither had knowledge that this would happen. It is argued therefore that Lord Steyn was correct in his dissent in *Bournewood* when he said that the suggestion that the claimant could go free was 'fairy tale' (p. 475).

The essence of false imprisonment is, as we have seen, the restraint of a person without lawful justification. In most cases this restraint will be of a person who is lawfully at large. A difficult problem is posed by the question whether a person who is lawfully imprisoned can ever complain of false imprisonment in relation to acts subsequent to his lawful imprisonment. This matter was considered by the House of Lords in *R* v. *Deputy Governor of Parkhurst Prison, ex parte Hague* [1992] 1 AC 58 (see Mullis, 1991, pp. 396–8). Allegations were made against the prison authorities by two prisoners. H alleged that in breach of the Prison Rules he had been transferred to another prison and there segregated from other inmates for 28 days. W alleged that he had been falsely imprisoned by being placed in a strip cell overnight. The House of Lords held that no action for false imprisonment could lie in these circumstances. The prison authorities had a complete defence by virtue of s. 12(1) of the Prison Act 1952 which provides that 'a prisoner ... may be lawfully confined in any prison'. This section, their Lordships said, provided a complete defence for the restraint of a prisoner within the bounds of a prison by the governor or someone acting with the governor's authority. Thus where the prisoner was locked up in a part of the prison with the governor's authority there was no room for an argument that the prison authorities were liable for false imprisonment based on any 'residual liberty' of the prisoner's. They further held that holding a prisoner in intolerable conditions could not give rise to liability for false imprisonment because this was to confuse the *fact* of confinement with the *conditions* of confinement. The tort of false imprisonment was confined to remedying the former. They did accept, however, that an action for negligence might lie if a prisoner suffered injury as a result of such confinement. (Even where there is no injury, the prison authorities may now be liable under the Human Rights Act for violating the prisoner's art. 3 right not to be subjected to inhuman or degrading treatment: see *Keenan* v. *UK* (2001) 33 EHRR 913.) While no action lay on the facts of this case, the House of Lords did not wholly reject the possibility of an action being brought by a person who is lawfully imprisoned. The court said that if another prisoner, or a prison officer who acted in bad faith, locked up within the confines of a prison a person who was lawfully imprisoned, this could amount to false imprisonment.

Although no action for false imprisonment lies by reason of the conditions under which a prisoner is kept, a prisoner who is detained beyond his sentence may sue the person responsible for the detention as, once the sentence has expired, the defence of lawful authority ceases to apply. This is so even where the prison governor has acted in good faith and on the basis of existing law. Thus, in *R* v. *Governor of Brockhill Prison, ex parte Evans (No 2)* [2001] 2 AC 19 the House of Lords held that a prison governor who had incorrectly calculated the applicant's release date was liable in false imprisonment from the date on which the prisoner should have been released. This was the case even though the governor had calculated the release date by reference to judicial decisions that were only overruled when the applicant's application for judicial review of the decision fixing her release date was successful.

Can a person (A) be liable for false imprisonment where it is not him but another (B) who imprisons the claimant? Where B is A's employee or agent and is acting under his instructions there is little doubt that A, as principal or employer, would be liable for the imprisonment. More difficult, however, are cases where B is neither A's agent or employee, but, acting on information given by A, B detains the claimant. The paradigm example of this is the case where a police officer arrests a person on the basis of information given to him by a member of the public. In such a case, could either the person who gave the information or the arresting officer be liable for false imprisonment? This was considered by the Court of Appeal in *Davidson* v. *Chief Constable of North Wales* [1994] 2 All ER 597, which held that it would only be in very rare circumstances that a person who gave information to the police would be liable for any subsequent imprisonment. This is surely correct. A decision by a police officer to arrest involves the exercise, on the part of the officer, of an independent discretion. The police officer does not in any real sense act as the informant's agent and the arrest decision is his. Sir Thomas Bingham MR made clear, however, that, if the informant went beyond the mere laying of information before the police for them to take such action as they thought fit and he took steps which, 'amounted to some direction, or procuring, or direct request or direct encouragement that they should act by way of arresting these defendants', then the informant may be liable.

16.5 Intentional Infliction of Physical Harm Other than Trespass to the Person: *Wilkinson v. Downton*

In *Wilkinson* v. *Downton* [1897] 2 QB 57 the defendant, by way of a practical joke, falsely represented to the plaintiff that her husband had met with a serious accident. The plaintiff, believing the story, suffered a violent shock to her system and subsequently became ill. She brought an action against the defendant claiming damages for her psychiatric injury. Wright J held that where a person wilfully does an act calculated to produce an effect on the plaintiff of the kind which was actually produced then a cause of action would arise in the absence of any legal justification. On the facts it was clear that the defendant had to be treated as having intended to induce the plaintiff's illness and, therefore, the plaintiff's claim succeeded.

There have been few cases in English law in which the principle of *Wilkinson* v. *Downton* has been applied. In one (*Janvier* v. *Sweeney* [1919] 2 KB 316) the defendants, who were private detectives, told the plaintiff that unless she produced certain letters then in the possession of her employer they would disclose to the authorities that her fiancé was a traitor. She suffered a 'nervous illness' as a result of these statements. The Court of Appeal held, applying *Wilkinson* v. *Downton*, that her action for damages succeeded. In the more recent case of *Khorasandjian* v. *Bush* [1993] QB 727 the defendant subjected the plaintiff, a former friend, to a campaign of harassment over a period of months. The plaintiff suffered considerable stress as a result of the defendant's behaviour and sought a *quia timet* injunction preventing him from, 'using violence to, harassing, pestering or communicating with' her. At first instance the judge granted the injunction and, by a majority, the Court of Appeal upheld the award. Such an injunction was justified according to the court on the basis, *inter alia*, of *Wilkinson* v. *Downton* which 'established that false words or *verbal threats* calculated to cause and uttered with the knowledge that they are likely to cause and actually causing physical injury to the person to whom they are uttered are actionable' (per Dillon LJ, at 676; see also *Burris* v. *Azadani* [1995] 1 WLR 1372).

What then, in the light of these authorities, is the extent of the principle recognised in *Wilkinson* v. *Downton*? Clearly within the principle are those cases where the defendant makes a *false* statement intending to cause the claimant a psychiatric illness and where such an illness is in fact caused. It also applies to illness caused by verbal threats intended to frighten or terrify the claimant (*Khorasandjian* v. *Bush* and *Janvier* v. *Sweeney*). Although the injury in *Wilkinson* v. *Downton* resulted from a false *statement* there is no reason in principle why the rule should not extend to *acts* (*Khorasandjian* v. *Bush*).

Proof of intention to cause such harm does not appear to be indispensable. Such an intention may be inferred where the consequences which result are the natural and probable result of the defendant's conduct (*Wilkinson* v. *Downton*). However, mere foreseeability that physical or psychiatric injury is likely to occur is not sufficient. What is required is knowledge that the words or conduct are likely to cause, that is to say subjective recklessness as to the causation of, physical or psychiatric injury (*Home Office* v *W* [2001] EWCA Civ 2081, para. 80, per Buxton LJ). There seems to be little reason to confine the principle to cases where a 'nervous' or psychiatric' illness is caused. Thus, if the defendant were to shout at a person riding a bicycle intending to cause him to fall off, any *physical* injury suffered in the subsequent fall would give rise to liability. Further, although some injury must be suffered (so mere distress would not be actionable: *Wong* v. *Parkside Health NHS Trust* [2001] EWCA Civ 1721) a court may issue a *quia timet* injunction in order to prevent the occurrence of the tort in the future where there is 'an *obvious risk* that the cumulative effect of the continued and unrestrained further harassment' would cause a recognisable psychiatric illness (*Khorasandjian* v. *Bush* [1993] QB 72, 736, per Dillon LJ).

The rule in *Wilkinson* v. *Downton* is descended from the action on the case and is not a form of trespass. It is for this reason that the claimant must prove actual loss. What then is the rule's relationship with the trespassory torts (assault, battery and false imprisonment)? At least three views appear tenable. First, liability under *Wilkinson* v. *Downton* should be confined to cases of intentionally but *indirectly* inflicted physical or emotional harm. Thus, it should be seen as a residuary form of liability for intentionally caused personal injury supplementing the trespass torts. Secondly, the tort recognised by *Wilkinson* v. *Downton* should be seen as a separate nominate tort broadly equivalent to the tort of intentional infliction of emotional distress recognised in the USA in Restatement Second of Torts, s. 46. Under that provision, which represents the law in the majority of states in America, liability is imposed where a person intentionally or recklessly inflicts emotional distress upon another and (a) the actor's conduct is extreme and outrageous, (b) the harm intended is severe, and (c) the actual resulting emotional harm is also severe. Although such a view has its attractions in that the well-developed American law on the subject could provide a basis for the development of English law (see Givelber, 1982), little in the existing case law suggests that such a development is likely. Finally, there is the possibility that *Wilkinson* v. *Downton* will be treated as giving rise to a general principle of liability for all intentionally inflicted harms (including economic losses) whether directly or indirectly caused. Such an approach would require a radical restructuring of the existing law and this appears unlikely. For the moment, therefore, it seems likely that the principle will continue to be treated as a separate complementary form of liability covering cases of intentionally but indirectly caused *physical* harm.

16.6 **Protection From Harassment Act 1997**

The common law did not recognise a tort of harassment (*Wong* v. *Parkside Health NHS Trust* [2001] EWCA Civ 1721). Yet harassment, in the sense of something intended to annoy, upset or distress, can cause considerable hurt to its victim. Some types of harassment will of course constitute an assault, battery, trespass to land or some other actionable tort. Thus, if A threatened B on several occasions with immediate violence, B would have an action against B in assault. Other types of behaviour, potentially just as hurtful or frightening for the victim, may not, however, fall within the ambit of an existing nominate tort. Thus, a series of silent telephone calls or the persistent following of another while upsetting and distressing would only rarely be actionable at common law (e.g. where they are intended to result, and do result, in psychiatric illness: *Khorasandjian* v. *Bush*). It is true that remedies had been developed within family law to protect against harassment but these only gave protection to a limited class of people. Growing public concern in the 1990s about harassment and the apparent inability of the law to provide a remedy led Parliament to pass the Protection From Harassment Act 1997 (PHA 1997). Section 1 of the Act makes it an offence to pursue a course of conduct which the defendant knows or ought to know amounts to harassment and by s. 3 of the Act this is civilly actionable. Where a claim under the Act is successful, the victim may recover damages for (among other things) 'any anxiety caused by the harassment and any financial loss resulting from the harassment' (s. 3(2)). Furthermore, while the Act does not expressly provide the court with the power to restrain harassing conduct by injunction, s. 3 allows for a 'claim' in civil proceedings to be brought and this will include the grant of an injunction.

For a claim to succeed under s. 3, there must be a 'course of conduct' which amounts to harassment of another and which the defendant knows or ought to know amounts to harassment of the other. For behaviour to constitute a 'course of conduct' it must involve 'conduct on at least two occasions' (s. 7(3)). There is no requirement that there be any particular period of time between harassing acts. Thus, in theory, two acts of harassment several years apart might constitute a 'course of conduct'. However, the fewer the incidents and the further apart in time they occur, even if they ostensibly arise out of the same quarrel, the less likely it will be that a finding of harassment can reasonably be made (*Lau* v. *DPP* [2000] Crim LR 580). The Act does not provide a definition of harassment. However, in order to constitute harassment, not only must the defendant's conduct (which includes speech: s. 7(4)) be such that a reasonable person would conclude that it amounted to harassment but the defendant must himself either have known or ought to have known that his conduct amounted to harassment of another. A person whose course of conduct is in question ought to have known that his conduct amounted to harassment 'if a reasonable person in possession of the same information would think the course of conduct amounted to harassment of another' (s. 1(2)). Thus, the fact that the defendant intended his conduct as a joke would not prevent an action arising if a reasonable person would have thought that the intended 'joke' amounted to harassment. Obviously within the definition of harassment would be any course of conduct intended to frighten another or put him in fear of violence. However, harassment clearly goes well beyond this and may embrace persistent following, 'door-stepping' by a journalist, silent telephone calls, abusive or offensive letters and even persistent teasing.

It is a defence to show that the course of conduct was pursued for the purpose of preventing or detecting crime (s. 1(3)(a)), or under any enactment or rule of law, or to comply with any condition or requirement imposed by any person under any enactment (s. 3(1)(b)), or that in the particular circumstances the pursuit of the course of conduct was reasonable (s. 3(1)(c)). Whether conduct is reasonable will depend upon the circumstances of the particular case and this may require a court to have regard to article 10 of the European Convention on Human Rights (right to freedom of expression). Thus, a court should be slow to find that political protest or legitimate discussion, even if intemperately phrased, of matters of public interest amount to harassment (see, for example, *Huntingdon Life Sciences* v. *Curtin* (1997) Times, 11 December; *Thomas* v. *News Group Newspapers Ltd* [2001] WL 1535397).

16.7 Damages

Unlike negligence, where proof of damage is an essential element in the cause of action, trespass to the person is actionable *per se* (without proof of any damage). Substantial damages may, therefore, be awarded even where there is no physical injury simply for invasion of the right itself. Thus, a person who is falsely imprisoned is entitled to damages for the loss of his liberty regardless of whether the imprisonment caused him any physical or economic harm and a person who is the victim of a battery is entitled to damages for the invasion of his bodily integrity even if he is not harmed but only affronted, upset or embarassed. Additionally, exemplary damages may be awarded where the trespass occurred either as a result of arbitrary conduct by a government official, or as a result of a deliberate or reckless breach of the law done with a view for gain (see 22.2). The fact that exemplary damages can be awarded in respect of arbitrary conduct by a government official gives trespass an important role in the protection of the liberties of the citizen against infringement by the state.

16.8 Defences to Trespass to the Person

Once the claimant has proved the direct interference that constitutes the trespass, it is for the defendant to justify his action by reference to one of the defences. There are a number of defences to trespass to the person of varying degrees of practical importance. Thus, a parent who punishes a child by locking him in his room or by slapping him, may be entitled to rely on the defence of lawful discipline provided that any steps taken in punishing the child are reasonable. Whether a parent's right to control and discipline its child has been affected by the Human Rights Act is not entirely clear. In *A* v. *United Kingdom* (1998) 27 EHRR 611 the European Court of Human Rights held that English law was incompatible with the

Convention in so far as it failed to protect a child, who had been hit by his stepfather, from inhuman or degrading treatment. However, the decision concentrated on the burden of proof in criminal law and made no adverse comment on the civil law position. Moreover, parental control and discipline are recognised as being part of family life and are therefore protected by art. 8 of the Convention. Although teachers act *in loco parentis* their power to use corporal punishment in disciplining children has been abolished (Education Act 1996, s. 548). Statutory authority can also be a defence and so, in limited circumstances, can contributory negligence (see 11.5) and illegality (see 11.6). The fact that criminal proceedings have already been taken against the defendant may also, in certain circumstances, relieve him of civil liability (Offences Against the Person Act 1861, ss. 42–5). Probably the most important defences in practice are the powers of arrest conferred on police officers, and the more limited powers conferred on private citizens, by the Police and Criminal Evidence Act 1984. Where a police officer or a private citizen carries out a lawful arrest he will commit neither a false imprisonment nor a battery. Reference should be made to texts on constitutional law or civil liberties for details of the powers of arrest. Three defences – consent, self-defence and necessity – are considered in more detail below.

Consent

Where a person consents either expressly or impliedly to a trespass to his person no action will lie. There is some debate over the question whether consent is strictly speaking a defence at all because a defence is something that it is for the defendant to prove. In *Freeman* v. *Home Office (No 2)* [1984] QB 524 McCowan J held that the burden of proving absence of consent was on the claimant thereby implying that absence of consent is an essential element of trespass to the person. While this is probably the prevailing view in English law today (cf. the view in Australia, where McCowan's view has been rejected), it is suggested that Rogers (Winfield and Jolowicz, 2002) is correct when he says (p. 845) that 'as a practical matter, however, the defendant may need to lead evidence to lay a foundation from which the court will infer consent and in modern pleading he would have to raise consent as a specific issue in his defence to the particulars of claim'. In this sense, therefore, consent may be treated as a 'defence'.

Consent can be given expressly, for example, where a patient signs a consent form to an operation. Alternatively, consent may be implied. An example of implied consent can be found in the old American case of *O'Brien* v. *Cunard* (1891) 28 NE 266 where the court held that by standing in line and holding out her arm the plaintiff impliedly consented to being vaccinated (but see Shalleck *et al.*, 1992). Similarly, participants in 'violent sports' impliedly consent to the risks ordinarily incidental to such sports. They do not, however, consent to excessive violence or to deliberate unfair play. The line between the two is, however, by no means easy to draw.

The relevance of consent in a civil action may differ from that in criminal proceedings. While certain consensual activities may be considered so contrary to public policy that they are treated as criminal, it might nevertheless be wrong to allow one consenting participant to sue another. Thus, in the infamous case of *R* v. *Brown* [1992] 2 All ER 552 the Court of Appeal held that the participants in homosexual sado-masochistic 'games' could not rely on the defence of consent to negate their criminal liability. Much stress was laid by the court on the public interest that people should not injure each other for no good reason. While this is clearly a relevant matter when considering a criminal prosecution it is less clear that it is relevant in a civil action where the court is primarily concerned with the reciprocal rights and liabilities of the parties *inter se* (Skegg, 1988, pp. 38–40). Thus, had one of the participants in the activities brought an action for battery it is suggested that his consent should amount to a complete defence. A more difficult question is whether a 16 year old man successfully prosecuted for having 'unlawful sexual intercourse with a girl under the age of sixteen' (Sexual Offences Act 1956, s. 6), to which consent is not a defence, could rely on the defence if sued for battery. The purpose of making such an act criminal must, at least in part, be to protect the girl from her own consent. Should this, therefore, be a case where the defendant cannot rely on consent as a defence? (See Restatement Second of Torts, s. 892C.)

For consent to be valid it must be genuine. Thus, consent obtained by duress would be no defence. So, for example, consent to sexual intercourse obtained by threats of violence would not be valid. But the mere fact that the claimant may feel under 'pressure' to give consent does not necessarily mean that any consent given will not be valid. In *Freeman* v. *Home Office (No 2)* [1984] QB 524, for example, the Court of Appeal held that the consent given by a prisoner to medical treatment was genuine. The institutional pressures imposed in those circumstances were held not to negative the consent given.

Consent will not be valid unless the claimant understands the nature and purpose of the touching. However, as Bristow J made clear in *Chatterton* v. *Gerson* [1981] QB 432, 'once [a person] is informed *in broad terms* of the nature of the procedure which is intended and gives her consent, that consent is real'. The difficulty is to determine what information is relevant to the 'nature' and 'purpose' of the touching and what is merely collateral to it. In circumstances where the consent was induced by deceit or given under a misapprehension as to the nature and purpose of the touching the courts have held that the consent was vitiated. In *R* v. *Williams* [1923] 1 KB 340, for example, it was held that there was no valid consent by a woman to sexual intercourse where she was told that this was therapy for her voice. There the deceit was as to the nature and purpose of the touching.

More uncertainty surrounds the situation where the claimant is aware of the nature and purpose of the touching but unaware of its harmful consequences. This issue was considered in *R* v. *Clarence* (1888) 22 QB 23. The defendant had sexual intercourse with his wife with her consent.

Unknown to the wife, the defendant had gonorrhoea and she became infected. The defendant was charged with 'assault occasioning actual bodily harm' and 'unlawfully and maliciously inflicting grievous bodily harm'. Thus, it was necessary to prove that the defendant's wife had not consented to the touching. The court held that the woman's consent was valid even though she had no knowledge of her husband's condition.

Despite, or perhaps because of, its antiquity this case has attracted much academic criticism. Grubb and Pearl (1990) have argued that the case should be narrowly confined. *Clarence* was a decision relating to a criminal prosecution for a serious offence and the result that was reached was not surprising given the prevailing social and sexual mores of the time. It should not, however, be treated as authority for the proposition that in a civil action for trespass to the person consent to a touching will always be valid if the person touched knows the nature and purpose of the touching but does not know of its potentially harmful consequences. It is suggested that two situations need to be distinguished. Where, *unknown to the claimant*, the defendant intends to cause the harmful consequences, or where he is reckless or negligent as to those consequences, then consent should not be a defence. However, where the harmful consequences are not a reasonably foreseeable consequence of the consented-to touching then the defendant should be able to rely on the defence of consent. Thus, if A, knowing he has Aids, has intercourse with the claimant intending to infect him, consent to the sexual act should not bar recovery by the claimant. However, if when A and B are indulging in 'horseplay', something 'snaps' when A picks B up causing B to be paralysed, then consent should amount to a defence to any action brought by B against A. Unless it could be said that B was negligent as to the consequences caused, B's consent to indulge in the 'horseplay' should bar his recovery (see *Hellriegel* v. *Tholl* (1966) 417 P 2d 362).

Finally, something should be said about consent in medical cases as this is probably the most important area of the defence's operation. As a general rule, the principles explained above apply equally to medical cases. Indeed, many of the leading authorities involve medical treatment. Thus, provided the broad nature of the proposed operation is explained to a patient any consent given will excuse what would otherwise be a battery (see, for example, *Chatterton* v. *Gerson*). Particular difficulties arise, however, in medical cases in three types of case: the treatment of children, the treatment of the mentally disabled or ill and the treatment of the unconscious. In the case of children, s. 8 of the Family Law Reform Act 1969 provides that a minor between the ages of 16 and 18 can give an effective consent to surgical, medical or dental treatment as if he were an adult. As regards a child who has not reached his sixteenth birthday, the House of Lords held in *Gillick* v. *DHSS* [1986] AC 112 that a child can give effective consent to medical treatment providing he has the ability to understand what is involved in the medical procedure proposed. In *Gillick* itself, Lord Scarman said that in relation to contraceptive advice and treatment this would involve not only understanding the reasons for the doctor touching the child and the purposes behind the touching but also an understanding of the wider social and moral implications. In the case of a very young child, consent must be sought from a proxy (usually a parent) in order for the touching to be lawful. Even where a child is competent, its power to consent to treatment is concurrent with that of its parents and a parental consent may render lawful treatment to which the child objects (*Re R* [1991] 3 WLR 592). Where, however, a child is competent to give a valid consent and does so, the parents' objections to the child's treatment will not invalidate the consent (*Re W* [1992] 4 All ER 627). In all cases involving a minor, the court may in the exercise of its inherent jurisdiction override a child's consent to, or refusal of, treatment.

So far as the treatment of adults is concerned, the starting point is that everyone has the capacity and right to decide whether to consent to or refuse medical treatment. The central importance of individual autonomy means that this presumption is a heavy one to rebut. Once it is established that a person did have the capacity to make a decision, then that is conclusive of the consent issue even if he made his decision for 'religious reasons, other reasons, for rational or irrational reasons or for no reason at all' (*Re MB* [1997] 2 FCR 541, 553). The authoritative test for capacity to consent was set out by the Court of Appeal in *Re MB* (pp. 533–4):

'The inability to make a decision will occur when
(a) The patient is unable to comprehend and retain the information which is material to the decision, especially as to the likely consequences of having or not having the treatment in question.
(b) The patient is unable to use the information and weigh it in the balance as part of the process of arriving at the decision.'

Where a person is suffering from a mental disorder or is mentally ill, the mere fact of that disorder does not of itself mean that the person is unable to give a valid consent. Whether he is able to give a valid consent depends upon whether the test in *Re MB* is satisfied. Where a mentally ill person is incapable of giving consent, treatment may, however, be justified on the grounds of necessity. This defence is considered below. A person who is unconscious will be unable to make a decision within the test in *Re MB*. As in the case of the mentally ill who are unable to give a valid consent, medical treatment may be justified on the grounds of necessity. In *F v West Berkshire Health Authority* [1990] 2 AC 1 the House of Lords held that treatment of the unconscious or mentally ill could not be justified by any extension of the notion of implied consent; it would be a pure fiction to suggest that such patients impliedly agreed to medical treatment in their best interest. English courts have also resisted adopting the American concept of 'substituted consent' whereby the courts seek to ascertain from the evidence what the person would himself do if competent (*Airedale NHS Trust* v. *Bland* [1993] AC 789).

Self-Defence

Where a person hits another in defending himself from an attack by that other person he may be able to plead self-defence as a justification. The defence may succeed even where the aggressor has not actually touched the defendant. So, for example, if a person threatens another with a gun the defence would succeed if the threatened person sought by force to disarm the aggressor. A reasonable apprehension of threatened aggression is all that is required to justify the use of reasonable force in self-defence. Provocation is not, however, a defence but may be relevant either to show the defendant believed he was being attacked or in mitigation of damages (but see Lord Denning MR in *Murphy* v. *Culhane* [1977] QB 94).

In addition to proving that he was justified in using force to defend himself, the defendant must also prove that the force used was reasonable. This is in essence a question of fact and the answer given will depend on such factors as the degree of violence threatened, its immediacy and whether any weapons were used. It was held not to be self-defence in *Cook* v. *Beal* (1697) 1 Lord Raym 177, for example, for the defendant to draw his sword and cut off the hand of a person without a weapon who had merely struck him. Having said that, the use of even lethal force may be justified if the initial attack is sufficiently violent. Although in many situations the best form of defence is retreat, there is no *duty* on the defendant to retreat in the face of an assault. The fact that the person attacked did not retreat is however a factor to be taken into account in determining whether the action he took was reasonable.

In addition to the right to defend oneself if attacked, a trespass to the person may be justified if the defendant acts in defence of other persons or even to protect his property. It is clear that a person may defend any member of his family. As with self-defence the force used must be reasonable. It is submitted that it is also legitimate to use force in protection of persons other than one's own family. Nobody should have to stand idly by and watch a person seriously assault another because he is afraid of a civil action being brought against him for trespass.

A similar principle applies in relation to protection of property. A person is entitled to use reasonable force to defend land or chattels in his possession. So, for example, an occupier of land may use reasonable force in ejecting a trespasser. As with the defence of another person, the force used must be reasonable. In *Collins* v. *Renison* (1754) Say 138 Ryder CJ held that overturning a ladder on which the plaintiff was standing in order to eject him from the defendant's property was not justifiable. As the judge put it: 'the overturning of the ladder could not answer the purpose of removing the plaintiff out of the garden; since it only left him upon the ground at the bottom of the ladder, instead of being upon it'.

Necessity

In *F* v. *West Berkshire Health Authority* [1990] 2 AC 1 Lord Goff acknowledged that English law recognises a principle of necessity that 'may justify action which would otherwise be unlawful'. The cases on necessity, he said, could be conveniently divided into three different categories. First, there are cases of public necessity. A typical example of this category would be where a person pulls down another man's house in order to prevent the spread of a catastrophic fire. Secondly, there are cases of private necessity. Typically these occur where a person damages another's property or inflicts injury on another in order to save his own person or property. Finally, there is a series of cases concerned with action taken as a matter of necessity in order to assist another person without his consent. As an example of this category Lord Goff suggested the case of a man who forcibly seizes another to drag him from the path of an oncoming vehicle. As Fleming (1998) has pointed out, the defence of necessity involves 'more obviously than any [other] a hard choice between competing values and a sacrifice of one to the other' (p. 102). Its basis lies in a mixture of altruism, public protection and the maintenance of 'solid' social values. As a result, determining when it applies will be no easy task.

Most of the cases on public necessity are cases that justify trespass to land or to chattels and are, therefore, not compelling authority on the question whether public necessity justifies a trespass to the person. In principle, however, there seems to be no reason why, given an appropriately strong case, it should not. For example, consider the case of a fire chief who, in attempting to prevent the spread of a fire to a hospital, orders that a burning house causing most danger to the hospital be pulled down. He knows that there are three people trapped in the house and that if he pulls down the house they will almost inevitably be killed. Would the inevitable killing of the three occupants in the house be justified by the saving of the patients? Can the taking of one or more lives ever be justified on the ground that it is neccesary to save others? It is suggested that, provided the fire chief's action was reasonable in all the circumstances, he should be able to rely on the defence of public necessity (cf. *Re A (conjoined twins)* [2001] Fam 147).

Yet, even if it is accepted that the fire chief's decision can be justified by necessity, it might be asked whether, in such a case, the 'community' should not have to make good the claimant's loss. It is surely wrong in principle to force one individual to suffer for public purposes without just compensation. Such a conclusion has been reached in a number of states in the USA. Thus, in *Wegner* v. *Milwaukee Mutual Insurance Co* (1991) 479 NW 2d 38 the Supreme Court of Minnesota held that damage done to the plaintiff's house by the police when attempting to arrest a suspect who had fled there was compensable. The court commented that, 'in situations where an innocent party's property is taken, damaged or destroyed by the police in the course of apprehending a suspect, [it] is for the *municipality* to compensate the innocent party for the resulting damages. The policy considerations in this case center around the most basic notions of fairness and justice ... We do not believe that the imposition of [the whole] burden of the loss on the innocent citizens of this state would square with the underlying principles of justice.' (p. 48, *per* Tomljanovich J). Whether a similar approach would be taken by English law is less clear. It was held in *Burmah Oil Co Ltd* v. *Lord Advocate* [1965] AC 75 that the Crown must pay compensation for property destroyed when acting under its prerogative powers during wartime. However, the effect of this was largely removed by the War Damage Act 1965 which provides that no compensation is payable by the Crown in respect of damage to or destruction of property caused by lawful acts of the Crown during or in contemplation of war. Today any claim against a local authority in respect of damage to or destruction of property is likely to involve consideration of art. 1 of the First Protocol to the European Convention on Human Rights which prohibits the deprivation of property except 'in the public interest and subject to the conditions provided for by law and by the general principles of international law'. Whether this would require that compensation must be paid by a local authority that destroys property when acting under necessity is, however, by no means certain.

As with public necessity, cases of private necessity justifying the infliction of harm are very rare. Most of the cases on private necessity concern trespass to land or chattels carried out to protect the defendant's own land or chattels. In principle, however, private necessity may justify a trespass to the person except that the circumstances in which the defence will succeed are likely to be more limited than for public necessity. The courts are less likely to be sympathetic to one who acts for wholly selfish reasons rather than for the benefit of the general public. For example, a person who pulls an innocent third party in front of him as a shield against an attack by another is extremely unlikely to be able to rely on necessity. While necessity may, in limited circumstances, justify what would otherwise be a trespass, it is submitted that a person who causes injury to another for his own benefit should have to compensate the other for any loss caused to that other. The compensation payable in such a case could be assessed either on the basis that the defendant has been unjustly enriched at the claimant's expense and he should therefore be obliged to hand over the value of the unjust enrichment or on the basis of the value of the damage caused to the claimant.

Finally, there are the cases where the defendant acts for the purpose of protecting the claimant's own health or property. As we have seen, any unconsented-to touching is prima facie, actionable. Yet in some cases respecting a patient's wishes may mean having to stand by and watch that person die. Does the principle of sanctity of life allow the patient's wishes to be overruled? It is beyond the scope of this book to consider this very difficult issue in any detail, but two situations are illustrative. First, if a prisoner determines to refuse medical treatment or to go on hunger strike and the prison authorities forcibly treat or force-feed him, should they be able to rely on the defence of necessity if sued for battery? Notwithstanding some dicta to the contrary, the prevailing view in English law prior to the coming into effect of the Human Rights Act 1998 was that the forced feeding or treatment of a competent person was not justified (see, for example, *Secretary of State for Home Department* v. *Robb* [1995] 1 All ER 677). Thus, a prisoner fed or treated without his consent could sue for damages. Where, however, the prisoner was not capacitated or competent then, at common law, such treatment was justified provided that it was medically necessary and in the prisoner's best interests. The European Convention on Human Rights prohibits, in art. 3, any inhuman and degrading treatment, and it might be thought therefore that force-feeding or forcible treatment would in all circumstances be prohibited under the 1998 Act. However, the European Court of Human Rights has held that force-feeding to preserve life does not invariably constitute a breach of the Convention (*Herczegfalvy* v. *Austria* (1992) 15 EHRR 437). Provided therefore that the treatment carried out or force feeding is medically necessary, in the best interests of the prisoner and does not constitute inhuman or degrading treatment contrary to art. 3 of the European Convention on Human Rights, forcible treatment or force-feeding of an incompetent person may be justified (*R (on the application of Wilkinson)* v. *Medical Officer Broadmoor Hospital* [2002] EWCA Civ 1545, [2002] 1 WLR 419).

A second difficult situation arises where a pregnant woman refuses a Caesarean section for religious or other reasons, in circumstances where without such an operation both she and the unborn child will undoubtedly die. Would a doctor who performed a Caesarean section in such circumstances be able to rely on the defence of necessity if sued for battery? In *Re T (Adult: refusal of treatment)* [1992] 4 All ER 649 Lord Donaldson left open the possibility that the law might ignore the woman's refusal in such a case. However in more recent cases (e.g. *Re MB* [1997] 2 FCR 541; *St George's Healthcare NHS Trust* v. *S* [1999] Fam 26) the Court of Appeal has firmly rejected any suggestion that a competent woman's right to refuse treatment is modified by the fact that she is pregnant. As Judge LJ explained in *St George's Healthcare NHS Trust* v. *S* [1999] Fam 26, 48:

'While pregnancy increases the personal responsibilities of a woman it does not diminish her entitlement to decide whether or not to undergo medical treatment. Although human ... an unborn child is not a separate person from its mother. Its need for medical assistance does not prevail over her rights. She is entitled not to be forced to submit to an invasion of her body against her will, whether her own life or that of her unborn child depends on it. Her right is not reduced or diminished merely because her decision to exercise it may appear morally repugnant.'

The defence of necessity may also have an important role to play in the case of treatment of incompetent (including unconscious) patients. In *F* v. *West Berkshire Health Authority* the House of Lords upheld a declaration made by a judge allowing the sterilisation of a mentally incompetent woman. Such treatment, although not consented to, could be justified on the principle of necessity. Lord Goff said that for the defence to succeed there must have been (a) a necessity to act in circumstances where it was not practicable to communicate with the assisted person and (b) the action taken must have been such as a reasonable person would in all the circumstances take, acting in the best interests of the assisted person. In determining what is in the best interests of the assisted person, Lord Goff said that in non-medical cases the test was that of the reasonable man. In medical cases, however, the principles set out in *Bolam* v. *Friern Hospital Management Committee* [1957] 2 All ER 118 should be applied (see also 8.4). Provided a doctor acts in accordance with a responsible and competent body of medical opinion, he will not be liable.

Summary

16.1 The modern trepass to the person torts – assault, battery and false imprisonment – are derived from the ancient writ of trespass which provided a remedy for directly inflicted intentional interference with the person.

16.2 A cause of action will only lie in trespass where a person *intentionally* applies force directly to another. Where force is applied negligently the action is in negligence (cf. Diplock LJ in *Letang* v. *Cooper*).

16.3 Where a person intentionally and without the other's consent applies force directly to another, that is a battery. Where a person intentionally makes a threat that causes another reasonably to apprehend the immediate infliction of a battery on him, that is an assault. Directness is a requirement in both assault and battery. A touching will only amount to a battery where it falls outside the category of generally acceptable physical contacts. For there to be an assault some conduct is usually required to cause the plaintiff to apprehend the infliction of a battery.

16.4 The tort of false imprisonment is committed when the defendant intentionally and without lawful justification restrains a person's liberty within an area delimited by the defendant. The restraint must be total, though it is not necessary for a person to be locked up in a prison. A person may impose reasonable conditions on the manner in which an entrant leaves his premises. It is not necessary that the imprisoned person knows that he is imprisoned. A change in the conditions of a lawful imprisonment cannot render the imprisonment unlawful.

16.5 Where a person intentionally, but indirectly, inflicts physical harm on another, that person may be liable on the basis of the principle in *Wilkinson* v. *Downton*.

16.6 The Protection from Harassment Act 1997 creates a new statutory tort of harassment. By section 3 of the Act, a course of conduct which the defendant knows or ought to know amounts to harassment is actionable and a successful claimant can recover damages which may include damages for 'any anxiety caused by the harassment and any financial loss resulting from the harassment' (s. 3(2)).

16.7 The trespass torts are actionable without proof of damage.

16.8 A number of defences that apply generally in the law of tort apply equally to trespass to the person. Thus, illegality and statutory authority are both defences to trespass to the person. The use of reasonable force in defending oneself, one's property or another person may also justify a trespass. Probably the most important defences in practice are the arrest powers contained in the Police and Criminal Evidence Act 1984, consent, self-defence and necessity.

Exercises

16.1 If A negligently touches B's breasts, does this give rise to an action in trespass? If A touched B's breast deliberately but honestly thought that all women liked being touched in that way, would he be liable to B?

16.2 Is Lord Denning MR's judgment in *Letang* v. *Cooper* preferable to that of Diplock LJ in the same case?

16.3 A persuades B, who is 16 years old, to pose naked for him. A tells B that he intends to use the photographs to try to win a prestigious art prize. In taking the photographs A touches B's leg to show him how to pose. A subsequently publishes the photographs in a pornographic magazine. Would B have any action against A? (cf. *Kaye* v. *Robertson* [1991] FSR 62.)

16.4 Was the infliction of harm in *DPP* v. *K* direct? Could the directness requirement safely be abandoned?

16.5 A took his gun to a field where his family grew hay. A large amount of hay was piled up and A fixed a target to it and began firing. A had no way of knowing that B was asleep in the haystack. B was seriously injured. Is A liable?

16.6 A was sitting up a tree taunting B. B shook the tree causing A to fall. A was seriously injured. Is B liable?

16.7 A points a purple water pistol at B, and B, wholly unreasonably, is terrified. Is this an assault?

16.8 A's house has been burgled several times. He hears noises in his garden and goes outside with his gun to investigate. In the darkness he sees two boys in the south side of his garden. Intending to frighten them he points the gun in a northerly direction and fires. Unfortunately, A hits B, one of the boy's friends, of whom A was wholly unaware. Is A liable to B?

16.9 In *Robinson* v. *Balmain New Ferry Co Ltd* would the result reached by the court have been different if, instead of the vessel going on a short journey, it had been bound for America? What would the result have been if the defendant had demanded £5 from the plaintiff before he could exit? How long could the defendants in *Herd* v. *Weardale Coal and Coke Co Ltd* have left the plaintiff down the mine? Are these two cases reconcilable with *Sunbolf* v. *Alford* (1838) 3 M & W 247?

16.10 A is walking down a road when he hears a cry from a house. 'Let me out', the voice says. A does nothing. B, the person who had cried out, sued A as well as the person who originally imprisoned him. Is A liable to B?

16.11 A goes to his doctor for a blood test for glandular fever. Without A's consent the doctor tests the blood for the HIV virus. Would the doctor be able to rely on the defence of consent?

16.12 Are there any circumstances in which a doctor should be able to treat a competent person against their express wishes?

Part III

Interference with Land

17 Interference with Land: Introduction

17.1 Property, Tort and Crime

A number of torts can be seen as an adjunct to the law of real property. Speaking in broad terms, we can say that legal rules relating to interests in land may be grouped under three headings. First, there are rules that determine who has precisely what interest in land. Secondly, there are rules that serve to protect those various interests in land against interference. Thirdly, there are rules that govern the passing on of those interests to others, for instance by sale or by inheritance. Rules under the first and third headings are primarily the concern of books on land law; those under the second, however, are the preserve of the law of tort. The torts of trespass and nuisance, in particular, are the means by which those with interests in land prevent their enjoyment of those interests being eroded unlawfully. In performing this function, the torts of trespass and nuisance also add flesh to the skeleton furnished by land law's list of interests in land: where land law specifies who has what interest in land, tort law specifies what in practice those interests entitle one to do.

Trespass is concerned with 'direct' encroachments on land; nuisance with interference that is 'indirect'. If I step on your land without your permission or deliberately place something on it (e.g. my rubbish) that is a trespass, whereas if I pollute your land with noise, smells and fumes, or let things inadvertently escape from my land onto yours (as where my wall falls down through disrepair), that is a nuisance. 'Nuisance' is used here in a technical sense to denote the unreasonable interference with the use and enjoyment of another's land.

Sometimes this tort is called 'private nuisance' in order to distinguish it from 'public nuisance' which is a crime of ill-defined scope: the courts have the power to label any conduct that causes annoyance to a substantial portion of the community a 'public nuisance' (see Spencer, 1989). Public nuisances need not have any impact on the use and enjoyment of land. Examples have included making a telephone bomb hoax, selling food that was unfit for human consumption and holding an ill-organised pop festival. A public nuisance, though primarily a criminal offence, will give rise to a concurrent tortious liability where an individual suffers 'special damage' as a result of the conduct in question. In view of the nebulous nature of public nuisance, our discussion of it is confined to its most common manifestation: obstruction of the highway (see 18.7).

A third type of nuisance is 'statutory nuisance'. Statutory nuisances, like public nuisances, are criminal offences. Under the Environmental Protection Act 1990, Part III, a number of activities that are harmful to the environment are listed as statutory nuisances, and the courts are empowered to order the cessation of those activities. The creation of these offences is a crucial prong of environmental policy. Unlike public nuisance, there is no rule that a person who suffers special damage as the result of a statutory nuisance may bring an action for damages in tort. The facts that give rise to a criminal liability for statutory nuisance may, however, give rise to an independent tortious liability for public or private nuisance if they satisfy the requirements of those causes of action.

17.2 **Trespass, Nuisance and Negligence**

As elsewhere in the law, the expansion of the tort of negligence has had an impact on the more established torts, particularly the tort of nuisance. Many claims which involve the competing rights and duties of neighbouring landowners, and which historically would therefore have been viewed as the concern of the law of nuisance, are today brought under negligence. This tendency was most noticeable in relation to liability for the acts of third parties and natural hazards on one's land (see 18.5). In both these areas, liability in nuisance was slow to develop and negligence, which was thought for a time to treat the foreseeability of harm to the claimant as the sole criterion of liability (see 3.2), seemed to offer claimants better prospects of success. It is now clear that foreseeability is not enough to establish liability in negligence in such cases. There is no advantage to be gained from framing one's action in negligence rather than nuisance (see *Goldman* v. *Hargrave* [1967] 1 AC 645). Nevertheless, the liability of landowners for the acts of third parties and natural hazards on their land is now an established part of the tort of negligence (see 6.6) and has substantiated what Markesinis (1989) views as negligence's 'unstoppable tendency to subsume under its heading the role of older nominate torts'.

The effect of the rise of negligence is not only that negligence is in practice tending to take over the role of nuisance: it is also the case that doctrines of nuisance law have been infused with the 'fault principle' which negligence embodies. Areas of nuisance law in which liabilities had been imposed irrespective of fault (e.g. under the rule in *Rylands* v. *Fletcher*: see ch. 19) – or, conversely, in which liability did not arise however reprehensible the conduct in question – came to be regarded as anomalous. Consequently, the courts took every opportunity to enlarge the category of cases in which liability turned upon the reasonableness of what was done and to stress that liability should not be imposed without proof of fault (see 18.3). Some commentators have responded to these developments by arguing that, in reality, 'nuisance is a branch of the law of negligence' (Williams and Hepple, 1984, p. 124; see 18.8). Nevertheless, the primary remedy for a nuisance is an injunction and the tort may therefore be regarded as more forward-looking, and more concerned with regulating a continuing relationship, than can negligence whose concern is only to compensate a loss that has already occurred.

The tort of trespass to land also pursues a range of objectives quite distinct from the goal of compensation for losses incurred (indeed, it shares with other types of action in trespass the characteristic that it is actionable without proof of loss). Today, its chief practical significance is as a means of maintaining the privacy of one's home against unwanted intrusion and of settling boundary disputes with one's neighbours, purposes for which the tort of negligence is not suitable.

Summary

17.1 The torts of trespass to land and private nuisance provide protection against interference with the use and enjoyment of land. Trespass deals with 'direct' interferences, private nuisance with interferences that are indirect. Private nuisance should not be confused with public nuisance, a crime that may incidentally give rise to tortious liability if 'special damage' is suffered as a result. Public nuisances need not be connected with the use of land.

17.2 Notwithstanding the tendency of the tort of negligence to subsume the role of the older nominate torts, it appears that trespass and nuisance perform independent roles as means to vindicate interests in land against interference and to regulate the continuing relationship of neighbouring landowners.

---

18 Private Nuisance

18.1 The Nature of Private Nuisance

The tort of private nuisance is 'primarily concerned with conflict over competing uses of land' (Fleming, 1998, p. 457). It is remedied by the award of damages, or by the granting of an injunction, or both (see ch. 23). Alternatively, the claimant can take steps to abate the nuisance herself, and recover the reasonable costs of what she has done from the defendant (*Delaware Mansions Ltd* v. *Westminster City Council* [2002] 1 AC 321: underpinning of flats destabilised by encroaching tree roots). The task of mapping out the precise contours of the tort, however, has frustrated the legal mind from the early days of the common law. Confusion has undoubtedly been caused by a failure clearly to distinguish private nuisance, with which we are concerned here, from public nuisance, the crime of ill-defined scope which may exceptionally give rise to liability in tort (see 17.1). But even considered on its own, in isolation from public nuisance, private nuisance suffers from a lack of doctrinal clarity. One of the most ancient actions in the law of tort, it retains hints of its history in the days of the forms of action and many pockets of caselaw falling under the general rubric 'nuisance' strike us today as anomalous; the tort has yet to be united under a coherent thread of general principle, albeit that steps have been taken towards this goal.

The classic definition of private nuisance is given in Winfield and Jolowicz, 2002, p. 508: 'Private nuisance may be described as unlawful interference with a person's use or enjoyment of land, or some right over, or in connection with it'.

This formulation gives rise to a number of questions:

(a) What rights and interests associated with the use and enjoyment of land are protected by the tort of nuisance?
(b) When will interference with those rights and interests be treated as unlawful?
(c) Whose rights and interests are protected (i.e. who can sue for a private nuisance)?
(d) Who can be held liable for the unlawful interference?
(e) What defences might be raised to an action in private nuisance?

We now consider these questions in turn.

18.2 Protected Rights and Interests

The tort of nuisance protects a variety of aspects of the use and enjoyment of land. As such, it may be regarded as a necessary complement to the law of real property. Whereas the law of real property deals with the creation and transfer of interests in land, the tort of nuisance provides a mechanism by which those interests may be protected. It performs this function in tandem with the tort of trespass to land. While trespass to land only protects against the direct invasion of the claimant's property, nuisance deals with indirect interference.

As a rough generalisation, we may say that the tort of nuisance protects three aspects of the use and enjoyment of land (see *Hunter* v. *Canary Wharf Ltd* [1997] AC 655, 695, per Lord Lloyd). First, it guards against indirect physical invasions of the claimant's land. (Remember that direct invasions are dealt with as trespasses.) A simple example would be where branches from the defendant's tree overhang the claimant's land (see *Smith* v. *Giddy* [1904] 2 KB 448). Secondly, it provides a remedy in cases of physical damage on the claimant's land, even in the absence of physical intrusion, for example, where a cistern is dislodged by vibrations from the defendant's electricity generator next door (see *Malone* v. *Laskey* [1907] 2 KB 141, considered below at 18.4). Lastly, it safeguards the claimant's so-called 'amenity interests'. The nature of such interests calls for further elaboration.

Interference with the use and enjoyment of land can take many forms and need not involve any physical invasion or physical damage. Owners and occupiers of land may suffer personal discomfort and inconvenience in various other ways in respect of which the tort of nuisance offers a remedy. The law thereby enables landowners to enjoy the amenities associated with their ownership of land. It has long recognised liability for interference with the enjoyment of land by smell (see *Wheeler* v. *JJ Saunders Ltd*, below at 18.3) and by noise (see *Kennaway* v. *Thompson* [1981] QB 88). Yet it must be remembered that nuisance is a tort to land, not to the person, and that liability for noise, smell and other things causing personal discomfort arises only where the claimant's use and enjoyment of her land is adversely affected: the law of nuisance does not directly compensate for the discomfort or inconvenience suffered by individuals on the land (*Hunter* v. *Canary Wharf Ltd* [1997] AC 655).

It cannot be assumed, however, that all aspects of the use or enjoyment of land are capable of protection in the tort of private nuisance. According to a celebrated dictum of Wray CJ, for example, no action lies for blocking a pleasant view or prospect because 'the law does not give an action for such things of delight' (*Bland* v. *Moseley*, 1587, unreported). Although it has been suggested that this justification is 'more quaint than satisfactory' (*Dalton* v. *Angus* (1881) 6 App Cas 740, 824 per Lord Blackburn), the rule remains in the modern law. Its more convincing rationale is that to treat loss of prospect as a nuisance would unduly inhibit the construction of new buildings; indeed, as '[a] right of prospect ... would impose a burthen on a very large and indefinite area' (ibid.), it could be used to frustrate all large-scale property development. As Lord Hardwicke LC famously remarked in response to a submission that English law recognised a right of prospect, 'Was that the case, there could be no great towns' (*AG* v. *Doughty* (1752) 2 Ves Sen 454).

Wray CJ's dictum that the law recognises no action in respect of 'things of delight' may be thought, despite the doubts expressed above, accurately to express the law's unwillingness to protect the merely recreational aspects of the use or enjoyment of land (at least in cases where there is no damage or physical intrusion). In *Bridlington Relay* v. *Yorkshire Electricity Board* [1965] Ch 436, Buckley J noted that he had been referred to no case in which interference with a purely recreational facility had been treated as a nuisance. In his view, '[c]onsiderations of health and physical comfort and well being appear to me to be on a somewhat different level from recreational considerations' (p. 447). Nevertheless, he declined to hold that interference with purely recreational facilities and activities could never amount to a nuisance.

The law's reluctance to protect purely recreational interests is evident in the cases which consider whether interference with a television signal can constitute an actionable nuisance. In the *Bridlington Relay* case, Buckley J treated domestic television viewing as an almost entirely recreational matter, notwithstanding the educational or political content of some programmes, and held that it could not be regarded as so important a part of an ordinary householder's enjoyment of property that its disruption would amount to a nuisance (nor a fortiori would the commercial relaying of television signals). But this decision was given only qualified support by the House of Lords in *Hunter* v. *Canary Wharf Ltd* [1997] AC 655. Their Lordships were required to rule whether damages could be obtained in nuisance for interference with domestic television viewing caused by the construction of the tower at Canary Wharf (currently the UK's tallest building). They held that where, as here, the interference resulted from the presence of a 'tall and bulky' building or other physical obstruction there could be no private nuisance. The court was impressed by an analogy with the cases on 'loss of prospect': the same concern lest construction work be unduly inhibited arose where it was alleged that television interference was caused by the erection of a building in the line of sight between a television transmitter and the land affected. The court, however, reserved its opinion on the question whether interference caused *mechanically* or *electrically*, as in the *Bridlington Relay* case, could ever amount to a nuisance. (It should be noted that a Canadian court has declined to accept the *Bridlington Relay* principle in such circumstances: *Nor-Video Services Ltd* v. *Ontario Hydro* (1978) 84 DLR 3d 221.)

Does the tort of private nuisance protect interests in privacy by recognising a right to be let alone within the boundaries of one's own property? Although *entry* into property is actionable as trespass, violation of the right to seclusion can take other forms, for example, the surveillance of property with electronic devices or the publication of photographs taken with the aid of powerful zoom lenses. An official report by Sir David Calcutt QC (1993) recommended the creation of a statutory liability for harm caused by such means, but there are currently no plans to implement the proposal (see further 20.1). It may be, however, that the tort of nuisance can be developed to provide some protection, especially now that the Human Rights Act 1998 has come into effect. Indeed, there were signs that nuisance might be developed as a remedy in respect of invasion of privacy even prior to the implementation of the Act. Admittedly, it was well-established that it was not a nuisance to erect a building which gave a view of the hitherto unobservable activities of a neighbour (see *Browne* v. *Flower* [1911] 1 Ch 219). But in more recent times Griffiths J had suggested that the harassment of constant surveillance of the claimant's house from the air, accompanied by the photographing of his every activity, might well constitute a nuisance (see *Lord Bernstein of Leigh* v. *Skyviews and General Ltd* [1978] QB 479; as this case involved a single incident, it could not give rise to liability). Furthermore, in *Khorasandjian* v. *Bush* [1993] QB 727, the Court of Appeal had ruled that the disturbance to domestic life caused by a telephone pest was actionable in nuisance. However, prior to the passage of the Human Rights Act, the effectiveness of this remedy against invasions of privacy was limited by the requirement that the person bringing the action had to have an interest in the land affected (see 18.4). Whether the new Act will induce the courts to relax that requirement, the better to protect the right to respect for private and family life under art. 8 of the European Convention, will be considered further below.

Another area where the law of nuisance seems already to provide protection against intangible harm is where the defendant's activities are liable to cause distress or alarm to those on neighbouring land. Liability may arise not only where the distress or alarm arises from actual physical interference with the ordinary amenities of land ownership, for example, where distress is caused by the impingement upon the senses of unpleasant smells or loud noises (see above), but also where the physical harm is only prospective, for example, where alarm is generated by the reasonable fear of contagion (see *Metropolitan Asylum District* v. *Hill* (1881) 6 App Cas 193). Additionally, it seems that the law also provides protection against activities that cause purely mental distress or alarm. In *Thompson-Schwab* v. *Costaki* [1956] 1 WLR 335, the plaintiffs complained of the defendants' use of a neighbouring townhouse as a brothel. They alleged that the defendants, both prostitutes, used the house as a so-called 'resort' to which they would return with customers whom they had attracted from nearby streets. The house, although not far distant from streets with an unsavoury reputation, was in a good-class residential street. The Court of Appeal upheld the award of an interlocutory injunction pending full trial of the matter. It provisionally rejected the submission that a nuisance must affect the reasonable enjoyment of premises in a physical way and held that the perambulations of the prostitutes, and their use of the building as a brothel, constituted a prima facie private nuisance even if their conduct could not be shown to be criminal. One could well imagine, declared Romer LJ, the effect of that activity on the minds of young people in the plaintiff households, to say nothing of the feelings of visitors. It is submitted that, while mere upset should not give rise to liability in nuisance, a response of righteous outrage might well indicate an interference with the reasonable enjoyment of premises.

18.3 **Unlawful Interference**

The rights and interests recognised by the tort of private nuisance are only protected against *unlawful* interference. The question of when interference with the use and enjoyment of land becomes unlawful is much disputed. Confusion has arisen from a tension between the apparent tendency of early common lawyers to lay down rights and duties in black-and-white terms and the modern urge to infuse all areas of the law of tort with the concept of reasonableness.

The early common lawyers seemed little concerned with notions of reasonableness and fault. Their maxim was 'sic utere tuo ut alienum non laedas' (use your property in such a way that you do not injure anybody else's). The rule was expressed in absolute terms, apparently leaving no room for a defence that the defendant had acted reasonably. Since at least the nineteenth century, however, there has been an increasing tendency to employ a reasonableness formula to balance the competing rights and interests of claimant and defendant. The picture today is something of a mess. Pockets of strict liability remain (see, e.g., *Wringe* v. *Cohen* [1940] 1 KB 229 and 18.7), as do instances of cases in which a person has an absolute and unqualified right to interfere with a neighbour's use and enjoyment of land and in which, therefore, there can be no liability in any circumstances (see, e.g., *Mayor of Bradford* v. *Pickles* [1895] AC 587). Many of these pockets concern what land lawyers know as 'natural rights' and easements; so-called 'water rights' and 'rights of support' are among the most important in practice (for more detailed discussion, see the first edition of this work at pp. 178–81). Such anomalies have, however, been greatly reduced in number over the course of time and the concept of reasonableness has emerged as the central pillar of the modern law of nuisance. In the modern law of nuisance, unlawfulness tends to be equated with unreasonableness.

A notable example of this trend relates to interference with the use or enjoyment of land caused by the forces of nature. For centuries, the courts denied that liability could arise where a landowner failed to prevent land in its natural condition, or wild animals on it, causing damage to neighbouring property. Thus in *Giles* v. *Walker* (1890) 24 QBD 656 it was held that it was no nuisance if thistle seeds were blown from A's land to B's, where they took root and did damage. Lord Coleridge brusquely dismissed the claim with the words: 'I have never heard of such an action as this' (p. 657). Times, however, have changed and the rise of the concept of reasonableness has made the courts more willing to impose liability for 'natural nuisances' that landowners might reasonably be expected to prevent. In *Leakey* v. *National Trust* [1980] QB 485, the Court of Appeal accepted this principle for the first time and held the owner of hill-top land liable when rocks and other debris fell naturally onto property below (see 18.5). It is disputed whether the earlier caselaw justified the court in *Leakey* in adopting a general rule of liability for natural nuisances (see Wedderburn, 1978); nevertheless it is undeniable that the tendency of the law – exemplified by *Leakey* – has been to discard the old classifications of specific rights and duties relating to the use of land, expressed in absolute terms, and to increase the role played by the standard of reasonableness. A recent illustration of this process is provided by the case of *Marcic* v. *Thames Water Utilities Ltd* [2002] EWCA Civ 64, where the Court of Appeal, relying upon *Leakey*, declined to follow the old common law rule (see *Glossop* v. *Heston and Isleworth Local Board* (1879) 12 Ch D 102) that a water authority was not liable for nuisances resulting from its failure to enlarge or improve the sewage system in response to increased usage. On the facts before the court, the claimant was entitled to damages from the defendant water company whose sewers had repeatedly overflowed and flooded his home at times of heavy rain. The defendant had taken no steps to remedy the situation and it had not demonstrated that spending money on the claimant would unreasonably inhibit its discharge of its statutory responsibilities.

Whereas in the tort of negligence the question of reasonableness surfaces in enquiring whether the defendant exercised reasonable care, in nuisance we ask whether there was *unreasonable interference* with the *claimant's* use and enjoyment of land, or (which amounts to the same thing) whether the *defendant* was engaged in an *unreasonable use or user* of land. The courts apply 'a rule of give and take, live and let live' (*Bamford* v. *Turnley* [1860] 3 B&S 62, 84 per Bramwell B) and seek 'the balance of convenience and inconvenience' as between the competing rights and interests of the two parties to the action (*Dalton* v. *Henry Angus & Co* [1881] 6 App Cas 740, 824 per Lord Blackburn). Although there is no limit to the circumstances which may be taken into account in determining whether there has been an unreasonable interference or user, the following factors have attracted particular attention and warrant separate treatment.

The Extent of the Interference

The more intrusive and longlasting the interference, the more likely it is to be considered a nuisance. Physical damage is a graver form of injury than mere discomfort or inconvenience, and some commentators go so far as to deny that the reasonableness of the defendant's user of land can ever excuse physical damage (see, e.g., Spencer, 1987). But private nuisance ought not to be treated as if it were divided into two torts, one dealing with physical damage and the other with discomfort or inconvenience (see *Hunter* v. *Canary Wharf Ltd* [1997] AC 655, 705–6 per Lord Hoffmann), and the distinction between the different types of nuisance is best seen as one only of degree. Interference which results in physical damage is more likely to be regarded as unreasonable than that which causes purely intangible harm but ultimately everything should turn on a flexible application of the reasonableness test (see Salmond and Heuston, 1996, p. 57; cf. 'locality', below).

Nuisance's rule of give and take, live and let live assumes particular importance where the complaint is of intangible harm. As a certain amount of noise and smell, for instance, must be tolerated as part of everyday life, the discomfort which the claimant alleges must be substantial. According to the much-quoted formula of Knight Bruce VC in *Walter* v. *Selfe* (1851) 4 De G & Sm 315, 322, the question to ask is:

> 'Ought this inconvenience to be considered in fact as more than fanciful, more than one of delicacy or fastidiousness, as an inconvenience materially interfering with the ordinary physical comfort of human existence, but according to plain and sober and simple notions among the English people?'

Often the duration of the interference will be a material factor. Many nuisances involve intrusions that continue for a significant period of time, but this is not to say that an isolated incident cannot give rise to a cause of action. Nevertheless, where the claimant complains of a single occurrence, it is necessary to demonstrate that the incident was attributable to a continuing state of affairs on the defendant's land (see *British Celanese Ltd* v. *AH Hunt Ltd* [1969] 1 WLR 959).

Locality

In *Sturges* v. *Bridgman* (1879) 11 Ch D 852, 856 Thesiger LJ famously remarked: 'What would be a nuisance in Belgrave Square would not necessarily be so in Bermondsey'. The point he was making is that the reasonableness of any use to which land is put will depend on, among other things, the character of the neighbourhood the land lies in ('the locality'): factories billowing out smoke might be all right in an industrial estate but not in an idyllic rural village. This approach has the advantage that '[s]ocial friction is ... most effectively minimised by compelling newcomers to accommodate themselves to the prevailing conditions of the neighbourhood' (Fleming, 1998, p. 469), unless of course these go beyond what a person in such a locality could reasonable tolerate. (It is no defence in such a case that the claimant 'came to the nuisance': see 18.6, below.) But the consequence may also be that existing inequalities in residential utility are entrenched and magnified, as those in poor, working-class districts, often adjacent to the factories for which they once supplied the labour, are left to bear the brunt of environmental pollution. As Tuckey LJ unapologetically made clear in a recent case, '[o]ccupiers of low cost, high density housing must be expected to tolerate higher levels of noise from their neighbours than others in more substantial and spacious premises' (*Baxter* v. *Camden London Borough Council (No. 2)* [2001] QB 1, 10, aff'd [2001] 1 AC 1).

This 'locality principle' applies only to cases of intangible harm, not to property damage. This was decided by the House of Lords in *St Helens Smelting Co* v. *Tipping* (1865) 11 HLC 642. In that case, noxious vapours from the defendant's smelting works damaged trees and shrubs on the plaintiff's land. The defendant alleged that, as almost the whole neighbourhood was devoted to copper smelting or similar manufacturing activities, those activities could be continued with impunity. Lord

Westbury LC disagreed. In his view, it was necessary to distinguish two types of case, the first being where the nuisance produces what he refers to as 'material injury to property' or 'sensible injury to the value of the property', and the second being where it merely produces 'personal discomfort'. Locality was relevant only in relation to the latter: 'If a man lives in a street where there are numerous shops, and a shop is opened next door to him ... he has no ground for complaint, because to him individually there might arise much discomfort from the trade carried on in that shop' (p. 650). In relation to the former, however, locality was of no significance. It followed that the injury to the plaintiff's trees and shrubs in the case before him gave rise to a cause of action in nuisance, irrespective of whether the pollution from the defendant's works was exceptional for the locality.

Lord Westbury's ruling has been criticised on a number of grounds. First of all, the precise meaning of what he says is obscure. He talks of 'sensible injury to the value of property' and distinguishes this from 'personal discomfort', yet if land becomes uncomfortable to live on then its value will surely be diminished. Perhaps it is best to assume that Lord Westbury merely intended to draw a line between cases of physical damage and those of intangible loss. A more substantial criticism is that the apparently rigid distinction between material damage to property and purely intangible harm prevents a flexible application of the standard of reasonableness and might produce arbitrary or undesirable results. Where, for example, the parties live on an isolated mountainside on which rock falls are regular, it might be appropriate to expect landowners to put up with a certain amount of damage caused by falls from land higher up the mountain (see Buckley, 1996, pp. 9–10).

The character of a locality may be changed very rapidly by large-scale property development. Where this is carried out lawfully, with the relevant planning permission, the reasonableness of any interference with the use or enjoyment of land will be assessed in the light of the neighbourhood's new character. Planning permission does not, however, act as a defence analogous to that of statutory authority (see 18.6). In *Gillingham Borough Council* v. *Medway (Chatham) Dock Co Ltd* [1993] QB 343, local residents complained of disturbance arising from traffic passing to and from the defendants' dockyard. The local council sought an injunction under the Local Government Act 1972, s. 222, to stop what it alleged was a public nuisance arising out of the private nuisance suffered by the local residents. Ironically, the council had, some nine years previously, granted planning permission to the defendants to develop a port at the site of the dockyard, even though it was fully informed as to the likely disturbance to local residents. (It seems that the council's legal action was motivated by a desire to avoid the payment of compensation for revocation of the permission.) Buckley J denied that planning permission acted as a defence in the same way as statutory authorisation but held that 'where planning consent is given for a development or change of use, the question of nuisance will thereafter fall to be decided by reference to a neighbourhood with that development or use and not as it was previously' (p. 361).

It must be noted, however, that not every grant of planning permission will serve to alter the character of a neighbourhood. In *Wheeler* v. *JJ Saunders Ltd* [1996] Ch 19, the Court of Appeal approved the decision of Buckley J in the *Gillingham* case but distinguished it from the case at hand. Granting permission for a project on the scale of a commercial dockyard, as in the *Gillingham* case, might indeed effect a change in the character of the neighbourhood, but this would not be the case where the development was small-scale and involved merely an increase in the levels of an existing activity rather than a wholly new use. Thus where, as in *Wheeler*, the defendants had merely been given permission to erect additional buildings to continue their pig rearing business, this could not be said to have effected a change in the character of the locality. It did not allow the defendants to create a fouler stench than that permitted before the grant of the planning permission.

Hypersensitive Activities

In the words of Lord Robertson, 'A man cannot increase the liabilities of his neighbour by applying his own property to special uses, whether for business or pleasure' (*Eastern and South African Telegraph Co* v. *Cape Town Tramways* [1902] AC 381, 393). It follows that one cannot complain about interference with abnormally sensitive activities where ordinary activities would not be affected, albeit that, where there is unreasonable interference with the ordinary use of land, this will justify liability even to an abnormally sensitive user (see *McKinnon Industries Ltd* v. *Walker* [1951] 3 DLR 577). The rule was applied by Buckley J in *Bridlington Relay Ltd* v. *Yorkshire Electricity Board* [1965] Ch 436 in deciding that interference with the signals received by a television broadcast relay station, caused by a nearby electricity power line, did not amount to a nuisance. The judge pointed to the abnormal nature of the plaintiff's business which, if it were to prosper, required an exceptional degree of immunity from interference. This was not a case of interference with ordinary domestic television reception. (As an alternative, he was prepared to rule that television reception was not so important a part of the ordinary enjoyment of land that it should be protected at all: see 18.2.)

An exception is made to this rule where the claimant complains of interference by something which is inherently noxious. In *Cooke* v. *Forbes* (1867) LR 5 Eq 166, the plaintiff was in the business of making coconut matting which was hung out to dry after it had been bleached. He alleged that emissions of hydrogen sulphide from the defendant's premises dulled the colours of the matting, requiring it to be dyed again at considerable expense. The court disregarded the fact that the matting required such unusually delicate handling that the fumes might impair its value and concluded that the defendant was liable in nuisance. The later case of *Robinson* v. *Kilvert* (1889) 41 Ch D 88, however, makes it clear that the crucial factor in that case was the noxious nature of the interference; in other cases, the hypersensitivity of the claimant's activities would be a good defence. The plaintiff kept stocks of brown paper which he sought to sell at a profit; the defendant occupied the premises below in which he made paper boxes, for which he required heat and dry air. The heat passed into the plaintiff's premises and dried out his paper, causing it to lose weight; as the paper was sold by weight, the plaintiff suffered a loss of profit. The Court of Appeal viewed the plaintiff's business as exceptionally sensitive, for ordinary paper would not have dried out in the same way. Accordingly his action failed. *Cooke* was distinguished on the grounds that the hydrogen sulphide emitted from the defendant's premises was 'inherently noxious': this made the hypersensitivity of the plaintiff's activity irrelevant. (Note also that interference with a hypersensitive use of land may also give rise to liability where the defendant acts with 'malice': see *Hollywood Silver Fox Farm* v. *Emmett* [1936] 2 KB 468, below.)

Fault

In the modern law of private nuisance, 'fault of some kind is almost always necessary' in order to establish liability (*The Wagon Mound (No 2)* [1967] 1 AC 617, 639 per Lord Reid); it appears that his Lordship inserted the word 'almost' to take account of the exceptional instances of strict liability, e.g. in cases involving natural rights and dangers adjacent to the highway). For this reason, nuisance adopts the same rule of remoteness as applies in negligence and the defendant is only liable for the foreseeable consequences of her unreasonable use of land (ibid.). In nuisance, 'fault' need not involve the element of carelessness alleged in most negligence actions; more often, the defendant's user of land is deliberately continued in full knowledge of the claimant's objections to it, and the question for the court is whether the 'balance of convenience and inconvenience' favours the former or the latter. Nevertheless it seems to be legitimate to ascribe fault to the deliberate continuation of an interference which the law regards as unreasonable.

'[I]f the user [sc. of land] is not reasonable, the defendant will be liable, even though he may have exercised reasonable care and skill to avoid it' (*Cambridge Water Co Ltd* v. *Eastern Counties Leather plc* [1994] 2 AC 264, 299 per Lord Goff). In such cases, the defendant's fault consists simply in pursuing a user of land that should not in the circumstances be pursued at all (or pursued at the same level of intensity). This is not to say that the exercise of reasonable care is irrelevant to an action in nuisance, for an activity carried out carelessly may give rise to liability when none would arise if due care had been employed. The principle was clearly stated by Vaughan Williams J in the context of disturbance caused by demolition work (*Harrison* v. *Southwark and Vauxhall Water Co* [1891] 2 Ch 409, 413–14):

'[A] man who pulls down his house for the purpose of building a new one no doubt causes considerable inconvenience to his next door neighbour during the process of demolition; but he is not responsible as for a nuisance if he uses all reasonable skill and care to avoid annoyance to his neighbour by the works of demolition. Nor is he liable to an action, even though the noise and dust and the consequent annoyance be such as would constitute a nuisance if the same had been created in sheer wantonnesss.'

If the defendant's wanton or thoughtlessly inconsiderate behaviour makes it hard to justify her disturbance of the claimant, her case is even weaker if she acts maliciously out of a desire to harm the claimant. This is made plain by *Christie* v. *Davey* [1893] 1 Ch 316. The plaintiffs' was a musical family. Mrs Christie and her daughter were music teachers; her son was a cellist. Mr Christie seems not to have been a musician and, as the judge remarked dryly, 'perhaps fortunately for himself is very deaf'. The defendant, who occupied the adjoining house, was disturbed by the noise, particularly of singing which he claimed was hard to distinguish from the howling of a dog. He wrote to the Christies in protest (this entertaining correspondence is well worth reading in the law report), but his complaints were ignored. In retaliation, he decided to pursue his own brand of musical studies. Whenever he heard the sound of music coming from the Christies' house, he would begin to bang on the wall, beat on trays and blow a whistle. North J found that this behaviour constituted a nuisance on account of the fact that the defendant had acted maliciously, for the purpose of annoying the Christies. The judge contrasted the noise made by the latter: their music-making had been a legitimate use of their house.

Mayor of Bradford v. *Pickles* [1895] AC 587 is a case that has given rise to controversy in this area. The source of the problem is a dictum of Lord Halsbury LC that 'Motives and intentions ... seem to me to be absolutely irrelevant' (p. 594). This should not be taken as laying down a rule for the law of nuisance as a whole; indeed, Lord Halsbury expressly limited it to cases of the same type as that before him. The case arose out of the defendant's action in draining his land. This threatened to diminish the supply of water available for the domestic use of the inhabitants of Bradford, for a proportion of this supply was drawn from water that percolated under the defendant's land. The plaintiffs alleged that the defendant had acted maliciously, as his intention was to get the city to pay for the water. This motive was rightly held to be irrelevant, for this was a case involving 'natural rights', more specifically 'water rights', and it was well established that a landowner has an absolute natural right to abstract water percolating under his land no matter how unreasonable his behaviour appears to others. The decision dealt with one of the anomalous pockets of nuisance law in which the test of reasonable user or interference has no application (see above).

This was acknowledged in *Hollywood Silver Fox Farm* v. *Emmett* [1936] 2 KB 468. In that case, the defendant threatened to fire his gun during the fox breeding season – saying 'I guarantee you will not raise a single cub' – if the farm continued to advertise its breeding activities which the defendant feared would put off potential purchasers of his land. When the farm refused to comply, the defendant carried out his threat with the result that some vixens ate their cubs and others did not mate at all.

McNaughten J held that the defendant's malice made the disturbance actionable as a nuisance, rejecting the contention that *Mayor of Bradford* v. *Pickles* had any bearing on cases such as that before him; it was not applicable to cases in which unreasonable user or interference was the test of unlawfulness.

18.4 Who Can Sue?

In order to complain of a private nuisance, it is necessary to show an interest in the land affected by the defendant's unreasonable user. This rule, propounded in the leading case of *Malone* v. *Laskey* [1907] 2 KB 141, was recently put in question by the Court of Appeal but has been affirmed by the decision of the House of Lords in *Hunter* v. *Canary Wharf Ltd* [1997] AC 655. In *Malone* v. *Laskey*, the plaintiff lived in a house belonging to her husband's employer; she herself had no interest in the property. While she was making use of the lavatory, the cistern was dislodged by vibrations from the defendant's electricity generator next door and fell on top of her. The Court of Appeal held she could not sue in nuisance in respect of her personal injuries as she lacked any interest in land (neither could her husband sue in lieu).

Two later decisions of the Court of Appeal declined, however, to recognise the 'interest in land' requirement advanced in *Malone*. In *Khorasandjian* v. *Bush* [1993] QB 727, Dillon LJ (with whom Rose LJ agreed; Peter Gibson J dissented) stated:

'To my mind, it is ridiculous if in this present age the law is that the making of deliberately harassing and pestering telephone calls to a person is only actionable in the civil courts if the recipient of the calls happens to have the freehold or a leasehold propriety interest in the premises in which he or she has received the calls ... The court has at times to reconsider earlier decisions in the light of changed social circumstances ... If the wife of an owner is entitled to sue in respect of harassing telephone calls, then I do not see why that should not also apply to a child living at home with her parents.'

This bold decision was subsequently followed by a differently constituted Court of Appeal in *Hunter* v. *Canary Wharf Ltd* [1996] 1 All ER 482, where Pill LJ (who gave the principal judgment) submitted that it was enough that the plaintiff could demonstrate a 'substantial link' with the property in question; the occupation of property as a home was therefore sufficient to enable the occupier to sue in private nuisance.

This decision was reversed by the House of Lords. Their Lordships (Lord Cooke dissenting) insisted that nuisance was 'a tort against land' (p. 702, per Lord Hoffmann), i.e. 'a tort directed against the plaintiff's enjoyment of his rights over land' (p. 688, per Lord Goff); an action might therefore be brought by the owner or tenant of the land affected, or even by a person who enjoyed exclusive possession of the land (approving

Foster v. *Warblington UDC* [1906] 1 KB 648), but not by a licensee without exclusive possession. To recognise the latter's right to sue would be to effect a fundamental change in the nature and scope of the tort of nuisance and would give rise to practical difficulties. In the first place, the category of those enjoying a substantial link with the land was 'not easily identifiable' (p. 693, per Lord Goff): would it extend to a lodger or an au pair, and would it apply to workplaces as well as residences? Secondly, the efficacy of voluntary arrangements by which potential conflicts between neighbouring landowners might be avoided would be threatened, because it might be impracticable to reach agreement with every person whose occupation of the property was substantial (ibid.). Lastly, the extension of nuisance that was countenanced would transform it into a tort to the person and render redundant the sensible restrictions on the right to sue for personal injury that were imposed in the tort of negligence, for example, by allowing liability for mere discomfort without damage (ibid.). Their Lordships therefore preferred to overrule *Khorasandjian* v. *Bush* in so far as it held that a mere licensee could sue in private nuisance (it retains authority as a case on intentional harassment under the principle in *Wilkinson* v. *Downton*: see 16.5).

With the passage of the Human Rights Act, there may be a case for revisiting the 'interest in land' requirement in order to secure fuller protection of the right to respect for private and family life under art. 8 of the European Convention. Lord Cooke, who dissented on this issue in *Hunter*, considered that various international human rights standards, including art. 8 of the European Convention, militated in favour of residence in the property affected as entitling a person to sue in nuisance. More recently, in a striking-out application, the High Court found it arguable that the courts' obligation to develop the common law under the Human Rights Act required an extension of the right to sue in nuisance so as to comply with art. 8 (*McKenna* v. *British Aluminium Ltd*, Times, 25 April 2002, Neuberger J).Yet the law already provides considerable protection for the claimant who complains of intrusions into her domestic life, even in the absence of an interest in the land. Section 3 of the Protection from Harassment Act 1997 imposes liability upon any person who pursues a course of conduct which causes alarm or distress to another person, or otherwise amounts to harassment, and damages may be awarded for (amongst other things) any anxiety suffered as a result. It is immaterial whether the harassment occurs in the claimant's home or anywhere else. Admittedly, the liability is limited by the requirement of a 'course of conduct', meaning conduct on at least two occasions (s. 7(3)). But it is submitted that the distress or alarm caused by a solitary invasion of a person's privacy is not in itself such as to warrant the fundamental re-conceptualisation of private nuisance that would be entailed by relaxing the 'interest in land' requirement. Of course, should the defendant seek to publish or make other use of information or images derived from a solitary invasion of another's privacy, the claimant may well have a legal remedy – but that would be for breach of confidence, not nuisance (see 20.1).

18.5 Who Can Be Liable?

Those whose activities cause unlawful interference with another's use or enjoyment of land will be liable in nuisance. For these purposes, the activities of an occupier of land include not only those carried out personally or by employees, but also those carried out by independent contractors, at least where the activities involve 'a special danger of nuisance' (*Matania* v. *National Provincial Bank* [1936] 2 All ER 633). This represents an exception to the normal rule of vicarious liability, which requires proof of a contract of employment before responsibility will arise (see ch. 21). In *Matania*, the defendants employed independent contractors to make extensive alterations to their flat. The plaintiff's flat underneath was affected by dust and noise which gave rise to an actionable nuisance. The defendants were held liable for the actions of the contractors, whose activities were found to involve a special danger of nuisance, it being inevitable that the noise and dust would interfere with the plaintiff unless precautions were taken.

The liability on those who 'create' a nuisance extends beyond those in occupation of land themselves, however, and covers those who create nuisances while on somebody else's land or even on the public highway. Although doubts have been expressed on the latter score (see *Esso Petroleum Ltd* v. *Southport Corporation* [1954] 2 QB 182, 204 per Devlin J, [1956] AC 218, 242 per Lord Radcliffe; *Hussain* v. *Lancaster County Council* [2000] QB 1, 23 per Hirst LJ) most of the authorities assume that a nuisance need not emanate from private land. Thus it has been held that striking workers mounting a picket in the road outside a factory may be liable in private nuisance (*Thomas* v. *NUM (South Wales Area)* [1986] Ch 20), as may the owners of an oil refinery in relation to the noise of lorries approaching and leaving the refinery on a road running by the plaintiff's house (*Halsey* v. *Esso Petroleum* [1961] 1 WLR 683).

An occupier of land may be liable for interference caused by trespassers and natural hazards on her land as well as for interference caused by her own activities (or those of her employees and independent contractors). In the idiosyncratic language of the tort of nuisance, she may face liability not merely for a nuisance she 'creates', but also for one that she 'adopts' or 'continues'. She adopts a nuisance if she makes any use of the thing that constitutes the nuisance; she continues it if she allows it to remain after she knew, or ought to have known, of its existence and when she could reasonably have put an end to it.

Acts of a Third Party

The leading case on liability in nuisance for the acts of a third party is *Sedleigh-Denfield* v. *O'Callaghan* [1940] AC 880. The defendants owned property on which they located a religious commune. The plaintiff owned the adjoining property. At the boundary between the two properties, there was a ditch which belonged to the defendant. Local authority workers laid a drainage pipe in the ditch, in so doing trespassing on the defendants' land which they had no permission to enter. The workers neglected to place a grid at the mouth of the pipe to keep it clear of refuse. All these activities were observed by the defendants' representative at the commune, Brother Dekker. Some three years later, after a heavy rainstorm, the pipe had become so obstructed with refuse that rainwater overflowed from the ditch and flooded the plaintiff's land. The House of Lords held the defendants liable for they had both continued and adopted the nuisance, either of which alone would have been sufficient to make them liable. Viscount Maugham explained the application of the principles to the facts of the case (p. 895):

> 'After the lapse of nearly three years, they must be taken to have suffered the nuisance to continue, for they neglected to take the very simple step of placing a grid in the proper place, which would have removed the danger to their neighbour's land. They adopted the nuisance, for they continued during all that time to use the artificial contrivance of the conduit for the purpose of getting rid of water from their property without taking the proper means for rendering it safe.'

Whether the *Sedleigh-Denfield* approach applies where the nuisance is created by a person with permission to be on the defendant's land remains a matter of some uncertainty. The Court of Appeal has twice ruled that landowners can be liable for nuisances created by Gypsies or travellers camping on their property (*Page Motors* v. *Epsom and Ewell Borough Council* (1982) 80 LGR 337; *Lippiatt* v. *South Gloucestershire County Council* [2000] QB 51). But it is unclear whether this liability arises where the landowner merely continues the nuisance, or only where the landowner is deemed to have adopted it: in both *Page Motors* and *Lippiatt*, the defendant councils were found to have adopted the nuisance because they had provided facilities (e.g. fresh water and waste disposal) for the encampments.

Where the nuisance is committed by the defendant's tenant, as opposed to a mere licensee, it appears that the circumstances in which liability may arise may be even more restrictive. Traditionally, the liability of landlords for nuisances created by their tenants arises where the landlord lets out the premises (a) for purposes which the landlord knows will entail the creation of a nuisance, as in *Tetley* v. *Chitty* [1986] 1 All ER 663 in which a local authority let land for the specific purpose of go-karting which was inevitably going to disturb local residents; or (b) with the knowledge that a nuisance already existed at the date of the lease; or (c) retaining the right to enter and repair the premises if a nuisance arises. (With regard to the last category of case, an additional claim is now possible under section 4 of the Defective Premises Act 1972, which requires landlords who have a right to repair to take reasonable care to ensure that those who might be affected by defects in the state of the premises, whether on or off the premises, are reasonably safe.) In *Smith* v. *Scott* [1973] Ch D 314, there was an attempt to extend the landlord's liability to a case where a local authority gave council accommodation to an unruly family, the Scotts, in premises adjacent to the claimant, even though it knew that the Scotts were likely to engage in anti-social behaviour. The Scotts proceeded to make life so intolerable for the claimant that he was driven to vacate the premises and live with relatives. The council, notwithstanding the claimant's protests, did nothing. Without referring at all to the *Sedleigh-Denfield* decision, Pennycuick VC found that the council could not be held responsible for the Scotts' conduct. It had not authorised the Scotts to act as they had done; indeed, the tenancy agreement expressly prohibited the commission of a nuisance. In the subsequent case of *Hussain* v. *Lancaster County Council* [2000] QB 1, the Court of Appeal affirmed the correctness of Pennycuick VC's decision, and reached the same conclusion in a case where the plaintiffs, whose shop was on the defendant's housing estate, were subjected to severe harassment by a number of the defendant's tenants on the estate, who would congregate outside the plaintiffs' shop, shout abuse at them, and commit acts of violence against their property. It may be that the decision was justified on the narrow ground that the acts in question were not truly linked to the occupation of council housing by those who committed them. This at any rate was the basis on which *Hussain* was distinguished shortly afterwards by a differently-constituted Court of Appeal in *Lippiatt*, where the council's land was effectively used as a base or launching pad for acts of trespass onto the plaintiff's property. But it must surely now be admitted that the landlord's responsibility extends to the taking of reasonable precautions to control unruly tenants, at least where their acts are connected with the land that is under lease to them. To limit liability to the traditional categories appears inconsistent with the House of Lords' decision in *Sedleigh-Denfield* v. *O'Callaghan* and may also be regarded as contrary to public policy, for it is not always realistic to expect individuals to bring their anti-social neighbours to court: bringing pressure to bear on the landlord may be more likely to produce a satisfactory outcome (see Morgan, 2001, p. 404). In any case, even if the common law fails to evolve in this area, it seems that local authorities may be held liable under the Human Rights Act 1998 itself if they fail to take reasonable steps to protect the right to respect for private and family life of those who have to endure intolerable interference from their neighbours in council housing.

Natural Nuisances

For some time after the House of Lords' decision in *Sedleigh-Denfield* v. *O'Callaghan*, it was questioned whether the same duty of positive action on the part of an occupier of land might arise in the context of natural hazards rather than the acts of third parties. Such a duty was finally recognised to be part of English law in the case of *Leakey* v. *National Trust* [1980] QB 485. The natural hazard in that case was debris in the form of rocks, soil, tree roots and the like that fell from the steep banks of a hill owned by the National Trust, Burrow Mump in Somerset, onto the plaintiff's property below. The falls threatened to damage houses on that property. The Court of Appeal held that a nuisance had been established. Megaw LJ, who delivered the leading judgment, said that it would be a grievous blot on the law if such a duty were not recognised. He countered fears that this might result in injustice where those affected by the hazard were much wealthier than those on whose land it arose by saying that the scope of the duty imposed on the latter was limited. In contrast to the objective standard of care generally imposed in the tort of negligence (see 8.2), the standard proposed by Megaw LJ was that of what the particular occupier could be expected to do. Where physical effort was required to avert an immediate danger, the standard would reflect the occupier's age and physical condition; where the expenditure of money was required, it would reflect her means. Megaw LJ even went so far as to suggest that the duty on the defendant might depend upon what it was reasonable to expect the plaintiff to do to protect herself, for instance by erecting a barrier on her own land or by paying for repairs on the defendant's. It appears that the same rule limiting the scope of an occupier's duty of positive action will apply whether cases like *Leakey* are argued in nuisance or, as they might very well be, in negligence. This at least was the view of Lord Goff who, in *Smith* v. *Littlewoods Organisation Ltd* [1987] AC 241, 274 doubted whether there could be any material difference between what was required of the occupier in nuisance and what was required in negligence (see also *Delaware Mansions Ltd* v. *Westminster City Council* [2002] 1 AC 321, 333 per Lord Cooke).

Following *Leakey*, the courts have on several occasions recognised a duty to take reasonable steps to abate a natural nuisance. Hence, a water authority must take reasonable precautions to guard against the flooding of an individual's property caused by the overflowing of its sewers at times of heavy or prolonged rain (*Marcic* v. *Thames Water Utilities Ltd* [2002] EWCA Civ 64), while the owner of a tree whose roots encroach on neighbouring land, causing subsidence, must remove the tree or undertake reasonable works to underpin the land (*Delaware Mansions Ltd* v. *Westminster City Council* [2001] UKHL 55; [2002] 1 AC 321). A positive duty of this nature was also recognised in principle in *Holbeck Hall Hotel Ltd* v. *Scarborough Borough Council* [2000] QB 836, where the claimants' cliff-top hotel fell into the sea as a result of coastal erosion affecting the bottom of the cliffs, which were the property of the defendant council. But here no liability arose on the facts, apparently because there was nothing that the council could reasonably have been expected to do which would have prevented the landslips responsible for the damage.

18.6 Defences

Prescription

No liability arises if the defendant has acquired a prescriptive right to commit a nuisance after having done so without objection from the claimant for a period of 20 years. This only applies to interferences which can develop into easements. It is possible to acquire an easement to discharge rainwater from your eaves onto your neighbour's land, or to send smoke through flues in a party wall, but it is doubtful whether the right to disturb your neighbour by smell or noise can be acquired as an easement (see Clerk and Lindsell, 2000, para. 19–124).

Statutory Authority

No liability will arise if the defendant is empowered by statute to carry out a certain activity of which the unavoidable consequence is interference with the claimant's use and enjoyment of land. Such interference is regarded as impliedly authorised even if it is not expressly permitted. In *London, Brighton and South Coast Railway* v. *Truman* (1886) 11 AC 45, a railway company was empowered to purchase station yards to accommodate cattle that were to be carried by rail. When it did so, occupiers of nearby houses complained of the noise of the cattle and drovers. The House of Lords held that a yard such as the defendants' had inevitably and of necessity to be located close to stations which in turn had to be located close to centres of population; in consequence, the yard would have been a nuisance wherever located and Parliament must have been taken to authorise that nuisance. Planning permission does not act as statutory authority, although it may prevent liability in nuisance arising by changing the character of the locality in question (*Wheeler* v. *JJ Saunders Ltd* [1996] Ch 19; see 18.3).

The policy behind the defence was described by Lord Roskill in *Allen* v. *Gulf Oil Refining* [1981] AC 1001 in the following terms (p. 1023):

'The underlying philosophy plainly is that the greater public interest arising from the construction and use of undertakings such as railways must take precedence over the private rights of owners and occupiers of neighbouring lands not to have their common law rights infringed by what would otherwise be an actionable nuisance. In short, the lesser private rights must yield to the greater public interest.'

In that case, the plaintiffs urged that, although Gulf Oil had been authorised to build a refinery on land acquired by compulsory purchase, the relevant statute said nothing about putting the refinery to use and, if it could not be operated without unreasonable disturbance of neighbouring landowners, then it should not be operated at all. Lord Diplock responded wryly: 'Parliament can hardly be supposed to have intended the refinery to be nothing more than a visual adornment to the landscape in an area of natural beauty. Clearly the intention of Parliament was that the refinery was to be operated as such' (p. 1014). Nevertheless, the House of Lords agreed that it was still open to the plaintiff landowners to prove that the interference caused by Gulf Oil's refinery was in excess of that which was the inevitable consequence of the operation of any refinery whatsoever on the land.

By virtue of s. 3(1) of the Human Rights Act 1998, any legislation authorising the commission of a nuisance must so far as possible be read and given effect in a way that is compatible with the Convention rights, including the right of respect for private and family life (art. 8). The right under art. 8 is not absolute, and interference with private and family life may be justified under art. 8 § 2 where it is in pursuit of a legitimate aim (e.g. public safety or national economic well-being), in accordance with the law, and necessary in a democratic society. To establish that such interference is indeed necessary, the authorities may have to demonstrate that they have conducted a proper inquiry into how the environmental effects of the activity causing the interference can best be minimised (*Hatton* v. *United Kingdom* (2002) 34 EHRR 1). It is immaterial whether or not the interference itself is directly attributable to the activities of a public authority, as the state has a positive obligation to take reasonable measures to secure the human rights of its citizens (ibid.). If legislation authorising the commission of a nuisance cannot be read compatibly with art. 8 § 2, however, all a domestic court can do is to issue a declaration of incompatibility under Human Rights Act 1998, s. 4. Its decision does not affect the validity, continuing operation or enforcement of the legislation found to be incompatible (except in the case of subordinate legislation where removal of the incompatibility is allowed by primary legislation). In order to recover compensation in such a case, it may be necessary to undertake proceedings in the European Court of Human Rights (as in *Hatton*: compensation for local residents affected by night-time flights at Heathrow airport).

Claimant's Act

The defendant may be able to defend an action for nuisance by pointing out that the claimant was responsible for all or some of the injury she suffered. If the claimant, by word or deed, has shown her willingness to accept the interference, then a defence of voluntary assumption of risk would bar her claim; if she carelessly contributed to her own loss, then a defence of contributory negligence might reduce any damages payable to her. These defences will only avail a defendant if the claimant has done something unreasonable and the courts have been adamant that those who move to a previously inhospitable environment have done nothing unreasonable: it is no defence that the claimant 'came to the nuisance' (*Bliss* v. *Hall* (1838) 4 Bing NC 183). Those who move to inhospitable areas must, however, put up with whatever degree of personal discomfort, though not physical damage, is appropriate in the locality (see 18.3).

18.7 **Nuisances On or Adjacent to the Highway**

The public interest in freedom of passage along the highway has resulted in the courts imposing liabilities of exceptional stringency on those who impede that passage. Obstruction of the highway amounts to the criminal offence of public nuisance, and it may give rise to tortious liability if an individual suffers 'special damage' as a result. This liability was first recognised, and the special damage requirement explained, by Fitzherbert J in *Hikkys* v. *More* (1535) (see Baker, 2002, p. 434). The judge considered a case where the highway was obstructed by a ditch dug across it. In his view, no one could complain about mere delay caused by the obstruction but, if a man fell into the ditch, he should be allowed to sue the person who had dug it in respect of this special loss. This liability is anomalous because, in contrast with cases in which a moving vehicle causes a collision, where negligence must be proved, the defendant will be liable if she intentionally caused the obstruction whether or not she could reasonably have foreseen damage to the claimant (see Newark, 1949). It is also anomalous in that the claimant may be able to recover pure economic loss resulting from the obstruction, – for example, where, as in *Rose* v. *Miles* (1815) 4 M&S 101, she has to pay for alternative transport – thus evading the limitations on such recovery in the tort of negligence.

Another area in which ordinary principles of liability have been cast aside relates to the collapse of artificial structures adjacent to the highway. In *Wringe* v. *Cohen* [1940] 1 KB 229, 233 Atkinson J laid down the following rule:

'if, owing to a want of repair, premises upon a highway become dangerous, and, therefore, a nuisance, and a passer-by or adjoining owner suffers damage by their collapse, the occupier ... is answerable, whether or not he knew, or ought to have known of the danger'.

He went on to exclude liability in cases where the collapse was caused by the act of a trespasser or 'a secret and unobservable act of nature, such as a subsidence under or near the foundations of the premises'. The liability arises even where the plaintiff suffers injury not on the highway but on private property. This indeed was the case in *Wringe* in which the Court of Appeal found the defendant liable when his wall collapsed and fell on to the roof of the plaintiff's shop next door. Once again, it seems unreasonable to have one rule when the nuisance is a threat to users of the highway and another when it is not.

18.8 The Relationship Between Nuisance and Negligence

Much controversy attends the issue of whether nuisance is best regarded as a branch of the law of negligence or as a wholly separate tort. The former view finds particularly persuasive advocates in Williams and Hepple (1984), pp. 123–7. To see whether they are right, we now consider a number of claims made by those who insist that negligence and nuisance are very different entities. As will be seen, the differences between the two are in many respects more apparent than real.

Nuisance Protects a Wider Range of Interests than Negligence

Admittedly, there are many interests not protected by a duty of care in negligence that are recognised in nuisance. Whereas negligence generally limits liability to cases of physical damage, nuisance can be employed to prevent interference of an intangible nature by ensuring, for example, freedom from unreasonable noise and smells. Williams and Hepple, however, argue that this is simply a matter of terminology: 'Why should we not say that people are under a duty of care not to be noisy and not to allow a noxious escape of such a nature that the plaintiff cannot reasonably be expected to tolerate it?'. In other words, nuisance might be encompassed within negligence if we were just prepared to recognise that unusually extensive duties of care are owed to owners and occupiers of land.

Liability in Nuisance is Strict Whereas Liability in Negligence Depends on Proof of Fault

We should at the outset make it clear that there are indeed cases of strict liability (i.e. liability irrespective of fault) that fall under the general heading of the tort of nuisance. But they are anomalies in the modern law, arising only in a few, narrowly confined areas, for example, in relation to 'natural rights' (see 18.3) or dangers on the highway (see 18.7). In the vast majority of cases, interference with the use and enjoyment of land will only be regarded as actionable if it is unreasonable, and we have taken the view that this requirement of unreasonable user entails fault on the part of the defendant (see 18.3: 'Fault'). This position is supported by some distinguished legal figures: in *Sedleigh-Denfield* v. *O'Callaghan* [1940] AC 880, 904 Lord Wright insisted that the 'liability for a nuisance is not, at least in modern law, a strict or absolute liability' and, in *The Wagon Mound (No. 2)* [1967] 1 AC 617, 639 Lord Reid argued that 'fault of some kind is almost always necessary' for liability to arise.

One persistent source of confusion in this regard is a remark made by Lindley LJ in *Rapier* v. *London Tramways* [1893] 2 Ch 588. Delivering judgment for the plaintiff in an action for nuisance in respect of the smell coming from the defendant's excessively large and overcrowded stables, he commented (pp. 599–600): 'At common law, if I am sued for a nuisance, and the nuisance is proved, it is no defence on my part to say, and to prove, that I have taken all reasonable care to prevent it'. (In the *Cambridge Water* case, Lord Goff made the same point: see 18.3: 'Fault'.) As Williams and Hepple point out, however, this does not mean that liability was being imposed without fault, for, if all else failed, the only reasonable course left to the defendant would be to close his stables down. This was clearly in the mind of Lindley LJ, because he says, 'If the defendants are right in saying that they cannot concentrate their stables to such an extent as is desirable without committing a nuisance to the neighbourhood, then they cannot concentrate their operations to such an extent' (p. 602). Their failure to cease or cut back their operations itself amounted to fault.

In summary, then, we can say that an interference will be regarded as unreasonable only if the defendant was at fault either in the way an activity was carried out or in carrying on with the activity at all. For this reason, it is appropriate to rely upon the *Wagon Mound* test of remoteness of damage in nuisance as well as negligence (*The Wagon Mound (No 2)*; see ch. 10).

'[T]he distinguishing aspect of nuisance, as compared with other heads of liability like negligence, is that it looks to the harmful result rather than to the kind of conduct causing it.' (Fleming, 1998, p. 458)

In negligence actions, we put the question: 'Did the defendant take due care?'; in nuisance actions, we ask: 'Was there unreasonable interference with the claimant's use and enjoyment of her land?' Despite this difference in emphasis, it would be wrong to conclude that negligence looks only at the defendant's conduct, and nuisance only at the claimant's injury. In fact, both torts look both at the nature of the damage suffered by the claimant and at the nature of the defendant's conduct. In negligence, the court compares the extent of the risk faced by the claimant with the ease with which the defendant might have eliminated that risk before deciding whether the latter took reasonable care. If the foreseeable risk to the claimant is greater than that to ordinary people (as in *Paris* v. *Stepney Borough Council*: see 8.3) then the defendant will be expected to alter her behaviour accordingly. Similarly, in nuisance, the court enquires not only into the extent of the interference with the claimant, but also into the motive with which the defendant acted: what might be reasonable if done with care might be a nuisance if done wantonly (see 18.3).

The Function of Negligence is to Allocate Losses after One-off Accidents Whereas the Function of Nuisance is the Provision of Guidelines to Neighbours in a Continuing Relationship

Neighbouring owners and occupiers of land are in a continuing relationship that is very different from the relationship between those involved in the paradigmatic instances of negligence, accidents on the roads and the like. They need much clearer guidelines as to how they should conduct their affairs than the simple injunction to take reasonable care not to injure their neighbours. In response to this need, categories of the law of nuisance have grown up in which the limits of what one can do with one's land are spelt out in black-and-white terms; the vague but appealing standard of reasonableness is put on one side (see 18.3). Consider the question of 'water rights'. The law provides that you may stop up your neighbour's water supply by abstracting that water as it percolates under your land no matter how ill your motive (*Bradford* v. *Pickles*); on the other hand, you may not take water from a stream that passes through your land to supply your factory if the result is that your neighbour's supply is diminished, irrespective of the importance of your business and the difficulty of obtaining another supply (*Chasemore* v. *Richards* (1859) 7 HLC 349). To this extent, the law of nuisance gives occupiers and owners of land very clear guidelines as to what they can and cannot do with their land.

Yet in the majority of cases neighbours can get no clear guidance as to how they may use their land, for all is left to the court's view of what is reasonable in the circumstances. Admittedly, once the court has given its view, then the parties are bound to continue their affairs in accordance with this view, at least until the character of the neighbourhood changes sufficiently to justify a reassessment. But this is no more than what happens in many cases in negligence, for the parties to a negligence action may well be in a continuing relationship, such as that between employer and employee: a decision that it was negligent not to provide safety goggles or the like to employees may serve to lay down a standard for the future for a whole industry. In this, as in the other respects already highlighted, nuisance and negligence perform a common function in setting down legally-recognised standards of reasonable conduct.

Summary

18.1　The tort of private nuisance is primarily concerned with conflict over competing uses of land; it is remedied by the award of damages in respect of losses already incurred and by the grant of an injunction to prevent interference in the future.

18.2　The tort of nuisance protects a variety of aspects of the use and enjoyment of land, including freedom from physical intrusion or harm; particular difficulty arises in respect of the protection of so-called 'amenity interests'.

18.3　Where the reasonableness of an interference is relevant, this is assessed after consideration of its extent, the locality in which it takes place, the sensitivity of the claimant to interference of that kind, and the fault (if any) exhibited by the defendant.

18.4　The traditional requirement that the claimant in a nuisance action must have an interest in the land affected has recently been reasserted, precluding nuisance actions by those who merely reside on the property in question.

18.5　Liability is imposed on those who create, adopt or continue a nuisance, whether by their own acts or the acts of their independent contractors. In certain circumstances, landlords may be liable in respect of nuisances created on land they have let out, although the courts have so far taken a restrictive view of their responsibilities.

18.6　Various defences may be raised to an action in nuisance, notably prescription and statutory authority. Although the unreasonableness of the claimant's conduct may give rise to a defence of contributory negligence or *volenti*, it is no defence that the claimant 'came to the nuisance'.

18.7　The public interest in free passage along the highway has resulted in the imposition of liabilities of exceptional stringency on those who cause obstructions. Such liabilities arise in the tort of public nuisance rather than private nuisance, as there is no interference with the use or enjoyment of any private property. Liability in public nuisance depends on proof of special damage. A stringent liability is also imposed under the rule in *Wringe* v. *Cohen* in respect of the collapse of structures adjacent to the highway.

18.8   It is a disputed question whether nuisance is best regarded as a branch of the tort of negligence or as an entirely independent tort. Careful analysis of the alleged differences between the two suggest that these are often more apparent than real.

Exercises

18.1   To what extent is nuisance a tort of strict liability?

18.2   What is the test of 'reasonable user'? Is it relevant in all cases of nuisance? What factors determine whether a user of land is reasonable?

18.3   What is the significance of *St Helen's Smelting* v. *Tipping*? Do you agree with the views of Lord Westbury LC in that case?

18.4   Can *Mayor of Bradford* v. *Pickles* be reconciled with *Christie* v. *Davey*?

18.5   Who may sue in the tort of nuisance? Is the law satisfactory on this issue?

18.6   In what circumstances will liability in the tort of nuisance be imposed on one who has not personally created the nuisance?

18.7   Will the mere fact that a defendant has statutory authority to carry out a particular activity absolve her of any liability in nuisance?

18.8   Is it a defence that the claimant 'came to the nuisance'? Should it be?

18.9   Should obstruction of the highway be any of the following: (a) a crime; (b) a tort; (c) the tort of private nuisance?

18.10 Is nuisance in reality nothing more than a branch of the tort of negligence? (For a problem on nuisance and the rule in *Rylands* v. *Fletcher*, please see the end of Chapter 19.)

---

19 The Rule in *Rylands* v. *Fletcher*

19.1 **Introduction**

Rylands v. *Fletcher* (1866) LR 1 Exch 265, (1868) LR 3 HL 330 lays down a rule of strict liability for harm caused by escapes from land applied to exceptionally hazardous purposes. Although historically it seems to have been an offshoot of the law of private nuisance, and was treated as a form of nuisance by the House of Lords in *Cambridge Water Co Ltd* v. *Eastern Counties Leather plc* [1994] 2 AC 264, it appears to differ from nuisance in that its concern is with *escapes from* land rather than *interference with* land. Accordingly, some authorities hold that there is no requirement – like that in the tort of nuisance – that the claimant be the owner or occupier of the land affected by the escape, though the point is far from uncontroversial (see 19.5). If this is so, the rule in *Rylands* v. *Fletcher* may be thought to have a role in protecting not just interests in real property but also interests in the person and in personal property. But its possible development into a general principle of strict liability for ultrahazardous activities has been obstructed by a number of limitations on its scope, notably the requirement of an escape.

The case concerned the flooding of the plaintiff's mine with water from the defendants' recently constructed reservoir. A coal seam had previously been worked on the site of the reservoir and, although the mine shaft had been filled up, water from the reservoir was able to escape down the shaft and from there to the plaintiff's mine. The existence of the disused shaft had not been discovered before the reservoir was filled with water and thus no precautions had been taken to guard against the risk which eventuated. The fault for this lay with the independent contractors the defendants had engaged to construct the reservoir; the defendants were not personally to blame. Furthermore, the general rule is that, while one may be vicariously liable for the acts of an employee, one is not responsible for the acts of an independent contractor (see ch. 21). This difficulty, though, was avoided in the case by treating the defendants as personally liable irrespective of fault.

In the Court of Exchequer Chamber, Blackburn J set out the rule to be applied in such cases, together with the defences to it (his formulation was subsequently approved by the House of Lords in the same case):

> '[T]he person who, for his own purposes, brings on his land, and collects and keeps there anything likely to do mischief if it escapes, must keep it in at his peril, and, if he does not do so, he is prima facie responsible for all the damage which is the natural consequence of its escape. He can excuse himself by showing that the escape was owing to the plaintiff's default, or, perhaps, that the escape was the consequence of vis major, or the act of God.'

This formulation makes it clear that there are two essential ingredients of *Rylands* v. *Fletcher* liability: first, the bringing of a dangerous thing onto one's land so as to apply it to a 'non-natural use'); secondly, the escape of that thing.

19.2 **Non-natural Use of Land**

The requirement that the defendant must bring something onto his land was inadvertently transformed in the House of Lords by Lord Cairns. He paraphrased Blackburn J 's words, saying that the rule applied only to a 'non-natural use' of land, not to a case in which a substance had accumulated naturally on the land. Yet there is an ambiguity in the word 'natural' and, although Lord Cairns meant to exclude from the scope of the rule only those things which were present on the land in its natural state, 'the law has long departed from any such simple idea, redolent of a different age; and . . . natural use has been extended to embrace the ordinary use of land' (*Cambridge Water Co Ltd* v. *Eastern Counties Leather plc* [1994] 2 AC 264, 308 per Lord Goff; see also Newark, 1961). Hence no liability will arise in respect of a man-made object or accumulation so long as they could be described as 'ordinary' ('ordinary' here being a synonym for 'natural'). What will be regarded as ordinary and natural will depend on the exact circumstances of the case. Changes in perceptions brought about by the passage of time must be taken into account: keeping a motor-car in one's garage might be unremarkable in the twenty-first century, but a hundred years ago it might have been thought unusually dangerous (see *Musgrove* v. *Pandelis* [1919] 2 KB 43). So too must more transient shifts in community standards: in *Read* v. *Lyons* [1947] AC 156 it was held that it was 'natural' to use land for the manufacture of explosives at time of war.

An influential examination of the non-natural use requirement is to be found in the speech of Lord Moulton in *Rickards* v. *Lothian* [1913] AC 263, 280. In his view, '[i]t must be some special use bringing with it increased danger to others and must not merely be the ordinary use of the land or such a use as is proper for the general benefit of the community'. This requirement effectively robbed the rule in *Rylands* v. *Fletcher* of its primary justification, for strict liability is premised upon the belief that the rights of individuals should not be sacrificed in the furtherance of the public interest (see 12.2). It is precisely where land is put to 'such a use as is proper for the general benefit of the community' that strict liability should be imposed, as a 'licence fee' to be paid by those who are permitted to pursue the activity in question. Furthermore, Lord Moulton's view that hazardous activities could give rise to liability under *Rylands* v. *Fletcher* if beneficial to the community left the (supposedly) strict liability derived from that case hard to distinguish from liability in negligence: exposing others to danger without generating a countervailing benefit should, as a matter of legal logic, amount to negligence.

Although Lord Moulton's words have been cited with approval on many occasions, the House of Lords has recently cast doubt upon his approach. In *Cambridge Water Co Ltd* v. *Eastern Counties Leather plc* [1994] 2 AC 264, 308, Lord Goff (who delivered the only substantial speech) criticised his suggestion that no liability could arise in respect of uses of land that are 'proper for the general benefit of the community': this threatened unduly to restrict the scope of the liability. Accordingly, on the facts before them, their Lordships rejected the view that the benefit to the local community provided by the provision of employment opportunities at an industrial leather tanning works precluded the operation of the doctrine. The defendants' operations involved the storage of substantial quantities of chemicals on industrial premises, which was 'an almost classic case of non-natural use' (p. 309 per Lord Goff). His Lordship added: 'I find it difficult to think that there could be any objection to impose strict liability for damage caused in the event of their escape'. Although the claim failed on other grounds (see below), the approach taken by the House of Lords to the issue of non-natural use will please advocates of strict liability because it presages a greatly increased role for *Rylands* v. *Fletcher* compared with that envisaged by Lord Moulton.

19.3 Escape

The requirement that the thing brought onto the land must have escaped from the land was authoritatively laid down by the House of Lords in *Read* v. *Lyons* [1947] AC 156. The plaintiff was injured in her employment as an inspector of munitions in the defendant's arms factory when an artillery shell exploded on the production line. Their Lordships held that the rule in *Rylands* v. *Fletcher* had no application to her case as she had been injured on the defendant's land: the shell had not escaped and injured her on neighbouring land.

Fleming has commented that '[t]he most damaging effect of the decision in *Read* v. *Lyons* was that it prematurely stunted the development of a general theory of strict liability for ultra-hazardous activities' (1998, p. 383). Such a theory has been adopted in many US jurisdictions (see Restatement of the Law of Torts, 2nd, ss. 519–25), but the Law Commission (1970a) has recommended against its adoption in the UK in the light of fears that key terms such as 'especially dangerous' or 'ultra-hazardous' might prove uncertain of definition and give rise to practical difficulties in their application. In the *Cambridge Water* decision, Lord Goff noted these misgivings but indicated in any case his provisional view that the courts should not take it upon themselves to develop such a theory. The decision whether and how to introduce strict liability for high-risk activities was better left to Parliament, which could by statute define the activities to be affected with greater precision than was possible at common law.

19.4 **Remoteness of Damage**

The claimant must prove that damage resulted from the escape from the defendant's land. In the *Cambridge Water* case, the House of Lords decided that the damage resulting from the escape must be foreseeable, though the escape itself need not be foreseeable. Their Lordships applied the rule of remoteness recognised in *The Wagon Mound (No 2)*, holding that it was necessary to ensure consistency with the tort of nuisance from which the rule in *Rylands* v. *Fletcher* was originally derived (see 18.3). The case concerned the spillage of a chemical solvent used by the defendants, a long-established leather manufacturer, in its tanning process. The solvent seeped through the soil and contaminated water percolating below, which was the source of the water extracted from the plaintiff's borehole some 1.3 miles away. The solvent took approximately 9 months to reach the borehole. On these facts, it was not foreseeable that the seepage of the solvent into the soil would cause harm to the plaintiffs; as foreseeability of harm was a prerequisite of liability under the rule in *Rylands* v. *Fletcher*, no liability could arise. Notwithstanding this decision, liability under the rule in *Rylands* v. *Fletcher* remains strict and may even arise where the defendant is engaged in a reasonable use of land which cannot be restrained by way of injunction.

19.5 **Parties**

The primary liability under the rule in *Rylands* v. *Fletcher* is upon the owner or controller of the thing that escapes. The escape need not be from that person's own land but can be from land she is merely licensed to use or indeed from the highway. In *Rigby* v. *Chief Constable of Northamptonshire* [1985] 1 WLR 1242, 1255 Taylor J said that he could 'see no difference in principle between allowing a man-eating tiger to escape from your land on to that of another and allowing it to escape from the back of your wagon parked on the highway'. The owner or occupier of land on to which the thing is brought may also be held liable (*Rainham Chemical Works* v. *Belvedere Fish Guano Co* [1921] 2 AC 465), though she may have a defence where the actions are those of a stranger (see 19.6).

It is clear that the owner or occupier of the land affected can sue in relation to the damage to her property. Two significant areas of doubt arise, however, when we consider the question to whom the liability is owed. First, it is not clear whether it is possible to claim in respect of personal injuries as opposed to property damage. In *Read* v. *Lyons*, Lord Macmillan said that 'an allegation of negligence is in general essential to the relevancy of an action of reparation for personal injuries' and would not countenance *Rylands* v. *Fletcher* as an exception to that general rule. Yet the point cannot be regarded as decided, for none of the other judges in *Read* was prepared to express a view on the issue and the Court of Appeal had previously awarded damages for personal injury under the rule, for example, in *Hale* v. *Jennings Bros* [1938] 1 All ER 579 where the plaintiff, the tenant of a shooting gallery at a fairground, was injured when a chair, with its occupant, became dislocated from the defendant's rotating 'chair-o-plane' ride. Secondly, different opinions have been expressed as to whether the claimant must have a proprietary interest in the land invaded. Again, the courts have on several occasions awarded damages to those who had no interest in the land on which they were injured, for example, the plaintiff in *Shiffman* v. *Order of St John* [1936] 1 All ER 557 who was injured in Hyde Park when the defendants' flag-pole fell on him. Having regard to such decisions, one judge has declared that it is not open to the Court of Appeal to limit the rule to cases of interference with a proprietary interest (*Perry* v. *Kendricks Transport Ltd* [1956] 1 WLR 85, 92 per Parker LJ). But the House of Lords in the *Cambridge Water* case treated the liability under *Rylands* v. *Fletcher* as a form of private nuisance, and it may therefore be that the cause of action is subject to the same restrictions, in which case it can be invoked only in respect of interferences with the use and enjoyment in land, and only by a person with an interest in the land affected (see 18.4).

19.6 Defences

Blackburn J indicated three defences to liability under *Rylands* v. *Fletcher* in the passage extracted above (19.1). First in his list was default of the claimant. In extreme cases, no liability at all will arise, as where it was the plaintiff's mining operations beneath the defendant's canal, performed with full knowledge of the likely consequences, that caused water to escape and damage his mine (*Dunn* v. *Birmingham Canal Co* (1872) LR 7 QB 244). More mundane instances of fault can be dealt with through the apportionment provisions of the Law Reform (Contributory Negligence) Act 1945 (see 11.5). The second defence indicated by Blackburn J was *vis major*, which in this context refers to cases in which the escape was caused by the independent acts of a third party. The act of a third party will be considered 'independent' unless it would not have occurred without the negligence of the defendant. Hence, in *Perry* v. *Kendricks Transport Ltd*, the Court of Appeal declined to hold the defendants liable when a motor-coach in their car park was set on fire by young boys: the motor-coach was not left in such a condition that it was reasonable to expect that children might meddle with it and cause the fire. Lastly, the defence of Act of God will arise where the escape was caused by some wholly unforeseeable natural event (e.g. an earthquake or hurricane). The question of whether exceptionally heavy rains or violent winds give rise to this defence is a matter of degree (compare *Nichols* v. *Marsland* (1876) 2 Ex D 1 with *Greenock Corporation* v. *Caledonian Railway* [1917] AC 556).

In addition to the defences listed by Blackburn J, the defendant may be able to rely upon the defences of necessity (see 16.8), consent to the non-natural user of land and statutory authority (see 18.6).

19.7 **Fire**

Notwithstanding the narrow approach to *Rylands* v. *Fletcher* liability evident above, the courts have shown some flexibility when it comes to cases in which things brought onto land catch fire and the fire escapes to neighbouring land. Although Blackburn J's words, taken literally, would seem to require the thing that escapes to be the same as the thing brought on to the land, in *Mason* v. *Levy Auto Parts of England* [1967] 2 QB 530, McKenna J accepted that the same rule of strict liability applies where the non-natural thing catches fire and it is the fire that escapes from the land.

Section 86 of the Fires Prevention (Metropolis) Act 1774 confers a tortious immunity in respect of fires beginning accidentally on the defendant's land. This does not apply, however, when liability can be established on *Rylands* v. *Fletcher* principles or indeed in negligence (*Musgrove* v. *Pandelis* [1919] 2 KB 43). Even where a fire begins without any negligence or non-natural user, the defendant may lose her immunity under the Act if she negligently allows the fire to spread. Thus, in *Musgrove*, the defendant was held liable after the engine of his motor car caught fire on being started up in his garage; the crucial factor in the case was that the spread of the fire to the plaintiff's premises above the garage would not have occurred without his servant's negligence. (An alternative ground for the decision was that keeping the car was a non-natural user of land which itself deprived the owner of any immunity: see 19.2.) The converse is true when a fire is lit intentionally but in a controlled environment and subsequently spreads from the defendant's land without any fault on her part. In such circumstances, the statutory immunity may be raised. Hence, in *Musgrove*, Warrington LJ considered that if a lump of coal should jump unexpectedly from a fire lit in a domestic hearth the resulting conflagration should be regarded as having begun accidentally and the statutory immunity would apply.

A similar rule to that under *Rylands* v. *Fletcher* governs the liability of those engaged in dangerous operations involving the creation of fire. The leading case is *Honeywill and Stein Ltd* v. *Larkin Bros (London's Commercial Photographers) Ltd* [1934] 1 KB 191, in which contractors engaged to work in a cinema themselves employed photographers to record their handiwork on film. The primitive flashlights used by the photographers set fire to the cinema. The contractors were held liable for the fire damage, even though they were not personally at fault, because they had instigated the dangerous operation. This liability differs from that under *Rylands* v. *Fletcher* in three main respects. First, it applies even in the absence of a non-natural user of land. Secondly, there is no requirement of any escape from the land on which the dangerous operations are carried out. Lastly, it seems that the liability is not properly regarded as strict but a hybrid form of liability for which negligence must be shown, even if it is the negligence of an independent contractor (see ch. 21).

Summary

19.1   *Rylands* v. *Fletcher* lays down a rule, originally formulated by Blackburn J in the Court of Exchequer Chamber, of strict liability for harm caused by the escape of dangerous things accumulated on land.

19.2   The defendant must be engaged in a 'non-natural use of land'.

19.3   The claimant must be injured by an escape from the defendant's premises: no liability under the rule can arise when she is injured on those premises.

19.4   It must be reasonably foreseeable that the claimant will suffer damage as a result of the escape, though the escape itself need not be foreseeable.

19.5   Both the owner or controller of the dangerous thing and (if they are not one and the same) the owner or occupier of the land from which it escapes may be held liable under the rule.

19.6   Defences which may be raised against the imposition of liability under the rule include default of the claimant, the independent act of a third party and act of God.

19.7   The escape of fire may give rise to a liability analogous to that under *Rylands* v. *Fletcher*. The tortious immunity conferred by the Fires Prevention (Metropolis) Act 1774 does not apply to cases that fall within the rule, or indeed to cases where a fire was started negligently. Even when fire does not escape from premises, something approaching strict liability may be imposed under the rule in *Honeywill and Stein* v. *Larkin Bros*.

Exercises

19.1   What are the ingredients of liability under the rule in *Rylands* v. *Fletcher*?

19.2   Is the imposition of liability without fault justifiable? To what extent have the courts paid heed to the objectives of strict liability in developing the rule in *Rylands* v. *Fletcher*?

19.3   Can liability for fire damage ever arise in the absence of negligence? If so, when?

19.4   D and E are neighbours in Meadow Lane. Four weeks ago, F started to sell roasted chestnuts from a mobile stall in the lane outside D and E's houses. Many passers-by have been inconvenienced by the fact that F's stall gets in their way; D and E have more particular grievances. D alleges that she can no longer host her regular wine appreciation evenings as the smell from the stall overwhelms the bouquet of the wines. E, who is trying to sell her property, has been told that the fact that 'a dirty old tramp' has set up a stall in the vicinity, 'spoiling the view' and 'making a terrible smell', means that she will have to reduce the price considerably. When E asks F to move on, the latter replies: 'There've been stalls like mine in the area for hundreds of years. You should value your heritage. Besides, I'm only here a couple of hours a night.' Angered by E's attitude, F starts to burn an even more pungent fuel than before. Yesterday sparks from F's stall set fire to D's hedge. D's gardener, G, who comes to work for D one afternoon a week, tried to put out the fire with the garden hose. However, her efforts to direct the jet of water at the fire were ineffectual as she is elderly and suffers greatly from arthritis. As a result, a fire spread to D's rubbish tip and thence to E's property where it burnt down an outhouse. Despite this damage, F vows to continue selling chestnuts from the same place in the future. Advise the parties as to their rights and liabilities in tort.

Interference with Reputation

20 Defamation

20.1 Interference With Personality Generally

How much protection should English law give to 'interests in personality'? Should people, for example, have a remedy when others make untrue statements about them that affect their sense of dignity or honour? What if those statements are true but deeply embarrassing? Should there be any remedy for the person who is photographed without his consent or who has people listening in to his telephone calls? What if those photographs are sold to a magazine specialising in stories about people in the public eye? Should someone be able to bring an action where another appropriates his name or picture for commercial use without his permission? These are difficult questions that have troubled lawyers, both practising and academic, for several hundred years. In this chapter we will look principally at the way in which a particular interest in personality – a person's reputation – is protected by the law of defamation. As we shall see, defamation is primarily concerned with providing a remedy to a person who has been the victim of an untrue statement which lowers his reputation in the estimation of others. Yet, 'interests in personality' extend far beyond an individual's interest in preserving his good reputation and the law of defamation leaves most of these unprotected. In particular, it provides almost no protection in respect of what might compendiously be called a person's right to privacy. There is no remedy in defamation when *true* but private information is published by one person about another. Nor does defamation provide a remedy to the person who has been the victim of unwanted surveillance or intrusive photography, or where one person for commercial purposes exploits another's name or image for financial gain. Before turning to look at the law of defamation, therefore, it is worth spending a little time considering the many other ways in which English law protects 'interests in personality'.

The Interest in Reputation

The interest in reputation, though chiefly protected by the tort of defamation, may also be protected by the torts of negligence and malicious falsehood. Thus, in *Spring* v. *Guardian Assurance plc* [1995] 2 AC 296 it was held that in writing a reference about an employee, an employer owed him a duty of care. As Lord Goff said:

> 'the employer is possessed of special knowledge, derived from his experience of the employer's character, skill and diligence in the performance of his duties while working for the employer ... Furthermore, when such a reference is provided by an employer, it is

plain that the employee relies upon him to exercise due care and skill in the preparation of the reference before making it available to the third party. In these circumstances, it seems to me that all the elements requisite for the application of the *Hedley Byrne* principle are present.'

Recognition that an action lies in negligence in such a case is of considerable significance for those inaccurately characterised in a reference. As we shall see, the law of defamation recognises that statements made on certain occasions may be 'privileged' (20.10–11). Statements made in references have always been assumed to be protected by qualified privilege. If, therefore, the action were brought in defamation the claimant would not succeed unless he could establish that the defendant was actuated by malice. But privilege is not a defence to negligence.

A person's reputation may also be vindicated by an action for malicious falsehood. Such an action will lie where false words are maliciously published in circumstances where they are calculated in the ordinary course of things to produce, and do produce, injury to a person in his trade, property or business. Although the tort of malicious falsehood primarily protects a claimant's interest in his property or trade, it may in limited circumstances be utilised by a claimant to protect his reputation. Thus, in *Joyce* v. *Sengupta* [1993] 1 All ER 897, the defendant newspaper published an article alleging that the plaintiff lady's maid had stolen letters from her employer, the Princess Royal. Rather than proceeding in defamation, which as the Court of Appeal accepted was the obvious action, the plaintiff sued for malicious falsehood, for which legal aid was available. Clearly, the plaintiff's reputation had been lowered but she had also been injured in her trade, that of lady's maid. The Court of Appeal held that to pursue a claim for malicious falsehood rather than defamation, for which legal aid was not available, was not an abuse of process. Many causes of action overlap and, where they do, there is no requirement that the claimant pursue all claims or the most 'appropriate' one. Although the two causes of action frequently overlap in relation to the same set of facts, not every case of malicious falsehood is a case of defamation. Defamation as a tort protects a person's reputation while malicious falsehood protects his interest in exploiting his business or commercial interests. Words may injure a person's ability to exploit his business or commercial interest without damaging his reputation and in such a case an action will lie for malicious falsehood only.

The Interest in Informational Privacy

Unlike the position in a number of common law jurisdictions, there is at present no nominate tort of infringement of privacy. As Glidewell LJ put it in *Kaye* v. *Robertson* [1991] FSR 62, 65: 'It is well known that in English law there is no right to privacy, and accordingly there is no right of action for breach of a person's privacy' (see also *W* v. *Home Office* [2001] EWCA

Civ 2081). Moreover, the tort of defamation will only rarely be of much help in vindicating the interest in informational privacy. Defamation only protects a small part of that which is personal to the individual: his reputation. Much personal information is not discreditable and therefore no action for defamation will lie for its disclosure. Even if it is discreditable, the tort of defamation provides no protection where the information disclosed is true. There are, however, several other ways in which interference with informational privacy may be actionable.

First, there are a number of situations in which Parliament has enacted legislation to create a statutory duty not to disclose information without consent, expressly imposing civil liability if that duty is breached. By way of example, such a duty is found in the Data Protection Act 1998 which by s. 13(1) entitles a person to compensation where personal information held by a 'professional' in computer or structured manual files is disclosed to another.

Second, it is possible that the tort of negligence might be used to protect the interest in informational privacy. This might at first sight seem strange because the disclosure of confidential information will almost invariably be deliberate. However, the tort of negligence may give rise to liability for the unintended consequences of an intentional act, for example, where the intentional disclosure of confidential information causes psychiatric injury to the claimant (see *Furniss* v. *Fitchett* [1958] NZLR 396). In addition, an action might possibly lie, albeit infrequently, under the tort recognised in *Wilkinson* v. *Downton* [1897] 2 QB 57 where the deliberate disclosure of true confidential information by the defendant is calculated to cause the claimant injury and does in fact do so.

While an action in negligence and/or under *Wilkinson* v. *Downton* might occasionally give rise to a cause of action for unauthorised disclosure of confidential information, it is the action for breach of confidence that provides the widest protection for informational privacy. The elements of the cause of action for breach of confidence were stated by Megarry J in *Coco* v. *AN Clark (Engineers) Ltd* [1969] RPC 41, 49 to be: (1) the information has the necessary 'quality of confidence about it'; (2) the information was conveyed in circumstances importing an obligation of confidence; and (3) the unauthorised disclosure of the information was to the disadvantage of the person who communicated it. Although it has been used chiefly to protect trade secrets and particularly against the exploitation of information by former employees, it has also been used in several cases in respect of the unauthorised disclosure of personal information (e.g. *Barrymore* v. *News Group Newspapers* [1997] FSR 600 (sexual proclivities); *Douglas* v. *Hello Ltd* [2001] QB 967 (wedding photographs); *Argyll* v. *Argyll* [1967] Ch 302 (sexual conduct)). Moreover, it appears from *Douglas* v. *Hello Ltd* that breach of confidence may also have a role in protecting an individual's right to the commercial exploitation of his private life (see following section). An action for breach of confidence can arise independently of any pre-existing relationship between the parties and may protect both the form and the content of information.

In the absence of a nominate privacy tort, it is the action for breach of confidence that is being utilised by the courts to develop a remedy for infringement of a person's right to privacy. Undoubtedly a catalysing factor in this development has been the enactment of the Human Rights Act 1998 which recognises the Convention right to respect for private life (art. 8). Rather than fashioning a new tort of privacy, the courts have given effect to this right by expanding the action for breach of confidence. Although the courts have, at least so far, resisted the temptation to recognise a separate privacy tort (though note the judgment of Sedley LJ in *Douglas* v. *Hello Ltd* [2001] QB 967, at [109]), the expansion of the ambit of breach of confidence, and in particular the abandonment of the requirement that a pre-existing relationship between the parties must have existed before such an action could lie, has meant that the action for breach of confidence has been moulded to fill perceived gaps in the protection of privacy that might otherwise have been filled by a privacy tort. Whether in the light of these developments the creation of a separate tort would fulfil any useful function must be questionable.

While the action has acquired added significance in recent years, uncertainty remains as to the appropriate classification of the action. In particular, is the action equitable or tortious? The point is important not least because, if it is a tort, a successful claimant would have an *automatic* entitlement to damages, including damages for any associated emotional harm, whenever the elements of the cause of action and a compensable type of injury were made out. The award of equitable remedies is of course within the discretion of the court though it should be noted that there are cases in which damages have been awarded not just for the financial loss caused by a wrongful disclosure of confidential information but also for the emotional harm resulting from that disclosure (e.g. *Prince Albert* v. *Strange* (1849) 41 ER 1171). Notwithstanding its equitable origins, there has been some judicial support for the view that breach of confidence is a tort (see, for example, Butler-Sloss P in *Venables* v. *News Group Newspapers Ltd.* [2001] 1 All ER 908, 922). However, for the moment at least, the balance of authority is probably in favour of the action being an equitable one.

The Interest in the Commercial Exploitation of Personality

Some protection has been given to the interest in commercial exploitation of personality by the torts of defamation, malicious falsehood and the action for breach of confidence. In *Tolley* v. *Fry* [1931] AC 333, the court used the law of defamation to provide what looks, in essence, like a remedy for the unauthorised appropriation of another's personality. A caricature of a well-known amateur golfer with a bar of Fry's chocolate in his back-pocket was held to be defamatory of the golfer in that it implied that the plaintiff had agreed to appear in an advertisement and had thereby prostituted his reputation as an amateur. In reality, the plaintiff appears to have been given an action, under the guise of defamation, restraining the unauthorised use of his picture for commercial purposes.

Apart from this case, the courts have not shown themselves willing to allow an action for the unauthorised use of another's picture or name although, as Fleming (1998, p. 669) points out, '[t]he decision has potentially far-reaching implications and could be stretched to serve as a basis for restraining the unauthorised use of anyone's name or picture for commercial use under the guise of protecting reputation'.

Some protection for the commercial right to exploit one's own personality was also given in *Kaye* v. *Robertson* [1991] FSR 62. In this case, a reporter from the *Sunday Sport* took photographs and conducted an 'interview' with the plaintiff, a well-known actor, while he lay seriously ill in a hospital bed. The Court of Appeal held that as all the elements of the tort of malicious falsehood were made out, and as damages would not be an adequate remedy, the award of an injunction to prevent publication was appropriate. The effect of this was, as the court recognised, to protect the plaintiff's right to sell his own story and therefore to his right to commercially exploit his personality. As Glidewell LJ put it (p. 68):

'It needs little imagination to appreciate that whichever journal secured the first interview with Mr Kaye would be willing to pay the most. Mr Kaye thus has a potentially valuable right to sell the story of his accident and his recovery when he is fit enough to tell it. If the defendants are able to publish the article they proposed the value of this right would in my view be seriously lessened and Mr Kaye's story thereafter worth much less to him.'

The scope of protection provided to such commercial interests by the action for breach of confidence is evident from *Douglas* v. *Hello Ltd* [2001] QB 967. Here, the claimants, the film-stars Michael Douglas and Catherine Zeta-Jones, brought an action seeking an injunction preventing *Hello* magazine from publishing photographs of their wedding. It was unclear who had taken the photographs but it was clear that the claimants had not given their consent to the photographer as they had already signed an agreement with *OK!* magazine to sell them 'exclusive' pictures of the wedding. The real essence of the claimants' complaint was therefore not that their interest in seclusion had been infringed but that their interest in the commercial exploitation of their personality had been infringed. In these circumstances, the Court of Appeal discharged the injunction granted by the first instance judge. The claimants had sold the greater part of their privacy and thus their rights fell to be protected, if at all, as a commodity in the hands of *OK!* magazine. However, while an *injunction* was not necessary to protect the claimants' interests pending trial, damages might be awarded to compensate them for the losses that publication of the photographs in a rival magazine would cause.

The Interest in Seclusion

Finally, some protection is given to one's interest in 'seclusion' by, *inter alia*, the torts of trespass, nuisance and intentional interference with the person, and by the action for breach of confidence. Thus, an owner of land may be able to sue in trespass a photographer who sneaks onto his land to take photographs and an injunction may be issued against a campaign of harassment that is likely to cause another psychiatric illness (*Khorasandjian* v. *Bush* [1993] QB 727: see, further, 16.5). Additionally, a number of statutes (mostly of a criminal or regulatory nature) provide protection against interference with the seclusion interest. For example, s. 14 of the Post Office Act 1969 makes it an offence to open another person's mail without authorisation and s. 43(1)(b) of the Telecommunications Act 1984 makes it a criminal offence to make persistent telephone calls to annoy or cause needless anxiety. Of considerable significance in this area is the enactment of the Protection from Harassment Act 1997. In addition to creating two criminal offences – one to catch the most serious cases (where the victim fears for his safety; s. 4); the other to deal with less serious cases (s. 1) – the Act also creates a statutory tort of harassment (s. 3). This provision is widely drafted and allows a victim to obtain an injunction to stop not only behaviour that is already causing distress but also behaviour that may cause distress in the future. Breach of any injunction made is made a criminal offence, carrying the power of arrest (s. 3(3)) (see, further, 16.6).

Evaluation and Comparative Excursus

While English law does not have a nominate tort of infringement of privacy, it has been seen that interests in personality are protected in several different ways by English law. However, development of the law protecting personality interests has been somewhat piecemeal and, in relation to certain aspects of personality (e.g. the interest in informational privacy and the interest in the commercial exploitation of one's name or image), the law is in a relatively early stage of development. So far at least, Parliament has resisted legislating in this area, other than in a number of specific cases such as data protection and harassment, despite the fact that six private members bills have come before it. Moreover, recent cases such as *Douglas* v. *Hello Ltd* and *Venables* v. *News Group Newspapers Ltd* [2001] Fam 430 demonstrate that the courts have a sufficiently flexible tool in the action for breach of confidence if they wish to provide further protection to personality. The need for legislation is therefore not especially pressing. However, if the press continues to irritate politicians, other powerful public figures and members of the royal family by disclosing details of salacious gossip, it is likely that the case for legislative intervention will again be pressed. Politicians are notoriously cavalier about free speech where their personal interests are affected. Certainly, while the inconsistencies and inadequacies of the existing law remain it is unlikely that the issue will go away. How far the law should protect interests in personality is likely to remain an area of great controversy.

If the English law relating to privacy is in a relatively early stage of development, the same cannot be said of the United States where the law relating to the protection of privacy is relatively well-developed if erratically effective. Interestingly, the impetus for this development came from an academic article written in 1890 (Warren and Brandeis, 1890) in which the authors reviewed a number of (predominantly English) cases dealing with diverse issues of the law of property, contract, confidence and defamation and concluded that they were based upon a broader principle which protected the individual against the infliction of mental suffering through the invasion of his privacy. A common law tort of invasion of privacy flowing from natural law and the constitutional guarantees of personal liberty and security was recognised by the Georgia Supreme Court in 1905 (*Pavesich* v. *New England Life Insurance Co*, 50 SE 68 (1905)). By 1939 the new 'tort' was sufficiently well established to be included in the Restatement of Torts.

Today, the law in the United States encompasses four distinct kinds of invasions that together make up what might be called a right to privacy. The first form of invasion of privacy relates to the appropriation of another's name or likeness. Where, without the consent of the claimant, the defendant appropriates the claimant's name, picture or other likeness for his own benefit or advantage then an action will lie. While the action may protect the claimant's feelings, the effect of the decisions has been to 'create an exclusive right in the individual plaintiff to a species of trade name, his own, and a kind of trade mark in his likeness' (Prosser and Keaton, 1984, p. 854). The action has also been held to exist in relation to the appropriation of a catchphrase (*Carson* v. *Here's Johnny Portable Toilets Inc*, 698 F 2d 831 (1983)) and, in some states, to continue to subsist for the benefit of the estate after the plaintiff's death (*Memphis Development Foundation* v. *Factors Etc Inc*, 616 F 2d 956 (1980)).

Secondly, most states recognise a right to be free from 'unreasonable intrusions'. An action may lie where a person, whether by physical trespass or not, interferes with another's interest in solitude or seclusion, either as to his person or to his private affairs or concerns (Restatement Second of Torts s. 652B). The tort has been held to extend to such matters as eavesdropping on private conversations, bugging, and to persistent and unwanted telephone calls. Thirdly, if an individual makes public, to the world at large, private facts about another which would be highly offensive and objectionable to a person with ordinary sensibilities, and the public has no legitimate interest in having the information made available, then an action may lie. There are two potential defences. First, the defences of absolute and qualified privilege found in the law of defamation apply. Second, to accommodate the potential conflict between the right to privacy and other social values, such as freedom of speech and disclosure of iniquity, it is also a defence that the information is of legitimate public interest. The concept of legitimate public interest is 'inspired by the first amendment and therefore is interpreted expansively' (Markesinis and Deakin, 1999, p. 676). Pretty much anything that is 'newsworthy' has been treated as being of legitimate public interest provided that it does not offend against common decency. Thus, the public is usually legitimately interested in the goings on of public figures and officials, however salacious. So few claims against the media have been successful that one commentator has been prompted to call this privacy action a 'phantom tort' (Zimmerman, 1989).

Finally, an action may lie where a person is placed in a false light in the public eye. Such an action most typically exists where some view or utterance is falsely attributed to the claimant. Closely related to the tort of defamation, it is subject to constitutional limitations in the interests of preserving freedom of speech.

20.2 The Law of Defamation

The remainder of this chapter will look at the protection afforded to a person's reputation by the law of defamation. From the earliest times, the law has recognised the making of false statements about another as a wrongful act. The high value accorded to a person's reputation has led to virtually every legal system in the world affording it protection. In English law, this function is performed by the law of defamation. Yet, whilst a reputation is deservedly afforded substantial legal protection, the law must reconcile this with the competing demands of freedom of speech.

The right to freedom of expression under art. 10 of the European Convention on Human Rights is now – by virtue of the Human Rights Act 1998 – incorporated into English law. No system of law does or should offer absolute protection for reputation. This is particularly the case where the maker of the statement is discussing a matter of public interest. One of the concerns, therefore, of the law of defamation is to achieve a satisfactory balance between these two interests. It is in respect of this difficult balance between the right to reputation (recognised in arts. 8 and 10 of the European Convention on Human Rights (ECHR)) and the right to freedom of speech (art. 10 ECHR) that the common law has already felt, and is likely to continue to feel, the influence of the ECHR.

Although it is common to speak of the law of defamation, English law in fact recognises two separate causes of action in respect of publication of defamatory matter, namely, libel and slander. In general terms, libel is a defamatory publication conveyed in a permanent form, while slander is a defamatory publication conveyed in a non-permanent or transitory form. In order for liability to arise in libel or slander, a defamatory statement must be published about the claimant to a third person. Additionally, in the case of slander, actual injury must usually be proved. Each of these elements of the tort will now be considered in turn.

20.3 The Statement Must be Defamatory

A defamatory statement is one that adversely affects a person's reputation, that is, how others regard him. No single test has been said to be wholly adequate to define that which is defamatory. Thus, a statement has been said to be defamatory if it has a tendency to lower, or adversely affect, a person's reputation (*Sim* v. *Stretch* [1936] 2 All ER 1237, 1240, per Lord Atkin), or if it exposes a person to 'hatred, contempt or ridicule' (*Parmiter* v. *Coupland* (1840) 6 M & W 105, 108 per Parke B), or causes him to be 'shunned or avoided' (*Youssoupoff* v. *Metro-Goldwyn-Mayer Pictures Ltd* (1934) TLR 581, 587 per Slesser LJ), or injures his reputation in the conduct of his trade or business or professional activity (*Drummond-Jackson* v. *British Medical Association* [1970] 1 WLR 688, 698–9, per Lord Pearson). In most cases the question of whether a statement is defamatory is resolved by applying Lord Atkin's test from *Sim* v. *Stretch* ('Would the words tend to lower the plaintiff in the estimation of right thinking members of society generally?'). However, even that is not invariable and the other 'tests' may be used where more appropriate (see, for example, *Berkoff* v. *Burchill* [1996] 4 All ER 1008). To be defamatory a statement need only have the tendency to affect a person's reputation; it need not actually lower it. Thus, an imputation may be defamatory whether or not it is believed by those to whom it is published.

Vulgar abuse or insulting name-calling will not generally be defamatory because such behaviour is usually only insulting to a person's pride and does not affect his reputation. However, as the case of *Berkoff* v. *Burchill* [1996] 4 All ER 1008 illustrates, those who indulge in gratuitous insult must take care if their statements are not to be characterised as defamatory. In that case, the Court of Appeal by a majority held that statements made in an article that Mr Berkoff, the well known thespian, was 'hideously ugly' and looked a 'little like Frankenstein's monster without the bolts' were capable of being defamatory of him.

Reputation in this context is interpreted broadly as comprehending all aspects of a person's standing in the community. Thus, a statement may be defamatory if it impugns a person's mental competency, if it reflects adversely on his moral character, or if it comments adversely on his physical characteristics. Reputation is not, however, limited to a person's general character but extends to his reputation in his trade, business, calling or profession.

Whether or not a statement is capable of being defamatory is a question of law for the judge. Whether or not it is in fact defamatory is one of fact for the jury (Fox's Libel Act 1792). It is the tendency of the words themselves, however, that is important and not the intention of the maker of the statement. Thus, words may be held to be defamatory notwithstanding that no defamatory meaning was intended. In considering the standard to be applied when determining whether or not the words used are defamatory the courts have not been wholly consistent. However, the formulation most used is that of the 'right thinking person' or 'the good and worthy subject of the Queen'. The question asked is, therefore, whether the 'right thinking person' would construe the words in a way defamatory of the claimant. It may, of course, be a controversial question what the 'right thinking person' would think. For example, would he consider that an allegation that a woman had been raped, or that she was not a virgin when she married, lowered her in the estimation of society?

Similarly, would a 'right thinking person' consider that an allegation of insanity or alcoholism was defamatory? It may be that the courts in considering what the 'right thinking person' thinks are inclined to look to what he *should* think rather than what he does in fact think. A good illustration of this tendency is seen in the case of *Byrne* v. *Deane* [1937] 1 KB 818.

In *Byrne* v. *Deane*, police removed automatic gambling machines from a golf club where they were being kept illegally after someone had informed them of the machines' presence. A verse appeared soon after this on the notice board of the club. The last two lines of the verse read, 'But he who gave the game away, may he byrnn in hell and rue the day'. The issue for the Court of Appeal was whether the trial judge had been correct to leave to the jury the question of whether the words were defamatory of the plaintiff, Mr Byrne, in the sense that they meant he was guilty of underhand disloyalty to his fellow members. The court held that the words were not capable of a defamatory meaning as no 'good and worthy subject of the King' could consider such an allegation against a person to be defamatory. Thus the case should not have been left to the jury.

As Greene LJ admitted in his judgment, many people in the country would not consider any moral reprobation attached to the playing of gambling machines. Thus, for them at least, the allegation made against the plaintiff – whom they might regard as officious – could be defamatory. Why should not the question of whether the words are defamatory be judged according to what they think? The answer given by the court to this is that it is always possible to discover a small group in society who would not find the words complained of defamatory. For example, among certain groups, to describe someone as a 'professional thief' would be a compliment. The ordinary meaning of words cannot be left to such anti-social groups but must instead be considered by a more respectable body of opinion.

While it is surely not open to objection that the courts will not consider what effect the imputation would have on the claimant's reputation in the opinion of a small group with anti-social views, at least two concerns may be raised in relation to the 'right thinking person' test. First, the test asks what right thinking people *generally* would think. It assumes, in other words, that there is a shared community view on matters of right and wrong. Whether today such a shared view exists must be doubtful. Secondly, even if one concedes that we should not be concerned how the claimant's reputation is affected in the opinion of a small group of malcontents, not all 'small' sections of the community are disreputable. By way of example, it is probably the case that the majority of people in the UK no longer consider it insulting to say of a young woman that she was not a virgin when she married. Yet to say that of a woman from certain backgrounds or religious affiliations would be highly insulting and damaging. Are we to refuse her damages because the 'majority' no longer regard such an imputation as defamatory? There is much in the approach taken by the majority of American states in this respect, namely to consider whether the imputation has a tendency to lower the claimant in the esteem of any substantial and respectable group, even though it may be quite a small minority.

In deciding whether or not the words used are in fact defamatory the jury is asked to consider the meaning of the words in their 'natural and ordinary' sense. In many cases of course the words used only have one meaning and that meaning is clearly defamatory. However, a word may be capable in its ordinary usage of having more than one meaning. For example, in *Winyard* v. *Tatler Publications, The Independent*, 16 August 1991 it was accepted that the phrase 'international boot' was capable in ordinary usage of meaning either a type of footwear or a physically unattractive person ('an ugly old harridan'). A third possible meaning, that of a promiscuous person, was found only in a dictionary of slang and to be actionable it would have to be shown that it was published to a person who understood the word in that meaning. Where more than one natural and ordinary meaning is possible and pleaded it is left to the jury to decide which meaning the words have. Even though a publication may convey different meanings to different readers the jury is required to determine the *single* meaning that the publication conveyed to the notional reasonable reader.

In determining whether a particular statement is defamatory it must be read in context. Thus, no action will lie if one statement in a larger publication appears to be defamatory of the claimant when looked at in isolation but is evidently not defamatory when looked at in context: 'the bane and the antidote must be taken together' (*Chalmers* v. *Payne* (1835) 2 Cr M & R 156, 159, per Alderson B). But it is, of course, the case that not every reader reads with the same care. Reading a Sunday newspaper, for example, one's eye is inevitably drawn to some things and not others. Could a claimant written about in such a publication sue on the basis that *some* reasonable readers would conclude on reading part (for example, a headline) in isolation that it lowered the claimant's reputation? This question was considered but answered in the negative by the House of Lords in *Charleston* v. *News Group Newspapers Ltd* [1995] 2 AC 65. The court recognised that readers of newspapers read selectively but nevertheless held that it was a fundamental principle of the law of defamation that the publication must be read as a whole (see also *Cruise* v. *Express Newspapers plc* [1999] QB 931).

Innuendo

In some cases the claimant may wish to allege that the meaning to be attributed to the words is not their ordinary and natural meaning but is instead a meaning that can only be drawn by inference or implication, or perhaps only from the use of evidence separate from the statement itself. In both cases, apparently innocent words or statements may yet be found to be defamatory. Where the words do not speak for themselves, the claimant may, if he is to succeed, have to prove the necessary 'innuendo'. Innuendos are either 'true' or 'false'. A false innuendo is no more than an elaboration or embroidering of words without proof of extrinsic facts. It is an aspect of the ordinary meaning of words which includes inferential meanings that a reasonable reader would conclude that the words were capable of bearing. Unlike a true innuendo, it does not need to be separately pleaded. A true innuendo is one that depends on extraneous facts that the claimant has to prove in order to give the words a meaning separate from their ordinary and natural meaning. The meaning only arises by virtue of extraneous or extrinsic facts outside the words and it is these facts that give the words a defamatory meaning distinct from their natural and ordinary meaning (which may be wholly innocent). Thus, although a statement may appear innocent, knowledge of facts separate from the statement, may make it defamatory. Because a true innuendo constitutes a cause of action separate from any arising in relation to the words in their ordinary and natural meaning it must be separately pleaded.

An example of a false (or popular) innuendo can be seen in *Lewis* v. *Daily Telegraph* [1964] AC 234. Two newspapers published a story in which it was reported that officers of the London Fraud Squad were 'inquiring into the affairs of the R Co and its subsidiary companies'. Three possible meanings were considered by the House of Lords: first, that there was an investigation in progress; second, that the plaintiffs were suspected of fraud; third, that the plaintiffs were guilty of fraud. Lord Reid stated that, in determining the meaning to be given to the words, the question to be asked was what meaning would be conveyed to the ordinary person. Such a person 'does not live in an ivory tower and he is not inhibited by a knowledge of the rules of construction. So he can and does read between the lines in the light of his general knowledge and experience of world affairs'. Adopting this approach, their Lordships held that only the first two meanings were possible. It was impossible in this case, they said, for the statement that an inquiry was taking place to convey the impression that the subject of the inquiry was *guilty* of fraud. Acceptance of the second meaning, that the plaintiffs were suspected of fraud, involves a false innuendo. No extrinsic evidence is required for this meaning to be attributed, it is simply an implication that can be drawn or an impression that may be gained from a reading of the words themselves.

Where, by way of contrast, the meaning that the claimant is seeking to establish can only be ascertained by the use of extrinsic evidence this is known as a true innuendo. A good illustration of a true innuendo can be seen in the case of *Cassidy* v. *Daily Mirror Newspapers Ltd* [1929] 2 KB 331. In that case the defendants published a photograph taken of Kettering Cassidy, also known as Michael Corrigan, and another woman. Below the photograph were the words: 'Mr M. Corrigan, the race horse owner, and Miss X, whose engagement has been announced.' Mr Cassidy had told the photographer of this announcement. The action was brought by Mrs Cassidy, who was in fact the lawful wife of Cassidy. Although they lived apart, Cassidy occasionally visited her. She argued that the words and picture were capable of meaning that 'Corrigan' was a single man and that she, therefore, was living in immoral co-habitation with him. The Court of Appeal held that the publication was capable of bearing this defamatory meaning. On their own, the words and picture were not defamatory. However, in the light of the extrinsic evidence that Cassidy was in fact married, a defamatory meaning was possible. It did not matter that the defendant newspaper did not know of the extrinsic facts, provided that the paper had been read by those who did and who understood the statement to apply to the plaintiff.

20.4 The Statement Must be Published to a Third Person

The law of defamation is concerned, as we have seen, with the protection of a person's reputation. As a person's reputation is, in crude terms, the opinion or estimation in which he is held by others, it follows that unless the statement is published to someone other than the claimant there can be no damage to his reputation. If nobody but the maker of the statement and its subject know of the contents of that statement, how can it have affected the subject's reputation in the eyes of his fellows? Thus, English law requires that the defamatory statement must be published to someone other than the person whose reputation is impugned. An unexpressed defamatory thought or even the writing of such a thought on paper will not be actionable unless and until it is actually communicated to another. The publication must also be made to a person capable of understanding the defamatory meaning. Where, for example, the statement is not defamatory on its face but only when considered in the light of extrinsic evidence (a case of true innuendo) the hearer must know of the extrinsic facts that make the statement defamatory. More obviously, if a defamatory statement is written in a foreign language the reader must be able to understand that language.

It is not necessary for the claimant to prove that the publication was intentionally made. As long as he can show that the defendant ought reasonably to have foreseen that the statement would come to a third party's attention the requirement of publication will be satisfied. Thus in *Theaker* v. *Richardson* [1962] 1 WLR 151 the defendant addressed a defamatory letter to the plaintiff who was a married woman. The letter was contained in a manilla envelope similar to the kind used for distributing election addresses. The plaintiff's husband opened the envelope thinking it was an election address. At the trial the jury found there had been a publication of a defamatory statement and awarded damages to the plaintiff. On appeal to the Court of Appeal, Pearson LJ said that the question that should be asked was, 'Was his [i.e., the husband's] conduct so unusual, out of the ordinary and not reasonably to be anticipated, or was it something which could quite easily and naturally happen in the ordinary course of events?'. This was pre-eminently a jury question and as the jury had decided that the opening of the letter by the husband was something that could quite easily happen in the ordinary course of events the Court of Appeal would not interfere with its decision. By way of contrast, the Court of Appeal held in *Huth* v. *Huth* [1915] 3 KB 32 that, where a husband sent a defamatory letter to his wife, the fact that it had been opened and read by the butler did not constitute publication.

Lord Reading CJ observed: 'Fortunately, it is no part of a butler's duty to open letters which come to the house of his master or mistress addressed to them; and in this case there is nothing exceptional, save that his curiosity was excited by reason of the lady being addressed by her maiden name' (p. 38).

Every repetition of a defamatory statement is a new publication and creates a fresh cause of action in the person defamed. The person repeating the statement will be treated in the same way as if he had originated it. Further, a defendant cannot escape liability simply by putting a prefix such as 'it has been rumoured that ...' or 'I have been told that ...' before the allegation and then asserting that it was true that there was such a rumour or that he had in fact been told what he had then repeated. Such a 'hearsay' statement is treated as if it were a direct statement, so the person who repeats the rumour will have to prove the truth of the allegation to escape liability and not just that there was such a rumour in existence (see *Stern* v. *Piper* [1997] QB 123). This principle is sometimes known as the 'rumour' doctrine.

Although every repetition of the original defamatory imputation creates a new cause of action, common sense dictates that liability must cease somewhere. Whilst there may be good arguments of policy for holding liable those primarily involved in the publishing process (such as author, publisher and editor), less reason exists for imposing liability on those more tangentially involved in the 'publishing' process (such as libraries, printers and booksellers). Those only tangentially involved in the publishing process have little control over the content of any publication and often have no reason to suspect that any statement it may contain might be defamatory. To expect them to read for libel every line of all the material they distribute is clearly unrealistic. At common law, such so-called 'mechanical' publishers can rely on the defence of innocent dissemination. In *Vizetelly* v. *Mudies' Select Library Ltd.* [1900] 2 QB 170 the Court of Appeal held that a person who has been involved in the dissemination of a defamatory imputation is not liable if he can prove (a) that he was innocent of any knowledge of the libel contained in the work disseminated by him; (b) that there was nothing in the work or in the circumstances in which it came to, or was disseminated by him which ought to have led him to suppose it contained a libel; and (c) that when the work was disseminated by him it was not by any negligence on his part that he did not know it contained a libel.

While the decision in *Vizetelly* has been relied upon successfully by a porter delivering books and news-vendors, the exact scope of the defence was by no means clear and recent changes in technology have made it even less so. Section 1 of the Defamation Act 1996 was enacted with the intention of codifying the existing law while at the same time modernising it. In addition to those who would formerly have been treated as 'mechanical' publishers, the defence can now be relied upon by, *inter alia*, the broadcaster of a live programme which contains the statement, in circumstances where the broadcaster has no effective control over its content, for example, on talk radio (s. 1(3)(d)); the operator of, or provider of access to a communications system (such as the Internet) by means of which a statement is transmitted; and persons responsible for processing, making copies of, distributing or selling any electronic medium (such as CD-ROMs and floppy disks) in or on which the statement is recorded (s. 1(3)(c)). The conditions for the existence of the defence are found in s. 1(1) of the Act. This provides that a person shall have a defence if he shows that (a) he was not the author, editor or publisher of the statement complained of; (b) he took reasonable care in relation to the publication; and (c) he did not know, and had no reason to believe, that what he did caused or contributed to the publication of a defamatory statement. While the legislation does in the main merely represent a modernisation and codification of the common law, the new provision restricts the scope of the defence in one important respect. At common law, the defence had been available to a distributor who had no knowledge that the publication in question contained a *libel*. Under s. 1(1)(c) of the Act, however, the defence is only available if he did not know, and had no reason to believe, that what he did caused or contributed to the publication of a *defamatory statement*. The distinction is important because, while those such as newsagents and booksellers may be aware that publications they sell contain *defamatory statements*, they are frequently assured by the publishers that such statements are true; in other words, that there is no *libel*. As the common law defence is not abolished by the new section 1, the possibility for conflict exists.

A related question was considered by the Court of Appeal in *Slipper* v. *British Broadcasting Corporation* [1991] 1 QB 283: is the original maker of the statement liable for subsequent re-publications of his statement by others? The Court of Appeal held that the law relating to re-publication in defamation cases is simply an example of the rule of causation encapsulated in the Latin phrase 'novus actus interveniens' familiar throughout the law of tort (see ch. 10). Thus, in any case involving the repetition of a libel the following question should be asked: was it a foreseeable or natural and probable consequence of the libel that the third party to whom it was published would repeat it?

20.5 **Reference to the Claimant**

The third essential requirement to found an action for defamation is that the defamatory imputation referred to the claimant. Where the claimant is expressly mentioned by name there will usually be no difficulty. However, it is not essential that the claimant be expressly referred to. In *Morgan* v. *Odhams Press Ltd* [1971] 1 WLR 1239 the fact that the plaintiff was not expressly referred to was not held to be fatal to his claim. The defendants published an article which stated that a woman had been kidnapped by a dog-doping gang. The woman had in fact been staying voluntarily with the plaintiff around this time. At the trial the plaintiff produced several witnesses who said that they thought that the article referred to him. The House of Lords held that, in determining whether the article referred to the plaintiff, the test to be adopted was whether a hypothetical sensible reader, knowing what the witnesses knew, could reasonably come to the conclusion that the article referred to the plaintiff. Such a reader was not expected to read a newspaper article with the care that a lawyer would read an important legal document. It was accepted that he may read it quickly in order to get a general impression. What were important were the inferences that the reader would draw from the article. On the facts of the case, despite the fact that a close reading of the article would have made it clear that it could not refer to the plaintiff, their Lordships upheld the jury's verdict in his favour.

The fact that the defendant in making the statement did not intend to refer to the claimant has been held by the courts to be irrelevant. In *Hulton* v. *Jones* [1910] AC 20, Artemus Jones, a barrister, brought an action against the defendants in respect of a newspaper article which he claimed referred to him. The article referred to 'Artemus Jones', a church-warden in Peckham, and cast imputations on his moral behaviour at a motor festival in Dieppe. The defendants argued they had never intended the article to refer to the real Artemus Jones but instead had intended to create a fictitious character. The House of Lords held that the defendants' intentions were irrelevant. Lord Loreburn said 'a person charged with libel cannot defend himself by shewing that he intended in his own breast not to defame, or that he intended not to defame the plaintiff, if in fact he did both' (p. 23). The test to be applied was to ask whether a reasonable person would consider in all the circumstances that the article referred to the claimant.

In *Newstead* v. *London Express Newspaper Ltd* [1940] 1 KB 377, the Court of Appeal applied the principle of *Hulton* v. *Jones* to the situation where the defendant had intended to refer to a person about whom the statement was true but the claimant said that the statement also referred to him and was defamatory. Provided a reader of the article would reasonably think that the statement referred to the claimant, it is no defence for the defendant to prove that the words were intended to refer to another person of whom they were true.

While the harshness of the strict liability rule in this context may be mitigated by the new offer of amends procedure in s. 2 of the Defamation Act 1996 (see 20.14), it remains the case that the rule makes it almost impossible for a publisher to protect itself against unintentional defamation. With the incorporation into English law of the ECHR, it is almost inevitable that in due course the strict liability rule will be challenged on the basis of incompatibility with art. 10. An early indication of this came in *O'Shea* v. *MGN Ltd* [2001] EMLR 40, where the defendants published an advertisement for a pornographic website. The advertisement featured a photograph of a woman, E, whom the claimant alleged was her spitting image. Morland J accepted, as he was bound to do, that the test for reference was objective. That the publisher did not intend to refer to the claimant or even know of her existence was irrelevant. However, in Morland J's opinion, to apply the rule to a 'look-alike' situation would be incompatible with art. 10 and he therefore dismissed the claim as having no reasonable prospect of success. According to the judge:

> 'It would impose an impossible burden on a publisher if he were required to check if the true picture of someone resembled someone else who because of the context of the picture was defamed. Examples are legion: unlawful violence in street protest demonstrations, looting, hooliganism at football matches, people apparently leaving or entering court with criminal defendants and investigative journalism into drug dealing, corruption, child abuse and prostitution.'

Whether *Hulton* and *Newstead* were properly distinguishable, as the judge thought, on the ground that the existence of the claimants in those cases could 'theoretically' have been discovered, whereas it would be impossible to discover whether a 'look-alike' of the photograph of the real person existed, seems to us to be debateable. What seems certain, however, is that Morland J's will not be the last word on this important issue.

Defamation of a Group

Where words are spoken of a group or class of people, proof that the article refers to a particular member of that group is likely to be difficult. If a person were heard to say 'all lawyers are thieves', this would be unlikely to give rise to a cause of action on the part of any individual lawyer. As Lord Atkin explained in *Knuppfer* v. *London Express Newspapers* [1944] AC 116, 122:

> 'The reason why a libel published of a large or indeterminate number of persons described by some general name generally fails to be actionable is the difficulty of establishing that the plaintiff was, in fact, included in the defamatory statement, for the habit of making unfounded generalizations is ingrained in ill-educated or vulgar minds, or the words are occasionally intended to be a facetious exaggeration.'

However, the fact that proof of reference in such a case as this is difficult does not mean that defamatory imputations directed against a group of persons will never be actionable at the suit of a member of that group. There is no invariable rule to that effect and an action may lie where the words used may be reasonably understood to refer to every member of the class. Although it has been said that no special rules exist for group defamations, the smaller the group and the more specific the allegation, the more likely it is that it will be held that sufficient reference was made to the claimant. Thus, in *Knuppfer* v. *London Express Newspapers*, Lord Porter suggested that each member of a body, however large, could be said to be defamed 'where the libel consisted in the assertion that no one of the members of a community was elected as a member unless he had committed a murder.' However, on the facts of *Knuppfer* itself, the House of Lords concluded that, although the claimant was the leader of the relatively small group referred to, there was not sufficient reference to found a cause of action.

20.6 Damage: The Distinction Between Libel and Slander

English law draws a distinction between two forms of defamation: libel and slander. Each is a separate nominate tort, though in most respects the rules of liability are the same. In general terms, libel is a defamatory communication conveyed in some permanent form, most often, though not invariably, writing; slander is a defamatory communication conveyed in some non-permanent or more transitory form, such as the spoken word. In the case of libel, damage need not be proved as it is presumed: it is actionable *per se*. Save in four exceptional circumstances – imputations of criminal conduct punishable with imprisonment (e.g. *Gray* v. *Jones* [1939] 1 All ER 798); imputations that the claimant is suffering from a contagious or infectious disease (e.g. *Bloodworth* v. *Gray* (1844) 7 M & G 334); imputations of unchastity against a woman (Slander of Women Act 1891); and imputations calculated to disparage the claimant in any office, profession, calling, trade or business (Defamation Act 1952, s. 2)) – slander is only actionable on proof of special damage. 'Special' damage in this context means some pecuniary loss or some actual damage that is capable of being estimated in money. Thus, while loss of reputation and 'mere mental suffering or sickness' are not enough, the loss of a job or trade has been held to amount to special damage, as has the loss of membership of a club and the loss of hospitality of friends (but not the mere loss of their society).

Originally, the distinction between libel and slander lay in the difference between oral and written statements. However, as methods of communication have developed and changed this distinction is no longer wholly satisfactory, if it ever was. How, for example, should we classify radio defamation? Does it make any difference whether the programme is live or recorded? Are defamatory statements made on the Internet (see *Godfrey* v. *Demon Internet Ltd* [2001] QB 201), CD-ROMs, videotapes and television libels or slanders? Should an e-mail message be treated as libel or slander? Parliament has legislated in respect of some of these questions (see, for example, s. 166 of the Broadcasting Act 1990 and s. 4 of the Theatres Act 1968 which provide respectively that radio and television broadcasts and theatrical performances are libel) but where it has not, some 'test' must be sought to distinguish between the two.

Although there are statements to the effect that libels are conveyed to the sense of sight, whereas slanders are conveyed to the ear, it is suggested that the best view is that permanence is the gist of the distinction. As Lopes LJ said in *Monson* v. *Tussauds Ltd* [1894] 1 QB 671, 692: '[L]ibels are generally in writing or printing, but this is not necessary; the defamatory matter may be conveyed in some other permanent form. For instance, a statue, a caricature, an effigy, chalk-marks on a wall, signs or pictures may constitute a libel.' Further, as that case makes clear, while libels are most often written they need not be: a wax model of the plaintiff placed in an exhibition entitled 'the chamber of horrors' was held to be a libel.

Although the origin of the distinction between libel and slander lies in history, there have been a number of modern attempts to justify its continued existence. It has been argued that, as libels are in a permanent form, they are likely to remain in currency for longer, to be read by more people, and have more significance attached to them. It has also been suggested that a libel conveys the impression of a more deliberate and calculated attack on reputation than does slander. Slanderous remarks are often made in the context of heated conversations and once made may be immediately regretted. Libel, however, usually requires the defendant to have sat down and given some thought about what he is writing. While there is some truth in much of the above, it is suggested that a slander may have just as serious an effect on a person's reputation as a libel. For example, a well-placed remark at a board meeting of a large company concerning the personal proclivities of the company's chairman could be just as damaging as an article in a major newspaper. It is surely such factors as the status of the person making the statement, the statement's seriousness and the circumstances in which it was made that are important rather than the permanence of the statement or the means by which it is conveyed.

20.7 **Parties**

The general rule is that any legally-recognised person or entity except a governmental entity or political party can bring an action in respect of a libel or slander. Moreover, any legally-recognised person or entity may be sued for defamation. Where more than one person is involved jointly in the publication of a libel, all those responsible may be joined as co-defendants or any of them may be sued separately. The rules as to who can sue and be sued in the law of tort generally apply to the law of defamation. However, certain categories of cases give rise to particular problems. Of these it is worth mentioning that the dead can neither sue nor be sued, trading corporations can sue but only in respect of their trading reputation, and special rules apply to trade unions and bankrupts. Full discussion of these exceptions is beyond the ambit of this chapter, however, one particular category of case is worthy of more discussion and this is considered next.

While central government departments and local authorities are today engaged in many activities also pursued by trading corporations, they are different in the significant respect that they are democratically accountable. 'We the People' have the right every few years to decide whom to elect, a right we do not possess in respect of ordinary trading corporations. In *Derbyshire County Council* v. *Times Newspapers* [1993] AC 534, the House of Lords concluded that this essential difference between trading corporations and local authorities meant that the latter should not be allowed to sue in defamation. To hold otherwise would have an unnecessary 'chilling effect' on freedom of speech (p. 550, per Lord Keith):

'It is of the highest public importance that a democratically elected governmental body, or indeed any governmental body, should be open to uninhibited public criticism. The threat of a civil action for defamation must inevitably have an inhibiting effect on freedom of speech.'

Although the case concerned a local authority exercising governmental and administrative functions, it is clear that the same rule applies to any democratically elected governmental body, whether at central or local level, and to non-elected institutions of central and local government exercising governmental and administrative functions. Thus, neither central government departments nor the Crown can sue for defamation in respect of imputations that reflect on their governmental and administrative functions. However, their Lordships made clear that the decision did not affect the right to sue of an individual MP, councillor or officer or employee of a governmental body if the words spoken of the organ of government were capable of referring to the individual.

Subsequent cases have extended the scope of the rule. Thus, in *Goldsmith* v. *Bhoyrul* [1998] QB 459 it was held that the rule applied to prevent a political party, then seeking power at an election and putting itself forward for office, from suing in defamation in respect of allegations about the conduct of its election campaign. According to Buckley J, while it was true to say that a party seeking power at an election could not be equated with a government body that had power (pp. 270–1):

'the public interest in free speech and criticism in respect of those bodies putting themselves forward for office or to govern is also sufficiently strong to justify withholding the right to sue. Defamation actions or the threat of them would constitute a fetter on free speech at a time and on a topic when it is clearly in the public interest that there should be none.'

More controversially, in *British Coal Corporation* v. *National Union of Mineworkers* (unreported, 28 June 1996) it was held that the rule prevented the British Coal Corporation from suing in defamation over allegations that it had 'stolen' £450 million from the mineworkers' pension fund. That the British Coal Corporation, a creature of statute, was neither democratically elected nor exercising administrative or governmental functions does not appear to have been conclusive against the application of the rule. However, in *Steel & Morris* v. *McDonald's Corporation* (unreported, 1999) it was held that a multinational corporation did not fall within the principle recognised in the *Derbyshire* case and had as much right to sue in defamation as any other trading corporation, notwithstanding the enormous power possessed by such corporations.

Although it is clear that organs of central and local government cannot sue in the law of defamation, it is by no means clear how much further the courts will be prepared to go in preventing certain bodies, organisations or even individuals from suing. Thus far, the English courts have resisted adopting the approach taken in American law that only allows actions to be brought against 'public bodies' or 'public persons' on proof of 'actual malice' (*Reynolds* v. *Times Newspapers Ltd* [2001] 2 AC 127). Of course, in one respect, the approach taken by English law is even more protective of freedom of speech than the American approach, namely that actions against central and local government and political parties appear to be absolutely precluded whereas in the United States such actions will only fail if the claimant fails to prove 'actual malice'. In other respects, however, American law is wider; actions brought by both 'public bodies' *and* 'public persons' (and this would include politicians and other self-publicists) will only succeed on proof of actual malice. Whether the absolute bar preventing political parties and organs of central and local government from suing will survive challenge under art. 6 of the ECHR remains to be seen.

20.8 Defences

A person sued in defamation can seek to defend an action brought against him on the basis that the claimant has not made out a prima facie case. Thus, the defendant might argue that the words complained of were not defamatory of the claimant, or that they were not published to a third person, or that they did not refer to the claimant. The next few sections are not concerned with 'defences' in that sense. Instead they are concerned with the substantive defences, additional to the general defences considered elsewhere in the book, that may be raised to defeat a claim even where the claimant has made out a prima facie case, and in respect of which the onus of pleading and burden of proof is on the defendant.

20.9 Justification

Where a claimant succeeds in showing that he has been defamed by the words complained of and that they have been published to a third party, the law presumes in his favour that such words are untrue. However, to such a claim the defendant can plead justification. The essence of the defence of justification is that the words complained of are 'true in substance and in fact'. The policy behind allowing justification as a complete defence was well put by Littledale J in *M'Pherson* v. *Daniels* (1829) B & C 263, 272: 'The law will not permit a man to recover damages in respect of an injury to a character which he either does not or ought not to possess.' Unlike other defences, such as fair comment or qualified privilege, the motive of the defendant in making the original statement is irrelevant. Thus, save in cases covered by the Rehabilitation of Offenders Act 1974, even where the defendant makes the statement with the express intention of damaging the claimant's reputation, if the words are true the defendant will escape liability.

In order to establish the defence the defendant must prove that the defamatory matter complained of is true. However, it is not necessary that every 't' should be crossed and every 'i' dotted. As Lord Shaw said in *Sutherland* v. *Stopes* [1925] AC 47, 79:

'[T]he plea [of justification] must not be considered in a meticulous sense. It is that the words employed were true in substance and in fact ... all that was required to affirm the plea was that the jury should be satisfied that the sting of the libel or, if there were more than one, the stings of the libel should be made out.'

Thus, if A accused B of having stolen his car on 20 March from outside his house, proof that B had stolen A's car would justify the sting of the accusation. The fact that B stole the car on 21 March from outside A's office would not prevent reliance on the defence. Such minor inaccuracies in no way add to the seriousness of the charge against B.

In order for the plea of justification to be successful it must cover the meaning attributed by the jury to the words complained of. You will recall that the claimant may, and must if he wishes to rely on them, give particulars of defamatory meanings which arise by way of innuendo (see 20.3). In a similar fashion, a defendant who pleads justification must state the meaning that he seeks to justify. If the defendant fails to justify the meaning which the jury finds the words to have then the defence will fail: the fact that the defendant can prove some other meaning is irrelevant. Thus, in *Lewis* v. *Daily Telegraph*, the fact that the defendant could justify the literal meaning of the words – that the company was under investigation by the police – would not have justified the innuendo meanings – that the company was suspected or guilty of misconduct.

A defamatory statement may contain more than one charge. At common law, where more than one charge was alleged, a plea of justification to the whole would only have been successful where the defendant justified the sting of all the charges. If A says of some person that 'he has murdered his father, stolen from his mother and does not go to church on Sundays' and A can prove the first two allegations but not the last, A will remain liable in damages in respect of the last charge. The common law has now been altered by section 5 of the Defamation Act 1952. This provides:

'In an action for libel or slander in respect of words containing two or more distinct charges against the plaintiff, a defence of justification shall not fail by reason only that the truth of every charge is not proved if the words not proved to be true do not materially injure the plaintiff's reputation having regard to the truth of the remaining charges.'

Under this rule, in the example given above, failure to prove that the claimant does not go to church on Sundays would not be fatal to a defence of justification if it was felt by the jury that an allegation of failure to go to church on Sundays did not add to the gravity of the other charges.

The provisions of s. 5 are, however, only applicable in an action where the claimant relies upon a defamatory statement which contains two or more distinct charges. It would appear to be open to a claimant to complain simply of one allegation out of several made against him. Should he do so, the defendant would not be allowed to justify other defamatory allegations contained in the publication in the hope of persuading the jury that the defamatory statement was substantially true or to influence the jury to award lower damages. However, although the claimant may isolate one particular allegation in the expectation of being able to prevent the defendant justifying other allegations, the defendant will only be prevented from justifying other allegations where they are 'separate and distinct'. Where the allegations have a common sting the defendant will be allowed to adduce evidence of the truth of the other allegations in order to justify the common sting. In *Polly Peck (Holdings) PLC* v. *Trelford* [1986] 1 QB 1000, O'Connor LJ held that whether allegations are 'separate and distinct' or have a common sting is a question of fact and degree in each case. In *Khashoggi* v. *I.P.C Magazines Ltd* [1986] 1 WLR 1412 a magazine article contained what purported to be an account of the plaintiff's life with her husband, an international arms dealer, before and after the dissolution of their marriage. The article contained a series of allegations regarding her sexual behaviour. The plaintiff objected to one of the allegations in the article suggesting that she had committed adultery with a named friend of her husband. The Court of Appeal held that, although the defendants could not prove the allegation of adultery with that particular person, the article was capable of meaning that the plaintiff was guilty of promiscuity generally. Evidence of other 'affairs', therefore, was relevant in considering whether the common sting of the article could be justified.

20.10 Fair Comment

The defence of fair comment on a matter of public interest is, like justification, a complete defence to an action for defamation. The defence gives legal recognition to the legitimate public interest of members of the public honestly to express their opinion however 'cranky', 'irrational' or 'muddle-headed' it may be. This public interest is of such social importance that in the area covered by the defence it outweighs the competing claim that a person has to have an unblemished reputation. In order for the defence to succeed it must be shown: (1) that the words used are comment and not fact; (2) that the comments are on a matter of public interest; (3) that the comment is based on true facts; and (4) that the comment is 'fair'. If the defendant proves these elements, the defence will succeed unless the claimant can show that the defendant was actuated by malice.

Comments or Statements of Fact

In order to be able to rely on the defence the defendant must indicate with reasonable clarity that the statement is one of opinion as opposed to one of fact. Where there is any doubt as to whether the words are fact or comment the trial judge is required to decide whether the words are capable of being comment, the question whether they are in fact comment being left to the jury. How then are facts to be distinguished from comment? The distinction is often elusive but an approach which has some merit has been suggested by Sutherland (1992):

> 'Generally, the issue ... can be determined by examining the statement in isolation. If the statement is at least theoretically susceptible of proof by objective criteria, then it is a statement of fact. If, on the other hand, it represents the statement of a moral or aesthetic judgment, then it constitutes opinion or comment.'

Thus a statement that 'A is a convicted burglar and is, therefore, unfit for public office' is a statement of opinion that A is unfit for public office based on a statement of fact that A is a convicted burglar. More difficult is a statement that A has been guilty of 'disgraceful conduct'. This has been assumed by more than one judge to be a statement of fact. Yet it is difficult to see that such a statement is susceptible of proof by objective criteria. Is it not in reality a statement of moral judgment?

Based upon True Facts

A defendant must prove that his comment was based upon true facts. At common law failure to prove the truth of any material basic facts, as distinct from the comments on, or inferences drawn from, those facts, prevented the defendant relying on the defence. Thus, a reviewer who wrote excoriating a writer for treating adultery in a cavalier fashion in one of his plays was held not to be able to rely on the defence when there was in fact no adultery in the play: 'There is all the difference in the world between saying that you disapprove of the character of a work and that you think it has an evil tendency, and saying that a work treats adultery cavalierly, when in fact there is no adultery at all in the story' (*Merivale* v. *Carson* (1887) 20 QBD 275, 284).

This strict position has, however, been mitigated by s. 6 of the Defamation Act 1952 which provides:

> '[I]n an action for libel or slander in respect of words consisting partly of allegations of fact and partly of expression of opinion, a defence of fair comment shall not fail by reason only that the truth of every allegation of fact is not proved if the expression of the opinion is fair comment having regard to such of the facts alleged or referred to in the words complained of as are proved.'

Thus where it is said of A that he is unfit for public office because he is 'a liar, a thief and he has never held office before', failure to prove that the claimant has never held office before would not prevent the defendant relying on the defence. The comment is still fair comment having regard to such of the facts as have been proved. However, if the defendant had failed instead to prove that the claimant was a thief, s. 6 would probably not provide a complete defence.

Although the comment must be based on facts that are sufficiently stated or identified so as to enable the reader to identify the publication on which the defendant is commenting, there is no need for the commentator to set out the facts in full. In *Kemsley* v. *Foot* [1952] AC 345 the defendant wrote an article accusing the Beaverbrook Press of the 'foulest piece of journalism perpetrated in this country for a long time'. The defendant's article was headed 'Lower than Kemsley'. The plaintiff, a rival newspaper proprietor, alleged that the statement implied that his companies knowingly published false statements and that 'his name was a byword in this respect'. The defendant pleaded fair comment. The House of Lords held that a plea of fair comment could succeed provided there was a 'sufficient substratum of fact stated or indicated in the words which are the subject matter of the action'. On the facts there was a sufficient substratum of fact – namely, that the plaintiff was in control of the newspapers and that his conduct in this regard was in question – to justify leaving the defence to a jury.

Matter of Public Interest

The comment must be on a matter of public interest. A matter is of public interest 'whenever ... [it] is such as to affect people at large, so that they may be legitimately interested in, or concerned at, what is going on; or what may happen to them or others' (*London Artists Ltd* v. *Littler* [1969] 2 QB 375, 391, per Lord Denning MR). Discussion of national or local politics, the administration of justice, matters concerning public health, religion and education, and the fitness of a person to hold a public position clearly falls within this definition. So too does discussion of entertainment, literary and artistic matters, and the management of public companies and institutions.

Whilst comment on both the substance of public debate and the conduct and behaviour of those engaged in such debate is essential in any democracy, care must be taken not to stray from comment on a person's conduct in their public capacity to comment on their private life. The private character of a person is of interest only in so far as it affects their capabilities or qualifications for public office. The mere fact of being in the public eye does not legitimise comment on every aspect of a person's character.

The Comment must be 'Fair'

The question of the appropriate test to be applied in determining whether a comment was 'fair' had, until the decision of the House of Lords in *Telnikoff* v. *Matusevitch* [1992] 2 AC 343, become so shrouded with confusion that the two leading practitioner works on defamation suggested different answers. In *Telnikoff* the House of Lords, approving the judgment of Lloyd LJ in the Court of Appeal ([1990] 3 WLR 725), held that the test is a purely objective one: 'could any fair-minded man honestly express that opinion on the proved facts' (p. 740, per Lloyd LJ). It was for the defendant to prove that a fair-minded person could hold the view expressed but he did not need to go further and prove that he honestly held that view. However, proof by the claimant that the defendant did not honestly hold the view expressed is good evidence of malice and malice, as we shall see, defeats the defence. The objective test applied here does not require an investigation into whether a reasonable person could hold that opinion. The test instead appears to be whether any fair-minded, i.e. honest though possibly prejudiced, person could hold the view expressed. Thus, as well as protecting those commenting intelligently on matters of public concern, the test protects the views of the honest 'crank' and even those of persons whose opinions are exaggerated, intemperate and biased. However, although a wide latitude is allowed to the obstinate and prejudiced, there comes a time when what is being said 'passes out of the domain of criticism' and becomes unfair abuse: 'Criticism cannot be used as a cloak for mere invective nor for personal imputations not arising out of the subject-matter or not based on fact' (*McGuire* v. *Western Morning News Co.* [1903] 2 KB 100, 109, per Collins MR). Such is likely to be held to be the case where the commentator follows the claimant into domestic life for the purposes of slander or mounts an attack on the moral character of the claimant unconnected with the subject matter of the comment.

Once the defendant has established that the subject matter is a matter of public interest, the facts on which the comment is based are true and the comment is one any fair-minded man could make, he is entitled to rely on the defence unless the claimant can establish that the defendant was actuated by malice. As the question of malice arises in almost identical terms in relation to the defence of qualified privilege, the issue of what amounts to malice will be considered later.

20.11 Absolute Privilege

In a limited number of situations deemed to be of great social or political importance, the law allows a person to speak or write about others without fear of the usual legal consequences that attach in respect of defamatory communications. Where an occasion is deemed to be of sufficient importance, statements made on that occasion will be absolutely privileged. This is a complete bar to an action for defamation no matter how false the wording may be or howsoever malicious the defendant. Because the effect of the defence is so drastic, preventing as it does a person from vindicating his reputation, the number of absolutely privileged occasions is small. The defence is not, however, designed to protect abusers of such occasions. Instead the immunity is granted to protect the makers of statements on certain occasions from being forced to defend themselves against unjustified accusations that they were actuated by malice.

The following circumstances are occasions of absolute privilege.

Parliamentary Proceedings

Article 9 of the Bill of Rights 1688 provides that, 'the freedome of Speech and debates or proceedings in Parlyament ought not to be impeached or questioned in any court or place out of Parlyament.' This has been held to have the effect that any statement made by members of the Houses of Parliament in the course of debates or other parliamentary proceedings (including standing committees: *Rost* v. *Edwards* [1990] 2 All ER 654) is absolutely privileged. The privilege does not, however, attach to all statements made by MPs wherever made: it is only those made within the environs of the Houses of Parliament which are protected. By s. 13 of the Defamation Act 1996 this protection is extended in a number of respects.

While in the field of defamation parliamentary privilege has its main effect in preventing courts entertaining a case alleging that an MP is liable for defamatory statements made in the course of parliamentary proceedings, it is clear that its impact is much wider. As Lord Browne Wilkinson said in *Prebble* v. *Television New Zealand* [1994] 3 All ER 407:

'In addition to article 9 itself, there is a long line of authority which supports a wider principle, of which article 9 is merely one manifestation, viz. that the courts and Parliament are both astute to recognise their respective constitutional roles. So far as the courts are concerned they will not allow any challenge to be made to what is said or done within the walls of Parliament in performance of its legislative functions and protection of its established privileges ... As Blackstone said in his *Commentaries on the Laws of England,* 17th ed. (1830), vol. 1, p. 163: "the whole of the law and custom of Parliament has its origin from this one maxim, that whatever matter arises concerning either House of Parliament, ought to be examined, discussed and adjudged in that House to which it relates, and not elsewhere." '

It follows from this that the effect of parliamentary privilege may not only be to prevent an MP being sued for what he has said in Parliament but also to prevent both claimant and defendant from raising evidence where that involves challenging anything said or done in Parliament (see *Prebble* v. *Television New Zealand Ltd* [1994] 3 All ER 407). The privilege protected is that of Parliament itself and not its individual members and it does not matter therefore whether it is the claimant or the defendant who wishes to rely on what was said in Parliament. Where, however, a claimant's claim to parliamentary privilege would effectively exclude all the evidence necessary to establish a defence, a stay of action may be granted in order to prevent injustice (*Allason* v. *Haines* [1996] EMLR 143).

While a stay of action is only granted where the court is convinced that the assertion of privilege makes a fair resolution of the case appropriate, its effect may, of course, make it impossible for a politician to clear his name. Such a situation may exist where the defendant wants to lead evidence central to his defence that would infringe parliamentary privilege.

Not to grant a fair trial stay would be unfair on the defendant, yet its grant may be unfair on the MP who would thereby be prevented from clearing his name. Moreover, the problem cannot be solved by the MP waiving parliamentary privilege: the privilege is that of the Houses of Parliament and cannot be waived by an individual MP (*Hamilton* v. *Al Fayed* [2001] I AC 395, 407, per Lord Browne-Wilkinson). In an attempt to avoid this perceived unfairness to a libelled MP, Parliament passed section 13 of the Defamation Act 1996 which allows a person whose conduct in or in relation to proceedings in Parliament is impugned to *waive* 'the protection of any enactment or rule of law which prevents proceedings in Parliament being impeached or questioned in any court or place out of Parliament.' Such waiver operates so that evidence, cross-examination, submissions or findings made relative to the particular person whose conduct is in issue in, or in relation to, proceedings of Parliament, are not to be excluded by reason of parliamentary privilege (s. 13(2)(a)) and none of those things shall be regarded as infringing the privilege of either House of Parliament (s. 13(2)(b)).

Parliamentary Papers Act 1840

In addition to the protection afforded to the maker of the statement, section 1 of the Parliamentary Papers Act 1840 provides that the court is compelled to stay any action brought against the publisher of any reports, papers, votes or proceedings published by order of or under the authority of either House of Parliament. As yet there is no similar provision with respect to the televising of Parliament, although the broadcasting authority would certainly be protected by qualified privilege.

Judicial Proceedings

An absolute privilege attaches to all statements, whether oral or written, made in the course of judicial proceedings. All concerned in judicial proceedings, whether as one of the parties to the action, counsel, judge, members of the jury or witness are immune from an action for defamation. The privilege extends to 'tribunals' as well as courts properly so-called, and applies not only to the proceedings themselves but also in respect of certain work preparatory to those proceedings. Thus, statements made to a solicitor when taking a witness statement prior to the commencement of civil proceedings have been held to be protected by absolute privilege (*Watson* v. *M'Ewen* [1905] AC 480), as have statements made between police officers investigating a crime or possible crime with a view to a possible prosecution and to statements made by a person to an investigator even where that person is not intended to be called as a witness (*Taylor* v. *Director of the Serious Fraud Office* [1999] 2 AC 177). By s. 14(1) of the Defamation Act 1996, 'A fair and accurate report of proceedings before a court ... if published contemporaneously with the proceedings, is absolutely privileged.'

High Executive Communications

Where a statement is made by one high-ranking member of the executive to another, it will be protected by absolute privilege. In *Chatterton* v. *Secretary of State for India in Council* [1895] 2 QB 189 the Court of Appeal held that a statement made by the Secretary of State for India to an Under-Secretary of State was protected by absolute privilege. The court attached great importance to the need for independence in such officers and the interest of the public in allowing them to get on with their work unhindered by libel actions.

The scope of this head of privilege remains uncertain. Whilst communications between ministers of state or between ministers and high-ranking civil servants are clearly protected, doubt exists as to how high-ranking the official must be and what executive bodies might be covered. Should the privilege extend, for example, to high-ranking officers in the police force or army? Unfortunately the cases are by no means clear: communications between middle ranking army officers have, for example, been held to be protected (*Dawkins* v. *Lord Paulet* (1869) LR 5 QB 94) while communications between police officers of similar rank were not (*Richards* v. *Naum* [1967] 1 QB 620, 625). All that can be said with any certainty is that no blanket privilege protects communications between government servants.

Statements of Public Officials Protected by Statute

A number of statutes expressly provide that publications made by certain officials, such as the Parliamentary Commissioner for Administration (the 'Ombudsman') and the Director General of Fair Trading, are absolutely privileged. The underlying rationale appears to be that the nature of their work makes it likely that they will be subject to actions for defamation. To allow a defamation action against them would make their work impossible and leave them looking over their shoulder in fear of such an action. To avoid this, and to facilitate the proper discharge of official functions, an absolute privilege is needed.

20.12 Qualified Privilege

In addition to those occasions of sufficient social importance to justify the application of absolute privilege, there are others which, while not of the same importance nevertheless still merit qualified privilege. As with absolute privilege, the reason for allowing statements made on such occasions to be privileged is 'the common convenience and welfare of society'. Although reputation is an important and integral part of the dignity of the individual and its protection conducive to the good of society, other compelling public interests (especially freedom of expression: art. 10 ECHR) may outweigh that interest. Where an occasion justifies the protection of qualified privilege, but is not sufficiently important to justify absolute privilege, statements made on such occasions will be protected unless the claimant can show that the maker of the statement was actuated by malice.

The categories of qualified privilege, amounting as they do to no more than applications in particular circumstances of the underlying principles of public policy, are never closed, and changing social conditions may indicate the need to extend an existing category or even to create a wholly new one. Thus, it is impossible fully to categorise all the occasions on which qualified privilege arises. As Lord Nicholls explained in *Reynolds* v. *Times Newspapers* [2001] 2 AC 127, 195:

> 'In determining whether an occasion is regarded as privileged the court has regard to all the circumstances ... And circumstances must be viewed with today's eyes. The circumstances in which the public interest requires a communication to be protected in the absence of malice depend upon current social conditions. The requirements at the close of the twentieth century may not be the same as those of earlier centuries or earlier decades of this century.'

The following classifications of qualified privilege should, therefore, not be taken as exhaustive.

Statements made in Performance of a Legal, Moral or Social Duty

Statements made in the discharge of a legal, moral or social duty to a person who has a corresponding duty or interest in receiving them are protected by qualified privilege. The determination of whether a duty to communicate exists is a question solely for the judge. The state of mind of the maker of the statement is not relevant to this question. Honest belief in the existence of a duty cannot create a duty to communicate. Whether a legal duty to communicate exists is not usually a difficult question. Certain statutes may, for example, impose an obligation to make a statement or disclosure (see, for example, Human Fertilisation and Embryology Act 1990, s. 35). Disclosures made in order to comply with this section would in all likelihood be protected by qualified privilege. A legal duty to communicate may also arise under contract.

Problems have arisen in determining whether a social or moral duty to communicate exists. In *Stuart* v. *Bell* [1891] 2 QB 341, 350 Lindley LJ suggested the following test:

> '[T]he question of moral or social duty being for the judge, each judge must decide it as best he can for himself. I take moral or social duty to mean a duty recognized by English people of ordinary intelligence and moral principle, but at the same time not a duty enforceable by legal proceedings, whether civil or criminal.'

The circumstances in which courts have held a moral or social duty to exist are extremely diverse. Where the statement is made in answer to an inquiry, the courts appear to be more willing to hold that a duty to communicate exists. Thus, a reply to a request for a reference (*Gardner* v.

Slade (1849) 13 QB 796) and an answer to an inquiry about the creditworthiness of another (*London Association for Protection of Trade* v. *Greenlands Ltd* [1916] 2 AC 15) are protected. However, it does not follow that where there is no request there is no duty. For example, unsolicited warnings by one member of a family to another regarding the 'moral dangers' of a suitor have been held to attract qualified privilege (*Todd* v. *Hawkins* (1837) 8 C & P 88). The case of *Watts* v. *Longsdon* [1930] 1 KB 130 illustrates, however, that not all 'well-intentioned' interventions will be privileged. There, the unsolicited repetition by an acquaintance to the claimant's wife of unsubstantiated information concerning the claimant's sexual conduct was held not to be covered by privilege.

The existence of a duty to communicate is not enough of itself to attract the defence. In addition the statement must be made to a person who has a legitimate interest in receiving it. Without this reciprocity there can be no privilege. A person may have a legitimate interest in receiving the contents of a statement by virtue of some legal or social relationship. For example, an employer has an interest in receiving a complaint concerning the fitness of an employee to do his job and a solicitor has an interest in receiving his client's instructions. The interest may also arise by virtue of the public position of the receiver. A police officer has a legitimate interest to receive information regarding the alleged commission of an offence (but query whether after *Taylor* v. *Director of the Serious Fraud Office* [1999] 2 AC 177 the initial complaint to a police officer is protected by absolute or only qualified privilege). Similarly, it has been held that an MP is legitimately interested in the way a constituent was treated by a local solicitor (*Beach* v. *Freeson* [1972] 1 QB 514). Where, however, the statement is published in a newspaper or on television to the general public, the courts have been less willing to uphold the existence of the privilege (see 'Publication in the Media' below). Something out of the ordinary will be required to satisfy the courts that the public at large, and not just a section of the public, has sufficient interest in receiving the information. An example might be where the information relates to a public emergency such as a scare – later found to be unsubstantiated – over the safety of a particular food product (see *Blackshaw* v. *Lord* [1984] QB 1, 27 per Stephenson LJ).

Statements made in Furtherance or Protection of an Interest

Private Interest Where a person makes a statement in protection of his own personal interests to a person who has a reciprocal interest in receiving it, the statement will attract the defence of qualified privilege. As Lord Oaksey said in *Turner* v. *Metro-Goldwyn-Mayer Pictures Ltd* [1950] 1 All ER 449, 470:

> '[T]here is ... an analogy between the criminal law of self defence and a man's right to defend himself against written or verbal attacks. In both cases he is entitled ... to defend himself effectively, and he only loses the protection of the law if he goes beyond defence and proceeds to offence.'

Therefore, statements made in protection of one's personal or business reputation, provided not excessive, will be protected. For example, if A was accused of theft by a police officer, A's reply that B was the thief would attract qualified privilege. By accusing B, there is no evidence that A has gone beyond what is reasonably necessary to defend his reputation.

The case of *Watts* v. *Times Newspapers Ltd* [1997] QB 650 makes clear that the personal interest 'defended' will affect the latitude given to the speaker. In that case, the defendant newspaper published an article defamatory of the plaintiff. Unfortunately, it accompanied the defamatory article with a photograph of another person (A) who shared the plaintiff's name. The newspaper agreed to publish an apology to A and suggested a neutral form of words. A, however, insisted on a form of words which, while making clear that he was not the person referred to, repeated the allegation against the plaintiff. The plaintiff sued both the newspaper and A in respect of, *inter alia*, the defamatory apology. The court held that while A was protected by qualified privilege, the newspaper was not. A was entitled, as a person defamed, to defend himself. Provided he did not overstep the bounds of reasonableness and include wholly irrelevant and extraneous material any response he made would be protected even if it included material that was not objectively necessary. The newspaper was, however, in a different position. While it was under a duty to right the wrong it had done to A, it did not follow from that that it could publish matter defamatory of the plaintiff. To fulfil its duty it need have done no more than publish an apology in the neutral terms it had originally suggested. Because it chose to go further, it was not protected.

In order to attract privilege, the communication must be made to a person with a corresponding interest or duty to receive it. This point has already been discussed with regard to statements made in performance of a duty.

Common Interest   A communication on a matter in which the defendant and the recipient share a common legitimate interest is privileged. For the privilege to exist, both parties must be interested in some matter which concerns them both. Where the recipient's interest is mere idle curiosity or meddling in the affairs of others the defence will not be established. The common interest may be financial. All employees were said in *Bryanston Finance Ltd* v. *De Vries* [1975] 1 QB 703 to have an interest in the survival and prosperity of the business in which they are employed. Therefore communications made to them for the purpose of informing them about the affairs of the business would be privileged. Other examples include statements made to a trade or professional association by one member about another or by a member of the public about the conduct of a member of the association; and statements by an employer to his employees as to why he had dismissed one of their workmates.

Publication in the media

Prior to *Reynolds* v. *Times Newspapers* [2001] 2 AC 127 it was clear that, although no generic privilege existed for fair publication in the press on a matter of public interest, there were some situations in which a qualified privilege would attach to publications in the media. The exact circumstances in which such a privilege would exist were, however, somewhat unclear. In *Reynolds* v. *Times Newspapers*, Lord Cooke pointed out (p. 225) that, prior to *Reynolds*, 'the only publications to the world at large to which English courts have been willing to extend qualified privilege have been fair and accurate reports of certain proceedings or findings of legitimate interest to the general public'. Except perhaps in cases of the utmost emergency, qualified privilege was unlikely to apply unless the matter published was a report of facts which had been finally ascertained and adjudicated upon. However, 'where damaging facts have been ascertained to be true, or been made the subject of a report, there may be a duty to report them ... provided the public interest is wide enough'. Thus, in *Allbut* v. *General Council of Medical Education* (1889) 23 QBD 400, the privilege was held to attach to the publication of a book containing the minutes of a meeting of the Council recording that the plaintiff's name had been removed from the medical register for infamous professional conduct after an inquiry at which the plaintiff had been represented by counsel. Giving the judgment of the court, Lopes LJ expressly had regard in reaching his decision to the nature of the tribunal, the character of the report, the interest of the public in the proceedings and the duty of the Council towards the public. By contrast, where the allegations made were still under investigation or had been authoritatively refuted, no privilege was likely to attach. Thus in *Blackshaw* v. *Lord* [1984] QB 1 the court held that no privilege attached to the publication in a newspaper of information extracted from a government press officer of a story to the effect that the plaintiff, a senior civil servant, had been dismissed for inefficiency and incompetence in the management of public money. While the question of wastage of public money was a matter of public interest, the court was of the opinion that this did not justify the defendants publishing what were in effect 'half-baked' rumours.

Reynolds v. *Times Newspapers* arose out of a *Sunday Times* story in its English edition which accused Mr Reynolds, then Taoiseach (prime minister) of Ireland, of lying to the Dail (the Irish Parliament) on a matter of considerable public controversy. In a longer version of the story the Irish edition indicated that Reynolds had not misled the Dail deliberately. Reynolds sued Times Newspapers for libel and was met with the defence of qualified privilege. At first instance and in the Court of Appeal, the publication of the article was held not to be privileged. Further, both courts rejected any wide qualified privilege at common law for political speech. The defendants appealed.

Stated in its simplest form, the issue in the case was whether a libellous statement of fact published by the news media in the course of a political discussion was protected by privilege. The starting point for Lord Nicholls, who delivered the leading speech, was 'freedom of expression'. According to his Lordship, freedom to disseminate and receive information on political matters was essential to the proper functioning of the system of parliamentary democracy. The media played an important role in this process. Thus, without a free press, freedom of expression would be a hollow concept. However, protection of reputation was also an important public good: 'The crux of the appeal, therefore, [lay] in identifying the restrictions which are fairly and reasonably necessary for the protection of reputation' (p. 201).

Notwithstanding the importance of press freedom and freedom of expression generally, the House of Lords did not accept that political speech necessarily creates an occasion of privilege. Thus, their Lordships rejected the need for a generic qualified privilege to apply to political speech or information. The House of Lords also rejected the approach that had been taken by the Court of Appeal in the instant case. The Court of Appeal had held that, in addition to the duty and interest test, a 'circumstantial test' had to be satisfied: 'Were the nature, status and source of the material, and *the circumstances* of the publication, such that the publication should in the public interest be protected in the absence of proof of express malice (we call this the circumstantial test)' ([2001] 2 AC 127, 167; emphasis added). While the test had the advantage over the generic privilege in that it required attention to be paid to all the circumstances of the case, it was not well supported by authority and in Lord Nicholl's opinion 'gave rise to conceptual and practical difficulties and [was] better avoided' (p. 197).

Having rejected the generic qualified privilege, and the 'circumstantial test', the House of Lords held that the only sensible course was to go back to the traditional twofold test of duty and interest. This test was sufficiently flexible to embrace, depending on the occasion and the particular circumstances, a qualified privilege in respect of political speech published at large. The essential question that had to be asked in any case was whether the public was entitled to know the particular information. This required consideration of many matters including, but not limited to, the nature, source, tone and character of the report, any steps taken to verify the information, the urgency of the matter, whether the claimant had been given the chance to respond, and the timing of the publication. Thus, the fact that a newspaper relied on a source it knew from previous experience to be unreliable or biased would be a serious matter militating against the existence of qualified privilege. So too, the use of a highly emotive tone (e.g. *Grobbelaar* v. *News Group Newspapers* [2001] 2 All ER 437) or a failure by a newspaper to seek comment from the claimant or take other steps to verify the story, while not conclusive, make it less likely that a court would decide that privilege attached to the particular story. That the publication was not true is not, however, a relevant factor. Nor is it relevant to speculate on what further information the publisher might have received had he made more extensive investigations (*GKR Karate (UK) Ltd* v. *Yorkshire Post Newspapers Ltd* [2000] 1 WLR 2571). Applying this approach to the facts of *Reynolds* itself, the House of Lords concluded, by a majority, that the paper's failure to give its readers Mr Reynold's side of the story precluded an occasion of privilege arising.

Undoubtedly, *Reynolds* v. *Times Newspapers* expands the circumstances in which a qualified privilege will apply to communications made by the press to the general public. Although their Lordships held that the traditional duty/interest test remained the appropriate one to apply, it is clear that they viewed the environment in which it had to be applied as substantially changed: 'The starting point is now freedom of expression, a right based on a constitutional or higher legal foundation. Exceptions to freedom of expression must be justified as being necessary in a democracy. In other words, freedom of expression is the rule and regulation of speech is the exception requiring justification. The existence and width of any exception can only be justified if it is underpinned by a pressing social need' (p. 208, per Lord Steyn). So too, the emphasis placed by several of their Lordships on the fact that news is a perishable commodity suggests that more width will be given to the media when publishing matter of serious public concern.

While it is clear that *Reynolds* adopts a more media-friendly standard than has hitherto been the case, two important caveats ought to be entered. First, several of the factors identified by Lord Nicholls as relevant to the question whether the privilege exists require in essence that the *defendant* prove that he acted reasonably. The effect of this will be to shift the focus of a claim for privilege away from the test of malice (see 20.13) to a test based on reasonableness, with the burden of proving lack of negligence on the defendant instead of the present situation under which the *claimant* must prove malice. This undoubtedly imposes a much greater burden on the defendant than had heretofore been the case. Secondly, their Lordships clearly did not view the press as a wholly responsible 'watchdog' of people's liberties which could be trusted to regulate itself. As Lord Nicholls pointed out, 'the sad reality is that the overall handling of [the protection of reputations] by the national press, with its own commercial interests to serve, does not always command general confidence' (p. 202). In considering any claim to privilege, therefore, it seems likely that, in order to uphold responsible standards of journalism, the conduct of the newspaper leading up to publication will be carefully scrutinised.

Statements made in Certain Classes of Report

Reports of Parliamentary Proceedings While an absolute privilege attaches to reports, papers votes and proceedings of Parliament published by or under the authority of either House of Parliament, the publication of any extract from or abstract of such report, paper, vote or proceeding attracts a qualified privilege only (Parliamentary Papers Act 1840, s. 3).

Fair and Accurate Report of Judicial Proceedings A fair and accurate report of judicial proceedings, whether or not published contemporaneously is protected by qualified privilege. Contemporaneous reports attract absolute privilege (see 20.10).

Statements Privileged by Virtue of Section 15 and Schedule 1 of the Defamation Act 1996 Section 15 of the Defamation Act 1996 provides for a statutory qualified privilege defence to protect the publication of certain reports and other matters specified in Schedule 1 of the Act. The reports and other matters specified in the schedule fall into two categories:

  (a) statements having qualified privilege without explanation or contradiction (Part I, Schedule 1); and;
  (b) statements privileged subject to explanation or contradiction (Part II, Schedule 1).

Where the defendant publishes any report or other statement mentioned in Schedule 1 of the 1996 Act, whether in Part I or II, the publication is privileged unless it is shown to have been made with malice (Defamation Act 1996, s. 15(1)). Where the defendant publishes without malice a report or other statement mentioned in Part II of the Schedule, the publication is privileged unless the claimant shows that the defendant:

'(a) was requested by him to publish in a suitable manner a reasonable letter or statement by way of explanation or contradiction, and
(b) refused or neglected to do so.' (Defamation Act 1996, ss. 15(2)(a), (b))

The section does not apply to the publication of matter which is not of public concern and the publication of which is not for the public benefit (s. 15(3)) or to matter, the publication of which is prohibited by law (s. 15(4)(a)). No limitations exist on the types of publication protected by the 1996 Act. Under s. 7 of the Defamation Act 1952, the statutory qualified privilege applied only where the publication was made in a newspaper or broadcast. Nor is there any requirement that the publication must be contemporaneous with the events that are the subject of the report (*Tsikata* v. *Newspaper Publishing Plc* [1997] 1 All ER 655).

20.13 **Malice**

Malice is used in a number of different contexts in the law of defamation. At one time, malice was said to be the foundation of an action in defamation and it had to be pleaded as part of the statement of claim. However, that is no longer the case. Today it is said that where a person publishes a defamatory imputation the law presumes malice or that 'legal malice' is established by proof of publication of the defamatory words. 'Express malice', on the other hand, refers to a state of mind that, if affirmatively proved by the claimant to have actuated the publication, will defeat a defence of fair comment or qualified privilege.

This section is concerned with 'express malice' and in particular with what must be established in order to defeat the defences of qualified privilege and fair comment.

The leading case on the meaning of express malice is *Horrocks* v. *Lowe* [1975] AC 135 in which Lord Diplock, who delivered the leading speech, restated the law in respect of express malice in the context of qualified privilege. The following principles can be derived from his Lordship's speech:

1. 'Express malice' denotes a state of mind that, if proved, defeats the defence of qualified privilege. The burden of establishing malice is on the claimant.

2. Express malice may be established by proving that the defendant had an improper motive for publishing the words complained of. An improper motive will exist where the defendant misuses 'the occasion for some purpose other than that for which the privilege is accorded by law' (p. 150). The commonest case is where the dominant motive is to give 'vent to his personal spite or ill will towards the person he defames'. There may, however, be other instances of improper motives that destroy the privilege. Thus, a person may act with the dominant motive of obtaining some private advantage unconnected with the duty or interest which constitutes the reason for the privilege. If he does so he loses the benefit of the privilege.

3. Proof by the claimant that the defendant did not honestly believe that what he published was true is generally conclusive evidence of express malice. If the defendant publishes untrue defamatory matter 'recklessly', that is without considering or caring whether it be true or false, this is treated as if he knew it to be false. However, carelessness, impulsiveness or irrationality in arriving at a positive belief that it is true is not to be equated with indifference to the truth of what he publishes.

4. A positive belief in the truth of what is published – which is presumed unless the contrary is proved – will be sufficient to negative express malice unless it is proved that the defendant misused the occasion for some improper motive.

Although the actual decision in *Horrocks* v. *Lowe* related to the effect of express malice on the defence of qualified privilege, it is submitted that the principles stated in that case are equally applicable, subject to necessary limitations imposed by the nature of each defence, to the defence of fair comment. Thus, proof that the defendant's dominant motive in publishing the words complained of was an improper one will amount to malice and this is so even if the comment was objectively 'fair'. Similarly, the fact that the opinion expressed is not one that the defendant honestly holds will generally be conclusive evidence of malice.

Though it is clear that proof the defendant was careless as to the truth or falsity of the facts stated will not defeat malice, it appears, following *Reynolds* v. *Times Newspapers* [2001] 2 AC 127, that the defendant's carelessness may prevent the privilege arising in the first place, at least where the defamatory words are published to the public at large. Several of the factors stated by Lord Nicholls to be relevant to the question whether the necessary duty/interest existed amount in essence to tests of reasonableness. Thus, the fact that the defendant took no, or inadequate, steps to verify the information, used a source of information that a reasonable journalist would not have trusted or failed to solicit the claimant's side of the story may mean that the privilege is not established. The effect of *Reynolds* is, therefore, that unless the *defendant* establishes that he behaved as a reasonable and responsible journalist the privilege will not exist and there will be no need to consider the issue of malice. Of course, if the defendant does establish that, objectively, he behaved as a reasonable and responsible journalist, it is almost inconceivable that a jury would find him to be malicious. Thus, it would appear to be strongly arguable that the effect of *Reynolds*, at least in relation to publications in the media, is seriously to undermine the authority of *Horrocks* v. *Lowe*.

Where more than one person has been involved in the publication of the defamatory material difficult questions have arisen in relation to malice. Does the proof of malice against one co-publisher prevent the others from relying on the defences of fair comment or qualified privilege? In *Egger* v. *Viscount Chelmsford* [1965] 1 QB 248 the plaintiff sued all eight members and the secretary of a committee of the Kennel Club in respect of a letter written by the secretary on the instructions of the committee. The trial judge held that the letter was written on an occasion of qualified privilege and the jury found that five of the members were actuated by malice but that the other three and the secretary were not. The Court of Appeal held that the non-malicious members were not tainted by the malice of the malicious members. As Lord Denning put it, 'each defendant is answerable severally, as well as jointly, for the joint publication: and each is entitled to his several defence whether he be sued jointly or separately from the others'. Whilst *Egger* v. *Viscount Chelmsford* was concerned with the defence of qualified privilege, there seems to be no reason why the principle in the case should not apply to the defence of fair comment as well (but cf. Davies LJ).

20.14 Unintentional Defamation

Liability for a defamatory statement, as we have seen, does not depend on the intention of the maker of the statement. The fact that the writer or publisher intended to refer to a different person from the claimant, did not intend to refer to a living person and had no idea that what he said was defamatory is, at common law, irrelevant to liability. Liability for defamation is in general strict (though see *O'Shea* v. *MGN Ltd* [2001] EMLR 40). In an attempt to mitigate some of the difficulties this causes for writers, publishers and others, Parliament enacted a statutory offer of amends in s. 4 of the Defamation Act 1952. Unfortunately, s. 4 proved virtually unusable in practice. This was due, at least in part, to the twin requirements that the offer of amends had to be made as soon as practicable after the complaint was received (which effectively ruled out investigation) and that the defendant had to show that publication took place 'innocently'. Words were only treated as published innocently where the publisher took all reasonable care in relation to their publication and either (i) he did not intend to publish the words about the plaintiff and did not know of circumstances by which they might be understood to refer to him, or (ii) the words were not defamatory on their face and the publisher did not know of circumstances by virtue of which they might be understood to be defamatory of the plaintiff. In practice proof of innocent publication proved virtually impossible and the defence remained virtually unused.

The rules regulating the defence have now been substantially changed by ss. 2–4 of the Defamation Act 1996. By s. 2 a person who has published a statement alleged to be defamatory of another may make an offer of amends. An offer to make amends under the section is an offer (a) to make a suitable correction and sufficient apology to the person defamed, (b) to publish the correction and apology in a manner that is reasonable and practicable in the circumstances, and (c) to pay the aggrieved person such compensation (and costs) as are agreed or determined (s. 2(4)). The offer cannot be made after serving a defence in proceedings brought against him by the aggrieved person (s. 2(5)).

Where such an offer is made and *accepted*, the party accepting the offer cannot bring or continue proceedings in respect of the publication concerned (s. 3(2)). Where the parties agree on the steps to be taken in fulfilment of the offer, the aggrieved party may apply to the court for an order that the other party fulfil the offer (s. 3(3)). If the parties do not agree on steps to be taken by way of correction, apology or publication, the party making the offer may take such steps as he thinks appropriate and in particular he may make the correction and apology in open court with the approval of the court and give an undertaking to the court as to the manner of their publication (s. 3(4)). Where the parties do not agree as to the amount to be paid by compensation, it shall be determined by the court on the same principles as damages in defamation proceedings although the court shall take account of the terms of the offer and its suitability (s. 3(5)). Where an offer is made and *not accepted*, then the fact that an offer was made is a defence (s. 4(2)) unless the party making the offer knew or had reason to believe that the statement complained of (a) referred to the aggrieved person or was likely to be understood as referring to him, and (b) was both false and defamatory of that party (s. 4(3)). The person who made the offer of amends need not rely on it as a defence but if he does he cannot rely on any other defence (s. 4(4)).

There is not doubt that the new provisions are an improvement on the old. The fact that the defence is available even where the defendant knew the statement was defamatory but thought it was true, and that the burden – to defeat the defence – is on the *claimant* to show that the defendant had no reason to believe the statement referred to the claimant or was false and defamatory of him, will undoubtedly make the new defence more attractive than the old to newspaper defendants. However, the defendant can only rely on the defence where he makes an apology and agrees to pay damages. Clearly difficult decisions will arise as to whether to try to justify the story before a jury (and risk a finding of liability and *jury*-assessed damages) or whether to apologise and obtain a *judge*-assessed amount.

20.15 **Damages**

The primary remedy that the law provides for defamation is damages. In every action for libel and slander actionable *per se*, damage is presumed and does not have to be proved. Where, however, the slander is not actionable *per se*, a claimant can only recover if he can show that he has suffered special damage. Most exceptionally, defamation actions are usually still tried by a judge and jury and the assessment of the amount of damages is a matter for the jury. The primacy of the jury in this matter is well established and the courts have until relatively recently shown themselves unwilling to interfere with jury awards. However, the amounts awarded by juries during the 1980s and early 1990s evoked considerable judicial and a wider public concern. This led to changes in the advice given to juries in defamation actions in an attempt to introduce some measure of reality into the amounts awarded and to the granting to the Court of Appeal (by legislation) of a power to overturn jury awards of damages and substitute their own. Section 8(2) of the Courts and Legal Services Act 1990 and Civil Procedure Rules, 52.10(3)(a) and (b) empowers the Court of Appeal, on allowing an appeal against a jury award of damages, to substitute for the award of the jury such sum as might appear to the court to be proper. In *Rantzen* v. *Mirror Group Newspapers (1986) Ltd* [1994] QB 670, the Court of Appeal interpreted this provision as entitling it to substitute an award whenever the amount awarded by the jury was such that 'no reasonable jury could have thought that the award was necessary to compensate the plaintiff and re-establish his reputation'. There have now been some half dozen or so cases in which the Court of Appeal has substituted a sum for a jury award and in the majority of those the court has substituted a figure of £50 000 or less (see, for example, *Gorman* v. *Mudd* [1992] CA Transcript 1076, compensatory damages reduced from £150 000 to £50 000; *John* v. *MGN Ltd* [1997] QB 586, compensatory damages reduced from £75 000 to £25 000 and exemplary damages reduced from £275 000 to £50 000). However, it should be noted that in *Kiam* v. *MGN Ltd* [2002] EWCA Civ 43, the Court of Appeal (Sedley LJ dissenting) in upholding a jury award of £105 000 to a well-known businessman took a much more 'hands-off' approach. According to the majority, it was not for the Court of Appeal to interfere with a jury award unless it was 'out of all proportion to what could sensibly have been thought appropriate' (para. 53, per Simon Brown LJ). Moreover, the recent increase in damages awarded in personal injury actions as a result of *Heil* v. *Rankin* [2001] QB 272, the need to show deference to jury awards, and the startling percentage differential between juries' awards and those substituted for them in the few s. 8 cases there had been, all militated against interfering with a jury award even if it appeared to be on the high side. While the majority were careful to warn against the use of this case as 's. 8(2) comparable' (see below) in future cases, it would be unfortunate if *Kiam* were to signal the return to the telephone number figures that were awarded prior to *John* v. *MGN Ltd*.

In addition to the power to substitute its own award for that of the jury, the Court of Appeal has stated in *John* v. *MGN Ltd* [1997] QB 586 that the jury should be given substantial guidance in making their assessment decision. Thus, in addition to advice about the value of money, the jury should be referred to (a) sums substituted in other cases by the Court of Appeal in the exercise of their jurisdiction under s. 8(2) of the Courts and Legal Services Act 1990 (the so-called s. 8(2) comparable cases) and (b) awards for pain and suffering and loss of amenity in personal injury actions. Counsel and the judge should also be allowed to make suggestions as to the appropriate award. Mentioning figures, Sir Thomas Bingham MR thought, would induce a mood of realism: 'The plaintiff will not wish the jury to think that his main object is to make money rather than clear his name. The defendant will not wish to add to the insult by underrating the seriousness of the libel' (p. 616). Short of actually removing the function of assessing damages from the jury there is probably little else that can be done to limit the sums awarded. Whether juries will now get the hint remains to be seen (it should be noted that the Law Commission, 1995b, provisionally concluded that juries should continue to decide quantum (para. 4.100) but thought they ought to be provided with greater direction (para. 4.103)).

Damages in a defamation action are primarily intended to be compensatory. The jury is required to assess the sum required to vindicate the claimant's reputation and to compensate him for the injury to his feelings. However, in addition to compensatory damages, aggravated and exemplary damages may be available. The circumstances in which, and basis upon which, such damages are awarded is considered in Chapter 22 on remedies (see 22.2).

20.16 Injunctions

A court has the power to grant an injunction to prevent the anticipated publication of a defamatory statement and, after a trial at which the jury has found for the claimant, to prevent the re-publication of the statement. The court's power is discretionary and in exercising that discretion the court must be guided by the statutory constraint in section 37(1) of the Supreme Court Act 1981 that it should be exercised only where 'it appears to the court to be just and convenient to do so'. Where, at the trial of an action for libel, the jury finds for the claimant, the court may issue an injunction restraining any further publication of the offending material. An injunction will be granted 'in all cases where the court thinks it just and convenient' provided only that there is reason to believe that further publication by the defendant is likely.

The availability of an interlocutory injunction to prevent the threatened publication of material defamatory of the claimant is more limited than in other torts and, in practice, such injunctions are rarely granted. The reluctance of the courts to grant such injunctions derives from concerns about the chilling effect their grant may have on free speech. Thus, an interlocutory injunction will only be issued where (a) the statement is unarguably defamatory; (b) the claimant can prove that the statement is plainly untrue; (c) there are no other defences on which the defendant can rely; and (d) there is evidence that the defendant has threatened, or intends, to publish the defamatory words.

Summary

20.1 'Interests in personality' are protected by a number of legal mechanisms in English law. The primary tort in this area is the tort of defamation which protects a person's reputation. However, additional protection is provided by the torts of negligence, breach of confidence, malicious falsehood, trespass, nuisance and passing off. Additionally, a number of statutes protect interests in personality. English law, however, knows no tort of infringement of privacy.

20.2 The tort of defamation is committed when the defendant publishes defamatory material about the claimant to a third person.

20.3 A defamatory statement is one that lowers the claimant in the estimation of right thinking members of society generally. In applying this test the courts tend to look to what right thinking members of society *should* think, rather than what they actually think. Although words are frequently capable of having more than one meaning, the jury is required to decide what single meaning the words conveyed in the instant case. The intention of the publisher is irrelevant in this regard and the meaning of words should be judged objectively. Words should be given their natural and ordinary, and not a forced, meaning. However, it is open to either party to argue that, taken in context, the words convey an inferential meaning different from their ordinary meaning or even that the words can only be understood by having regard to extrinsic evidence.

20.4 The statement must be published to a third person. However, the statement need not have been intentionally published. It is sufficient that the defendant ought reasonably to have foreseen that the statement would come to the attention of a third person. Every repetition of a defamatory statement gives rise to a fresh cause of action. However, the original maker of the statement only remains liable for the repetition where it was foreseeable.

20.5 The defamatory statement must refer to the claimant. There is no need, however, for the claimant to be expressly referred to. It is sufficient that a reasonable reader with knowledge of the special facts would have thought that the statement referred to the claimant. A defamatory statement made about a group is not actionable unless the words can reasonably be understood as referring to all of the group or as referring to the claimant individually.

20.6 English law draws a distinction between libel and slander. Libel is actionable without proof of damage. Slander, unless falling within one of the exceptional categories, requires proof of damage. There is no single test for distinguishing between libel and slander. Generally, however, a statement made in a permanent form and conveyed to the sense of sight will be treated as a libel, while a statement made in transitory form and conveyed to the ear will be treated as a slander.

20.7 Any legally-recognised person or entity except a governmental entity or political party can bring an action for libel or slander.

20.8 In addition to certain general defences, such as voluntary assumption of risk and consent, the law of defamation has its own special defences.

20.9 Where a claimant succeeds in showing that the words complained of are defamatory, their falsehood is presumed. Justification or truth is, however, a defence. The essence of a plea of justification is that the words in their natural and ordinary meaning are true in substance and in fact. Where there are two or more distinct charges against the claimant the defence will not fail merely because one or more cannot be proved, provided the untrue words do not otherwise materially injure the claimant's reputation.

20.10 The defence of fair comment is, like justification, a complete defence. In order for the defence to succeed it must be shown (i) that the words used are comment and not fact; (ii) that the comment is on a matter of public interest; (iii) that the comment is based on true facts; and (iv) that the comment is fair. The claimant can rebut the defence by showing that the defendant was actuated by malice.

20.11 Some situations are deemed to be of such social or political importance that the law allows a person to speak or write about another without restraint. These are situations of absolute privilege and they include statements made by Members of Parliament in Parliament, statements made in judicial proceedings, high executive communications and statements made by certain officials.

20.12 Some occasions, although not of sufficient importance to attract absolute privilege, are nevertheless considered to be of sufficient importance to attract qualified privilege. Statements covered by qualified privilege are protected unless the claimant can show that the maker of the statement was actuated by malice. Statements attracting qualified privilege include: statements made in performance of a legal, moral or social duty; statements made in furtherance or protection of an interest; and statements made in certain classes of reports. There is no generic privilege for fair publication in the press or other media on a matter of public interest but untrue publications in the media may attract qualified privilege in the circumstances set out in *Reynolds* v. *Times Newspapers*.

20.13 Malice is used in a number of different contexts in the law of defamation. The type of malice that defeats the defences of fair comment and qualified privilege refers to a state of mind that may be established by proof that the defendant had an improper motive for publishing the words, or did not honestly believe that what he published was true.

20.14 A defendant may make an offer of amends (Defamation Act 1996, s. 2). Whether or not it amounts to a complete defence depends upon whether the conditions of sections 2–4 of the Act are satisfied.

20.15 Defamation actions are usually tried by a judge and jury with the assessment of damages left to the jury. Damages in a defamation action are primarily intended to be compensatory. However, exemplary damages may be awarded.

20.16 A court has the power to grant an injunction to prevent the anticipated publication of a defamatory statement and, after a trial at which the jury has found for the claimant, to prevent the re-publication of the statement.

Exercises

20.1 Should there be a statutory tort of breach of privacy? Who would benefit from the enactment of such a tort?

20.2 Is it defamatory to accuse someone of being HIV positive? (See *Bloodworth* v. *Gray* (1844) 7 Man & G 334.) Does the 'right-thinking person' provide a satisfactory yardstick against which to measure what is defamatory?

20.3   Was the House of Lords correct in *Lewis* v. *Daily Telegraph* to say that the words complained of could not convey the impression that the plaintiff was guilty of the allegations?

20.4   What is the difference between a true and a false innuendo?

20.5   Would an action lie against the maker of a television programme in respect of remarks made in a review in a newspaper which repeated the defamatory allegations made in the programme?

20.6   Should *Hulton* v. *Jones* and *Newstead* v. *London Express Newspapers Ltd* be followed today?

20.7   How satisfactory is the test for distinguishing between libel and slander? Should the courts continue to draw this distinction? Does the existence of the exceptional cases, where slander is made actionable *per se*, make it unnecessary to continue to draw the distinction?

20.8   A writes that B has a number of convictions for theft and robbery. Additionally, he accuses B of having been convicted of rape. B brings a libel action in respect of the allegation that he has been convicted of robbery. This is untrue, although the other allegations are true. Would A be able to rely on the defence of justification? Would your answer be different if B sued in respect of the rape allegation where this was untrue, although the other allegations were true?

20.9   A writes of B, a Member of Parliament, that he is a drunkard who beats his dog and that he is, therefore, unfit to represent his constituents. B beats his dog but is not a drunkard. Does B have any remedy?

20.10   Members of Parliament are so irresponsible that their historical right to say what they like in Parliament should be abandoned. Do you agree?

20.11   'The assessment of damages is too complicated for juries.' Do you agree?

20.12   Anarchy plc is the owner of *Your Investments*, a weekly magazine devoted to stock market comment and City gossip. Brian, a journalist on the magazine, was preparing an article about the takeover of Holy Securities Ltd by Satanic Securities plc, a company in which the principal shareholder was Robert, a well-known entrepreneur. The article, transcribed onto Brian's word-processor, alleged that Robert had obtained control of Holy for Satanic by 'strong-arm' tactics and by threatening to expose the extra-marital affair of David, Holy's principal shareholder, to David's wife, Edna. Felicity, an executive employed by Anarchy plc to manage the magazine's affairs, saw the final draft of the article on the word-processor screen when she went into Brian's office while he was out to lunch. Felicity was about to resign her job as she was unhappy with the way the magazine was being run. She was also a friend of Edna and decided to disclose the contents of the story to her and also to David's fellow shareholder, Gaynor. On receiving the information from Felicity, Edna became irate and telephoned a gossip magazine called *City Slicker*, informing the editor, Ian, that one of David's affairs was with a well-known rock singer whose name was 'synonymous with Satan'. These words appeared in a report in last week's *City Slicker*. In using the words Edna had intended to refer to a rock singer named Cyn with whom she thought David was having an affair. In fact David was having an affair with a rock singer called Devilla.

The edition of *Your Investments* containing the article was published last week. The allegations contained about Robert are untrue.

Advise the parties as to their rights and liabilities in tort.

Part V

General Principles of Tortious Liability

21 Vicarious Liability and Joint Torts

21.1 Introduction

As we have seen, liability in the modern law of torts is generally still dependent on proof of some notion of fault or blameworthiness. Liability will not, subject to certain well-known exceptions, be imposed on a person unless he has intentionally or negligently caused some loss or damage to the claimant. Thus liability is usually based on personal fault. However, a person may incur liability as a result not only of his own acts but also as a result of the acts of another. Vicarious liability is an example of just such a situation. Where certain criteria are satisfied, the law holds the defendant vicariously liable for the misconduct of another. This is the case even though the defendant is not himself in any way at fault. In this chapter we examine the criteria required to establish vicarious liability and look at the justifications for a rule of law that appears to run counter to two basic principles of English law, namely that a person should not be liable in the absence of fault and that a person should only be liable where his own act or omission caused the injury.

Vicarious liability may be defined as the liability imposed on one person (D) for the tortious act or omission of another (X) which causes loss to a third person (C). For one person to be vicariously liable for another's tort, certain requirements must be met. First, C must be injured or suffer loss as a result of a tortious act committed by X. This was for some time a source of judicial and academic debate in that some had argued that unless D himself owed C a duty of care, D could not be liable. X's acts were to be attributed to D, but D was not liable for them unless *he* owed C a duty of care. This view was known as the master's tort theory. It is clear today that the view expressed in the master's tort theory is not correct. All that is required is that X commits a tortious act which injures C. Second, some relationship must exist between the tortfeasor X and the defendant D. The relationship that most characteristically satisfies this requirement is that of master and servant or, as it would be more commonly called today, that of employer and employee. Third, there must be some connection between the tortious act and the relationship. This requirement is satisfied where the employee acts in the 'course of his employment'.

Where the requirements of vicarious liability are met the employer will be liable for the acts of his employee regardless of his own culpability and regardless of whether he owes the injured person any duty recognised by law. The liability of the employee in such a case is not extinguished but, for reasons of policy, the courts have considered it desirable to give the injured person an action against the employer. Vicarious liability is a form of joint liability, the employer may, either at common law or under the Civil Liability (Contribution) Act 1978 be able to recover some or all of the damages he has to pay from the employee. However, because the employee is unlikely to be able to satisfy any substantial claim, and because of the danger to good labour relations, an employer is unlikely to bring such a claim.

21.2 Justifications for Vicarious Liability

Despite vicarious liability being one of the longer established principles in English law, its existence is still considered by English lawyers to be somewhat exceptional and to require some special justification. The reason for this is, as we have seen, that the doctrine seems to run counter to two well-established principles of the law of tort. Various arguments of policy have been put forward from time to time to justify the doctrine's existence. Today the most accepted justification is that, as the employer derives an economic benefit from his employee's work, so he ought to bear any losses or liability incurred in the course of the enterprise. It is felt to be justifiable to impose liability on the employer, who in most cases is likely to have substantially greater means than his employee, because these losses are a normal incident of his business and he should therefore bear responsibility for them. He is also better able to spread the cost of the accident. Because the employer knows that he has to bear the cost of any accidents, he will usually take out insurance to cover such losses – indeed he is required to do so in respect of accidental injuries suffered by his employees for which he is liable (Employers' Liability (Compulsory Insurance) Act 1969) – and increase the price of his products to take account of the cost of the insurance. By this mechanism, rather than one person having to bear the whole of the loss, the loss is distributed among those who derive a benefit from either the sale or use of the product.

21.3 Employer and Employee Relationship

In order for a person to be vicariously liable for the tort of another the relationship between them must be governed by a contract *of* service. Where the person is employed under a contract *for* services the employer will not generally be vicariously liable for his torts. In the latter case the person employed is more properly known as an independent contractor and, in the absence of a personal non-delegable duty on the employer (see 21.5), the latter will incur no liability in respect of the torts of the independent contractor.

The courts have not found it easy to articulate a single test to answer the question whether a person is an employee or – which amounts to the same thing – whether a person is employed under a contract of service. The changing nature of employment, the increasing technicality of many jobs and professions and the complexity of corporate structures makes it considerably more difficult today, compared with one hundred years ago, to say of a person that he is definitely employed by a particular employer. For example, if a lawyer is seconded from his law firm to a government department, does he remain employed by his law firm? Similarly, is a consultant, who normally only does private work, an employee of the local health authority if he does an operation for the authority under the National Health Service? It might be thought that the answer to the question of whether a person is an employee or an independent contractor will depend upon how the parties themselves have classified the relationship. However, while any classification made by the parties will be taken into account by the courts, it can never be conclusive.

The conventional test used by the courts for distinguishing an employee from an independent contractor is the 'control' test. The test was well expressed by Bramwell B in *Yewens* v. *Noakes* (1880) 6 QBD 530, 532–3, where he said, '[a] servant is a person subject to the command of his master as to the manner in which he shall do his work.' An employee is, therefore, employed under a contract of service if his employer can tell him not only what to do but also how to do it. Such a test is, however, only satisfactory in an agricultural or primitive industrial society where the employer has at least as much technical knowledge as the employee and is able to instruct him in how to do the work. In a modern, complex industrial society it is doubtful whether the test is capable of any sensible meaning except in its application to the simplest of jobs. People are employed today in many cases precisely because they have the technical knowledge and skill that their employer does not have. If a hospital authority told a doctor how to resuscitate a patient or a warehouse owner told a fork-lift truck driver how to drive his truck they would probably be told, in no uncertain terms, to mind their own business.

While the courts continue to use the 'control' test in its traditional formulation where that is appropriate, they have not hesitated to hold an employer liable even where the work on which the employee is employed is highly technical and the method of its performance is something of which the employer is ignorant. In order to do so what they have done is to re-interpret the 'control' test so that what they now look for is 'not so much the power to direct *how* the work shall be done but instead the power to control the employee in relation to the incidental features of his employment – what has been termed the 'when' and the 'where' of the work' (Atiyah, 1967, p. 47). Thus the courts, in seeking to answer the question of who is in 'control', have taken into account a wide variety of factors, such as who has the power of appointment and dismissal, who pays the wages, where the 'employee' works, who provides the 'tools of the trade', who pays national insurance contributions or deducts tax and whether the contract itself makes any provision as to the parties' relationship (see also *Short* v. *J & W Henderson Ltd* (1946) 62 TLR 427, 429, per Lord Thankerton).

The case of *Ready Mixed Concrete (South-East) Ltd* v. *Minister of Pensions and National Insurance* [1968] 1 All ER 433 illustrates some of the factors the courts are likely to take into account in considering whether a contract of service exists. The case raised the question whether an owner-driver was employed under a contract of service for the purposes of s. 1(2) of the National Insurance Act 1965. Although not concerned with the question of vicarious liability it highlights the problem of identifying a contract of service in a modern 'atypical' employment context. A company organised a scheme for the delivery of ready-mixed concrete to its customers through so-called 'owner-drivers'. The contract with each driver provided, *inter alia*, that each driver was to buy the vehicle on hire-purchase terms from a finance company owned by the company; the driver was not to use the vehicle for any haulage business other than that of the company; the driver was not to make any alterations, change or sell the vehicle without the consent of the company; the driver was to make the vehicle available to the company at all times of the day and night and was generally to comply with all rules, regulations and reasonable orders given by the company. Mackenna J held, despite these provisions which were suggestive of a high degree of control by the company, that this was not a contract of service. While there were a number of provisions suggestive of such a contract, the fact that the driver owned the vehicle, was free to maintain the vehicle as he chose, to hire another driver in the event of holiday or sickness and to buy fuel where he chose were more in line with this contract being a contract of carriage. As Mackenna J put it, 'the ownership of the assets, the chance of profit and the risk of loss in the business of carriage are [the driver's] and not the company's.'

21.4 The Course of Employment

The existence of the relationship of employer and employee is not, however, a sufficient basis for liability in itself. The tort committed by the employee may have absolutely no connection with his employment and in such a case the employer will not be vicariously liable for his employee. For example, if an employee of an accountancy firm assaulted another person in a night club, the mere fact that he happened to be an employee is manifestly no ground for imposing liability upon his employer. In addition, therefore, to the requirement of a contract of service the employee must commit the tort in the 'course of his employment'.

Clearly, if the tort committed by the employee has been expressly authorised or ratified by the employer, the employer will be liable for the tort (though this will not be on the basis of vicarious liability but instead a distinct principle of agency that applies even outside the employment relationship). Such cases are probably rare and it is clear that the course of employment is not limited to such circumstances. However, articulating a clear test to determine whether a tort was committed in the course of employment is not an easy task. As Fleming points out (1998):

'[T]he course of employment is an expansive concept which provides ample scope for policy decisions and, despite the vast volume of case law, has failed to acquire a high degree of precision. No statistical measurement is possible, and precedents are helpful only when they present a suggestive uniformity on parallel facts.'

The standard starting point adopted by the courts is the test set out in Salmond and Heuston (1996, p. 443). The authors there state that a tort is committed in the course of the employee's employment: 'if it is either (a) a wrongful act authorised by the master, or (b) a wrongful and unauthorised mode of doing some act authorised by the master'. The test makes clear that the employer is liable not only for those wrongful acts that he has authorised but also for those acts which, although he has not directly authorised them, are nevertheless to be treated as wrongful and authorised modes of performing an authorised task. While few difficulties arise in respect of the first category, the distinction between cases where the employee's act amounts to an unauthorised mode of doing something authorised and those where he is doing something so unconnected which what he has been employed to do that he should properly be regarded as engaged in an independent act can sometimes be obscure and problematic. In particular, the issue of whether the employee was doing an authorised act in an unauthorised way is almost meaningless where the act of the employee amounts to an intentional tort. In *Lister* v. *Hesley Hall Ltd* [1992] 1 AC 215, [2001] UKHL 22 the House of Lords criticised the 'improper mode' approach and warned against applying it in an excessively literal manner. Instead, 'the test' should be regarded merely as a guide to the application of the law to diverse factual situations. According to their Lordships, the real issue in any case was 'the closeness of the connection between the employee's wrongful act and his employment'. An act will, therefore, only be within the scope of the employee's employment if it is sufficiently closely connected with the employee's employment such that it can properly be regarded as an unauthorised mode of doing something which is authorised. The underlying idea is that the injury done to the claimant must be an inherent risk of the employee's employment or characteristic of the employee's business such that it is just to make him bear the loss (Winfield and Jolowicz, 2002, pp. 712–13).

Whether the 'close connection' test is any more certain than the 'improper mode' approach is doubtful. Suffice to say in this regard that the Supreme Court of Canada divided four to three in *Jacobi* v. *Griffiths* (1999) 174 DLR (4th) 71 on whether its 'close and direct connection' test for vicarious liability was satisfied where an employee of a children's club sexually assaulted two club members in his house. Whatever 'test' is chosen, it is likely to remain a very difficult question in many cases whether conduct is or is not within the scope of employment. While it is certainly not a question of pure fact, it is not a question that lends itself to the imposition of a mechanical test. Much will depend in the end on whether in all the circumstances the court thinks that the employer ought to be held liable. While scientific classification remains impossible, the following sections give some idea of how the courts have approached the question of whether the employee is acting within the scope of his employment in several commonly recurring situations.

Frolics, Detours and Incidental Duties

In *Joel* v. *Morison* (1834) 6 C & P 501, 503 Parke B stated that an employee acts outside the course of his employment 'when embarking on a frolic of his own'. This clearly encompasses egregious behaviour entirely for the employee's own benefit. For example, if an employer instructs his employee to drive from London to Glasgow to deliver a parcel and the employee deviates via Land's End to pick up a friend it can be said that he has deviated from his route so extensively that he has gone on an entirely new journey and is acting outside the course of his employment. On the other hand if he stops off between London and Glasgow in order to buy himself lunch and negligently runs someone over in the restaurant car park he is likely to be treated as acting in the course of his employment. In this case the diversion from the most direct route would be likely to be treated as incidental to his employment. In *Century Insurance Co Ltd* v. *Northern Ireland Road Transport Board* [1942] AC 509 a petrol tanker driver lighted a cigarette while delivering petrol and then threw away the match causing an explosion which damaged the plaintiff's property. The House of Lords held that he was still acting within the course of his employment. Even though the act of lighting the cigarette was done purely for his own benefit and convenience and not for his employer's benefit, the act could not be treated as a wholly independent act but was instead an improper mode of doing that which he was employed to do.

Some difficulty has been experienced by the courts in dealing with cases of negligence committed by employees while on their way to work or while travelling between different workplaces on the instructions of their employer. In *Smith* v. *Stages* [1989] AC 928 the House of Lords, while recognising that it was impossible to provide for every eventuality, set out a number of presumptions. First, an employee travelling to or from work is, in ordinary circumstances, not acting within the course of his employment. Of course it may be said that in order to carry out a day's work he must travel to and from work and thus the travel should be seen as an incidental part of his work. The House of Lords was, however, of the view that, while a person was employed to work at his place of work, he was not in ordinary circumstances employed to travel from his home to his workplace. However, their Lordships recognised that, where a person is obliged to travel to work by means provided by his employer, he may be held to be acting within the course of his employment. Secondly, where an employee is instructed or required by his job (e.g. if he is a travelling salesman) to travel from one workplace to another or from his home to a succession of workplaces and he is paid for this travelling, he will usually be acting within the course of his employment. Finally, payment of wages while travelling or allowing the employee a discretion as to the mode and time of travel are factors to be taken into account but are not conclusive of the question whether a person is acting within the course of his employment.

Prohibited Conduct

If an employer expressly prohibits his employee from doing a particular act and the employee in breach of that instruction does that very act and injures another it might be thought that he would be acting outside the course of his employment. This is, however, not necessarily the case. Some prohibitions do, and some do not, take the employee outside the course of his employment. Whether or not a prohibition takes the employee outside the course of his employment depends on whether it limits the sphere of his employment or seeks only to deal with conduct within the sphere of employment (*Canadian Pacific Rly Co* v. *Lockhart* [1942] AC 591, 591 per Lord Dunedin). It is often a very difficult question which side of the line a prohibition falls, and fine judgements may be called for. In some cases the breach of a prohibition makes the employee's conduct so unconnected with his employment that he will be treated as acting outside the course of his employment. For example, if a company expressly forbade the drivers of its buses from racing other buses, an employee who caused an accident while racing a rival firm's bus would in all likelihood be treated as acting outside the course of his employment. On the other hand, if a company prohibits its employees from using their own cars for work unless they are properly insured, an employee driving his own, uninsured, car who causes an accident will not be acting outside the course of his employment as the prohibition merely affects the way in which he is to do his job. It does not restrict him in what he is employed to do (*Canadian Pacific Rly Co* v. *Lockhart*).

As a general rule prohibitions which affect the manner, time or place of performance are not held to affect the sphere of performance and, therefore, breach of the prohibition will not take the employee outside the course of his employment. In *Rose* v. *Plenty* [1976] 1 WLR 141 Mr Plenty was a milk roundsman employed by the defendants. His duties included driving a float on his round and collecting money. He was expressly prohibited by the terms of his employment from employing children in the performance of those duties. In breach of this prohibition, he invited the infant plaintiff to help him and the plaintiff was injured when Plenty drove the float negligently. The Court of Appeal, by a majority, held that Plenty was acting within the course of his employment. The judges held that the prohibition affected only the sphere of employment in that it went only to the manner in which the work was to be performed.

Intentional Misconduct

As with cases where the employer has expressly prohibited his employee from doing a particular act, it might be thought that if by intentional or wilful misconduct an employee injures or otherwise causes harm to another that would take the employee outside the course of his employment. By way of example, if an employee of an accountant's firm sexually assaulted a client or if a university lecturer was to assault a student who was annoying him, then in all likelihood the accountancy firm and the university would not be vicariously liable for their employee's torts. In neither case, could it properly be said that what was done by the employee was an improper way of doing that which they were authorised to do or that the employee's wrongful act was sufficiently closely connected with his employment such that the employer ought to be responsible. Having said that, there are cases where even intentional or wilful misconduct may be treated as falling within the scope of the employee's employment. Thus, where an employee stole a fur coat that had been sent to the defendant for cleaning, it was held that the defendants were liable (*Morris* v. *CW Martin & Sons Ltd* [1966] 1 QB 716). So too, fraud by an employee, even where the fraud is wholly for the benefit of the employee, may be within the scope of the employee's employment provided that the claimant was led by some statement or conduct of the employer to believe that the employee was acting within the scope of his employment (*Armagas Ltd* v. *Mundogas SA* [1986] AC 717).

Where the wrongful act amounts to an intentional tort against the person, then, unless the tort is directed against a person whose care has been entrusted to the employee, it will be comparatively rare for the act to be treated as being within the scope of the employee's employment. By way of example, an assault committed by a nightclub bouncer after he had ejected the claimant from the nightclub was held to be outside the scope of the bouncer's employment in *Daniels* v. *Whetstone Entertainments Ltd* [1962] 2 Lloyd's Rep 1. So too, in *Warren* v. *Henlys Ltd* [1948] 2 All ER 935 it was held that a petrol pump attendant who knocked the plaintiff senseless when the plaintiff threatened to report him to his superiors was acting outside the scope of his employment. Where, however, the intentional tort occurs as part of an over-enthusiastic but honest attempt to protect his employer's interests, a court is more likely to conclude that the employee was acting within the scope of his employment. Thus, in *Poland* v. *John Parr & Sons* [1927] 1 KB 236 H, an employee of the defendants, struck and caused serious injury to a boy whom he honestly believed was stealing sugar from his employer's wagon. The Court of Appeal held that H was acting within the course of his employment, though Atkin LJ did comment that the answer given by the court would have been different had he shot the boy.

Acts of sexual assault or abuse committed by an employee were at one time regarded as paradigm examples of acts outside the scope of the employee's employment. Thus, in *Trotman* v. *North Yorkshire CC* [1999] LGR 584 it had been decided that a deputy head teacher was not acting within the scope of his employment when he sexually abused a disabled teenager during a residential school trip. However, in *Lister* v. *Hesley Hall Ltd* the House of Lords overruled *Trotman* and held that the defendant children's home was liable for the acts of a warden who had systematically abused children placed in the home. The defendant had assumed a responsibility to the children when it placed them in the home and entrusted their care to the warden. There was therefore a sufficiently close connection between the sexual abuse of the children and what the warden was employed to do such that the defendant ought to be vicariously liable for the warden's acts. While it is clear from *Lister* v. *Hesley Hall Ltd* that acts of sexual abuse committed by an employee may fall within the scope of the employee's employment, it is clear that not all acts of abuse will do so. Where the employment merely provides the opportunity to engage in abuse (e.g., if in *Lister* the abuse had been perpetrated by a cleaner or groundsman) this will not attract vicarious liability.

21.5 Liability for Independent Contractors

As a general rule, employers are not liable for the acts of independent contractors whom they employ to do a particular task or series of tasks. The reason given for this qualification of vicarious liability is that the employer lacks detailed control over the independent contractor who is, in any event, better able to distribute the losses caused by his work than his employer. In many cases this is of course true. If a person hires a taxi to drive him from London to Heathrow he has little control over the way in which the driver drives and it is surely more appropriate to expect the taxi driver to insure against any losses caused by his negligence rather than the passenger. However, as McKendrick points out (1990), it may no longer be realistic to treat all 'independent contractors' in the same way. Some are without doubt large, well-organised businesses which are capable of including provision for insurance within their pricing policy. However, over the last few years there has been a vast increase in the number of home-workers and the 'self-employed'. Neither category may be 'employees' as that word has been defined by the courts and yet, unlike their employers, they may be unable to bear or shift any loss that may be caused by their negligence. This change in work patterns may suggest a need to re-evaluate the courts' traditional opposition to liability for independent contractors and indicate a need either for a wider view of who is an 'employee' or for a relaxation of the rules against recovery against an employer of an independent contractor.

Although the courts have traditionally refused to allow a claimant to recover damages against the employer of an independent contractor there are a number of exceptional categories where recovery has been allowed. In recent years the courts have shown themselves willing to expand upon these exceptions, though unfortunately they have not articulated the basis on which they have done so. The mechanism by which liability is imposed on an employer is that of the non-delegable duty. By saying that an employer owes such a duty, the courts mean that he cannot divest himself of liability by exercising reasonable care in choosing an independent contractor to do the work. As Glanville Williams has pointed out (1956), there is unfortunately no coherent theory that explains when a duty will be classified as non-delegable. Nevertheless, there are now a substantial number of duties that are classified as non-delegable and in the remaining part of this chapter we will seek to identify some of these.

Unsurprisingly, many of the duties that have been classified as non-delegable are strict duties. For example, there are a number of strict *statutory* duties that cannot be discharged by the employment of an independent contractor (see, for example, many of the duties placed on employers under industrial safety legislation). So also the duty imposed upon neighbouring landowners to prevent the escape of dangerous things imposed by *Rylands* v. *Fletcher* is a non-delegable duty, as are the strict duties to maintain premises abutting a highway and to provide lateral support for adjacent land (*Tarry* v. *Ashton* (1876) 1 QBD 314). An analogous case to *Rylands* v. *Fletcher* is the non-delegable duty owed by all those who engage independent contractors to do 'extra-hazardous' acts. In the leading case of *Honeywill and Stein Ltd* v. *Larkin Bros (London Commercial Photographers) Ltd* [1934] 1 KB 191 a cinema company engaged the plaintiffs to do some acoustic work in their theatre. The contractors employed photographers to take photographs of their work inside the theatre. At the time, the taking of flashlight photographs involved the ignition in a metal tray of magnesium powder which, on being ignited, flared up and caused intense heat. As a result of the negligence of the camera operator the magnesium ignited too close to the curtains and they caught fire causing damage. The Court of Appeal held that the contractors were liable for the harm done. Where, as here, an act 'in its very nature involved a special danger to others' the contractors could not discharge their liability simply by proving that they had hired a competent independent contractor.

In addition to the strict duties which the courts have classified as non-delegable, they have identified a number of situations in which breach of the non-delegable duty is dependent upon fault, albeit that of an independent contractor rather than an employee. In such cases, the duty is not merely to take reasonable care but to ensure that reasonable care is taken. Thus, proof by the employer that he took all reasonable care in selecting a competent independent contractor will not excuse him from liability if the independent contractor is careless. Examples of such duties include the obligation of employers to provide a safe system of work (*Wilson and Clyde Coal Co* v. *English* [1938] AC 57); of hospitals to care for their patients (*Cassidy* v. *Ministry of Health* [1951] 2 KB 343, per Denning LJ); and of school authorities to care for their pupils (*Carmarthenshire County Council* v. *Lewis* [1955] AC 549).

Finally, it must be pointed out that an employer is not liable for any 'casual' or 'collateral' acts of negligence of the independent contractor. The distinction between 'collateral' acts of negligence and those for which the employer is responsible is by no means clear. What appears to be meant is that the employer is liable only when the independent contractor commits the tort while engaged in doing that which he was actually employed to do. Thus, in *Honeywill & Stein Ltd* v. *Larkin Bros* the employer would probably not have been liable for the independent contractor had he managed to set fire to the curtains while throwing firecrackers.

21.6 **Joint and Several Liability: The Distinction Between Joint, Several Concurrent and Separate Tortfeasors**

Where damage is caused to the claimant by two or more tortfeasors he may be uncertain as to whom to sue. Must he sue all of them or can he sue one only? Can he recover the full amount in his loss from one of the tortfeasors or must he bring separate actions against each tortfeasor to recover from each their proportionate share of his loss? If the claimant is required to sue all those involved in causing him damage he may be faced with problems if, for example, one of the tortfeasors cannot be found or is uninsured or insolvent. On the other hand, if a claimant is allowed to recover all his loss from one tortfeasor, fairness would seem to dictate that that tortfeasor should have some right to contribution from the other tortfeasors. In the remainder of this chapter we examine some of the problems that arise where more than one tortfeasor causes damage to the claimant and also consider the rights of tortfeasors to claim contribution from each other.

There are three possible types of case where a person may suffer damage as the result of a tortious act committed by two or more tortfeasors. First, the same damage may be caused to the claimant by two or more tortfeasors acting in pursuance of a common design. This may happen in at least three classes of case; namely agency, vicarious liability and joint enterprise. Thus, for example, in one case where two people were looking for an escape of gas and one lighted a match thereby causing an explosion, it was held that they were engaged on a joint enterprise and were jointly liable for the damage caused (*Brooke* v. *Bool* [1928] 2 KB 578). Similarly, where an employer is vicariously liable for the tort of his employee, both are jointly liable for the damage caused by the employee's tort. Where two or more people *jointly* participate in causing the same damage the claimant may sue any of them separately for the full amount of the loss. Alternatively, he may sue all of them jointly in the same action. The liability of *joint* tortfeasors is, therefore, joint and several.

Secondly, two or more tortfeasors may cause the same damage to the claimant in circumstances where they are acting independently and, therefore, do not fall within the first category. In such a case the tortfeasors are known as several concurrent tortfeasors. Where, for example, two cars driven by A and B respectively crash into the claimant's car causing him 'whiplash' injuries, A and B are several concurrent tortfeasors. As with joint tortfeasors, each several concurrent tortfeasor is answerable in full for the whole damage caused to the claimant.

At common law there were two principal distinctions between joint tortfeasors and several concurrent tortfeasors. First, judgment against one joint tortfeasor, even if it remained unsatisfied, barred any subsequent action. Second, the release of one joint tortfeasor operated as a release of all. Neither of these rules applied to several concurrent tortfeasors. The first rule has now been abolished and the second much diminished in importance such that there is now little substantive distinction between joint and several concurrent tortfeasors.

Finally, where two or more persons not acting in pursuance of a common design cause different damage to the same claimant, they are treated as separate and independent tortfeasors. For example, as a result of A's negligent driving the claimant's wrist is broken and requires hospital treatment. At the hospital Dr B, who had been drinking heavily, bandages the claimant's wrist but does it so negligently that the claimant permanently loses all feeling in his arm. A may not be responsible for Dr B's negligence. A and Dr B are separate and independent tortfeasors who have caused different damage to the same claimant. The cases of *Performance Cars* v. *Abraham* [1962] 1 QB 33 and *Baker* v. *Willoughby* [1970] AC 467 (see 9.2) are also good examples of separate and independent tortfeasors. No special rules are required where two or more tortfeasors cause different damage to the claimant.

21.7 Contribution Between Tortfeasors

General Right to Claim Contribution

As a general rule the common law allowed no contribution to be claimed between joint or several concurrent tortfeasors even where one tortfeasor had satisfied the plaintiff's claim in full. This rule has, however, largely been reversed by statute. The rules relating to contribution are now found in the Civil Liability (Contribution) Act 1978. Section 1(1) of the Act provides that:

> 'Subject to the following provisions of this section, any person liable in respect of any damage suffered by another person may recover contribution from any other person liable in respect of the same damage (whether jointly with him or otherwise).'

The Act is not limited in its application to tort. It also applies where the legal basis of liability is 'breach of contract, breach of trust or otherwise'.

Who May Claim Contribution?

In order to be able to claim contribution, the person seeking contribution must either have been found by a court to have been liable or be able to show that liability could be established against him at trial (s. 1(6)). Where, therefore, no action could be brought against him because, for example, a limitation period has expired, his claim for contribution will fail. However, if one of the tortfeasors has paid the claimant, he is still entitled to contribution even if he has ceased to be liable to the original claimant provided 'he was liable immediately before he made or was ordered or agreed to make the payment in respect of which contribution is sought' (s. 1(2)). If one of the tortfeasors settles his claim with the claimant, without admitting liability, he will only be able to claim contribution if he could prove that he was legally answerable (s. 1(4)).

Where the claimant settles with one tortfeasor for an agreed sum, he is not necessarily precluded from further action against another tortfeasor. The claimant's right to recover against another tortfeasor is dependent on whether the original settlement was intended to compensate the claimant for his full loss or only part of it (*Heaton* v. *Axa Equity & Law* [2002] UKHL 15).

From Whom May Contribution Be Claimed?

Section 1(1) provides that contribution is recoverable from anyone who is liable for the same damage. A person may still be liable to make contribution even where he has ceased to be liable to the claimant (s. 1(3)). For example, a person may have ceased to be liable to the claimant because the claimant waived his claim against that person or because the claim was settled. More commonly, the period of limitation within which the claimant must sue the defendant may have expired. Provided, however, the person seeking contribution brings the action against his co-defendant within two years from the date of judgment or settlement an action for contribution may still lie.

Assessment of Contribution

Section 2(1) of the Act provides that 'in any proceedings for contribution under s. 1 above the amount of contribution recoverable from any person shall be such as may be found by the court to be just and equitable having regard to the extent of that person's responsibility for the damage in question'. The assessment of the amount of contribution payable is made by having regard only to the parties before the court: the negligence or contributory negligence of a party not before the court cannot be taken into account. In determining the 'responsibility for the damage' the courts have looked at both the blameworthiness of the tortfeasor and the extent to which that person's act directly caused the loss. Thus, the question of responsibility is assessed on the basis of fault plus causation and not simply moral blameworthiness.

Where the amount of damages payable by one of the tortfeasors to the claimant has been limited by agreement or by virtue of the operation of the Law Reform (Contributory Negligence) Act 1945 then the maximum amount recoverable in contribution is that limited or reduced amount (s. 2(3)).

Summary

21.1 Vicarious liability may be defined as the liability imposed on an employer (D) for the tortious act of his employee (X) that causes loss to a third party (C). For one person to be vicariously liable for the tort of another three conditions must be satisfied. First, the relationship of employer and employee must exist. Second, the employee must commit a tort. Third, the tort must be committed within the course of the employee's employment.

21.2 The most commonly accepted justification for the principle of vicarious liability is that as the employer derives a benefit from his employees' work so he ought to bear any losses or liability incurred in the course of the employment. Other justifications have, however, been put forward.

21.3 In order for the employer to be liable for the torts of his employee a contract *of* service, as opposed to a contract *for* services, must exist. Traditionally, the 'control' test was used to establish this relationship. However, the more modern approach is to look at all the terms of the contract and the surrounding circumstances in order to see whether a contract *of* service exists.

21.4 The tort must be committed by the employee *in the course of his employment.* Torts are committed by the employee within the course of his employment where they are so connected with acts which the employer has authorised that they may be rightly regarded as modes, albeit improper modes, of doing that which the employee was employed to do. The fact that the employee intentionally committed a tort, was doing something he had been prohibited from doing or committed a tort while on a frolic of his own are relevant factors in considering whether a servant was acting within the course of his employment. They are not, however, conclusive against the imposition of vicarious liability.

21.5 As a general rule an employer will not be liable for the acts of his independent contractors. However, in recent years the courts have held that an employer will be liable where he owes the claimant a non-delegable duty. The circumstances in which non-delegable duties have been found to exist are many and various.

21.6 Where two or more tortfeasors cause the same damage to a claimant, the claimant may sue any or all of them to recover his loss. In such a case the tortfeasors will either be joint tortfeasors (where they act in pursuance of a common design to cause the same damage) or several concurrent tortfeasors (where they act separately to cause the same damage). Where two or more tortfeasors act separately to cause different damage they are separate and independent tortfeasors and must be sued separately.

21.7 Joint and several concurrent tortfeasors may recover contribution from the other tortfeasors. The rules on contribution are contained in the Civil Liability (Contribution) Act 1978.

Exercises

21.1 In what circumstances will a employer be liable for his employees?

21.2 Is the principle of vicarious liability justifiable?

21.3 If a employer is liable for the torts of his employee why should he not be liable for the torts of his independent contractors?

21.4 A Ltd own a number of nightclubs. B Co hire out 'bouncers' for nightclub work. A Ltd hire Kevin, who is on B Co's books, for six months. B Co pay their 'bouncers' a nominal £25 per week when they are not employed by another company. Under the terms of the agreement between A Ltd and B Co, A Ltd agree to pay B Co £50 per week for Kevin's services. It is also agreed that A Ltd can dismiss Kevin for 'misconduct' and that A Ltd will pay Kevin £200 per week in cash (to avoid any tax problems). Kevin's contract with A Ltd describes him as self-employed.

A Ltd tell Kevin that under no circumstances must he drink on duty or strike a customer unless he is attacked first.

One night Kevin gets drunk in the club with a 'friend' of his, C. C, who is very drunk, starts to cause trouble. The manager of the club tells Kevin to

eject C. Kevin tries to persuade C to leave. C starts to leave but on his way out he turns around and calls Kevin a coward. Kevin chases after C and catches him. Kevin stabs C with a knife he carries for 'protection'. C is seriously injured.
Advise the parties as to their rights and liabilities in tort.

21.5 What is meant by the control test? Is it a satisfactory determinant of the question whether an employer–employee relationship exists?

21.6 Should an employer ever be liable where an employee does something that the employer has expressly forbidden him to do?

21.7 Why should an employer not be liable in respect of torts committed by an employee on the way to work?

21.8 Is there any coherent principle underlying the cases where the courts have held that an employer owes a non-delegable duty?

22 Remedies

The subject matter of this chapter is the remedies available to the victim of a tort. The main focus is on the principles governing the recovery of damages for personal injury and death. However, we also examine the rules governing the recovery of damages for the loss of or damage to property and the circumstances in which an injunction may be granted in the law of tort.

22.1 The Indemnity Principle

The general object of an award of damages is to give the claimant full compensation for the damage, injury or loss that the defendant's tort has occasioned him. Damages are generally awarded only to compensate the claimant and not to punish the defendant. A claimant is entitled to be compensated for both his pecuniary and non-pecuniary loss. Pecuniary loss is that loss which is essentially financial in nature and includes losses such as loss of earnings, the cost of medical treatment and loss of business profits. Non-pecuniary loss is loss that is essentially non-financial in nature and as such it is less readily quantifiable than pecuniary loss. Included within this category are losses such as pain and suffering and loss of amenities.

In contrast to the law of contract, where damages are generally awarded to put the injured party in the position he would have been had the contract been performed, the general principle applicable to both pecuniary and non-pecuniary loss in tort is that the court should award as damages a sum that will put the person who has suffered the loss in the position in which he would have been had the tort not occurred. As Lord Scarman said in *Lim Poh Choo* v. *Camden and Islington Area Health Authority* [1980] AC 174, 187, 'the principle of the law is that compensation should as nearly as possible put the party who has suffered in the same position as he would have been in if he had not sustained the wrong'.

22.2 Kinds of Damages

Although damages are ordinarily awarded in order to compensate the claimant for his injury that need not be the case. Awards of damages may be made which are non-compensatory in intent. Within this category are (a) contemptuous damages, (b) nominal damages, (c) exemplary damages and (d) restitutionary damages. A court may also award aggravated damages that, although often difficult in practice to distinguish from exemplary damages, are, in fact, compensatory in intent.

Contemptuous Damages

Although the claimant may succeed in his action, the court may indicate that it has formed a low opinion of the merits of his claim or of the claimant's conduct by awarding a derisory amount. Such damages are contemptuous and the amount awarded is usually 'the smallest coin in the realm'. An award of contemptuous damages may imperil the claimant's chances of recovering his costs. The reason for this is that, while costs usually 'follow the event' (i.e., are borne by the losing party), the award of costs is at the judge's discretion. Thus, although the award of contemptuous damages does not necessarily lead to the conclusion that costs will not be awarded to the successful claimant, the fact that the court awarded contemptuous damages only is a material factor for the court to take into account in exercising its discretion. Contemptuous damages are most commonly awarded in defamation actions.

Nominal Damages

Nominal damages may be awarded where a person's legal rights have been infringed but he has suffered no actual loss. Where, for example, a person succeeds in an action for assault (which is actionable *per se*) but cannot prove that he has suffered any injury or loss, the damages awarded are likely to be nominal only. The function of nominal damages is, therefore, to mark the fact that the claimant's rights have been vindicated albeit that he has suffered no damage. Additionally, nominal damages may be awarded where the fact of the loss is shown but the necessary evidence as to the amount of damage suffered is not established.

The award of nominal damages does not involve any finding that the claimant was guilty of any misconduct nor does it reflect on the merits of the claimant's case. However, as is the case with contemptuous damages, the fact that the court made an award of nominal damages is a material factor for the judge to consider in exercising his discretion in awarding costs.

Exemplary Damages

In *Rookes* v. *Barnard* [1964] AC 1129, the House of Lords referred to damages intended to punish, deter and convey disapproval as 'exemplary'. This terminology has become commonplace so that damages awarded with a punitive intent are now generally known as 'exemplary' damages. In *Rookes* v. *Barnard* Lord Devlin, with whom the other members of the House of Lords concurred, expressed the opinion that the availability of an exemplary award of damages in a civil action was anomalous because the punitive considerations which it incorporates properly belong to the criminal law. However, because of the weight of authority supporting them and the fact that they could, in rare circumstances, vindicate the strength of the law he preferred to restrict their availability rather than abolish them outright (pp. 1225–6).

Since *Rookes* v. *Barnard*, a claim for exemplary damages can only succeed when it falls within one of three categories. These are (a) oppressive, arbitrary or unconstitutional action by servants of the government, (b) wrongful conduct by the defendant which has been calculated by him to make a profit for himself which may well exceed the compensation payable to the claimant and (c) any case where such an award is authorised by statute. Additionally, the Court of Appeal had held in *A.B.* v. *South West Water Services Ltd* [1993] QB 507 that the cause of action (i.e., tort) upon which the claim was based must have been one in respect of which exemplary damages had been awarded prior to *Rookes* v. *Barnard* (the 'cause of action' test). However, the House of Lords has held in *Kuddus* v. *Chief Constable of Leicestershire Constabulary* [2002] 2 AC 122 that *A.B.* v. *South West Water Services Ltd* was wrongly decided and that the award of exemplary damages is not so limited. Even if the case falls within one of Lord Devlin's categories, a court is not *compelled* to award exemplary damages. As was made clear by the House of Lords in *Cassell & Co Ltd* v. *Broome* [1972] AC 1027, a court retains a discretion to refuse a claimant's claim; exemplary damages are discretionary, not mandatory. Each of these preconditions for the award of exemplary damages will now be considered in turn.

Oppressive, Arbitrary and Unconstitutional Executive Action

The first category – that of oppressive, arbitrary or unconstitutional action by a servant of the government – was derived from a series of eighteenth century cases that sought to protect the liberties of the subject from the power of the state. Although the category is limited to oppressive, arbitrary or unconstitutional abuses of *governmental* power, the House of Lords in *Cassell & Co Ltd* v. *Broome* [1972] AC 1027 made clear that 'servants of the government' should not be narrowly interpreted. Thus, it has been held to include not only crown servants, but also others who exercise government functions, such as police officers, soldiers and local government officials. It was said, however, not, to encompass the misuse of power by businesses and other powerful non-governmental bodies despite the fact that the former may exercise considerably more economic power than a small local authority and may also perform similar functions (see the speech of Lord Nicholls in *Kuddus* v. *Chief Constable of the Leicestershire Constabulary* [2002] 2 AC 122, 145 criticising this view).

Even where the defendant is a 'servant of the government', it must be shown that the act complained of was done in exercise of a governmental or executive power. In this regard, it is the nature of the functions or powers being exercised that is relevant. By way of example, in *A.B.* v. *South West Water Services Ltd* a nationalised body set up under statute for a commercial purpose, namely the supply of water, was regarded by the Court of Appeal as outside the first category because in conducting the commercial operations it was not engaged in performing governmental functions.

Wrongful Conduct by Defendant Calculated to Make a Profit

Lord Devlin's second category covers cases where the defendant's conduct has been calculated by him to make a profit for himself exceeding any compensation payable to the claimant. Once again, it is clear that a broad interpretation should be given to these words. Like the first category, the purpose of an award of damages under this category is, to use the words of Lord Hailsham in *Cassell* v. *Broome*, 'to teach the wrongdoer that tort does not pay'. Thus, it is not essential that the defendant should be seeking to profit in *monetary* terms. Nor is it necessary that the defendant calculate that the claimant's damages, if he sues to judgment, will be smaller than the defendant's profit: 'The defendant may calculate that the claimant will not sue at all because he has no money ... or because he may be physically or otherwise intimidated' (*Cassell & Co Ltd* v. *Broome* [1972] AC 1027, 1079, per Lord Hailsham). It is enough that the defendant was, for example, seeking to gain some property at the claimant's expense. Defamation cases provide many examples of awards in this category. In *Cassell & Co Ltd* v. *Broome*, where the defendant published a book containing grave imputations on the plaintiff's conduct, an award of £25 000 exemplary damages was upheld by a majority of the House of Lords. The book was only published after the publishers had been warned as to the defamatory material it contained. Further, there was, according to their Lordships, enough evidence for the jury to have reached the decision they did that the defendant had made a cynical calculation that the damages the company might have to pay would not exceed the profit it would make. That is not to say, however, that exemplary damages will be awarded in every case where defamatory material is published in a newspaper with a view to increasing the publication's circulation. In addition, it will have to be shown that the defendant made a decision to proceed knowing that it was wrong, or was reckless as to whether it was wrong, because he had calculated that the financial benefits outweighed any risks involved (*Cassell & Co Ltd* v. *Broome* [1972] AC 1027, 1079 per Lord Hailsham).

Express Authorisation by Statute

Lord Devlin's third category recognises the obvious fact that exemplary damages may be awarded whenever a statute allows such an award to be made. There are, however, few modern statutes that expressly authorise the award of exemplary damages. Further, it is not clear that those statutes that appear to allow the award of exemplary damages in fact do so. As the Law Commission has pointed out, 'it is possible that both of the statutes (s. 13(2) of the Reserve and Auxiliary Forces (Protection of Civil Interests) Act 1951 and ss. 97(2) and 229(3) of the Copyright, Designs and Patents Act 1988) which are often cited as falling within this category are actually examples of statutes which permit aggravated damages as opposed to exemplary awards' (Law Commission, 1993, para. 3.52; see also *Nottinghamshire Healthcare NHS Trust* v. *News Group Newspapers Ltd* [2002] EMLR 33). In any event, little use has been made of this justification in practice.

The 'Cause of Action' Test

In *A.B.* v. *South West Water Services Ltd* [1993] QB 507 the Court of Appeal held that exemplary damages should only be awarded in cases where the cause of action on which the claim was based was one for which exemplary damages were available prior to *Rookes* v. *Barnard*. The decision was heavily criticised on the basis that it introduced irrationality into the law, was not dictated by precedent (Burrows, 1993) and 'encouraged a tedious trawl through ancient authority in an attempt to unearth an award of damages that could be categorised as exemplary in a case based upon a particular cause of action' (*Kuddus* v. *Chief Constable of Leicestershire* [2002] 2 AC 122, 159 per Lord Scott). The House of Lords accepted the force of these criticisms in *Kuddus* and held that *A.B.* v. *South West Water Services Ltd* was wrongly decided and should be overruled.

After *Kuddus* therefore, the award of exemplary damages is no longer limited to causes of action in respect of which exemplary damages were awarded prior to 1964. Whether this means that exemplary damages will necessarily be available in respect of all torts simply because the case is shown to fall within one of Lord Devlin's categories is less clear. The non-availability of exemplary damages in, for example, the tort of negligence is long established and it can be argued that it would be a mistake to re-open the possibility of victims of negligent conduct being awarded exemplary damages. It may also be argued that exemplary damages should not be awarded in respect of torts created by statute unless the statute itself provides for such an eventuality. However, it should be noted that there was evidence in *Kuddus* of a willingness on the part of three of their Lordships to abandon the previous limitations altogether and to rationalise the law relating to exemplary damages in a way similar to that proposed by the Law Commission, namely that exemplary damages may be awarded where the defendant's conduct was outrageous or his disregard of the claimant's rights contumelious (see [45] per Lord McKay, [89] per Lord Hutton, and [26] per Lord Slynn). At this time, all that it is possible to say with certainty is that the cause of action limitation introduced by *A.B.* v. *South West Water Services Ltd* has been abandoned.

Overriding Discretion and Assessment

Even when the pre-conditions for the award of exemplary damages are satisfied it is still open to a court or jury to decide not to award them. The award of exemplary damages is discretionary and a court or jury may decide in its exercise of discretion that the case is not a proper one for their award. In considering whether to exercise the discretion several factors are likely to be relevant including the conduct of claimant and defendant, whether or not the defendant has already been subject to a criminal penalty for his actions, and whether the person who would have to pay the damages is the wrongdoer.

Where a court or jury decides that the case is an appropriate one for the award of exemplary damages, the amount to be awarded must be decided. As the purpose of an exemplary award is to punish, deter or condemn the defendant's conduct, the damages awardable should, in theory, be measured by 'the gravity of the defendant's conduct, by whatever sum is sufficient to deter it, or by a sum which represents an appropriate symbolic indemnification' (Law Commission, 1993, para. 3.87). Such considerations are of course very difficult to evaluate. However, a number of principles relevant to the assessment of exemplary damages have been developed by the courts. Thus, awards should be 'moderate' and take account of the wealth of the defendant and whether the defendant is the wrongdoer. Account must also be taken of any award of compensatory damages made. Only where that sum is inadequate to 'punish' the defendant for his outrageous behaviour can an award of exemplary damages be made. Where a claimant sues more than one defendant, the principle of proportionality in punishment means that the sum awarded should be the lowest that the conduct of *any* of the defendants deserves. In the case of multiple claimants, the jury should determine a single global sum for 'punishment' and this should then be divided among the claimants.

The fact that the amount to be awarded as exemplary damages is usually a matter for a jury has been the subject of considerable criticism. However, there has traditionally been a reluctance on the part of judges either to interfere with a jury award on the ground that it was excessive or to set arbitrary limits on the amount that might be awarded by way of exemplary (or compensatory) damages. The result was that disproportionately large sums were awarded in respect of both compensatory (where those were assessed by jury) and exemplary damages as 'juries lacked an instinctive sense of where to pitch their awards. They were in the position of sheep loosed on an unfenced common, with no shepherd' (*John* v. *MGN Ltd* [1997] QB 568, 608 per Sir Thomas Bingham MR). In order to bring some semblance of reality to the size of exemplary damages awards, the Court of Appeal in *Thompson* v. *Commissioner of Police of the Metropolis* and *Hsu* v. *Commissioner of Police of the Metropolis* [1998] QB 498, 517 set out effective maximum and minimum amounts that should be awarded in actions for false imprisonment and malicious prosecution:

> 'Where exemplary damages are appropriate they are unlikely to be less than £5000. Otherwise the case is probably not one that justifies an award of exemplary damages at all. In this class of action the conduct must be particularly deserving of condemnation for an award of as much as £25 000 to be justified and the figure of £50 000 should be regarded as an absolute maximum, involving officers of at least the rank of superintendent.'

So too, in defamation actions, while the Court of Appeal in *John* v. *MGN Ltd* [1997] QB 586 did not lay down any particular sum as an absolute maximum that may be awarded, it is clear from that case and others that excessive awards of exemplary damages in such actions will not be tolerated and that the Court of Appeal will, using its powers under s. 8(1) of the Courts and Legal Services Act 1990, interfere more readily than had hitherto been the case with what is considers excessive jury awards (cf. *Kiam* v. *MGN Ltd* [2002] EWCA Civ 43).

There are arguments both in favour and against exemplary damages. At the root of the arguments in favour is the claim that, while compensation may be the predominant aim of a civil award of damages, 'the pursuit of retributory, deterrent and condemnatory aims is in certain instances and under certain conditions a legitimate function of the law of civil wrongs' (Law Commission, 1993, para. 5.13). The award of exemplary damages may also lead to a better protection of rights, as well as vindicating the strength of the law. By way of example, serious interferences with interests of personality which give rise to such 'intangible' harms as insult, humiliation or degradation are difficult to assess in compensatory terms. Such wrongs may be more effectively remedied by a punitive model. The main arguments against their award are that they confuse the purposes of the civil and criminal law, import 'criminal'-type punishments into the civil law without any of the corresponding protections, provide the claimant with an undeserved windfall, and are difficult to assess and invariably excessive. Further, the opponents argue that since non-pecuniary harm is now freely compensable, exemplary damages are no longer necessary.

In its final report on exemplary damages (Law Commission, 1997) the Law Commission concluded in favour of the view that exemplary damages should continue to be part of English law and indeed that their scope should be extended. In addition to recommending the overruling of *A.B.* v. *South West Water Services Ltd*, which has now been achieved, the Law Commission recommended that exemplary damages should be available for any tort or equitable wrong (but not breach of contract) where the defendant had deliberately and outrageously disregarded the claimant's rights. The government has indicated, however, that it is not at present minded to legislate.

Aggravated Damages

Aggravated damages are typically awarded where the *manner* in which the tort was committed was such as to injure the claimant's proper feelings of pride and dignity, or gave rise to humiliation, insult or other distress. In theory, such damages are compensatory only. They are not, as are exemplary damages, awarded to punish the defendant but instead to compensate the claimant for any additional injury resulting from the high-handed way in which the defendant has behaved. The defendant's conduct is relevant only to cast light upon the claimant's injury and not to punish, condemn or otherwise deter the defendant. In order for an award of aggravated damages to be made, two elements must be satisfied. First, the defendant's conduct must be 'exceptional', i.e. particularly offensive or accompanied by malevolence or spite. Examples of such conduct would include the wrongful eviction of a tenant where that is accompanied by abuse or other forms of harassment, police misconduct, a particularly humiliating and vicious sexual assault and malicious libels. Such conduct must, however, be exceptional and aggravated damages are not therefore available for negligence even where the negligence is particularly serious. Conduct subsequent to the wrong may be sufficient to give rise to aggravated damages. In *Sutcliffe* v. *Pressdram Ltd* [1991] 1 QB 153, 184, the Court of Appeal viewed as aggravating in the context of a defamation action:

> 'a failure to make any sufficient apology and withdrawal; a repetition of the libel; conduct calculated to deter the plaintiff from proceeding; persistence, by way of a prolonged and hostile cross-examination of the plaintiff or in turgid speeches to the jury, of a plea of justification which is bound to fail; the general conduct either of the preliminaries or of the trial itself in a manner calculated to attract further wide publicity; and persecution of the plaintiff.'

The second requirement is of an injury to a personality interest. This requirement means that a company, which has no feelings, or a person who is unaware of the defendant's motives should not be able to recover aggravated damages. In *Cassell & Co Ltd* v. *Broome* [1972] AC 1027, the House of Lords thought that mental distress, injury to feelings, insult, indignity, humiliation, and a heightened sense of injury or grievance were sufficient to give rise to an award of aggravated damages. More doubtful, however, is whether aggravated damages are available in respect of feelings of anger and indignation excited by the defendant's conduct. A claim based on 'injury' of that nature was struck out by the Court of Appeal in *A.B.* v. *South West Water Services Ltd.* In the court's view, feelings of anger and indignation were not a proper subject for compensation. However, this would appear to conflict with previous law and the better view is that feelings of anger and indignation may be compensable. Where aggravated damages are appropriate the total figure for basic and aggravated damages should not exceed fair compensation for the injury the claimant suffered. Moreover, since *Thompson* v. *Commissioner of Police for the Metropolis*, where a jury considers an award of aggravated damages appropriate, they should be told to make a separate award apart from 'normal' compensatory damages thereby making it easier for the Court of Appeal to exercise control, through its power under s. 8 of the Courts and Legal Services Act 1990, over the amount awarded.

Restitutionary Damages

The branch of law concerned with 'unjust enrichment' is commonly called 'restitution'. As we have seen (ch. 1), the governing concern of this area of law is the restitution of benefits that the defendant received at the expense of the claimant. While some benefit-based remedies are generated by 'restitutionary' claims that are clearly independent of any tort, breach of contract or equitable wrong, there has been an increasing awareness that restitutionary claims may overlap with other types of claim. Of course, in the majority of tort claims there will be no such overlap. In a typical personal injuries action, the defendant acquires no benefit he only suffers a loss. However, that need not be the case. Restitutionary claims are particularly likely to overlap with tort claims where the defendant has benefited by the wrongful use of the claimant's property. This may commonly arise in what have been called the proprietary torts: trespass to land and chattels, conversion and the infringement of intellectual property rights. If, for example, the defendant wrongfully used the claimant's property he would be liable for trespass to land. In such a case, the defendant may also have, by the use of the land, wrongfully benefited at the claimant's expense (see *AG* v. *Blake* [2001] 1 AC 268, 279 per Lord Nicholls). However, outside the proprietary torts, there are other situations where normal compensatory principles have been displaced and a remedy awarded that deprives the defendant of benefits received at the claimant's expense. By way of example, where the defendant has calculated that he can make a profit from committing a tortious act, the courts have awarded exemplary damages, at least in part, to strip him of his profit.

There is much to be said, from the point of view of policy, for allowing restitutionary awards to be made in tort claims in certain limited circumstances. The restitutionary approach prevents the defendant from benefiting through his own wrong and also provides a method of deterring the deliberate exploitation of wrongdoing. It also provides a valuable means of vindicating the claimant's rights (especially property rights). Against that it might be argued that, at least in some cases, the claimant gets an undeserved windfall and that such awards may, in certain circumstances, inhibit enterprise and discourage economic activity (Law Commission, 1993, para. 7.18). Thus far the law has yet to recognise a general principle requiring the defendant to account for profit derived from his tortious conduct. How far the courts will go remains to be seen. The Law Commission in its final report on Aggravated, Exemplary and Restitutionary Damages (Law Commission, 1997) recommended against legislation stating comprehensively the torts in respect of which restitutionary damages could be awarded. Instead, it recommended that the development of restitutionary damages be left to incremental judicial development.

22.3 **Damages Recoverable Once Only**

The damages which the claimant is entitled to recover from the defendant can be recovered once only. This rule has two aspects to it. First, the claimant cannot bring a second action on the same facts simply because the initial loss turned out to be more serious than was thought when judgment was given in the first action. This rule was laid down in *Fetter* v. *Beal* (1701) 1 Ld Raym 339. The plaintiff recovered damages from the defendant in respect of a trespass to the person. After the judgment had been given 'part of [the plaintiff's] skull came out of his head'. The plaintiff sought to bring a second action in respect of the deterioration in his condition. The court held that the recovery in the first action for trespass barred the second action in respect of the subsequent loss.

The second aspect of the rule is that damages are awarded on a once-and-for-all basis and paid in the form of a single lump sum. This requires that the court make an assessment not only of what the claimant has lost between the accident and the trial but also of what he will lose in the future as a result of the accident. Future contingencies must therefore be translated into a present value. In the case of property damage this rarely gives rise to much difficulty in that future losses can usually be estimated with some accuracy. However, where personal injury has been suffered the difficulty of predicting whether the claimant will recover, and if so when and to what extent, has caused problems for the courts. There has, as a result, been a great deal of debate as to whether the system of once-and-for-all payments should be retained or whether some form of periodic payments should replace it (Pearson, 1978, paras. 555–571). The matter has recently been the subject of a Lord Chancellor's Department consultation paper ('Damages for Future Loss: giving the courts the power to award periodical payments for future loss and care costs in personal injury actions') which provisionally concluded that courts should have power to order that damages for future losses and care costs should be paid in the form of periodical payments. That power would be discretionary, and it would be for the courts to decide whether it was appropriate to make an order for periodical payments, based on the individual circumstances of each case.

Proponents of the existing system argue that it leads to finality in litigation, the defendant (usually an insurance company) can close its files and the claimant can concentrate on getting better. Further, the claimant is given a free hand in spending the money. Opponents argue, however, that these advantages – to the extent that they are advantages – are outweighed by the disadvantages of the existing system. First, as Lord Scarman acknowledged in *Lim Poh Choo* v. *Camden and Islington Area Health Authority* [1980] AC 174, 183 assessment of future losses is replete with problems:

> '[K]nowledge of the future being denied to mankind, so much of the award as is attributed to future loss and suffering ... will almost surely be wrong. There is only one certainty: the future will prove the award to be either too high or too low.'

Secondly, there is a danger that if the claimant fritters away his award the state will have to maintain him when the award runs out. Periodic payments would solve these problems to a large extent. Moreover, periodic payments more accurately replace what the claimant has lost, namely a series of periodic payments.

Although the general rule remains that the award must be made in a lump sum there exist a number of exceptions. The first is the award of provisional damages. Where there is a chance that at some definite or indefinite time in the future 'the injured person will, as a result of the act or omission which gave rise to the cause of action, develop some serious disease or suffer some serious deterioration in his physical or mental condition' (s. 32A(1) Supreme Court Act 1981), then a court may, by virtue of s. 32A(2) of the 1981 Act, award

'(a) damages assessed on the basis that the injured person will not develop the disease or suffer deterioration in his condition; and (b) further damages at a future date if he develops the disease or suffers the deterioration.'

The effect of this provision is that a court has the power to compensate a claimant whose condition deteriorates after the trial. In order to recover, the claimant must establish a 'chance' of developing some '*serious* disease' or suffering some '*serious* deterioration'. The legislation does not define the words 'chance' or 'serious', however, some guidance on their meaning can be gained from the decision of Scott Baker J in *Willson* v. *Ministry of Defence* [1991] 1 All ER 638. The judge held that in order to qualify as a chance it must be 'measurable and not fanciful' (p. 642). However, in the judge's view a 'slim' chance was a measurable one. As to 'serious deterioration', Scott Baker J held something 'beyond ordinary deterioration' was required. This was ultimately a question of fact but what was envisaged by the legislation was a severable risk rather than a gradual deterioration. Thus, on the facts of that case, the judge held that the possibility of developing arthritis was insufficiently serious because it was not a severable risk.

Secondly, where certain pre-conditions are satisfied a court may make an award of interim damages. Part 25.7 of the Civil Procedure Rules provides that a court may make an order for an interim payment only:

'If . . . the court is satisfied – (a) the defendant against whom the order is sought . . . has admitted liability to pay damages or some other sort of money to the claimant; or (b) the claimant has obtained judgment against that defendant for damages to be assessed, or for a sum of money (other than costs) to be assessed; or (c) . . . it is satisfied that, if the claim went to trial, the claimant would obtain judgment for a substantial amount of money (other than costs) against the defendant from whom he is seeking an order for an interim payment.'

Such an award can only be made against an insured person, the Motor Insurance Bureau, a public authority, or a person whose means and resources are such as to enable him to meet any interim payment. As to the amount to be awarded, this is at the discretion of the court but must not exceed a 'reasonable proportion' of the damages that are likely to be recovered by the claimant at trial.

Finally, there is the possibility of the parties, where the defendant has liability insurance, agreeing to a structured settlement. A structured settlement is 'an agreement settling a claim or action for damages for personal injury on terms whereby (a) the damages are to consist wholly or partly of periodical payments; and (b) the person to whom the payments are to be made is to receive them as the annuitant under one or more annuities purchased for him by the person against whom the claim or action is brought or, if he is insured against the claim, his insurer'

(Damages Act 1996, s. 5). Such a concept was, until the late 1980s, virtually unknown in the UK because it offered few advantages over the traditional lump sum payment. However, an agreement in 1987 between the Association of British Insurers and the Inland Revenue to the effect that certain forms of structured settlement are not liable to income tax boosted the use of such settlements. Structured settlements were given statutory recognition by the Damages Act 1996. Importantly, however, the Act does not give a court the power to order a structured settlement – although, to preserve the possibility of a structured settlement if the claim goes to trial, s. 2 of the Damages Act 1996 gives a court power to 'make an order under which the damages are wholly or partly to take the form of periodical payments'. Such an order may, however, only be made with the consent of the parties. The main purpose of the provisions was simply to 'rationalise and build on the existing voluntary system'. Thus, the Act does not represent a new start but rather an attempt to regularise the existing system and make it easier to administer and less complicated.

In practice, a structured settlement will usually consist of two parts: a lump sum to cover the past losses and existing needs of the claimant at the date of settlement, and a series of further instalments of the damages for which the defendant is liable. The parties agree how much the claim would have been worth according to conventional principles. Some discount on this figure, currently around 10 per cent, is likely to be agreed between the parties (Law Commission, 1994, para. 3.125) because of the fiscal advantages to the claimant of accepting a structured settlement. Part of the agreed sum will then be allocated to meet any existing needs and to compensate the claimant for past pain and suffering and any costs and expenses already accrued, leaving the balance to be structured. As to the periodic payments, the defendant insurer will fund its liability by purchasing a life annuity from a life insurer (Damages Act 1996, s. 5(1)). The Inland Revenue has given advance clearance in principle to structured settlements provided they incorporate one of four standard form periodic payment schedules (Law Commission, 1994, para. 3.4). Any variations require individual clearance.

The structured settlement has substantial advantages to both the defendant insurer and the claimant. So far as the insurer is concerned the main attraction is that, because the income from the annuity is not taxable in the hands of the claimant, it will be able to negotiate a discount to be made from the sum to be invested in the annuity. Although the Law Commission expressed some concern that the discounts typically negotiated sometimes exceed the amount of tax that would be payable in respect of the income from an ordinary annuity (Law Commission, 1994, para. 3.125), it was satisfied that there was at least some evidence to suggest that claimants also benefited from the favourable tax status (Law Commission, 1994, para. 3.126). In addition to the tax advantage, the main advantages cited for claimants are certainty and flexibility. So far as certainty is concerned, the claimant is relieved of the burden of having to manage a large sum of money, something of which he may have had little previous experience, and is protected from the possible dissipation of funds. Structured settlements also offer considerable flexibility. A settlement can be structured such that payments in some years are greater than others (s. 5(3)), or so as to take account of inflation (s. 5(3)(b)) and it can be linked to the life of the claimant so that the money does not run out before the claimant dies. It is also possible for a guarantee to be built into the structure whereby periodic payments are made for the lifetime of the claimant or for a guarantee period whichever is the longer (s. 5(2)). By this method, provision can be made for the claimant's dependants to benefit, rather than the insurance company, in the event of the claimant's premature death.

While the structured settlement does have considerable advantages over the traditional lump sum award, it also has its limitations. First, it does not avoid the need for forecasting. In fact, the process of assessing the future requirements of the claimant may place 'an undesirable emphasis on forward planning which is avoided where lump sums are used' (Law Commission, 1994, para. 3.20). In order to decide how to structure the periodic payments, a complex 'budget for life' will have to be prepared by the claimant's experts. Where damages are paid in a single lump sum, payments will be made by the claimant to meet his needs as required. The whole process of advance planning is thus avoided. Secondly, structured settlements do not completely remove the risk that the monies will be inadequate to meet the claimant's needs. Once the settlement has been agreed, changes cannot be made if the claimant's prognosis changes. Further, the claimant is still able to squander his periodic payments; there is nothing to guarantee that he will spend them on the purpose for which they were awarded. Finally, there is the possibility that the claimant will, despite the advantages of the structured settlement, want his damages paid in a single lump sum. As has already been mentioned, the structured settlement is a 'creature of negotiation': the Act makes no change to the existing practice that, if this is not agreed voluntarily, a court cannot order that any damages be structured.

22.4 Special and General Damages

'Special' damage has several meanings in the law of tort. Thus, in defamation, 'special' damage must generally be proved to sue for slander. A further important meaning of special damage arises as a matter of pleading. In this context, special damage is used in contra-distinction to general damage and refers to particular damage that would not ordinarily be assumed to flow from the wrong. Such damage has to be specially pleaded and proved. By way of contrast, general damages are presumed to flow from the wrong and therefore do not have to be specially pleaded. Examples of general damages would include loss of amenities, pain and suffering and loss of future earnings. Expenses incurred in travelling to and from hospital, the cost of an operation which the claimant has had done privately and pre-trial loss of earnings would, however, be classified as special damage.

22.5 **Damages for Personal Injuries**

Before examining the formal rules on the recovery of damages for personal injury something must be said by way of general introduction. It might be thought that for most people who have been injured as a result of an accident their most important consideration is how much can they get for their injury. Readers of newspapers cannot have failed to notice that awards of damages in excess of £1 million are becoming more common. Is this, therefore, the sort of award that a person who has been injured in an accident can expect? The answer to this is 'No'. First, studies have shown that only a small proportion of accident victims succeed in recovering any damages at all. Most people simply give no thought to attempting to recover any damages: they are concerned solely with recovering physically from their injuries. A survey done in 1976 by the Oxford Centre for Socio-Legal Studies (the Oxford Survey) showed that only one in seven accident victims reached the stage of consulting a lawyer and, of these, one out of seven failed to get any damages (Harris *et al.*, 1984). Thus most accident victims recover nothing at all.

Secondly, the vast majority of claims are settled out of court as a result of negotiations between the parties' representatives. In the Oxford Survey, for example, only two per cent of those who received some award of damages received these after a contested trial. In many ways this is a good thing. Parties to litigation should be encouraged to settle their differences quickly and as cheaply as possible. Staying out of court means that the lawyers' costs will be lower and the claim should be dealt with more expeditiously. Further, if all personal injury actions were actually litigated the courts would be totally overwhelmed with work and the time it takes to complete a personal injury action would be lengthened.

It must be borne in mind, however, that there are serious disadvantages to the settlement process. As Harris *et al.* (1984) have pointed out, the parties to a typical personal injury action are unlikely to have the same bargaining strength. The advantage almost invariably lies with the defendant which is usually an insurance company. For the claimant this is a one-off action that he cannot afford to lose. He may be without a job as a result of the accident and have no other source of income. He may have little or no recollection of the accident and will almost inevitably want to get the whole thing over as quickly as possible. Further, he may well have gone to his local high-street solicitor who may not have had much experience of personal injury litigation. For the defendant, however, this is likely to be one of many actions in which it is involved. The insurance company is interested not so much in the result of an individual case as with the aggregated results of all its cases (it is a 'repeat player'). It will also inevitably be represented by personal injury specialists, often members of its own in-house team. Further, while an insurance company will have to pay a claimant who is awarded damages interest for the time he was kept out of the award, this rate of interest is likely to be less than the rate the company can get by investing (or lending) the money itself.

The longer, therefore, it delays paying out to the claimant, the better. The pressures on a claimant to settle and to settle for less than a court may award are, therefore, very real. Only looking at sums awarded in contested trials distorts the picture and ignores the fact that the vast majority of cases are settled out of court for considerably less than the awards made in court.

Finally, even where cases do reach a court and are contested it is only in the most serious cases of disabling injury or death – and sometimes not even then – that a claimant is awarded a sum in excess of £1 million. Most actions for personal injury or death are for much smaller amounts as a quick glance at Kemp and Kemp, *The Quantum of Damages* will show (see also, Law Commission, 1994).

With this background in mind, we now examine the way in which the courts assess damages for personal injury or death.

22.6 Non-Pecuniary Loss

As we have already seen non-pecuniary losses are those losses that are essentially non-financial in nature. Such losses are less readily quantifiable than pecuniary ones, yet English law does seek to put a value on such losses. The problem arises, however, of how such losses are to be valued. What, for example, is the loss of a leg or an arm worth? How much money would compensate for the loss of the ability to play football, to dance or to play the piano? Inevitably any amount awarded must of necessity represent a conventional one. In assessing this amount, the guiding principle adopted by the courts is that the amount should be 'fair, reasonable and just' (*Heil* v. *Rankin* [2000] 2 WLR 1173, at [27], per Lord Woolf MR). What the claimant will do with the money is irrelevant to this assessment, as are the consequences any award would have on the defendant. However, the wider social and economic consequences of any award can be taken into account: 'Awards must be proportionate and take into account the consequences of increases in the awards of damages on defendants as a group and society as a whole' (*Heil* v. *Rankin*, at [36], per Lord Woolf MR). In order to avoid the danger of like cases being treated differently and to assist in the facilitation of settlements, the courts assess damages for non-pecuniary loss by reference to awards made in previous cases. Moreover, since 1992 judges, and practitioners who deal with personal injury cases, have also been able to refer to the Judicial Studies Board's *Guidelines for the Assessment of General Damages in Personal Injury Cases* (6th edition, 2000) which indicate the appropriate bracket of award and list features which might affect the level of the award within the bracket. In *Heil* v. *Rankin*, the Court of Appeal conducted a thorough reappraisal of the appropriate level of damages for non-pecuniary loss and concluded that at the highest level awards needed to be increased by approximately one-third but that there was no need for any increase in awards which were then (2000) below £10 000. Between those two levels, the extent of the adjustment should taper downwards.

The effective maximum amount that may be awarded to the most seriously injured claimants for non-pecuniary loss is therefore now in the region of £200 000.

Pain and Suffering

The court will award damages to reflect the pain and suffering felt as a consequence of the accident. In so far as 'pain' and 'suffering' can be separated, the Law Commission (Law Commission, 1995, para. 2.10) thought that 'pain' meant 'physical hurt or discomfort attributable to the injury itself or consequent upon it' while 'suffering' referred to 'the mental or emotional distress which the plaintiff may feel as a consequence of the injury'. Courts do not, however, usually distinguish between the two elements. Examples of matters that would be included under this head are pain attributable to the accident or to any subsequent medical treatment, embarrassment at facial or other disfigurement, and unhappiness associated with awareness of one's predicament. Prior to the Administration of Justice Act 1982, a separate claim for the shortening of life expectancy existed and a conventional sum was awarded in respect of this. Loss of expectation of life was abolished as a separate head of damages by s. 1(1)(a) of the 1982 Act. However, loss of life expectancy may still be relevant when assessing damages for pain and suffering. Where the knowledge that his life expectancy is reduced causes the claimant mental suffering or anguish, this may increase the damages awardable under the head of pain and suffering. The court is no longer restricted to awarding a conventional sum but should instead award an amount based on the claimant's particular circumstances and attitude to the fact that his life expectancy has been reduced.

Where the claimant is rendered permanently unconscious as a result of the accident, he will not be able to recover damages under this head. The courts have held, and this was confirmed by the House of Lords in *Lim Poh Choo* v. *Camden and Islington Area Health Authority* [1980] AC 174, that damages will not be awarded for pain and suffering where the claimant is unconscious or otherwise incapable of experiencing pain. As the Law Commission pointed out, pain and suffering is an 'inherently subjective head of non pecuniary loss' (Law Commission, 1995b, para. 2.12), and as such recovery under this head depends upon the claimant's awareness of it.

Loss of Amenities

An injury may deprive a claimant of his ability to do things that he could do before the accident. Thus, a claimant who is rendered deaf or blind by the accident can obviously no longer enjoy the experiences associated with those senses. The law allows damages to be recovered for losses of this type under the head 'loss of amenities of life'. Damages are recoverable under this head both for the loss of faculties or amenities which are inherent in the injury itself and also loss of any special amenities possessed by the claimant. Thus, a keen tennis player who loses his legs in an accident can recover damages both for the loss of his ability to walk and for his loss of ability to play and enjoy tennis. In addition to the loss of capacity associated with loss of, or damage to limbs or the body and loss of any of the senses, damages are also awardable under this head for, *inter alia*, loss of marriage prospects, loss of sexual function and even loss of pleasure in one's work.

Whether an unconscious claimant who is unable to appreciate that he has lost any of the normal 'amenities of life' should be able to recover damages under this head has been the subject of considerable debate. This question raises two separate issues. First, what is the purpose of an award of damages for non-pecuniary loss? Is it to put a value on what the claimant has lost (the 'diminution of value' approach)? Alternatively, is it to provide a claimant with sufficient damages to enable him to purchase substitute sources of satisfaction (the 'functional' approach)? If it is the latter, then an unconscious claimant should not be compensated for loss of amenity because he will not be able to benefit in any way from the damages awarded. Although the Pearson Commission thought that English law should adopt the 'functional approach' and damages should not be awarded to an unconscious claimant where they can serve no useful purpose (Pearson, 1978, vol. 1, paras. 393–8), this is not the approach that the courts have adopted. In *H West & Sons* v. *Shephard* [1964] AC 326, the majority of the House of Lords held that damages for loss of amenities were awarded for the fact of their deprivation. The court rejected the view that the appropriate method of assessing such damages was to ask what the claimant could buy to provide solace for the loss. Instead, the court should seek to put a value on what the claimant had lost.

Secondly, even if one takes the view that in assessing damages for non-pecuniary loss a court should seek to put a value on what the claimant has lost, that does not necessarily mean that an *unconscious* claimant should be able to recover damages for loss of the amenities of life. The question still arises as to whether such a loss should be assessed subjectively (through the claimant's awareness of it) or objectively (irrespective of the claimant's awareness of it). The current approach taken by English law is to assess the loss of amenities of life objectively. The House of Lords in *H West & Sons* v. *Shephard*, viewed the loss of amenities of life as a grave deprivation for which the claimant was entitled to be compensated regardless of whether he was or was not aware of the loss. As Lord Morris put it in that case, 'the fact of unconsciousness does not, however, eliminate the actuality of deprivations of the ordinary experiences and amenities of life which may be the inevitable result of some physical injury' (p. 349).

Although this approach has been criticised, the Law Commission has recently recommended that there should be no change in the law (Law Commission, 1999a, para. 2.19). In reaching this conclusion, the Commission was particularly attracted by the argument that it would be unjust to award lower compensation for catastrophic injuries than for less serious ones and also by concerns that the apparently irreversibly unconscious may have some awareness of their predicament or may recover a degree of consciousness. Moreover, as the Law Commission recognised, adoption of a subjective approach would be likely to lead to inconsistency and unpredictability in the assessment of damages with 'a premium put on protestations of misery' in order to increase the award for non-pecuniary damages. Whatever its merits, therefore, the functional approach is unlikely to become part of English law in the near future.

The Injury Itself

The injury itself is also a proper subject of a claim in a personal injury action. This claim is in addition to any amount that may be awarded for pain and suffering and loss of amenities. However, while in principle the claims are separate, it will be a rare case in which 'the plaintiff is compensated for the injury as distinct from its consequences (be they pain, suffering or loss of amenity)' (Law Commission, 1995, para. 2.20).

22.7 Pecuniary Loss

Although the amount awarded for non-pecuniary loss in a serious accident may be substantial, damages for pecuniary loss will usually make up the greater part of the claim. As we have seen, the usual practice is that damages are awarded on a once-and-for-all basis and paid in a single lump sum. In assessing the claimant's pecuniary loss the court must, therefore, award a sum to take account of both his actual pre-trial loss and also any future pecuniary losses he will suffer.

Where a seriously injured person is in employment, the largest part of any damages awarded for pecuniary loss is likely to be for loss of earnings. However, this is not the only head of damages awarded under pecuniary loss. Damages, as we shall see, can also be awarded for other losses suffered and expenses reasonably incurred, both before and after the trial.

Loss of Earnings

Damages for loss of earnings can conveniently be divided into two categories, pre-trial and post-trial. The assessment of pre-trial loss of earnings is relatively straightforward. The court will simply seek to ascertain the sum of money that the claimant would have been paid had he not been injured. Assuming, for example, that a claim comes to trial exactly three years after the accident and that the rate of pay for the claimant's job had not altered during that period of time, the claimant's pre-trial loss of earnings would be calculated in the following way. First, the claimant's net annual loss must be established. This is calculated by deducting from his gross annual income the amount he would pay in tax

(*British Transport Commission* v. *Gourley* [1956] AC 185), national insurance contributions (*Cooper* v. *Firth Brown Ltd* [1963] 2 WLR 418) and by way of employee pension contributions (*Dews* v. *National Coal Board* [1988] AC 1). In order to earn his annual income the claimant would have to pay tax and national insurance (and may also have to pay into a pension fund) and thus, to avoid over compensating him, these must both be deducted from his gross income. The sum remaining after these deductions is then multiplied by the number of years between the accident and the trial, thereby yielding the damages payable for pre-trial loss of earnings.

The calculation of post-trial or future loss of earnings is more complicated. As damages are payable at the time of the trial in a lump sum, it is necessary for a court to convert the claimant's future loss of earnings into a lump sum which reflects that future loss. This exercise is fraught with difficulty. To take some examples, how long would the claimant have lived if he had not had the accident? Would he have remained in the same job? Would he have been promoted or would he have been sacked? What will be the rates of wage and price inflation? Will the tax or national insurance rates change? Some or all of these problems are likely to arise in every claim for future loss of earnings. In the light of this, it might be thought that the courts would enlist the help of experts such as actuaries or economists to assist them. Actuaries do not, of course, have crystal balls in which they can see the future but, by turning to statistics of the experience of a similar class of people to the claimant, actuaries can offer statistical evidence as to probable mortality and other matters. For many years, however, the practice of the courts was to take no account of such evidence. Indeed in one case, Oliver LJ said 'the predictions of an actuary can be only a little more likely to be accurate (and will almost certainly be less entertaining) than those of an astrologer' (*Auty* v. *NCB* [1985] 1 WLR 784, 800).

The publication by the Government Actuary's Department of *Actuarial Tables with Explanatory Notes for use in Personal Injury and Fatal Accident Cases* (the 'Ogden' Tables) appears to have done much to change the practice. The purpose of the Ogden Tables is to provide those involved in personal injury litigation with data specifically geared to the assessment of damages in personal injury actions. Although, as recently as 1994, Lord Bridge warned against placing too much reliance on the Tables (*Hunt* v. *Severs* [1994] 2 AC 350), the House of Lords has now made clear in *Wells* v. *Wells* [1999] AC 345 that the Tables must be employed. Lord Lloyd put the point as follows (p. 379):

'I do not suggest that the judge should be a slave to the Tables. There may well be special factors in particular cases. But the Tables should now be regarded as the starting-point, rather than as a check. A judge should be slow to depart from the relevant actuarial multipliers on impressionistic grounds or by reference to a "spread of multipliers in comparable cases" especially when the multipliers were fixed before actuarial tables were widely used.'

The multiplier method

How, then, do the courts assess future loss of earnings? Bear in mind that the court is seeking to award a sum of money which, when invested, will produce annually out of income and capital a sum equivalent to the claimant's loss, for as long as that loss is expected to last, and no more. As Lord Oliver explained in *Hodgson* v. *Trapp* [1989] AC 807, 826:

> 'Essentially what the court has to do is to calculate as best as it can the sum of money which will on the one hand be adequate, by its capital and income, to provide annually for the injured person a sum equal to his estimated annual loss over the whole of the period during which that loss is likely to continue, but which, on the other hand, will not, at the end of the period, leave him in a better financial position than he would have been apart from the accident.'

The method of assessment used to achieve this is the 'multiplier method'. The starting point is to work out the multiplicand. This is, in essence, the net annual loss of income that the claimant suffers as a result of the accident, in other words the claimant's gross income less tax, national insurance and employee pension contributions. This sum is then multiplied by a 'multiplier' to reflect the fact that the claimant's annual loss will continue for some years.

The starting point for the assessment of the multiplier in respect of loss of earnings is the number of years over which the claimant's loss of earnings is expected to continue. This estimation is made as at the date of trial and may require medical evidence. However, to award as the multiplier the number of years during which the loss of earnings will continue would be to over-compensate the claimant as he would receive at the date of trial a sum representing income that, but for the accident, he would not have received until some time in the future. This sum could be invested yielding interest in the period between the date of trial and the date when he would, but for the accident, have received the earnings. As this is interest he would not but for the tort have received, the effect would be that he was over-compensated. What the court seeks to do therefore is to choose a multiplier that when multiplied by the multiplicand reflects the *present day value* of all the future streams of income. To calculate the present day value of the future streams of income that will be lost as a result of the accident, it is necessary to apply a discount rate to each stream of income. The choice of discount rate is obviously crucial for the assessment of the multiplier because the higher the discount rate, the lower the multiplier. Conversely, the lower the discount rate chosen, the higher the multiplier.

How then should the level of the discount rate be set? The level of the discount rate represents the rate of return assumed to be obtainable on the investment of the lump sum. For many years, courts assumed that claimants invested the sum awarded in a mixed fund of equities and gilts and that they would receive on that sum a *real* rate of return (i.e. a rate of return *after* taking out the effect of inflation and basic rate tax) of between

4 per cent and 5 per cent. Thus, the discount rate was conventionally assumed to be about 4½ per cent. However, the Law Commission in its report on *Structured Settlements and Interim and Provisional Damages* (Law Commission, 1995a, paras. 2.24–2.35) criticised this on the grounds that it assumed a rate of return that was difficult for an ordinary person to obtain. Instead the Law Commission recommended that the courts should assume that the claimant invested his lump sum in index-linked government securities (ILGS). ILGS constitute a virtually risk free alternative to investment in gilts and equities and, according to the Law Commission (1995a, para. 2.28), the rate of return on such an investment constitutes 'the best evidence of the real return on any investment where the risk element is minimal, because they take account of inflation, rather than attempt to predict it as conventional instruments do'.

The matter of the appropriate discount rate to apply came before the House of Lords in the three combined appeals, *Wells* v. *Wells, Thomas* v. *Brighton Health Authority*, and *Page* v. *Sheerness Steel Co* [1999] AC 345 (hereinafter *Wells* v. *Wells*). The House of Lords concluded that the discount rate should be based on the rate of return, net of basic rate tax, achievable by investing in ILGS. Their Lordships accepted that a court was entitled to assume that a claimant would behave prudently in the investment of the lump sum but denied that prudent investment meant investment in a mixed portfolio of equities and gilts. Even if investment in equities and gilts achieved a better long-term rate of return than investment in ILGS, and was therefore a 'better' investment for an 'ordinary' investor, that did not mean it was necessarily a suitable form of investment for the personal injury victim. In several respects, as Lord Lloyd explained (p. 366), personal injury victims are not in the same position as 'ordinary' investors:

'The ordinary investor may be presumed to have enough to live on. He can meet his day-to-day requirements. If the equity market suffers a catastrophic fall, as it did in 1972, he has no immediate need to sell. He can bide his time, and wait until the equity market eventually recovers. The plaintiffs are not in the same happy position. They are not "ordinary investors" in the sense that they can wait for long term recovery ... for they need the income, and a portion of the capital, every year to meet their cost of care ... Equities may well prove the best long-term investment. But their volatility over the short term creates a serious risk.'

Having concluded that the discount rate ought to be selected by reference to the rate of return available on ILGS, their Lordships decided upon 3 per cent as the appropriate net after tax return. This was selected on the basis that it represented the average rate of return on ILGS over the previous three years net of tax and was to remain in effect until the Lord Chancellor exercised his power under s. 1 of the Damages Act 1996 to prescribe a different rate or until there were significant changes in the ILGS rate. The Lord Chancellor has now exercised his power to prescribe a rate under the

Act and has lowered the discount rate still further to 2½ per cent (Damages (Personal Injury) Order 2001; see also 'Setting the Discount Rate Lord Chancellor's Reasons', Lord Chancellor's Department press release, 27 July 2001).

The impact of the decision in *Wells* v. *Wells* has been dramatic. Under the old 4½ per cent discount rate regime, the effective ceiling for multipliers, though rarely reached, was 18. Post *Wells* v. *Wells* multipliers in excess of 25 have been awarded and after the Lord Chancellor's decision to lower the discount rate to 2½ per cent are likely to rise still further (see 'Damages Act 1996, Analysis of the Impact of the Prescribed Discount Rate of 2.5%, Lord Chancellor's Department press release, March 2002).

Adjustments to the multiplier for contingencies

In addition to the discount for accelerated receipt of future streams of income, the courts have, as a matter of practice, made a further reduction to the multiplier to take account of the so-called 'hazards' or 'vicissitudes' of life. Such a reduction, which in some cases has been as much as 20 per cent, was justified on the basis that the claimant might die earlier than expected or might be made redundant or suffer some other accident rendering him unemployable. Yet, as was made clear by Lord Lloyd in *Wells* v. *Wells* [1999] AC 345, 378–9, the courts' insistence on making a deduction for the vicissitudes of life is misconceived. Where the multiplier is based on the expectation of life *agreed* by the doctors, there can be no justification for further reducing the multiplier on the possibility that prediction of the life expectancy might be wrong.

> 'In the case of life expectancy, the contingency can work in either direction. The plaintiff may exceed his normal expectation of life, or he may fall short of it ... There is no purpose in the courts making as accurate prediction as they can of the future needs if the resulting sum is reduced for no better reason than that the prediction might be wrong. A prediction remains a prediction. Contingencies should be taken into account where they work in one direction, but not where they cancel out. There is no more logic or justice in reducing the whole life multiplier by 15 per cent or 20 per cent on an agreed expectation of life than there would be in increasing it by the same amount.'

Although Lord Lloyd confined his comments to the calculation of cost of care damages, we would argue that the same principle should apply in loss of earnings claims where there is an agreed actuarial assessment of the claimant's probable working life. The contingencies in such a case can go both ways and no deduction for contingencies should be made in the absence of special circumstances.

The assessment of loss of earnings claims by children

Although there is no difference in principle between the approach taken by courts to the assessment of loss of earnings claims by children, two matters should be noted. First, considerable uncertainty may exist, particularly where the child was very young at the time of the accident, as to the likely net annual loss. Would, for example, the child have grown up to be an investment banker earning several hundred thousand pounds a year or would he have become a shop assistant earning rather less? In such a case the court must do its best to estimate the child's prospects and what he would have earned. Where there is little or no evidence of the abilities of the particular child, the court will pay particular regard to the parents' earnings and education. In several cases the courts have adopted the national average earnings as the appropriate multiplicand but considerably higher awards have been awarded. Thus, in one case, the Court of Appeal upheld an award of 2½ times the national average earnings to a young child of parents that the judge had accurately described as 'well-to-do' (*Cassel* v. *Hammersmith and Fulham HA* [1992] PIQR Q168).

Secondly, the multiplier chosen for the loss of earnings claim is likely to be lower than for loss of earnings claims by younger adults already working at the time of the accident. Where a child is young there will be several years before he would have been able to work. As a result a lump sum awarded to a young child can be invested for some years before the loss is deemed to accrue. Less capital will, therefore, be needed to compensate fully the child for the loss of future earnings.

The Lost Years

Where as a result of the accident the claimant's life expectancy is reduced, the question arises whether damages for loss of earnings should be awarded for the period of the post-accident life expectancy or for the period that the claimant's working life would have lasted but for the accident. One approach to this problem might be to say that as 'nothing is of value except to a man who is there to spend or save it' damages ought not to be awarded to the claimant for lost earnings in the lost years. To put it differently, because the claimant will not be there when the earnings he would have made in the lost years would have accrued, they are not a 'loss' to him and therefore his damages should be assessed on the basis of his post-accident life expectancy. Such an approach was, however, rejected by the House of Lords in *Pickett* v. *British Rail Engineering Ltd* [1980] AC 136. Their Lordships held that where an injury reduces the claimant's expectation of life, his *pre-accident* life expectancy should be used to assess the multiplier and not the post-accident life expectancy. Lord Wilberforce justified the approach adopted as follows (p. 149):

'To the argument that "[damages for lost earnings in the lost years] are no value because you will not be there to enjoy them" can he not reply, "yes they are: what is of value to me is not only my opportunity to spend them enjoyably, but to use such part of them as I do not need for my dependants, or for other persons or causes which I wish to support. If I cannot do this, I have been deprived of something on which a value – a present value – can be placed".'

Moreover, their Lordships were of the opinion that the effect of not allowing a claim in respect of the 'lost years' would mean that the claimant's dependants would lose out. Because the claimant's action would have been settled or he would have obtained judgment before his death no claim could be made under the Fatal Accidents Act 1976. Therefore, the effect of denying a claim in respect of the lost years would mean that the claimant's dependants would be uncompensated. Two responses might be made to this latter point. First, such an argument assumes that the claimant has dependants. If he does not its validity disappears (although the claimant still loses the opportunity to spend the earnings he would have made on other causes he would wish to support). Secondly, if the damages are intended to benefit the dependants, why not award them to the dependants? Such a result could be achieved either by allowing dependants to bring an action under the Fatal Accidents Act 1976 notwithstanding the fact that the claimant's action for damages for personal injury had been settled or he had obtained judgment before his death, or by allowing the dependants a cause of action for pecuniary loss where the person on whom they are dependant is injured as well as where he has been killed (see Burrows, 1994, pp. 201–2).

While the House of Lords accepted in *Pickett* that damages for lost earnings in the lost years are in principle recoverable, claims brought by those without dependants have not been met with great enthusiasm by the courts. Thus, claims brought by children under this head have generally failed. The reason given by the courts is that the valuation of a child's lost earnings in the 'lost years' simply involves too much speculation (*Croke* v. *Wiseman* [1982] 1 WLR 71). While claims by infant claimants for lost earnings in the lost years have generally been denied, the courts have left open the possibility of such a claim by a child prodigy or a case where the infant claimant is the heir to a large estate. Where claims have been brought by adult claimants without dependants, the courts have also refused to award any damages at all for lost earnings in the lost years on the basis that such an assessment requires too much speculation (*Kandalla* v. *British Airways Board* [1981] 1 QB 158), or, alternatively, they have dealt with such claims by a small adjustment to the multiplier (*Housecroft* v. *Burnett* [1986] 1 All ER 332).

In assessing damages for lost earnings in the lost years, a deduction should be made from the multiplicand of a sum to represent the victim's probable living expenses during those years. Such a deduction was said by Lord Wilberforce in *Pickett* to be justified because 'the basis, in principle, for recovery lies in the interest which [the claimant] has in making provision for dependants and others and this would be out of surplus' (p. 151). *Pickett* does not, however, give any further guidance as to the proper method of calculating the appropriate deduction. After a period of uncertainty during which at least three different solutions were adopted, the Court of Appeal in *Harris* v. *Empress Motors Ltd* [1983] 1 WLR 65 adopted the so called 'station of life' solution. Thus, the sum to be deducted as living expenses is the proportion of the victim's net earnings that he spends to maintain himself at the standard of life appropriate to his case. This should be contrasted with the position under the Fatal Accidents Act 1976 (see 22.13) where only the amount that the claimant would have spent exclusively on himself is deducted when assessing the loss of dependency. The reason for the difference is that lost years' damages are intended to compensate the claimant for his own loss while damages under the Fatal Accidents Act 1976 are intended to compensate the dependants for their loss.

Damages for Loss of Earning Capacity

Where a claimant is, as a result of his injuries, disadvantaged in the labour market – in the sense that were he to lose his current employment he would be at a disadvantage in getting another job or one as well paid – a court may make a separate award for his loss of earning capacity. Damage awards under this head derive from the decision in *Smith* v. *Manchester Corporation* (1974) 17 KIR 1, and are made not to compensate the claimant's actual loss of earnings but instead for his disadvantage in the job market. Damages for loss of earning capacity are not usually assessed by the multiplier method because of the many uncertainties involved. Instead the court will make a separate lump sum award as part of general damages. While no single formula exists for solving the problems involved in the assessment, helpful guidance as to the proper approach can be found in Stephenson LJ's judgment in *Moeliker* v. *Reyrolle* [1977] 1 WLR 132, 144:

'In assessing damages under this head the judge has to engage in a double speculation, to measure, first the plaintiff's chances of losing his job, and then his chances, if he loses it, of getting other employment ... [the judge] has to turn his assessment of the two risks into appropriate action ... into a suitable number of pounds sterling "plucked from the air". The extent of the risk varies with the circumstances of each case. If, as will be rare, both are negligible or fanciful (I avoid "speculative" because this head of damages can really be nothing else) ... If one or both are real or substantial, but neither is serious, the award should not be a token or derisory amount, but should generally be in hundreds of pounds ... If both risks are serious, the compensation should generally be in thousands of pounds.'

Medical, Hospital and Other Nursing Expenses

The claimant is entitled to recover all medical, hospital and other rehabilitation expenses that he has reasonably incurred, or will reasonably incur, as a result of the accident. Whether a particular expense is reasonable is a question of fact and will depend on such matters as whether the course of treatment claimed for has been recommended by the claimant's doctor, any scientific proof relating to the efficacy of the treatment proposed and whether the charges of the treatment provider chosen are in line with charges of other providers of the same services.

That the treatment preferred by the claimant is not the cheapest does not preclude recovery, provided that the preferred treatment is reasonable.

A claimant is not prevented from recovering the cost of private treatment if he could have used the National Health Service (NHS) but chose instead to have the necessary treatment done privately, thereby incurring expenses that he would not have incurred had he used the NHS. Section 2(4) of the Law Reform (Personal Injuries) Act 1948 provides that:

> 'In an action for damages for personal injuries ... there shall be disregarded, in determining the reasonableness of any expenses the possibility of avoiding these expenses or part of them by taking advantage of facilities available under the National Health Service.'

Courts have interpreted this provision to mean that when an injured claimant incurs expenses which are reasonable, the fact that he could have taken advantage of the services provided by the NHS and avoided the expenses altogether, is to be ignored (see, *Harris* v. *Brights Asphalt Contractors Ltd* [1953] 1 QB 617, 635 per Slade J). The fundamental argument in favour of the current position is that it would be inconsistent with the freedom of the individual to choose private treatment if the claimant were prevented from claiming the cost of it from the defendants. Yet, even conceding the general right of the individual to choose, it might be objected that, given the existence of universal national health care, the *public* (through the cost of liability insurance) should not have to subsidise those who want private treatment (Cane, 1999, p. 182). If *defendants* actually paid for the claimant's stay in a private hospital, an award might be justified. But *defendants* don't pay damages. It is the insurance company that pays from premiums collected from its customers. Effectively, therefore, it is the *public* that pay and it is not right to fix them with the cost of private health care. While it is suggested there is much in the arguments (see further Law Commission, 1996, paras. 3.7–3.17) of those opposed to the principle enshrined in s. 2(4), the Law Commission provisionally recommended (para. 3.18) that s. 2(4) should not be repealed or reformed. The objection discussed above was dismissed as a 'non-argument': 'as the central tort principle that the victim is entitled to be fully compensated by the tortfeasor means that damages should cover reasonably incurred private health costs, it is simply a non-argument to point to who ultimately may share the burden of those costs' (para. 3.17).

Recoupment of NHS Charges

Where a claimant is treated by the NHS, and does not incur any medical or hospital expenses, he cannot make any claim in respect of the cost of such treatment. So far as the claimant is concerned that is sensible; he has suffered no loss and therefore needs no compensation. Nor can a claimant recover for damages that he will not, on the balance of probabilities, incur. But where a claimant makes use of NHS services, expense is incurred by the NHS and the individual hospital. Neither the NHS nor the hospitals themselves have a general right to recover the cost of treatment from the tortfeasor. However, for some sixty years hospitals run otherwise than for profit have had the power under road traffic legislation (currently ss. 157 and 158 of the Road Traffic Act 1988) to require a defendant to meet some of the cost of the treatment where a person was treated for injuries sustained in a road traffic accident and that person subsequently made a successful claim for damages against the holder of a compulsory motor vehicle insurance policy. Until the enactment of the Road Traffic (NHS Charges) Act 1999 this provision was not supported by any central administrative arrangements for collection of the charges due and the performance of local hospitals in recouping these expenses was patchy. The 1999 Act puts in place a new administrative system to ensure that all cases in which recoupment of NHS charges is possible are identified and that the payments are collected and passed on to the hospitals which provided treatment. It also provides for the method of calculating the cost to the NHS to be changed by regulation in order to reflect more closely the actual costs of treatment.

Section 1 of the 1999 Act sets out the circumstances in which NHS charges are due. These are largely the same as those found in the Road Traffic Act 1988 but costs can now be recovered from the Motor Insurance Bureau. Under the pre-existing law, the power to collect the charges rested with hospitals. The 1999 Act transfers collection to the Secretary of State who will issue certificates of the charges that are due (s. 2). The basis on which those charges are calculated is set out in regulations. The work of collection is undertaken, on behalf of the Secretary of State, by the Compensation Recovery Unit, the unit that is also responsible for the recoupment of social security benefits, the intention being that the administrative procedures established to recoup NHS charges will so far as possible mirror the pre-existing procedures applying to social security benefits (see 22.9). However, as will be explained in more detail (22.9), in respect of benefit recovery the compensator is required to apply for a certificate of deduction *before* paying compensation and may reduce the compensation payable to the injured person to take account of this. In respect of NHS recovery, the amount payable to the claimant is unaffected by NHS charges claimed by the Secretary of State and the charges can be claimed both before and after a payment of compensation has been made. Section 2 therefore contains provisions allowing compensators to apply to the Secretary of State for a certificate of NHS charges before making a payment of compensation so that in cases where there is both benefit and NHS recovery the two recoveries can be handled together by both government and the insurance industry for administrative efficiency.

Loss of Earnings and Cost of Care: Avoiding Duplication

A potential problem is the duplication of loss of earnings and cost of care damages. Consider the case of a person who, as a result of an accident, will require round-the-clock care in a NHS hospital. If this person was working at the time of the accident he will, of course, be able to recover damages for lost earnings. However, if a court were to allow him to claim his full loss of earnings he would be over-compensated because, as he will be fully maintained by the state, he will not have to apply any of his earnings to living expenses. To avoid the duplication that would otherwise exist, the ordinary living expenses saved are deducted from the cost of staying in a private hospital and by s. 5 of the Administration of Justice Act 1982 any saving to the injured person which is attributable to his being maintained at public expense in a hospital, nursing home or other institution must be set against any lost earnings. An analogous problem arises in respect of private medical care: if the claimant recovers damages for the cost of residential accommodation at a private hospital as well as full damages for loss of earnings he will be over-compensated. To avoid this, the courts deduct the 'hotel' element from damages for the cost of private medical care (*Lim Poh Choo* v. *Camden and Islington Area Health Authority* [1980] AC 174).

Care Provided by Third Parties

Finally, consideration must be given to the question of nursing care provided by third parties. Where a professional nurse is employed, provided such employment is reasonable, there will be no problem in the cost being recovered. It is also clearly established that the claimant can, as a general rule, claim damages for gratuitously rendered nursing services. The latter claim requires some explanation. Why, it might be asked, if the claimant's partner provides the nursing services gratuitously should the claimant receive any compensation? Surely he has suffered no loss? If anyone has suffered any loss it is the person who gratuitously provides the nursing services. In *Donnelly* v. *Joyce* [1974] QB 454 Megaw LJ sought to reconcile the award with normal compensatory principles by treating the claimant's loss as the existence of the need for care rather than as the incurring of the nursing expenses. However, this view was rejected as unconvincing by the House of Lords in *Hunt* v. *Severs* [1994] 2 AC 350. According to their Lordships, the underlying rationale of awarding damages to claimants in this type of case is to enable the voluntary carer to receive proper recompense for his or her services. Where, therefore, the claimant needs nursing care and that care is provided gratuitously by another, the damages awarded are to be held on trust for the benefit of the provider of the services.

The facts of *Hunt* v. *Severs* involved a relatively common twist on the above situation. The plaintiff in that case suffered serious injuries in a motorcycle accident where she was a pillion passenger on a motorcycle driven by the defendant. The defendant, whom the plaintiff later married, admitted he was negligent but disputed the plaintiff's claim in respect of the caring services which had been and would continue to be provided by the *tortfeasor*. Of course, the action was defended by an insurer; the nominal defendant was actually rooting for the plaintiff. The House of

Lords agreed with the defendant and refused to allow the claim. Once it was established that a claimant in receipt of 'gratuitous care' could recover damages but should hold them on trust for the carer, it followed logically that where the carer was the defendant no damages should be awarded because damages would otherwise be recovered from and held on trust for the same person. Where, therefore, it is the tortfeasor who provides the gratuitous services, no damages will be paid to the claimant under this head.

Hunt v. *Severs* has been the subject of sustained and, we would argue, justified, criticism (see, for example, Matthews and Lunney, 1995; Kemp, 1994). Not only is the result in the case open to criticism, but the use by their Lordships of the trust concept raises several difficult and unanswered questions as to its application. What, for example, is the position if the claimant dies before the 'carer' damages are consumed? Are those damages to be returned to the tortfeasor on a resulting trust or is the carer to have the money on the basis that he was the intended beneficiary and he is ready and willing to provide the services? In the event of the claimant's insolvency, is the carer to have preferential status among the claimant's creditors? What are the claimant's responsibilities as trustee of the moneys? Is he, for example, under a duty to invest? It is hard to resist the conclusion that the use of the trust concept is not perhaps the panacea the House of Lords thought it might be. Apart from the difficulties associated with the trust concept, the actual result in *Hunt* v. *Severs* can be criticised. What if, in a *Hunt* v. *Severs*-type situation, the claimant and defendant separated or the defendant simply found it impossible to continue to provide the necessary nursing services? The claimant would then be left without any means of paying for the services and would either have to rely on the state or go short. Neither result is satisfactory and the only person who benefits is the tortfeasor, or, more likely, the tortfeasor's insurance company.

Perhaps because of such difficulties, the courts have in two more recent decisions resisted attempts to extend the trust approach outside the context of care and domestic services. In *Dimond* v. *Lovell* [2002] 1 AC 384, D's car was damaged as a result of an accident caused by L. D hired a car from a company under an agreement which provided that D could postpone paying the cost of her hire car until her damages claim had been concluded and that the car hire company would have conduct of any litigation. In proceedings against L, the House of Lords held that the agreement was a regulated consumer credit agreement falling within the Consumer Credit Act 1974. As it had not been properly executed it was unenforceable against L. Furthermore, the problem for the car hire company could not be resolved by allowing D to recover damages for it as trustee as the effect of doing so would be to confer legal rights on the company by virtue of an agreement which the Act has declared to be unenforceable. So too, in *Hardwick* v. *Hudson* [1999] 1 WLR 1770, the claimant, a car mechanic who ran a successful car repair and sales business, was held not to be entitled to recover damages for the gratuitous work done by his wife in the business. While encouraging a close relative or friend to look after an injured person represented a justified policy for the law to pursue, the same could not be said for the situation where the voluntary services were provided in a commercial setting. Thus, in the absence of any duty on the provider to provide the commercial services, no damages would be awarded.

In light of the criticisms directed against *Hunt* v. *Severs*, it is hardly surprising that the Law Commission has recommended its statutory reversal (Law Commission, 1999b, para. 3.76). Further, while it thought that damages should continue to be awarded in respect of care provided gratuitously to the claimant by relatives and friends, it recommended that the trust concept should not be used as the appropriate mechanism for remunerating the carer. Instead, in respect of care already provided prior to the trial, the claimant should be under a personal legal obligation to account for the damages awarded to the relative or friend who had provided that gratuitous care. In respect of future care, however, while the Law Commission thought damages should continue to be awarded, there should be no legal duty on the claimant to pay over the damages recovered.

Other Expenses

Any other expenses that the claimant can show he has reasonably had to incur as a result of the accident are recoverable. Thus, the cost of travel to and from hospital for appointments, the extra costs of running a specially-adapted car and the cost of necessary medical aids have all been held to be recoverable. The claimant can also recover the expenses of relatives and friends, though not those of the defendant, visiting him in hospital. Such damages would presumably have to be held on trust for the visiting relative.

22.8 Interest

Where a person suffers personal injury as a result of the negligence of another or where his property is damaged or destroyed, he may have to wait some years before his loss is made good. During that time, he is kept out of the sum to which he is entitled and which could have been earning interest if invested. The question arises, therefore, whether a claimant is entitled to an award of interest and, if so, at what rate and for what period of time.

The general power to award interest on an award of damages is contained in s. 35A of the Supreme Court Act 1981. In a series of cases, the courts have laid down guidelines in respect of the award of interest in particular circumstances. First, no interest can be recovered on damages for future pecuniary loss, whether cost of care, loss of earnings or loss of future dependency. As Lord Denning MR explained in *Jefford* v. *Gee* [1970] 2 QB 130, 147:

'Where the loss or damage to the plaintiff is *future pecuniary loss* ... there should in principle be no interest. The judges always give the present value at the date of trial, i.e., the sum which when invested at interest would be sufficient to compensate the plaintiff for his future loss, having regard to all contingencies. There should be no interest awarded on this: because the plaintiff will not have been kept out of any money. On the contrary, he will have received it in advance.'

Secondly, in respect of pre-trial loss, the rate of interest payable depends on whether the loss is pecuniary or non-pecuniary. Pecuniary loss attracts a rate approximately equivalent to half the normal short-term rate (i.e. the rate available on money paid into court and placed in the special investment account) for the period from the accident to the trial. The rate is halved to take account of the fact that while interest runs from the date of the accident, the losses have not all been incurred at that time. Where the loss is a non-pecuniary one, interest is awarded because the claimant has been kept out of money to which he was entitled from the date of the accident until the trial. However, as damages for non-pecuniary loss are calculated as at the *date of the trial*, and therefore any changes in the value of money from the accident to the trial are already reflected in the award, there is no need to award interest to 'inflation-proof' the damages. Thus, the interest rate awarded need only represent the rate of return after tax and inflation that an investor would receive if he invested in an investment with minimal risk.

22.9 Collateral Benefits

Schemes for the compensation of injury frequently operate alongside each other. Thus, a person injured as a result of the negligence of his employer may be entitled as a result of his injuries to tort damages, social security benefits, sick pay and an incapacity pension, and he may even receive an *ex gratia* payment from his employer or a third party. Given these, and other, potential overlaps, important policy decisions have to be made concerning the inter-relationship between the various 'compensation' schemes (see Lewis, 1998). In the context of personal injury litigation, two major questions arise: should the courts in assessing damages for personal injury take account of these 'collateral benefits' and reduce the damages payable by the tortfeasor accordingly; and should those who provide the additional source of compensation be able to obtain reimbursement for services they have provided or of the moneys they have paid out? This section deals mainly with the first of these issues, but also examines the circumstances where English law currently allows reimbursement.

The main source of compensation for accident victims is the social security system. Unsurprisingly, the question whether a claimant in receipt of social security payments should have to deduct such payments from any damages awarded has been a matter of considerable controversy. The position regarding the deductibility of most Social Security benefits was radically changed in 1989 by the enactment of the Social Security Act 1989. This has subsequently been amended and the law as to deduction and recoupment of social security benefits is now contained in the Social Security (Recovery of Benefits) Act 1997 and the Social Security (Recovery of Benefits) Regulations 1997.

The general position is that most social security benefits received by the claimant for the relevant period may be recouped by the Secretary of State from the compensator. The payment of benefits to the Department of Social Security takes place in advance of the payment of damages (which are assessed in the usual way disregarding the amount of any listed benefits paid or payable: Social Security (Recovery of Benefits) Act 1997, s. 17). Payment of the net amount to the claimant is treated as discharging his claim.

The Act applies to all cases where a person makes a payment to or in respect of any other person in consequence of any accident, injury or disease suffered by the other. By s. 4 of the Act, the 'compensator' must, before making a compensation payment, apply to the Secretary of State for a certificate of 'recoverable benefits'. This certificate specifies the benefits paid for the 'relevant period' to the claimant since the date of the accident. The 'relevant period' is defined in s. 3 of the Act. If it is a case of accident or injury, the relevant period is the period of five years immediately following the day on which the accident or injury in question occurred (s. 3(2)). In the case of disease, the relevant period is the period of five years beginning with the date on which the claimant first claims a listed benefit in consequence of the disease (s. 3(3)). Where, however, before the end of the five-year period a compensation payment is made in final discharge of any claim arising out of the accident, injury or disease or an agreement is made under which an earlier compensation payment is treated as having been made in final discharge of any such claim, the relevant period ends at that time (ss. 3(4)(a), (b)).

Section 8 of the Act deals with the issue of reduction of compensation payments. This provision is somewhat complicated because, unlike the position under Part IV of the Social Security Administration Act 1992 and the Social Security (Recoupment) Regulations 1990, it does not simply require a deduction in full of the recoverable benefits from the *total* amount of damages. The position under the 1992 Act was perceived to be unfair to claimants because the benefits received by claimants did not necessarily meet the same loss as the heads of tort damages. In particular, it was felt to be unfair that benefits received were deducted from damages for non-pecuniary loss since most social security benefits do not generally compensate for non-pecuniary loss. Under the 1997 Act, therefore, although the amount of recoverable benefits is repayable in full by the compensator, benefits are not deducted from heads of damage to which they do not relate, nor are they deducted from damages for non-pecuniary loss (for further detail see s. 8 and Sch. 2, columns 1 and 2).

Where the 'collateral benefit' paid or payable to the claimant is not a listed benefit, the common law continues to apply. The decisions in this area are often not easy to reconcile. However, it is possible to identify a number of factors that appear to have influenced the courts in reaching their decisions. Where the benefit received is the result of the generosity of others the courts have refused to allow deduction. Thus charitable or ex-gratia payments are not deducted (*Redpath* v. *Belfast and County Down Rly* [1947] NI 167). The reason behind this appears to be an under-standable reluctance to discourage charitable giving. Also, where a claimant has paid for, or in some sense earned his 'benefit', the courts have generally refused to deduct the 'benefit'. Thus, no deduction is made where a person benefits from a contract of insurance that he has taken out (*Bradburn* v. *Great Western Railway Company* (1874) LR 10 Exch 1) or where he receives payments under a pension scheme which he had set up himself (even where his employer contributed to the scheme: *Smoker* v. *London Fire and Civil Defence Authorities* [1991] 2 AC 502). By way of contrast, where the benefit is financed by taxation or by the defendant himself, the courts have tended to insist on deductiblity. Thus long-term sickness benefits payable under an insurance scheme run by the defendant employers have been held to be deductible, as have sick pay and wages.

22.10 Damages for Death

The death of a person can have two effects in the law of torts. First, it may affect existing tort actions in which the claimant is involved. Secondly, it may give rise to a cause of action in favour of the deceased's dependants. The first part of this section deals with the effect of death on existing causes of action. In the second part, the question of an action for dependency will be considered.

22.11 The Effect of Death on Existing Causes of Action: The Law Reform (Miscellaneous Provisions) Act 1934

At common law any cause of action in which the deceased person was involved, whether as claimant or defendant, died with that person. This rule was abolished by the Law Reform (Miscellaneous Provisions) Act 1934. This provides, in s. 1(1), that 'all causes of action subsisting against or vested in [the deceased] shall survive against, or, as the case may be, for the benefit of, his estate'. If, for example, a person is killed as the result of another's tort, the deceased's cause of action will survive *for the benefit* of his estate. So too, if a person is injured by another and that other person subsequently dies, the injured person's claim survives *against* the deceased's estate.

The Act sets out a number of limitations on the right of a claimant to sue or claim damages. First, by virtue of s. 1(2)(a)(ii), no claim can be made in respect of loss of income for the period after the deceased's death. This is to prevent a double liability existing to the dependants (who already have a claim under the Fatal Accidents Act 1976: see 22.12) and to the estate (suing in respect of the deceased's 'lost years'). Thus, where the claimant is killed instantaneously all the estate will be able to recover are the funeral expenses (s. 1(2)(c)). If, however, the victim dies some time after the accident but before the trial of any action against the tortfeasor, his estate will be able to recover damages for any earnings lost up to the date of death and also a sum of money in respect of any non-pecuniary losses suffered in that period. Where death is almost, but not quite, instantaneous, it appears from the case of *Hicks* v. *Chief Constable of the South Yorkshire Police* [1992] 2 All ER 65 that no damages for either pecuniary or non-pecuniary loss can be recovered. In *Hicks*, one of the several reported cases arising out of the Hillsborough football disaster, the House of Lords held that no claim could be made (under the 1934 Act) by the estates of spectators crushed to death at Hillsborough for either the fear of impending death or any pain and suffering experienced in the moments before they died from traumatic asphyxia. Secondly, s. 1(2)(c) provides that the damages recovered for the benefit of the estate are to be calculated without reference to any loss or gain to the estate consequent on the death of the deceased, except that funeral expenses may be included. Thus, an insurance policy that accrued to the benefit of the deceased's estate on his death would not be taken into account in calculating the damages payable under the Act. Finally, the damages recoverable for the benefit of the estate may not include exemplary damages and actions for defamation die with the deceased.

22.12 **Claims by the Deceased's Dependants: The Fatal Accidents Act 1976**

The original Fatal Accidents Act was passed in 1846, a time when, as a result of the Industrial Revolution, the number of industrial accidents was on the increase and increasing numbers of dependants were being left uncompensated for the loss of the family breadwinner. The purpose of the original Act was to remedy the perceived unfairness of the rule in *Baker* v. *Bolton* (1808) 1 Camp 493. This rule denied the existence of any claim on the part of dependants of a deceased person. In its original form, the Act gave actions to the surviving spouse, parents and children of the deceased only. However, subsequent Acts have widened the class of those entitled to bring an action for the loss of dependency.

The Act of 1976, which was a consolidating statute, gives 'dependants' an action for their loss of dependency provided certain criteria are met. The first requirement is that the death must have been caused by 'any wrongful act, neglect or default which is such as would (if death had not ensued) have entitled the person injured to maintain an action in respect thereof' (s. 1(1)). In other words, if the deceased would not have had an action, neither will his dependants. Thus, if A went for a joyride in B's light aircraft knowing that B was extremely drunk and the aircraft crashed killing A, A's action would be likely to fail on the ground that he had voluntarily assumed the risk (see 11.3). In such a case, A's dependants would also be barred.

The second requirement is that the person claiming must be within the class of dependants set out in the Act. Since the Fatal Accidents Act of 1846, the class of persons categorised as dependants has been widened considerably. Section 1(3) of the Act provides that not only are spouses, former spouses, and the legitimate children of the deceased within the class of dependants, but so too are: natural ascendants and descendants; any person treated by the deceased as his parent or child; adopted, illegitimate and step-children; brothers, sisters, and uncles and aunts and their issue; and any person who has been living as husband or wife of the deceased in the same household for at least two years prior to the death. Further, by section 1(5), '(a) any relationship by affinity shall be treated as a relationship of consanguinity, any relationship of the half blood as a relationship of the whole blood, and the stepchild of any person as his child, and (b) an illegitimate person shall be treated as the legitimate child of his mother and reputed father.' While the range of dependants is far wider than in the original Act of 1846, criticism has been directed against the existing list on the grounds of its arbitrariness and restrictiveness. Why for example, should an illegitimate child be within the range of potential claimants while a child not of the deceased but supported by him when he was engaged in a marriage-like relationship of long standing with the child's parent would not? Further, why should same-sex partners, co-habitants who do not satisfy the two-year rule and certain distant relatives supported by the deceased be excluded from the class of dependants? Surely the better approach, as the Law Commission has recommended (1999c, para. 3.46), is to allow anyone who can show that he was financially dependant on the deceased, other than as a business associate, to bring an action.

The third requirement is that the claimant's dependency must have been a financial or pecuniary one. No damages are awarded to dependants under this head for their own mental distress (they may, of course, have their own cause of action against the defendant for negligently causing them 'psychiatric injury') or for the loss of society of the deceased. A fairly broad approach has, however, been taken to what is a financial dependency. While loss of money brought into the household clearly constitutes a loss of a pecuniary benefit, other less tangible benefits may also constitute a pecuniary benefit and as such may be recoverable. Thus, for example, where the deceased did not bring money into the household but instead provided 'services' such as gardening, cleaning or child-care, the loss of such 'services' may constitute a recoverable loss. Similarly, it has been held that damages can be recovered for the loss of the services provided by a mother in looking after her children (see, for example, *Corbett* v. *Barking, Havering and Brentwood Health Authority* [1991] 2 QB 408), by a wife in caring for her disabled husband (*Feay* v. *Barnwell* [1938] 1 All ER 31), by a husband in providing various services around the house and garden (*Robertson* v. *Lestrange* [1985] 1 All ER 950), and by a husband and father for work on the family home (*Crabtree* v. *Wilson* [1993] PIQR Q24).

To be recoverable it is not necessary that the dependant was in receipt of the pecuniary benefit at the time of the deceased's death; all that is required is that the dependant had 'a reasonable expectation of pecuniary benefit' from the continuance of the deceased's life. Thus, in *Taff Vale Railway Co.* v. *Jenkins* [1913] AC 1 it was held that the parents of a young woman nearing the completion of her apprenticeship as a dressmaker could recover damages to compensate them for the loss of the prospective pecuniary advantage of which they were deprived by their daughter's death. However, the House of Lords in *Davies* v. *Taylor* [1974] AC 207 refused to allow a claim for loss of future dependency by a wife who had deserted her husband five weeks before his death in circumstances where, as the trial court found, there was no appreciable chance or expectation of reconciliation. In so holding, the House of Lords made clear that the test to be applied where one partner has left another is, whether there was a reasonable expectation of a reconciliation and not, as the trial judge had thought, whether a reconciliation was more likely than not. Thus, for example, if it could have been shown that there was a 25 per cent chance of reconciliation, the wife would have been able to recover damages for her loss, albeit only to the extent of 25 per cent of the loss had there been no marriage break-up.

The Act also recognises two further claims. First, a claim may be made for damages for 'bereavement' under section 1A of the Act. This provision allows for the payment of a fixed sum of £10 000 to the wife or husband of the deceased and, where the deceased was a minor, to the parents of a legitimate child and the mother of an illegitimate child. It is not necessary to prove any actual mental suffering: this is presumed by law. Secondly, a claim may be made in respect of funeral expenses.

22.13 Assessment of Damages for Loss of Dependency

Once the claimant has established that he falls within the category of dependants and that he has suffered a loss of dependency that arose solely from the familial relationship, the court will consider the appropriate measure of damages. The purpose of an award of damages in a fatal accidents claim is, in the words of Lord Diplock in *Mallet* v. *McMonagle* [1970] AC 166, 175:

'to provide ... the dependants of the deceased with a capital sum, which, with prudent management will be sufficient to supply them with material benefits of the same standards and duration as would have been provided for them out of the earnings of the deceased had he not been killed by the tortious act of the defendant.'

As in a personal injuries claim, damages are assessed using the multiplier method.

In assessing the multiplicand, the starting point for the calculation is the deceased's net earnings (i.e. the deceased's earnings after tax and national insurance have been deducted). To this must be added the value of any other services, such as cleaning or gardening, provided by the deceased to his dependants. From this figure must be deducted the amount the deceased would have spent exclusively on himself. The deceased's share of the joint expenses, such as rent or mortgage payments, the cost of running a car and other general household bills are not deducted. The sum left after deducting the claimant's personal expenditure from his net earnings is what is left for the dependants. In practice, unless there is compelling evidence to the contrary, the courts simply deduct a conventional percentage from the net earnings to represent the claimant's personal expenditure. Where the family consists of husband and wife, a deduction of one-third is made to represent the claimant's personal expenditure. Where there are children the deduction for personal expenditure is reduced to one-quarter.

Once the multiplicand has been calculated the court proceeds to assess the appropriate multiplier. In calculating the multiplier the court is seeking to arrive at a figure which, when multiplied by the multiplicand, will yield a lump sum that when invested in index-linked government securities (ILGS) will, out of capital and income, provide annually for the dependant a sum of money that is equivalent to the estimated annual loss over the period during which the dependency would have been likely to continue had the deceased not been killed, and no more. However, unlike a personal injuries action where the multiplier is assessed as at the date of the trial, the multiplier in a Fatal Accident Act claim is generally assessed as at the date of death. Why should the date generally chosen for assessment of the multiplier in actions under the Fatal Accidents Act be different? Assessing damages is, as we have seen, a somewhat inexact 'science'. Knowledge of the future being denied to them, the courts have to make the best guess that they can based on such information as is available. In an ordinary personal injury action, the court does at least know what has happened to the claimant between accident and trial. Thus, the multiplier is assessed as from the date of trial. In an action brought under the Fatal Accidents Act, however, everything that might have happened, had the deceased not died, after the date of the death is uncertain. Nothing is gained in terms of certainty, therefore, by postponing the time of assessment of the *multiplier* until the time of trial. Thus, the multiplier is assessed from the date of death. Where, however, there is a substantial delay between the date of death and the trial, some adjustment to the multiplier may be appropriate to take account of the fact that one element of a dependency calculation is now less speculative (i.e. the continued survival of the dependant: see *Corbett* v. *Barking, Havering and Brentwood Area Health Authority* [1991] 2 QB 408).

In assessing what multiplier should be awarded in the case of a fatal accident there are, as Purchas LJ pointed out (pp. 422–3) in *Corbett* v. *Barking, Havering and Brentwood Health Authority*, at least five essential elements that must be considered: first, the likelihood of the provider of the support continuing to live; secondly, the likelihood of the dependants being alive to benefit from that support; thirdly, the possibility of the providing capacity of the provider being affected by the changes and chances of life either in a positive or in a negative manner; fourthly, the possibility of the needs of the dependant being altered by the changes and chances of life, again in a positive or negative way; finally, the discount necessary to take account of (a) the immediate receipt of compensatory damages in advance of the date when the loss would actually have been incurred, and (b) the requirement that the capital should be exhausted at the end of the period of the dependency. Once the multiplier has been assessed the sum awarded is divided into special damages and general damages. Special damages are awarded for the pre-trial loss and attract interest at the same rate as pre-trial damages for pecuniary loss in a personal injuries action. General damages are awarded for the loss thereafter and do not attract interest.

So far we have dealt with the general approach taken by the courts in assessing the sums awardable in a fatal accident case. Some comments must now be made as to particular difficulties that arise in fatal accident claims. First, by virtue of s. 3(3) of the 1976 Act, the benefits accruing to a wife as a result of the prospects or fact of re-marriage are not to be taken into account when considering a wife's claim in respect of her husband's death. This provision has, in relation to actual re-marriage, been the subject of some criticism. The point has been made that where, after the death of her husband, a woman remarries a richer man it is somewhat unsatisfactory to compensate her on the basis that she suffered a loss as a result of her husband's death. To the contrary, she may be said to have gained from his death; she is now financially better off than she was before. While there is force in this objection, the provision can be justified on the basis that it accords with the general principle expressed in s. 4 of the Act that 'benefits which ... accrue to any person from the deceased's estate *or otherwise as a result of his death* shall be disregarded' (emphasis added).

Secondly, claims by children of the deceased, although assessed using the same general approach as above, raise a number of different issues. In most cases the child's dependency will be presumed to continue until the child would be expected to leave school. Where a child is likely to proceed to tertiary education the multiplier will be adjusted accordingly. Claims by children also give rise to problems in the assessment of the multiplicand. Where a child is deprived of one or more of his parents, he will of course suffer a readily assessable financial loss. However, he will also be deprived of their services. By way of example, a child who is very young needs a constant child-minding service. A child who is ill needs to be nursed. So too, older children 'require' a laundry and taxi service. These services have a value. How do the courts value such losses? In a sense it depends upon the loss in respect of which damages are claimed. Where a very young child is deprived of its mother, courts will often value the loss as the cost of a full-time nanny. This may be subject to an uplift to take account of the fact that a parent does not work set hours and is in constant attendance.

However, older children do not require such full-time attendance. In their case, therefore, damages may be limited to the cost of child-minding after school. So too, it has been held that where the mother is in full-time employment and could only care for the children on a 'part-time' basis a discount may be made to the multiplicand.

22.14 Apportionment Between Dependants

Section 2(3) of the Fatal Accidents Act 1976 provides that 'not more than one action shall lie for and in respect of the same subject matter of complaint'. Thus, an action under the Act must be brought by the executor or administrator of the deceased's estate in the name of the dependants. As to the apportionment of any award, ss. 3(1) and 3(2) of the Act provide that such damages may be awarded as are proportioned to the injury resulting from the death to the dependants respectively and shall be divided among the dependants in such shares as may be directed. In practice, the compensation paid to the spouse of the deceased will be the larger amount; the children, if any, will receive smaller shares.

22.15 Deductions in Dependency Cases

Unlike the situation in a personal injuries claim, the general position in respect of a claim by dependants is that no deductions will be made in respect of collateral benefits accruing either to the estate or to dependants directly. This is made clear in s. 4(1) of the Act which provides that 'the benefits which have accrued or will or may accrue to any person from [the deceased's] estate or otherwise as a result of his death shall be disregarded'. Thus, it seems clear that insurance monies, pensions, gratuities and social security benefits that accrue to the dependants as a result of the death are not deductible. Further, it is also clear from *Stanley* v. *Saddique* [1992] 1 QB 1 that s. 4 is not to be narrowly construed and extends beyond direct pecuniary benefits to include non-pecuniary benefits that accrue as a result of the death. In *Stanley* v. *Saddique* itself, the Court of Appeal held that the trial judge was correct in his decision that the (non-pecuniary) benefits accruing to the infant plaintiff as a result of his absorption into a family unit consisting of his father and stepmother and siblings should be wholly disregarded for the purposes of assessing damages.

In the light of *Stanley* v. *Saddique*, the Court of Appeal's decision in *Hayden* v. *Hayden* [1992] 1 WLR 986 was somewhat surprising. In *Hayden*, the plaintiff's mother was killed in a diving accident caused by her father's negligence. The father subsequently gave up work to look after the plaintiff full-time. By a majority, the Court of Appeal held that the father's services should be taken into account in the assessment of the plaintiff's damages. For Parker LJ, the daughter had suffered no loss: her mother's services had been replaced by those of her father's. Because she had lost nothing, she could recover nothing. For Sir David Croom-Johnson, the father's services were not a benefit resulting from the death because the father was doing no more than fulfilling his existing parental obligations. Neither explanation is entirely satisfactory, or easy to square with existing caselaw. To conclude that the plaintiff had suffered no loss is inconsistent with a line of cases in which it had been held that loss of a parent's services even if replaced gratuitously was a compensable loss. Moreover, the conclusion that s. 4 did not apply because the benefit did not result from the death should have led the court to apply the common law rule that a benefit that does not result from the death is equally to be disregarded.

In *R* v. *Criminal Injuries Compensation Board, ex parte K* [1999] QB 1131 the Divisional Court reconsidered this issue. The Criminal Injuries Compensation Board (CICB) had held, applying *Hayden* v. *Hayden*, that the claimant children had suffered no loss of *general* parental care because their aunt and uncle provided them, after their mother's death, with at least equivalent care. The Divisional Court quashed the CICB's decision and applied *Stanley* v. *Saddique*, distinguishing *Hayden* v. *Hayden* on the grounds that (1) the defendant in *Hayden*, as the provider of the substitute services, was himself the tortfeasor so to make him pay would effectively be awarding double damages against him and (2) the duties that the father took on after the mother's death were simply an extension of the existing parental duties of the father and hence did not arise as a result of the death. Although this reconciliation is not entirely satisfactory, it does have the merit of confining *Hayden* v. *Hayden* to its relatively uncommon facts. The result of the three decisions appears, therefore, to be that, where caring services are replaced by a third party, the benefit accruing to the claimant thereby is not to be taken into account in the assessment of damages. Where, however, a surviving parent, provides increased care, this 'extra' care is as a result of his ordinary parental duties and the dependant's claim is reduced either because the dependant has suffered no loss or because the loss does not result from the death.

As will have been apparent from the discussion above, s. 4 does not obviate the need when dealing with benefits received by the dependant to consider whether the dependant in fact suffered a loss at all. The courts have continued to draw a distinction between the ascertainment of the loss and the assessment of damages. The point is well illustrated by *Auty* v. *NCB* [1985] 1 WLR 784. In that case the plaintiff claimed damages for the loss of her husband's support and for the loss of the widow's pension to which she would have been entitled, under the scheme to which her husband had belonged, had he survived to retirement. She argued that the pension she was receiving under her husband's death-in-service scheme should be ignored in assessing damages for *both* of these losses. The Court of Appeal agreed that s. 4 required the pension to be ignored in the assessment of her claim for loss of her husband's services but held, in respect of the claim for loss of the pension she would have received, that she had suffered no loss since she was in receipt of precisely the pension she would have received had her husband died in retirement.

22.16 **Property Damage and Economic Loss**

The basic principle for the assessment of damages, that the claimant should be put in the same position as if the tort had not occurred (*restitutio in integrum*), applies as much to the recovery of damages for loss of, or damage to, property and the recovery of damages for pure economic loss, as to the recovery of damages for personal injury. What is required to give effect to the principle *restitutio in integrum* when goods are destroyed is usually the award of the market value of those goods at the time and place of destruction. This will usually enable the claimant to purchase replacement goods for those destroyed. So, for example, if due to the defendant's negligence the claimant's car was damaged beyond repair, he would be entitled to recover in damages an amount which would enable him to replace his lost car valued as at the time the loss occurred. Further, it is of no relevance that the replacement value of the goods is considerably greater than the price originally paid for the goods by the claimant. Thus, in *Dominion Mosaics Co Ltd* v. *Trafalgar Trucking Co* [1990] 2 All ER 246, owners of machines destroyed in a fire were held to be entitled to recover the full replacement cost of those machines even though they had originally purchased the goods at a particularly favourable price and had no intention of replacing the goods.

Where the chattel destroyed is profit-earning, the claimant is also entitled to recover damages for profits lost as a result of the tort. In *Liesbosch Dredger* v. *S.S. Edison* [1933] AC 449, 463–4 Lord Wright explained the rule as follows:

> 'The true rule seems to be that the measure of damages in such cases is the value of the ship to her owner as a going concern at the time and place of the loss. In assessing that value regard must naturally be had to her pending engagements, either profitable or the reverse.'

In the *Liesbosch* case itself where the plaintiffs' dredger was sunk while under a dredging contract in Patras harbour, the plaintiffs recovered in addition to the market price of a comparable vessel in substitution: the costs of adaptation, transport and insurance of the substitute vessel to Patras; compensation for disturbance and loss in carrying out their contract over the period of delay between the loss of the *Liesbosch* and the time at which the substituted dredger could reasonably have been available for use in Patras; and, overhead charges, expenses of staff and equipment thrown away.

Where the claimant's property is merely damaged and can be repaired, damages may be assessed either by reference to the diminution in value of the property or the cost of cure. Diminution in value is usually assessed by taking the difference between the market price for damaged and undamaged property. The cost of cure is assessed by reference to the cost of repair or reinstatement. Useful guidance on the choice between the two measures in the context of damage to real property can be found in

Donaldson LJ's judgment in *Dodd Properties* v. *Canterbury City Council* [1980] 1 All ER 928. After identifying the two measures, he said (p. 938):

'Which is appropriate will depend on a number of factors, such as the plaintiff's future intentions as to the use of the property and the reasonableness of those intentions. If he reasonably intends to sell the property in its damaged state, clearly the diminution in capital value is the true measure of damages. If he reasonably intends to continue to occupy it and to repair the damage, clearly the cost of repairs is the true measure. And there may be in-between situations.'

Where a claim is made in relation to damage to real property there is no invariable practice as to which measure is used. Each case depends upon its own facts. However, courts have awarded damages on the basis of the cost of cure notwithstanding that the amount claimed was considerably in excess of any diminution in the value of the property. Such an approach is understandable, particularly in relation to domestic property, where the claimant will often want to repair the damage caused by the tort in order that he can go on living there. Where a claim is made in respect of damage to goods, the almost invariable basis of assessment of such loss will be cost of cure. This reflects the general practice that goods are usually owned for use rather than sale. However, if it could be shown that the damaged goods were owned for sale rather than use or that the repair costs were considerably in excess of any diminution in their market value, then the diminution in the market price should be the appropriate measure. Thus, in *Darbishire* v. *Warren* [1963] 1 WLR 1067 the plaintiff was held not to be entitled to claim damages assessed on the basis of the cost of repair because the cost of repairing his car (£192) greatly exceeded the market value of a similar replacement (£85) and although the plaintiff may have acted reasonably as far as he was concerned in having his car repaired, the reasonableness of his actions had to be judged according to whether he acted reasonably as between himself and the defendant. On the facts, there was nothing special about the car and because the cost of repairs greatly exceeded the market value of a similar replacement, damages were assessed in the basis of the car's market value and not the cost of repairs.

Where the costs of repair claimed are reasonable, the fact that by doing the repairs, the chattel will be more valuable than before does not usually justify reducing the damages by the amount that the repairs will increase the value of the chattel. As was explained in *The Gazelle* (1844) 2 Wm Rob 279, 281:

'The right against the wrongdoer is *restitutio in integrum* and the restitution he is bound to make without calling upon the party injured to assist him in any way whatsoever ... If that party derives incidentally a greater benefit then mere indemnification, it arises only from the impossibility of otherwise effecting such indemnification without exposing him to some loss or burden, which the law will not place upon him.'

The fact that the repairs have not been carried out at the date of trial or indeed will never be carried out, because, for example, the damaged goods have been sold, does not prevent the claimant recovering the cost of repair.

Where as a result of the defendant's tort the claimant is deprived of the use of his chattel while it is being repaired, he is entitled to be compensated for that loss. The measure of damages recoverable will depend upon the use to which the chattel would have been put, but for the tort, and whether any profits would have been earned by the use of the chattel. Whether or not the goods are profit-earning the claimant will usually be entitled to claim the reasonable costs of hiring a substitute while his chattel is being replaced or repaired. Where, however, the goods are profit-earning, damages may also be recovered for profits lost while the chattel was being repaired. The damages recoverable for loss of profits are not necessarily limited to the profits that would have been earned while the chattel was being repaired but may include damages for loss of future profits.

Where a chattel is non-profit-earning and the claimant does not hire a substitute during the period of repair, damages may still be recovered for loss of use. As Earl Halsbury LC explained in *The Mediana* [1900] AC 113, 117:

> 'What right has a wrongdoer to consider what use you are going to make of your vessel? More than one case has been put to illustrate this: for example, the owner of a horse, or of a chair. Supposing a person took away a chair out of my room and kept it for twelve months, could anybody say you had a right to diminish the damages by shewing that I did not usually sit in that chair, or that there were plenty of other chairs in the room? The proposition so nakedly stated appears to me to be absurd.'

Economic Loss

As we have seen, the English law of tort only rarely allows a claimant to recover in respect of a pure economic loss. Where, however, such loss is recoverable then, as with any other type of harm, the basic principle for the assessment of damages in respect of such a loss is that the claimant should be put in the same position as if the tort had not occurred. It is beyond the scope of this book to discuss in any detail the issues that may arise in relation to the assessment of damages relating to such loss but one particular issue of general interest will be mentioned here.

Lay people often seek the advice of professionals before entering into particular types of transaction. Thus, a solicitor may be consulted about legal problems likely to arise in relation to the sale of a company and a surveyor is almost always asked to value a house before it is purchased. A difficulty may arise in such cases in ascertaining the extent of the professional's liability if the advice which he gives is negligent. Is the professional in such a case liable for all the foreseeable consequences which flow from the advisee entering into the transaction or just for the consequences of the advice being incorrect? By way of example, in *South Australia Asset Management Corporation* v. *York Montague Ltd* [1997] AC 191, a valuer engaged by a lender to value a property on which the lender was considering making a loan, negligently over-valued the property. The lender relying, *inter alia*, on the valuation, lent money to a borrower on the security of the property. Had the lender known the property's true valuation it would not have lent at all. Soon after the loan was made property prices collapsed, the borrower defaulted on the loan and the security proved inadequate to repay the loan. The lender sued the valuer claiming that had it known the true value of the property it would not have entered into the transaction at all and, therefore, that it was entitled to recover damages for *all* the consequences that flowed from its having entered into the transaction. In other words, the lender was claiming that in a case such as this the valuer would bear the whole risk of a transaction which but for its negligence would not have happened, *including* any loss attributable to the market fall.

The Court of Appeal agreed with the lender. Where the lender would not, absent negligence, have entered into the transaction (the so-called 'no transaction' cases) the valuer should bear the whole risk of any transaction going wrong. However, if, absent negligence, the lender would have gone ahead but would have lent less or on different terms (the 'successful transaction' cases), the lender could only recover as damages the difference between what he actually lost and what he would have lost if he had lent the lesser amount. In the House of Lords, Lord Hoffmann held that the Court of Appeal had started at the wrong point. As his Lordship pointed out, 'before one can consider the principle on which one should calculate the damages to which the plaintiff is entitled as compensation for the loss, it is necessary to decide for what kind of loss he is entitled to compensation'. A duty of care, as we have seen, does not exist in the abstract. Not only must the claimant establish that a duty was owed to him but also that it was a duty in respect of the kind of loss which was suffered. Until the scope of the duty is established, damages cannot be assessed because a defendant is only liable for the consequences of his breach of duty. What then was the scope of the defendant's duty in this case? It was, according to Lord Hoffmann, to provide information to the lender to help it decide whether to lend money on the property or not. It was not a case where the adviser undertook a duty to advise the plaintiff whether to enter into a particular transaction or not. The valuation was simply one of the factors to be considered by the plaintiff in deciding whether to lend money on the property. Thus, the extent of the valuer's liability was limited to the consequences of the advice given being wrong. The consequence of the valuer's advice being wrong was that the lender had less security than it thought it had. The consequences did not, however, include the market fall; that would have happened regardless of the valuer's negligence.

The case is by no means an easy one but we would suggest that the principles on which it is based are correct. Prior to any assessment of damages, the scope of the defendant's duty must be established in order to ascertain whether the defendant undertook merely to *supply information* or whether he undertook to give the claimant advice on whether to enter into a transaction or not. If the duty undertaken is only to *supply information*, the professional must take reasonable care to ensure that the information is correct but if he is negligent he is liable *only* for the consequences of that information being incorrect. He is not responsible for all the consequences that flow from the lender entering into the transaction. Again, where the adviser's duty is to give the advisee advice as to whether to enter into a transaction, the adviser is liable for all the consequences of his advice being incorrect. In these circumstances, a foreseeable consequence of the defendant's negligence would be that the claimant would enter into a transaction that he would not otherwise have entered into. The claimant would, therefore, be entitled to compensation for all the consequences of that. Of course, in any particular case, it may be a difficult question as to whether the defendant has undertaken to advise generally upon the wisdom of entering into the contract or whether he has merely undertaken to provide information on the basis of which the claimant could take a decision (see, for example, *Aneco Reinsurance Underwriting Ltd* v. *John & Higgs Ltd* [2002] UKHL 51).

22.17 Injunctions

Instead of, or sometimes in addition to, the award of damages a court may grant the claimant an injunction. An injunction is an order of the court restraining the commission of some wrongful act or ordering the defendant to take some positive steps to rectify a wrongful act. Originally an injunction, as an equitable remedy, could only be issued by the Court of Chancery; however, today any division of the High Court may do so. As an equitable remedy an injunction is never available 'as of right'. Instead the issue of an injunction lies within the discretion of the court. In this section we will look in outline at four different types of injunction. These are: prohibitory, mandatory, interlocutory and *quia timet* injunctions.

A **prohibitory injunction** is, as its name suggests, an order of the court that restrains the defendant from committing or continuing a wrong. Injunctions are commonly sought to prevent or stop a nuisance or in cases of continuing or repeated trespasses. However, there seems to be no reason why an injunction should not issue to prevent the commission or continuation of other torts. Where liability has been established and where there is a likelihood of recurrence or continuation the claimant will nearly always be granted this type of injunction. In rare cases (considered below) damages may be awarded in substitution for an injunction.

A **mandatory injunction** differs from a prohibitory injunction in that, instead of preventing or restraining the defendant from doing a wrongful act, it orders the defendant to take positive steps to rectify that which he has already done. In *Redland Bricks Ltd* v. *Morris* [1970] AC 652 the House of Lords held that a mandatory injunction would only issue where three criteria are satisfied. These are (1) damages are not a sufficient or adequate remedy; (2) the defendant has acted wantonly or unreasonably; and (3) the terms of the injunction can be stated clearly such that the defendant can know what it is he has to do.

An **interim injunction** is a provisional and temporary injunction that is designed to restrain the commission or continuance of an activity pending the final settlement of the claim. In *American Cyanamid Co* v. *Ethicon Ltd* [1975] AC 396, the House of Lords held that for an interim injunction to issue there must be a serious question to be tried but not necessarily a prima facie case. If there is a serious question to be tried, then the court must decide whether, on the balance of convenience, to issue an injunction. In considering whether the balance of convenience lies in favour or against interim relief the court should take into account whether damages would be an adequate remedy for the claimant, whether the claimant's undertaking in damages gives the defendant adequate protection if the claimant loses at trial and whether the preservation of the status quo is important enough to demand an injunction. Where, after considering these factors, the court is of the opinion that the balance of convenience is 'even' the court may consider the relative merits of the two parties' cases.

Usually an injunction will only issue where a tort has already been committed. However, where, to use the language of Lord Upjohn in *Redland Bricks Ltd* v. *Morris* [1970] AC 652, 664 'the plaintiff shows a very strong probability on the facts that grave damage will accrue to him in the future', a *quia timet* **injunction** may issue. *Quia timet* injunctions are, therefore, ordered to prevent threatened torts. Lord Upjohn, however, made clear that a *quia timet* injunction would only issue where the threatened or intended damage was imminent and where damages would be an inadequate remedy.

As has already been mentioned, the injunction is a discretionary remedy. However, in the context of prohibitory injunctions, the claimant's entitlement becomes almost absolute if he makes out an actionable interference with his rights (*Redland Bricks Ltd* v. *Morris* [1970] AC 652, 664 per Lord Upjohn). Nevertheless, there are certain established grounds on which a court may decide not to grant an injunction, Thus, an injunction may be refused: where damages are an adequate remedy (*Pride of Derby and Derbyshire Angling Association Ltd* v. *British Celanese Ltd* [1953] Ch 149, 181 per Evershed MR); on the grounds that the claimant acquiesced in the defendant's infringement of his legal rights (*Gaskin* v. *Balls* (1879) 13 Ch D 324); where the claimant delays unreasonably in enforcing his rights (*Sayers* v. *Collyer* (1884) 28 Ch D 103); where the claimant has used fraudulent or other deplorable means to protect his interests (*Armstrong* v. *Sheppard & Short Ltd* [1959] 2 QB 384); where the issue of an injunction would require the defendant to do something impossible or illegal (*Pride of Derby and Derbyshire Angling Association Ltd* v. *British Celanese Ltd* [1953] Ch 149, 181, per Evershed MR); and, where the award of an injunction is unnecessary (because the defendant is willing to give an undertaking in the same terms as the injunction the claimant seeks) or would be ineffective (*Wood* v. *Sutcliffe* (1851) 2 Sim

NS 163: injunction to stop defendants polluting a river was refused as the area was so polluted that pollution of the river was inevitable).

Lord Cairns' Act (now the Supreme Court Act 1981, s. 50) allows damages to be awarded 'in addition to, or in substitution for, an injunction'. However, as we have seen, the general rule is that, where a claimant can show that his legal rights will be violated by the defendant, he will be entitled to the grant of an injunction. Section 50 of the Act was not intended to alter that. But it must not be forgotten that the award of an injunction is, like any equitable remedy, discretionary. In many cases an injunction will be granted almost as 'of course', but one will never be granted if this would cause 'injustice' or 'be oppressive' (see the judgments of Millet LJ and Sir Thomas Bingham MR in *Jaggard* v. *Sawyer* [1995] 1 WLR 269). It is in such cases that the award of damages in substitution for an injunction may be appropriate. The court in *Jaggard* v. *Sawyer* accepted that the well-known passage from the judgment of Smith LJ in *Shelfer* v. *City of London Electric Lighting Company* [1895] 1 Ch 287, 322–3 provided a good working rule to the exercise of the discretion. In *Shelfer* Smith LJ said:

'(1) If the injury to the plaintiff's legal rights is small, (2) And is one capable of being estimated in money, (3) And is one which can be adequately compensated by a small money payment, (4) And the case is one in which it would be oppressive to the defendant to grant an injunction: – then damages in substitution for an injunction may be given.'

Summary

22.1   The purpose of an award of damages in tort is to put the injured person in the position he would have been had no tort occurred. The overriding principle of the law is to compensate the claimant fully for his loss.

22.2   In certain circumstances the purpose of an award of damages may not be to compensate the victim. Awards of contemptuous, nominal, exemplary and restitutionary damages may be made for purposes other than to compensate the claimant. Aggravated damages are, however, intended to be compensatory.

22.3   Damages are recoverable once only. This rule has two aspects. First, the claimant cannot bring a second action on the same facts simply because his injury turned out to be worse than he had originally thought. Secondly, damages are payable in a lump sum once and for all. There exist three exceptions to this: an award of interim damages; an award of provisional damages; and structured settlements. Only the payment of interim and provisional damages can be ordered by the court. A settlement requires the agreement of the parties.

22.4   Where a court makes an award of damages the amount will be divided between special and general damages.

22.5   Newspapers often report the conclusion of litigation involving the award of a very large sum of money by way of damages but most people who are injured as a result of a tort do not pursue legal action and, of those who do, the vast majority of their claims are settled out of court for comparatively small sums of money. The formal rules of damages must be set against that background.

22.6 Non-pecuniary loss is loss that is essentially non-financial in nature. As such it is less readily quantifiable than pecuniary loss. Pain and suffering, loss of amenities and the injury itself are examples of non-pecuniary loss. An award of damages for loss of amenities is made for the fact of their deprivation, while an award of damages for pain and suffering is made only when the claimant actually experiences the pain and suffering. Although it is obviously difficult to put a figure on these non-pecuniary losses, the courts assess damages by having regard to previous cases and the guidance provided by the Judicial Studies Board's *Guidelines for the Assessment of General Damages in Personal Injury Cases.*

22.7 Pecuniary loss is that loss which is essentially financial in nature and includes losses such as loss of earnings, the cost of medical treatment and loss of business profits. Damages for loss of earnings are divided into pre-trial and post-trial loss. For post-trial losses the court seeks to award a sum of money which when invested will produce annually out of capital and investment income a sum equivalent to the total earnings that the claimant has lost, and no more. This is assessed by the multiplier method. In calculating the appropriate multiplier it is assumed that the lump sum awarded will be invested predominantly in index-linked government securities (ILGS).

22.8 Interest is payable on all pre-trial losses. The rate of interest payable depends upon the type of loss suffered. No interest is payable on post-trial losses.

22.9 Charitable payments and payments under an insurance policy are not to be taken into account in assessing the damages payable to the claimant. Virtually all other benefits that accrue to the claimant as a result of the tort must be taken into account in some way. The law as to deduction and recoupment of social security benefits is now contained in the Social Security (Recovery of Benefits) Act 1997 and the Social Security (Recovery of Benefits) Regulations 1997.

22.10 The death of a person can have two effects in the law of torts. It may affect existing causes of action in which the claimant is involved and it may give rise to a cause of action in favour of the deceased's dependants.

22.11 Section 1(1) of the Law Reform (Miscellaneous Provisions) Act 1934 provides that any cause of action subsisting against or vested in the deceased survives for the benefit of, or against, the deceased's estate. No damages are payable under the Act in respect of loss of income for the period after the deceased's death.

22.12 The Fatal Accidents Act 1976 gives a cause of action to 'dependants' (defined in s. 1(3)) for loss of a dependency. In order to recover, a 'dependant' must show that he was financially dependent on the deceased and that that dependency arose from a familial relationship. A more limited class of persons can recover damages for bereavement (s. 1A). Funeral expenses are also recoverable under the Act.

22.13 The purpose of an award under the Fatal Accidents Act 1976 is to provide the dependant with a capital sum which will be sufficient to supply him with material benefits of the same standard and duration as would have been provided for him out of the earnings of the deceased had he not been killed. The method of assessment is again the multiplier method, appropriately modified.

22.14 An action under the Fatal Accidents Act 1976 is usually commenced on behalf of the dependants by the deceased's executor or administrator. Each dependant recovers such damages as are proportioned to the loss suffered as a result of the death.

22.15 By virtue of s. 4 of the Act, any benefit accruing to a person as a result of the deceased's death is not to be taken into account when assessing damages. The courts have held that s. 4 is not just confined to direct pecuniary benefit but instead applies to all forms of material benefit.

22.16 Where property has been totally lost, the usual measure of damages is the market value of the lost property assessed at the time and place of the loss (ie the replacement value). Where the claimant's property is only damaged, a court may award damages based on either diminution in value or cost of cure. Damages may be recovered for any consequential loss.

22.17 Where a tort is threatened or likely to be repeated or continued, a court may grant an injunction. An injunction is an order of the court restraining the commission of some wrongful act or ordering the defendant to take some positive steps to rectify a wrong. The injunction is an equitable remedy and is never available as of right. Four types of injunction are considered in the text. These are prohibitory, mandatory, interim and *quia timet*. Damages may sometimes be awarded in addition to or, rarely, in substitution of, an injunction.

Exercises

22.1 What is the purpose of an award of damages in tort? Is the basis on which damages are assessed in tort the same as that for breach of contract?

22.2 When are exemplary damages available in a tortious action? Is the existing English law satisfactory? In what circumstances, if at all, should the victim of a tort be able to recover exemplary damages?

22.3 When are aggravated damages awarded? Should damages be recoverable in respect of such intangible injuries as injury to feelings, injury to dignity or indignation?

22.4 What is a structured settlement? Why has it been described as 'the greatest advance in personal injury law of recent times' (Lewis, 1988)? Should a court have the power to order a structured settlement?

22.5 Should damages be available for non-pecuniary losses? How do the courts assess damages for non-pecuniary loss? Was the Court of Appeal in *Heil* v. *Rankin* justified in raising substantially in amount the damages recoverable for such losses? Why should an unconscious claimant be able to recover damages for loss of amenities?

22.6 How do the courts assess damages for loss of earnings? Was the House of Lords in *Wells* v. *Wells* justified in its decision to apply the rate available from investment in ILGS instead of the existing 4.5 per cent rate? What was the effect of its decision on the size of awards?

22.7 Should a claimant be able to recover damages for earnings lost during the 'lost years'?

22.8 Why are the multipliers awarded for loss of earnings in cases of personal injury to young children lower than those typically applied to young adults?

22.9 A's partner gives up her job as a partner in a City solicitor's office to nurse him. She was earning £100 000 per annum. Can A recover this amount in respect of cost of nursing? Should A have to hold the damages awarded on trust for his partner? What alternatives exist to this approach?

22.10 Why should the cost of private medical care be recoverable? Why should the NHS be able to recover the cost of medical treatment in road accident cases?

22.11 Why are benefits received generally deducted in actions for personal injuries when they are not taken into account when assessing damages in respect of actions for death? Is there an underlying rationale for the different treatment of different benefits in a personal injuries action?

22.12 Why are no damages recoverable under the Law Reform (Miscellaneous Provisions) Act 1934 in respect of loss of income in the period after the deceased's death?

22.13 Is the current list of 'dependants' in the Fatal Accidents Act 1976 satisfactory? How do the courts assess damages under the Act of 1976? Should the fact of re-marriage be taken into account when assessing damages for loss of a dependency?

22.14 What are: prohibitory injunctions, mandatory injunctions, *quia timet* injunctions and interim injunctions? When will damages be awarded in lieu of an injunction?

22.15 A car crash leaves a number of people dead or injured. Liability for the accident was not disputed. Advise the following parties on the damages they may recover.

(i) Alpesh, aged four, was left unconscious in a coma from which it is feared that he will never recover. His life expectancy is reduced as a result of the accident and is now only 30 years. He is being treated in a private hospital. All the costs of the private care are covered by a health insurance policy.

(ii) Bettina, a 32 year-old bus driver and keen fun-runner, lost a leg in the accident. Before the accident she was earning £10 000 per annum. Afterwards, she was unemployed for two years while she recovered but was then able to take a clerical job earning £8 000 per annum. For the first 18 months of her recovery Bettina's partner, Cynthia, is given unpaid leave from her job at a bank to nurse Bettina back to health. A year after the accident, the Department of Social Security agreed to pay Bettina £20 per week in severe disablement allowance. Her case on quantum is heard 4 years after the accident.

(iii) Deborah was killed instantaneously in the accident. She is survived by Edward, her boyfriend of the last several years, and their two young children. Following an argument, Deborah and Edward had lived apart for the four months preceding the accident; however, hopes of a reconciliation were high. Deborah was 36 at the time of the accident and earned £150 000 per annum as a partner in a major solicitor's firm. Edward, also a solicitor, had left work to bring up the children, but expects to return to work after a couple of years. Just before the trial on quantum, Edward married Fiona, who had just inherited £2 million. Fiona wants to stay at home and look after the children full time.

How would your advice have been different if Deborah and Edward had been married?

408

Bibliography

Alexander (1972) 'The Law of Tort and Non-Physical Loss: Insurance Aspects', 12 *JSPTL* 119.
Allen *et al.* (1979) *Accident Compensation after Pearson* (Sweet & Maxwell).
Anderson (1994) in Markesinas & Deakin, *Tort Law*.
Atiyah (1967) *Vicarious Liability in the Law of Torts* (Sweet & Maxwell).
Atiyah (1972) 'Res Ipsa Loquitur in England and Australia', 35 *MLR* 337.
Atiyah (1995) *An Introduction to the Law of Contract*, 5th edn (Oxford University Press).
Baker (2002) *An Introduction to English Legal History*, 4th edn (Butterworths).
Baker and Milsom (1986) *Sources of English Legal History* (Butterworths).
Bell (1983) *Policy Arguments in Judicial Decisions* (Oxford University Press).
Beyleveld and Brownsword (1991) 'Privity, Transivity and Rationality', 54 *MLR* 48.
Birks (1985) *An Introduction to the Law of Restitution* (Oxford University Press).
Birks (1991) 'Civil Wrongs: A New World', *Butterworths Lectures 1990–91*.
Bishop (1980) 'Negligent Misrepresentation through Economists' Eyes', 96 *LQR* 360.
Bishop (1982) 'Economic Loss in Tort', 2 *OJLS* 1.
Bowman and Bailey (1986) 'The Policy Operational Dichotomy – A Cuckoo in the Nest', 45 *CLJ* 430.
Buckley (1996) *The Law of Nuisance*, 2nd edn (Butterworths).
Burrows (1993), 'The Scope of Exemplary Damages', 109 *LQR* 358.
Burrows (1994) *Remedies for Torts and Breach of Contract*, 2nd edn (Butterworths)
Buxton (2000) 'The Human Rights Act and Private Law', 116 *LQR* 48.
Calabresi (1970) *The Costs of Accidents* (New Haven, CT).
Calcutt (1990) *Report on Privacy and Related Matters* (HMSO), Cmnd 1102.
Calcutt (1999) *Review of Press Self-Regulation* (HMSO), Cm 2135.
Cane (1989) 'Economic Loss in Tort: Is the Pendulum out of Control', 52 *MLR* 200.
Cane (1996) *Tort Law and Economic Interests*, 2nd edn (Oxford University Press).
Cane (1999) *Atiyah's Accidents, Compensation and the Law*, 6th edn (Butterworths).
Clerk and Lindsell (2000) *Torts*, 18th edn, ed. A. Dugdale (Sweet & Maxwell).
Coote (1998) 'Chance and the Burden of Proof in Contract and Tort', 62 *ALJ* 761.
Coote (2000) 'Damages, *The Liesbosch*, and Impecuniosity', 60 *CLJ* 511.
Cornish and Clark (1989) *Law and Society in England 1750–1950* (Sweet & Maxwell).
Craig (1999) *Administrative Law*, 4th edn (Sweet & Maxwell).
Dewees and Trebilcock (1992), 'The Efficiency of the Tort System and its Alternatives: A Review of the Empirical Evidence', 30 *Osgoode Hall LJ* 57.

Dewees *et al.* (1996) *Exploring the Domain of Accident Law: Taking the Facts Seriously* (Oxford University Press).

Dias (1967) 'Trouble on Oiled Waters: Problems of the Wagon Mound (No. 2)' [1967] *CLJ* 62.

Dworkin (1986) *Law's Empire* (Fontana).

Dziobon and Tettenborn (1997) 'When the Truth Hurts: The Incompetent Transmission of Distressing News', 13 *PN* 70.

Fleming (1988) *The American Tort Process* (Oxford University Press).

Fleming (1989a) 'Probabilistic Causation in Tort Law', 68 *Can Bar Rev* 661.

Fleming (1989b) 'Property Damage–Economic Loss: A Comparative View', 105 *LQR* 508.

Fleming (1990) 'Requiem for Anns', 106 *LQR* 525.

Fleming (1998) *The Law of Torts*, 9th edn (The Law Book Co).

Furmston (ed.) (1986) *The Law of Tort: Policies and Trends in Liability for Damage to Property and Economic Loss* (Duckworth).

Gearty (1989) 'The Place of Private Nuisance in the Modern Law of Torts', 48 *CLJ* 214.

Genn (1987) *Hard Bargaining: Out of Court Settlement in Personal Injury Actions* (Oxford University Press).

Gilmore (1974) *The Death of Contract* (Ohio State University Press).

Givelber (1982) 'The Right to Minimum Social Decency and the Limits of Evenhandedness: Intentional Infliction of Emotional Distress by Outrageous Conduct', 82 *Columbia Law Review* 42.

Goodhart (1966) Note, 82 *LQR* 444.

Government Actuaries Department *Actuarial Tables with Explanatory Notes for Use in Personal Injury and Fatal Accident Cases* (The 'Ogden' Tables).

Grubb (ed.) (2002) *The Law of Tort* (Butterworths Common Law Series).

Grubb and Mullis (1991) 'An Unfair Law for Dangerous Products: The Fall of Anns' [1991] *Conv* 225.

Grubb and Pearl (1990) *Blood Testing, Aids and DNA Profiling: Law and Policy* (Jordan).

Harris *et al.* (2002) *Remedies in Contract and Tort*, 2nd edn (Butterworths).

Harris, Maclean, Genn, Lloyd Bostock, Fenn, Corfield and Brittan (1984) *Compensation and Support for Illness and Injury* (Oxford University Press).

Harris and Veljanovski (1986) 'Liability for Economic Loss in Tort', in Furmston (1986), 45.

Hart and Honoré (1985) *Causation in the Law*, 2nd edn (Oxford University Press).

Hedley (1995), 'Negligence – Pure Economic Loss – Goodbye Privity, Hello Contorts' [1995] *CLJ* 27.

Hepple *et al.* (2001) *Tort: Cases and Materials*, 5th edn (Butterworths).

Hitcham (1986) 'Some Insurance Aspects', in Furmston (1986), 191.

Holmes (1881) *The Common Law* (London).

Honoré (1983) 'Causation and Remoteness of Damage', *Int Enc Comp L*, XI, *Torts*, Ch. 7.

Howells (ed.) (2000) *The Law of Product Liability* (Butterworths Common Law Series).

Huber (1988) *Liability: The Legal Revolution and its Consequences* (Basic Books).

Jaffey (1985) 'Volenti Non Fit Injuria', 44 *CLJ* 87.

Jolowicz (1987) 'Product Liability – Directive and Bill', 46 *CLJ* 16.

Judicial Studies Board (2000) *Guidelines for the Assessment of General Damages in Personal Injury Cases.*

Kemp (1984) 3 *CJQ* 120.

Kemp (1985) 101 *LQR* 556.

Kemp (1994) 'Voluntary Services Provided by the Tortfeasor to his Victims', 110 *LQR* 524.

Kemp and Kemp (1985) *The Quantum of Damages*, 4th edn.

Kennedy & Grubb (1994) *Medical Law*, 2nd edn (Butterworths).

Kennedy (1995) *Note* 3 *Med LR* 189

Kodilinye (1986) 'Public Nuisance and Particular Damage in Modern Law', 6 *LS* 182.

Kodilinye (1989) 'Standing to Sue in Private Nuisance', 9 *LS* 284.

Law Commission (1969) *The Interpretation of Statutes*, Law Com No 21.

Law Commission (1970a) *Civil Liability for Dangerous Things and Activities*, Law Com No 32, Cmnd 142.

Law Commission (1970b) *Civil Liability of Vendors and Lessors for Defective Premises*, Law Com No 40, Cmnd 184.

Law Commission (1976) *Report on Liability for Damage or Injury to Trespassers and Related Questions of Occupiers' Liability*, Law Com No 75 (HMSO).

Law Commission (1993) *Aggravated, Exemplary and Restitutionary Damages*, Consultation Paper No 132 (HMSO).

Law Commission (1994) *Structured Settlements and Interim and Provisional Damages*, Law Com No 224 (HMSO).

Law Commission (1994b) *How Much is Enough? A Study of Compensation Experiences of Victims of Personal Injury*, Research Report No 225 (HMSO).

Law Commission (1995a), *Liability for Psychiatric Illness: A Consultation Paper*, Consultation Paper No. 137 (HMSO).

Law Commission (1995b) *Damages for Personal Injury: Non-Pecuniary Loss*, Consultation Paper No 140 (HMSO)

Law Commission (1996) *Damages for Personal Injury: Medical, Nursing and Other Expenses*, Consultation Paper No 144 (HMSO).

Law Commission (1997) *Aggravated, Exemplary and Restitutionary Damages*, Law Com No 247 (The Stationery Office).

Law Commission (1998) *Liability for Psychiatric Illness*, Law Com No 249 (The Stationery Office).

Law Commission (1999a) *Damages for Personal Injury: Non Pecuniary Loss*, Law Com No 257 (The Stationery Office).

Law Commission (199b) *Damages for Personal Injury: Medical, Nursing and Other Expenses; Collateral Benefits*, Law Com No 262 (The Stationery Office).

Law Commission (1999c) *Claims for Wrongful Death*, Law Com No 263 (The Stationery Office).

Law Commission (2000) *Damages Under the Human Rights Act*, Law Com No 266 (The Stationery Office).

Law Commission (2001) *The Illegality Defence in Tort*, Consultation Paper No 160 (The Stationery Office).

Lewis (1988) 'Pensions Replace Lump Sum Damages: Are Structured Settlements the Most Important Reform of Tort in Modern Times?', 15 *JLS* 392.

Likierman (Chairman) (1989) *Professional Liability Review* (HMSO).

Lord Chancellor's Department (1991) *Compensation for Road Accidents.*
Lord Chancellor's Department (1993) *Infringement of Privacy.*
Lunney (1996–7), 'Chances of Recovery in Tort' 7 *KCLJ* 101.
McKendrick (1990) 'Vicarious Liability and Independent Contractors – A Re-examination', 53 *MLR* 770.
McKendrick (2000) *Contract Law*, 4th edn (Palgrave).
Maitland (1936) *The Forms of Action at Common Law* (Cambridge University Press).
Markesinis (1987) 'An Expanding Tort Law – the Price of a Rigid Contract Law', 103 *LQR* 354.
Markesinis (1989) 'Negligence, Nuisance and Affirmative Duties of Action', 105 *LQR* 104.
Markesinis and Deakin (1992) 'The Random Element of their Lordships' Infallible Judgement: An Economic and Comparative Analysis of the Tort of Negligence from Anns to Murphy', 55 *MLR* 619.
Markesinis and Deakin (1994) *Tort Law*, 3rd edn (Oxford University Press).
Markesinis and Deakin (1999) *Tort Law*, 4th edn (Oxford University Press).
Matthews and Lunney (1995) 'A Tortfeasor's Lot is Not a Happy One?, 58 *MLR* 395.
Milmo (1996) 'Fast Track or Gridlock', 146 *NLJ* 222.
Morgan (2001) 'Nuisance and the Unruly Tenant', 60 *CLJ* 382.
Mullany and Handford (1993) *Tort Liability for Psychiatric Damage* (The Law Book Co).
Mullis (1991) 'Review of Tort Cases', *All England Rev* 396–8.
Mullis (1993) 'Wrongful Conception Unravelled', 1 Med LR 320.
Mullis and Oliphant (1991) 'Auditors' Liability', 7 *PN* 22.
Mullis (1997) 'Compounding the Abuse? The House of Lords, Childhood Sexual Abuse and Limitation Periods', 5 *Med LR* 22
Newark (1949) 'The Boundaries of Nuisance', 65 *LQR* 480.
Newark (1961) 'Non-Natural User and *Rylands* v. *Fletcher*', 24 *MLR* 557.
Newdick (1985) 'Strict Liability for Defective Drugs in the Pharmaceutical Industry', 101 *LQR* 405.
Newdick (1988) 'The Development Risk Defence of the Consumer Protection Act 1987', 47 *CLJ* 455.
Nolan (2002) 'Product Liability', in Grubb (ed.) (2002).
North (1972) 'Breach of Confidence: Is There a New Tort?', 12 *JSPTL* 149.
O'Dair (1991) '*Murphy* v. *Brentwood District Council*: A House with Firm Foundations?', 54 *MLR* 561.
Ogus, Barendt and Wikeley (1995), *The Law of Social Security*, 4th edn (Butterworths).
Oliphant (1996) 'Tort', 49 *CLP (Part I Annual Review)* 29.
O'Sullivan (1995) *CLJ* 241.
Owen (1996) 'Defectiveness Restated: Exploding the "Strict" Products Liability Myth', *Univ. Ill L Rev* 743.
Pearson, Lord (Chairman) (1978) *Royal Commission on Civil Liability and Compensation for Personal Injury* (HMSO), Cmnd 7054.
Posner (1992), *Economic Analysis of Law*, 4th edn (Little, Brown & Co.).
Priest (1987) 'The Current Insurance Crisis and Modern Tort Law', 96 *Yale LJ* 1521.
Prosser (1953), 'Palsgraf Revisited', 52 *Mich L Rev* 1.
Prosser (1955) 'False Imprisonment: Consciousness of Confinement', *55 Columbia Law Review* 847.

Prosser and Keaton (1984) *On Torts*, 5th edn (West Publishing Co.).

Salmond and Heuston (1996) *The Law of Torts*, 21st edn by R. F. V. Heuston and R. A. Buckley (Sweet & Maxwell).

Schlechtriem (1989) 'Presentation of a Product and Products' Liability under the EC Directive', 9 *Tel Aviv Studies in Law* 33.

Shalleck *et al.* (1992) 'Five Approaches to Legal Reasoning in the Classroom: Contrasting Perspectives on *O'Brien* v. *Cunard*', *Missouri LR* 351.

Skegg (1988) *Law, Ethics and Medicine* (Clarendon Press).

Smith and Burns (1983) '*Donoghue* v. *Stevenson* – the Not So Golden Anniversary', 46 *MLR* 147.

Spencer (1987) 'Flooding, Fault and Private Nuisance', 46 *CLJ* 205.

Spencer (1989) 'Public Nuisance – A Critical Examination', 48 *CLJ* 55.

Stanton (1986) *Breach of Statutory Duty* (Sweet & Maxwell).

Stapleton (1986a) *Disease and the Compensation Debate* (Oxford University Press).

Stapleton (1986b) 'Products' Liability Reform – Real or Illusory?', 6 *OJLS* 392.

Stapleton (1988a) 'The Gist of Negligence: Part I (Minimum Actionable Damage)', 104 *LQR* 213.

Stapleton (1988b) 'The Gist of Negligence: Part II (The Relationship between Damage and Causation)', 104 *LQR* 389.

Stapleton (1989) 'Software, Information and the Concept of Product', 9 *Tel Aviv Studies in Law* 147.

Stapleton (1991) 'Duty of Care and Economic Loss: A Wider Agenda', 107 *LQR* 249.

Stapleton (1994) *Product Liability* (Butterworths).

Stapleton (1995) 'Duty of Care: Peripheral Parties and Alternative Opportunities for Deterrence', 111 *LQR* 301.

Stapleton (1995a) 'Tort, Insurance and Ideology', 58 *MLR* 820.

Stapleton (1997) 'Negligent Valuers and Falls in the Property Market', 113 *LQR* 1.

Stauch (2001) 'Risk and Remoteness of Damage in Negligence', 64 *MLR* 191.

Stevens (1964) '*Hedley Byrne* v. *Heller*: Judicial Creativity and Doctrinal Possibility', 27 *MLR* 121.

Sutherland (1992) 'Fair Comment by the House of Lords?', 55 *MLR* 278.

Tan (1981) 'A Misconceived Issue in the Tort of False Imprisonment', *MLR* 166

Tunc (1983) 'Introduction', *Int Enc Comp L*, XI, *Torts*, Ch. 1.

Trindade (1996) 'Nervous Shock and Negligent Conduct', 112 *LQR* 22.

Wade (2000) 'Horizons of Horizontality', 116 *LQR* 217.

Warren and Brandeis (1890) 'The Right to Privacy', 4 *Harvard Law Review* 193

Wedderburn (1978) 'Natural Nuisances Again', 41 *MLR* 589.

Weinrib (1975) 'A Step Forward in Factual Causation', 38 *MLR* 518.

Weinrib (1995), *The Idea of Private Law* (Harvard University Press).

Weir (1989) 'Government Liability' [1989] *PL* 40.

Weir (1990) 'Statutory Auditor not Liable to Purchaser of Shares', 49 *CLJ* 212.

Weir (1991) 'Fixing the Foundations', 50 *CLJ* 24.

Weir (1992) *A Casebook on Tort*, 7th edn (Sweet & Maxwell).

Weir (1996) *A Casebook on Tort*, 8th edn (Sweet & Maxwell).

Weir (1996b) 'Swag for the Injured Burglar', *CLJ* 182.

Weir (2000) *A Casebook on Tort*, 9th edn (Sweet & Maxwell).

Wheat (1998) 'Liability for Psychiatric Illness: The Law Commission Report' [1998] *JPIL* 211.

Whittaker (1989) 'European Product Liability and Intellectual Products', 105 *LQR* 125.

Williams (1951) 'The Aims of the Law of Tort', 4 *CLP* 137.

Williams (1960) 'Penal Legislation in the Law of Tort', 23 *MLR* 232.

Williams and Hepple (1984) *Foundations of the Law of Tort*, 2nd edn (Butterworths).

Winfield and Jolowicz (2002) *Tort*, 16th edn, ed. W. V. H. Rogers (Sweet & Maxwell).

Wright (1985) 'Causation in Tort Law', 73 *Cal L Rev* 1737.

Wright (2001) *Tort Law and Human Rights: The Impact of the ECHR on English Law* (Hart Publishing).

Index